The People's University

The People's University:
A History of the California State University

Donald R. Gerth

2010
Berkeley Public Policy Press
Institute of Governmental Studies
University of California, Berkeley

Copyright © 2010 by the Regents of the University of California. All rights reserved.

Library of Congress Cataloguing-in-Publication Data

Gerth, Donald R.
    The people's university : a history of the California State University / Don Gerth.
       p. cm.
    Includes bibliographical references and index.
    ISBN 978-0-87772-435-3 (alk. Paper)
 1. California State University—History. 2. State universities and colleges—California—History. I. Title.
    LD729.5G473 2010
    378.794—dc22

                                                          2009043178

Since the adoption of the Master Plan for Higher Education in 1960, one of California's best ideas of itself as a democratic experiment has been the California State University system. In this comprehensive history, a veteran educator explores how the benefits of higher education have been extended to millions of Californians through a unique twenty-three campus system expressive of that hope for a better life that is today struggling to survive as part of the California Dream.

—Kevin Starr
Author of *Golden Dreams: California in an Age of Abundance, 1950–1963*

As Donald Gerth recognizes, the California *1960 Master Plan* for *Higher Education* was a successful, rational plan for growth, and the basis for collecting the then virtually independent state colleges into an almost unique, statewide institution with shared values. The *Master Plan* was well suited for the political and economic conditions of the 1960s. His wonderfully detailed book, *The People's University,* is about the California State University, but in the context of educational, political, economic, and demographic changes since that time. He contrasts the initial success of the 1960 plan to today's complete lack of rational planning for growth by the state or the universities and colleges. He urgently calls for a new master plan for growth to be negotiated, one that will reflect today's realities and explicitly include both educational and financial policy. I can only hope that someone in the corridors of power will heed his call.

—Patrick M. Callan
President, National Center for Public Policy and Higher Education

Don Gerth's love for California State University (CSU) is reflected in this comprehensive history. Through trials and triumphs, the "people's university" has evolved from a small and relatively minor player to an institution with twenty-three campuses that are culturally rich and comprise a significant economic force in California. This volume helps the reader understand the story behind this well respected institution and how it is changing so that its core values—to provide access, affordability, and quality to the state's diverse populations in pursuit of American dream of a college education—are perpetuated. Gerth gives great insight into CSU's complex past and its promise as "a major vehicle for building the future."

—Molly Corbett Broad
President, American Council on Education

For Bev

Contents

List of Photographs		xi
Foreword		xiii
Preface		xvii

Part I. Creating the California State University
Chapter 1	The Early Years: 1857–1950s	1
Chapter 2	The California State Colleges and the Master Plan	71
Chapter 3	From Campus Autonomy to System Integration—1960 to 1970	105

Part II. The Work of the California State University
Chapter 4	Academic Planning: Purpose and Direction	189
Chapter 5	Graduate Programs and the Doctorate	221
Chapter 6	Teacher Education—the Origins	241
Chapter 7	International Programs	269
Chapter 8	Information Technology	287

Part III. The People of the California State University
Chapter 9	Who Attends the California State University—Students and Alumni	309
Chapter 10	Faculty and Staff—Collective Bargaining	341

Part IV. The Support of the California State University
Chapter 11	Organizing the Future of Governance	391
Chapter 12	From Orange Book to Compact: Financing in the California State University	481
Chapter 13	Capital Outlay: Building Programs	519
Chapter 14	In Sacramento and Washington	539

Part V. The Mission, Master Plan, and an Agenda for the Future
Chapter 15	The Promise of the People's University: Promises Realized, Promises to be Fulfilled.	595

Appendix 1. Timeline: The Years of the CSU	619
Appendix 2. Interviewees, Participants in Focus Groups, and Contributors	633
Appendix 3. Trustee Appointments	635

Appendix 4. Chancellors of the California State University 641
Appendix 5. Enrollment in Five Year Intervals from 1935–36 to 2008–09 643
Appendix 6. Statewide Academic Senate Chairs 645

Index 647

List of Photographs

1. Members of the San Jose State Normal School "Tennis Club," 1893 — 13
2. Chico State Normal School, 1894 — 13
   Courtesy, CSU Chico Meriam Library, Special Collections and the Bidwell Mansion State Historic Park
3. San Jose State University, students in chemistry laboratory, 1917, Special Collections — 14
4. San Jose State University, students in lecture room, circa 1917, Special Collections — 14
5. Cover of the Master Plan for Higher Education in California, 1960–1975 — 70
6. Governor Edmund G. "Pat" Brown — 76
7. Assemblywoman Dorothy Donahoe, California Blue Book, 1958, Office of State Printing — 97
8. Senator George Miller, California Blue Book, 1958, Office of State Printing — 97 97
9. Donald Leiffer, University Archives Photograph Collection, Special Collections and University Archives, San Diego State University — 107
10. Louis Heilbron — 114
11. News clipping of Buell G. Gallagher's resignation — 128
12. News clipping of Glenn Dumke's appointment as chancellor — 134
13. President John F. Kennedy receiving the first California State Colleges honorary doctorate; from left, Governor "Pat" Brown, Chancellor Glenn Dumke, Kennedy — 147
14. Governor "Pat" Brown signing legislation to establish CSU Dominguez Hills; from left, Senators Joseph Kennick and Stephen Teale, Brown, and Les Cohen, Director of Governmental Affairs — 154
15. President Julian McPhee, Mrs. Dorothy Dumke, Mrs. Alma McPhee, and Chancellor Glenn Dumke, California Polytechnic State University, Special Collections — 159
16. Statewide Academic Senate Advisory Committee on Consortium — 202
17. Dedication of the Archives of the CSU, Dominguez Hills; from left, Donald Gerth, "Pat" Brown, Glenn Dumke, Helene Whitson, John O'Connell, and Louis Heilbron — 224
18. Trustee Herbert Carter and Chancellor Reed at Super Sunday — 317
19. Graduating and celebrating — 319
20. Campus protest — 366
21. Dr. Claudia Hampton — 394
22. Glenn S. Dumke Trustees Conference Center — 397

xi

List of Photographs

23. Clark Kerr, Barry Munitz, Trustee Chair Anthony Vitti; joint meeting of trustees and regents, October 13, 1993, Assembly Chamber — 398
24. Statewide Academic Senate Leadership, 1978; David Elliott, chair; Helen Gilde, Judson Grenier — 405
25. Trustee William Hauck — 408
26. Students outside the State Capitol "Protect the Future of California" — 410
27. The California State Student Association — 412
28. Proclamation by Governor George Deukmejian, February 1986 — 429
29. Governor Deukmejian Proclaims March 9–15, 1986, "California State University Silver Jubilee Week," Governor George Deukmejian, Chancellor W. Ann Reynolds, Trustee Chair Roy Brophy — 430
30. Chancellor Charles Reed, Trustee Chair Martha Fallgatter, Chancellor Barry Munitz, November 1997 — 451
31. Seated left to right: Author Hughes, President, University of San Diego; Patrick Callan, Executive Director, California Postsecondary Education Commission; W. Ann Reynolds, Chancellor; standing: Gerald Hayward, Chancellor, California Community Colleges; Bill Honig, Superintendent of Public Instruction; David Gardner, President, University of California — 465
32. Charles Luckman — 524
33. Artist's rendering of California State University Trustees and Chancellor's Building, 1998 — 536
34. Governor Ronald Reagan signing legislation creating California State University and Colleges, November 1971 — 546
35. Capitol Fellows Alumni, June 8, 2007 — 583
36. Donald Leiffer, Administrative Officer, 1960–1961, University Archives, Photograph Collection, Special Collections and University Archives, San Diego State University — 643
37. Buell Gallagher, Chancellor, 1961–1962 — 643
38. Glenn Dumke, Chancellor, 1962–1982 — 643
39. W. Ann Reynolds, Chancellor, 1982–1990 — 643
40. Ellis E. McCune, Acting Chancellor, 1990–1991 — 644
41. Barry Munitz, Chancellor, 1991–1998, Photograph, Ted S. Warren — 644
42. Charles B. Reed, Chancellor, 1998– — 644

All photos provided courtesy of the CSU Archives, unless otherwise noted.

Foreword

The California State University is an educational invention of the mid-20th century. It also is a result of the civic leadership of Californians in the years immediately after California became a state—leadership that has been sustained and built upon by the generations that have followed.

The investment that Californians in the 19th century made in education grew over the years—from state normal schools, to state teacher colleges, to state colleges, to the California State University. One normal school in San Francisco in 1857, founded in a frontier society, has grown to 23 California State University campuses with more than 450,000 students. This book is the story of the growth and development of the California State University system that has come to be admired nationally and internationally.

The California State University system provides a model for orchestrating a diversity of comprehensive universities to serve the needs of individuals and a state. As state colleges, many of them teacher colleges all over the country, made the transition to state universities a half century ago, they could look to California which made the transition from disparate campuses to an integrated system. Nationally, the California State University has been important in leading the way, building a sound and productive system of comprehensive universities. Internationally, the California State University has been visited and studied by educational leaders from every continent and a multitude of nations.

The California State University has served the people and the economy and culture of California for more than 150 years. CSU has given national leadership to the transformation of teacher colleges and technical institutes into comprehensive universities. Over many generations, it has helped to shape the field of teacher education. In 1999, when I was the U.S. Secretary of Education, I made a key policy speech on teacher education at California State University Long Beach. More teachers are educated in the CSU system than any other in the United States.

In the last 50 years, California State University has brought programs in the liberal arts and sciences and all of the professions, except law and medicine, to the ever growing and diversifying people of the state. Faculty members, deans, and presidents have played significant roles in the development of many academic programs nationally.

In the years since World War II, the California State University has been a model in bringing together institutions that were quasi-independent public colleges into a multicampus system, with campuses, each quite different, but at the same time, sharing a set of values and mission in the service of California. The California State University works in partnership with the University of California, founded in 1868, and the California Community Colleges, first founded in

1910, all within a larger context of public and private schools and California's private colleges and universities.

Each chancellor, beginning with the Master Plan in 1961, has brought leadership and has built upon the strengths of the previous systemwide administration. Glenn Dumke, for all practical purposes the founding chancellor, spent twenty years leading the creation of what is known today as the California State University. My friend, Charles Reed, has been chancellor since 1998 during complex budget and demographic changes in California, and the California State University continues to move forward.

State-based university systems like the California State University are central to the future of this country. We are well beyond understanding that we live in a learning society, and that education is at the heart of a country's capacity to build a good future for its people, as well as a healthy economy and culture. We can learn from what the California State University has accomplished—and what it has not.

Teaching universities emphasize access and quality in academic programs. The primary focus of the faculty is on students. Yet research, which usually is applied research and often with students as partners, is characteristic of the California State University. This is a model built within the CSU that has been useful to others throughout public higher education.

What would California be like without the CSU? What will California be like without continued access to the California State University, without continued affordability of higher education, and without the continued quality of sound and productive programs? These are fundamental public policy questions that California addressed 150 years ago, and again 50 years ago with the California Master Plan for Higher Education.

Don Gerth joined the California State University in 1958 as a young faculty member and administrator at San Francisco State College When he came to California, he was completing a Ph.D. in political science at the University of Chicago; he soon would be writing about the government of public higher education in California. When the idea of a "master plan for public higher education in California" was proposed in 1959, the first year of Governor Edmund G. "Pat" Brown's eight years of superb leadership in California, Don was invited to help with the research and preparation of papers.

Don has lived the invention and the development of the California State University system. In 2003, he "retired" after forty-five years, during which he served for twenty-seven years as a CSU president—first for eight years at the then young CSU Dominguez Hills campus in southern California, and subsequently for nineteen years at California's capitol campus, California State University Sacramento.

Don's career of teaching and administration in California was marked by a succession of policy formulating roles, chairing groups on many subjects of importance to healthy colleges and universities. Thus, this book is a combination of history and memoir.

Perhaps the most important aspect of *The People's University* can be found in using history to consider the years ahead. We all have been told often that looking to the future through the prism of the past informs the future—what can be learned and used. History does not confine or restrict vision; rather it is a rich source of information feeding our creativity in thinking about the future.

The most consequential investment any society can make is in its own people. This work is about California's investment in people in good times and bad.

Richard W. Riley
U. S. Secretary of Education, 1993–2001

Preface

The great tradition in higher education is one which is essentially humane. It is one which is skeptical, inquiring, searching, and evaluating about society and all of its institutions, about man, about culture, and about the natural world. In the language of today, the great tradition in higher education may have had and, indeed has had throughout history, a career component. But fundamentally the great tradition has sought to bring out the best in people. The great tradition is a thousand years and more of history in our culture, and it is representative of the best in all the cultures known on this earth.

Why would one call it a great tradition? This tradition in higher education has provided the opportunity for millions of individuals to live lives which are humane, civil, and full. This tradition is responsible for much, if not all, of the scientific and technological progress we have known.

What is a people's university? The people's university is available to people. The people's university reaches out and provokes the spark of human potential in all of the citizenry, directly or indirectly. The people's university is accountable to people for quality and for the choices of resources committed to its support in contrast with other basic human needs. But the people's university is no mean servant. It leads in society.

For example, it asks how our society can adjust to the demands of peace, a peace that is overwhelming and unambiguous fact. It asks how our society and our people can master, rather than serve, science and technology. It asks how our most pressing public problem, the arrangement and administration of public and private demands, can be pursued. It asks how the most revolutionary society in the history of the world—this nation—can survive. It asks about the human condition itself. . . . The people's university is an affirmation of a number of things in our society and in this state. It is an affirmation that higher education must be committed to quality and to the humane tradition. It is an affirmation of the concept that higher education must be widely available and not an accident of place or time in life. It is an affirmation of a commitment to human development in a broad sense.

The Great Tradition and the People's University, 1975[1]

This work is all about the past. It is really all about the future.

The California State University has developed over one hundred and fifty years. Its contemporary development dates from 1960 and the California Master Plan for Higher Education. In the fifty years since 1960, it has evolved into a new kind of institution—devoted to teaching by scholars, research that impacts communities and regions and the world, engagement with societal change in every sense, and civic and global leadership.

The history of the California State University is a story that can be understood in several ways. It is the evolution of a single institution and a concept—education of teachers for the frontier. It is institutional responsiveness to social need, sometimes within the context of making public policy, sometimes with the leadership of individuals and groups who had to overcome public policy. It is the history of a kind of higher education institution, with a richness over all of its years, that has become a national and global model. It is a reflection and a part of the building of a nation-state, California. It is a stunning story of organizational change in the context of the needs of the greater society, change propelled externally and internally, change propelled by the circumstances of California from a frontier that was already a diverse culture, and by the leadership of persistent and often visionary educators as well as external political, economic, technological, and cultural leadership.

Some person, unknown to me, wrote "without history, there is no identity," or perhaps I am paraphrasing. That is what this work is all about—the history that gives the identity to the California State University, an identity which is central to the people of California and to the future of California, an identity from which those in the present and future continue to build.

* * *

The architecture of this work is both a narrative and the careful examination of specific dimensions of the California State University story.

We begin at the very beginning, 1857, and the establishment in San Francisco of a training school for elementary school teachers. In 1862 this training school became the California State Normal School. In 1871, this first California State Normal School moved to San Jose. The first section of this book addresses the "early years." These years, spanning just over a century, saw the establishment of normal schools around the state, evolution into teachers' colleges and then state colleges with a major focus on teacher training, and finally with the advent of the GI Bill after World War II, the beginning of an emergence into comprehensive state institutions of higher education. These "early years" reached a culmination point in the 1950s as California's political and educational leadership concluded, first separately and then together, that California needed a design for higher education, a strategy and a plan.

The development of the normal schools/teachers' colleges/state colleges did not occur in a higher education vacuum. In 1868, eleven years after the founding of an "Evening Normal School" in San Francisco, the California legislature established the University of California as a land grant institution, following the Morrill Act which Abraham Lincoln signed in the midst of the Civil War. The University of California grew and in turn established campuses beyond Berkeley in this same time period. In 1919 the Los Angeles State Normal School became the Southern Branch of the University of California and in 1927 the University of California at Los Angeles. Similarly, during World War II the Santa Barbara State College was absorbed by the University of California. The junior college (as they were called in the early years) movement began in California early in the twentieth century, initially as an extension of secondary or high school programs into the first years of a college program. The first junior college in California was established in Fresno on a campus shared with Fresno State Normal School; not only were the buildings shared, but so were the faculty and administration for some years as well. By the 1950s junior colleges, later to become community colleges, were widespread in the state.

The second major segment of the book addresses the development of the California Master Plan for Higher Education. In the 1950s both educational and political leaders realized that some kind of orderly growth plan and structure was essential, especially facing the "impending tidal wave of students," a popular phrasing at that time not only in California but nationally, expected in the 1960s. Demographics made their great growth prediction a certainty. The story to be told about the development of the Master Plan is a story of leadership and considerable courage on the part of some, a story of political deals and trading and compromise, and ultimately a story of rather shrewd visionary leadership on the part of some of the participants. The three major components in the public sector, the junior colleges (then simply a statewide series of junior colleges in local districts), the University of California, and the California State Colleges were defined in the Master Plan. This was in every sense a rebirth, a re-founding of the state colleges away from teacher education as a de facto if not de jure primary mission, to become comprehensive public colleges within a single system. The legislature and governor enacted the Master Plan in 1960, and in doing so created the Board of Trustees of the California State Colleges which in turn created the position of chancellor.

The 1960s were years of consolidation of "the system," years of bringing together institutions that had been autonomous in major ways; a considerable number were in fact, if not in theory, committed to teacher education as a primary mission. These were years of defining mission, substance, and processes. Years ago I learned that a major function of leadership, particularly new leadership, is "authorizing the details of the organization." These early years, the 1960s, were also the years of the Free Speech Movement, the Vietnam War protests, the beginnings of a new civil rights movement, and considerable campus turmoil and conflict across the nation. As the 1960s drew to a close, in a sense some of the tensions became institutionalized, at least in the context of the California State Colleges, and a sense of direction and purpose began to emerge in this newly created "system."

The work of the California State Colleges, soon in the 1970s to become the California State University and Colleges and then in the early 1980s simply the California State University, is complex and has undergone substantial change in one sense while remaining the same in terms of core values over the years. Thus a series of chapters or sections will address the period from the "rebirth" or re-founding of the California State Colleges in 1960 to the present. There are many stories to be told. The first has to do with students. The Master Plan called for a reduction in the range of eligibility of high school graduates in both the state colleges and the University of California. This was accomplished by 1965. Over the years, the relationship of secondary school curriculum and standards to collegiate curriculum and standards has changed rather greatly whether one looks at the

American or California scenes. Institutional programs have also changed as well. Thus, the selection of student bodies has had to change. This has happened, one could even say responsibly, within the California State University. As the population of California has become more diverse, so have the students in the CSU. This change has been complex for both educational and political reasons, but it also has been productive.

Similarly, there has been a change in undergraduate programs. General education is a continuing topic. Majors go in and out of fashion; new programs emerge with social and technological change. Even more dramatic than undergraduate program change is graduate program change. It was only in the late 1950s that the then governing board, the State Board of Education, authorized the granting of a master's degree without a teaching or other education credential. Joint doctorates (with the University of California and private California campuses) were authorized by the Master Plan, though this approach has not been a success by any criterion. At this writing, only recently the independent doctorate in one field, education, has been authorized by the legislature—a change to the Master Plan. One of the early actions of the then new board of trustees was the creation of academic master planning.

An early initiative of Chancellor Glenn Dumke at the beginning of the 1970s was the "1000 Mile campus" and the opportunity for extended education programs to play a major part in the lives of many Californians. Research has been a major topic of growth and development. New and expanded professional programs and the refinement of programs in the arts and sciences have been ongoing over the years. A major international program initiative was launched soon after the Master Plan. It is alive and well, though not nearly large enough. Its faculty founder became the chair of the Foreign Affairs Committee in the House of Representatives. Student affairs programs have been rebuilt; *in-loco parentis* disappeared about the time of the Master Plan. Student affairs administrators have learned from both educational and social change. The campuses without exception have incorporated major programs addressing the diversity of California's population and the resulting needs for change and addition to student programs and curriculum.

The presence of CSU campuses in communities and regions and the role of campuses in economic and educational and social development have become over time major factors in the work of CSU faculty, the mission of campuses, the roles students play, and the role that institutions as institutions serve. Public service is a part of the work of many, if not all, faculty. Alumni of the CSU are everywhere—omnipresent in the life of the state and its regions and communities—and for that matter, the world. Universities have a public life, just as other social and cultural and economic institutions do, and that public life is not only political but more than that.

The faculties and staffs of the now twenty-three campus California State University give a significant character to the CSU and to each campus. One can assert that there is a CSU culture, but one can also assert that there are twenty three separate cultures, formed by many variables. "Recruitment and retention of a quality faculty," phrasing which emerged in the 1970s, has been a major push over time, and faculty character has changed over almost fifty years of the CSU. The character of administrative leadership has differed. Collective bargaining, which became a reality in the 1980s, continues to have a major impact.

Technology and the California State University grew up together, and both are still changing. The impact of technology could have been, almost from the beginning of the CSU in its present form, a major instrument used to create a "system," to bring the campuses together in harmonious and productive ways. It was not to be so, however, until the early to mid 1990s. Significant progress has occurred in the past dozen to fifteen years, and the momentum clearly continues.

Earlier we noted that the California State University does not exist in a higher education vacuum. Over the years since the Master Plan, relationships with the now California Community Colleges, not a system in any orderly and structured sense, and the University of California, have had a major influence on the growth and character of the CSU. California has a different balance between the public and private sectors of higher education than many eastern states. Indeed, the private-public balance shifts toward the public as one moves westward across the United States. The Master Plan created a coordinating mechanism. This mechanism, originally the Coordinating Council for Higher Education and now the California Postsecondary Education Commission, has changed over time, but has not been the kind of success some had hoped for. Relationships with the public and private schools, K-12, now pre K-12, have changed dramatically.

Governance has changed in extraordinary ways, both in the early years up to the Master Plan of 1960 and in the years since 1960. By the time of the 1950s, the closest mechanism the then California State Colleges had to a governing board was the monthly meeting of the State College presidents and top officials in the State Department of Education. This changed, suddenly but not easily, in 1960 and 1961. Faculty had virtually no role in governance prior to the Master Plan. Presidents were supreme and in many instances authoritarian in substantial measure on campuses. A genuine and working role for a chief administrative officer for the campuses collectively did not exist. The evolution of roles in governance of trustees, presidents, faculty, students, staff, and the chancellor and his/her staff is a remarkable story. Centralization and decentralization, the work of a system or central office under the trustees, is a factor. Decision-making driven by internal and external priorities has changed over time.

The financial administration of the California State Colleges was, prior to the Master Plan, subject to all of the same controls as any other state agency—the Department of Finance, the State Personnel Board, General Services, and the like. This greatly circumscribed the work of the campuses and created bureaucratic (in the negative sense of the word) procedures and often blocks. One rather distinguished State College president, J. Paul Leonard at San Francisco State, left his post in 1957 for another presidency, a "good" one as presidencies are commonly understood, with the very public comment that he was simply tired of junior budget analysts in the State Department of Finance making educational policy decisions—the size of classes, teaching methods, and the like—for his campus. The administrative history of the California State University since the 1960 Master

Plan is the story of the evolution of financial and other forms of administration from a state agency to a university system with a financial integrity, authority, and responsibility as well as accountability. This evolution has had its ups and downs, good years and bad years, often associated with the leadership styles of governors and other public officials, legislators, chancellors and vice-chancellors, presidents, and the wisdom of trustees, individually and collectively. The balance of public and private funding has shifted markedly. Capital outlay programs, totaling billions over the years, were a major factor in pulling the campuses together and into a "system" in the initial years of the trustees. One could argue that the absence of addressing seriously the financing of public higher education in California was a failure of the 1960 Master Plan.

The California State Colleges in 1960 had no collective presence in the state capital. Presidents, and in a few instances others, had an individual presence in Sacramento. One campus president, Julian McPhee at Cal Poly, a long time president from 1933 to 1966, was among a small number of the most influential lobbyists on the state scene. A "system" presence had to be built. This was an early effort of the board of trustees and the chancellor. There was no presence whatsoever in the nation's capital. This too had to be built. The creation of Sacramento and Washington representation is an important dimension of the building of the California State University.

So what does all of this mean? Since the mid-1960s, some, now many, have called the California State Colleges and the California State University the "peoples' colleges" and the "peoples' university." The CSU has gone through enormous change, some of it formal such as the change in names from the California State Colleges to the California State Universities and Colleges, and now to the California State University. The CSU has emerged from being a relatively minor player in California, not well known or a "player" nationally or beyond the United States, to a major presence in the lives and economy and culture of the people of California and the world of higher education nationally and more recently globally. The CSU is a multicultural and diverse institution in a multicultural and diverse state. The CSU is populated by more than 450,000 students, more than 23,400 staff, and nearly 23,600 faculty. The CSU has well over two million living alumni.

What is the culture of the California State University—is there a single fundamental culture? What are the core values of the California State University? Have core values carried the California State University from 1960 to 2009? Can core values carry the California State University into the future? How do core values play out with the growth and increasingly diverse population of California in a very competitive world? What are priorities? What are potentials unrealized?

There are such things as social inventions, and the California State University is a major social invention of the last half of the 20th century.

* * *

The process of putting this book together has gone through several stages.

I was concluding forty-five years in the California State University on four campuses and a year (1963/64) in the chancellor's office. During those years, I had the privilege of being a faculty member in political science and serving in various administrative positions. First I did an overview of where I might find materials: the Archives of the California State University at the CSU Dominguez Hills campus, the Bancroft Library at UC Berkeley (which I greatly underestimated at the beginning), my own quite extensive collection of CSU papers from my involvement over a forty-five year period, and a number of other sources. The collection of oral histories at the CSU Archives was particularly helpful. This continued for well over a year, as my wife, Bev, and I also enjoyed the pleasures and time afforded by partial retirement.

A strength that I can bring to this work is my involvement personally with so many issues in the building of the California State University. I soon realized that this strength could be replicated many times over. Thus we began a series of focus groups on particular topics about the growth and development of the California State University. Many of the active participants from the very beginning of the CSU in 1960 are alive and had much to contribute. The first focus group had to do with the selection and admission of students, a story beginning with the Master Plan and continuing to this day. Other focus groups have included the evolution of the role of the board of trustees (seven trustee chairs participated, five in one group ranging from Louis Heilbron, the first chair of the board of trustees to Roberta Achtenberg, the 2006-08 chair, and two individual interviews), the evolution of the role of presidents, the development of faculty participation in governance (this group included the first chair of the Statewide Academic Senate, Leonard Mathy, and other Statewide Academic Senate chairs serving over the years). Bev recorded these groups and has subsequently transcribed them. We began these groups in late 2004.

I did many individual interviews, and in the same vein found oral histories in a variety of places. A listing of the contributors in the focus groups and the individual interviews is to be found in the appendices.

Friends and colleagues have given us access to papers and notes, more than we ever expected. So in a very real sense this story of the building of the California State University is a story told by participants. Many, particularly those who participated early on in the 1960s and 1970s, did so when they were professionally young and were certainly committed to the building of the "system." Thus, this work is not just my story and my understanding of the meaning of things, but our stories and our understandings. I am indebted to all those who have contributed to these focus groups and interviews and given access to their papers. In one sense the CSU has always been for the professionally young of whatever age.

* * *

What is the purpose—what is the point of this work? It is to tell a story—the story of the building of a new kind of university. This kind of university has been key to the development of California in every sense—economic, cultural, social, and educational—especially for all of the years since World War II. The normal schools, state teachers colleges, and state colleges, from the beginning of the state to the mid-twentieth century, created the education base and culture for the state from the beginning. These institutions were for many the access to further and higher education.

Like any important institution, the California State University is under pressures of many kinds to adjust to change. Some pressures are in the name of tradition: become more like a "regular" university. Some pressures are economic: can the state afford higher education for so many people, or can the state fund the Master Plan commitment to access? Some pressures are demographic: can the CSU bring the diverse populations of California into the mainstream of education and thus the economy, the changing culture which the more diverse population must shape, the socio-political life of the state? Some pressures are internal: here I think of young faculty, new to the CSU. It does not look like or taste like the universities from which they recently received doctorates. Inevitably some pressures have to do with leadership: do new members of the board of trustees understand what the CSU is all about? Do new administrators, high and low, understand the mission and values? (I will observe that this was a concern in the first ten or fifteen years after the Master Plan, and still is on occasion.)

This work is not to develop the proposition that the California State University should not change. The CSU is all about change, and observably that change has accomplished the definition and redefinition of core values, while in a fundamental sense these core values remain constant.

Therein lies the purpose of this work. Is there an audience for an understanding of the history of the CSU and most particularly the core values of the CSU—the importance not only of the institution but of the model?

The intended audiences begin with the insiders—the faculty and students and staff and alumni of the California State University. The audience certainly includes trustees, presidents, and members of the many citizens' advisory groups on campuses and at the state level, members of the chancellor's staff over the years, other players in higher education in California and nationally. The audience must include the California legislature and the governor. Perhaps it is useful to list audiences I have thought about as I researched and listened: historians; current California college/university chancellors and presidents and aspirants to these positions; national and state-level policy makers (elected and administrative); an international audience represented by the many individuals and groups from other nations who have come to California to study and observe, not the least of which is the OECD project of the late 1980s; members of institutional and system governing boards and aspirants; graduate students, libraries; new and present CSU faculty, administrators, staff, and students, especially at the graduate level; emeritus faculty and staff and administrators; newspaper and magazine writers and editors; higher education advocacy associations, organizations, and institutes; foundations; writers and consultants about higher education.

In the last analysis, the work is all about higher education policy and the audience is those who affect policy.

* * *

My background for writing this book is relevant.

My wife and I came to California and San Francisco State College in 1958. I had been a student in the PhD program in political science at the University of Chicago (where I had earlier received baccalaureate and master's degrees). Since receiving the baccalaureate in 1947, I had been in several staff positions at Chicago (with one year away to serve as Field Representative for World University Service in Southeast Asia and subsequently almost five years of active duty in the Air Force, much of it related to Southeast Asia); most recently I had been part-time on the staff in the Office of Admissions as a counselor, and had just undertaken at the request of the dean who oversaw admissions and student recruitment the establishment of a kind of admissions/recruitment-focused institutional research program. My work in the Department of Political Science had focused, to the extent then possible, on Asian politics. I had just passed the "prelims" for the PhD, so my course work was concluded and I was developing a thesis topic on Indian politics—specifically something having to do with political elites.

One day a dean I knew well and had once worked for asked me if I would meet two visiting California State College presidents who were doing their annual national faculty recruiting trips—a custom at that time. My response was that I was not looking for employment; I hoped to have a Ford Foundation Fellowship to go to India. My dean friend asked me to do him a favor and meet the two presidents anyway—no commitment. Young faculty were in short supply in 1958. The first visiting president was Guy West, the founding president of what was then Sacramento State College. We had a pleasant conversation, and toward the end he said he would like to talk about a position. I did not give him any encouragement, and that was the end of it. A few days later, I met with Glenn Dumke, the then new president of San Francisco State College. Dumke, as I learned, was the first non-teacher educator in the memory of anyone in a California state college presidency (he was a published historian) and, as it became clear, he was also a believer in faculty consultation, then not a common California State College practice. We had a wide ranging and good conversation and then parted. Perhaps two weeks later I had a call from President Dumke on a snowy Chicago afternoon. He had a dean on the phone with him and he offered me a faculty position. As I was probably stammering, he made it clear that he was offering an associate dean position to be responsible for admissions (an area which I was very familiar with from my part-time job while working full time on the PhD program and supporting my wife and infant daughter) and the building of a student body. He had made it clear in our earlier conversation that he was at San Francisco State to build a changed college. I would also be able to teach. I promised to get back to him in a day or two after consulting my wife. Two days later I/we accepted.

There is a point to this story. I told my department chair I had accepted the position at San Francisco State. He was not happy and observed that the political science department at Chicago did not educate PhDs to go to state colleges, especially west of the Mississippi. More to the point, the next day the department secretary suggested we have coffee and a conversation. She told me that 70 percent of the PhD candidates who leave without the dissertation completed or nearly completed never finish. She urged me to change my dissertation topic to one where everything I would need for research could be found in the Bay Area, principally in the Berkeley and Stanford libraries, etc. I took her advice. About that time I was reading a book by a California political scientist, Lyman Glenny, *The Autonomy of Public Colleges*, and from this I thought of writing about the government of higher education in California. Research about the idea suggested that few social scientists had written about higher education—this had been the province of those in colleges and schools of education. So I moved ahead with my topic and research, and with the position at San Francisco State College.

When we arrived in California in 1958, I discovered a fair amount of ferment and more than only lively discussion about higher education. By January of 1959, a newgovernor, Edmund G. "Pat" Brown, assumed office. In the next few months the idea of a study of California higher education, particularly public higher education, emerged. A structure and process were established. Then President Glenn Dumke emerged as the principal State College player. As he became more involved in the development of what many were beginning to call a "Master Plan," he recalled my dissertation topic and enlisted me for some back room research. He would on occasion invite me to come to meetings. He involved me with the issues, particularly the issue of the selection of students. I came to know all of the participants and the issues in the Master Plan discussions; one assignment would follow another.

I attribute my career in the California State University first to Glenn Dumke opening the opportunities for my involvement in this fundamental public policy discussion as a 29-year-old graduate student without the degree, and second to the wise and observant department secretary's advice to change my dissertation topic.

In my forty-five year career in the California State University, I was always a professor and enjoyed the classroom teaching even during the years as an administrator. It gave me an insight into the lives and needs of students from whom I learned much. I had what is now clearly the good fortune to be involved in many of the policy discussions and decisions within California higher education and beyond from the beginning, 1958, and during eight years as president of the California State University, Dominguez Hills campus, and nineteen years as president of California State University, Sacramento.

In the spring of 2008 it was 50 years since Bev and I met Glenn Dumke. When a young couple are ages 26 and 29, they do not often make decisions for a lifetime, but we did, unknowingly. Our time with the California State University has been more than satisfying. It has been the opportunity to be builders, to participate with so many others in the creation of one of the important social inventions of our time. I will always think of the California State University as "the Peoples' University," affording an opportunity at reasonable cost for people from all walks of life to study and learn and to create a good life for themselves and their families and good policy for the greater society.

We are deeply grateful for the opportunity to spend a professional lifetime—and personal lifetimes—in the California State University.

* * *

Many individuals have contributed to this work. The appendices list those persons who did interviews and those who participated in group focus sessions. This work is not the work only of an author; it is the distilled experiences of many who participated, directly and indirectly, in the building of the CSU. There are hundreds of people with whom I have worked over the years, all of them teachers about the work of the CSU and about higher education as a social institution. I am indebted to each one.

Each of the five chancellors with whom I have worked over the years has been important. I had no forethought to interview Glenn Dumke directly for the book; he died in 1989. I did interview his wife, Dorothy, now beside Glenn, and his oral histories and papers are in the CSU Archives. I was able to interview Ann Reynolds, Ellis McCune, Barry Munitz, and Charles Reed. All were insightful and generous with their comments and each played a different leadership role. I did not interview Buell Gallagher, now long deceased, the first chancellor whose tenure was a brief seven months; I did hear him deliver a major address at San Francisco State College, and I had one meeting with him and Don Leiffer, whom I subsequently came to know well and respect.

When I started interviewing individuals for this work, the first person I asked was Louis Heilbron. When Pat Brown took office as governor in January of 1959, one of his early appointments was Louis Heilbron to membership and the chair of the State Board of Education. In that role Heilbron became an occasional advisor to Brown, and later a key advisor about the formulation of the Master Plan. Somehow I believe I should be calling him Mr. Heilbron, though he was known as Louis to all. He was not a tall man, but he was a formidable figure in California higher education. He was founding chair of the Board of Trustees of the California State University. He served two terms in that role, and remained on the Board for nine years. Louis and his wife, Delphine, had two sons, John and David. Louis' wife died in the early 1990s. An attorney in the Heller Ehrman law firm in San Francisco, he served on the Advisory Board of San Francisco State for years. He was the first chair of the California State University Archives Board. Louis Heilbron's thoughtful interviews and conversations and his wise counsel to California State University leaders over the years make him a very major figure in the history of the California State University. I am indebted to him. Louis died on December

20, 2006, at the age of 99. John and David Heilbron have placed Louis' CSU-related papers in the CSU Archives.

The California State University Archives were established by the board of trustees in 1979 at the Dominguez Hills campus. It is a rich, but not as yet complete, source of materials about the history and policies and operations of the CSU. The current Dean of the Library, Sandra Parham, and Gregory Williams, the Director of the Archives, are giving significant attention to the organization of the holdings so that they are accessible. Greg has been continuingly helpful for this work.

At the time of the establishment of the CSU Archives at the Dominguez Hills campus in 1979, one of the enthusiastic faculty members was an accomplished participant and established historian, Judson Grenier. Jud and I did a monograph together at that time about the history of the then California State University and Colleges. We have remained close colleagues over the years, and Jud has been a frequent advisor about this work.

In 1965, when I was a rather young dean of students at the Chico State College campus, I was able to secure a position for an administrative assistant. A young graduate student at San Francisco State named Robert Jones was recommended to me by some close friends. He was another political scientist, very sharp and bright, and I invited him to visit the Chico State campus to meet others. Shortly thereafter, I offered Robert Jones the position, and we worked together for the next 38 years, from Chico State to Dominguez Hills and finally to Sacramento, with the exception of a few years he "took off" for further graduate work and a position with David Gardner when David was a vice-president of the University of California. In my years at CSU, Sacramento, Robert worked with me as Vice President for University Affairs. Over all of these years he has been a fearless and tough critic of my writing, and never hesitated to critique my decisions. When I announced I would do this book after leaving the presidency, Robert offered once again to read my writing and be a critic. He has read each chapter and made extensive comments as to its clarity. Robert retired in 2004, ran for the Los Rios Community College Board, and won the election with an overwhelming majority vote. He is a man who has lived a lifetime in higher education just as I have. He has been a student in all three segments of public higher education in California, in a community college, the California State University, and the University of California. I value his criticism as I value his friendship and I am grateful to him. We've worked as a team for so many years that he reads my thoughts.

Over the years in administrative roles, I have worked with many talented individuals—I'll begin with secretaries—assistants, staff, faculty and faculty leaders, administrative colleagues, and certainly students. They made things happen, and together we worked as a team. A campus is like a city in many ways. As I reflect, it is astonishing to me how much I learned from their counsel and insight. I won't attempt to mention all of the names. *They know who they are.* But I want to take this time to write my personal thanks to the many wonderful colleagues for the years we worked together. In my years at the Sacramento campus, I was fortunate to work with two able immediate assistants. Joyce Longacre knew the Sacramento campus and its people, and she was indispensable to the transition in 1984 and the following years until her retirement. Karyn Domich worked with Robert Jones from the beginning of the transition in 1984 and later came to the president's office in 1999 with her extraordinary talents with people and her understanding of the issues and the context and meaning of the issues. Karyn is a graduate of CSU Sacramento. Without naming others, I have been very fortunate to have had colleagues in my administration who were trustworthy and congenial, sharing knowledge among one another, allowing all to work together as a team for the good of the university, the faculty, staff, students, and the community.

Writing this work was first suggested to Bev and me in 1995 by then Chancellor Barry Munitz. The idea became fixed on our agenda. When we actually set a retirement timeline for the summer of 2003, I first talked with Chancellor Charles Reed in August 2002 about leaving the presidency. I told him I wanted to write the history of the CSU as a part-time retired professor. Chancellor Reed agreed and he made available resources to complete the job. The Center for California Studies became my organizational home. Its Director, Tim Hodson, took me in. The Center's administrative analyst—really the operations manager—Sandra Bernard, handled finances, payment for the focus group meetings and the like, ordered supplies I needed, and helped in many ways. She was important and indispensable for accomplishing this work. Similarly, as the work progressed, I am grateful for the continuing advice and counsel from Executive Vice-Chancellor/Chief Financial Officer Richard West. He was Chancellor Reed's confidant, and he was always available to listen and be helpful. As I approached retirement and the reality of writing this history without "staff" set in, my colleagues told me that I needed to become computer literate. As president, I wrote all of my speeches in long hand or spoke into my dictaphone for the office staff to decipher. After lessons during my last months in the presidency from a wonderful support staff, two individuals from the University Computing Services stepped in. Scott McGown, Doris Ozuna, and the very competent and able students at the University Help Desk have kept our computer ticking away when we experienced computer problems. Without them I don't believe this book would have come to fruition.

As the work on the manuscript progressed, I explored publishing. Tim Hodson at the Center for California Studies suggested the Institute of Governmental Studies at the University of California, Berkeley, and the IGS Berkeley Public Policy Press. Ethan Rarick, the very able director of the press, and Bev and I met for perhaps two and a half hours and agreed to work together. Ethan is a published author; his biography of Pat Brown is superb. He and his colleague, Maria Wolf, have been excellent—we could not have asked for a better working relationship. We needed to gather some photographs, not many, of the campuses, students and chancellors, and others. Colleen Bentley, the experienced head of the public affairs staff in the chancellor's office and now Director of Special Projects helped us, and as we address publishing the book is working with us on marketing. Colleen introduced us to a very talented graphic artist, Katie Covington, who did an initial set of designs for the cover—the design chosen is an adaptation of her work.

Those with whom I worked in the California State University over the years, from the beginning in 1958, know that Bev and I come as a team. This was even true when our two daughters were young. It was certainly true at the Chico campus in the years when I was a dean of students and then vice-president for academic affairs, and at Dominguez Hills and Sacramento during the two presidencies. Bev was "Bev" to everyone on the campus and in the community. I may have been "President Gerth" or "Dr. Gerth," but she was "Bev." And so it is with this book. Without her, this would not have happened, from the initial three-way conversation with Barry Munitz in 1995 about the idea, to the decision to "retire" and do the book, to more than five years of work. She taped and transcribed the focus groups, used the computer endlessly to put drafts together, and we worked together going through what must have been hundreds of boxes of papers in the Bancroft Library, the CSU Archives, and the private papers of many. And she is still working. I am deeply indebted to my wife, Bev, for a lifetime of love, her efforts and support and encouragement throughout my career.

* * *

This book is a story; it is a history. But I am a political scientist, not an historian. The book is also a recitation of my involvement with the founding and growth and maturing of the California State University. I have been fortunate, from the day I was appointed to the faculty at San Francisco State to my retirement in 2003 after 27 years in two presidencies, to have been often at the center of things. Thus this work includes substantial material from my papers, documents, and experiences.

A fair amount of what is in this volume is a recounting of my part in all of these activities over the years. Unfortunately I did not keep a diary. I did keep for myself, in addition to the papers I left upon leaving various positions, many file cabinets of documents, reports, important correspondence, and the like. I kept all of my appointment books with notes from 1963, and all of my papers, addresses, and articles from about 1970. When the book is complete, these will be deposited in the CSU Archive along with the other materials and documents I have acquired in this writing project.

There are opinions and judgments in this work. Without exception, I am responsible for these, not the individuals named in this preface or the many individuals interviewed in the focus groups.

Notes

[1] Donald R. Gerth, "The Great Tradition and the People's University," commencement address, Area and Interdisciplinary Programs, California State University Chico, May 25, 1975.

Part One:
Creating the California State University

Chapter 1

The Early Years: 1857 to the 1950s

Education was on the minds of California's founders. At the state's first constitutional convention, convened in 1849, the legislature and governor were given the right and obligation to address financial, structural, and policy matters for public schools. The constitution created an elective office, superintendent of public instruction. Provision was made for common or traditional public schools and the establishment at some future time of a state university.[1]

In the 1850s, education was a priority in the major city of the new state, San Francisco, as well as in communities and rural areas. The idea was not organized in any systematic way, but early efforts were underway. By the mid-1850s, efforts to educate and prepare teachers were initiated.

To select a specific date for the founding of the first institution is necessarily arbitrary. But current conventional wisdom is that California's oldest public university or public higher education institution, San Jose State University, was founded in San Francisco in 1857 (it would be moved by the legislature to San Jose more than a decade later). This development was followed, in 1868, by the establishment of the University of California, with the implementation of the constitutional provision for a state university, and with the assistance of the national government's Morrill Act of the mid–Civil War years. The university was originally placed in Oakland, and then permanently located in Berkeley.

The first century of the California State University can be understood in three periods of formation and growth, all related to the economic and social maturing of the state and its people. The period from the 1850s to World War I was formative, with eight institutions founded. Additionally, although San Francisco/San Jose State Normal School had been originally conceptualized as a statewide institution, by the 1880s the state normal schools had become the institutions of the people of communities and regions. Early on, these institutions found their missions expanded, not by legislatures and governors, but by the people of the regions and communities they served and desires for economic and social growth.

The second period essentially spans from the end of World War I to the end of World War II. During this period the state normal schools continued to be driven by the people of the communities and regions where the normal schools were located (with the exception of the Los Angeles State Normal School, which had become a branch of the University of California in 1919, clearly against the will of most regents and faculty of the Berkeley-located University of California), driven to become institutions offering a more broad collegiate education and beyond the normal school/teachers college model. This became reality. Seven normal schools became teachers colleges and then state colleges in seven regions of the state.

The third period covers roughly a dozen years, from the end of World War II to the election of Edmund G. (Pat) Brown as California's governor in 1958. The end of the Second World War saw preparation for a period of postwar adjustment and growth, growth in numbers and in the economic and social fabric of the state. It was a time when people pressure, population pressure, and, thus, political pressure to add programs and degrees and build new campuses were great. This was a period of huge enrollment increases, and the establishment of new campuses. Virtually all agreed that the governance of the state colleges needed to be rationalized, as for the most part, the state colleges had simply grown, one by one, into a collection of institutions. The University of California, which was periodically but rather consistently negative about normal school/technical school growth and program development, and, to some extent (though in a very positive and different way), the junior colleges, were both factors very relevant to the state colleges. It was time for an assessment of the California State Colleges and of all of the California higher education enterprise, for serious study and action.

The story of the development of the California State Colleges up to the time of the Master Plan in 1960 is extraordinarily complex. In some ways it is like a puzzle without a frame, understood in terms of its parts but not as a whole. In the years before the Master Plan, each campus was created independent of the others. A major difference between the California State Colleges and the University of California is that as a set of campuses the university was created from the center of the circle moving out, with Berkeley as its capital. The state colleges were created from the circumference of the circle; there was no capital. The disparity in mission and in the structure and functioning of these two public higher education systems inevitably required some kind of rationalization of public higher education in California in the growth years after World War II.

* * *

By 1851, a number of both public and private schools had been established. In April 1853, State Superintendent J. G. Marvin remarked in a report to the legislature, "No apparent necessity for a Normal School has yet arisen. The supply of competent teachers in California is more than equal to the demand."[2]

San Francisco was California's largest city and the cultural and economic center of the state in the 1850s. In 1855, a citizens' committee with responsibility for reviewing the public schools in San Francisco recommended the establishment of "weekly normal exercises, to be attended by all the assistant teachers." Shortly thereafter, weekly meetings were scheduled for teachers. They were required to attend sessions each Saturday morning, and applicants for teaching positions were required to take an examination at the school.[3] The San Francisco newspaper, the *Daily Alta California*, reported that a "normal school" existed.

Visitors often addressed these Saturday meetings. One such visitor was John Swett, who over the years was to have great influence on the growth and development of education in California. In his remarks, he stated:

> We constitute the advance guard on the shores of the Pacific, cut off from the main body of American teachers. Let us organize and work together. Let us make our influence felt in leading public opinion in school affairs. The press is open to us, let us use it. All we need is common sense and uncommon energy.[4]

This first effort at creating a normal school ended one year later.

During 1856–1857, a new effort was initiated. This time, the goal was to create a full normal or teacher training school as part of the city schools. The San Francisco Board of Education had already created a high school at the opening of that school year. Again, weekly sessions for teachers were held. In 1857, San Francisco Superintendent Henry James proposed to the board of education that a normal class be started within the San Francisco High School until the time when the state would provide for a full normal school. The curriculum that he and others developed included "grammar and analysis, writing, general exercises and declamation, United States history, descriptive and political geography, mental and written arithmetic, reading, and physical geography."[5] Classes met weekly; teachers were required to attend. The principal was George Washington Minns, and the school was known to San Franciscans as Minns Evening Normal School.

Minns, who would later become principal of the California State Normal School, was a graduate of Harvard. While an undergraduate, he and a fellow student had exploded some gunpowder in a dormitory room. The Harvard faculty, responsible for student discipline, "rusticated" Minns and his fellow student for two years. Minns then returned, received the baccalaureate, enrolled in Harvard Law School, and received the bachelor of law degree. He practiced law in Boston for a number of years, sailed for California in 1854, and practiced law briefly in San Francisco, before being caught financially in a widespread economic downturn in 1855. He became a San Francisco grammar school teacher and, very soon, a principal. Minns was a public person, and a sought-after lecturer.

The evening normal school flourished. By 1860, it formally became the San Francisco Normal School. All San Francisco teachers were required to attend; in later years this would be referred to as "in-service" education or training. The school enrolled prospective teachers as well, and outstanding high school students were invited to enroll. Individuals who wished to become teachers could apply for admission to the San Francisco school superintendent and be admitted. School was not full time, but once a week for two and a half hours.

In 1856, Andrew Jackson Moulder was elected state superintendent. He had been a college faculty member in Virginia before he came to California to seek his fortune as a miner; he subsequently became a newspaper editor. In reports to the legislature in 1859 and 1860, he recommended the establishment of a state normal school. Around the same time, the San Francisco school superintendent recommended that a state normal school be established, and, in 1861, the San Francisco school board asked the legislature to establish a normal school, offered land (a building lot, not acreage), and volunteered to finance both a normal school and an experimental school for two terms.

Moulder followed through. In 1861, the first state teachers institute, a several-day program, was held in San Francisco; two hundred and fifty individuals participated. Moulder gave the keynote address, at which he stated:

> We must have the Legislature educated to have more faith in the public schools. . . . When our legislators believe with Horace Mann that every invasion upon the domains of ignorance is an invasion upon the domains of crime, they will not haggle at expending as much upon schools as upon the State Prison.[6]

The message is a familiar one, to this day. Moulder then sent a proposal to the legislature:

> Every year this necessity (for a normal school) is becoming more apparent and more urgent. It is rare, indeed, that the educated man possesses the art of teaching. He may be as learned as a collegiate education can make him, and yet lack the ability to impart this information. Long experience in other states has established the great superiority of those teachers who have received a normal school education. . . . In all other professions and trades a long apprenticeship is considered necessary; within our State, it too often happens that the imprudent pretender who has failed in all other pursuits betakes himself to teaching as a last resort to avoid hard labor. Of this, the State Superintendent has had frequent proof in the wretched chirography and equally wretched orthography and grammar of the communications addressed to him.[7]

Moulder went on to request five thousand dollars, a modest appropriation, for the San Francisco Normal School, hitherto entirely municipally supported, to make it available to applicants from all counties in the state.[8]

On May 2, 1862, the legislature sent Governor Leland Stanford a proposal to establish the California State Normal School in San Francisco. Stanford was a strong supporter of education, as he would demonstrate in his later life. The legislation created the State Normal School's board of trustees, which consisted of the state superintendent of public instruction and three superintendents of schools from "major cities"; the first three superintendents were from Sacramento, Marysville, and San Francisco. The trustees were authorized to maintain a normal school in San Francisco, open to all citizens of California, free of any charges, "prescribe curriculum and text books, appoint and fix salaries of teachers, and examine and award diplomas."[9] The trustees had discretionary authority to acquire the San Francisco Normal School (albeit with a very modest budget) and to negotiate with the San Francisco Board of Education to establish an experimental school. The school term was five days a week for a five-month period each year.

The statute addressed admission to the state normal school. Males must be eighteen years old and females fifteen to be admitted. Applicants must furnish a written statement of intent to teach "permanently" in California schools. Enrollment was to be apportioned to students by region proportionate to membership in the legislature. Diplomas would be granted based upon student performance in courses, in practice teaching, and in school government. Diplomas were to be very specific about the grades and subjects the graduates might teach.[10] The final appropriation for the first year was three thousand dollars.

The first meeting of the board of trustees was held in the governor's office in Sacramento on May 23, 1862. Governor Stanford presided. The board decided to accept the San Francisco Board of Education's offer of a location. The number of students for the first term was set at sixty, with at least one student from each county. The board also decided that all applicants must take an entrance examination covering reading, spelling, writing, grammar, geography, and arithmetic. Based upon test performance, applicants would be placed in basic or advanced courses. Applicants would also be required to submit references addressing "good intellectual capacity and high moral character and principles."

The members of the board and initial faculty defined a curriculum to cover two years. Each year would have a five-month term, from mid-July to mid-December. Many of the students were already teachers, and would teach for the remainder of the year when they were not at the normal school. The curriculum is of interest, given the status of teacher education in the state. The complete two-year curriculum included orthography, reading, elocutionary exercises, grammar, composition, rhetoric, writing, mental and written arithmetic, algebra, geometry, geography (mathematical, political, and physical), map drawing and the use of the globe, human physiology, the laws of health, natural philosophy, astronomy, and "the science and art of teaching."[11]

In a period of six years, Minns Evening Normal School of 1857 became San Francisco Normal School in 1860, and then the California State Normal School in 1862. This was California's first public venture into higher education. Earlier, in the 1850s, two private institutions had been founded at the southern end of the San Francisco peninsula, a Jesuit college, now Santa Clara University, and a Methodist college, now the University of the Pacific.

Start-up was slow. Six students appeared the opening day. But more applicants emerged, and by the end of the first term of the California State Normal School in December 1862, there was sufficient momentum for the leadership of the board to ask the legislature to finance another term beginning in January. The legislature responded positively, and the second term began in mid-January 1863, ending that June. By 1866, enrollment had increased to 384, and there were 108 graduates. In 1868, San Francisco experienced a strong earthquake. While there was substantial damage in the city, the only damage at the normal school was the destruction of a manikin that had been purchased in Europe to be used for the human physiology class. It was sent to Paris to be repaired.[12]

The earthquake became the occasion for opening a discussion about moving or changing the normal school. The board asked Oscar Fitzgerald, the state superintendent of public instruction, to explore merging the normal school into the newly established (1868) University of California. That exploration was brief, and went nowhere; the normal school was more mature than the university at this point. Public discussion emerged around the question of a normal school being located in a city other than San Francisco; some referred to San Francisco as a "city of sin." Other communities began to compete to have the normal school relocated, among them San Jose, Santa Clara, Vallejo, Stockton, Martinez, and Oakland. The students, when polled, favored remaining in San Francisco. State Superintendent Fitzgerald wrote to the legislature in 1870 and recommended San Jose: "San Francisco is not the place, for all experience proves that a school of this character cannot flourish in a great commercial city. To locate the Normal School in San Francisco would be dropping a piece of literature into an ocean of mammon. . . . San Jose . . . is the proper location for the State Normal School."[13] Finally, the legislature acted. The state senate and assembly held a joint session and chose to move the school to San Jose.[14] Subsequently, a new comprehensive law for the state normal school emerged from the legislature and was signed by the governor. The law created a new board consisting of the governor, the superintendent of public instruction, and five gubernatorial appointees. The act authorized the board to move the normal school from San Francisco to San Jose and to select a site, build a structure for offices and instruction, build dormitories (boarding houses, in the language of the time), and the like. Entrance ages for applicants were changed, sixteen for women, seventeen for men; a nonresident fee was established for students from other states, a one-time payment of one hundred dollars. A two-year appropriation of twenty-four thousand dollars was included in the new law, and a tax of two cents on every one hundred dollars of taxable property was levied to create a "State Normal School Building Fund."[15]

Members of the board looked at several sites in San Jose and selected a park, Washington Square. The city deeded the park to the state. One Washington Square is the address of San Jose State University today.

The San Jose campus opened June 14, 1871. In 1873, a new principal was appointed, Charles H. Allen, and he would provide the first long-term stability for the normal school. He remained the school's principal until 1889. In 1873, the position of preceptress, (dean of women) also was established. The board, at this point, removed itself substantially from the management. Allen was given authority to appoint faculty, and he recruited nationally. The curriculum became more complex and was extended to three years. Allan established a "training school," where normal school students could teach under supervision; the families of students in the training school paid tuition, and it was self-supporting.

Beginning in the early 1850s, several attempts were made to establish a statewide organization of teachers. None of these lasted for more than a year. In the early 1860s, three teachers institutes were held in San Francisco at the state normal school; these did not continue. In 1875, Principal Allen persuaded the normal school board to join in issuing an invitation to all the teachers of California to come to a conference. Many came. On June 10, 1875, the California Teachers Association was founded on the California State Normal School campus in San Jose. The CTA built strength and has been for years among the two or three most powerful lobbying groups in the state capitol, influencing public policy about education and many other matters.

* * *

The second California Constitutional Convention convened in September 1878 and concluded in March 1879. Two heated debates developed about Article IX, the education article in the original constitution. The University of California had been established in 1868 in the context of the Morrill Act, the extraordinary legislation authored by Senator Justin Morrill of Vermont and signed by President Abraham Lincoln in the midst of the Civil War. The Morrill Act was specific: funding was provided to create in each state an agricultural and mechanical arts institution. The 1878–1879 convention was in some measure a populist reaction to all of state government. There was a floor battle about whether the University of California program was too intellectual and insufficiently practical, an argument that had been brewing for at least a half dozen years. An education committee reported to the convention in January 1879 that the university should be a public trust and removed from the immediate surveillance of the legislature. The proposal was much debated; the friends of the university narrowly prevailed and Article IX, Section 9 of the constitution was reformulated to make the university a constitutionally independent entity.[16]

Another bitter debate occurred about normal schools. The drafting committee for education included normal schools within the public school system. The net effect of that would have been to allow normal schools to be established by cities, counties, and special districts. It is not clear whether that outcome was consciously proposed, although numbers of the Workingmen's Party argued strongly for it. The very fact of the 1878–1879 convention was a result of restlessness in the California population about the possibility of the government and its programs becoming more distant from the mass of people in the state—farmers, laborers, and workers of all kinds. The end result of this argument is that the constitution of 1879 simply used the term "normal school" and dropped the language including normal schools within the public school system.

The new constitution did not address secondary or high schools; support was provided only for elementary schools. In 1883, Anthony Caminetti, an assembly member, authored successful legislation extending elementary schools upward for four years, with the avowed purpose of preparing students for university entrance. This legislation remained in effect until 1891, when the legislature made provision for secondary schools and some support.[17] Further legislation in 1903 gave additional support to high schools. This was an important issue for the normal schools and the University of California. Admission to both was predicated on secondary school graduation. For UC, this meant that admission, at least in theory, was only available to applicants from communities that spent local tax money to support high schools. For the normal schools, this caused the development of four-year programs, in which the first two years covered what was essentially a secondary school curriculum; and participation at a normal school "preparatory curriculum" was used to qualify for admission either to UC or to the conventional teacher education curriculum.

In early 1880, fire struck the San Jose campus. The main building, which had been completed for the princely sum of $285,000, was burned to the ground. The library, laboratories, equipment, and furniture were destroyed. The normal school missed one day of classes and then resumed instruction in borrowed, temporary facilities; the building was replaced within a year.[18]

* * *

In January 1881, a resolution was introduced in the state senate to establish a "Branch State Normal School" in Los Angeles. Pressure for a normal school had been mounting in Los Angeles, and in 1880, a Los Angeles senator had introduced a bill to move the state normal school from San Jose to Los Angeles. The 1880 bill went nowhere, but the 1881 bill passed in both houses quickly, and in March, Governor George Perkins signed the legislation for the branch school's creation. The trustees of the California State Normal School in San Jose were also to be the trustees of the southern Los Angeles campus. They were empowered to select a site and appoint a principal and faculty. The legislature had appropriated fifty thousand dollars for a building, and the appropriation assumed that the Los Angeles City Council would provide a site. The city council refused. A citizen's campaign developed and resulted in raising eight thousand dollars for purchase of a site that the San Jose trustees selected.

The Southern Branch State Normal School opened in 1882 with sixty-four students. Within a few months enrollment increased to nearly one hundred. The populist spirit of the constitutional convention had not disappeared. In 1886 the legislature authorized the Southern Branch State Normal School to become Los Angeles State Normal School, and almost immediately thereafter it changed the name of the San Jose school to San Jose State Normal School. The legislature then changed the governance structure and provided for each institution to have a board of five members appointed by the governor from among the local citizenry; the governor and state superintendent of public instruction would be ex-officio members. The two institutions would continue to function administratively under the state superintendent of public instruction.[19]

The legislature was not finished with normal schools. On March 9, 1883, the legislature passed and sent to the governor a bill to establish a northern California normal school. The action was the result of substantial political pressure of the citizenry, the newspapers, and, consequently, a drive from regional legislators for a normal school and higher education in the Central Valley and foothills and mountains from Sacramento to the Oregon border. Competition was strong among communities to become the location for a normal school. Seven communities became bidders. Two Butte County legislators, Senator A. F. Jones of Oroville, and Assemblyman Allen Henry of Chico, were Chico's advocates. The contest finally came down to three communities, Redding, Red Bluff, and Chico. The bill that finally passed in the legislature provided that the northern branch would be located north of Marysville, and provided fifty thousand dollars for construction. The competition became more heated. A Red Bluff citizen's group allegedly sent spies to Chico to learn Chico's strategy. One of Chico's two newspapers, the *Chico Enterprise*, did an economic analysis and reported that the Normal School would generate sixteen thousand dollars of salary income, two thousand for each home purchased by faculty, and at least one hundred students spending one hundred to one hundred and fifty dollars each year for room and board. At the last minute, the town of Henleyville weighed in (a town that cannot be found on maps today).[20] The statute empowered the California State Normal School trustees, about to become the San Jose State Normal School trustees, to select a site.

The trustees visited Redding, Red Bluff, and Chico. They were met with large crowds and discussions with the most influential individuals in each city. The trustees met in the law office of Governor Washington Bartlett in San Francisco at the conclusion of their trip. It took thirteen ballots for the trustees to make a decision. Chico was selected. The decision was influenced by the donation of an eight-and-a-half acre plot of cherry orchard by General John Bidwell. Bidwell was a California pioneer who had led an immigrant group to California in 1841, served as a general in the Civil War, and was a major rancher and farmer in the Sacramento Valley. He became a United States senator, and was a candidate of the Prohibition Party for the presidency of the United States. His wife outlived him by many years and was the national president of the Women's Christian Temperance Union for a period.

After the site selection, the editor of a Red Bluff paper published a poem, patterned from the concluding lines of "Casey at the Bat":

> Somewhere the sun is shining, and
> Somewhere hearts are light.
> Somewhere folks are laughing, and
> Somewhere the day is bright.
> Somewhere no rain is falling,
> but this is to our knowledge—
> There ain't no joy in Red Bluff, since
> Chico stole the College![21]

Construction of Chico State Normal School began in 1888, and classes began in September of 1889 with ninety students enrolled. The first class graduated in 1891. The Bidwell influence was strong. In the early years, some faculty and two principals were dismissed for drinking alcohol or smoking. Following the practice developed at San Jose, there were both two- and four-year programs. The four-year programs were for students who had completed grammar or elementary school. The two-year programs were for students who had completed additional studies, or were otherwise judged to be ready. The fact that California had very few high schools meant that every applicant with any accomplishment beyond grammar school would be separately assessed by the faculty. Placement examinations were standard.

An early catalog spelled out student discipline:

- The regular study hours of seven to ten p.m. should be unremittingly observed all days except Friday and Sunday.
- All unnecessary promenading upon the public streets should be avoided.
- Absence or tardiness, except in the case of sickness, should be entirely unknown.
- Keeping the company of the opposite sex is, as a rule, inconsistent with strong work at school.
- The habit of speaking of teachers, pupils, or others in complaining or uncomplimentary terms is harmful to the well-being of the speaker, and should be oppressed in its incipiency.
- It is the duty of everyone to be cheerful; to avoid worrying, to be just, to be healthy. Hence each student should be regular in all aspects of exercise, diet, sleep, and study.[22]

Student housing was in supervised boarding facilities. The principal and preceptress were responsible.

The curriculum included language, mathematics, science, and miscellaneous subjects (penmanship, morals and manners, vocal music, drawing, and calisthenics). Training in the art of teaching was central. Like San Jose and Los Angeles, students had to sign a statement: "I hereby declare that my purpose in entering the school is to fit myself for teaching; that I intend to teach in the public schools of the State of California."

1. Members of the San Jose State Normal School "Tennis Club," 1893.

2. Chico State Normal School, 1894.

3. San Jose State University, students in chemistry laboratory, 1917.

4. San Jose State University, students in lecture room, circa 1917.

Now with three state normal schools, each with i̇s own local board, and the governor and state superintendent as common members, the legislature took another step and required that the trustees must meet together in a joint formal session each year. At this session they were to specify a uniform curriculum and textbooks to be used on the three campuses. At the first of these meetings in 1887, the group also developed a common calendar (two terms) and a postgraduate curriculum to prepare students for admission to the University of California for further study (with advanced standing), which would allow them to teach in high schools. In 1888, the joint meeting resulted in a calendar change from two to three terms in a year. Then, in 1889, the faculties presented a proposal that was far-reaching both substantively and procedurally, to return to two terms a year and adopt a curriculum that would work with a two-term system. This curriculum centered in the first year on languages, mathematics, and science, and included drawing, geography, history, and study of the United States Constitution. In the second year, students concentrated on pedagogy and studied manners, morals, and psychology. In the third year, the students moved to practice teaching and studied school law and government. The joint meeting of the trustees accepted these recommendations. Faculty participation in governance had emerged, a first and important step.[23]

The 1890s saw new working relationships develop, as the three institutions and their governing boards worked together. The principals/presidents pointed out to the boards that faculty workload in the normal schools was more than double that of the University of California, and that enrollment growth had created severe space shortages. The principal at San Jose negotiated an agreement with the University of California to admit normal school graduates without examination.[24] Admissions standards were being raised gradually. The first community/regional economic impact study was completed at the San Jose campus: "more than $100,000 [is] annually thrown into business circulation in San Jose...." In 1891, after years of neglecting secondary school education and focusing on grammar or elementary schools, the normal schools, and the University of California, the legislature adopted a number of measures about secondary or high schools. Then, in 1896, the normal schools began to urge high school graduation for admission.[25]

Also in 1896, the most overt act of political interference with the normal schools up to that date occurred. Governor James Budd and the principal at San Jose, Charles Childs, had been in conflict over a number of issues. In 1889, Childs had been the first graduate of the San Jose State Normal School to become principal. He had been instrumental in moving normal school programs forward on all three campuses. Childs was not reappointed in 1896. Ambrose Randall, a friend of the governor, was appointed, and remained principal for three years. Childs, meanwhile, remained on the San Jose faculty. In 1898, he was elected president of the California Teachers Association.

Following on the change in leadership at San Jose, the legislature moved to create a new governing group, the Joint Board of Normal School Trustees. The joint board was given authority to appoint presidents, though two years later that authority returned to the campus boards. The title of principal was changed to president at this point. The joint board also had authority to dismiss faculty (but not to appoint, adopt curriculum or textbooks, or set admissions standards). That same year, the course of study in the normal schools moved to four years—though the decision to do that had been made in 1893, prior to the joint board. Enrollment ceilings were proposed for the campuses. San Jose was to limit enrollment to six hundred individuals.

* * *

The state's population continued to grow and, thus, so did the social fabric and character of California's communities and emerging cities. San Diego and the surrounding area experienced booming growth in the 1880s, and the leadership and the people of San Diego wanted a college. Two abortive efforts were made in the late 1880s. A number of citizens, with the leadership of the San Diego superintendent of schools, had attempted to create a private "College of Letters." Another group had tried to create a branch of the University of Southern California in conjunction with the construction of a new community or subdivision. A downturn in San Diego's economy and an attendant population drop from forty thousand to seventeen thousand had defeated both of these efforts.[26]

In 1894, the movement to secure a normal school for San Diego began. San Diego had a young, vigorous, and entrepreneurial mayor, William Carlson, elected at age twenty-nine. A local businessman, John Spreckels, became involved and offered land (the name Spreckels reappears in Californian and Hawaiian history). The two forces that converged in this movement were clearly community development and a genuine need for trained teachers. In the 1894 city council elections, bringing a normal school to San Diego was a cause.

The legislature did not move quickly. Fresno too wanted a normal school. The three existing normal schools wanted more funding. In 1895, Wilfred Guy, an assemblyman from San Diego, carried a bill that passed in both houses of the legislature. It was vetoed by Governor Budd. In 1897, Assemblyman Guy tried again, and this time he succeeded. On March 13, 1897, Governor Budd signed the legislation, which provided for the creation of a board of trustees to select a site, build a building, and start the San Diego State Normal School. The appropriation for the start-up was fifty thousand dollars.

A site was selected, among the many offered. There is some evidence that the selection was influenced by builders of a new housing development.[27] The selection of a president took even longer. The trustees could not agree on a candidate. Finally, in September 1898, agreement was reached on the appointment of Samuel Black, then the state superintendent of public instruction. The San Diego State Normal School opened in the fall of 1898 in temporary quarters, with eighty-three students. President Black, who arrived on October 1, 1898, was to stay until 1910. Thus, unlike the three earlier normal schools, which experienced frequent changes of leadership, San Diego had stable and strong initial leadership for twelve years. Among the founding faculty was a young David Prescott Barrows, later to become president of the University of California.

San Diego did some pioneering in these early years. For example, the first summer session in any California higher education institution was at San Diego in 1899, followed four years later by San Jose. The campus began early an outreach program to the community and the region. A publications office was developed and materials were developed and published for elementary and secondary schools. In a sense, the San Diego campus had the advantage of the experience of the three earlier campuses. Members of the faculty were involved from the beginning in the development of educational policy.

The curriculum in the normal schools as the San Diego campus developed included two- and four-year programs. To enroll in a four-year program, an applicant must have completed grammar school. (California was slow to develop secondary schools for reasons that had nothing to do with educational policy and were related to the political forces in play at the time of the second constitutional convention in 1878–1879. Supportive legislation for high school or secondary education was implemented only in the 1890s.) The two-year program required high school graduation. In 1902, the faculty and President Black established an admissions policy for the two-year program. To be admitted, an applicant must be eligible for admission to the University of California. That required the completion of fifteen full-year high school courses, including English, mathematics, history, and the sciences.[28] The leadership of the normal school at that time argued that this move brought more students.

The next state normal school to be founded was in San Francisco, in 1899. To understand the establishment of San Francisco State Normal School in 1899, one must go back to the 1850s and the origins of San Jose State Normal School. The families of San Francisco had available for their children a small number of grammar, or elementary, schools. The teachers in these schools had no education or training for their roles. Many had been educated only through grammar school themselves. City leaders and officials decided that some effort needed to be made to train teachers. Thus began, as noted earlier, the series of Saturday morning classes for teachers. The instructor was John Swett, later to become a historic figure in the growth of public education in California through the early years of the twentieth century. Swett's Saturday classes evolved into Minns Evening Normal School, then the California State Normal School, and then moved to San Jose in 1871. This was the end of the first incarnation of a normal school in San Francisco.

But San Francisco was a rapidly growing city. Its need for teachers far exceeded the graduates of the State Normal School. San Francisco was one of the few communities in California that had established public high schools prior to the 1890s. In 1864, the board of supervisors created Boys' High School and Girls' High School. In 1867, the principal of Girls' High School initiated a teacher training program. The obvious assumption was that most, if not all, grammar school teachers were and would be women. The institution became Girls' High and Normal School and continued, after the state normal school moved to San Jose. The high and normal schools separated in 1895, and San Francisco Normal School was a stand-alone institution for four years. The normal school graduated more than fifteen hundred students in the thirty-two years of its existence, 1867 to 1899, and surpassed the normal school at San Jose in staffing grammar schools in the Bay Area.[29]

Politics and corruption in San Francisco (and many other places in California) were rough in the last third of the nineteenth century. Positions as teachers were frequently given to political favorites. The Girls' High and Normal School had been somewhat insulated by a long-serving principal, John Swett, and his successor, Mary Kincaid. When the San Francisco Board of Education separated into two schools the Girls' High and Normal Schools in 1895, Mary Kincaid resigned. The board named Laura Fowler as principal of the San Francisco Normal School, a very unpopular choice. Enrollment dropped, necessitating lowered admission standards. Many school districts declined to employ the San Francisco graduates. The school board decided in 1898 to close the normal school, which set the stage for the founding of the San Francisco State Normal School.

An alliance of civic leaders, San Francisco Normal School faculty, politicians, and even students (a foretaste of events to come) systematically lobbied the legislature and others in Sacramento, asking for $200,000 to create a new San Francisco Normal School. The legislature cut the amount to $150,000, then diminished it to $45,000, and finally to $20,000. The bill passed by a very small margin. The San Francisco State Normal School was created, and the first local board, including the governor and the state superintendent of public instruction, was appointed. The board's first action was to appoint a president, in order to secure the opening of classes in 1899. The appointment was an important one for the new institution as well as for teacher education in California and beyond. The board chose Frederic Burk, a relatively young educator and superintendent of schools in Santa Rosa. He had been a teacher; he had earned a master's in child development at Stanford, and a doctorate in psychology at Clark University. Burk came to the presidency and stayed until his death in 1924.

At the very beginning of the new normal school, some asserted that there were sufficient institutions in California and, thus, no need for a new one in San Francisco. Burk's response was that the San Francisco institution would concentrate on quality. San Francisco implemented admission standards higher than any others of the four normal schools of the time, and then moved the curriculum to a new level. Burk's influence was pervasive, and he brought around him a faculty of some note over the years; John Dewey was a frequent visitor. The campus developed what was then a new model of collegiate instruction for would-be teachers, "individual instruction," in which the students in a class would not be treated as a single unit, but, rather, individually. The model spread, becoming important in California, on the national scene, and in many other countries.[30]

A press was developed using the state printer (a requirement that applied to all CSU campuses until the 1990s), and thousands of instruction booklets were printed and were widely available. Among those displeased with the individual instruction model were education staff in state government, and in 1914 they succeeded in forbidding the curriculum and forcing a return to conventional teaching. The state printer was ordered to cease printing the material that the campus had used and that was widely available in other institutions and schools.

When Burk died in 1924, he was succeeded by a close associate who died soon after his selection. Mary Ward, another close associate and an early graduate of the school, became acting president for a year and, thus, became one of the first two women to be a president, albeit acting, in what is now the California State University. (It was not until 1974 that a woman was regularly appointed to the presidency of a California State University.) In its founding early years, San Francisco State had the stability of sustained leadership and, for its time in American higher education, a marked intellectual level, which Frederic Burk gave to the institution and, ultimately, all the state normal schools in the nascent system.

* * *

Railroads in California were a significant factor in the development of the state, economically, politically, and culturally. Railroads also influenced the establishment of normal schools. The campuses at San Jose, Chico, and San Diego were located where they were, in part, because of railroads. In 1894, the railroad from the north came to the agricultural community of San Luis Obispo; in 1901, it reached San Luis Obispo from Los Angeles in the south. In 1894, the *San Luis Obispo Tribune* began a campaign to establish a normal school in San Luis Obispo for California's central coast region. In 1897, Senator S. C. Smith introduced a bill in the legislature to establish the "Normal School at San Luis Obispo." The bill passed, but the governor did not sign it. San Luis Obispo and San Diego were in competition for the next normal school.[31] San Diego opened its normal school in 1898.

San Luis Obispo resident Myron Angel, a writer and frequent contributor to newspapers, proposed that the community change its goal and establish a state polytechnic school. Angel used Cornell University and the Pratt Institute in Brooklyn as models for his proposal. Senator Smith introduced a bill to establish a California State Polytechnic School in 1899, and again in 1901. There was opposition. The University of California saw competition and opposed a polytechnic, given its own intention to establish an agricultural branch at Davis.

Adjacent to Los Angeles, the private Throop Polytechnic Institute (later, the California Institute of Technology) had already been established in Pasadena and opposed a new polytechnic. Nonetheless, the 1901 bill passed and was signed by Governor Henry Gage on March 8 of that year. The California State Polytechnic School came into being on January 1, 1902, with a fifty thousand dollar appropriation for land acquisition, buildings, and equipment. It was in many ways an unusual institution, neither a college nor a secondary school.

Admission assumed only grammar school graduation, though its students were generally older, many in their late teens.

The governance of the polytechnic institution was similar to that of the normal schools. The governor and the state superintendent were trustees, and the governor appointed five additional trustees. The trustees were responsible for picking a site, although there was no question but that it would be in San Luis Obispo. They were also responsible for selecting and appointing a founding director. One of the governor's appointees to the trustee group, E. J. Wickson, was a professor of horticulture at UC Berkeley. Wickson had had a conversation about curriculum with Leroy Anderson, a colleague and the chair of the Department of Animal Husbandry, during which Anderson had suggested the concept "learn by doing"; to this day that concept is a basic principle for the Cal Poly curriculum. Anderson became the school's first director in 1902.[32]

Enrollments in Cal Poly's early years reflected the diverse ethnicity of that day, unlike the normal schools. Director Anderson and his family lived in the dormitory. In these very early years foreign student exchange programs developed, particularly around agriculture. The curriculum evolved in three areas: agriculture, mechanics, and domestic science.

An early guest at Cal Poly and in San Luis Obispo was President Theodore Roosevelt. In his address, he remarked about Cal Poly:

> I am glad to learn that the State of California is erecting here the polytechnic institute for giving all the scientific training in the arts of farm life. More and more people have awakened to the fact that farming is not only a practical but a scientific pursuit, and that there should be the same chance for the tiller of the soil to make his a learned profession that there is in any other business.[33]

Director Anderson was asked in 1907 to return to UC Berkeley as a professor of agriculture and to be, once again, a founding director, this time at the "university farm" at Davis (now the University of California, Davis). Anderson's successor at Cal Poly, Leroy Smith, was a Cornell graduate and a member of the Cal Poly faculty in English, history, and economics, not in any of the applied fields. Smith was director for six years, 1908–1914, until he too left for the University of California. Both Smith and Smith's successor, Robert Ryder, a University of California alumnus who headed Cal Poly's Department of Mechanics, devoted their attention to building the curriculum. Smith introduced a humanities curriculum, attended to building the library, and established the position of librarian. He added a year to the three-year curriculum for a four-year program to graduation and provided for the award of diplomas. Ryder addressed course content, particularly in the humanities and social sciences, and more advanced work in mathematics, making it possible by 1916 for Cal Poly graduates to be eligible to move on directly to colleges and universities for more advanced study.

The post–World War I years were difficult. The end of war brought an influx of veterans seeking applied education. Then in 1919, a worldwide influenza epidemic occurred. San Luis Obispo was particularly hard hit, and the campus closed for a time. When it did reopen, students, faculty, and staff all wore face masks. A new governor, Friend Richardson, was elected. He regarded Cal Poly as outmoded and costly, and its generous budget was cut in half. The early 1920s also brought a change in Cal Poly's governance. The institutional trustee board was abolished, the title of director was changed to president, and the president reported to the state superintendent of public instruction, as did the presidents of the normal schools; the designation of the normal schools was changed at this time to state teachers colleges.

The significance of the founding and early years of Cal Poly is in curriculum. Unlike the other campuses that became colleges and then universities over time, Cal Poly had a broader curriculum, albeit vocational, and this became a base, or rationale, for other colleges to move into applied programs as Cal Poly was more fully merged into in the system in the 1940s.

* * *

The Santa Barbara State Normal School of Manual Arts and Home Economics was established in 1909, built upon a manual training school that had been founded there in 1893. Its focus was on training teachers for applied programs, an initial move to prepare individuals for secondary school teaching. The Santa Barbara campus remained part of this system until 1944, when it became Santa Barbara College of the University of California.[34]

* * *

The community of Fresno was founded in the Central Valley of California in 1872. It grew rapidly and soon became a hub of the valley. It established a first school in 1873; by 1900, it had become a city and had a modest school system. Teachers, especially those with professional education, were difficult to recruit. The San Jose State Normal School was the nearest source and provided only a small number of teachers. In 1899, Charles McLane became superintendent of public schools in Fresno. McLane soon took up the issue of recruiting teachers.

The Fresno County Chamber of Commerce initiated a campaign to secure a state normal school. A committee was created, including a state senator, two assembly members, and a number of prominent citizens. The committee marshaled facts and brought a proposal to the 1909 legislature. The proposal included five possible sites for a normal school, each offered free of charge to the state. The bill's defeat in the assembly was attributed to the governor, who was then James Gillette. Neither the press nor the people of Fresno had supported Gillette's election. Superintendent McLane wrote at the time, "[H]e [Governor

Gillette] told me personally that it gave him a great deal of satisfaction to see that Fresno should receive no favors at this session."[35] McLane was the leader of this political effort because of his professional role in education as superintendent of Fresno schools. He was very aware that in 1907 the legislature had enacted (and the governor had signed) provisions for a junior college, an "upward extension law." He believed this to be helpful to the cause of securing a state normal school.

The junior college movement in the United States was born in the late nineteenth century, an idea related to conversation of that time that the first two years of university, often today called general education, were really an extension of secondary school studies. The first junior colleges in the United States were developed and encouraged by William Rainey Harper, the founding president of the University of Chicago. The very first few were private, and then Harper persuaded the public school leadership in Joliet, Illinois, to establish a junior college. This was shortly followed by public junior colleges in Peoria and Morgan Park, both in Illinois. These were to feed graduates into the University of Chicago. In California, Dean Alexis Lange of the University of California was a leader of the junior college movement, as were David Starr Jordan and Ray Lyman Wilbur, presidents of Stanford.

In 1907, Senator Anthony Caminetti of Amador County introduced legislation permitting high school districts to extend their programs upward. Caminetti had been a leader for education in the legislature for years. It was his continuing effort, beginning in 1883, after the 1879 constitutional convention had made no provision for high schools, to introduce state support for secondary school education. He had been successful in that effort earlier, and once again, in 1907, he was successful in getting the state to make the first moves toward junior colleges. The statute read:

> The Board of Trustees of any city district . . . may prescribe post-graduate courses of study for the graduates of high school . . . approximating the studies prescribed in the first two years of university courses. The board . . . may charge tuition for pupils living without the boundaries of the district wherein such courses are taught.[36]

The legislation did not use the phrase "junior college." No state financial support was provided.[37]

The 1907 law was permissive. After the 1909 effort to establish a normal school failed, Superintendent McLane developed a proposal for a two-year postgraduate course to be offered at the Fresno High School. He worked closely with his community allies from the normal school effort, and with the leadership at Stanford and Berkeley. Dean Lange at Berkeley was particularly helpful. The postgraduate course was to include mathematics, English, Latin, modern languages, history, economics, and technical subjects. The Fresno board of education adopted McLane's proposal. The postgraduate program opened in September 1910. This was California's first junior or community college, the first of well over one hundred campuses throughout the state. Thus did the efforts to establish a normal school and California's first junior college begin to merge.

The election of 1910 gave California a new governor, Hiram Johnson. Johnson was a reformer in every sense, and he was a supporter of education. McLane and his colleagues in Fresno immediately renewed their efforts to secure a normal school. The chamber created a committee in November, immediately after the election. The proposal created by McLane and his committee went beyond the earlier version. The new proposal addressed the need for a normal school that would teach agriculture, a high school curriculum subject that would move the normal school to train teachers for high schools. The proposal was accompanied by an offer of land for the agricultural program and school district facilities for the normal school in the short run and several free sites for a permanent campus.

The legislature passed the measure, Governor Johnson signed it, and the Fresno State Normal School opened September 11, 1911. On its first day one hundred and fifty students enrolled. A first among the normal schools to that date was the offering of courses in "manual training, domestic art, science, and agriculture"; all of these subjects in the high school curriculum that would lead to teaching in high schools. This was a significant breakthrough, for it was not until 1946 that state colleges would be generally authorized to grant secondary teaching credentials. The governor established the customary board of trustees, five citizens from the region to serve together with the state superintendent of public instruction and himself. A temporary site offered by the Fresno schools was accepted, and a permanent site was selected shortly after.

The most important strategic move made by the board was to appoint Charles McLane to the presidency of the normal school and place it for the first years in the same building with the junior college. McLane was president of both institutions. He proceeded to combine the curricula of the normal school with that of the junior college. The state regulations and agreements among the presidents and joint board members provided that high school graduates would have a two-year curriculum. McLane went further, and from the beginning provided a third year in agriculture, household economics, manual training, and drawing; again, he pushed a capacity for the normal school to prepare teachers for secondary schools. The faculty was jointly paid from the normal school budget and the junior college (Fresno public schools) budget. McLane himself received a salary of fifteen hundred dollars from the normal school and two thousand dollars from the Fresno schools.

McLane was an ardent advocate of a broad liberal education for teachers. In his semiautobiographical account of Fresno State, he included the following:

> Modern conditions demand that the teacher be first an educated person. Therefore, a teacher's college may well be part of a liberal arts college. The time will soon come when the point of differentiation into the various professions will be at the completion of the four-year academic course.[38]

In order to make this approach workable within the common framework for all of the normal schools, McLane established placement examinations, and these made it possible for most students to have room for liberal arts courses.[39] The junior college and the normal school had parallel schedules, making it easy for students to move back and forth.

Clearly, McLane was ahead of his time. He defined education for the profession of teaching and, later, for all professions, based on a liberal education and the environment of a liberal arts college.

When the normal school moved to temporary buildings on its permanent site, the relationship with the junior college became more difficult, but it was sustained; in 1921, the two institutions were formally merged. This merger had long-term implications for the state colleges after the redefinition of the normal schools to state teachers colleges and then, in 1935 to state colleges, and especially in the growth years subsequent to World War II.

The significance of the founding of a semimerged pair of institutions, the normal school and the "upward extension," was most likely not foreseen in 1911. It was to have great meaning up to the time of the Master Plan. The junior college created the circumstance for the institution to offer the full range of conventional university lower-division curriculum. That was exactly what the supporters from the Berkeley and Stanford campuses wanted. It also created the circumstance in which the normal schools and their successor institutions, the state teachers colleges and the state colleges, could offer to the people of their regions a full range of options for university study at the lower-division level.

This is exactly what happened over time. In 1923, the teachers colleges gained baccalaureate degree-granting authority, and in 1935, they were redefined as state colleges. With one exception, each of the original seven normal schools established over time a junior college function and used this for program development. Particularly in the years immediately up to and after World War II, this was used as a way to introduce new degree programs in areas beyond the liberal arts. Engineering would be a notable example. This introduction of the lower division provided a means for the normal schools and then the teachers colleges to respond to the variety of regional demands for programs well beyond the education of teachers.

* * *

Governor Hiram Johnson's administration brought a new era to Sacramento politics. Johnson was not long in office before the legislature passed and he signed the bill to create Fresno State Normal School. That event brought to the attention of the leadership of the Eureka Chamber of Commerce the possibility of creating a normal school for California's north coastal region, a region isolated from much of the rest of California, even to this day. In 1911, the nearest accessible normal schools were in Ashland, Oregon, and San Francisco. Practical travel to Chico did not exist. The chamber leadership undertook a study of teachers in the region and discovered that 65 percent, perhaps more, of the teachers in the region had not received any training. The Eureka chamber established a three-person committee in 1911 to pursue the idea of a normal school, create public support, and begin exploration with the state government in Sacramento.[40]

The campaign began. A new group was created, the Federated Commercial Bodies of Humboldt County, which gave strong support to the campaign. In December 1912, two Humboldt County legislators, State Senator William Kehoe and Assemblyman Hans Nelson, introduced legislation to establish a "Humboldt County Normal School, for the training and education of teachers and others in the art of instructing and governing the public schools of this state."[41] The legislative process was relatively quick and easy, especially when compared with those of the earlier normal schools. The actual establishment proved to be more difficult. The governor appointed the conventional board for that time: five local citizens, with himself and the state superintendent of public instruction bringing the number to seven. Humboldt County had three cities or towns: Eureka, the county seat and far the largest with a population of almost twelve thousand, and Arcata and Fortuna, in declining order of size. Three of the five gubernatorial appointees were residents of Eureka, and the common assumption was that the normal school would be located in Eureka. The initial funding for the normal school was to be ten thousand dollars, and the community was required to provide a two-year lease without cost for a building.

The five regional members of the board met for the first time on November 6, 1913. They instructed one of their members, Charlotte Gale, a Eureka resident, to send letters to the chambers of commerce in Arcata, Eureka, and Fortuna, notifying them that there would be a board meeting on November 13 to receive proposals to site the normal school. All three chambers responded. Eureka and Fortuna's leaders presented oral proposals. Arcata's leaders had organized, with the aid of George Burchard (one of the 1911 three-member Eureka exploratory committee, who had since moved to Arcata), and they presented a carefully drawn written proposal with a two-year free lease on an existing building (the Arcata grammar school) and twelve thousand dollars in pledges for added support beyond the ten thousand dollars appropriated by the state. The board accepted the Arcata proposal. One of the three Eureka trustees, Charlotte Gale, voted with two trustees, one each from Arcata and Fortuna. The board also appointed a founding president, Nelson Van Matre, the superintendent of schools in Eureka and a graduate of the University of Chicago, and set January 5, 1914, as the opening date for the Humboldt State Normal School.

It was not to be so simple. The Eureka board members appealed to the California attorney general on the grounds that the full board, including the governor and the state superintendent of public instruction, had not participated in the meeting. The attorney general ruled that the November 13 action was invalid. The board then gave the governor and state superintendent three dates for a meeting in Humboldt County. None of the dates were acceptable, so the board members traveled to Sacramento. The Eureka chamber group prepared a written proposal. The governor and state superintendent attended the board meeting. Charlotte Gale responded to pressure of her fellow citizens of Eureka, but the governor and state superintendent both voted for Arcata; the vote was four to three for Arcata. The Humboldt State Normal School opened there on April 6, 1914, with sixty-two students.

President Van Matre, newly in office at the Humboldt campus, leaned toward vocational preparation for the students, and he also followed the path created by the Fresno campus with advanced programs in agriculture, horticulture, domestic science, manual training, and music. The campus followed the general administrative pattern of the other California normal schools. Students were required to be at least sixteen, and could be in one of four programs: "a one-year course for experienced teachers, a two-year course for high school graduates, a three-year course for students with two or three years of high school, or a four-year course for grammar school graduates."[42]

The normal schools, like other higher education institutions, experienced significant enrollment decline as the US entered World War I; Humboldt's enrollment declined by two-thirds, to fifty-nine students. The state financial agency did a cost study at the end of the war and found that operating costs for Humboldt were higher than those of other campuses: $753 per student, contrasted with an average of $291 per student. The state board of education, which had only recently become the governing board, considered canceling the funding of the first permanent building and discussed closing the campus. President Van Matre went to Sacramento. Hans Nelson, by then a senator, succeeded in retaining funding for the building and maintaining the institution.

By 1914, there were eight normal school campuses. From north to south, these were: Humboldt, Chico, San Francisco, San Jose, Fresno, Santa Barbara, Los Angeles, and San Diego. There would be no additional normal schools or state teachers colleges or state colleges in California until after World War II and the return of the veterans. Moreover, two normal school campuses were moved to the University of California. The Los Angeles campus became the southern branch of the University of California in 1919 and, subsequently, UCLA in 1927; and the Santa Barbara campus became the Santa Barbara College of the University of California in 1944 and, subsequently, UC Santa Barbara.

* * *

The California State Board of Education had gone through a remarkable evolution over the years. The 1849 constitution did not mention a state board of education. In 1852, the legislature created a state board in the same legislation that created the possibility of local school districts. The first state board members were the governor, the state superintendent of public instruction, and the surveyor general. In 1864, board membership was changed by the legislature to include the superintendents of schools from major counties (none of them in the south) and to remove the surveyor general. The board was given authority to select textbooks, a factor that had major meaning for the normal schools some years later. In 1870, there was yet another change in membership to add the principal of the state normal school (only one in 1870), six designated county superintendents (Alameda, Sacramento, San Francisco, San Joaquin, Santa Clara, and Sonoma), and two teachers. Then the 1879 constitutional convention greatly diminished the modest role of the state board and moved most authority to county boards of supervisors. As noted earlier, this move did not include the normal schools, as the convention did not include the normal schools in the category of public schools in the final document. As a practical matter, the state board exercised little authority over the normal school (soon to be several schools). The revised constitution did leave the state board in existence with only the governor, the state superintendent, and the principal of the normal school. As more normal schools were established, their principals became members. In 1884, the state board reacquired responsibility for selecting textbooks for schools. In 1890, the president of the University of California also became an ex-officio member. The board's major function was to serve in an advisory role to the state superintendent.[43]

In 1899, the first state study of higher education occurred. It made several recommendations about the normal schools, and these were adopted by the legislature. Each campus would have a board of five members appointed by the governor and in addition, the governor and the state superintendent of public instruction. These boards were to be in some sense responsible to the state board of education (at that time, the members of the state board were the governor, the state superintendent, the presidents of the normal schools, and the president of the University of California, who had been added in 1890).[44] The state board was responsible for approving courses of study and setting admissions standards. The local boards had all remaining authority—to select presidents and appoint faculty and staff (all of whom served at the pleasure of the appointing board)—and fiscal responsibility.[45] An examination of actual key decision making suggests that relationships with the state board were loose and flexible, and the institutions broadly interpreted their authority, even with respect to curriculum and admissions, the latter of which varied campus by campus and administration by administration over the years, though in 1903, the state board and the joint board of trustees acted to require a high school diploma for admission to all campuses. Otherwise, the emphasis once again was on the normal schools serving the people of a region.

In 1912, the governance structure of the normal schools again changed. Conflict had gradually been developing over the issue of selecting textbooks for the public schools; both the state superintendent and the state board of education members believed they had that authority. A constitutional amendment titled "Free School Text Books" was introduced for the 1912 election. The amendment provided that textbooks be furnished in the public schools free of charge. Only brief mention was made of the provision in the amendment to reorganize the State Board of Education; the real purpose of the proposal was to change the state board. The amendment provided that the legislature would determine the method of appointing members of the board. The amendment passed. In 1913, the legislature gave the governor power to appoint a board of seven members, none of them professional educators. The superintendent would be the secretary of the board and would be responsible for implementing "general rules and regulations as the state board of education may adopt, the work of all assistant superintendents of public instruction, and such other appointees and employees of the board as may be provided by law." The redefined board was given limited powers of governing all state education operations except the University of California and was charged with advising the legislature, governor, and state superintendent. The elected superintendent continued to be the administrative head of all educational operations except those of the university.[46]

Also in 1913, the legislature gave the normal school boards the authority to create programs for high school teachers in subjects that the University of California and the private colleges had not addressed. These included art (drawing), music, physical education (physical culture), and all commercial, technical, and industrial programs.[47] The new campuses of that decade, Fresno and Humboldt, moved immediately to start these programs. The Fresno campus had been instrumental in causing this to happen.

In 1915, the state normal schools were placed under the governing structure of the state board of education for some purposes. Curriculum, admissions standards, transfer rules, and graduation standards were specifically placed under the jurisdiction of the state board. The local boards retained the authority to appoint presidents and faculty and were responsible for financial matters.[48] In 1916, the state board, in its annual report to the governor addressed the normal schools.

> California has reason to be proud of her Normal Schools, and of her generosity in providing, equipping, and supporting them. Our eight California Normal Schools represent an investment of $2,696,140. Their total annual budget for 1915–16 was $995,508.98. Their faculties numbered 267. They had in training last year 7,789 students. . . . A larger percentage of the teachers of California than any other state have had the advantage of normal training, and this fact is, without doubt, largely due to the efficiency of the Normal Schools and the superior advantages they afford.[49]

The board took its responsibilities seriously, and in 1917 it addressed admission standards. Over the years there had been some agreement among the trustees of the several campuses and the principals/presidents about admissions requirements. The pattern that had emerged was for elementary school graduates to go into a four-year program, an approach necessitated by California's late entry, among the states, to a statewide network of high schools. High school graduates were admitted to a two-year program and, in the immediate years before 1917, a longer specific program to prepare to teach a limited range of subjects at the high school level. In fact, campuses and presidents varied in their uses of admissions standards. Some presidents were more rigorous than others in applying standards, and presidents responded to the regional availability of potential students. In 1917, the board and then the legislature enacted a common admissions standard for all of the campuses: high school graduation with an 80 percent or higher grade point average, and a personal recommendation by a high school principal.[50]

The 1917 legislation also modified the governance structure. The State Board of Education was given comprehensive authority for governance, and the individual campus boards lost the power of appointment and financial administration. The presidents were invited to attend state board meetings. The local boards, devoid of authority, gradually disappeared.[51]

* * *

As Los Angeles emerged as the major urban center in Southern California, pressure gradually mounted to create a second state university in the city. In 1915, a bill was introduced in the legislature to establish a separate university with its own board of regents. The regents and administration of the University of California did not want a second university, and Benjamin Ide Wheeler, then the longtime president of the university, testified against the bill. It was defeated. But President Wheeler made a public commitment, in a regents meeting, to move "one step at a time," to make the programs of the university available to the citizens of Los Angeles and the surrounding region. In 1916, the university opened an extension center in Los Angeles. A Los Angeles civic group proposed that the university establish a two-year branch in Los Angeles. An extension center would offer courses; a two-year branch would offer whole programs. The regents rejected this. A new bill was introduced in the legislature but again did not pass. Then the Teachers Association of Southern California asked for a summer session in Los Angeles. Wheeler opposed this. The regents were convinced by Edward Dickson, a newspaper publisher and their one member from Southern California, to consider the request seriously, and Wheeler subsequently took it to a faculty committee. The committee members recommended against this. However, despite this, the regents approved the request and President Wheeler was instructed to implement the summer session.[52]

Wheeler had assumed the presidency in 1899 and had been a very strong leader, but by 1917, his health was failing. He designated a number of individuals, successively, to work with civic leaders, educators, and others in the Los Angeles area to find a reasonable—from the standpoint of the university—solution to the matter. None were successful. In 1917, the presidency of the Los Angeles State Normal School became vacant. This was early in the year, shortly before the legislation to transfer the power of appointing presidents from the trustees of the individual campuses to the state board of education had become effective. The Los Angeles normal school trustees appointed Dr. Ernest Moore, a Harvard professor, as president. In the selection process, the trustees had made

Moore aware of the desires of the leadership in Los Angeles and Southern California generally to establish a public university.

Shortly after President Moore arrived in Los Angeles, he was visited by Regent Dickson. They discussed the move of the normal school to the university. Both liked the concept. Dickson saw it as a solution to the establishment of a campus within the existing UC structure, in Los Angeles, and Moore saw it as the opportunity to expand the normal school program to conventional college and university work. Dickson took the matter to the regents. Negotiations ensued involving the faculty and administration of the UC, the regents, the faculty and administration of the normal school, and Southern California leadership. The negotiations were tedious and not productive. The regents had become aware of a young accounting graduate, Robert Sproul, who was then assistant comptroller and seemed to be performing well in this role, and was especially able to work with people in difficult situations. Sproul was appointed to chair a faculty-administration group, all the members of which were senior to him, and he personally handled the negotiations in Los Angeles. The situation was complex, as generally UC faculty, administration, and some regents were negative.

Eventually the university found itself boxed in. Either there would be a southern branch or the legislature and governor would most likely create a second state university. Regent Dickson went to the governor and the governor agreed to present the matter to the legislature. The governor proposed transferring the normal school, and the legislature agreed. The enabling legislation was passed and the Los Angeles State Normal School became the Southern Branch of the University of California in 1919. Ten years later Robert Gordon Sproul became president of the University of California.[53]

The University of California saga did not end in Los Angeles. In 1919, President Wheeler retired. The regents appointed David P. Barrows, a Berkeley political science professor, to the presidency. Barrows had begun his career at the San Diego State Normal School, now San Diego State University, and then moved to the University of California. He was in the army reserves, and during World War I had been on active duty and risen to the rank of major general. In 1920, Barrows sent an emissary, Dr. Robert Leonard, to Fresno to meet with the president of the normal school there, Charles W. McLane. The topic was bringing the Fresno State Normal School "under the control and management of the university . . . [with] the same relationships as now exist between the southern branch and the university at Berkeley."[54] McLane invited Leonard to meet with a local group of citizens, and the citizens supported the idea and asked for a study. A proposal was presented to the faculty, and the faculty formally approved it. President Barrows came to town and addressed a group of citizens, who applauded the idea. A Fresno legislator introduced a bill to move the normal school to the University of California. The bill died in committee.

* * *

World War I brought a decline in normal school and university enrollment, and enrollment did not increase with the end of the war, as California's economy offered attractive opportunities for employment. There was a significant elementary and high school teacher shortage. A new state superintendent, Will Wood, took office in January 1919. Wood was to play an important role in the decade ahead. The state senate created a special legislative committee to report on "the problem of meeting the needs of and furnishing support for the schools and educational institutions of the state."[55] Senator Herbert Jones of San Jose became chairman of this committee, which then selected Professor Ellwood Cubberly of Stanford to be its consultant. Cubberly wrote the report after hearings, and would become a major figure in American education.

The Jones report, as it was known at the time, covered much territory. It recommended the formation of a state department of education, which would have, among many responsibilities, administrative control of the normal schools. The report also recommended that the normal schools become four-year teachers colleges and confer degrees upon graduates. This redefinition was quite basic, for it defined the first two years of the curriculum as college-level instruction. The law also limited total time to four years, which translated to programs for elementary and only some high school fields for teachers as teaching in traditional high school subjects such as English and mathematics required preparation beyond a four-year degree program. The report removed the requirement, effective since 1862, that applicants for admission sign a declaration of intent to teach. The concept of teachers colleges was amended into the California constitution in 1920. The legislature established the California Department of Education in 1921, and the state superintendent became ex officio the director of education. The legislature also passed bills, which the governor signed, formally changing the name "Normal School" to "State Teachers College, formally abolishing local boards of trustees, and creating a position, deputy director of education, to administer the financial operations of the normal schools.[56]

Additional legislation authorized the newly defined teachers colleges to offer the bachelor's degree. The first degrees were awarded in 1923. Similarly, some of the colleges that had developed junior college programs were now de facto community colleges and could offer community college certificates, which were accepted at the University of California and by private colleges and universities.

The writer recalls a conference about the development of public higher education in California in the 1960s. One of northern California's most prominent lawyers discussed his college and university education. He was a small-town high school graduate in the mid-1920s. He attended Chico State Teachers College, essentially built his own pre-law major, received a bachelor's degree, applied to and was admitted to the law school at UC Berkeley, and went on to build a very distinguished career. The story is illustrative of the role of the regional colleges that the normal schools were becoming.[57]

Not long after all of these changes, a long-anticipated confrontation between the State Board of Education and the state superintendent of public instruction occurred. The state superintendent is a constitutional officer, accountable only to the electorate. The state board is appointed by the governor and accountable to the governor. In 1922, voters reelected Will Wood, an accomplished and respected educational leader, as state superintendent. The voters also elected Friend Richardson, an ardent conservative, to the governorship. Richardson appointed individuals like-minded to him to the state board. The statutes governing the teachers colleges provided for the superintendent to nominate individuals for presidencies and the board to confirm. In 1924, Frederic Burk, the founding president of the San Francisco State College campus, died in office. Shortly after, in early 1925, the president at the San Jose campus, Edwin Snyder, also died in office. Superintendent Wood nominated individuals for each of the presidencies. The governor did not like either nominee, though he was not part of the process; but a majority of the board agreed with the governor and refused to confirm both nominations. The conflict lasted for two years, until a new governor, Clement Young, took office in 1927. At that time the legislature increased membership on the board from seven to ten, and the new governor immediately made appointments. The impasse was broken and life continued on the two campuses.[58] When Wood resigned not long after being elected to a third term, Governor Young appointed the San Jose presidential nominee, William Cooper, to be state superintendent. Subsequently, Cooper was appointed to the position of U.S. commissioner of education.[59]

* * *

In 1929, the California legislature and governor established the California Nautical School. The context for this was federal legislation authorizing the US Navy to supply ships (1874) and funds (1911) to states for the establishment of nautical schools. At the time, there were three nautical schools in the country, all on the east coast. The 1929 California legislation was specific about the objective "to give practical and theoretical instruction in navigation, seamanship, steam engines, gas engines, and electricity, in order to prepare young men for service as officers in the American merchant marine."[60] The governance of the institution, initially and for many years, was through a board of governors appointed by the governor. The school was given a training ship; federal funds, with some added by the state, supported the institution. During the height of the Depression, the school experienced substantial financial trouble and, not unlike some of the teachers college campuses, faced threats of closure. In 1933, in order to save money, all of the students/cadets and faculty/officers held classes and lived on the ship.[61]

In a sense, the nautical school was a stepchild among the California institutions. It was only somewhat like the teachers colleges or the polytechnic institute, but its academic structure evolved in a parallel way. It had its own governing board but no significant constituency. Legislators were aware, in a general sense, of its economic value to the state. Simply for practical reasons, perhaps on the theory that everything has to be someplace, the nautical school was attached to the State Department of Education and its head met with state college presidents for some periods. The head was not responsible to the state superintendent and the school's budget was separate.

The nautical school became the California Maritime Academy in 1939. Beginning in 1940, graduates received the bachelor of science degree. The academy was administratively in and out of the structure of the State Department of Education and the California State Colleges/California State University until the 1990s, when it became the twenty-second campus of the California State University. This development was in part a result of the regional accrediting commission demanding reforms in governance and accountability and in part a byproduct of tight state budgets in the early 1990s

* * *

The Depression years were difficult for the teachers colleges. Some campuses were threatened with closing. The Santa Barbara campus was struggling to maintain enrollment. The Chico and Humboldt campuses were the smallest, and they were also struggling. At Humboldt, faculty wives sponsored a "Poverty Ball" in 1933 to establish a student loan fund.[62] At the Chico campus, the faculty banded together and took a voluntary pay reduction to avoid lay off.[63]

As the teachers colleges gathered strength in the liberal arts—because they were serving as either actual junior colleges (the Fresno model, adapted on several other campuses) or de facto junior colleges—interest in becoming comprehensive colleges grew. By 1927, the seven state teachers colleges were in agreement on two issues. There should be a four-year curriculum for an elementary school credential and separate comprehensive curricula leading to bachelor's degrees in the arts and sciences and some other fields. The four-year credential was achieved. In 1930, the state superintendent had a study done about preparing teachers for secondary schools. One of the study's conclusions was to authorize the teachers colleges to have presecondary school teaching curricula. This, and the reduction of the education course requirement to twelve units for granting the baccalaureate, would lead to an increase in enrollment, particularly on campuses in urban areas, such as San Francisco, San Jose, Fresno, and San Diego. A spokesman for the University of California criticized the teachers colleges "for losing sight of their proper functions and aspiring to become regional colleges offering courses of study parallel to those of the university."[64]

In 1927, after the impasse between the state superintendent and the State Board of Education and governor, Alexander Roberts became president of San Francisco State Teachers College. He began a campaign to transform a teachers college to a state college. Some of his efforts had to do with campus life, making activities and events available to students, faculty, and the community comparable to events and activities in a conventional college or university. Some of his efforts addressed curriculum and the offering of degrees beyond the field of education. He wanted the reality of a state college. Roberts became a leader in this effort, but it cut across all seven of the campuses and over the years gathered community and legislative support.

In 1932, the legislature and governor commissioned the Carnegie Foundation for the Advancement of Teaching to study all California tax-supported higher education institutions. The group was chaired by Dr. Henry Suzzalo, the president of the foundation; the group's report is commonly known as the Suzzalo report. The teachers college leadership thought the study to be a promising move in their efforts to become state colleges, and they hoped for recognition of the very substantial accomplishments of the normal schools and state teachers colleges over the years—just a few years prior to the study, for example, California had become the first state in the nation to require a baccalaureate degree for elementary teachers, an action largely due to the leadership of the normal school faculties and presidents and the state superintendent.

The Suzzalo report was a disappointment to the state college leadership. The report was critical of the teachers colleges for offering courses and programs in the liberal arts and for doing the equivalent of upper-division work without the permission of the University of California. The report did not address qualitative matters. The solution to the "problem" identified in the report was to transfer control of the teachers colleges from the State Board of Education to the regents of the University of California. The report embodied an impoverished view of the substance of teacher education, falling back in time to teacher training rather than teacher education. The faculties and administrators of the teachers colleges, virtually to a person and with the strong leadership of the state superintendent, wished to remain with the state board and maintain their independence. They were successful in this.[65]

By 1935, the teachers colleges had reached an enrollment above seven thousand students. They continued to be strongly identified with their areas, as regional institutions, and regional populations and legislators clearly regarded their campuses as their own. The Suzzalo report may have had an unintended result. Vierling Kersey, the state superintendent of public instruction, took on the mission of changing the functions and name of the teachers colleges, and in 1935, the California State Teachers Colleges became the California State Colleges. The legislature and governor went further: the campuses were authorized to go beyond teacher education and offer undergraduate liberal arts majors in those fields that were commonly taught in secondary schools. For many purposes the state colleges were simply liberal arts colleges with a fairly comprehensive curriculum. Clearly this is how alumni of that time viewed the campuses.[66]

With this change, the colleges began growth in enrollment, growing from more than 8,000 in 1936 to nearly 12,000 in 1940–41. They declined to 5,034 at a low point during World War II, but bounced back to 20,753 in 1946–47.[67]

* * *

The California State Polytechnic Institute campus had been changing as well, but with a different mission. The institution was redefined as a junior college in 1927, but then in 1933, its existence reached a crisis point. In the 1920s, Governor Friend Richardson, a very conservative and willful leader, had proposed the abolition of the campus. Richardson took the public position that the state did not need a technical institute at any level. The legislature responded with a generous budget for the Polytechnic. Richardson cut the budget to less than half. The campus and the community fought back, but the budget cuts stood. Cal Poly's president resigned. The vice president, Margaret Chase, became acting president and joined Mary Ward, at San Francisco State, as one of the two first women to become campus presidents albeit on interim appointments. The campus struggled financially, and then the depression hit, and Cal Poly was in serious financial trouble. Talk in Sacramento was about converting it to a prison. The senator from San Luis Obispo County, Chris Jespersen, asked Vierling Kersey, the state superintendent, to have the chief of agricultural education study the campus and report on its future. The state superintendent complied, and sent a young Julian McPhee to prepare a report. McPhee recommended that the institution remain open, but with major program changes. The state superintendent accepted the report and then appointed McPhee to the presidency. However, Kersey did not want to lose McPhee, so he proposed to the governor and the legislature that McPhee hold each position, president and chief, half-time. All agreed.

A new era began for Cal Poly. Curriculum was overhauled. McPhee changed the junior college to a two-year technical college. A third year was added in 1936, a fourth year, and the capacity to confer the baccalaureate degree, in 1940. McPhee addressed the substance of curriculum and introduced many changes. One notable alteration was the introduction of the "upside-down" curriculum: students work in their major field beginning in the freshman year, while general education for the most part comes later. McPhee's quest for the capacity to confer the baccalaureate degree ran into serious opposition from the University of California, which took the position that it was the land-grant institution for California as it had been created in the context of the Morrill Act. McPhee did not dispute the UC status and programs, but rather took the position that Cal Poly's practical approach to agriculture and technical education was also needed. The legislature agreed with McPhee.

In 1938, the Voorhis School for Boys site in the Pomona area east of Los Angeles became available. President McPhee learned that Charles Voorhis, the philanthropist who had funded the residential school for underprivileged boys in 1928, wanted to donate the property and the buildings on it to some useful purpose. Voorhis had founded and built the school for his son, Jerry, to be the headmaster. Jerry was elected to Congress in 1936. Charles Voorhis had made a fortune as a founder of the automobile manufacturing company that became Pontiac when it was acquired by General Motors. McPhee visited Voorhis early in 1938; Voorhis became interested in the Cal Poly approach to education, asked for time to learn more, and in July 1938 gifted to Cal Poly 157 acres with a complement of education buildings and dormitories. The actual cost of the property and the buildings to Voorhis had been about two million dollars. The new campus opened in September 1938 as a branch of Cal Poly, with eighty students and three faculty members from the San Luis Obispo campus. The curriculum focused on agriculture.

W. K. Kellogg, the breakfast cereal magnate, had visited Pomona many times to see a favorite niece. He especially liked to get away from Battle Creek, Michigan, in the winter, and he liked the climate in Southern California. He purchased three parcels of land and created a ranch with beautiful buildings, and began to gather a collection of Arabian horses. Kellogg used the ranch as his winter home during his sixties.

As Kellogg turned seventy, his eyesight began to fail and he concluded (erroneously) that he might not have long to live. He wanted to preserve the Arabian horses and establish a center where the breed might be popularized in the United States. He thought of donating the ranch to the University of California. At first the university was not interested. Then Kellogg offered a sizeable endowment, six hundred thousand dollars, and the university agreed to accept the property and maintain the horse ranch. In May 1932, the university accepted the property, but it did not maintain the property to Kellogg's satisfaction. An extremely testy relationship developed between Kellogg and President Sproul, and Kellogg wanted to get the ranch away from the university. He used the occasion of World War II to do so, and, with the aid of connections in the state and national governments, he succeeded in transferring title to the property to the War Department as a cavalry training center. The quid pro quo for the university was keeping the endowment.

The army did no better than the university in maintaining the ranch. At the end of the war, the ranch was declared to be surplus and turned over to the United States Department of Agriculture, which explored the idea of selling the property. The leadership of Pomona Junior College (now Mt. San Antonio College) sought the property because their postwar enrollment was booming, as was the enrollment at the branch Cal Poly campus. President McPhee learned of Kellogg's interest in restoring and maintaining the ranch. He visited Kellogg, and Kellogg was impressed by McPhee's description of the Cal Poly approach to higher education. McPhee was attentive to Kellogg's Arabian horse interest, and made clear that Cal Poly would maintain the Arabian horse program. Together, Kellogg and McPhee worked through newly elected Congressman Richard Nixon (who had defeated Jerry Voorhis in the 1946 general election) to transfer the property back to the state of California and to Cal Poly. Kellogg used his access to the White House and President Truman to assist in securing congressional action to complete the transfer. The transfer of the 813-acre property became final in 1949. With the transfer, the Voorhis and Kellogg properties together became the 970-acre Kellogg-Voorhis branch campus of Cal Poly and later Cal Poly–Pomona, a separate institution.

In 1945, the name of the parent San Luis Obispo campus had been changed to California Polytechnic State College, and from this point onward Cal Poly developed with the group of state colleges.[68]

* * *

There was an interesting ambivalence among state college presidents and other leaders about the meaning of the name change from state teachers colleges to state colleges. The presidents and faculty leaders and state superintendents had fought hard for this for more than a decade, and they finally were successful. Once the designation of state teachers colleges was dropped and authority was gained to grant the baccalaureate, there was no question about student interest. Students in numbers who might have attended the University of California or private campuses in California, or colleges and universities out of state, moved to state teachers colleges and then state colleges, simply to get the bachelors degree. But the presidents and at least some faculty were not so certain. In 1939, the Council of State College Presidents adopted a mission statement that embodied this ambivalence:

The purposes and objectives of the state colleges are functions of their organic status in the public school system and are summarized as follows:

> The primary function (is) supplying the state public school system with teaching, supervisory, and administrative personnel needed for all levels included in kindergarten, elementary, junior high, and special senior high positions.
>
> Since this primary function can be performed only on a foundation of basic liberal arts curricula extending through both the lower and upper division, the curricula provided can be used to prepare our youth for such life and public services as: homemaking, social service, child guidance and parent education, municipal, county, and state government service, youth agency service, personnel service, journalism, nursing and public health, library service, etc. The curricula can also serve as foundations for advanced work in professional and learned fields. Thus the state colleges can contribute directly to two general types of young people, namely those who seek to find their adjustment to community life directly from the state college and those who will continue their formal education in graduate institutions.[69]

This ambivalence did not end soon or easily. It was a pattern of thought and behavior that persisted through the war and the tremendous growth after World War II, and was an underlying factor in the 1950s. In a sense, the question was: are the state colleges essentially teachers colleges that offer liberal arts programs that fit with teacher education (the message of the president's statement above), or are they essentially liberal arts colleges, comprehensive in nature, that offer a variety of programs including professional programs such as teacher education?

The issue was not lost on others in California's higher education leadership. The presidents of the four major universities in California had formed the California Conference on Higher Education. When they met in December 1939, President Ray Lyman Wilbur of Stanford, President Robert Milliken of the California Institute of Technology, President Rufus von KleinSmid of the University of Southern California, and President Robert Gordon Sproul of the University of California, considered a sole agenda item: the role and future of the California State Colleges. They were unanimous in their conclusion: the state colleges should be placed under the control of the regents of the University of California, and they should function as regional institutions. World War II intervened and the proposal did not get to the legislature.[70]

In the late 1930s, the campuses were to a great extent preoccupied with growth and building programs. Two of the campuses, San Diego and San Francisco, had outgrown their sites and were searching for new ones. San Diego was successful and began a move in the late 1930s. San Francisco was successful only in the abstract, as an agreement reached just prior to the World War II was delayed in its implementation by the war. At the close of the war, a substantial battle with two brothers over land acquisition and development took some years to resolve. The Stoneson brothers wanted to acquire and develop a major piece of land in southwest San Francisco near Lake Merced, the ocean, and a golf course; the land was to be developed into a large shopping center and apartment complexes. World War II brought about substantial enrollment decline on all state college campuses, just as on all college and university campuses in the country. It was in the aftermath of the war that the first GI Bill brought explosive growth to every campus. The new president of San Francisco State, J. Paul Leonard, organized political allies and students, mostly veterans, for an invasion of city hall. San Francisco State secured the necessary land, and the Stoneson brothers had to be content with a smaller development, known today as Stonestown.

In 2007, San Francisco State acquired a portion of the development for faculty and student housing. Like San Francisco State, other campuses throughout the state, having seen their enrollments spiral upwards, found a need to move out into the communities to enlarge their campuses for additional classroom buildings, parking, housing, and the like.

* * *

In 1933, the legislature forwarded a bill to the governor creating a state council for educational planning and coordination. Signed on June 10, 1933, at the height of the depression, the bill established a nine-member board, jointly appointed by the State Board of Education and the regents of the University of California. The charge to this council was "to study problems affecting the relationship between the schools of the public school system and the University of California, and to make recommendations thereon jointly to the State Board of

Education and the regents of the University of California through the superintendent of public instruction and the president of the University of California."[71] In some measure this effort was a result of the Carnegie Foundation study and an alternative to the study's recommendation that the state teachers colleges be incorporated as colleges into the University of California structure under the regents.

In 1944, Santa Barbara State College was poised to become the Santa Barbara College of the University of California. The transition was accomplished only with serious conflict. Some of the college's faculty, its president, and some Santa Barbara community leaders wanted the move, and first raised the issue in the late 1930s. Neither the regents of the University of California nor President Sproul had responded positively. As pressure continued, Sproul became more openly supportive of the move. Community pressure and the aspirations of two local legislators resulted in the introduction of a bill in 1939 (with Fresno State College included) and again in 1941; both attempts failed in the legislature. By this time, Sproul was clearly in favor of the transfer. His concern had to do with the growing significance of the state colleges. In 1943, the two legislators once again introduced legislation, this time addressing only the Santa Barbara campus; the bill passed both houses. Governor Earl Warren asked his old friend and Berkeley classmate for advice. Sproul handled the situation carefully, as the regents were split on the matter by this point. But Sproul also quietly advanced the idea that acquisition of the Santa Barbara campus could be an initial step to the regents' acquisition of the state colleges one at a time. Governor Warren signed the bill in June 1943, and nine months later, the regents approved a transition plan.

The move backfired. A new state superintendent, Roy Simpson, urged by the state board and others, proposed a constitutional amendment prohibiting the transfer of any state college. Simpson put together a formidable coalition and the amendment was adopted by the voters, with a wide margin, in November 1946.[72]

As the war drew to a close in 1945, serious planning for the postwar period was underway in California. In January 1945, prior to a meeting of the State Board of Education, an informal discussion occurred among a number of board members. Out of this came a proposal that some kind of arrangement be created so that members of both boards could participate in joint discussions of matters that affected both the university and the state colleges. A few state board members who originated this were determined to at least try to avoid a continuation of conflict with the regents. Shortly after the formal meeting, a second informal meeting took place, this time with members of the state board and the regents. This group concluded that a joint committee, created by both boards without legislative action, could be productive. Each board took action to create a joint group, although the regents moved immediately and the state board, with some members angry over Santa Barbara, delayed action for a time. The regents' motion used the wording "liaison committee," and the state board resolution spoke of "plans for the coordination of education in California . . . to promote public understanding ... and at the earliest possible moment to secure their acceptance by the legislature."[73]

The first action of the newly formed Liaison Committee was to ask for a study of the need for a four-year college or branch of the university in Sacramento. That study resulted in a recommendation that a statewide study of the organization of public higher education be done. Both the state board and the regents approved this recommendation, and the legislature and the governor launched the study, which began in mid-1947 and concluded with a report submitted to the legislature on March 1, 1948. This study, *A Report of a Survey of the Needs of California in Higher Education*, more commonly known as the Strayer report after George Strayer, an emeritus professor from Columbia University and the chair of the group that assembled the report, was influential in great measure for setting the stage for what would happen in California in the 1950s.[74] One of the recommendations in the Strayer report was to maintain the Liaison Committee and fund it to make possible a small staff to do studies and reports. The state board and the regents continued the Liaison Committee and, in 1951, began to fund it modestly, thus creating a capacity for thoughtful studies and analyses about California public higher education.

* * *

As this long-term planning was being initiated, the return of great numbers of veterans from the war began to exert pressure on the existing campuses. The greatest pressure for the creation of a state college was in the Los Angeles basin and in the Sacramento region. The pressure for a state college in Los Angeles was so substantial that no prolonged political campaign was necessary. The junior colleges in Los Angeles had absorbed the mass of veterans as they returned in 1945 and 1946. In the Los Angeles basin there were several private colleges and two substantial universities, the University of Southern California, and UCLA (the first Los Angeles state college, as it was until 1919). The state college function, a degree-granting institution with broad access, was missing. In January 1947, the Los Angeles Board of Education, which was the governing board of the then Los Angeles junior colleges, proposed the expansion of Los Angeles City College into a four-year degree-granting institution. This joined the issue of a state college for the Los Angeles basin. Student lobbyists, who were essentially veterans, went to Sacramento and the legislative halls in the capitol to advocate for the establishment of a state college. In the ensuing months the legislature acted, and on July 2, 1947, Governor Earl Warren signed the act creating Los Angeles State College. The founding president was to be P. Victor Peterson, a longtime faculty member at San Jose State College who had recently become a dean on that campus. Peterson was also appointed to the presidency of Los Angeles City College. The new state college was established on the Vermont Avenue campus of the Los Angeles City College. The campus itself has a history. It had been the campus of the Los Angeles State Normal

School, then part of the Southern Branch of the University of California (which would become UCLA), and then the community college. The Los Angeles State College (in 1949 renamed the Los Angeles State College of Applied Arts and Sciences), remained on the junior college campus in temporary buildings until the mid-1950s.

In September 1947, two months after the state college was created, six faculty members welcomed 136 students to the institution. It offered only upper-division courses and programs; lower-division courses and programs were provided by the city college. The state college would grow rapidly. Enrollment grew from 238 in 1947–48 to 3,696 in 1950–51, and then to 8,424 in 1955–56.

It was clear from the beginning that the city college location could be only temporary, but selection of a permanent site was not easy. In 1951, the state college was denied accreditation by the regional accrediting body for lack of a campus. President Howard McDonald, who had succeeded President Peterson in 1949 (Peterson went on to found the Long Beach campus that year) devoted much of his time to surveying sites. One site seriously considered, Chavez Ravine, became the home of the Los Angeles Dodgers. In 1953, a decision was made to build on a 140-acre site in the Crenshaw area, and purchase of the property by the state got as far as escrow. The University of Southern California, Loyola, and Pepperdine universities, all relatively near the site, went together to members of the legislature and succeeded in stopping the land purchase. Finally, a decision was made to locate the campus bordering East Los Angeles on its present site, on land already owned by the state. Ground was broken on the site in May 1955, eight years after the campus enrolled the first students.[75]

* * *

The Sacramento City Unified School District established Sacramento Junior College in 1916, soon after the founding of California's first junior college in Fresno. It focused almost entirely for the first dozen years on the lower-division curriculum of the University of California. In the late 1920s, "occupational training for those who cannot or should not aspire to higher levels of training" was introduced.[76]

The quest for a four-year public institution in Sacramento also began in the late 1920s. A first bill was introduced in the legislature in 1927, and subsequent bills were introduced in 1929, and in the 1930s. Opposition by the University of California to the establishment of a state teachers college or a state college in California's capital city was strong. President Robert Gordon Sproul personally testified against one proposal in a legislative hearing. City leaders and the chamber of commerce attempted to mollify the UC leadership with a proposal to make the institution a degree-granting technical and trade school. The University of California stood its ground. Its position was enhanced by the 1934 Carnegie Foundation Suzzalo report that recommended that all of the state teachers colleges be brought within the UC framework and under the regents as regional liberal arts colleges.

The end of World War II and the return of veterans—essentially the GI Bill—changed the playing field. Support, which built into a campaign, for the establishment of a four-year public college was strong in the media, in government and education groups, and among local legislators. Support diverged on one issue: Should the new institution be limited to the last two undergraduate years, and be either an extension of the junior college or solely an upper-division college? Or, alternatively, should it be a separate four-year college? In late 1946, Senator Earl Desmond introduced legislation to charge the State Board of Education and the regents to do a joint study of the provisions for public higher education in the Sacramento Valley. The legislation passed and the study was completed in May 1947. The study recommended that a four-year college be established in Sacramento, but not made permanent until a comprehensive study of the whole state was completed. The study also recommended that the junior college be maintained as a separate institution.

Desmond then introduced legislation to create a "four-year state institution of higher education" in Sacramento. The legislation did not specify that the new college be within the framework of the state colleges, and it provided for the new institution to be located on the campus of the junior college, and for courses and programs initially to be at the junior and senior levels. Governor Earl Warren signed the bill on July 1, 1947. Though the legislation did not call for the new institution to be within the state college structure, the top leadership in the California Department of Education behaved as if this was a new state college. The head of the Division of State Colleges and Teacher Education, Dr. Aubrey Douglass, took the leadership to select a president and get the campus underway. The state board, upon the recommendation of Dr. Roy Simpson, then a relatively new state superintendent of public instruction, appointed Dr. Guy West, a dean and former registrar at Chico State College, as the founding president. West would remain president for eighteen years. On September 22, 1947, two hundred and thirty-five students registered for classes. In June 1948, the first commencement was held: John J. Collins, a transfer student from the Berkeley campus, received his degree in history.

As the selection process for a permanent site for the new college got underway in early 1948, the Sacramento school board renamed Sacramento College as Sacramento Junior College, in order to avoid confusion with the new state college. This name change triggered anxiety for some reason, and initiated a campaign to keep the new state college on the existing junior college campus. Other sites were considered, including the state fair grounds, then being abandoned by the fair for a new site. The campaign to locate the state college on the junior college site was quite intense. Belle Coolidge, the first woman mayor of Sacramento and a former vice president of the junior college, weighed in. The final decision was the responsibility of the State Public Works Board. A site next to the American River in the east of Sacramento was chosen.[77] With the site selected, Senator Desmond introduced legislation to recognize Sacramento State College as a part of the state college network.

The early years of "Sac State" were growth years. Enrollment increased from 235 in fall 1947 and 594 in spring 1948 to 1,894 in 1950–51, and 4,404 in 1955–56. The curriculum in these years was developed with a heavy emphasis on teacher education, due in part to a regional demand for teachers as a result of Central Valley growth, and in part to the interests and inclinations of President West and those he selected to be on the founding and early staffs. The college's rapid growth crowded the junior college campus; it became time for the state college to move. In 1951, construction on the American River campus began on a hop farm purchased from a local family. The physical move took place in 1953; its slogan was "Go East With West."

* * *

In this period of great growth in the state colleges a number of significant events occurred. In 1945, with the end of the war, colleges were authorized to give a fifth year of instruction, essentially to prepare teachers for all subjects in secondary schools. This move was followed in early 1948 by authorization to grant the master's degree, though this was limited to degrees granted in conjunction with education credential programs.[78]

The Strayer report went to the legislature in March of 1948.[79] The report had been written and assembled while the new campuses in Los Angeles and Sacramento were being opened. The legislature had asked that five issues be addressed: "an evaluation of the current and future needs . . . for education beyond . . . high school; an analysis of each area of the state for higher education facilities . . . ; an analysis of the needs of varying types of . . . institutions; consideration of desirable changes in the organization of public higher education; and (financial) support."[80] The report addressed a number of aspects of the state colleges, including minimum and maximum enrollments. Limitations on the capacity of smaller campuses, with twelve to fifteen hundred students, to offer comprehensive programs, were noted. Enrollment at the Chico and Humboldt campuses was expected to be stabilized at no more than fifteen hundred, with emphasis on teacher education and a small number of "occupational curricula." The campuses in urban areas were expected to grow to a maximum of five thousand students, and not beyond; the report argued that "experience shows that when a student body grows to more than five thousand, it becomes unwieldy. This size would permit these larger campuses to offer "a wide array of specialized curricula."[81]

While the study was underway, legislation was passed that defined the functions of the state colleges:

> The primary function of the state colleges is the training of teachers. State colleges also may offer courses appropriate for a general or liberal education and for

responsible citizenship, offer vocational training in such fields as business, industry, public services, homemaking, and social service, and offer the preprofessional courses needed by students who plan to transfer to universities for advanced professional study. Courses in military science and tactics may be given in conformance with the laws of the United States made and provided with reference to ROTC units in educational institutions.[82]

The Strayer group noted without comment that the state colleges, in offering "vocational training," included fields such as nursing, engineering, and journalism. These areas, particularly engineering, were sensitive with the University of California. Because of this, the report urged that engineering in the state colleges be limited to "practical engineering," and that a special study group be established by the University of California and the California State Colleges to "set up precise definitions of the distinctive aims and programs carried on by the University and the state colleges." A similar concern was expressed about journalism.[83]

Perhaps the most important dimension of the Strayer report was an emphasis on the allocation of functions among the junior colleges, the University of California, and the state colleges. The Fresno, San Jose, Chico, and Humboldt campuses included a junior college function (the San Diego campus had ended its junior college function shortly before the writing of the report). Fresno and San Jose had contracts with local school districts to do this. The Strayer report recommended that these campuses withdraw from the junior college function. The report made an exception for the Chico and Humboldt campuses, as the regions surrounding the campuses did not have junior colleges and did not have a population base to support the establishment of junior colleges. Similarly, the report addressed the linkage of the state colleges to the University of California, and carefully limited the state college role. "The state colleges are not responsible for graduate work involving research, nor for education for the professions with the exception of teaching."[84]

What the report did not do was discern the impact that the junior college function being carried out by many of the state colleges had had on state college programs and, ultimately, mission. The mixture of the junior college function, going as far back as the founding of the Fresno State Normal School in 1911, had provided some of the state colleges the opportunity to develop a full range of liberal arts programs. After the transition to state college status in 1935, many of the campuses used the junior college function to develop professional programs, first at the lower-division level, and then for the award of baccalaureate degrees. As mentioned above, engineering was the most sensitive of these developments and was the occasion of studies and some serious issues between the University of California, which sought to limit growth in engineering and the state colleges in the 1950s.

The Strayer report also addressed discrepancies in the application of the rules for admission; these varied among the state college campuses in 1947. The formal rules stated that high school graduates (and others deemed to have equivalent preparation) could be admitted on the basis of "fitness to profit by college instruction, such fitness to be shown by previous scholastic records, by evidence of good moral character and personal qualifications, and by a satisfactory score and standard college aptitude test."[85] In fact, from their earliest years as normal schools, the state colleges had had varying practices not only among campuses but on each campus, practices that changed over time and with campus administrations, as enrollments were sought or contained. The report recommended that "stricter admission requirements" be put in place and implicitly that these be uniform, but it did not propose what those requirements might be.

The report responded directly to the legislature's request to determine the need for additional institutions. From time to time the idea of expanding one or another junior college to a four-year degree granting institution would be proposed. The report bluntly opposed this for any junior college. The survey committee working with the authors of the report concurred with the action of the legislature to establish state college campuses in Sacramento and Los Angeles. The report went one step further and recommended the establishment of an additional campus in southeast Los Angeles or northern Orange counties. On the more general question of establishing new four-year institutions elsewhere in the state, the report concluded that there would be no need for any additional campuses of either the state colleges or the University of California until at least the early 1960s.

The Strayer group also addressed the governance and administration of the state colleges. No change was proposed in the governing board structure, although the importance of the annual meeting of the State Board of Education largely devoted to the state colleges was emphasized. The relevant statute required that each president, or a member of the faculty, attend or participate in this special meeting. The role of the state superintendent/director of education was emphasized. The report was forceful regarding the need for a central staff in the Department of Education to plan for and administer, in a general policy sense, the state colleges. The report pointedly addressed the need for this central office to have financial responsibility, held up to that time by the Department of Finance, the governor's budget arm.

The importance of the Liaison Committee, whose first action had been to ask the legislature to authorize the Strayer study, was stressed emphatically. The report clearly stated that it would be unrealistic to expect the many matters of public higher education in California to develop productively without some coordinating body. The recommendation was to continue the Liaison Committee and give it a budget. Finally, in a closing section titled "The State of California Has Ample Resources to Meet Its Educational Responsibilities" the report simply asserted what the section title stated: California had more than enough money "to finance the entire educational program, from kindergarten through graduate work."[86]

The Strayer report referred to the need to strengthen a central administrative structure for the state colleges. Shortly before the report was written, the state superintendent and the state board had created a new office and position, that of associate superintendent for the Division of State Colleges and Teacher Education. The first associate superintendent, Aubrey Douglass, was a strong and thoughtful administrator and a forceful advocate for the state colleges. He was central to the establishment of the new campuses in Sacramento and Los Angeles in 1947, and personally identified the presidents. For the first time a central office, very small in size and with a modest professional staff, was in a position to look at the state colleges as a whole. The associate superintendent worked with the presidents, and began to address statewide concerns with the group of state colleges. A paragraph in the Strayer report reflected this new sense of the character of the campuses and the shared values of the institutions.

> Whatever the legal and administrative ethics of the situation, the fact remains that the state colleges have developed into institutions responsive to the educational problems and demands of the areas they serve. Although the student body of a state college will contain students from outside the local area, and although training will be offered which has general as well as local appeal, a state college is primarily concerned with the region it serves. The state colleges have strong local support.[87]

The report noted that the California Polytechnic College was the exception, as an institution whose fundamental statewide mission and programs were unique to that campus.

Clearly, the Strayer group understood, accepted, and urged the regional and popular base of the campuses. The report and the creation of the new office in the State Department of Education was an early indication of a needed transition from what was a group of separate colleges into a system. The report created a new understanding of the state colleges. They were no longer to be single campuses located around the state; they would instead be institutions with shared missions, though not identical programs, and organized to be a part of publicly provided higher education in California.

In 1949, the legislature established a structure for local campus advisory boards. Each campus would have a board of citizens, seven to thirteen in number, nominated by the campus president and appointed by the state superintendent/director of education. The advisory boards had no authority. Individual presidents used them differently; some involved boards heavily in internal affairs and in building community relations, while others virtually ignored them and their members. The one campus exception to the requirement for advisory boards was Cal Poly. As in many matters, the education code would have two sections, one section for all of the campuses except Cal Poly and the other section for Cal Poly alone. This distinction was a result of Cal Poly's unique statewide mission and the extraordinary political strength and ability of Julian McPhee, the campus president from 1933 to 1966 and the man who built the modern Cal Poly, a strong and stable campus. To this date, McPhee is the longest serving California State University president, and only a few others have come close.

The Strayer group's recommendation for a new campus in Southwest Los Angeles–Northern Orange County was positively received, the enrollment pressure in the Los Angeles Basin pushing the issue. The legislature acted by appropriating one hundred and twenty-five thousand dollars to start a new state college, and Governor Earl Warren signed the legislation on January 27, 1949. P. Victor Peterson was appointed president; two years earlier he had been appointed the founding president of the Los Angeles campus. The site for the new campus had not been selected. This was left to Peterson and ultimately the State Public Works Board.

As with other new state college campuses, competition for the location of the new campus arose. The area it was to serve included a number of developing communities, among them Fullerton, Lakewood, and Santa Ana, in addition to Long Beach. A Long Beach developer, Lloyd Wheley, was building housing tracts with apartments and homes in Rancho Los Alamitos area of Long Beach, and he approached President Peterson about making temporary space available. Peterson accepted the offer. Classes began on September 26, 1949, in the temporary quarters, comprising converted apartments, garages, and the like.

The college's initial emphasis was on the education of teachers, and faculty appointments reflected this. On the first day of classes, 169 students were taught by nineteen faculty members. As with Los Angeles and Sacramento, Long Beach opened offering classes only for the last two years of undergraduate instruction. The first graduation was in June 1950, with thirty-one students receiving baccalaureate degrees.

During this first year, the state began a search for a permanent campus location. Two communities seriously entered the competition, and put measures on the June 1950 primary election ballot to support the purchase of a campus site. Voters in Fullerton turned down a four hundred and fifty thousand dollar bond measure. Voters in Long Beach approved one million dollars, to come from the city's revenue from oil at Signal Hill in mid–Long Beach. In addition, the Bixby Estate donated land for a campus. The Long Beach site, 320 acres in East Long Beach at Los Alamitos, was selected. The name of the college was changed to Long Beach State College. In the opening 1949–50 year, enrollment grew in the second semester from 169 to 694 students; in 1950–51, enrollment was 1,058; and in 1955–56, it rose to 5,568.[88]

* * *

The 1950s saw a pattern of growth both in student numbers and in program and organization throughout the system. With the three new campuses, the number of institutions totaled ten. Nine of the campuses were still significantly the heirs of the teachers college model, while the tenth, Cal Poly, which had come out of a vocational education model, was a polytechnic institution. The presidents of the other nine campuses—Humboldt, Chico, Sacramento, San Francisco, San Jose, Fresno, Los Angeles, Long Beach, and San Diego—were from the field of teacher education. Most of the senior academic administrators were as well.

The presidents met monthly in Sacramento. Their meetings were chaired by the associate superintendent. In late 1949, the presidents had asked the director of the State Department of Finance and his staff to undertake a study of the organization of the state colleges. The first segment of the study was completed in the summer of 1950, and James Dean, Finance's director, sent it with a transmittal letter to the state superintendent/director of education on October 5, 1950. The study outlined a model organization for a state college campus. It also addressed the Maritime Academy.[89]

The Maritime Academy occupied an ambiguous position in California government, from its founding in 1929 until the 1990s. In many ways it was treated like a state college, and its president met with the state college presidents monthly, though this was sporadic over the years, and the Maritime Academy had its own statutory governing board, appointed by the governor. Perhaps the great equalizer was the Department of Finance, that unit of California government reporting directly to the governor and holding the purse strings. In California state government, the governor sends "the governor's budget" to the legislature, and it is the Department of Finance that prepares the budget. Thus it is not surprising that Finance would include the Maritime Academy in a study of campus administration.

The organizational structure for the campuses was to be uniform. Significantly, the preamble to the study stated unambiguously that "the scope of activity of the colleges has changed significantly until they can now be classified as large liberal arts colleges."[90] The study was imaginative, and in a way anticipated events to come. "It appears that the appreciation of the effect of these changes is noticeably less at each level in the administrative hierarchy, beginning with the colleges themselves, and going through the departments of Education and Finance, and the legislature and its committee . . . they have developed into . . . regional institutions. . . . The Education Code neither prohibits nor recognizes this situation."[91] To address this, the study recommended a standard pattern of organization for most of the campuses, with four deans and a business manager reporting to the president, and specific positions reporting to each of the five members who constituted a president's leadership team. This kind of very specific approach is typical of the Department of Finance of that time.

The study anticipated large campuses (five thousand or more students) and two small campuses (three thousand or fewer students). The study also recognized that there would need to be "minor variations" and addressed these: for the Los Angeles campus, which emphasized student internships, staff to develop and monitor these; for the Fresno campus, which had an agriculture program, an extra dean for agriculture; for Chico and Humboldt, the "small campuses," fewer management positions; for the Maritime Academy, emphasis in labeling positions using an educational vocabulary.[92]

The study, in some ways, was ahead of its time. It recommended an administrative council for each campus, not an unusual recommendation in higher education, though it did go so far as to suggest which dean (by title) should chair it so that the president could play a free and inquiring role. It also recommended a "faculty council," not an unusual recommendation in the academic world. The campuses were born from a normal school–teachers college model, even the three new campuses, and the resistance of presidents to an elected faculty council was unanimous and persistent. This was to be a theme and an issue for years to come.[93]

Finally, the study acknowledged the existence of college foundations, or corporations, "for the purpose of facilitating the operation of functions which are impossible or difficult to achieve under state procedures." Two types of activity were at that time typically administered by foundations. The first included business activities such as bookstores, food service, farms supporting the agriculture programs, and the like, all of which needed flexibility. The second was defined as the purchase of land when state funds were not available. Finance described a set of commonsensical rules that legitimized a range of freedom and activity for campuses and created moving room for institutional development.[94]

This study was important for the development of all of the campuses. The leadership on the campuses understood this variously. The principal author of the implementing report for this study, Everett Chandler, was immediately appointed to a dean's position created by the report at the Cal Poly campus; President Julian McPhee was, as always, ready to move the Cal Poly campus forward and in new directions.

* * *

In 1951, the legislature, prompted by campus presidents, established a state college council. This was to be a lay group, appointed by the governor and including one member from each campus advisory board, one member of the board of governors of the Maritime Academy, and one member appointed upon the nomination of the president of the California State Polytechnic College. The state superintendent/director of education was an ex-officio member. The council's specific charge was to "study and make recommendations for the improvement of the organization and administration of the state colleges and the California Maritime Academy."[95] The appointments made by Governor Earl Warren were on the whole distinguished and included Theodore Meriam of Chico, a future chair of the yet-to-be-created board of trustees of the California State Colleges. The members of the council took their work seriously. The full council met with all of the presidents, most of the campus business managers, state officials, and the like. Individual council members met with campus members and community groups.

The council recommendations were generally cautious, given the magnitude of the developing state colleges and the need for clarity about the work of the junior colleges, the University of California, and the state colleges. The principal recommendation was for the creation of a "State College Board to be appointed by the Governor, and under the jurisdiction of the State Board of Education, to give adequate attention to the responsibilities, the activities, and the development of the state college system."[96] This was not the first time this approach had been discussed; a legislative committee had proposed it in 1949. The proposal was the recognition of the fact that as the state colleges had grown over the years, the State Board of Education had not functioned as a governing board.

Other council report recommendations included the designation of the state superintendent/director as the chief executive officer of the proposed board; provision for at least two joint meetings each year of the State Board of Education and the proposed state college board; a change in the state constitution to provide for the State Board of Education to appoint the state superintendent (this had been proposed many times over the years, and it was a politically unwise proposal in this context). In its concluding statement, the report rather ambiguously walked both sides of the street about the autonomy of the campuses and the need for statewide coordination and organization.[97]

The presidents of the state colleges responded carefully, but, essentially, they did not support the report. They did not want to see their local influence and authority diminished. With the growth of enrollment in the colleges, the institutions and their presidents had become important political factors in their regions and with members of the legislature. In the churning atmosphere of public higher education of the time, the report more or less disappeared, while it became a piece of the puzzle, the overall pattern and complexity of activities that would eventually lead to the Master Plan.

The presidents had their own group. The Council of State College Presidents had been formed in the 1930s during the period of the transition from state teachers colleges to state colleges.[98] The council's formation was an early recognition that the state colleges had some linkages and some commonality. The Strayer report as well as the work of the Liaison Committee greatly reinforced the presidents' sense of a need to work together, at least on some matters. In 1952, the presidents completed, with help from the State Department of Education staff, a codification of their roles. In fact, it was a description of how state colleges functioned. Perhaps the most telling paragraphs are early in the document.

> Neither state laws nor state regulations have attempted to outline in detail the procedures to be followed in administering the colleges at the local level. Even the administration of the local institutions is a matter which is to be governed by prevailing practice in the profession of school administration, . . . it is obvious that California state laws and regulations assume a high degree of local autonomy in the administration of state colleges. The president is responsible for selecting and recommending all personnel for appointment, for organizing, directing, and supervising the faculty and staff, for maintaining satisfactory relations with the students and the public, and for reporting to and taking directions from the appropriate state authorities.[99]

The presidents clearly had in mind the authority they and their institutions needed. It fell into three categories: financial administration, personnel administration, and the building program. The level of detailed bureaucratic control from state agencies such as the Department of Finance over the campuses was substantial. Among the most egregious control excesses was out-of-state travel. After a request was considered at the campus level, if approved, it would go to the State Department of Education, and then, if there were no objections, to the governor's office. All personnel actions, such as appointments, tenure, civil service status for the staff, and promotions, had to be approved by the superintendent/director and the State Board of Education; on personnel matters, the process was only pro forma, but it nonetheless had to be followed. All capital outlay projects down to the smallest detail, even after inclusion by the legislature and governor in the budget process, had to be approved by the Department of Education, the Department of Finance, and the State Public Works Board, and then be designed by the state architect and staff. The presidents were requesting more autonomy and administrative flexibility and less second-guessing and micromanagement.

Yet the presidents and their colleagues functioned well for the most part. Beginning at about the turn of the twentieth century, the history of the normal schools, state teachers colleges, and state colleges is one of great local autonomy regarding the substance of educational programs. The very early years, the nineteenth century, saw interference with the campuses; for the most part this was political—pitting local boards (which then had the power of presidential, faculty and staff appointment) against the governor and state superintendent who had always been players. It was in the years after World War II, the era of growth, that the need for collaborative administration and some measure of governance and action came to the fore. This is when the presidents as a group emerged with some force. Presidents, who were universally out of teachers college, public school, and education disciplinary backgrounds, did not on the whole want to cede power.

For all practical purposes, the Council of State College Presidents was the governing board of the state colleges. State Department of Education leadership was preoccupied with the administration and leadership of a mushrooming public K-12 system. For a time, there was a strong associate superintendent, and he used his strength to collaborate with the presidents. State Board of Education actions were perfunctory, for the most part, even to the point of approving the superintendent's selection of presidents and certainly the approval of new academic program and degree proposals. Moreover, the campus presidents and their staffs were independent lobbyists in Sacramento, each president lobbying for campus buildings and programs and budgets.

* * *

The years of the early 1950s also saw extraordinary activity on the campuses. Enrollments were growing substantially. From 1950 to 1953, enrollments increased by one-third.[100] New faculty members were recruited, and the greatest number of these were in the arts and sciences, and in newly emerging professional fields such as business, nursing, and engineering.

In 1951, the Liaison Committee acquired professional staff, one from the University of California and one from the State Department of Education (the latter to represent both the state and junior colleges). This development resulted from a request unanimously made by the committee, which was made up of members of both the regents and the state board. It was clear that these two staff members were to work together, and while each was responsible to their superiors, the president of the university and the state superintendent, as a team they were responsible to the two boards (regents and state board) and their executive officers.

These two professional positions became the joint staff. The initial two interim staff members were drawn from existing faculty; one from the UCLA law faculty and the other from Sacramento State College. A recruitment process was initiated and two individuals subsequently were appointed. These individuals were to have substantial impact on events as they unfolded. Dr. Thomas Holy was brought from Ohio State University, where he had been the director of the Bureau of Educational Research, to be the University of California staff member. Dr. Hubert Semans, previously the dean of liberal arts at Cal Poly, was named the State Department of Education staff member. The two began their work together in September 1952. The regents and state board had both approved all recommendations of the Liaison Committee to this point (save one about scholarships, on which the regents took no action). Both boards largely implemented these actions.[101]

One of the early actions of the joint staff was a proposal to the Liaison Committee that the study of higher education be resumed. The committee members agreed and took the proposal to their respective boards, which also agreed. The legislature was asked to appropriate funds and did so, allocating one hundred and twelve thousand dollars.[102] The proposal that had gone to the legislature called for the appointment of a full-time "chief consultant," with other staff consultants and advisory committee members as needed. The appointment went to T. R. McConnell, the chancellor of the University of Buffalo and a respected individual in the national higher education community.[103] The assumption that faculty and staff from the University of California, the junior colleges, and the state colleges would be available to assist this effort was made explicit by both boards. Thus was born "A Restudy of the Needs of California Higher Education." The legislature called for the restudy to be completed and reported by 1955.

The two joint staff members and the chief consultant prepared a plan and submitted it to the two boards. Four major areas were to be studied: (1) enrollments in all of California higher education, public and private, by 1955, 1960, and 1965, and the resulting facilities needed; (2) the "functions, organization, and educational programs for all of California higher education, the three public segments and the private institutions with particular reference to such differentiation of function as seems appropriate" within the three types of publicly supported institutions; (3) the government and administration of public higher education; and (4) the financing of both public and private higher education. Individuals from private education were immediately brought into significant roles in the restudy.

A number of assumptions for the restudy were made explicit. These included:

1. "Existing enrollment predictions are conservative;
2. The state will continue to make higher education available at low cost;
3. Governance of public higher education will continue to be divided, not consolidated;
4. A differentiation of functions, so far as possible, of the three segments of public higher education, namely the University of California, the state colleges, and the junior colleges, is imperative if unnecessary and wasteful duplication is to be kept at a minimum;
5. The coordination of all of higher education will be voluntary;
6. The public junior college system should continue to be developed and receive support;
7. Private colleges and universities should continue to be a significant part of all higher education in California;
8. Both the University of California and the state colleges should be integrated systems;
9. The major responsibility for research should continue to belong to the University of California;
10. Student housing and state scholarships should be developed to open access for students living beyond commuting range of existing campuses; and
11. Another review of all California higher education should be accomplished in 1960."[104]

The restudy was submitted to the legislature on February 7, 1955. Its recommendations were intended to be substantive and to provide a blueprint for the continuing development of higher education in the state. The first recommendation was clear and straightforward stating that: "No new state colleges and no new campuses of the University of California be established before 1965, and the potential enrollment be cared for by expanding the facilities of the present institutions. . . ."[105] This recommendation noted that enrollment ceilings at both the University of California and state college campuses should be lifted. The UC and state colleges were asked to reduce lower-division enrollments in favor of upper-division and graduate enrollments, and to support the most substantial growth of the junior colleges and their preparation of lower-division students for transfer.

The functions of the state colleges were addressed carefully and with considerable vision for the colleges' changed nature. The mission of the state colleges that the members of the restudy team saw was not a product of a political compromise, but a substantive educational mission. The report acknowledged the legislature's 1949 action of restating teacher education as the colleges' primary function, and from this premise built an analysis of what the state colleges do—the variety among the campuses, the wide range of programs offered, and the impact of the University of California's "highly selective" admission standards. Flexibility for the campuses, a capacity to address changing circumstances, and public needs for higher education were noted, and for the first time the importance of faculty scholarship was seriously identified.[106] The vocabulary of the day included the phrase "occupational education," and this translated into a variety of undergraduate professional programs and the beginning of these programs at the master's degree level. The telling paragraph was:

> The state colleges have functions to perform in the State's diversified program of public higher education that are distinct from those of the junior colleges on the one hand, and from those of the University of California on the other. Some degree of overlapping among all three types of institutions is, of course, inevitable and desirable.... But the differences should be cultivated as well as the similarities, if the widely varied needs of the commonwealth and the equally diverse needs of students are to be effectively and efficiently served.[107]

The report went on to address the master's degree in occupational or professional fields as well as in the liberal arts and sciences. The restudy team joined the issue and recommended that the master's degree might be conferred by state colleges in occupational/professional fields, following a careful and defined process. Earlier policy about master's degrees had been based on developing curricula in areas taught in high schools, and the degree was accompanied by a credential. The report asked that the governing board of the state colleges study how to create the capacity to confer master's degrees in the liberal arts and sciences without the education courses requirement.[108]

At the time of the restudy, in 1954 and 1955, the state colleges were actively examining freshmen admission standards. There were two issues to address. The first was the defined admissions standards to be used by all campuses for freshmen admission (Chico and Humboldt, the campuses retaining a junior college function, theoretically could admit students either to their junior college or the state college). The second issue was the widely varying application of admissions standards (in the California Administrative Code) by the campuses. The restudy recommended a review and raising of the standards, and this was done by the colleges in late 1955, and ultimately approved by the State Board of Education.[109] The report noted that data about student performance was minimal, and the governing board needed to cause serious studies of student performance and many other matters.

The restudy report tackled the politically sensitive matter of statewide governance of the state colleges. Essentially, the restudy group had found that there were few, if any, systematic approaches to governance at the state level. There were no formal procedures for the approval of curriculum—not simply courses, but entire degree programs.[110] The restudy staff did an analysis of minutes of meetings of the State Board of Education for a four and one-half year period, and of verbatim transcripts for one of those years. The analysis revealed that what little time was spent on state college matters was devoted mainly to routine required approvals, and that the rare policy discussions were mostly superficial. The report concluded that the real governing board was the Council of State College Presidents. "So far, without a great deal of planning, the state colleges have changed from two-year normal and teacher training schools to large five-year liberal arts colleges offering numerous specializations in liberal arts and occupational fields. These changes have generally come about because of local and statewide pressures on the individual colleges and on the authorities in control of the institutions as a group."[111]

The report analyzed several models of governance, including one developed by the legislatively created State College Council of 1951, the proposal for a state college board to be responsible to the State Board of Education. All of the models that were essentially adaptations of the existing structure were found wanting. Moreover, the practical working relationships of the colleges with the state superintendent/director of education as the theoretical chief executive officer for the state colleges were found wanting, as were those of the small Division of State Colleges and Teacher Education in the State Department of Education with both the colleges and the state superintendent. The Council of State College Presidents had simply moved—"drifted" might be a better word—into a vacuum of leadership and procedure. The restudy proposed that a new nine-member state board be created to govern the state colleges; eight members were to be appointed by the governor, with the state superintendent as an ex-officio member. The State College Board would appoint a "chief administrative officer," who would in turn create a central administrative office to address educational policy and programs, financial matters, and the general operations of the campuses.[112] This was the first formal proposal for a separate state college board and administration responsible to the legislature and the governor.

A repeated theme through the restudy was that the state colleges should be understood as and should function as an entity, not as a collection. Unlike the University of California, which grew from a single institution branching out through the state, each state college had been established separately and had its own constituency, and presidential and political behavior. With the exception of Cal Poly, each of them had a strong, central base in their regions; Cal Poly's base was statewide, in the agricultural community and, to a very substantial extent, in the strong relationships the institution's longtime president, Julian McPhee, had cultivated with the legislature and with its members individually.[113] Bringing the state colleges together as an entity was to be a central issue for discussions and actions about the state colleges for the 1950s and 1960s. The restudy did not suggest that an individual state college abandon its regional base, but rather that the regional bases be built upon to create also a coherent whole.

The restudy had an impact. It made one hundred and forty recommendations. The Liaison Committee adopted eighty-nine of these. The state board, in turn, approved seventy-eight of these, and the regents approved thirty-five. The restudy had sought to bring the principles of differentiation of function spelled out in the Strayer report into concrete reality by applying them to curricular fields.[114] The overriding factor at that moment in 1955 was the explosion of enrollment and of programs. The most significant impact of the restudy was to further set the scene for the Master Plan study in 1959, and to explicitly put on the table the comprehensive mission of the state colleges and the issue of their governance.

* * *

At the end of World War II, the San Fernando Valley was still an area of orchards, horse ranches, and agriculture, not yet a bedroom community for Los Angeles. As John Broesamle, the author of a history of California State University, Northridge, stated, "The building explosion that transformed the San Fernando Valley into suburbia largely followed World War II. The automobile was the fuse."

The Los Angeles State College of Applied Arts and Sciences was established in 1947 as an upper-division and graduate institution. For its initial years it was in temporary quarters. After five years, funds were appropriated to purchase a site. There was competition among communities in the Los Angeles Basin for the location of the campus. The State Department of Education had excluded the San Fernando Valley as a site. When a site finally was selected in 1952 in the Baldwin Hills area of Los Angeles, intense opposition developed. Assembly Member Julian Beck, a member from the San Fernando Valley and the Democratic floor leader, introduced an assembly concurrent resolution (ACR), a move that is designed to express the sense of the body on an issue. This resolution asked the State Public Works Board to rescind its earlier site selection of the Los Angeles campus and reopen the process, specifically including the San Fernando Valley. The ACR passed with a good margin in both the assembly and state senate. The State Public Works Board rescinded the Baldwin Hills selection, and then selected a San Fernando Valley site, only to be overruled by the director of finance, who had chosen the earlier Los Angeles site, located not far from "downtown" Los Angeles, the present site of California State University Los Angeles.

The president of the Los Angeles campus, Howard McDonald, had previously been president of Brigham Young University and was experienced in working with a community. McDonald sought permission to open a branch of the college in the San Fernando Valley. At the same time, he asked Warner Masters, the Los Angeles campus business manager, to arrange a dinner with the greater Los Angeles legislative delegation. The goal was explicit: to acquire a site for yet another state college campus in the Los Angeles area. On December 21, 1954, Masters and several of his colleagues hosted a dinner at the Brown Derby for twenty-one members of the assembly and two senators. At the conclusion of the dinner, the legislators agreed to sponsor legislation in the next regular session, in 1955, to acquire a site for another campus. Coincidentally, on December 21 the State Department of Education gave permission to Los Angeles State College to start a branch in the San Fernando Valley.

The members followed through. Legislation to create a branch campus passed in 1955, and the legislation provided for purchase of a site. In the meantime, the Los Angeles campus began classes at the San Fernando High School in rented quarters. President McDonald appointed Delmar Oviatt, an administrator from the Los Angeles campus, as dean for the San Fernando Valley campus. Oviatt was to play a major role for the next dozen years in defining the character of the campus, though he did not become its president. McDonald also had faculty and administrators at the Los Angeles campus rough out curricula. With a site purchased for a branch, groundbreaking occurred in January 1956.

Julian Beck, the legislator who had started this process, was appointed to the bench in 1954. He was succeeded in the legislature by Allen Miller, his former law partner. In 1957, Miller introduced legislation to create San Fernando Valley State College. It passed both houses easily and quickly, and Governor Goodwin Knight signed it. The new state college was to come into being July 1, 1958. The selection of a founding president was the responsibility of State Superintendent Roy Simpson, with the approval of the State Board of Education. The common wisdom was that the dean of the branch, Delmar Oviatt, would be the appointee. Earlier, President McDonald had said he wanted the position, but he backed away. Oviatt was personable and liked by many, but he was also authoritarian, particularly with respect to finances and budgets, and he evidenced a strong leaning to the tradition of state colleges with an emphasis on teacher education.

Simpson surprised everyone, picking a junior college president, Ralph Prator of Bakersfield College. Prator had a strong academic background for that time, with bachelor's and master's degrees in history from the University of Colorado and teaching and administrative experience on that campus; among other roles, he had been director of admissions at Colorado. Along the way, he had completed a doctorate in educational administration at UC Berkeley.

Prator started working at the campus five months before he assumed formal responsibility, and kept around him key administrators who had come from the Los Angeles campus, including Oviatt. San Fernando Valley State College officially opened July 1, 1958. The values of the new college had been importantly affected by its initial establishment as a branch of the Los Angeles State College of Applied Arts and Sciences. President McDonald had been very open and emphatic that the San Fernando campus would not have the business-industrial-vocational bias that Los Angeles had had at its beginning. Many thought of the San Fernando Valley campus as a liberal arts college, but it developed virtually from the beginning with a blend of liberal arts and professional programs. Unlike the Los Angeles campus, the new college opened with a full lower-division and general education program. Faculty from the Los Angeles campus were given the option of moving to the new campus. Almost one hundred volunteered and about thirty were selected. In the opening year of the new college, the student population was 3,658—a sizeable institution from the first day.[115]

* * *

In the 1955 legislative session, bills were introduced to establish nineteen new state colleges. In 1956, the Liaison Committee of the regents and the State Board of Education undertook a study, formally titled, "A Study of the Need for Additional Centers of Public Higher Education in California." The study went to the legislature and others in 1957.[116] Not as firm in its conclusions as the 1955 restudy, this study focused on the importance of the differentiation of functions, a need for additional junior colleges, and adequate support for existing institutions.[117]

Pressure for additional state colleges continued. The idea for one in Orange County had been under discussion since the late 1940s. The legislation that established the Long Beach campus had specified that it be in Orange County or southwestern Los Angeles County, and there had been strong expectation, especially among people in Orange County, that it would be in Orange County. The idea did not go away. In 1957, numerous bills for new campuses were again introduced. One of the most persistent advocates was Senator John Murdy of Orange County. In the give and take of the legislative session, a rivalry developed between Orange County and a coalition of San Bernardino and Riverside counties. Murdy prevailed and the bill to establish Orange County State College passed and was signed by Governor Knight.[118]

In some measure it was a product of rivalry between the northern and southern parts of the state. The north had San Francisco, San Jose, Sacramento, Chico, and Humboldt state colleges. Fresno and Cal Poly, in the central part of the state, were north of the Tehachapi Mountains. The south had San Diego, Los Angeles, Long Beach, and a Cal Poly branch at Pomona. There was a drive to establish another campus in the San Francisco Bay Area, in the East Bay. The broker in the legislative debate was Senator Nelson Dilworth of Riverside County. Riverside and San Bernardino were then not populous counties, and Riverside already had a University of California facility, an agricultural station. Dilworth proposed to Murdy that he join with the East Bay forces and pair establishment of two new campuses. That strategy would turn out to be successful.

State Superintendent Roy Simpson moved quickly to establish the new Orange County college. There had been strong opposition from the University of California to the creation of the campus. Simpson phoned Dr. William Langsdorf, then the president of Pasadena City College, to offer him the presidency. Langsdorf asked for time to think about the offer, and he ultimately accepted. A significant factor for Langsdorf in accepting the position was his understanding that the state colleges had moved beyond the teachers college phase; he would be building a college focused on the liberal arts and education for the professions.

As usual, the site selection process was competitive. The position that the campus should be located in relationship to the Long Beach and Pomona campuses prevailed, and a site in Fullerton was selected. Langsdorf took charge of the establishment of the new campus quickly. The initial appropriation to start the campus in the 1959–60 year was very small and did not contemplate having students the first year. Langsdorf thought that idea unwise for a variety of reasons, among them the opposition of the University of California. Superintendent Simpson and Langsdorf were in agreement, and went to the newly elected governor, Edmond G. (Pat) Brown for support. The UC pressured Brown to delay the campus opening, but Brown sided with the new state college. The college opened with only a short planning period of a few months.

As Langsdorf recruited faculty, he sought a deliberate break with convention. He did not recruit faculty from other state colleges, as he saw the established campuses still locked in, to some extent, to the past. He did not recruit from the University of California (with two exceptions), as he saw a disdain prevalent in the university for the state colleges (he had earned his PhD in history at UCLA). Instead, he recruited from public and private institutions across the country, the first state college president to follow this deliberate approach to faculty recruitment. The new Orange County State College (which would become California State College, Fullerton), opened in temporary quarters in September 1959 with 466 students.

* * *

Early in the 1950s, another set of communities had begun the drive for a state college. In the San Francisco Bay Area, the East Bay refers to Alameda and Contra Costa counties, and thus includes Berkeley, the home of the University of California. In 1954, the Hayward Chamber of Commerce formally launched a campaign to establish a state college in the East Bay. The Hayward area was among the most rapidly growing in California. A powerful member of the legislature, Carlos Bee, represented the area. Bee was a former high school teacher and Hayward city councilman. He moved rapidly and introduced legislation in the 1955 regular session to establish Alameda County State College. The bill passed in the assembly and then failed in the senate. Its failure only served to fuel the desire and the work to create the college. In the next regular session, 1957, Bee reintroduced the bill. Again it passed in the assembly. At the same time, the effort was underway to create Orange County State College; it had the support of the senate, but less support in the assembly. The leaders of these two efforts made common cause, and two new state colleges were established.

As noted earlier, the process of site selection and the establishment of the new college in Orange County went smoothly. In Alameda County, a two-year struggle had just begun. Shortly after the bill signing in July 1957, the State Department of Education issued a public statement about the general location of a new campus within a sixty-four-square mile area south and east of Oakland. It was followed shortly by a public statement by Governor Knight that the State Public Works Board (chaired by his appointee, the director of finance) would consider any site and any proposal in southern Alameda County, a different geographic approach. Twenty proposals were received. The staff of the State Public Works Board studied them and held hearings for two years. Twenty sites were cut to seven and then three. Pat Brown took office as governor in January 1959, and a new director of finance, Bert Levit (the father of parking fees on CSU campuses), became chair of the Public Works Board. When the board cut the sites down to three, a protest group went to Governor Brown. Brown asked the board to reconsider. It did, and selected a site in Pleasanton, then a small bedroom community. The state superintendent of public instruction weighed in on the necessity of staying within the 1957 legislation's $10,150,000 appropriation. The Hayward City Council launched what they called a counterattack, and actually generated more than forty thousand letters to Sacramento, the Public Works Board, and the governor. The board selected another site; this time with contingencies about zoning and cost sharing. The zoning contingency was not satisfied. The Hayward City Council came forward with money. Finally, in December 1959, three months after the campus had first opened in rented quarters, the State Public Works Board selected one of the three original sites, high on hills in Hayward, overlooking the San Francisco Bay.

In January 1959, State Superintendent Simpson selected Dr. Fred Harcleroad as the founding president. Harcleroad had been the dean of instruction, the chief academic officer, at San Jose State College. Prior to that, he had been a professor of education and administrator in two western states. Simpson had selected two presidents, with backgrounds in the liberal arts, both historians. He would soon cause the appointment of another individual, not a teacher educator, to the presidency of an existing campus. The selection of Harcleroad was, in a sense, a resumption of the pattern of years of presidential and academic leadership from teacher educators, and this became a factor in the early years of the college's development. Alameda County State College opened in September 1959 with an enrollment of 293 students.[119] In 1963, the college was renamed California State College, Hayward and again renamed, in 2005, as California State University, East Bay.

* * *

In 1957, State Superintendent Roy Simpson asked the Department of Finance, the governmental agency that provides administrative oversight for a governor over all other state agencies and operations, to do a study of the organization and coordination of the state colleges at the state level. In an early paragraph the study's report notes the changed circumstances of the state colleges:

> While the state colleges remained few in number, had small enrollments, and offered limited academic programs, the need for planning for their activities collectively was limited. The expansion of their numbers, the tremendous growth of enrollment and diversification of programs made it apparent that provision must be made for insuring that their collective efforts adequately meet the statewide needs of the public.[120]

The Department of Finance study identified four major areas for attention: planning of academic programs; financial operations and budgeting; physical facilities' planning and use; and leadership and administration. The author of the Finance study indirectly observed that neither the legislature nor state control agencies (such as Finance) had the time or the competence to be a governing board or a statewide administration. The report defined the problem. It did not offer a resolution.

In 1957, J. Paul Leonard, the president of San Francisco State College, resigned to take the presidency of the American University in Beirut. In his twelve years as president in San Francisco, he had proved to be a president with major competence and had provided substantive academic leadership beyond the ordinary. When he resigned, he publicly addressed the governance of the California State Colleges—one could paraphrase Leonard "the absence of academic governance and the substitution of state controls." Roy Simpson's appointment of Glenn Dumke as J. Paul Leonard's successor surprised everyone, including the appointee.

Dumke was the dean of the faculty (chief academic officer) and a professor of history holding a named chair at Occidental College, a respected and nationally known liberal arts college at Eagle Rock in the Los Angeles basin. Dumke and Simpson had come to know each other slightly when Dumke chaired the regional accrediting commission earlier in the 1950s, at the time when the new Los Angeles State College of Applied Arts and Sciences was denied accreditation. Simpson phoned Dumke one day early in 1957 and offered him the presidency of San Francisco State College. Dumke told him he needed to think about it and asked for time. Simpson told him he had a week. In addition to talking with his wife Dorothy, Dumke flew to San Francisco and spent time anonymously on the campus. He discussed the offer with President Arthur Coons of Occidental College, already a well-known figure in California and national higher education, and later to become an important figure in the development and implementation of the California Master Plan. On the eighth day, Dumke phoned Simpson and accepted the offer.[121]

The Dumke appointment was initially not well received on the San Francisco State campus. The campus was already on the way to becoming the most internally politicized among the state college campuses. The issue was not

Dumke, but the fact that Simpson made the appointment with absolutely no consultation with faculty. There was a faculty outcry. Dumke was in the middle, and had second thoughts about leaving Occidental, an institution where he had "grown up" (Dumke was an alumnus; after receiving his baccalaureate there, he had attended UCLA for the master's and PhD degrees in history, and then returned as a faculty member to Occidental). The leader of a faculty group protesting Simpson's action was Frank Fenton, an English professor. While opposition to Simpson was strong, Fenton changed his position and argued that the faculty should nonetheless welcome Dumke because he was from the liberal arts and could be a leader in moving the campus (and perhaps the state colleges) to a new orientation and mission. Many faculty reacted positively to Fenton's appeal. Dumke stuck to his decision and came to San Francisco. The faculty in teacher education and related fields were hardly pleased. The seeds of later conflict were sown, and this conflict would have an important meaning for all of the state colleges in the years to come.

Simpson seemed to understand, however reluctantly, that the teacher education era of the state colleges was ending, and that there was a need to build the state colleges as comprehensive liberal arts institutions. He made six presidential appointments from 1957 to 1960. Four were in the liberal arts tradition and two in the teacher education tradition. One of the two, the associate superintendent who had been responsible for the soon-to-be-defunct Division of State Colleges and Teacher Education, was appointed in 1960 as the founder of a new campus in the Central Valley community of Stanislaus. As events would show over the next years, the Dumke appointment to San Francisco would have significant consequences for the California State Colleges, as the Langsdorf appointment had for Fullerton.

Nineteen fifty-eight was an important year for all of California higher education. Robert Gordon Sproul retired after almost thirty years as president of the University of California. He had been a dominant figure in all of California education, although he did not succeed in one of the most critical of his major efforts, to limit the development of the state colleges toward becoming comprehensive liberal arts and sciences institutions and their further development of professional programs. Roy Simpson was elected to his announced final term as state superintendent, and would in a few years close out seventeen years of leadership, albeit of varying character and strength, of the California State Colleges. Both Sproul and Simpson had participated in or presided over a major series of events and studies that had set the stage for the coming era in California public higher education.

At San Francisco State, Dumke began to build his team and exert leadership among the state college presidents, a marked change from the past. In July 1958, Clark Kerr succeeded Sproul. In the November 1958 California gubernatorial campaign, Pat Brown, one of the candidates, spoke more than once about the need to reassess California higher education and plan for major growth in the near future to accommodate the growth already in elementary and secondary schools. Brown took office in January 1959. In that month, as a new session of the legislature convened, twenty-three bills, three resolutions, and two constitutional amendments were introduced calling for new campuses and for changes in the structure of public higher education in California. The setting for the development of the Master Plan was complete.[122]

* * *

The early, pre–Master Plan years of the California State University can be understood now as falling into three distinct periods. The first phase, from the founding of the initial normal school to the time of World War I, was the formative era, during which each campus was founded locally, and the base of support for each was local. The normal schools received state funding and the amounts varied over time. Governance was primarily local, though with effort a governor or state superintendent could intervene. Curriculum and admissions standards varied; there was some framework for cooperation among the campuses, variously used. Professionalism of faculty and principals/presidents varied and began to develop at about the turn of the century. Cal Poly was an exception among these schools, founded as a vocational high school at the time when the state was beginning to recognize the importance of establishing and supporting high schools and filling the gap between elementary schools and colleges. Conflict between the normal schools and the University of California was rare, although there was some over the establishment of Cal Poly.

The second phase, the time from World War I to the end of World War II, was a period of substantial growth in professionalism within the faculties and among presidents and the limited number of other administrators. The State Board of Education became the sole governing board for all of the campuses. The State Department of Education became a minor factor in the leadership of the colleges, although the state superintendent was a major figure with the practical power of designating a nominee, whom the state board would appoint to a vacant presidency. In 1921, the name change, to state teachers colleges, followed in 1923 by degree-granting authority, made a major difference. Students with no interest in becoming teachers (though on many campuses they were still required to sign a form saying they wanted to become teachers, as a condition of admission) began to use the state teachers colleges as regional campuses to obtain the baccalaureate. The further name change, to state colleges in 1935, and the events leading up to this were the occasions of more serious conflict with the University of California. The move of the Los Angeles State Normal School to the University of California did not occasion serious conflict, but the move of the Santa Barbara State College to the University of California became a culmination point for conflict, which had begun with degree-granting authority in the 1920s and picked up substantially in the early 1930s with the name change to state colleges. The outcome was a 1946 constitutional amendment that prohibited any further moves of state colleges to the University of California.

The third phase began with the end of World War II and the influx of veterans and other students on the campuses. Both individually and collectively, the colleges became so substantial in numbers of students that attention was forced on their future. The Strayer report and the restudy defined the issues, having to do with governance, growth, and the broadening of mission. The restudy offered a solution regarding governance, but not really for growth or the broadening of mission. In the meantime, the founding of additional state colleges became a focal point in the political arena. For many legislators, the biggest prize one could bring home to the district was a new campus. For waves of new liberal arts and professional faculty, the goal had become a change of mission, not just the broadening of the existing one. For presidents, the goal was the stature and status and support of their campuses; presidents in great measure were independent of each other and operated on campuses as if they were fiefdoms. For state government, the issue was to achieve some measure of control and governance that would be functional and coherent.

At that moment, when it was becoming clear that a master plan for higher education in California was what was needed next, Pat Brown became governor.

Notes

[1] California Constitution of 1849 art. 9, sections 1 and 2. This chapter also uses three previous works: Donald R. Gerth, "The Government of Public Higher Education in California" (unpublished doctoral dissertation, University of Chicago, 1963); Donald R. Gerth, James O. Haehn, and associates, *An Invisible Giant: The California State Colleges* (San Francisco, New York, London: Jossey-Bass, 1971); Gerth and Judson A. Grenier, "A History of the California State University and Colleges" (monograph, Carson, Calif.: California State University, Dominguez Hills, 1981).

[2] William W. Ferrier, *Ninety Years of Education in California: 1846–1936* (Berkeley, Calif.: Sather Gate Book Shop, 1937), 327.

[3] Benjamin Franklin Gilbert, *Pioneers for One Hundred Years: San Jose State College 1857–1957* (San Jose, Calif.: San Jose State University, 1957), 2.

[4] *Ibid.*, 3.

[5] *Ibid.*, 4.

[6] *Ibid.*, 15.

[7] Ferrier, *Ninety Years*, 327–28.

[8] Gerth, "The Government," 91.

[9] Gilbert, *Pioneers*, 17.

[10] *Ibid.*, 18.

[11] *Ibid.*, 19–23.

[12] Gerth, "The Government," 92; Ferrier, *Ninety Years*, 43.

[13] Ferrier, *Ninety Years*, 333.

[14] Gilbert, *Pioneers*, 45, 49–50.

[15] *Ibid.*

[16] Calif. Const. 1879, art. 9, sec. 9; Gerth, "The Government," 65.

[17] Gilbert, *Pioneers*, 72.

[18] *Ibid.*, 78.

[19] Gerth, "The Government," 92–93; Gerth and Grenier, *"A History,"* 7–9; Gilbert, *Pioneers*, 79–80.

[20] "Prologue and Past" (Chico: California State University, Chico, n.d., ca. 1991); Gilbert, *Pioneers*, 81–82.
[21] W. H. Hutchinson, "When Chico Stole the College," in *A Precious Sense of Place: The Early Years of Chico State* (California State University, Chico, Friends of the Meriam Library, 1991), 10–21. This section about the founding and early years of the Chico campus is heavily dependent upon the essays in *A Precious Sense of Place*. A major contributor to *A Precious Sense* is Clarence McIntosh, in his essay, "Chico Normal."
[22] *Ibid.*, 36.
[23] Gilbert, *Pioneers*, 82–83; Gerth and Grenier, *A History*, 9.
[24] Gilbert, *Pioneers*, 92.
[25] *Ibid.*, 95–97.
[26] Raymond Starr, *San Diego State University* (San Diego, Calif.: San Diego State University Press, 1995), 15–31. The story of the creation of San Diego State Normal School is told well in that work, and this segment is drawn from it.
[27] *Ibid.*, 18.
[28] *Ibid.*, 21.
[29] Arthur Chandler, *The Biography of San Francisco State University* (San Francisco: Lexikes Press, 1986), 13–35. This section about San Francisco State Normal School is heavily dependent upon Chandler's work, which goes into considerable detail about the early history of San Francisco State University.
[30] *Ibid.*, 47–53.
[31] Robert E. Kennedy Library, California Polytechnic State University, *Cal Poly: The First Hundred Years* (Santa Barbara, Calif.: Companion Press, 2001), 14–15. This section, about the establishment of Cal Poly at San Luis Obispo, is heavily drawn from the above volume and from Robert E. Kennedy, *Learn by Doing: Memoirs of a University President* (San Luis Obispo, Calif.: California Polytechnic State University, 2001).
[32] *Cal Poly*, 15–17.
[33] *Ibid.*, 13.
[34] J. Burton Vasche, "The California State Colleges," California Schools, vol. XXX, no. 1, January 1959.
[35] Charles L. McLane, "The Growth and Development of the Fresno State College for the First Twenty Five Years 1925–1936" (unpublished manuscript, California State University, Fresno Library, 1937), 17. This section, about the founding of Fresno State Normal School, also uses Fred P. Hogan, "The History of the Fresno State Teachers College" (master's thesis, Stanford University 1930); Eugenia Rowland, "Origin and Development of Fresno State College" (PhD dissertation, University of California Berkeley, 1949).
[36] California Statutes, chap. 69, 88 (1907).
[37] Gerth, "The Government," 111–13.
[38] McLane, "The Growth," 49–50.
[39] *Ibid.*, 52.
[40] William R. Tanner, *A View from the Hill: A History of Humboldt State University* (Arcata, California: Humboldt State University, 1993) 1, 3–4. This section about the founding of Humboldt State Normal School draws substantially from Tanner's work.
[41] *Ibid.*, 3.
[42] *Ibid.*, 9.
[43] Murray Haberman, "A Double-Headed System" (Sacramento: California State Library, 1999), 2–3.

[44] Morgan Odell, "Distribution of Authority within the California State College System," (PhD dissertation, University of Southern California, 1967), 101.
[45] Haberman, "Double-Headed," 4.
[46] Gerth, "The Government," 93; Gerth and Grenier, *A History*, 12.
[47] Ferrier, *Ninety Years*, 333.
[48] Haberman, "Double-Headed," 2. Haberman's recitation of the evolution of the state board is definitive and is the basis for these paragraphs.
[49] Haberman, "Double-Headed," 4; Gerth, "The Government," 93.
[50] Gilbert, *Pioneers*, 133.
[51] *Ibid.*, 134.
[52] Gerth, "The Government," 69–70. This story is told in a number of places, including University of California records; Haberman, "Double-Headed"; and the memoirs of Regent Dickson and Dr. Moore.
[53] *Ibid.*
[54] McLane, "The Growth," 89–90.
[55] Gilbert, *Pioneers*, 134.
[56] Gilbert, *Pioneers*, 134–40; Gerth, "The Government," 94–95.
[57] Personal file of writer, author's notes on Grayson Price.
[58] Haberman, "Double-Headed," 6–7; Gerth "The Government," 95.
[59] Gilbert, *Pioneers*, 145.
[60] Douglas Peterson, "California Maritime Academy, A Brief History" (unpublished draft).
[61] *Ibid.*
[62] Tanner, *A View*, 37.
[63] Conversations between the author and Dr. Hugh Bell, longtime faculty member and dean at Chico, 1964–66.
[64] Odell, "Distribution," 103–05.
[65] Carnegie Foundation for the Advancement of Teaching, *State Higher Education in California*, New York: Carnegie Foundation for the Advancement of Teaching, June 24, 1932 (Archives of the California State University, CSU Dominguez Hills Archives); Odell, "Distribution," 105–07.
[66] Gerth, "The Government," 95–96.
[67] "Statistical Abstract," the California State University.
[68] Donald H. Pfeuger, *California State Polytechnic University, Pomona: A Legacy and a Mission* (Spokane, Wash.: Arthur H. Clark, 1991), 41–46, 77–89; Gerth "The Government," 96–97.
[69] Minutes of the state college presidents, December 4–5, 1939, California State Department of Education, 41.
[70] Odell, "Distribution," 107–08.
[71] Joint Staff for the Committee and the Technical Advisory Committee, "The Origin and Functions of the Liaison Committee of the State Board of Education and the Regents of the University of California," August 1957, Archives of the California State University, 1.
[72] John Aubrey Douglass, *The California Idea and American Higher Education* (Stanford, Calif.: Stanford University Press, 2000), 157–63.
[73] "Origin and Functions"; Douglass, *The California Idea*; in this history of higher education in California, Douglass notes that a state board member conceived this idea out of concern that tensions were rising between the two segments of higher education.

[74] *A Report of a Survey of the Needs of California in Higher Education*, The University of California, Berkeley, The California State Department of Education; George Strayer, Monroe E. Deutsch, Aubrey A. Douglas, 1948, Archives of the CSU.

[75] The story of California State University, Los Angeles, is found in two volumes: Donald O. Dewey, *That's a Good One: Cal State L.A. at 50* (California State University, Los Angeles, 1997); and *Being Here: An Autobiography of California State University, Los Angeles* (California State University, Los Angeles, 1987). The enrollment numbers are from the Statistical Abstract of the California State University.

[76] George S. Craft Jr., *California State University Sacramento, The First Forty Years: 1947–1987* (Sacramento: California State University, Sacramento, 1987), 9. Craft's book is the source for these paragraphs, along with the personal knowledge of this writer, a former president of CSUS.

[77] In February 1986, severe rainstorms hit northern California. Rivers overflowed their banks in many areas. A coffer dam burst in the mountains, and the American River rose uncontrollably. Folsom Lake filled to almost the top of the dam. Water released from the dam brought the American River within about six inches of the top of the levee. While all of this was going on, I was informed that the gates under the railroad tracks to the west of the campus were being oiled, and that the high embankment on which the tracks sat was a secondary levee to keep downtown Sacramento from being flooded. This banter, as I thought it was, went on for probably a day and a half. I was in my second year on the campus. Why would anyone locate a college or university campus in an area to be flooded deliberately to protect a city downtown area (and the state capitol)! I didn't believe it. Finally I decided to see for myself; it was true. The gates were being oiled. I phoned the city manager. Together we walked the primary levee. I closed the campus that evening for one day. The rains stopped in another 36 hours, the campus was saved, and my common sense began to recover.

[78] Gerth, "The Government," 97.

[79] *Report of a Survey*, 1.

[80] *Ibid.*, 19–20.

[81] *Ibid.*, 21.

[82] *Ibid.*, 28–29.

[83] *Ibid.*, 22.

[84] *Report of a Survey*, 34.

[85] *Report of a Survey*, 81–82.

[86] *Report of a Survey*, 132.

[87] *Report of a Survey*, 33.

[88] David Bernstein and Kaye Briegel, "California State University Long Beach, A Historical Overview: 1949–1989" (unpublished paper, Department of History, California State University, Long Beach, 1989).

[89] California State Department of Finance, "Organization of the California State Colleges, September 1, 1950," California State Department of Finance, Archives of the CSU.

[90] "Organization of the California State Colleges," 1.

[91] *Ibid.*, 2.

[92] *Ibid.*, 37–42.

[93] *Ibid.*, 13–14.

[94] *Ibid.*, 30–31.

[95] California State Department of Education, *Report of the State College Council to the Governor and the Legislature of California*, State Department of Education, March 1, 1953, 1.

[96] *Ibid.*, 19.

[97] *Ibid.*, 25–26.

[98] Odell, "Distribution," 113.

[99] California State Department of Education, *Handbook of Administrative Policies and Procedures for California State College Presidents*, State Department of Education, Sacramento, April 1952 (Archives of the CSU), 8.

[100] Statistical Abstract, 3.

[101] T. C. Holy and H. H. Semans. *A Restudy of the Needs of California in Higher Education*, Joint Staff of the Liaison Committee of the Regents of the University of California and the California State Board of Education, California State Department of Education, 1955, 1.

[102] "Origin and Functions," 5.

[103] Now the State University of New York, Buffalo. McConnell later became the director of the Center for the Study of Higher Education at UC Berkeley. This center was to become greatly influential in policy matters for all of American higher education. McConnell was a mentor to this author in some ways, first for the completion of my doctoral dissertation, and in the author's work and interests for a time.

[104] Holy and Semans, *Restudy*, 5–6.

[105] *Ibid.*, 47.

[106] *Ibid.*, 68.

[107] *Ibid.*, 71

[108] *Ibid.*, 96–101.

[109] Holy and Semans, *Restudy,* 111–13; Dr. Arthur Hall, interview by author, March 1, 2005. Hall was director of institutional research at San Francisco State College with then President Glenn Dumke, was an active participant in Master Plan committees, and was subsequently state college dean of institutional research from 1962 to 1970.

[110] Holy and Semans, *Restudy*, 263.

[111] *Ibid.*, 271–73.

[112] *Ibid.*, 285–88.

[113] McPhee was appointed in 1933 and maintained a Sacramento role part time as chief of the Bureau of Agricultural Education until 1945, and then as state director of vocational education until 1949; Robert E. Kennedy, *Learn by Doing*, 21.

[114] Gerth and Grenier, *A History*, 17.

[115] John Broesmale, *Suddenly a Giant: A History of California State University Northridge* (Northridge: California State University, Northridge, Santa Susana Press, 1993), 1. This section about the establishment of California State University. Northridge, is drawn from Professor Broesmale's work and this writer's conversations with Dr. James W. Cleary, the third president of CSUN.

[116] H. H. Semans and T. C. Holy, *A Study of the Need for Additional Centers of Public Higher Education in California*, California State Department of Education, 1957.

[117] "Origin and Functions," 9–11.

[118] The story of the founding of the Fullerton campus is found in "From the President to Vice-Chancellor," the oral history of William B. Langsdorf, Archives of the CSU. There were three interviews : January 12 and 18, 1984, and August 27, 1987. This section is based on pages 1–11 of the consolidated transcript.

[119] The information about the early years of California State University, East Bay (first Alameda County, then Hayward) is from papers sent by the office of the president to the writer in the autumn of 2003, and from the Statistical Abstract of the California State University.

[120] California State Department of Finance, "Management Survey for the Department of Education, Division of State Colleges and Teacher Education," Department of Finance Survey 855, September 3, 1957, 6, Archives of the CSU.

[121] These events and the reactions at the San Francisco campus are discussed in four oral histories. Glenn S. Dumke, three interviews in April and June of 1984 and July of 1986, Regional Oral History Office, Bancroft Library, University of California, Berkeley; Dumke Oral History, July 18, 1981 and March 27, 1987, CSU Archives; Dorothy Dumke, November 28, 2003 by Donald R. Gerth, CSU Archives; Glenn P. Smith, April 1, 2004, by Gerth, CSU Archives.

[122] Gerth and Haehn, *An Invisible Giant*, 15.

5. Cover of the Master Plan for Higher Education in California, 1960–1975.

Chapter 2

The California State Colleges and the Master Plan

The years 1958 though 1960 were major transition years for the California State Colleges. In 1958, a new governor, Pat Brown, was elected. In the election campaign, Brown had made it clear that he was aware of the unrest and lack of stability in all of the state's higher education structures, the University of California, the California State Colleges, and the junior colleges. Brown also knew that his administration would have to face the need for expansion of public higher education on the order of hundreds of thousands of new students, while the plentiful funds that had accumulated in the state treasury in World War II and its aftermath were gone.

    The causes of the unrest varied among the segments. All could agree on the need for funds, as new student populations cascaded onto campuses. The junior colleges were pushed by growth and uneven support in the many districts across the state. The University of California was genuinely alarmed by what its leadership saw as out-of-control mushrooming growth in the state colleges, where six new campuses had been created in the last ten years, with at least two more campuses expected in the years immediately ahead, and more sites identified in the 1957 study of additional campus sites. There also were ever more frequent and forceful demands for university status. The state college presidents and faculties wanted full university status, with doctorates, research, funding parity with the University of California, and an effective governance structure— given the histories of the colleges, had they thought through a description of that structure, presidents and faculties would doubtless have come to different conclusions about what *effective* might mean.

The state colleges were beginning to grow a new generation of leaders. While a division was emerging between two groups of presidents, those in the teacher education tradition and those more identified with the concept of the liberal arts and professions as the base of undergraduate education, the presidents were united in a judgment that the existing system of governance was a failure, and that there was a need for governance separate from the State Department of Education, which was simply inadequate for the tasks of leadership and governance. The unit for the state colleges in the department was small, three professional or academic staff, in addition to an associate superintendent position that was weak. This small office was unable to protect the campuses from interference and micromanagement of state agencies, not only with respect to amounts of funding, but to the details of the use of funds, the micromanagement of personnel processes, building design and construction, and the like. The academic staff of the Department of Education did not have the intellectual heft of their many opposite numbers in the University of California. Finally, the superintendent was protective of the past and of the status quo, although willing to do what he could be convinced was politically necessary to maintain the status quo. He supported growth and new campuses, but gave no leadership to their establishment; that leadership came from members of the legislature. He appointed a number of presidents with backgrounds outside of teacher education, but gave no substantive academic leadership to the campuses.

Five of the presidents were leaders in a move for change: John Wahlquist of San Jose, Arnold Joyal of Fresno, Malcolm Love of San Diego, Julian McPhee of Cal Poly, and Glenn Dumke of San Francisco. Malcolm Love cut across the ideological line; while he was from the field of education, prior to his presidency at San Diego he had been president of the University of Nevada, which conferred the PhD and had a research program. Love was the most vigorous advocate for the state colleges to become state universities and initiate doctoral programs, at a minimum the doctorate in education, and provide for research. These five presidents galvanized action, and in 1958, they went public in Sacramento with a proposal for a separate board for the state colleges and doctoral programs in education.[1] The fact that this leadership came from a group of presidents is a product of the history of the colleges, founded separately, and for the most part developed separately. They were regulated by state agencies, but not governed. The parts were the whole, both in terms of academic program and, for many purposes, politics. A coalition of presidents pressed for changes, reflecting the somewhat organic and decentralized history of developing the colleges in contrast with the UC centralized structure and leadership.

The presidents also addressed engineering education, which had been the focal point of UC opposition to the development of professional degree programs beyond teacher education. Programs in engineering had grown out from the junior college function many of the state colleges still carried from the time of the amalgamation of the junior college function with Fresno State Normal School in 1911. As the state colleges acquired more freedom and moving room in the years after World War II, a number of the campuses simply developed engineering programs without going through the customary formal action to create a program. There was no legislative interference with these independent actions, and local and regional legislators were happy with this program development. It was a mixed group of programs; some were serious engineering programs, others more like industrial arts. The University of California had blocked efforts to have these programs accredited, and the Department of Education had not intervened on behalf of the campuses. The presidents' 1958 initiative included this issue and proposed authority for the state colleges to move ahead with professional accreditations. It is notable that, neither State Superintendent Roy Simpson, nor the State Board of Education, actively supported or opposed this presidential initiative.[2]

The role of Roy Simpson as state superintendent and the responsible chief officer for the state colleges through this period appears to be an ambivalent one. In fact, early in his superintendency in the mid-1940s, he had taken part in a successful campaign to prevent the University of California from acquiring any additional state colleges beyond Los Angeles and Santa Barbara. He took obvious pride in having the state colleges among his responsibilities, yet he gave them short shrift in terms of attention, care for significant issues, and leadership. His two principal deputies for the state colleges were opposites in administrative style. Aubrey Douglass was a competent and caring administrator and worked productively with the colleges and the presidents. J. Burton Vasche, who succeeded Douglass, was passive as associate superintendent of public instruction and chief of the division of state colleges and teacher education. As events in Sacramento and the successive studies of the '40s and '50s increasingly demonstrated, the colleges needed cohesive leadership. There was none, beyond that of the presidents when they acted together. Simpson seemed to sense the need for change in the leadership of the colleges from a "teacher education with liberal arts and some professional programs focus" to a "liberal arts and professional programs, including teacher education focus." His appointments to the presidencies in the 1950s did reflect this awareness, to some extent. He did not discourage or organize opposition to the efforts of the presidents finally to break loose from the Department of Education, although it was clear he did not want this to happen. He did cooperate with Clark Kerr and others in the ongoing work of the Master Plan. His selection of Glenn Dumke to lead the state colleges in the development of the Master Plan was a break with the past. Simpson apparently did not confide in anyone about his choice of Dumke. One can only speculate that he acquiesced to Clark Kerr as an easy way out of a potential conflict and with some confidence that Dumke's academic stature and values would make him as effective as possible in negotiations.

Clark Kerr assumed the presidency of the University of California from Robert Gordon Sproul on July 1, 1958. The event was made a notable one by the regents and the faculty leadership.[3] Sproul had been president for twenty-eight years. His influence on all of education in California had been cumulative and had become enormous over the years.[4] He had firmly guided the University of California through a period of substantial growth and program development, and put in place the building blocks and early initiatives for a great research university. He had just as firmly tried to limit the programmatic growth of the state colleges. He had used the Liaison Committee of the regents and the State Board of Education to guide, to the extent possible, the expansion of California's colleges and universities in the '40s and '50s. In some ways he was grounded in the past. Moreover, the sheer numbers of students and resulting growth in numbers of state colleges simply overwhelmed conventional efforts to protect the university's turf as Sproul saw it, and contain the expansion of higher education. Kerr assumed the presidency not only with new energy, but with a sense of academic diplomacy that would change relationships in all of California higher education. The University of California, not unlike higher education institutions in general over the years and up to the present, was a very conservative institution about its own affairs.

Kerr clearly sensed the need for a collaborative working relationship with the state colleges and their leadership, as well as with the junior colleges. Only a few months into his presidency, the state college presidents' group launched the initiative in Sacramento to redefine the state college role and the relationship between the state colleges and the university. Shortly after the presidents' move, Kerr attended his first meeting of the Liaison Committee as president of the university. He made a number of conciliatory moves toward the state colleges, and then proposed yet another study and made it clear that he was open to change within the context of a strategic study and resulting agreement about working relationships.[5] He proposed a joint meeting of the regents and the State Board of Education. Kerr's cards were now on the table.

What were the causes that contributed to the willingness of many individuals, often with conflicting interests, to come together and consider seriously the present and future condition of higher education in California? The idea of change was in the air. The concept of a master plan came at the right moment. Leaders in higher education knew that change must come, from within the higher education enterprise or from without.

In the first month of the 1959 legislative regular session,[6] twenty-three bills, three resolutions, and two constitutional amendments were introduced, calling for the establishment of new University of California or state college campuses, for changing the functions of existing institutions, or for changing the governance structure of public higher education.[7] Legislative members, and particularly the leadership, were trying to make sense of public higher education. The leadership of the legislature had changed parties; it, as well as the governor's office, had moved from Republican to Democratic control as a result of the November 1958 election. The call among members of the legislature for the leadership in higher education to fix its own house, or houses, was clear; this call and its refrain were to be heard with frequency over the next year as well from the governor. Moreover, Governor Brown was addressing his first budget with limited resources.

Kerr's proposal for a joint meeting of the two boards was accepted by all groups. Two joint meetings were planned for the spring of 1959. Immediately after the Liaison Committee had agreed to the two meetings and to the concept of a joint study, a vice president of the University of California, James Corley, had scheduled a meeting with Assemblywoman Dorothy Donahoe. Then in her second term as a representative from the Bakersfield—Kern County region of the state,

Donahoe had just become chair of the assembly's Committee on Education. She was no stranger to the field of education, having been for some years a school administrator in Bakersfield, on the nonacademic side of the house. She had been open with her concerns for adequate support for junior colleges and regarding the expansion of state colleges without any plan or coherent strategy. Corley, a familiar figure to many legislators, was an experienced lobbyist for the University of California and had been close to President Sproul.

The Donahoe-Corley meeting marked the beginning of what would become the Master Plan. Corley proposed a study, to be called the Master Plan for Higher Education, and he had a written proposal for Donahoe to consider. Corley was the emissary of Clark Kerr, without a doubt. He asked Donahoe to introduce a resolution requesting the regents and the State Board of Education to prepare jointly a plan for the ongoing development of the university and the state colleges. Donahoe agreed to carry the proposal. She subsequently speculated about the wisdom of carrying the proposal, given her relative newness to the legislature, and consulted a number of colleagues, notably State Senator George Miller, the chair of the Senate Finance Committee, whom she had come to know. Miller encouraged her, and his support was important. Donahoe moved ahead and introduced a resolution in early March.[8] In the meantime, the first of two meetings of the regents and the State Board of Education was scheduled for March 14.

The first joint meeting was held at the UC Berkeley campus. It was attended not only by all members of the state board and most regents, but by senior staff from the University of California and the State Department of Education, state college presidents and UC chancellors, the director of finance (perhaps the key lieutenant to the governor at that time, outside of his immediate staff), and at least one legislative staff member. The chair of the board of regents opened the meeting as host and then asked the chair of the State Board of Education to preside. Though the governor was not present, as he was out of the state, he sent a clear written message, which was read by a personal representative. The message was to the board members and educational leaders: achieve coordination and reasonable working relationships, or the state government will do it for you. This message was often to be heard in the next year from many sources.

Dorothy Donahoe, in her role as chair of the Assembly Committee on Education also delivered a message: the legislature would defer all bills on higher education until the boards agreed on "a unified program for higher education in California."[9] She raised the question of a separate board for the state colleges, but also mentioned the idea that the regents assume responsibility for all of public higher education; she was clear that the two boards had on the whole worked productively separately. She was open in her concerns for the junior colleges and their importance. After her meeting with Corley, she had authored Assembly Concurrent Resolution 88 (ACR 88), which called for a master plan. She addressed ACR 88 and the importance of placing on hold for two years proposals for new campuses and new programs, while the work on a master plan would be completed. The 1957 report about possible new UC, state college, and junior college campuses had addressed thirteen possible to likely sites for new state colleges (the le-

6. Governor Edmund G. "Pat" Brown.

gislature had already acted on two of these) and three new UC campuses (all three were established shortly after the adoption of the Master Plan).

President Kerr and Superintendent Simpson made presentations. Kerr and Simpson had both supported the concept of a study and the need for coordination, but Simpson surprised almost all the participants. Once again, shifting his position about the state colleges and change, his only reference to the mission of the state colleges was to emphasize the importance of teacher education. The heart of his statement was a call for a dramatic expansion and the addition of seven state college campuses. He stated a need to double state college enrollment in five years, and he asked for immediate action. This was a rebuff for those in the legislature seeking order and some control of budgets, though for legislators hoping to bring home a campus to their districts, this had an appeal. The proposal for new campuses was not realistic in the context. The impending enrollment increase was clear, though not its magnitude. Actually, enrollment doubled in the eighth year. Simpson's proposal underscored the need for the study.

For the Liaison Committee meeting of March 3, less than two weeks before the joint meeting of the two boards, the joint staff had prepared a set of four resolutions for action by the boards. The Liaison Committee, composed of four State Board of Education members, Simpson, and five regents including Kerr, approved these draft resolutions. The resolutions provided for the continuing work of the Liaison Committee and a set of studies and discussions, which would result in a master plan. Essentially, these studies and deliberations would accomplish the goals of ACR 88.

Regent Donald McLaughlin proceeded to move the resolutions agreed to on March 3. A key piece of the Liaison Committee agreement was a two-year moratorium on the establishment of new campuses, unless approval was given by both boards, the regents, and the State Board of Education. State Board of Education member (and Liaison Committee member) Raymond Daba then moved a substitute resolution on the issue of the moratorium and asked for the establishment of additional state college campuses, which had been Simpson's proposal earlier in the meeting. Daba argued that growth in numbers of students could only be accommodated by the establishment of new campuses, and that Superintendent Simpson's timetable for seven new state college campuses (beyond Orange County and Alameda County, opening in 1959, and the North Bay and Stanislaus campuses, authorized but not yet established) must be followed immediately. This move threw the meeting into heated and even angry discussion. The Simpson approach would clearly have had the impact of derailing ACR 88, and the development of a comprehensive plan or even planning process. The result of this discussion was to refer the whole matter back to the Liaison Committee, and defer action until the second meeting of the joint boards. The next meeting was scheduled for April 15 in Los Angeles. It was agreed that the Liaison Committee would meet in Sacramento before April 15, at a time and place that made it easy for members of the legislature to attend. Dorothy Donahoe had the last word, stating, "[T]he members of the legislature would like to feel that they are members of the team working toward a satisfactory solution to the problem," and she inquired into the mechanics for making this possible.[10] She wanted a "definitive program."

The Liaison Committee met on April 2, in the offices of the State Department of Education in Sacramento. Eleven people attended. Not all were there to advocate for the approach of ACR 88. Some were there to advocate for new campuses in their districts. A compromise was proposed by William Blair, the chair of the State Board of Education. The state board would agree to a moratorium, provided that site acquisition for the Simpson list of sites (drawn from the additional centers study of 1957) could proceed. The next step was the joint meeting of the boards on April 15.[11]

The April 15 meeting was approached carefully by both Governor Brown and his staff, and President Kerr and the regents. Going into the meeting, Brown did not reveal his hand. Members of the legislature and others were flown to Los Angeles in the personal planes of regents. Regent Edwin Pauley, a former ambassador to Australia and a significant figure both in California and nationally, hosted a dinner on the evening of April 14 for the members of the boards, legislators, and others. Brown used the occasion of the dinner to make it clear that he wanted a result from this meeting.[12] He simply wanted to see some sensible resolution of the continuing conflict, and the institutionalization of stable and coordinated administration and leadership among the higher education institutions.

The attendance at the meeting was rather extraordinary, but so was the meeting itself. In attendance were most members of the State Board of Education, a greater number of regents than at the March meeting, including the governor and the Speaker of the assembly (Ralph Browne), state college campus presidents and University of California campus chancellors, the legislative analyst (Alan Post), the director of finance (Bert Levit), the chair of the Assembly Ways and Means Committee (Jesse Unruh), Dorothy Donahoe and eight members of the legislature, accompanied by key staff. Two new State Board of Education members, Louis Heilbron and Thomas Braden, were at the meeting; both were to be heard from often. They had been appointed by Brown with a deliberate intent to change the state board's approach to educational policy. Both were accomplished and experienced civic leaders and outstanding in their professions, Heilbron an attorney in a major San Francisco law firm, and Braden a newspaper publisher.

Governor Brown presided. A member of the Liaison Committee reported on the April 2 meeting. A resolution embodying the Blair compromise about state college site acquisitions was introduced and adopted (once the Master Plan was adopted the site acquisitions did not happen; the establishment of additional campuses proceeded one by one). The major discussion that ensued focused on the timeline for reporting the results of a master plan study. The proposed resolution called for a report in 1961, the next regular session of the legislature. Regents, State Board of Education members, and legislators all participated, and a sense of urgency about the timeline emerged. Someone proposed that the report be completed in time for consideration at a 1960 special session, and the governor was asked about his willingness to call a session for the specific purpose of addressing higher education. While he was cautious about making a commitment, it became clear in the discussion that he was favorably disposed to do so. State Board of Education member Blair, the author of the compromise, spoke strongly in support of it. In some ways, the compromise was a way out for both Board of Education members and regents, a way out from the effort of Superintendent Simpson to derail the process at the earlier meeting. The resolution passed unanimously. The compromise acknowledged the work and conclusions of the additional centers study of 1957. For all practical purposes, the compromise acknowledged the state college campuses being established or to be established at Orange County, Alameda County, North Bay, Stanislaus, and San Bernardino—Riverside Counties, and three new UC campuses to be established at San Diego, Southeastern Los Angeles—Orange Counties (Irvine), and the Monterey—Santa Cruz area, though the UC campuses were not explicitly part of the Blair proposal. Subsequently, the members of the two boards unanimously endorsed ACR 88. Accompanying these actions was a resolution to charge the already existing Joint Advisory Committee (composed of three sitting chancellors/presidents from the UC, the state colleges, the junior colleges, and the private sector of colleges and universities, and one staff member from each segment) to work with the Liaison Committee.

Governor Brown then proceeded to invite further discussion, especially from members of the legislature. First he turned to Dorothy Donahoe, who addressed the request that had been made by the Liaison Committee's joint staff for a two hundred and fifty thousand dollar special appropriation to finance the higher education study. She made it very clear that the detailed studies envisaged by the joint staff were exactly what was not needed: "while it is proposed in ACR 88 that a study be made, it should be a dynamic one and rapidly prepared—not another long-range plan as has been done in the past—but a master plan which will outline a cooperative and coordinated program for higher education."[13] The funding request was dropped.

Assemblyman Harold Sedgwick of San Diego, whose district included the San Diego State College campus, next spoke about Assembly Bill 392, which proposed a state college board. This was the first bill in the legislature to propose a state college board. He indicated that the bill was already in hearings and would be difficult to delay. His remarks had an impact opposite to the one he sought. Senator George Miller, Assembly Member Jesse Unruh, and newly appointed State Board of Education member Louis Heilbron urged moving ahead with ACR 88 and a master plan. One week after this second meeting of the two boards, ACR 88 was adopted by the legislature. The Master Plan was underway.

The Joint Advisory Committee had already been meeting. Malcolm Love, then president of San Diego State College, had circulated a paper calling, among other matters, for the state colleges to become universities, to award the PhD, and to establish a research function, and the group accepted the paper. This was clearly unacceptable to the University of California, and was rejected. Both sides of this debate were angry; the state college presidents because many of them wanted other changes, and Kerr and his advisors because the three UC chancellors on the joint board acquiesced to Love's insistence. As a result, the Joint Advisory Committee was simply sidelined. In the weeks after the joint meeting of the two full boards, Kerr and Simpson reached agreement on a structure to accomplish the goals of ACR 88 and prepare a "master plan." At its June 3, 1959 meeting, the Liaison Committee established a Master Plan study committee (later renamed the Master Plan Survey Team). The composition of the group would include a chairman selected by the state superintendent and the president of the university; subsequently a representative of the private institutions, selected by the Association of Independent California Colleges and Universities, was added.[14]

The Liaison Committee responded to the call from the legislature; ACR 88 asked the Liaison Committee "to prepare a master plan for the development, expansion, and integration of the facilities, curriculum, and standards of higher education, in junior colleges, state colleges, the University of California, and other institutions of higher education of the State, to address the needs of the State during the next ten years and thereafter. . . ."[15] Specifically, the committee asked the survey team to address (1) the size of student enrollments and how enrollments should be distributed among the public and private institutions of California, (2) admission requirements, (3) enrollment projections for the state colleges and the university and how the Master Plan would modify these, (4) the differentiation of functions among the three public segments, (5) the establishment of new state college and university campuses and the need for new junior college campuses, (6) a series of questions about costs and finances, with particular attention to shifting students to junior colleges and consequent costs to the locally financed junior college districts, (7) student fees and the underlying question of who should pay for public higher education, (8) the state's ability to pay, and finally (9) the governance of public higher education in California.

The process of selecting individuals for the survey team was quickly underway. Simpson and Kerr agreed on a chair, Arthur Coons, the president of Occidental College in Los Angeles. Coons was a nationally known educational leader. He had not been involved with the issues underlying the need for a master plan. He had recently been the president of the Association of American Colleges, and he had been a member of President Eisenhower's Committee on Education Beyond the High School.

The various appointing authorities also acted quickly to fill out the membership of the survey team. The junior colleges selected Henry Tyler, the executive secretary of the California Junior College Association. Kerr and the regents chose Dean McHenry, a political science professor at UCLA and a longtime friend and close confidant of Kerr. McHenry was later to become the founding chancellor of the University of California at Santa Cruz. The Association of Independent California Colleges and Universities chose Vice-Provost Robert Wert of Stanford, later the president of Mills College. The joint staff members appointed were Thomas Holy, of the University of California, Arthur Browne of the Division of State Colleges and Teacher Education, and Howard Campion, a retired associate superintendent of the Los Angeles Unified School District, which at that time included the Los Angeles junior colleges.

The selection of the state college appointee was key, from the standpoint of the presidents and faculties. By this time the advent of the Master Plan process had drawn the attention of faculty leadership and faculties on all of the state college campuses. The presidents had been attentive from day one and had played a major role in bringing about the circumstances for the process. There was unanimity among the presidents about the need for change, but not about what needed to change and how. The general perception of the time on the campuses was that San Diego President Malcolm Love was the choice of some presidents and that Simpson and Kerr discussed Love. Love had been responsible, in the weeks prior to the April 15 meeting of the boards, for the Joint Advisory Committee proposal to change substantially the role of the state colleges, including university status, granting of the doctorate, provisions for research—in effect a major and preemptive move on the key issues that the University of California wanted to negotiate. Love was aggressive in style. It was thought that Kerr objected forcefully and that Simpson backed away from proposing Love to the state board members. Simpson proposed Glenn Dumke, the relatively new president of San Francisco State. Dumke, though new (he had been at San Francisco State for two academic years at this point), was known for some of his views, especially the centrality of the liberal arts and sciences to undergraduate education. He had been supportive of many of the moves of Love and others about graduate education and research, but he also had been diplomatic in working with others inside and out of the state colleges. Simpson nominated Dumke and the state board approved Dumke's appointment. It is not at all clear that there was any effort to understand that the playing field was not level between the state college and UC members of the survey team. The UC member, working with Kerr, could count on the entire UC organization to be with him. The state college member was on his own and had to be persuasive with presidential colleagues, the state superintendent, faculty, and others. Again, the phenomenon of the history of the state colleges, the fact that there was no "center," played a role.

The Liaison Committee and the survey team organized quickly to address the questions posed by the legislature in ACR 88. Timing was important. A report to the boards and a proposal to the legislature were due in approximately six months. At a July 8 meeting, the Liaison Committee established six technical committees, each to be responsible to the survey team, which in turn reported to the Liaison Committee, which was a creature of the two boards. The structure was set. The technical committees were to address enrollment projections, the selection and retention of students, the state's ability to finance higher education, the costs of higher education, institutional capacities and area needs, and adult education. Each technical committee included representatives of all four segments (the independent colleges and universities were treated as a segment) and in a few instances, others. In addition, the Liaison Committee formally extended invitations to selected members of the legislature, the legislative analyst, Alan Post, and the director of finance, who was represented by his chief deputy.[16]

Early after she became chair of the Committee on Education, Dorothy Donahoe had identified a young legislative intern (a position later renamed Assembly Fellow) to whom she assigned major responsibilities to work on the master plan project. This intern, Keith Sexton, remained on the staff of the Education Committee when his internship concluded. He had been "on the inside" virtually from the beginning of the Master Plan phase, and he became also a consultant to the survey team.[17] He would play a major role bringing individuals and points of view together, and later was to play a significant role in follow through on the Master Plan and the coordinating council that it created.

* * *

Everyone involved with this process had a stake in the outcome. There were no disinterested parties. Kerr and the regents and the University of California wanted the status quo with respect to the university, protection of its monopoly on advanced graduate and professional education and research, and, especially, containment of the state colleges. The university had an interest, shared by all, in adequate funding; their definition of adequate funding went well beyond the costs of instruction and was based on the certain knowledge that the University of California was each year becoming more a major research university in the nation and in the world. Key elements of the research role of the university were in the nuclear sciences, medicine, the agricultural sciences, all in the nation's interest. Kerr prepared a careful analysis of UC–state college relationships for the regents. He observed that board to board, relationships had not been negative. "The problem has not been to obtain agreement, but rather to secure adherence to agreed and prescribed policies and programs."[18]

The junior colleges wanted recognition of their work as a clear part of the higher education enterprise in California. The junior colleges were governed, then as now, by local boards in local districts. The shift to junior college districts, independent of public school districts, was just beginning. There was no central state office with any responsibility or authority, and the junior colleges did not want a statewide governance structure with authority. They did want state funding, particularly for capital outlay and the construction of facilities to handle burgeoning growth.

The independent colleges and universities wanted more support, and support that would not in any way compromise their carefully guarded independence. The state had initiated, in 1955, a scholarship program that made funds available to students, funds that could be used in the independent colleges and universities. The independents hoped for an increase in this support, and they achieved this.

The state colleges, their leadership, their faculties and staffs, their communities and advisory boards, were the major seekers for a new era in California higher education, seekers of change. Virtually all agreed on a need for a governing board only for the state colleges. There was no interest in moving to a single governing board for all of higher education, without or with the junior colleges; the assumption was that the state colleges would be second-class citizens in a university dominated by the regents and the campuses of the University of California, especially Berkeley and Los Angeles. Virtually all agreed that it would be desirable and important for the state college board and the colleges to have constitutional status and autonomy parallel to that of the University of California (Article IX, Section 9 of the 1879 constitution). Presidents and other administrators and knowledgeable faculty and advisory board members wanted freedom from state agency control, beginning with the Department of Education. The line-item budget control exercised by the Department of Finance, the legislative analyst, and the legislature was more than onerous, and genuinely got in the way of reasonable administration and rational operation of the campuses; there was no campus capacity to move funds from one function or line item to another. Other state agencies were often problems, including the State Personnel Board, the State Architect (design and construction of all buildings), and the like. The disparity in funding between the University of California and the state colleges was an issue for all; the perception and the reality of the difference, though not always accurate, led faculties and administrators to find common cause on this issue. All one had to do was compare UC and state college campuses to drive the point home. The teaching loads were considerably different, for example: twelve units were standard in the state colleges, while in the UC, the average unit load was seven.

Presidents, faculty members, and involved community leaders all wanted change and further development of academic programs, though there was certainly not unanimity about the direction. The issue of whether the institutions had as a central focus a liberal arts and sciences/professional programs base, with teacher education and related programs for counselors and administrators among the professional programs, or a central focus on teacher education in a context of liberal arts and sciences and other professional programs, was hardly resolved. This would continue to be an issue in the 1960s, and was more divisive on some campuses than others. There was substantial but not universal agreement about further development of graduate programs, the ability to offer the doctorate, and research. The faculties, presidents, and community business and civic interests wanted unfettered program-development capacity, with or without the doctorate and medical or law schools.

There was also a subset of faculty, staff, and union advocates among the faculties who wanted a capacity for unionization in the conventional sense, and for collective bargaining. This was not a major factor and was only present at that point on some campuses, most notably San Francisco State. It had not been carefully thought through. It was not visible in any consistent way, but it was a piece of the puzzle for some, and did become significant on some of the campuses with the implementation of the Master Plan in the 1960s.

For those in state government in Sacramento, there were additional issues. The new governor wanted stability, a sensible, collaborative agreement about the growth and development of higher education for at least the next eight years; and, as negotiations went on, a legacy. He wanted a plan that was financially viable, including cost containment. Leaders and members of the legislature wanted peace and cooperation between the state colleges and the university, an end or at least a reduction of the long-standing strife. They too wanted a sensible plan for growth and development that was financially sound and would not cause a problem with taxes, while at the same time it would satisfy their constituents. They also wanted cost containment, given the explosive growth of the time. Many were torn by loyalties to the University of California, either because they were alumni or because they admired the work of a research university. Of the one hundred and twenty members of the legislature (eighty in the assembly and forty in the senate), the elected members in the 1959 and 1960 sessions included more than fifty university alumni and three alumni of a state college.[19]

At this stage in the development of higher education generally in the country, there was not a widespread understanding of the work of comprehensive colleges and universities. This dimension of higher education was only beginning to form, in California as well as nationally. Clearly and unambiguously, however, major legislative leaders, most notably Senator George Miller, did not like the fact that in major ways the University of California was beyond the reach of state government, and were determined that this would not be replicated with the state colleges. For Dorothy Donahoe, the Master Plan was an important and essential public policy issue. It was to be her legacy.

Finally, in Sacramento there were many state agencies invested in various ways in the Master Plan outcome. In some measure this was a function of the personalities, values, and aspirations of those in various roles. For some in state agencies, it was a matter of providing for the responsibilities assigned to various units of state government. For others it was a matter of providing for the orderly growth and development of public higher education in California. And for others it was jobs, and the preservation of both positions and responsibilities. For the small staff in the State Department of Education actually concerned with the state colleges, the focus for the most part was adequate provision for the state colleges. Superintendent Roy Simpson was an inconsistent and ambivalent figure. He was simultaneously protective of the role of superintendent, reluctant to see any change in structure and power, willing to support uncoordinated growth of the state colleges; yet when cornered politically, he was sometimes willing to work with Clark Kerr (in theory his opposite number) to move the Master Plan process forward. From Simpson's perspective, it was not uncoordinated growth—it was a way to provide more educational access to individuals throughout the state. He had seemed to understand the changing mission of the state colleges with several presidential appointments, yet here again was ambiguity: two of his last presidential appointees had die-hard commitments to the colleges' teacher education past and style and were not prepared for the newly emerging world of the California State Colleges. No one was really ready for the work needed to bring about a clear and cohesive articulation of the state college system in contrast with the UC. As has been outlined above, the state colleges initially emerged as regional institutions, and the ability to envision them as a "comprehensive institution" was in the years ahead.

* * *

The initial direction of ACR 88 and the analysis of the Master Plan survey team listed a substantial set of issues to be addressed. The survey team members organized to address all of these, but there were key issues that the Master Plan was all about. The central issue was ironing out the relationship of the state colleges and the University of California, and differentiating the functions of the two. This was true from all perspectives, save the junior colleges and the privates. The legislature and the governor had a second key issue, cost containment.

The concept of differentiation of function was not a new one. It was to be found in the 1899 study; it was implicit in the Jones report of 1919 and in the Carnegie report of 1933, and it was explicit in the 1948 Strayer report and the 1955 restudy.[20] In the early 1900s, differentiation of function had had to do with the founding of an agricultural institute to become Cal Poly, at the time when the university was moving to the founding of "the Farm" at Davis. In the years from 1911 to the 1920s, the issue shifted focus when some of the normal schools/state teachers colleges used their responsibility for the junior college function to create lower-division liberal arts programs. In the later 1920s and 1930s, as the schools all became state colleges, the issue of differentiation became the colleges' open and widespread development of the liberal arts, and again, after the 1935 name change, the point of contention shifted to the colleges' awarding of baccalaureate degrees in selected liberal arts majors. Then, during the growth years immediately after World War II, the colleges pursued professional education, again to some extent built on use of the junior college function by some campuses and graduate education including education for the professions and the awarding of masters degrees, and they began a modest push toward modestly comprehensive institutions.

The lack of any real resolution of the UC–state college relationship, the lack of any serious follow-through of the 1948 Strayer report and the 1955 restudy, and the continuing uncoordinated development and growth of state college campuses, provided the circumstance for the emergence of a new set of issues. A major factor certainly was the growth of state college enrollments and campuses in a context of weak and inconsequential governance through the State Department of Education and State Board of Education.

Thus, the core issues of the Master Plan process, where some firm and practical agreement had to be reached, were only a few. On this short list were graduate work, the doctorate and research; the governance of the state colleges, which included the matter of constitutional status; admissions, and some measure of control of enrollment growth within the context of California's historic implicit commitments to access and reasonable cost containment; and the definition of some kind of mechanism or process to address the continuing relationships and work of all segments of higher education. The heart of the matter, however, was differentiation of functions, then and into the future.

As the work of the survey team got underway, the composition of the State Board of Education began to change. Appointed by the governor and confirmed by the senate, State Board of Education members served four-year terms. The board consisted of ten members. Thus Governor Brown had the almost immediate opportunity to bring new thinking to the board membership, and he accomplished that with great thought and deliberation. He wanted public policy change, and he appointed individuals who wanted change, not only in the state colleges, but in all of education. Brown personally held them accountable, and he was not reluctant to call them to task, whether for missing meetings or avoiding hard issues. Among his earlier appointments, Louis Heilbron and Thomas Braden would play major roles in the actual beginning of a new governance structure. Heilbron became an activist immediately, and participated, not only in state board discussions about the work of the survey team, but in meetings, especially with the governor.

The survey team went to work immediately. The work of the technical committees was determined, and the survey team tackled the key issues. The chair of the team, Arthur Coons, played the role of manager of the process—sometimes an exasperated manager. The two major members of the survey team would be Glenn Dumke and Dean McHenry. McHenry had the less complex of the roles. He began as a confidant of Clark Kerr. Kerr was, at that time, in such complete control of the university, and had the confidence of the regents and internal university leadership that it was relatively easy for McHenry to function in a straightforward way in the survey team. The university had a clear and focused agenda.

Dumke had many masters, or perhaps clients. Theoretically, Roy Simpson was in charge; he was Kerr's "opposite number," but not really, other than by occasional exercise of his authority. It was clear that Simpson would prefer that the whole Master Plan idea would go away. Heilbron and Braden, new state board members, clearly wanted change, as did other board members, some new and some from earlier appointments. Simpson never had worked closely with the board and the board had developed the practice of generally agreeing with his proposals. With Brown's appointees, who wanted new policy directions and change, Simpson lost his board.

The presidents pressured Dumke for change, but not the same change. The most difficult was Malcolm Love. Love wanted the doctorate and university status; the one point where he converged with virtually everyone was on the matter of a new board independent of the Department of Education. The teacher education issue was alive and well among the presidents, and there was division among them. The state colleges were in a condition of internal evolution with respect to mission and values. Dumke had in reality two opposite numbers, Kerr and McHenry, without the support system both had; he had to build an agenda, and he had to engage in the give and take of the negotiations, and adjust the agenda as the process moved along. The contextual environments for Dumke on the one hand, and Kerr and McHenry on the other hand were astonishingly different.

Faculty leaders on various campuses were pushing for a variety of specific changes. The faculty at San Francisco State kept up substantial pressure on Dumke, who was often away from the campus as a member of the survey team. Essentially the San Francisco faculty pressure was to secure for the state colleges and especially that campus the same status, degree-granting authority, budget, and the like that the university had. No one who was remotely realistic expected this, but it did set a tone. Dumke was a relatively quiet and reserved individual. He did not handle this easily, and mistakes were made by a variety of individuals, including Dumke, in the internal politics of the San Francisco campus; these made some matters more difficult.[21] Dumke pushed very hard, without bringing faculty along, for conventional liberal arts content and organization in the curriculum; San Francisco State was not a conventional place.

In July 1959, Simpson wrote to all of the state college presidents after a Liaison Committee meeting that the survey team is "off to a good start," and that Dumke (and Arthur Browne, the state college staff member), "are [giving] very able representation." He reported on the actions of the Liaison Committee, essentially procedural to that time.[22]

At its first meeting in June, the survey team went into substantial issues. Dumke joined the issue of the doctorate, but only in the field of education. His argument was not dissimilar from arguments that continued for years, that the state colleges had special competence, given their history in teacher education. The agenda for the meeting had been set by the chair, Arthur Coons. After two meetings focusing on the doctorate, Coons backed away and changed the agenda. Coons had wanted a single board for the university and the state colleges from the beginning, something neither group wanted for differing reasons. Nevertheless, he persisted in a quest for the single board.[23]

Dumke again took the lead. He countered with a two-pronged proposal for a separate state college board and a coordinating group that would work with both the UC and the state colleges (and the junior colleges, though they were incidental to the discussion at that point). Both the separate state college board and the desirability of a coordinating mechanism had been in the mix of discussion for some time; now they were on the table. A Sacramento State government professor, Lyman Glenny, had been doing research on the governance of public institutions and had also been involved with the earlier 1950s restudy. He was invited to meet with the survey team (Roy Simpson had previously stated that he did not want state college people talking with Glenny about the Master Plan study). Glenny, who was at that time emerging as a major researcher on higher education and government, met with the survey team and argued, in the Master Plan discussions and in his published work, that coordinating boards could only be useful when lay members were a majority of the membership.[24] The survey team committee concluded in October, after several months of discussion, that there should be a separate state college board and a coordinating group to bring the segments together. The coordinating group, however, would only have individuals representing higher education.

* * *

The work of the survey team was followed closely by presidents, other administrators, and faculty leaders within the state colleges. In August, President Love, as a member of the Joint Advisory Committee that had been effectively sidelined by Kerr with Simpson's cooperation months earlier, used the Joint Advisory Committee as an arena once again to start a discussion about the doctorate and research. Correspondence among some of the presidents was supportive. In turn, Dumke wrote to all of the presidents and convened a Saturday meeting in mid-September in Sacramento to go over progress, little at that point, of the survey team. Simpson and Vasche were notified but not invited. Dumke posed a series of questions and asked for advice on tactics and the substance of issues.[25] Neither Love's moves nor Dumke's request for advice caused anything of note. The presidents were simply not together on any issues beyond governance, a separate board, constitutional independence, and parity with the University of California. The doctorate and research were divisive issues. Dumke was on his own.

The interest of faculty leadership was a different matter. In the years after World War II, with the growth in enrollments and the appointment of many faculty members in the arts and sciences and newly emerging professional fields on the state college campuses, faculty interest in participation in the governance of campuses was rising. Some campuses were developing faculty councils or other bodies. None were mature. As an alternative, many other faculty and staff groups formed, some around issues as straightforward and limited as insurance programs. Among the presidents, Dumke was the most articulate supporter of faculty participation in governance. His Occidental College experience had been in a setting in which faculty participation was conventional and assumed. Dumke called for two meetings of state college faculty representatives in the fall months while the Master Plan negotiations were underway.

The first was in Sacramento on September 28, two weeks after a presidents' meeting. The meeting was well attended. Each of the thirteen campuses was invited to send four faculty members; the participants had been variously selected, some by faculty organizations, some by presidents. The discussions were lengthy and substantive, and essentially covered the range of topics that the technical groups and the survey team were addressing. The day's work was brought back to the campuses, and was widely circulated; some faculty teams reported in writing to their entire faculties, some arranged for general faculty meetings; on at least one campus, both happened. On a few of the campuses, there was little administrative support for faculty involvement and awareness. One manifestation of this was reimbursement of travel expenses. One president offered each of his four faculty representatives a dollar, but indicated that he would attempt to find money for travel to the second meeting, which would be at the other end of the state from their campus.

Faculty interest at the colleges was high and it was about the issues. The faculty wanted a state college governing board; they wanted parity in funding and salaries and workload with the University of California; some also wanted to be able to grant the doctorate and to have supported research. These issues became rallying points, and an internal politicization within state college faculties began. The organizations of state college faculty, some allied to national groups such as the American Association of University Professors or unions, some only internal such as the Association of California State College Professors, were in a sense, galvanized by the Master Plan negotiations and the statewide faculty interest.[26] The faculty participants in the first meeting agreed to poll faculty on the campuses about the issues, and the polling resulted in a report to the subsequent meeting. Nine of the thirteen faculties favored a separate board. All campuses asked for more independence from state controls. Six campuses favored creation of a coordinating group. Six campuses also pushed for the doctorate. Generally, the faculties favored retaining the proportions of high school graduates eligible for admission to the three segments: 100 percent for the junior colleges; 45 percent for the state colleges; 15 percent for the university.[27] In fact, the ranges of admissions eligibility for the state colleges and the university were somewhat higher than published statements in catalogs at that time.

A second meeting of faculty representatives was held in Los Angeles on November 14, this time with eleven of the thirteen campus presidents also in attendance. At the same time, the survey team and the Liaison Committee were struggling with the most difficult issues of the Master Plan discussions—

constitutional status, the doctorate, research, essentially the core issues about differentiation of function. The faculty representatives at the meeting continued to meet after the presidents departed. They adopted a set of resolutions addressed to the survey team, the Liaison Committee, both governing boards, and members of the legislature. The resolutions supported a separate governing board; fiscal, program, and personnel autonomy; the doctorate and research; further study of any admissions changes; and a coordinating body. The resolutions were widely circulated on the campuses and became a basis for much faculty understanding of the issues in the Master Plan negotiations; the faculty leadership was generally frustrated with the work of the survey team. But there was no comprehensive state college leadership talking about the reality of the process.[28]

* * *

Agreement having been reached on governance, a separate board for the state colleges, and a coordinating council, a next major area to be addressed was the selection of students and related questions about allocation of student spaces among the segments. The distribution of student spaces had major budget implications for the state. Costs per student varied enormously between the state colleges and the university. The funding of student spaces in the junior colleges was principally a local district responsibility; state subsidies were a minor fraction of junior college budgets. Arthur Browne, the State Department of Education joint staff member of the Master Plan Survey Team, joined the issue with a counterproductive argument about costs between the university and the state colleges; he argued about the actual expenditures of the university in lower-division instruction. Dumke backed away from Browne's argument and took the position that both the university and the state colleges could usefully reduce their respective zones of freshman eligibility and shift a significant number of students to the junior colleges. This was an important breakthrough in the negotiations for the legislature and the governor, as it addressed cost containment.

The technical committee on selection and retention of students was already underway. The committee was chaired by Herman Spindt, a revered and veteran figure in California higher education and the longtime director of admissions at UC Berkeley. The state college member of the committee was Ralph Prator, the new president of the San Fernando Valley campus, who had earlier in his career been director of admissions at the University of Colorado. The members of the survey team were to be disappointed with the work of this committee. The technical committee did not argue for fixed standards, but rather for admissions officers to work with individual students and guide individuals toward what might be best for them. The committee also called for continuing studies of admissions criteria and a longer term development of new standards for admission.

Within the state colleges there was a clear split on the issue of admissions criteria. Dumke and others among the newer presidents and administrators and faculty wanted criteria related to a college preparatory curriculum, and they wanted clear published standards to be generally used. The campuses, until the time of the Master Plan negotiations, had varied widely in the actual application of criteria to individual applicants; the variations ranged from little use to firm use of the published criteria. The criteria in effect in 1959 used grades of A and B in all high school courses except physical education and ROTC, and a standardized test score for marginal candidates. The survey team simply moved beyond the work of the technical committee.

The technical committee on the costs of higher education was developing data about relative costs among the segments. The survey team explored a redefinition of the composition of the undergraduate student bodies at both the university and the state colleges; in both entities, undergraduate enrollment was split almost evenly between the upper and lower divisions. Dumke proposed to direct more lower-division students to the junior colleges, as a viable approach to both financial issues and a tightening of admissions standards. McHenry agreed. Certainly, the junior college representative did also. Using data from the technical committee on costs and on enrollment projections, they agreed on a 60/40 balance of undergraduate enrollment, 60 percent of student spaces in the upper division, 40 percent in the lower division. This would mean significant enrollment increases for the junior colleges, and in turn this triggered work on state subsidies to districts for operating expenses related to enrollment.

The chair of the technical committee on enrollment projections, Carl Frisen, was a highly respected economist and did population and other projections for the State Department of Finance. The question was simply put to him: what should be the zones of eligibility, given the data available, for admission with freshman standing to the University of California and the state colleges to achieve the 60/40 balance? Frisen's response and the ultimate recommendation of the technical committee, was the top 33 1/3 percent for the state colleges, the top 12½ percent for the University of California. This became the recommendation, though there was serious disagreement within the state colleges among those who were committed to being as close as possible to an open-door admissions approach. A sizeable minority of presidents, if not a majority, wanted no change in admissions standards. Within the state colleges, the lines on this issue were largely drawn by longevity—the more senior faculty and administration tended to favor standards that were inclusive and did not focus on college preparatory curriculum. Faculty and administrators who had joined a state college more recently tended to favor standards that were not exclusive—that was not the point—but that did focus on a college preparatory curriculum. There were disciplinary differences about this also; faculty and those relatively few administrators out of a liberal arts and sciences background tended to support a college preparatory curriculum.[29]

The word "top" was not defined. Each segment was given the responsibility to define it. For Glenn Dumke and newly appointed members of the State Board of Education, the issue was to build admissions standards upon college preparatory programs, and that was an issue to be addressed after the implementation of the Master Plan.

* * *

The deadline for preparation of a Master Plan proposal, its review and action by the Liaison Committee, and then submission to a third joint meeting of the boards, was mid-December. By November, there was agreement on a separate board for the state colleges, a coordinating council, the distribution of student spaces among the segments, admissions standards, and a variety of other matters. The technical advisory committees for the most part were productive in preparing reports with important background information. But with five to six weeks before the joint board meeting, the most important issue of the whole process, differentiation of function and how it would be handled, was still unresolved. The mid-November meeting of faculty representatives, presidents, and State Department of Education staff had not helped Dumke, and throughout the months of negotiations, he remained the man in the middle. Clearly, the majority of state college people in all categories wanted the doctorate, research, constitutional status, and funding.

Others entered into the conversation with the survey team. Alan Post, the legislative analyst, for many years the most generally respected figure in California state government, had been brought in from the beginning. Post was a superb public administrator with some background in higher education as a faculty member at Princeton, where he was for a time a department chair. He could focus on budgets and numbers and at the same time on the intellectual and cultural dimensions of colleges and universities. Post was also an Occidental alumnus; he and Dumke had known each other as students. Post made an early proposal to Dorothy Donahoe in the spring of 1959 about the dimensions of what turned out to be the Master Plan study. His role was often a conciliatory one, bringing the parties together. He played that role in November and early December 1959. He was cognizant of George Miller and Dorothy Donahoe's exasperation with the lack of resolution regarding the related issues of governing boards and differentiation of function. Miller, Donahoe, and others were in conversation about introducing a bill simply to put all of higher education under a single board, presumably the regents, and resolve everything.[30]

One of the advisors in Pat Brown's campaign for governor was a professor of political science at San Diego State College, Donald Leiffer. Leiffer was a Californian by adoption. He had completed the baccalaureate at UCLA in its early years and gone on to do the doctorate at Harvard. For a time he taught at Boston University and became chair of political science there, and the holder of an endowed professorship. He was interested in returning to California. He taught a summer session at UCLA in 1947 and the following year was offered a professorship at San Diego State, specifically to start a graduate program in public administration, the first of its kind in the state colleges. In a very real sense he was one of the key faculty pushing the border between the state colleges and the University of California in the growth years after World War II. The Strayer report, the work of the Liaison Committee, and the restudy, and various other reports and actions spelled out the rules of the game, more often than not in ways subject to interpretation. Leiffer came to push a border—graduate work in a field that itself was just developing as a distinctive area of professional study.

Leiffer was an activist at heart. He quickly became a campus leader in the California State Employees Association and in the Association of California State College Professors. He also became politically active. His particular field of interest at that time was local government. The Brown campaign had asked Leiffer to prepare several position papers for the gubernatorial race about metropolitan government. Not long after Brown took office, Leiffer was invited to Sacramento to visit with Brown. He was offered the formal position of research secretary (Leiffer described it as a euphemism for speechwriter). Then Brown asked him to develop a plan for the reorganization of state government. In this context, he began to represent Brown at various board meetings, including those of the regents and the State Board of Education. He was not Brown's education staff member; at that point Brown did not have anyone in that role. The Master Plan process was not part of his assignment, but he had great interest in it and gradually became involved. As a side note, when university officials learned of Leiffer's appointment as research secretary, they asked for a UC professor also to be added to the staff. They did not want to be left out. Professor Harry Girvetz of the philosophy department at Santa Barbara joined the governor's staff. He did not become involved in the Master Plan work, although later he became a sideline critic of the state colleges.

Leiffer was asked to represent the governor at some critical survey team and Liaison Committee meetings, and gradually became more involved. In a sense as a UCLA alumnus and a San Diego State faculty member he had a foot in both camps. In late November, he reported to Brown that the survey team was mired in an argument about the doctorate, research, and how this would play out in terms of differentiation of function and a constitutional amendment. Leiffer was to subsequently play a major role in the implementation of the Master Plan. Brown's reaction was that he and members of the legislature could and would write legislation and do whatever was necessary to bring an end to conflict between the university and the state colleges. This was a threat to both systems.[31]

It was at this point that Kerr went to four of the state college presidents and proposed that their campuses be absorbed into the university. Fresno, San Diego, San Jose, and San Francisco were each invited to become UC campuses. Each president, Arnold Joyal of Fresno, Malcolm Love of San Diego, John Wahlquist of San Jose, and Dumke at San Francisco turned the offer down, and they did so independent of each other. Dumke's reasoning at the time was that San Francisco State would become a second-class citizen within the UC family. He was aware of the experience of the Santa Barbara campus as it moved to the University of California, and it was not a positive one.[32]

Arthur Coons was concerned. He wanted the survey team to succeed in developing a workable solution. He convened a special meeting of the team in early December. Dumke proposed a compromise: the doctoral and research issues would be referred to the proposed coordinating council after the implementation of the Master Plan. This was agreed to by the survey team members. The council would address the unresolved issues of differentiation of function, in addition to their previously agreed-upon role of budget coordination. Kerr was not present at the meeting. When told of the compromise, he rejected it, and, in turn, he said that without agreement on differentiation of function the university would not support a separate board for the state colleges.

The final meeting of the Liaison Committee was December 7–9, 1959, on the Berkeley campus, just a few days prior to the joint meeting of the State Board of Education and the regents. This meeting had an audience. It was attended by the media, legislators and others from Sacramento, and some regents and state board members who were not on the Liaison Committee. For two days the members worked through noncontroversial issues in the proposed report. At the end of the second day, Arthur Coons put on the table the fact that agreement had not been reached in the survey team about the key issues, differentiation of function and governance. He also announced that he would present his recommendations on these issues the next morning.

Kerr invited the two board chairs, McLaughlin and Blair (who would soon leave the role), Coons, Simpson, Dumke, and McHenry to his office. In the meeting the discussions were candid. Two versions, at least, exist of this meeting Kerr called and both reflect a meeting with candid discussion. Kerr's memoirs and Dumke's oral history each claim responsibility for the idea of the joint doctorate; Dumke's oral history addresses the agreement on research related to instruction as a proposal he made to start the state colleges moving more formally to faculty research. The important point, however, is that an agreement was reached. The agreement defined a new phenomenon for California higher education, the "joint doctorate," a degree awarded by two campuses, one UC campus and one state college campus. Research related to instruction would be included in the state college functions. All agreed to support a separate board for the state colleges, written into the constitution, to be parallel in legal status to the provisions for the University of California in Article IX, Section 9. The functions of each of the three public segments would be in the new Article IX, and thus fixed.[33]

The next morning Coons presented to legislators, the people of all three segments, civic leaders, and the media, a master plan proposal to which all had agreed. The Master Plan was initially defined, and the boards adopted the proposal soon thereafter.

* * *

The development of the Master Plan was not over. As the contents were discussed and became clearer, disagreement emerged. Governor Brown had to call a special legislative session for consideration of the Master Plan proposal in the spring of 1960. President Kerr and Superintendent Simpson forwarded the plan, on behalf of the regents and the State Board of Education, to the senate and the assembly. Their letter of February 1, 1960, was addressed to Glenn Anderson, the lieutenant governor and president of the senate, Ralph Browne, the speaker of the assembly, and members of both houses. They recited briefly the charge from ACR 88, and then wrote, "We are glad to inform you that these recommendations ... were unanimously approved in principle by the Regents of the University of California and the State Board of Education meeting in joint session on December 18, 1959."[34] They wrote that only some of the sixty-four substantive recommendations needed legislative action. As both boards had passed all of the recommendations, Simpson and Kerr wrote that they "would proceed without delay" to implement the many other recommendations.

Within the three segments, almost immediately after the joint meeting of the board on December 18, the leadership began to promote the agreement; clearly the agreement was a compromise about the doctorate and research, and this was well understood. Dumke did not even wait for the joint meeting on December 18, but moved ahead, anticipating the holidays, to be in touch with presidents and faculty before the campuses went into recess. He and Art Browne wrote a memorandum to the state college community celebrating the compromise that had been reached and touching on the many recommendations that would improve the lot of the colleges. In a sense, the Master Plan discussions had been mostly about the state colleges. They focused on the proposed constitutional amendment establishing a board of independent trustees parallel to the university.

The memo was candid about "some concessions on the part of the state colleges." Dumke and Browne were specific: "the price was the writing of differentiation of function into the Constitution. . . . Some faculty research . . . would be permitted . . . open door [is] left for doctoral programs." Research related to instruction and joint doctorates were provided for in the constitutional draft language. They noted that the state board, the state superintendent, and the state college presidents were "standing unanimously behind the proposed agreement."[35]

On the whole, individuals associated with the junior colleges were satisfied. Among the recommendations were promises of additional support, most especially for the sizeable number of students to be "diverted" (a new term in California's higher education vocabulary) from the state colleges and the university to the junior colleges. The university people were content for the most part; the status quo seemed to be maintained with respect to the things they treasured, the constitutionally independent board, the doctorate, and major research. There was no thoughtful analysis of long-term implications for the university. The media were generally supportive, and editorials in support appeared around the state.

Two arenas were not satisfied. Resistance in the state colleges varied from mild to vociferous. Resistance in the legislature focused on a few key points. Dorothy Donahoe and George Miller were supportive on the whole, but clearly were not in agreement with all of the details, some of which were major ones.

The state college faculty organizations were unanimous in their disagreement about the doctorate and research; they wanted both, with all of the support and opportunities the UC had. Many of the state college presidents, most especially those who had been in office for a while, had been reserved in their support for a Master Plan while the process was underway. It had not been difficult in 1959 for faculty and others to get presidential messages and lack of enthusiasm. By January, and through the legislative discussions in the ensuing months, the messages were less subtle; discussions were focused around the doctorate and research. A considerable amount was about admissions—cutting the zone of eligibility for freshmen admissions from the 45 percent to 33⅓ percent, and the promise of vigorous administration of admission rules. (Up until this time, the "top 45 percent" of high school graduates were automatically eligible for state college freshman admission, and the Master Plan proposal cut this "zone of eligibility" to the "top third—33⅓ percent" of high school graduates.)

Research done for Dumke at the time of the Master Plan discussions made clear that some campus practices were far from the published standards. Some campuses were still exercising the junior college function, 100-percent access to the lower division. One of the recommendations in the report would terminate the junior college function on those two campuses (Chico and Humboldt, in the north) authorized to do the junior college function, due to a lack of junior colleges in the far north of the state. The new requirements were to take effect in 1964. Assemblyman Bruce Allen, from the San Jose area, began a negative public campaign about the proposed admission cuts in the UC and state colleges, and he achieved a fair amount of media coverage. Allen's theme—in large block letters in newspapers—was, "Does your child plan to go to college?"[36]

In the state colleges the Master Plan discussion became the occasion and the opportunity for issues about the faculty role in governance to emerge. In the 1950s, there was a rising call and a rising level of frustration about governance. Senior faculty, who perceived that they had suffered through years of benign, paternal, or just plain autocratic rule, were often quietly resigned to the status quo. More recently appointed faculty, joined by a number of intense senior faculty, pressed for change and a faculty role in governance. Dumke had made some early moves toward increasing faculty involvement in governance at San Francisco, as had Malcolm Love at San Diego, and a few others. But there was still no statewide administrative leadership on the issue. The majority of the Council of State College Presidents came out of an earlier era and tradition. The Master Plan discussions did not address either internal campus governance or internal system governance. The cumulative discontent in the state colleges had little or no impact on legislative action; but it did set the stage for significant discussions and actions in the implementation of the Master Plan.

The legislature was another matter. Dorothy Donahoe and George Miller were in general support, but they and many others expressed serious reservations about particular aspects of the proposal. The basic issue was placing the California State Colleges in the state's constitution. Some form of constitutional action was an imperative. The 1879 constitution made it clear that the State Board of Education was responsible for the "common schools" and the normal schools; this had been reinforced by a constitutional amendment adopted in 1912. At a minimum, if the Master Plan recommendation about a separate board was to be accomplished, the constitution must be changed to remove the state colleges from State Board of Education control. Many members of the legislature were more than just discontented with the constitutional independence of the University of California, the "fourth branch of government." This was not a new issue, as it went back virtually to the adoption of the 1879 constitution. George Miller was particularly sensitive to this, as a result of his experience as chair of the Senate Committee on Finance. He wanted as little as possible about the state colleges in the constitution. He and many others saw no reason for the statement about differentiation of function in the constitution. The statement presented in the proposed Master Plan addressed policy matters that the legislature should discuss and control.

The issue of the coordinating council, again a constitutional issue, was perhaps more subtle. Sacramento State faculty member Lyman Glenny, whose book *The Autonomy of Public Colleges* had been published in 1959, was a known figure and credible in the legislature. Glenny opposed the form of the council, with only members from the three public higher education segments and the private sector,[37] while legislators were also opposed to placing the council in the constitution.

The Master Plan proposal was formally presented to the legislature in the special session called by Governor Brown on February 29, 1960. This was followed by both houses of the legislature, assembly and senate, convening jointly as a committee of the whole to hear a presentation about the plan. Members of the survey team and others made presentations and responded to questions. In anticipation of this, the state superintendent's office asked the presidents to begin an information campaign with members of the legislature—lobbying by another name. Each president received a list of members to contact along with a request to contact others beyond the list, if personally known, for support. The letter outlined three points to cover: "more efficient use of public colleges for more students through better coordination, a separate State College System to meet its growing needs, and state aid to the junior colleges." The letter was clear in asserting that each president would endorse the Master Plan.[38]

Alan Post, the legislative analyst, came into play at this point. He had followed closely the work of the survey team and the Liaison Committee. Higher education was a consistent interest of his over the years, and he was involved with the humanities and the arts at the Berkeley campus. (Post and his wife are

7. Assemblywoman Dorothy Donahoe   *8. Senator George Miller*

both accomplished artists, he in oil, and she in sculpture). Post had been wary of creating constitutional status for the state colleges parallel to that of the University of California. He and Miller were in essential agreement about not placing the state colleges in the constitution. Post personally wrote for Miller legislative language that would amend the constitution to move the state colleges from the public school jurisdiction of the state board, but go no further.[39]

In the midst of this, the chair of the State Board of Education changed from William Blair, a longtime member of the board who had worked with Simpson over the years, to Louis Heilbron, a member of only one year, appointed by Brown. Heilbron, a Berkeley alumnus, was close to many of the major actors, including Brown and Kerr. He was a formidable figure, with or without the chair role. He had weighed in at the joint meetings of the boards in favor of the proposed Master Plan, and he remained consistently supportive.

Miller announced that he would introduce substitute legislation for the Master Plan. The plan as presented by the regents and the state board had been introduced as a senate constitutional amendment early in March. Miller, in statements to the senate education committee and then to the media, indicated that his legislation would only move the state colleges from the state board and place most of the remaining recommendations in statutory law.[40] Miller's substitute legislation was adopted by the Senate Education Committee and the senate, and Dorothy Donahoe then shepherded the Miller bill through the assembly.

The governor called for a meeting in his office with Kerr and the chair of the regents, Donald McLaughlin, state board chair Louis Heilbron, Senator George Miller, and a few others. Dumke was not present. Kerr made a forceful presentation about the importance of the Master Plan proposals being placed in the constitution. The issue was confirmation of the state college role, locking in the differentiation of function and constitutional status parallel to the university.

Miller made it clear that there was no way this would be acceptable in the legislature; it would not happen. Kerr suggested the university might back out of the Master Plan. At this point, Brown intervened and suggested that in addition to all of Miller's reasons about ultimate legislative authority, there needed to be a long-term view of higher education. Surely societal and economic circumstances would change, and higher education and the state colleges would need to change.[41] Brown went on to urge that all agree on placing the contents of the master plan proposal in statute. Shortly thereafter, McLaughlin, Kerr, Heilbron, and Simpson coauthored a letter that appeared in the press, expressing regret that the Master Plan provision would not be placed in the constitution, but supporting the adoption of the proposals in statutory form.[42]

Miller's bill had already passed in the senate. Donahoe scheduled a Monday meeting of the assembly education committee, which she would chair. She had not been well for a few days, but returned to Bakersfield in her district for the weekend to participate in a function. Her health over the years had not been strong, and she had chronic asthma to the extent that she kept with her a device to assist with breathing. Over the weekend she developed pneumonia, and Monday morning she died suddenly in Bakersfield. The education committee met later on Monday without her, unaware of her death. The proposal was adopted, subsequently went to the floor, and passed.

George Miller renamed his bill the "Donahoe Higher Education Act," and in that form it was adopted by both houses. On April 14, 1960, Governor Brown signed the Donahoe Higher Education Act.

The Master Plan had more than sixty recommendations. Only a small number of these were addressed by the legislature; the remainder were the responsibility of the Board of Regents of the University of California, the Board of Trustees of the California State Colleges, and the Board of Education (for the junior colleges) and junior college district boards to implement. In their joint letter to the legislature of February 1, 1960, President Kerr and Superintendent Simpson assumed responsibility for the public systems to implement the recommendations. Many were implemented, and the passage of time and events have had their impact, as has also been the case with the legislative actions.

In November 1960, the voters approved a constitutional amendment removing the state colleges from the State Board of Education, and establishing the California State Colleges and a Board of Trustees with eight-year member terms. The Master Plan, the Donahoe Higher Education Act, became reality.

*   *   *

The most important accomplishment of the Master Plan for the state colleges is something that had not been on anyone's wish list. The state colleges became an entity, not a collection of institutions. The California State Colleges were in the constitution with a board of trustees. The California State Colleges were in statutory law with defined functions, albeit not including the freestanding doctorate and open-ended research. The trustees and their chief executive officer succeeded to all of the responsibilities and authority of the State Board of Education and the state superintendent of public instruction with respect to the state colleges.[43] Legislative intent was clear that the trustees of the state college system were to have "a large degree of flexibility in determining the most effective use of funds available for higher education in the state colleges," and that "it is the desire and intention of the legislature that budget bills hereafter enacted shall provide for the state college system certain exemptions from fiscal and budgetary controls similar to those exemptions presently granted to the University of California."[44] This senate concurrent resolution about fiscal flexibility was resisted by state agencies and by the legislature itself, and there would be a long uphill road to secure its obvious intent.

For many in the state colleges who had envisioned an overnight transformation to becoming universities with freestanding doctorates and major research functions, the Master Plan was a disappointment. That disappointment and even anger, often directed at Dumke as he had been the principal in the negotiations, is understandable. Expectations had been created at the very beginning of the process, expectations that were unrealistic and, from the standpoint of time, ill advised. The implementation of the Master Plan was to be a new beginning—the opportunity to build a system of state colleges not at all like the system of the University of California campuses just then emerging beyond Berkeley and UCLA.

The California State Colleges did secure an opening to the doctorate, but it was to take more than forty years to move beyond that opening. The colleges also secured a recognized, limited, research capability, and it would take twenty-five to thirty years for that to flourish. Regarding student admissions, a major issue, a pattern was set that survives to this day.[45] There were other forward steps on lesser issues.

There was great disappointment among virtually all in the state colleges that all of the Master Plan language about the state colleges was not placed in the constitution. In fact, however, Governor Brown and Senator Miller, whatever the reasons, actually did public policy and the future students and faculties of the California State Colleges—the future California State University—a great service by not placing the particulars in the constitution. Because of this, there was room to grow and develop, to adapt a mission to meet the changing economic and sociopolitical and cultural circumstances of a changed world.

Two gaps in the Master Plan stand out. The first is the lack of coordination among the three segments of public higher education, to allow them to move forward together and resolve differences. The legislature did provide for a "Coordinating Council for the Higher Education," and Lyman Glenny's efforts were productive; not only were the three public segments and the independent segment each represented by three members, but the governor was to appoint three members representing the general public. Yet the council had no real authority. Unlike the Supreme Court, which has been in some measure an instrument to resolve great and potential conflict and permit the nation to move forward (with a few strategic misjudgments), the council had no teeth. This was a serious oversight evident from the beginning.[46]

The second gap had to do with the funding of higher education. The Master Plan did address an immediate fix. The 60/40 balance in undergraduate enrollment and the projected shift of fifty thousand lower division students from the university and the state colleges to the junior colleges provided substantial cost savings in the early years after the implementation of the Master Plan, and does to this day in a sense. But the survey team and the two boards, the legislature, and the governor did not address the fundamental problem of financing higher education in a learning society, as it was seen by some in the 1960s, or a knowledge-based society, as it would be understood in the years ahead. The Master Plan was explicit about public higher education in California being tuition free. The matter of financing public higher education was a gap that would become more serious as a public policy question in the years to come.

Glenn Dumke, the state college representative on the survey team, became the central state college negotiator. It was not an enviable role. A fundamental fact is that the University of California and the state colleges were asymmetrical as organizations; factually, it would be an exaggeration to call the state colleges of the 1950s an organization. One element of the Master Plan negotiations shared by the university and the state colleges is that neither wanted a single board; neither wanted to be in the same tent with the other. The university did not want to dilute its mission and its "destiny" (even though on a few occasions Kerr used this as a threat). The state colleges did not want to be second-class citizens in a large organization whose principal mission they would not share. The issue was more complex than this rough description. One element of the negotiations, perhaps the only one, shared by all within the state colleges except Superintendent Simpson and his close associates (none of whom did serious battle on the matter) was the desire for a separate state college governing board, seemingly without any serious understanding or analysis of what this would mean for the campuses.

Dumke's role was to try to move the state college group together, as well as possible, and secure the establishment of the state colleges as more than a collection. In the almost yearlong saga, he had to try to keep as many of the leaders and groups together as possible to secure status and recognition for the state colleges. He embraced the substantive agenda of presidents and faculties and others to do that. For the most part, the public substantive agenda was not achieved—the freestanding doctorate, open-ended research, constitutional status as a fourth or fifth branch of government. What was achieved, however, was the creation of a structure, the California State Colleges, that would impact millions of lives and the culture and economy of California over the years ahead. The opportunity to build came with the implementation of the Master Plan.

Notes

[1] Minutes of the Council of State College Presidents, April 8–9, 1958.
[2] Dorothy M. Knoell, interview by the author, March 14, 2005.

³ I attended a formal academic ceremony at the Berkeley campus, one of many, as a representative of San Francisco State College.

⁴ Sproul's role became clear to me years ago. In the spring of 1958, as a new arrival in California and soon to be dean responsible for admissions and relations with schools at San Francisco State, I was invited by President Glenn Dumke to accompany him to the spring articulation conference. Then held twice each year, the articulation conferences provided a setting for representatives and leaders of all of California public higher education to meet. The gathering was in President Sproul's large conference room on the Berkeley campus, around a large rectangular table. Sproul sat at one end of the table; on either side of him were Grace Bird, the UC director of relations with schools, (a former junior college president), and Herman Spindt, the UC director of admissions. At that time, the individuals responsible for a given function on the Berkeley campus were, for the most part, responsible for that function university-wide. Around the table were the UC campus heads, the state college presidents, and most of the junior college presidents of the state (this was 1958 and there were many fewer junior colleges in California than there are today). Each campus head could bring one staff member; the staff members sat in chairs against the wall. Sproul chaired the meeting. Grace Bird had the agenda with all of the supporting papers. The issues had to do with curriculum and transfer, and how the campuses related to each other—should, for example, anthropology XYZ at ABC junior college be considered as transferable and, if so, is it physical or social anthropology? How does the engineering curriculum at XYZ state college relate to the engineering program at ABC? Bird would introduce the item. It would be discussed around the table. At some point Sproul would observe that it seemed clear that the matter should be resolved as whatever, and he would state the resolution, hit the gavel on the table, and ask Bird for the next agenda item. It was a different way of transacting business then.

⁵ Minutes of the Liaison Committee of the Regents and the State Board of Education (hereafter cited as the Liaison Committee), December 11, 1958.

⁶ The California legislature convened in regular session in the years after general elections, the odd-numbered years; during that year, there was no limit or boundary on subject matter for bills introduced. During the even-numbered years, the second year of each two-year legislature, only budget matters could be addressed, unless a special session on a specific topic or topics was convened by the governor. This was revised in 1966, with a constitutional change establishing a full-time legislature.

⁷ *A Master Plan for Higher Education in California, 1960–1975*, prepared for the Liaison Committee of State Board of Education and the regents of the University of California, California State Department of Education, Sacramento, 1960.

⁸ Keith Sexton, interview by the author, January 26, 2007.

⁹ The references for this quote and the story of the March 14 joint meeting are from "Minutes of the Joint Meeting of the State Board of Education and the Regents of the University of California," March 14, 1959, Berkeley, California.

¹⁰ "Minutes of the Joint Meeting," March 14, 1959, 322.

¹¹ Minutes, Liaison Committee, April 2, 1959.

¹² Sexton, interview.

¹³ The references for this quote and the story of the April 15 joint meeting are from "Minutes of the Joint Meeting of the State Board of Education and the Regents of the University of California," April 15, 1959, Los Angeles, California.

¹⁴ *A Master Plan*, 21–22.

¹⁵ *Ibid*, 19.

¹⁶ *Ibid.*, 23–24.

[17] Sexton, interview.

[18] Memorandum to regents, May 19, 1959; a copy is in the Archives of the CSU.

[19] Glenn Dumke, then president of San Francisco State College, asked me, then a young associate dean at SFSC, to check the higher education backgrounds of the members. As has been my custom with many matters over the years, I have kept notes, though at that time I had no anticipation of preparing this manuscript. At that time I was preparing a dissertation, "The Government of Public Higher Education in California," which addressed the pre–Master Plan situation. My notes say: "50+ university alumni."

[20] The contents of this chapter are drawn from a substantial number of interviews, oral histories done in previous years, memoirs, papers, and the like. Most of these sources are available (including all of the interviews and oral histories) in the Archives of the CSU, at the Dominguez Hills campus. I also draw upon my papers, notes, calendars, and files, which I have maintained over the years since joining the faculty and my appointment at San Francisco State College in 1958.

[21] Sexton, interview; Glenn Smith (he was assistant to Dumke, 1958–1961, and later vice president at San Francisco State and chancellor, San Mateo Community College District), Gerth interview April 1, 2004; Dumke, oral history, April–June 1984, Regional Oral History Office; Dumke, oral history, July 18, 1981, and March 27, 1987, Archives of the CSU; Glenn S. Dumke Collection, Archives of the CSU.

[22] Dr. Roy Simpson, personal letter to each state college president, July 16, 1959.

[23] Arthur G. Coons, *Crises in California Higher Education: Experience under the Master Plan and Problems of Coordination, 1959–1968* (Los Angeles: Ward Ritchie Press, 1968). The minutes of the survey team meetings are at the office of the California Postsecondary Education Commission, Sacramento.

[24] Lyman Glenny, oral history, June 24, 1988, Archives of the CSU; Lyman A. Glenny, *Autonomy of Public Colleges* (New York: McGraw-Hill, 1959).

[25] Malcolm A. Love, letter to state college presidents, memorandum about "revision of the functions statement and a basic statement of functions of higher education," August 17, 1959; Glenn S. Dumke, memorandum to state college presidents, August 12, 1959, Archives of the CSU.

[26] Glenny, *Autonomy of Public Colleges*, 26–38.

[27] "Summary of Faculty Opinions Concerning the Master Plan Survey," November 13, 1959; document proposed for November 13, 1959 meeting of presidents and faculty representatives, Archives of the CSU.

[28] "Resolution of the Faculty Representatives for the Master Plan Survey Team," November 14, 1959; conference notes, faculty representatives, state college presidents, division of state colleges staff meeting, November 14, 1959, Los Angeles State College, all at the Archives of the CSU.

[29] Arthur Hall, interview by Gerth, March 1, 2005. Hall was a significant figure in the development of the system. A mathematics faculty member at San Francisco State, Hall represented the state colleges on the technical committee on costs of higher education; he was a major informal advisor for Dumke through the Master Plan negotiations and into implementation; and he became state college dean for institutional research in 1961, a position he held for ten years.

[30] A. Alan Post, oral history, Donald Seney, California Oral History Project, April 23 to June 4, 2002; interview by author, February 28, 2006.

[31] Donald Leiffer, oral history, November 24, 1980 and March 26, 1987, 5–6; Archives of the CSU.

[32] Dumke, oral history, July 18, 1981, 8. Dumke recounted this to me at the time it happened.

[33] Minutes, Liaison Committee, December 7–9, 1959; Dumke, oral interview; Clark Kerr, *The Gold and the Blue*, vol. I (Berkeley and Los Angeles: University of California Press, 2001), 180–82.

[34] *A Master Plan*, iii.

[35] Glenn Dumke and Arthur Browne, "Memorandum to presidents and faculty representatives, December 11, 1958, Archives of the CSU.

[36] Bruce Allen, "Does Your Child Plan to go to College?" Press release, February 11, 1960.

[37] Glenny, *Autonomy of Public Colleges*.

[38] Roy Simpson, letter to presidents, February 24, 1960, Archives of the CSU.

[39] Post, interview.

[40] *San Francisco Examiner*, March 9, 1960.

[41] Interviews, Donald Leiffer, Louis Heilbron, Sexton; Ethan Rarick, p. 151; the author has pieced together the contents of this meeting from a number of sources.

[42] *San Francisco Chronicle*, March 29, 1960.

[43] California Education Code, sec.1, div. 16.5, chap. 3, secs. 22600–607.

[44] California Legislature, Extraordinary Session of 1960, Senate Concurrent Resolution 16.

[45] The admissions matter will be discussed extensively in later chapters.

[46] The issue of coordination will also be addressed later in this work.

Chapter 3

From Campus Autonomy to System Integration—1960 to 1970

This chapter covers the major events of the Master Plan transition years, and the creation of a coherent system of institutions, related to each other in an overarching mission and yet each individually distinctive.

Governor Brown signed the Donahoe Higher Education Act on April 14, 1960, and the Master Plan for Higher Education in California became a reality. The years from the end of World War II in 1945 to 1960 had been difficult in many ways for the leaders of public higher education in California. Tensions had often been high and relationships strained, yet hundreds of thousands of students had been educated. From the end of World War II in August 1945 to the spring semester of 1960, when the Donahoe Act was signed, the California State Colleges had awarded 99,269 degrees; of these, 11,306 were master's degrees. What had been hundreds of faculty and staff in 1945–46 had become several thousand in 1959–60, all working to educate these students.

A Transition Year

Governor Pat Brown and the legislature helped to set the stage for the state college transition, with a 7½ percent faculty pay increase for 1960–61. The raise was not only supported by the usual cost of living and price indices, but was also a gesture of confidence and expectations. Forming the system was the work of the 1960s. The beginning of this period was marked by the first meeting of the Board of Trustees of the California State College System, on August 12, 1960; its end was signaled in late 1970, with Chancellor Glenn Dumke's set of addresses, "New Approaches," first given to the board and then around the state generally.

Between August 1960 and fall 1970, the trustees, chancellors Buell Gallagher and Glenn Dumke, and many others methodically assembled a state college system, piece by piece, issue by issue. There were many achievements and, from a long-term point of view, there was remarkable progress. There were also stumbling points, and there was resistance, from those who perceived correctly the loss of the autonomy enjoyed during the previous era, and from those who wanted a new autonomy—a system whose purpose would be to funnel money and provide for conditions and a mission identical, at least, to those of the University of California. Then, beginning in the mid-1960s, there was the student and faculty unrest, which surely had an impact on the shaping of the system and the values of those who witnessed it or participated in it.

After becoming chancellor, Glenn Dumke convinced members of the legislature to drop "System" from the title of the institution, and let it be called the California State Colleges. Dumke thought the word conveyed a poor message about the nature and properties of an academic community. Though it was dropped as a part of the legal name, this work will continue to use the word on occasion, for lack of a better one (in fact, it has continued in common parlance, over the years).

* * *

The Donahoe Act provided that the board of trustees of the California State Colleges would assume full and legal responsibility for the colleges on July 1, 1961. The act provided for a twenty-one-member board, sixteen of whom were to be appointed by the governor, and five of whom were ex officio: the governor, the lieutenant governor, the speaker of the Assembly, the superintendent of public instruction, and "the person named by the Trustees to serve as the Chief Executive Officer of the System." The act provided however, that ten of the sixteen first gubernatorial appointees would be the ten members of the State Board of Education then sitting, and the governor could appoint an additional six members. The sixteen would draw for term lengths ranging from one to four years.[1]

The legislature and the governor placed on the November 1960 general election ballot Senate Constitutional Amendment 1, which separated the state colleges from the State Board of Education and established the Board of Trustees of the California State College System, and the colleges as an entity within California state government. The amendment, which passed overwhelmingly, provided eight-year terms for the appointed trustees, and required that the appointed members again draw for terms, this time all eight-year terms.[2]

9. *Donald Leiffer.*

The board of trustees was to have a planning year prior to assumption of legal responsibility. The State Board of Education and the superintendent of public instruction would be legally responsible through June 30, 1961, but the same individuals supplemented by the six new gubernatorial appointees and the ex-officio members would be responsible for planning the takeover. This was an ingenious design as it provided for both continuity and change.

On April 4, 1960, Dr. Donald Leiffer, the on-leave San Diego State College political science professor who was working as a member of the governor's staff, wrote to Fred Dutton, a senior member of the governor's staff, about education budgets. Leiffer's assignment had not been higher education originally, but in the final months of the Master Plan he had become involved in negotiations on behalf of the governor. Leiffer made special note of the necessary increase in budgets for the state colleges and the University of California, and he described that increase, not for new programs but for enrollment only, from $49,038,000 to $70,900,000 for the state colleges, and from $95,239,000 to $118,360,000 for the University of California, over three years of budget cycles. He also noted a need of $93,000,000 for capital outlay for both the CSC and the UC; at that time capital outlay was funded from the state general fund, not a special fund or bonds.[3]

Leiffer was asked to help with the transition to the board of trustees. On July 13, 1960, he wrote to the governor, reminding him that the organizational first meeting of the new board of trustees would be August 12, a date chosen so that the governor could attend. The governor was ex-officio president of the trustees (as he was of the regents). Leiffer's memo was a five-page summary of higher education issues on the governor's plate, and he addressed not only the trustees' meeting and agenda, but the forthcoming November election and the constitutional amendment that would formally establish the trustees separate from the State Board of Education, and provide for eight-year terms (the California Constitution limits terms of members of state boards of all kinds to four years, so a special constitutional provision needed to be made, as it had been in the previous century for the regents). Leiffer also addressed the need to give a strong start to the soon to be established Coordinating Council for Higher Education, to new campuses for both the state colleges and the University of California, and to financial support, especially for faculty salaries and for the junior colleges, as they would gain lower-division enrollment from the state colleges and the University of California under the terms of the Master Plan.

Governor Brown appointed six trustees in late July 1960. The board met for the first time on August 12, 1960, in the governor's council room in the state capitol. All seats were filled, save only one constitutional member, "the person named by the Trustees to serve as the Chief Executive Officer of the System." In his role as president of the board, the governor opened the meeting. He remarked on the historic nature of the meeting and the pioneering responsibility of the first board members, to build from fifteen colleges with almost 95,000 students to 170,000 students in 1975 (by 1975–76, there were in fact more than 312,000 students on nineteen campuses). Brown addressed the importance of the November 1960 election and a favorable vote, to increase the terms of board members to eight years and place the board and the colleges in the constitution. Finally, he talked about the importance of cooperation among the segments of higher education and the newly established Coordinating Council for Higher Education. He announced that one of his initial trustee appointees, Warren Christopher, would resign before the end of the meeting to accept an appointment to the council. A few weeks later, Christopher became the founding chair of the Coordinating Council (he would later become U.S. Secretary of State).

The members of the board elected Louis Heilbron as chair and Thomas Braden as vice-chair. They determined terms by lot. In preparation for the meeting, Leiffer had purchased sixteen empty capsules in a nearby drugstore, and with a staff member in the office, he tore paper into sixteen small pieces and wrote down four sets of terms, from one to four years, all expiring on March 1, from 1961 to 1964. He stuffed a piece of paper in each capsule, placed the capsules in a hat, and passed the hat. Heilbron drew a one-year term (actually six and one-half months), until March 1, 1961. He was subsequently reappointed to a full eight-year term after the constitutional amendment passed in November.

Heilbron, after thanking his colleagues for their trust in him, observed "the challenge in this present phase of higher education in California is to bring the fifteen State Colleges into an integrated system with high standards and uniform procedures. The most important of the immediate tasks is the selection of a top flight executive officer."

Superintendent Simpson remarked that he appreciated the need for change and that during his administration the state colleges had more than doubled in enrollment. The members set dates and places for meetings through June 1961; two of the meetings, in the spring of 1961—budget time in the legislature—were to be at Sacramento State College. Warren Christopher moved that the chair be asked to appoint three committees: the first would address the selection of a chief executive officer to assume office on July 1, 1961, and interim personnel required for the planning period to June 30; the second would address budget and finance; the third organization and rules; the chair would serve ex officio on all committees. Representatives to the Coordinating Council were selected.

Warren Christopher then officially resigned from the board; and the governor seated his replacement, Charles Luckman, who was also at the meeting. Thus Christopher and Luckman were both present at the beginning; Luckman would prove to be second only to Heilbron in leading the establishment of the board of trustees as an effective and powerful agent in transforming a set of mostly autonomous institutions to a cohesive entity.[4]

When the August 12 meeting adjourned, Leiffer retreated to his office in the governor's complex. Shortly the members of the selection committee were at his door, to offer him the position of secretary to the board, the board's chief administrative officer, for the interim or planning period through June 30, 1961. Leiffer's response was that he "could not visualize that role and that title," and he urged that whoever was in that role "should have a more responsible assignment than was suggested by that title." He had no opinion about what the title should be, but he told the members he did have an opinion about salary. "If I were to be selected, I would request a salary of at least $100 more than the top salary paid to any state college president." He was clear that the position needed to be defined in relation to the presidents "[w]ho were a pretty independent group, or he would be ineffective in the role." The committee did not disagree; they had not thought the matter through, and it was clear they were not prepared to agree.[5]

Leiffer had completed his leave from San Diego State; he returned to the campus. "[M]y son enrolled as a freshman ... and I enrolled as a returning alien in the faculty corps." Not long after, Louis Heilbron phoned Leiffer and asked Leiffer to come to San Francisco to meet. Leiffer agreed. He then phoned John Carr, the state director of finance, later to be a trustee. He asked Carr about support for the planning year; two hundred and fifty thousand dollars had been allocated. Carr asked what Leiffer would need, and Leiffer's response was "at least one million." Carr said he would find the money. Leiffer then asked to borrow, at least for the year, two individuals from the Department of Finance staff; one was Jim Whitsel, who had been responsible for the budgets of the University of California and the state colleges, and the second was George Normington, who had worked in Finance with most other state agencies. Carr agreed.

Leiffer came to San Francisco, met with Heilbron and with two additional trustees, Tom Braden and Ted Meriam, and Carr. Heilbron offered the position to Leiffer, all agreed on the title, administrative officer, and the salary was exactly one hundred dollars more than the highest state college presidential salary.

Leiffer accepted. The board met at the San Jose State campus on September 16, and Leiffer was appointed.

At the end of the meeting Superintendent Roy Simpson came to Leiffer and offered him office space for the planning group in the State Department of Education building on the mall a few blocks from the capitol. Leiffer responded with what he called his first decision: "Thank you very much Roy, but I believe that when a man has divorced his wife, he shouldn't go to bed with her again, and we'll find quarters on our own."[6] Leiffer, who had found his way around state government for a year on the governor's staff, turned to a unit in the Department of Finance that located space, and he secured offices immediately across the street from the capitol.

Shortly after the September board meeting, trustee chair Heilbron was invited to testify before the Assembly Ways and Means Committee. He accepted the invitation and reviewed with the members the tasks to be done in the planning year and the details of the transition. While making clear that at this early stage he spoke only for himself, Heilbron addressed in some detail educational policy for the newly minted California State Colleges—"first-rate teaching colleges"—and he provided a definition, "a college that stresses high standards of instruction and emphasizes instruction." He did address common curricula between the state colleges and the University of California, and graduate degree programs; he emphasized master's degree programs, which he characterized accurately as having "lost their luster" in many fields and institutions. He talked of admission standards and the need to emphasize college preparatory courses: "[M]ore solid stuff…. [T]he right to enter cannot be based on some pleasant social custom or easy qualifying courses." Finally, he addressed expansion, and the need to address faculty status and faculty-administration relations. He made it clear that faculty viewpoints needed to be heard not only on campuses, but at the statewide administration and the board. "The State Colleges have come of age in [a] period of growth … they will be coordinated into a system under the new Chief Executive Officer and the Trustees … the direction of the State Colleges seems clear."[7]

* * *

In the months after the governor signed the Donahoe Act, the presidents were almost adrift. Legally, their reporting relationship to the state superintendent remained intact. Other than for the routine of operations, however, that relationship was ending. The state superintendent would, in the new life of the state colleges, be on the governing board, as one among twenty-one. The ten members of the State Board of Education would be, at least initially, on the new board of trustees. But prior to July 1, 1961, when the trustees would assume legal responsibility, each of the State Board of Education members would have to make a choice: either go with the trustees of the state colleges, or remain with the state board for the remainder of their appointed term.

As a practical matter, the presidents had no one in authority to report to or talk with. The presidents met as a group a few days in advance of the August 12 organizational meeting of the trustees. They prepared a twelve-page memorandum to Superintendent Simpson. The memorandum opened with a three-part statement that offered support for the new board of trustees and its executive officer, and assistance in the transition, hope that they would individually and collectively work closely with the new governing board and its executive officer, and strong support for "the maximum autonomy of each state college consistent with the requirements of the statewide organization." The document presented statements and, in some instances, resolutions on a variety of matters. The presidents expressed support for the creation of a representative body of faculty on each campus, and repeated verbatim a state board resolution inviting campuses to submit to the board proposals for the establishment of more effective cooperation and participation. On a very positive note, the presidents suggested a statewide conference of faculty representatives, the executive officer to be appointed, and the presidents to "discuss the implications of the Master Plan."

A set of proposals for legislation to supplement the Master Plan was presented in the form of resolutions, all adopted unanimously by the presidents. These addressed shifting authority from various state agencies to the trustees, clarifying the Master Plan, and various personnel matters such as tenure, salaries, leaves, promotions, and faculty communications with the legislature. They were very specific on one matter: end the practice of administrators (all but presidents) holding tenure in their administrative positions, a practice that had made change on campuses difficult since the postwar years. At the beginning of a fourth year, faculty and those in academic administrative positions—coordinators, associate deans, deans, vice presidents—received tenure. When promoted, whether in academic rank or to an academic administrative position, they acquired tenure in their new position. The group also went in some detail into the responsibilities of presidents.

This remarkable document was addressed to Simpson. Clearly, the intended audience was the board of trustees and at least whatever interim administration would be established. The document ended on a note of caution about "over centralization," and the regional autonomous base of each campus was a consistent theme. No staff member in a new central office was to have any authority to issue a "directive."[8] The minutes of the board of trustees for 1960–61 do not reflect any discussion of this document, though it surely helped set the stage for the transition.

* * *

Immediately after becoming administrative officer, Leiffer set about organizing a small transitional office. The first professional appointees were borrowed from the Department of Finance: James Whitsell, to prepare a budget for the 1962–63 year, and George Normington, to work with the state agencies that the colleges needed for various financial, personnel, and other purposes. The extraordinary growth rate of the colleges underscored the need to maintain a sizeable capital outlay budget. Leiffer borrowed Harry Brakebill, the executive dean at San Francisco State, for one year, to develop capital outlay budgets for 1961–62 and 1962–63. Typically, the governor's budget for the coming fiscal year is completed in December for submission to the legislature in early January. There was not much time to prepare a budget for 1961–62, and for the most part the individual campus budgets were used, while a budget for a central office was needed. The office had no designated legislative advocate. President McPhee of Cal Poly offered a senior staff member, Harold Wilson, who was credible and widely known in Sacramento, as an interim advocate. Wilson played this role until a Sacramento office was created later.

In October 1960, the trustees made the decision that the chief executive officer to be recruited would be given the title of chancellor. In a sense the juxtaposition of titles between the University of California and the state colleges reflected the histories of each. The university, a single institution, had a president; campuses grew from the center and were administered by chancellors (a title first used by the university in 1952). With the state colleges, which had grown independently, the center grew from the campuses. Thus, the campuses had a history of chief executive officers, or presidents, and the chancellor's role emerged from that.

Faculty interest in this transition year was high. Glenn Dumke, then president of San Francisco State, wrote to Leiffer in October about the importance of paying attention to faculty organizations. The immediate occasions were two. The regents had, in their budget proposal for 1961–62, a 1.8 million dollar request to establish group life and health insurance programs for their twenty-one thousand employees. Dumke pointed out that such insurance was available to state college employees only through faculty and staff organizations. The previous weekend, the presidents and chairs of all faculty council–senate groups from all campuses met in San Francisco. Their objective was to move the trustees to establish some form of statewide organization. The leadership of the faculty group had consulted Dumke about their agenda, and Dumke noted to Leiffer that he had urged them not to be impatient, as the trustees necessarily had "organizational tasks before they can come to grips with some of the basic problems." Dumke concluded that "the push is on and I feel a comment is not out of order."

Dumke's recommendations to Leiffer included inviting representatives of faculty groups and councils to work with the board and presidents' committees to develop a proposal, as "any attempt to impose an organization unilaterally from above will meet with little cooperation." He urged that the trustees not delegate final policy authority on any matters either to a faculty council or senate, or to the presidents—in essence, not to copy what the regents of the University of California had done in earlier years, immediately after World War I. Finally he pressed for the trustees to take immediate leadership.

Dumke had a faculty-centric view, and he wanted and urged consultation; he was firmly opposed to delegated power. "I am embarrassed at urging haste, but there are so many people and so many organizations eager to step into the breach that I am fearful of serious complications unless the Trustees assume the position of being the champions of the state college faculties.... It is more a question of attitude than of techniques, but the attitude, believe me, is most important." Dumke copied his letter to board chair Louis Heilbron and to Roy Simpson, who was, in theory, still the chief administrator of the colleges.[9]

At their December 1960 board meeting, the trustees formalized a five-committee structure. This would include committees on educational policy; campus planning, buildings and grounds; finance; faculty and staff affairs; and gifts and public affairs. The trustees also discussed convening a meeting of presidents, faculty representatives, and the board to discuss the transition, the future, governance—essentially, the mission of the California State Colleges— and the work to be done. The State Board of Education, in the spring of 1960, before the trustees had come into being, had already addressed the importance of a faculty role in governance; Heilbron was in the chair of the state board by that time. In an interview years later, Don Leiffer noted that in the autumn of 1960 "anyone could sense separateness in the air."[10] The potential for strife was building.

On March 4, 1961, ten trustees, ten presidents and five representatives of presidents, thirty faculty representatives, and nine individuals from the administrative office (virtually the entire staff) convened at Fresno State College for a daylong conference. Governor Brown addressed the group about his hopes for the state colleges. He was specific about growth. Don Leiffer, who chaired the meeting, noted that faculty councils and presidents had provided the trustees with criteria for the selection of a chancellor. He joined the matter about the importance of establishing fully representative faculty senates and councils. Louis Heilbron was the most substantive speaker. He presented an eight-point agenda emphasizing "mature liberal arts programs . . . reasonable provision for research . . . teacher education with an emphasis on academic subjects rather than on teaching methods . . . [and] the development of new admission standards." Heilbron also addressed the faculty role in governance of campuses and put on the table the question of whether there should be a "statewide representative faculty body." Heilbron's address was widely distributed on the campuses.

The group broke into three small mixed discussion groups chaired, respectively, by a faculty member, a president, and a trustee. The small-group reports were fairly consistent and addressed faculty recruitment, retention, and working conditions; faculty participation in governance and, to a lesser extent, how campus planning and development could improve academic programs; and the mission of the state colleges. Heilbron closed the day with the comment, "[T]he day

10. Louis Heilbron

provided a foundation for common understanding, and the need and importance for a second meeting."[11]

At the meeting when a chancellor would be appointed, on April 6, 1961, the trustees passed the following resolution: "Resolved, that it is the policy of the board of Trustees of the California State Colleges that a representative faculty body be established at each state college for the purpose of participating in the determination of educational and professional policy."[12] A second meeting did take place, after the chancellor was appointed and again at the Fresno campus. The new chancellor, Buell Gallagher, was to preside and speak. About an hour before the meeting was to begin, the chancellor walked through a glass door and had to be taken to a hospital. The meeting was less significant than the first gathering, understandably, given the circumstances.

The various faculty associations, membership groups apart from the councils and senates being established formally on the campuses, were vying for the role of spokesperson for the state college faculties with the legislature and governor. In late April 1961, the California College and University Faculty Association, in conjunction with the California Teachers Association, wrote to Governor Brown about "salary policy development and salary schedule and policy in California State Colleges." The twelve-page document was specific and provided wording for a proposed trustee resolution about salary levels and the method to be used in setting salaries. Attached to the memorandum was a third item on "faculty-administration relations." Similarly, Professor Arthur Bierman of the philosophy department at San Francisco State, who was representing the California State Federation of Teachers, wrote regularly through the 1960–61 academic year to several legislators about the importance—indeed, necessity—for the trustees to delegate a wide range of matters to faculty bodies.[13] The Association of California State College Professors joined the discussion, with a request that there be legislative delegation of authority to faculty bodies on each campus, on a wide range of matters to faculty.[14]

* * *

During the 1960–61 year, two new state college campuses were established. These had been authorized by the legislature as the Master Plan discussions were underway. In each instance the state superintendent and the State Board of Education were legally responsible for the appointment of a president and the establishment of the campus.

The first proposal for a campus in Stanislaus County had been made in 1949. Assembly Member Ralph Brown of Modesto (later to be Speaker), and Senator Hugh Donnelly of Turlock introduced bills to establish a state college in Stanislaus County. They reintroduced legislation in 1953, and again in 1955. Finally, in 1957, they succeeded in joining the proposal to fund the purchase of a state college site with a bill to purchase sites for campuses in Orange County, Alameda County, and the North Bay area (Napa and Sonoma counties). This was at the time of the activity leading up to the Master Plan. The establishment of campuses in Alameda and Orange counties was pursued immediately, but the North Bay and Stanislaus campuses were deferred, not out of any decision to do so, but simply because the necessary machinery and procedures were not set in motion quickly, and the actual establishment was caught up in the work of the Master Plan. The Liaison Committee of the regents and the state board had addressed these four potential campuses first in 1953.

The legislation authorizing a state college for Stanislaus County passed in 1959, and was signed by the then newly elected Governor Edmund G. Brown. Funds for purchase of a site had been appropriated two years earlier. Quickly, strenuous competition between the cities of Modesto and Turlock developed, and soon reached to Sacramento, where the decision was to be made by the State Public Works Board, a group chaired by the director of finance. A stalemate developed. Modesto was the larger of the two communities and had a junior college that was known for many of its programs. Turlock was a small community with no visibility. Members of the Public Works Board and others, including the state architect, visited a number of sites in the county. A final hearing was set.

Not long before the hearing, Governor Brown's first director of finance, Bert Levit, resigned to return to the private sector. He was replaced by John Carr; Carr became ex-officio chair of the State Public Works Board. (Carr would later play a pivotal role in the transition of the state colleges from the State Board of Education to the trustees of the state colleges, after which time he became a trustee.) At the State Public Works Board hearing in Sacramento, a sizeable group of interested parties, citizens and community leaders of Modesto and Turlock, state agency staff members, including architects, members of the legislature, gathered. Superintendent Simpson was represented by Dr. J. Burton Vasche, the associate superintendent responsible for the Division of State Colleges and Teacher Education. Vasche recommended the Turlock site. Ralph Brown, by then Speaker, was present. Even though he was from Modesto, he did not weigh in to the discussion. Carr did, and he supported Turlock strongly, and a Turlock site was chosen.

In May 1960, as the negotiations were completed and Governor Brown formally signed the Master Plan, a request for a fifty-six million dollar appropriation for construction of a permanent campus in Turlock went to the legislature. Shortly thereafter, Superintendent Simpson proposed to the State Board of Education the appointment of Vasche to the presidency of Stanislaus State, and the board approved. Vasche's position of associate superintendent would soon disappear, as would the division for which he was responsible. Vasche's appointment helped to move along the transition of the state colleges from the State Department of Education to the newly forming trustees. Vasche assumed the presidency on July 1, 1960.

The first task was to assemble a founding faculty and staff and find temporary quarters for the new institution in order to open the doors for students in September 1960. Vasche brought with him Gerard Crowley, an experienced and still relatively young state government administrator from Sacramento. Crowley, not an academic, had a background in financial and land and building development for the state, and Vasche named him executive dean in charge of the campus building program. Vasche also recruited an academic dean, a librarian from another state college, and faculty members. Perhaps because of the short time and the shortage of faculty nationally then, Vasche recruited many young faculty with newly acquired doctorates as well as a fair number still working on the degree; these young faculty built the campus from the ground up. The September 1960 opening of classes was planned and budgeted for 300 students, or 160 FTE (full time equivalent students, fifteen semester units). The first registration brought 756 students, shortly to increase to just over 800 students, and the FTE for the first year was 321.

Crowley's task was to find quarters for the institution. The Stanislaus County fairgrounds were in Turlock, a few miles from the chosen campus site. Crowley negotiated the rental of a portion of the fairgrounds, the section customarily used for turkey exhibitions. (Stanislaus County was, and is still for the most part, a rural agricultural county. It is known for turkey ranches.) The inevitable happened—Stanislaus State College became "Turkey Tech." When President John Moore arrived in 1985, in his address at the opening of the academic year, he announced that he never wanted to hear the words "Turkey Tech" again. The college had actually been named for the county rather than the community, to help pacify the leaders of Modesto. The name "Stanislaus" caused many to inquire about its origins. St. Stanislaus was bishop of Krakow, Poland in the eleventh century. One of the early California Franciscan Missions, located to the west of California's central valley along the coast, had converted to Roman Catholicism most members of an entire Indian tribe. Traditional Christian names were given to the converts; the chief was named Estanislao. Later the tribe revolted and the entire tribe migrated to the central valley. In the 1840s Mexican troops were sent to bring the tribe back to the area of the mission. A battle was fought. The Indian tribe won, the Mexican military retreated, and subsequently General John Fremont named the local river for the chief, Stanislaus River. Thus, Stanislaus County, Stanislaus State College, and California State University Stanislaus.

Stanislaus State College opened its doors in the 1960–61 academic year. The early years of Stanislaus State were not easy. In 1961, President Vasche was diagnosed with incurable cancer, and not long afterward, he was confined to his home. Dean Crowley was chosen by Vasche to represent him on the campus and in Sacramento. For about eighteen months, Crowley had the unenviable task of meeting with Vasche and Vasche's wife, who was caring for him at home, to receive instructions, and then working with the campus leadership, Sacramento offices, community leaders, the new administration in the transition—the entire range of people involved in one way or another with the establishment of a new state college. Crowley accomplished this skillfully and won the respect of all.

Vasche formally retired in early May 1962 and died at the end of that month. Glenn Dumke, who had only weeks before become chancellor, moved immediately to request the board of trustees to appoint Crowley as acting president for a year. Afterward, Crowley would remain at the Stanislaus campus as executive dean until the mid 1980s. He built the original physical campus and was a major positive player, especially in providing continuity in the development of the college.

The campus grew steadily but not explosively through the 1960s. It experienced more than a fair share of presidential change, from Vasche to Crowley to a new president in 1963, who resigned in 1968, and to another president in 1969. In the 1970–71 academic year, the number of students was just short of 2,600. The establishment of the Stanislaus campus was understood at the time to be a political and personal decision, a going-away gift for Ralph Brown, a longtime assembly member, who had become speaker in his last few years before his announced retirement.[15]

* * *

San Francisco State had built a strong extension and continuing education program in the years after World War II. Three campuses were in some measure the result of these activities: Hayward, Sonoma, and Stanislaus. Dr. Leo Cain, a San Francisco State dean who was the leader of these activities, would later become the first vice president at San Francisco State and then be appointed the founding president of the Dominguez Hills campus in Southern California.

Pressure for a separate campus, from communities in the northern Bay Area and Sonoma and Napa counties, had built during the middle and late 1950s. The

Santa Rosa Off-Campus Center of San Francisco State was established in 1956. It was a stopgap measure, in a sense, although those at San Francisco State who were involved did not see it that way. San Francisco faculty were offered the opportunity to move to the Santa Rosa Center. George McCabe, a faculty member from San Francisco State, was appointed director. McCabe served in this role until 1961; he would later lead some of the California State Colleges' most important initiatives in the 1970s. McCabe and his colleagues occupied rented quarters and proceeded to build a set of academic programs.

On the last day of the 1960 special legislative session, during which the Master Plan was enacted, Senator Joseph Ratigan introduced SB 43, a bill calling for the establishment of Sonoma State College. It passed in both houses that day. Governor Brown signed the bill on May 2, 1960. The Santa Rosa Center would remain in operation through the 1960–61 academic year. The need for a state college in the North Bay area had been identified by the Liaison Committee in the 1950s, and funds had been appropriated for purchase of a site in 1957. The purchase had not happened, not as a result of any specific decision, but simply because it was caught up in all of the activities leading up to the Master Plan. The 1957 appropriation also included funds for Alameda and Orange County campuses, and these were given priority because of population and political pressures. Ratigan seized an opportunity in the legislature. He and his family would later become involved in site selection and purchase.

A president was needed. There were no provisions for a faculty role in presidential selection at this point in the development of the state colleges. State Superintendent Simpson consulted Don Leiffer about the appointment and then recommended Dr. Ambrose Nichols to the state board. Nichols, a professor of chemistry of some note at San Diego State, had been a close colleague of Leiffer at the San Diego campus. In February 1961, Dr. Nichols was appointed the founding president of Sonoma State College. The faculties at the San Francisco Santa Rosa Center were offered the opportunity to remain at Sonoma State or return to San Francisco State. Most, including McCabe, remained.

Nichols began his active leadership of this new college in the summer of 1961, parallel in time with the assumption of responsibility by the board of trustees. Nichols quickly captured the support of the faculty, the students, and the community, and he became known to all as Amby. Perhaps the most important thing Nichols did was to make clear from his first day that Sonoma State College was a liberal arts college. He was unwavering with this message, which was not perceived as controversial or a challenge to the colleges' teachers college history by anyone, including, notably, the teacher education faculty. The 1961–62 year opened with the college in temporary rented quarters in Rohnert Park. A permanent site was soon selected, and the college moved to it in 1966.

The initial academic plan for the college was influenced by the early academic planning work of the newly established chancellor's office. The academic plan included the liberal arts and sciences and two professional fields, business and teacher education. The faculty wanted more than the conventional fields, and with the leadership of Nichols it developed a wholly new type of academic plan around the concept of cluster schools. The initial centerpiece of this plan was the Hutchins School of Liberal Studies, named for Robert Maynard Hutchins who had been president of the University of Chicago and a forthright leader of the liberal tradition in higher education. Hutchins was still alive when this naming happened in 1969. Nichols took the plan to the trustees and they adopted it.

Nichols resigned the presidency in 1969 amid considerable controversy. The student revolution of the last half of the 1960s was underway, though Sonoma State had been little affected. However, the culture of the campus was affected; students elected to the student body presidency a convicted felon who was about to be released. An uproar followed, and the trustees became involved—although this was a sideshow, compared to what was underway at San Francisco State. The trustees moved to force the removal of the student body president, and Nichols did not agree; he wanted to resolve the conflict. Nichols consequently elected to step aside, as he did not see trustee support for his sense of freedom of action on the campus. He returned to teaching chemistry, where he remained, admired until his retirement and death many years later. The Sonoma campus retained much of the character impressed on it by Nichols over the years. By the 1970–71 academic year, the student body had increased to 4,122.[16]

Both the Stanislaus and Sonoma campuses were the product, not unlike the earlier campuses, of a combination of general population growth in the state and specific political pressure. The institutions that developed were, and are, different in character, in large part as a result of direction—or lack of it—from the founding president in the early years.

The First Chancellor

One of the most important responsibilities of the new board of trustees, in the 1960–61 transitional year, was the selection and appointment of a chief executive. In an initial action in August 1960, the board had created a committee to accomplish this and several other transitional tasks. In October, the board settled on the title of chancellor. The board's chair, Louis Heilbron, soon designated a core group of three members to work on the selection. The members of this group were Thomas Braden, a newspaper publisher in Southern California, Theodore Meriam, a department store owner in Chico, and Heilbron himself; Braden was chair. The trustees discussed at length the criteria for selecting a chancellor. In an oral history in the 1980s, Heilbron talked of the selection process. The trustees had wanted someone with a liberal arts orientation; with a "track record for meeting somewhat critical situations," and with experience in a large institution, "[S]o that he or she could come into the picture in our system and not be awed by his or her responsibilities."[17]

The trustees solicited widespread input about criteria and nominations or suggestions from faculties and presidents, students and staff, the Sacramento government community, the public, and nationally renowned figures. All of the major national higher education organizations and offices were encouraged to nominate individuals. The board received many nominations and input of all kinds. The group of three, Braden, Meriam, and Heilbron, sifted through these, checked out, at least initially, every nomination, and carefully discussed candidates with other members of the board. While candidacies from California were not excluded, interviews and records make clear that the emphasis in the search was on a national pool. Most campus presidents and faculty leaders expressed the opinion that an individual from California would bring complicated relationships to the role. The large pool of candidates—dozens—was narrowed in discussions among board members, and then the three-person committee prepared to undertake interviews.

California's new venture in higher education attracted national interest. The short list included two cabinet members from the Eisenhower administration (which had ended in January 1961), a very distinguished admiral (who had some background in higher education), one individual about to become a cabinet member in the Kennedy administration, and an individual who would later become a president of the University of Wisconsin.

The three trustees embarked on a nationwide trip to interview the narrowed-down pool of candidates. At this point the pool was not large. One of the candidates interviewed was Buell Gallagher, then the president of the City College of New York. City College of New York at that time was viewed as a premier and important public institution nationally, both within higher education and by the media. For years it had been an important intellectual center for the country. Clearly it was an institution open to a great variety of ideas and political activity. Gallagher had been president for nine years, was highly regarded by faculty and students, and he had enjoyed good press. Heilbron, Braden, and Meriam met with him on the CCNY campus, interviewed him, and then interviewed others about him on campus and in the city. The Gallagher interviews were the last in New York. Heilbron recounts a conversation with his colleagues in the taxi on the way to the airport from the interview. The three of them agreed that it was not clear whether they interviewed Gallagher or Gallagher interviewed them.

Gallagher was invited to come to California to meet with the full board. He did so, and the members were suitably impressed and voted to offer him the chancellorship. After considerable discussion with board members, especially with Braden, about the terms of the appointment (a factor to be major in ensuing months), Gallagher accepted the position, and the board announced the appointment at its meeting on April 6, 1961, the same meeting at which Heilbron announced that every campus should have a faculty senate. Gallagher immediately asked Leiffer to remain as administrative officer and work with him through the next steps of the transition. Leiffer agreed. Trustee chair Heilbron sent a telegram to his counterpart, the chair of the CCNY board. *The New York Times* editorial of April 8, 1961, was titled "The City Loses Dr. Gallagher";

New York loses more than a fine college president in the resignation of Dr. Buell G. Gallagher whose inspiring leadership has contributed to the improvement of City College for nearly a decade. It loses also one of its finest citizens, an exemplar of and spokesman for civil liberties, academic freedom, and high moral principles, who has left his impress on the mind and heart of the community.... As the first Chancellor of California's State College System, soon to comprise sixteen colleges, Dr. Gallagher will have under his administration the higher education of nearly 100,000 students. His election will surprise no one acquainted with Dr. Gallagher as a man or as an educator. New York, grateful for what he has done here, regrets his departure. No one is indispensable but it will be hard to find his replacement.[18]

The first board meeting Gallagher attended as chancellor convened on July 7 at the San Diego campus. The board began a practice, used to this day, of asking that the first substantive item on the agenda of the full board meeting (after committees) be a report from the chancellor. After a few words, Gallagher deferred to Leiffer, and Leiffer effectively summarized, in a detailed statement, the state of the California State Colleges, as the board and chancellor had just assumed responsibility and control July 1, seven days earlier. Much had been accomplished in the eleven months since the first meeting of the board on August 12 of the previous year. A budget for 1961–62 had been prepared. The state colleges were in the new budget year as of July 1. The first trustees' capital outlay budget had gone to the legislature and been funded for an initial year. Many meetings and discussions had been held about governance of the state colleges. Initial moves had been made by the trustees to develop campus academic plans, a new concept to most of the campuses, as the starting point for capital outlay planning and funding.

One of the routine activities, but a very important one, undertaken by Leiffer's small staff in the spring of 1961 was to comb California statutes and the administrative code for references to the state colleges and identify all those that needed to be changed, as a result of the change in the governance structure. The trustees were able to act almost immediately after assuming legal responsibility on a broad range of changes for the code, and to request legislative action on statutes in the state colleges legislative program.

When Leiffer finished his report, Gallagher added some of his own thinking about governance. He made it clear that substantial decentralization would be one of his administrative objectives. He also made clear his support for freedom of inquiry and his willingness to live with "the possibility of error" to be corrected by "exposing error to truth in a free and open debate." At the conclusion of the meeting, the trustees set in motion planning for the investiture of the chancellor, in a ceremony that would achieve "the widest possible coverage."[19]

When Gallagher flew in to California just before July 1, 1961, to assume his new office, he was met by reporters and photographers, and a barrage of questions. Many of the questions were about his political views and actions over past years, his educational background, and his professional history. Gallagher had received an education conventional for an academic of his time, a baccalaureate degree, and a PhD from Columbia University. Along the way he had attended the Union Theological Seminary in New York, received the bachelor of divinity degree, and been ordained in the Congregational Church. He had authored a number of books about race relations, and his Columbia dissertation was titled *American Caste and the Negro College*. During his presidency at CCNY, he had stoutly defended freedom of speech for all, including Marxists and professed Communists. The members of the news media probed him hard as he stepped off the plane. One result was a photograph on the front page of the *San Francisco Chronicle* accompanied by the quote, "I have not come to California to preside over subversion of the California State Colleges. . . ."

Almost immediately after the announcement of the Gallagher appointment, various extreme right-wing groups had begun a campaign opposing the appointment. The John Birch Society, then near the height of its activity, launched a campaign of accusations, letter-writing to the governor and other public officials, to the trustees as a group and individually, and attacking Gallagher in the media. A Bakersfield group calling itself the Student Research Committee circulated material over the state. Governor Brown's papers at the Bancroft Library at the Berkeley campus of the University of California contain hundreds of letters, some clearly from friends and acquaintances, opposing the appointment and asking that Gallagher be removed. Brown answered every letter, and he was supportive of Gallagher, as were the trustees.

Gallagher fought back. At the August 4, 1961 meeting of the board of trustees at the San Jose campus, Gallagher made a major statement about his political views and the subject of Communism. By this time, the efforts of the Birch group and others were common currency in the media and on the campuses, even in the summer. Gallagher denied that he was an agent of the Communist Party or linked in any way to Communist programs and movements. Again and again, he repeated the statement, "I have not come to California to preside over subversion."

Gallagher's background was one of a man of strong, deep convictions. He had identified himself with many humanitarian efforts over the years. After receiving his theological degree in 1929 from the Union Theological Seminary, he had served for ten years as president of Talladega College in Alabama, a liberal arts college serving a black student population; Gallagher was white. After leaving Talladega, he served as a professor of Christian Ethics at the Pacific School of Religion at Berkeley. He served as United States Chairman of World University Service, an international organization headquartered in Geneva, Switzerland, dedicated to rebuilding universities in the years after World War II.[20] In a very real sense, Gallagher was a perfect target for the Birch group and others who were attacking many of the conventions of U.S. civil society in the 1960s.

The faculties on the campuses of the state colleges in general had responded positively to Gallagher's appointment, and faculty senates and councils had passed resolutions of support. Gallagher had a public record at CCNY, and it was one that appealed to faculty. His doctorate from Columbia University was in education, so the teacher education faculties were satisfied. His work at Talladega had focused on the development of a liberal arts institution. For the presidents and other administrators, it was a time to wait and see; the presidents were supportive and cooperative, but most held their own counsel as controversy surrounding Gallagher developed.

Shortly after the July board meeting, Glenn Dumke wrote a remarkable letter to Buell Gallagher. It was strongly supportive to Gallagher and what he had said to the board and others about academic leadership and administration. The eight-page private letter walked Gallagher through some decision-making and other relevant issues in the creation of the Master Plan. He addressed the "fallout" from the Master Plan that would require early attention from the board and chancellor, the issues relevant to the concept of differentiation of function, which was the core of the Master Plan. In a key sentence he wrote, "I do not think that the [University of California's] greatness depends either upon 'keeping the state colleges in their place,' or upon building an undergraduate empire, and it seems to me to have an unfortunate desire to do both." The letter addressed "a wide and deep schism which has grown up over many years between faculty and administration, a sense of dichotomy which has had, and will have, if uncorrected, serious effects on our future." He urged in strong terms the creation of a statewide faculty representative body. "You have a magnificent opportunity to move into this system as the champion of all those high aspirations which both faculties and presidents hold to be important."[21] Dumke's letter to Gallagher was private, not shared with board members, presidents, or others. Dumke had explicitly removed himself from consideration for the chancellorship months before, as the trustees had initiated the search. He viewed his presidency at San Francisco State to be important, though it was difficult and would become even more so in the future.

At the August 4 board meeting, Gallagher submitted to the trustees a "Statement of General Principles in the Delegation of Authority and Responsibility." The document was comprehensive and covered academic (including faculty and administrative appointments and student affairs) and fiscal affairs. The document did not propose radical change, but did include some clear mandates about the establishment on each campus of grievance procedures and a faculty senate or council, with some definition of the scope of faculty consultation. The proposal also included a delegation to the chancellor of the authority to make all appointments in the chancellor's office except vice-chancellors, and the authority and responsibility to establish the organization of the headquarters office. The trustees reserved to themselves all authority not delegated in their action.

The August 4 meeting was a definitive one for the time in many ways. The most important action of the meeting addressed academic programs. The board adopted as stated policy "an initial complement of liberal arts and science offerings and certain professional programs for each state college." The list included specific degree programs and courses in the humanities, the social sciences, the sciences and mathematics, physical education, and the professional fields of business administration and education. This action had been triggered by the need perceived by the trustees, especially Charles Luckman, to have a programmatic base for the building program.

The Master Plan provided for California State College and University of California campuses to award joint doctoral degrees. The trustees approved the establishment of a ten-member joint graduate board, five individuals from each segment, to develop basic policy for awarding joint doctorates. This board would make the first policy recommendations to the trustees and the regents. Finally, the trustees approved a motion to establish the headquarters of the trustees in the Los Angeles area. At this meeting, the trustees acted on matters both major and minor; a fair number of the actions were about the details of the operations of the state colleges. The trustees were in charge.[22]

Gallagher was to some extent caught up in the political issue of Communist leanings and ideology from the day of his arrival. Subsequent to the August board meeting, the issue intensified. Both Governor Brown and trustee chair Heilbron had substantial correspondence on the matter and both supported Gallagher; Gallagher went to groups over the state, his theme consistently as he had stated it when he arrived ("I have not come to California to preside over subversion").

As Gallagher had given considerable assistance to the US military during World War II, the idea of recognizing him for his service came up, and was welcomed by the trustees and by Gallagher as well. A formal military ceremony was arranged for the San Jose campus, where there was a large ROTC program. The ceremony was held in October 1961. The commanding general of the 6th Army, then located at the Presidio of San Francisco, gave Gallagher an award on behalf of the Department of Defense. The day was one of formal military ceremony with many state leaders, Trustees, and others present. Gallagher spoke about American values. The anti-Gallagher activity continued unabated nonetheless. While support for Gallagher from the governor and trustees as well as campus faculties and students continued to be strong, the matter had clearly gone beyond the level of a mere distraction.

Gallagher continued his work within the state colleges. He began the process of staffing his office. He and the trustees had agreed that there would be three vice-chancellors: an executive vice-chancellor, a vice-chancellor for academic affairs, and a vice-chancellor for finance. Gallagher turned to Don Leiffer, who had shepherded the trustees and the new system through the transition year, and was still moving mountains of issues and material through the system administration, the trustees, and the campuses. Gallagher offered Leiffer his choice among the three vice-chancellorships; Leiffer chose executive vice-chancellor. At the same time, Leiffer suggested that an individual "acceptable around the system by the faculty and with leadership potential" be appointed to the academic vice-chancellorship. In addition, Leiffer recommended John Richardson to fill the financial vice-chancellorship role. Richardson had been in the Bureau of the Budget, had been vice-president of the Asia Foundation, and director of finance for the state of Oregon. Gallagher recommended Richardson to the board, and the board appointed him.

Gallagher approached Glenn Dumke. This became either known or assumed. There was what might be characterized as grumbling resistance from the faculty organization leaders and some presidents. At this point it became clear why the board had received pressure from some faculty leaders and presidents to go outside for the appointment of a chancellor. Dumke did not respond immediately to the offer from Gallagher. Dumke had been quietly approached about going to Oregon as the chancellor for public higher education in that state. The previous chancellor had accepted an offer to come to California as executive director of the California Post-Secondary Education Commission. Dumke had a San Francisco State staff member quietly gather information about Oregon, but after much thought, he accepted Gallagher's offer to become vice-chancellor for academic affairs.

Gallagher made two additional key appointments in the fall of 1961. For chief of personnel, he brought in Mansel Keene, whom he had come to know in his New York years, and who was then a senior US civil service administrator. To be chief of institutional research, he chose Arthur Hall, a professor of mathematics at San Francisco State who had done much of the detailed research for Dumke on the Master Plan survey team. Richardson needed chiefs for the budget and capital outlay, and he recommended George Clucas, an experienced administrator with years in the State Department of Finance, to be chief of the budget division. He recommended Harry Harmon, at that time number two person in the planning office at UCLA, as chief of physical planning and development. Clucas would eventually move to San Luis Obispo and become a dean. Harmon would become executive vice-chancellor, fourteen years later. Gallagher favored the title of "chief" for those reporting to vice-chancellors, and for lesser positions reporting to him, notably the personnel position.

Dumke was to have three chiefs: academic programs (later to be academic planning), student affairs, and institutional research. Art Hall was already in position in institutional research. James Enochs, a staff member from the Division of State Colleges in the Department of Education, was by this time at Los Angeles State College, and was borrowed to help in the academic programs position for an interim period. Enochs was a quite competent individual, certainly knowledgeable, but with political baggage from the past. He ultimately went to the new Sonoma State College as an academic dean.

The first priority in student affairs was to implement the Master Plan admissions provision for freshmen—the top one-third of high school graduates. Clark Kerr had already written to Gallagher about the state college failure, as he saw it, to implement the top one-third provision, and the correspondence had a sharp edge to it. Dumke attempted to bring in an administrator at San Francisco State College who had worked closely with him. The individual was asked to come to Sacramento for an interview with Leiffer. Gallagher dropped in to the interview briefly and listened. After he left, Leiffer explained to the interviewee that it was not practical to appoint anyone who had been close to Dumke to the chief position. The position was lost in the shuffle for another year and the admissions issue fell to the small institutional research office.[23]

Gallagher toured the state speaking to various interest and civic groups. He also toured the campuses, meeting with key administrators and others. He made a major address on each campus at a convocation of faculty. The participants in the formal convocation were faculty and administrative officers and Gallagher, all in cap and gown. The address Gallagher gave on the campuses was of a general philosophical character. There was no question but that he had enormous faculty support on the campuses. The support was related to his record, and to faculty anticipation for his administration. In his address at the San Jose campus, he argued the position that individual faculty in classrooms as well as institutions should be able to take positions on political and social matters, rather than simply encouraging students to have an open mind on political and social issues. The convocations were open to students and staff and the public but received little public notice, in contrast to the media coverage of allegations of Gallagher's pro-Communist stance and his addresses to community groups about his values and American values.

As the fall 1961 academic term began, the question of a schedule of presidential meetings arose. Gallagher let it be known that he believed that the presidents had great responsibility, particularly given the delegations to the presidents in the trustee actions of August 4, and that he did not want to intrude and take them away from their campuses with any frequency. He also informed presidents that he saw no need for them to spend time attending meetings of the board of trustees; presidents should feel free to attend trustee meetings when they were near their own campuses. The presidents received this message with concern about their roles in the newly emerging governance structure.

At the August 4 meeting, the trustees had made a decision to move their headquarters to Los Angeles. No specific site had been chosen. There was general agreement that the headquarters would not be on a campus, in order to avoid the perception that there was a "premier campus." However, the issue was not really settled. Substantial political pressure to remain in Sacramento emerged. Don Leiffer, now executive vice-chancellor, expressed his opinion that he felt it wise to stay in Sacramento; his alternative suggestion was to locate the office near the Los Angeles or San Francisco airports. Gallagher, who had spent ten years teaching ethics and theology at the Pacific School of Religion in Berkeley, wanted the office to be in or adjacent to San Francisco. At one point, as it appeared that the August decision for Los Angeles would stand, Gallagher pulled all of his headquarters office staff together and asked for a show of hands: who would join him in resigning in protest against a Los Angeles move? Only one staff member (a young individual on loan from the Department of Finance who had no intention to stay with the state colleges) raised his hand.[24] Board members eventually held firm, and Governor Brown did not intercede on behalf of the various state agencies and some legislators who wanted the headquarters in Sacramento. The move to Los Angeles took place in mid-December 1961. The "chancellor's office," as it is known internally to this day, was in rented quarters near the airport. The address was 2930 Imperial Highway in Inglewood, perhaps a ten-minute drive at that time from the Los Angeles Airport, and in the district of Jesse Unruh, the relatively new Speaker of the assembly. Unruh had advocated to the board and others very strongly, to have the office located in his district. The chancellor's office instantly became known, of course, as "imperial headquarters," and the name stuck, until a move a number of years later to another rented facility, considerably more adequate, on Wilshire Boulevard in Los Angeles (both facilities were owned by the California Federal Savings and Loan Association).

January 1962 brought more pressure about Gallagher's position on Communism as well as restlessness on the part of presidents and other campus administrators about working relationships. A meeting of the board of trustees was scheduled for mid-January at the San Luis Obispo campus, and the night before the meeting, many of the trustees gathered for dinner. Gallagher attended, but excused himself as dinner was ending to go to his room and prepare for the board meeting the next morning. After the dinner, as the trustees were leaving for their motel, Heilbron suggested that they gather for conversations in two groups, to avoid the appearance of an unscheduled illegal meeting, contrary to California's then-new open meetings statute. The trustees followed Heilbron's suggestion. They did not anticipate a member of the press following them for the evening. In one of the groups they talked about the Soviet Union; Tom Braden, the newspaper publisher trustee, had just returned from several weeks there. In the other group, trustees simply visited with informal conversation. There was some movement back and forth between the two groups. The headline in the *San Francisco Examiner* newspaper the next morning was about the trustee's illegal meeting to discuss Gallagher's status. In fact, there had been no discussion of Gallagher.

On the following day, Gallagher discussed with the board his positions about academic freedom and the invitation of speakers to campuses. There was no specific instance that prompted the discussion, which was general in character. He had earlier taken the position that presidents were responsible for speaker policies on their individual campuses. The coincidence of these two stories, one about an event that never happened, sharpened the issues swirling around Gallagher.

When Gallagher was appointed in April 1961, he asked for a "chancellor's house," a "generous discretionary and entertainment fund," and the transfer of his pension fund to California. There was no chancellor's house, and Gallagher was told so. He was not promised a home. Soon after the Gallaghers arrived in California, and the chancellor's office had been located in Los Angeles, President McPhee offered the Gallaghers a home at the Kellogg-Voorhies Campus of Cal Poly, but Mrs. Gallagher declined, stating that it would be too distant from the city, Los Angeles. (Mrs. Gallagher had been a New York City resident, and Pomona then seemed to her to be in the country.) Discretionary funds were limited. Trustee Braden, who dealt with Gallagher on these matters, told him to discuss pension transfer with the Department of Finance. Gallagher did, and re-

11. News clipping of Buell G. Gallagher's resignation.

reported that he was satisfied. By January, Gallagher had learned that his pension could not transfer. Mrs. Gallagher was unhappy with their situation and made that perfectly clear to others. She simply stated that she did not like California. Meanwhile, trustee Heilbron had initiated a campaign, raising approximately one hundred thousand dollars to purchase a chancellor's house, and that was on the list of things to be done. In the meantime, the Gallaghers lived in a home loaned to them by a trustee, on the Palos Verdes peninsula.

The invitations to the inauguration of Chancellor Gallagher had been mailed in early January to universities and colleges and a substantial constituency in the United States and abroad. The inauguration was to be a major event in downtown Los Angeles in March 1962; a procession leading from a major hotel to Philharmonic Hall was planned. An inauguration committee had been formed: Raymond Rydell, a dean at the San Fernando Valley campus was to chair, assisted by Thomas McGrath, a dean from the Kellogg-Voorhies campus. Both devoted almost full time to this. (Rydell later became vice-chancellor for academic affairs and then executive vice-chancellor; McGrath became a member of the chancellor's staff, then assistant executive vice-chancellor and, subsequently, president of Sonoma State College.)

In February 1962 Gallagher scheduled himself to participate in a conference in New York City. Mrs. Gallagher accompanied him. Unbeknown to the trustees, Gallagher had been in quiet conversation with members of the CCNY board for some time about returning to his previous position. Trustees would learn of this after Gallagher's departure. Gallagher met with members of the governing board of the City College of New York. His previous position had not been filled; CCNY had been operating with an acting president since Gallagher's departure the previous summer. Gallagher accepted an offer to return to the CCNY presidency. The chair of the board sent Heilbron a telegram, duplicating what Heilbron had telegraphed him the previous April, and wryly thanked Heilbron and the other trustees for giving Gallagher seven months of experience in California. Gallagher phoned Heilbron at home in the evening of the day he accepted the offer to return to New York and told him of his resignation. It was too late to notify other trustees, and most learned it from the morning newspapers on the next day. Leiffer was in Sacramento for a meeting when he received a call—too late for the last plane for Los Angeles.

Gallagher's explanation to the media focused on a loss of $8,000 per year in his pension. Heilbron, though publicly accepting of this, quietly checked the numbers and concluded that the difference would be a loss of about one thousand dollars per year, had Gallagher stayed to conventional retirement. The Gallaghers did not return to California at the time, but asked that their possessions be packed and shipped to New York. The Gallaghers had not moved any of their personal belongings to California, beyond clothing.

Gallagher remained at CCNY to retirement. After his death, Mrs. June Gallagher left New York to live near, and eventually with, their only child, a daughter. Ironically, given Mrs. Gallagher's strong and expressed dislike of California, the Gallaghers' daughter and her family lived in San Jose, and Mrs. Gallagher lived out her life there.[25]

The period of Gallagher's ten months, from his appointment in early April 1961 to resignation in mid-February 1962, was something of a roller-coaster ride for the California State Colleges. In many ways the new statewide structure was carried by Leiffer and those he brought in to help with the transition, and by the board of trustees. It was a united board, and there were a number of natural leaders in the group; Heilbron, Luckman, Meriam (the only Republican) and others, were strong and purposeful. The several staff appointments made in the late months of 1961 were important. The appointment of Dumke, certainly supported by the trustees, brought both substantial knowledge of the detail of the system's operations as well as a firm, if controversial, point of view about curriculum and the liberal arts and sciences and other matters as well. John Richardson, for all practical purposes selected by Leiffer, was a competent and seasoned administrator, albeit new to the state colleges. The presidents carried on, without benefit of their monthly gatherings, but they stayed in touch among themselves informally. In later years Heilbron speculated aloud in several oral histories about whether Gallagher came prepared to stay. Heilbron thought it likely that, given the convergence of controversy about Gallagher's values, the failure to obtain the pension and sizeable discretionary funds he requested, as well as his request that the CSC purchase a chancellor's home and his wife's negative reaction to living in California rather than in New York City, at some point Gallagher simply decided he should return to New York.

A Second Beginning

Gallagher's departure, most especially its sudden and unanticipated nature, was a shock to the faculty and staff, students, trustees, and presidents of the California State University, as it was to the governor, the legislature, and other state figures. Heilbron quickly consulted other trustees and an initial decision was made to not appoint an acting chancellor, but to have Don Leiffer simply remain in charge as executive vice-chancellor. The body of the discussion focused on what to do next. The choices explored included a new national search, or a search within California. The consensus was to look at candidates within California and, especially, within the California State Colleges. To paraphrase Louis Heilbron, from one of the oral histories: among twenty-five million people in California there must be at least one person who could fill the role. Candidates were discussed including Vice-Chancellors Dumke and Leiffer, and President Malcolm Love of San Diego State. The board concluded that some thought and informal consultation was needed.

In fact, there was no mystery about what was going on, at least in the minds of faculty leaders and presidents and political leaders, including members of the legislature and the governor. The most frequently mentioned name, by far, was Glenn Dumke's. During the earlier search that had produced Gallagher, much speculation had focused on Dumke. That speculation tapered off as the search went on, and its national character became known. In fact, Dumke privately told the trustees at the outset of the search that he would not be a candidate. When Dumke was nominated by Buell Gallagher to the board for the vice-chancellor for academic affairs, there had been resistance from some faculty and from some members of the legislature. Dumke was a known Republican and had been a delegate to the 1956 Republican presidential nominating convention. Some Democratic legislators brought pressure on the governor to insist that the chancellor be a Democrat. Brown resisted, but finally asked Heilbron to prolong the period of informal consultation and conversation among trustees by a month. Heilbron had hoped to have a board decision by early to mid-March. At the governor's request he postponed a decision to April.

The more significant opposition to Dumke came from within the state colleges. Dumke had baggage from his years in the presidency at San Francisco State. He had moved deliberately to change a central focus from teacher education to the liberal arts and sciences. He had encountered especially strong opposition to his emphasis upon the arts and sciences from the faculty in the Division of Education, and this became almost hostile. He had made some controversial appointments, in terms of the positions he created, some of the individuals he chose, and some due to the fact that formal and stylized consultation procedures had not been developed at San Francisco State, or any of the state colleges, at that time. By way of example, the college had two English departments. One was in the Division of Humanities and was in the conventional tradition of English departments, focusing on literature and the like. The other was in the Division of Language Arts, focusing on creative writing and contemporary poetry; in this latter department there were faculty with national reputations, and not just a few. Both departments taught freshman English, the bread-and-butter courses. The chair of the Division of Language Arts was also chair of English in that division—that, for the most part, was the division—and she was strong and widely admired, not only by her own faculty, but by many others. San Francisco State had at that time perhaps four points of nationally recognized excellence, all helped by the fact that it was in San Francisco; the Division of Language Arts was one of these points.

At the beginning of his third academic year as president, Dumke announced the merger of the two English departments into the Division of Humanities, and, at the same time, announced national searches for the chair of the division and of the English Department. He had consulted principally within his administration. Most of the advice he received was negative: don't do it. He was strongly convinced that the issue was one of academic integrity, and he moved ahead. The controversy was immense and the issue followed him for years.

From a political standpoint, the more important campus controversy was about governance and, for some faculty leaders, legislators, and others, about collective bargaining. The state colleges were coming out of the dark ages in terms of governance. This was clear in the last years leading up to the Master Plan negotiations, and was an underlying factor in advances made by faculty groups to members of the legislature during the year of transition. Only two campuses among the state colleges had made any significant progress toward a faculty role in governance to the time of the Master Plan, San Diego, under the leadership of President Malcolm Love (who had come to San Diego from another public presidency in 1952), and San Francisco, under the leadership of Glenn Dumke (who had come to the presidency in 1957 from the academic dean's position at the relatively small, respected, and traditional Occidental College). By 1961, faculty participation in governance on both campuses was in early stages of development, by conventional standards, but it existed. The strongest boost really had come from the State Board of Education in the spring of 1960, repeated by the trustees in the transition year. There was much naiveté among the faculty generally, while some members were seriously maneuvering for power. Some members of the legislature became involved, either for their own purposes or due to faculty pressure.

Dumke was perceived by virtually everyone as the front-runner for the newly vacant chancellorship because of the combination of his role in the Master Plan (essentially as Clark Kerr's opposite number) and his subsequent appointment as vice-chancellor. Some Trustees talked with him about the position immediately after Gallagher's sudden departure. Heilbron met with Dumke, and Dumke said he would be willing to undertake the responsibility.

Gallagher's resignation had come on February 13. Heilbron scheduled a closed meeting of the board for March 1–2, 1962. The meeting was in Sacramento, partly on the Sacramento State campus and partly in the capitol. The sole topic was selection of a chancellor. Governor Brown and Lieutenant Governor Glenn Anderson were both ex-officio trustees. Brown was scheduled to be out of state. He informed Heilbron that it was simply too early to make a decision. The day before the meeting, Brown had a letter delivered to Heilbron restating this. Anderson also stated publicly that he favored delay, and he participated in an evening meeting in the capitol that lasted beyond one o'clock in the morning. The matter was given widespread publicity in the newspapers, most particularly the San Francisco papers. Three days before the trustees' meeting, the executive committees of the three principal faculty organizations at San Francisco State— the Association of California State College Professors, the California Teachers Association, and the California Federation of Teachers—issued a joint public statement urging that the trustees delay an appointment and engage faculty groups in more consultation. Dumke's name was not mentioned in this statement or in any of the statements of groups on other campuses. The locus of the controversy was at San Francisco State.

The board met for two days in closed session. Dumke was invited to meet with the trustees on both days. Some trustees, including Tom Braden, who had chaired the search committee that recommended Gallagher, and still chaired the personnel committee, openly supported Dumke in the media. Speaker Unruh clearly supported Dumke. As to Dumke's politics, the governor said he thought the board should appoint the best person, Republican or Democrat. At the conclusion of the closed meetings, the board held a brief open session to announce that they would need more time and wished to consult with the presidents and the officers and representatives of faculty groups and organizations. Chair Heilbron stated that the board had set a thirty-day time schedule for an appointment to be made.

The board scheduled closed meetings with both groups. The presidents' meeting was not eventful. The meeting with faculty representatives was characterized as "difficult and tense," by one faculty member in a later news report. The faculty, forty-eight individuals from the sixteen campuses, met in advance of the meeting with the trustees. They adopted a resolution asking the board to lift the thirty-day time limit for an appointment, and requested a screening committee with equal representation from both the trustees and faculty members. The individual selected to be presented to the board would necessarily be acceptable to a majority of each group. The trustees declined to accept the faculty proposal. The remainder of the meeting focused on qualifications for the appointment. A proposal that some faculty groups had made in the first search, that the new chancellor should not come from the state colleges, the University of California, or any California education circumstance, was not accepted by either trustees or faculty at the meeting.

Postponing a board decision for a month to April provided time for a substantial amount of political activity. Jesse Unruh, speaker of the assembly and a trustee, (and the individual most responsible for the location of the chancellor's office in his district in Los Angeles) advised Heilbron, after he had agreed with the governor to postpone appointing a chancellor to April, that doing so had opened the board to political pressure that might well run away with the issue. Something resembling a campaign opposing Dumke's appointment developed. The issue of collective bargaining, or some form of unionization, complicated the issue on governance. This was being urged by some, especially the leaders in the already existing union affiliate. There was no question where Dumke stood on faculty participation in governance; he was forthrightly supportive and took the position that no healthy college or university could exist without faculty involvement. His definition of involvement, however, did not include formal and final delegation. Many faculty leaders cited as a model the delegation by the UC regents of final authority on some matters, a delegation that over time had become more symbolic than real. Quite apart from Dumke, the board, especially Heilbron, had already made it clear that there was no interest in final delegation. Not long after the move from Sacramento to the new Los Angeles offices (and well before Gallagher's unanticipated departure), Dumke, still using a large packing crate as a desk in his windowless office, held a number of informal discussions about how to move along the creation of a statewide faculty consultative body.

Collective bargaining and faculty unions were another matter. Dumke had no interest in these, and was genuinely opposed. (Though his style was a quiet one, it was not difficult for others to figure out his position.) This issue would not become a major one in the understanding of the faculty generally until the mid-1970s, but it would be a constant political factor in the years to that point.[26]

The board's next scheduled meeting was April 5–6, 1962, at the San Fernando Valley campus. The first item on the agenda was the appointment of a chancellor. Heilbron, as chair of the selection committee, reported that it had met four times; it had met with the presidents and with representatives of faculty from each of the sixteen campuses, and with a faculty committee of five selected from the group of sixteen campus faculty senate chairs. The selection committee received more than thirty names. Additionally, they reviewed the sixty individuals that remained after screening down from a list of one hundred and eighty nominees that had been in the earlier selection process from which Gallagher had been chosen.

Heilbron stated that the committee got to a "blue ribbon list" and had come to "the considered conclusion that the man who properly heads the list is Dr. Glenn S. Dumke." Dumke was appointed in a resolution adopted unanimously. Dumke, who had not been present for the report, was invited to address the meeting; he noted the "challenging and inspiring assignment," promised to "do

12. News clipping of Glenn Dumke's appointment as chancellor.

his best," and was seated. He was forty-three years old at that time. The board proceeded with a regular meeting.[27]

On the morning after the appointment, Dumke sent a letter to all faculty and staff in the California State Colleges. The letter was in a sense humble, and he observed that he would do his best to fill a role that demanded much. He wrote about a substantive agenda for the new system and about consultative procedures and mechanisms to be established.[28]

In the week after the board meeting, Dumke called a meeting of the presidents. The group had not met with regularity for almost one year. Dumke made it clear that he wanted the group to meet monthly, certainly before each meeting of the board of trustees, and that he wanted the group to have some structure. After discussions, the group determined that it would be called the Chancellor's Council of State College Presidents. Later it would have a committee structure parallel to that of the board. As chancellor, Dumke would preside or ask others to do so. The group would function by consensus. He stated for the record that "the Chancellor and Presidents would be the line administrative staff of the colleges." He asked three presidents, Love, Langsdorf, and McPhee, to serve as an agenda committee; he chose carefully. The minutes of the meeting reflect serious discussion of working relationships. The conclusion of this discussion was that written guidelines would help; McPhee volunteered to prepare a draft. He had it ready in less than three weeks.

Later in this meeting, Dumke reviewed all of the major staff studies underway and those soon to be initiated. These included curricular master plans defining the core programs to be offered by all new institutions, and a related study of high-cost programs; a study addressing the need for additional state colleges; budget and support for research; faculty councils/senates (a report to be available in two months); data processing; implementation of the Master Plan recommendations on admissions, and a joint UC–California State College study on eligibility of high school graduates; initial moves toward joint doctoral programs; evening and extension programs (a point of sensitivity with the University of California); and salaries. The plate was full, and action was underway.[29]

Don Leiffer, the first person employed systemwide by the board of trustees in 1961, decided he would return to San Diego State. He did not wish to continue and thought it time to make the break. He remained for a few weeks to work with the new chancellor. Leiffer's contribution to the establishment of the California State Colleges was enormous and the impact has been a lasting one. He played a secondary but important role in the Master Plan and the establishment of the board of trustees, though he was there, with insider's knowledge, to quietly advise Brown and others. He set the stage and defined the agenda for the first meeting of the board on August 12, 1961. He was the chancellor without title for ten months, while the search for a chancellor was conducted. Perhaps the most difficult task of all was guiding the state colleges through the seven months of Buell Gallagher's chancellorship, when Gallagher was effectively distracted from his responsibilities, and Leiffer's steady hand of guidance minimized the confusion that could have resulted from Gallagher's abrupt departure and the two-month hiatus in the chancellorship.[30] There were in fact two indispensable individuals through this period, Louis Heilbron and Don Leiffer.

Leiffer returned to the political science department at San Diego State, but soon was offered a post by the US government under the Kennedy administration as advisor to the president of Egypt, Gamal Abdel Nasser, for the reorganization of local government in that country. Leiffer remained in Egypt for a number of years, and eventually returned to the faculty at San Diego State, from which he retired. He remained a strong and thoughtful supporter of the California State Colleges, and of The California State University, in his later life and to his death.

Dumke moved relatively swiftly and brought in to the vacant vice-chancellor position Donald Muchmore. Muchmore was an Occidental College graduate and common wisdom at that time was that Dumke had known him as a student. Muchmore's assignment was very specific: he was to build a coherent and organized governmental relations program. Up to this time each college had represented itself in Sacramento. The president of each campus and those he designated, typically the campus chief financial officer, would work with state agencies, the legislators geographically associated with the campus, and other members the president might know. The institution with a statewide legislative constituency at that time was Cal Poly, and President Julian McPhee had carefully created this. Muchmore asked each campus president to designate a primary individual and an alternate to assume campus responsibility for legislative affairs, and to work with him and his office on legislative matters.

One of Muchmore's tasks was to build a Sacramento office to represent the California State Colleges. He also was to create a public affairs office to work with the media. He took for himself the task of building relationships with various groups over the state. Muchmore was an almost mysterious figure on the state colleges campuses. He had no presence on any campus. He came to perform a set of tasks, stayed for two years, and departed. A first major task he undertook was the development of a campaign for a capital outlay bond on the November 1962 ballot. He worked with the legislature to develop the proposal and then began a first campaign (there were many to follow) to secure passage by the electorate of the bond proposal.[31] The bond proposal passed.

The position of vice-chancellor for academic affairs was vacated when Dumke was appointed chancellor. This is a position of importance, not only to presidents, but to faculty on the campuses. In this formative stage of the state colleges, it was urgent that the position be filled quickly. Using the group of campus senate chairs as a consultative body, Dumke selected Raymond Rydell, the San Fernando Valley dean who had been loaned to the chancellor's office to plan the inauguration of Buell Gallagher. Rydell, an historian, was among the first faculty at the Los Angeles campus, and became chair of the Division of Liberal Arts. As he pointed out in his oral history, the position had no standing in Sacramento in the 1940s and early 1950s, as it was not recognized by the Department of Finance. When the Los Angeles branch in the San Fernando Valley was established, Rydell moved and, with the formal establishment of the San Fernando Valley State College, became dean of educational services and summer sessions, a position responsible for extension, outreach, and summer programs, and often used in the period from 1945 to at least the 1970s as a cutting-edge position for the development of innovative academic programs, depending on the style of the campus president.

Coming Together

Rydell's immediate responsibilities as vice-chancellor were to address the trustee demand for serious academic planning on each campus, and to give some leadership, along with a biology faculty member on leave from San Jose State, to the definition of the faculty role in governance. Rydell was well suited for both of these responsibilities. He saw himself as a member of the faculty and made that clear. He was a strong appointee. As a person he was quiet, had a capacity for explaining even the most complex matters clearly, and was quite firm about the mission of the state colleges.

While formal consultation bodies and procedures did not exist, Dumke asked the chairs of campus academic senates and faculty councils to meet with him periodically to consult about these and other appointments. When asked about scheduling an inauguration or investiture ceremony, Dumke declined to have one.

One reason for Dumke's quick move to appoint Rydell as vice-chancellor for academic affairs was the need to move firmly on an overall academic planning strategy. The trustees' first move on academic planning, in December 1961, was to ask for a master curricular plan for the system that would address both the basic core of programs to be offered on all campuses and the identification of high-cost programs, to avoid unnecessary duplication among the individual campuses. To do this, each campus had to develop for itself a comparable academic plan. The months from January to July 1962 had been filled with the impact of the controversy around then Chancellor Gallagher, and then his resignation and sudden departure, the selection of a second chancellor, and the inevitable effort and activity to restore some sense of order. Through all of this period, Dr. James Enochs, the Los Angeles dean who had been borrowed earlier to work on academic programs (and former State Department of Education senior staff member, essentially its leading academic) had worked with individuals on the campuses. Enochs, and sometimes one or two colleagues (the chancellor's office staff was very small at this time), had visited each campus and met at length with presidents, academic deans, and other administrators as well as with the constituted faculty councils and senates, many as yet in their infancy. He had not met with the several campus faculty organizations (which were at varying stages of development), other than to the extent their members or leaders were in the constituted faculty councils or senates. Each campus had provided a master curricular plan or a statement about a plan in development. Academic planning was just beginning on the campuses, except for a few that had developed plans in earlier years, most notably Cal Poly in the late 1940s and San Diego State in the early 1950s.

The trustees' December 1961 request had been for a master curricular plan to be presented in July of 1962. A well-developed document that went into some detail about existing programs on the campuses, the plan was in the board agenda and of course had been seen by those on the campuses, which received the agendas just as trustees had. At the July board meeting, there was an outcry from faculty organization representatives about insufficient consultation, dictatorship by the board and chancellor's staff, and the like. The leader of this protest was John Hensill, a biologist from San Francisco State. He had support from other campuses. Uncharacteristically, trustees talked back. Heilbron, a man of calm and judicious character, called the protests "intemperate." Harry Harmon, the head of the chancellor's staff campus planning unit, doubtless added fuel to the debate when he observed that ten buildings could be eliminated or reduced in size as a result of the Master Curricular Plan. The discussion was characterized as harsh by the media. Dumke played a conciliatory role and suggested that the document be approved in principle, but that a six-month process be undertaken to review the matter again with each campus faculty and leadership. The board agreed.[32]

At a meeting of the presidents on August 23, 1962, Rydell and Dumke reviewed the issue and proposed a strategy. One president, Cornelius Siemens of Humboldt State, suggested that individual academic master plans be prepared for each campus. There was general agreement that master plans for each campus would be developed, but the first priority, set by the trustees, was to be a plan for the system to identify a basic core of subjects that would be offered by all colleges, and at the same time identify high-cost programs to avoid unnecessary duplication. The Dumke-Rydell approach was to have a team—Rydell and James Enochs—visit each campus and meet with all faculty councils, senates, curriculum committees, and the campus leadership.[33]

Rydell and Enochs began their "pilgrimage" to the campuses. The meetings were productive, and the context may be best characterized by Ray Rydell, in his oral history:

> The feeling out in the colleges was, now that the Donahoe Act passed, we had new institutions coming along, a good budget, promises of plenty of budgetary support, that this was a rich opportunity for all of us. After all these years of being held down as teacher training schools . . . we were going to have the opportunity to do whatever we wanted. . . . We really—and I was as guilty as the rest of them—had no idea where we were going. The presidents, in particular, after having been held down, so to speak, by the State Department of Education all of these years, suddenly had an opportunity to do anything they wanted. . . . All of a sudden during one of these early meetings Charles Luckman shocked the whole system by asserting, and he made it stick, that there wasn't going to be any building of instructional facilities of any kind until there were, as he called them, master curricular plans for each institution. Moreover, that no institution was going to be all things to all people."[34]

Academic master plans clearly were needed. At the time there was speculation that Heilbron, Luckman, and Dumke were in collusion, along with trustee Ted Meriam, who had become chair of the Educational Policies Committee in 1961. Luckman, who was central to this effort, was by profession an architect, and a very successful one. He had learned that designing and building something must necessarily be based upon the substance of a program.

Emerging from the fall 1962 round of campus visits, Rydell and Enochs reformulated the process of academic planning. Phase I was "the identification of the basic complement of arts and sciences as the foundation program of the colleges; accomplished March 1962"; the result was the controversial document that went to the board on July 1962 and that was acknowledged. Phase II was the "review, evaluation, and recommendations concerning specialized programs; to be accomplished March 1963"; the result was a major and comprehensive document, including the substance of the document that went to the board in July 1962, and results of the Enochs-Rydell visits to the campuses in the subsequent months. The board adopted "A Master Curricular Plan for the California State Colleges" on March 8, 1963. The first sentences to the preamble state: "The Master Curricular Plan for the California State Colleges shows the responsibility of the colleges for meeting the higher educational needs of the state. Since these needs are gradually shifting, the Master Curricular Plan must be under continuous study."[35] Phase III was still to come: "Development of master curricular plans for each campus, to include review and evaluation of current programs, plus a tentative projection of programs for the future." Rydell's April 6, 1963, memorandum to the presidents spelled out all of this and became the basis for the long-term development of academic planning.[36]

Jim Enochs left the chancellor's staff in the summer of 1963, for a dean's position at Sonoma State, before retiring several years later. The new statewide Academic Senate was forming, and Dumke and Rydell were able to consult with the group. Rydell, who was from the San Fernando Valley campus, was placed in charge of the process of securing a dean of academic planning. He invited Ellis McCune, the newly appointed dean of letters and science at the San Fernando campus, to be a candidate. McCune was known to the chancellor's office, trustees, and many others, as he had chaired the committee that had brought the statewide Academic Senate into existence. Prior to his new deanship, he had been a professor of political science and president of the faculty (an unconventional title for the role more commonly called chair of the Academic Senate) on the San Fernando campus. Rydell invited at least one other senior campus administrator to be a candidate. Consultation with the leaders of the faculty group at the final stages of forming the statewide senate yielded strong support for McCune, and he was appointed as state college dean of academic planning, to begin his new role on October 1, 1963.

McCune inherited a secretary and a small professional staff of two. He proceeded to replace the professional staff with three individuals with substantive faculty experience on three state college campuses. Together, they set about implementing Phase III of the trustees' adopted Master Curricular Plan.[37]

Faculty and Governance

From the beginning of the Master Plan discussions in 1959, the issue of the faculty role in governance of the state college campuses had been on the table. The central question in Master Plan discussions was structure and mission; governance was a quiet issue on the side at the state level. On the campuses, the matter was not a quiet one on the side. No campus had academic or faculty senates with a sufficient amount of authority to satisfy many faculty leaders.

The model that many faculty worked from, as they thought about the faculty role in governance, was the University of California. Immediately after World War I, Benjamin Ide Wheeler, who had been a strong and authoritative president of the university for most of twenty years, retired; he had been in failing health the last few years in office. The regents appointed as his successor David Barrows, a faculty member who was returning from military service with the rank of major general. Barrows had begun his California career as a faculty member at San Diego State Normal School. He was not a strong president. In the transition from Wheeler to Barrows, there occurred what some have called a "faculty revolution," and the regents delegated to the faculty direct authority for many academic matters relating to curriculum, personnel, and academic and admissions standards. This approach worked well over the years, for the most part. Robert Sproul, the almost thirty-year president of the university, worked easily with faculty leadership on the whole. In addition, the University of California culture was a product of the longtime sole campus, Berkeley, and benefited from a single and coherent culture shared by most of its people, giving Sproul most often a free hand. The California State Colleges, as we have witnessed, did not have a single and coherent culture. The campuses had started independently of each other; each had been affected by the styles and values of its presidents and faculty leaders. There were as many patterns of governance as there were campuses.

The first steps to involve the faculty directly in policy formulation at the state level took place as the Master Plan was being developed. President Dumke, the state college representative on the team, visited each of the campuses, some more than once, seeking faculty input. Once the Master Plan was enacted in the spring of 1960, the members of the State Board of Education, soon to be also the Board of Trustees, with the strong leadership of chair Louis Heilbron, issued a firm statement supporting faculty participation. During the transition years, the trustees held a conference in early March 1961 at the Fresno campus with faculty leaders and presidents from each campus. The conference resulted in a resolution supporting faculty participation:

> Resolved, that it is the policy of the Board of Trustees of the California State Colleges, that a representative faculty body be established at each State College for the purpose of participating in the determination of educational and professional policy.[38]

In December 1961, faculty representatives and presidents from each college met again in Fresno with the trustees to discuss faculty personnel rules. The sudden departure of Chancellor Buell Gallagher soon after that meeting created a crisis in governance, in the largest measure due to the controversy surrounding Dumke, as a possible replacement for Gallagher. In the month after Gallagher's resignation, the trustees invited the chairs of each campus faculty senate, or a designee, to meet with them for a day at Los Angeles State College to discuss the selection of a chancellor. The chair of the board of trustees then invited five of the sixteen faculty representatives, selected from among themselves, to sit with the five-member trustee committee to select the second chancellor. This group of sixteen campus senate chairs continued to function as a consultative group, and individuals from the group were invited by the new chancellor to sit with search committees. The pattern continued until the statewide Academic Senate was established.

All was anything but peaceful. The faculty organizations continued to press for more involvement and for delegations of authority from the legislature and the trustees. Four faculty organizations were significant: the Association of California State College Professors, the California College and University Faculty Association, the California Teachers Association (made up mostly of education faculty, many of whom were concerned about the liberal arts orientation of the trustees), and the California State Federation of Teachers (AFL-CIO). The organizations found a sympathetic ear from some legislators; faculty members vote and some faculty organizations had money to contribute to campaigns. The issues used to keep stirring the pot included the appointment of Gallagher's successor as chancellor, and other appointments; the trustees' request for campus academic plans (characterized as an extreme invasion of academic freedom); and faculty personnel policies (most of the old policies had been automatically rendered obsolete with the move of authority to the trustees) and the like. These issues were tools in the struggle for power.

After his appointment to the chancellorship at the April 5–6, 1962 trustee meeting, Dumke met first with the presidents and then, on April 14, with the sixteen campus faculty senate chairs. He made clear his intention that each campus would have a faculty senate. He made a commitment to select presidents and vice-chancellors from lists of potential candidates developed by faculty consultative committees, and set in motion the planning of a statewide academic or faculty senate. Dumke appointed a group comprising three faculty representatives, three college presidents, and a member of his staff, to propose "principles and concepts" for a statewide faculty organization and outline the steps to be taken to create the organization. The presidents in this group were William Langsdorf and Ralph Prator, both recent presidential appointments, and Fresno's Arnold Joyal, a temperate member of the teacher education group. The faculty members were three campus faculty senate chairs, Ellis McCune from San Fernando Valley, Jordan Churchill, a philosophy professor from San Francisco State, and John Francis, a Cal Poly faculty member, who had a law degree. The group was chaired by Langsdorf, an individual in whom all parties had confidence.

This group became known as the Phase I Committee. The group reported to a joint meeting of campus senate chairs and presidents in exactly three months. The recommendation was positive—to create a statewide senate with three specific purposes spelled out: to provide the CSC with "a wide base for the development of policies," to provide the chancellor with "a recognized source of faculty advice, and recommendations on system-wide policy matters," and to "provide the faculties with an avenue for participation." After a few minor changes, the faculty chairs and presidents unanimously adopted the report.

Dumke immediately created a "Phase II" committee. He appointed two presidents, Langsdorf and Prator, and asked the sixteen faculty senate chairs to select five of their number. Ellis McCune became chair. Jordan Churchill and John Francis were joined by two other campus senate chairs as members. This second committee was to write a constitution, consult broadly on the campuses, and conduct a statewide faculty vote to secure ratification. The committee moved quickly. First, it formally designated an interim faculty consultative body—the sixteen campus senate chairs. An ambitious and purposeful schedule was set forth: drafting committees; identification of key questions to be presented to the campus faculties; compilation of the results; writing a draft of a constitution; presentation of this draft to the faculties, presidents, and trustees; further modification based on the presentation and consultation. Finally, a statewide faculty vote would follow; if the vote was favorable, the trustees would act.

There was some opposition to a statewide senate. Except for Langsdorf, Prator, and Ambrose Nichols at Sonoma State, most presidents opposed it vigorously; they were worried about centralization, and loss of local autonomy as well as presidential authority. Some faculty also opposed it out of concern about centralization and local autonomy. The faculty membership organizations wanted a piece of the action—in the case of the union-related group, they did not want conventional faculty governance, but union based relationships.

The legislature weighed in as the planning for a statewide senate went on. Senator Albert Rodda of Sacramento introduced a resolution calling for the creation of an academic senate. He wrote to Heilbron that "many individuals in the Legislature and in the field of higher education are watching carefully the steps that are being taken in the evolution of arrangements for faculty involvement in the state college system operation."

The calendar was followed. An October questionnaire that went to all faculty yielded substantial feedback. Using this, McCune and Churchill did the bulk of drafting the constitution. On the whole, reaction was positive to the document. McCune visited all of the campuses, often accompanied by Churchill, and spent time with faculty members explaining the reasons for creating the constitution as proposed. The vote of the faculties statewide was overwhelmingly positive. The first statewide Academic Senate meeting was held in May 1963, and the senate became fully functional in the autumn of 1963. It has had a major impact on the development of the California State University. It is not conceivable that the California State University or any comparable higher education enterprise could function with integrity and in good health without a faculty representative body in a significant and respected governance role.[39]

* * *

One of the by-products of the Master Plan process was the concept of year-round operations and a drive to change both the University of California and the state colleges to the quarter system. Year-round operation and the quarter system are not necessarily the same. The then recently established Coordinating Council for Higher Education pushed this idea, and the council's chair, Warren Christopher, was a strong supporter of the proposal. The primary motivating force behind it was to save money on capital outlay (construction) and the building program. Clark Kerr supported year-round operations strongly. Dumke did not; he was concerned about too much change at once, and he thought this to be expendable. However, the pressure to do it was great, and Dumke finally agreed to move toward a year-round calendar.

Properly, discussions were initiated in the statewide Academic Senate and with the presidents. While initially, in September 1963, the statewide senate favored the quarter system, strong resistance emerged with both the faculty and the presidents. In the University of California, the issue was worked through on campuses and with the Academic Senate. The university converted to the quarter system over the course of several years, beginning in 1963. In the state colleges, the issue was among the first to be considered by the new statewide Academic Senate. Campus senates individually reviewed the issue.

State college faculty leaders and presidents were often feeling besieged by change during this period. Probably the most difficult was the advent of academic planning. Many presidents, new and old alike, were feeling pushed to absorb much change in a relatively short period. The chancellor's staff had one state college dean assigned principally to the year-round operations issue, for purposes of policy discussions with the academic senate and campus faculty groups. Bruce Fisher had been appointed state college dean of institutional relations and student affairs early in the 1962–63 academic year. He was appointed following a selection process in which a committee of the interim group of campus faculty senate chairs identified a list of candidates, and the chancellor or vice-chancellor then selected an individual from the list. Fisher came to the deanship from the faculty of the Fresno campus. He was a psychologist and had no higher education administrative or faculty leadership experience. Fisher took on year-round operations (YRO). The principal staff work was done by the newly appointed general counsel, Norman Epstein, and by Lois Feldheym, the deputy to Assistant Chancellor Mansel Keene.

Ultimately, four campuses elected to move to the quarter system: San Bernadino and Dominguez Hills were new and had only planning staffs; Hayward was relatively new, and the president pushed it through; and Los Angeles had a new president, and he simply made the decision to change as he started in the presidency. His faculty resisted, but he prevailed. Cal Poly had long been on the quarter system. The statewide senate, which became heavily involved, which had initially supported it, withdrew its support and resisted vigorously. YRO became a cause. Ultimately, the effort was defeated, beyond the experiment on the four campuses and Cal Poly. From the standpoint of faculty self-interest, such a result is surprising. YRO with funding clearly saves money in the building program. Equally clear, it affords members of the faculty considerable flexibility in scheduling their time, and the opportunity to increase their income in some instances. But the reaction to an overload of change prevailed, and in a sense should have been read as a signal. The issue was not helpful to building a sense of common purpose in the new system.[40]

Building Practice and Policy

As the chancellor's office organization was being built, there was a need for legal counsel. This had been true from the beginning in 1960. The administrative officer, Don Leiffer, and the subsequent chancellors, Gallagher and Dumke, had turned to the attorney general and his staff for help, and it was forthcoming. In 1961, Louis Heilbron met with the attorney general, Stanley Mosk, to prepare the way for the establishment of an independent counsel for the state colleges. Mosk, not surprisingly, refused, stating that "the attorney general is your lawyer." Norman Epstein, a young deputy attorney general in the attorney general's Los Angeles office, was assigned part time to the trustees and state colleges when the office moved to Los Angeles in December 1961.

In the coming months, Mosk relented, and a recruiting process began. Several individuals applied, two with strong legal-establishment support. None of the applicants were acceptable to Dumke, now chancellor, or to Heilbron, who interviewed each one. Epstein was invited to apply for the role. He was reluctant as he was very young, both in age and experience. He had graduated from the UCLA Law School in 1958, and passed the bar in January of 1959. Nevertheless, he was interviewed by Heilbron and Dumke, and offered the position. After a week of thought, Epstein accepted the position, which had been given the title assistant vice-chancellor and administrative advisor.

As with many other things in the state colleges, building the office was building from the ground up. Epstein's goal was to create an office "analogous to a good small private law firm." He emphasized "preventive law," a new idea for the campuses and, at that point, for higher education. Attorneys had been very distant organizationally from state college campuses. Epstein defined preventive law as "the idea of an attorney giving advice before one thing or another had been done, and dealing with malleable facts rather than facts that had become cold, so that you are now trying to pick up the pieces." The preventive law approach led to the involvement of legal staff in many policy and operational matters, and became in some measure a way of life for the state colleges. In a sense, it became the basis for individual campus development of a legal capability, a movement that started two decades later. Epstein built a strong staff, and he and that staff served the campuses and the chancellor's office and trustees well, though not without controversy.[41] Epstein was a mature attorney, perhaps beyond his years, and brought a well-developed sense of the law and the mission of the state colleges to the roles of attorney and advisor. At times administrators and others were not prepared to listen to carefully reasoned advice. He remained with the chancellor's office until an appointment to the bench in 1975. He became in relatively short time an Associate Justice in the state appellate court system.

***

A major provision of the Master Plan was the decision for the state colleges to admit freshmen from the top 33⅓ percent of high school graduates, and the University of California to admit from the top 12½ percent. As mentioned previously, the word "top" was not defined; it was left to the segments. This decision was not based on research, but on finances and a division of labor among the university, the state colleges, and the junior colleges.

Implementation of this provision was not at the top of any list as the state college system's organization began on July 1, 1960. Neither Leiffer, as administrative officer, nor Gallagher, as chancellor, were attentive to this. The University of California, on the other hand, moved relatively quickly to implement the top 1/8 percent standard. The university had the advantage of long-set admissions standards, initially only for their single campus, that related high school curriculum to university study—essentially a university preparatory curriculum. At one point, in late 1961, there was a sharp exchange of correspondence between Clark Kerr and Buell Gallagher about what Kerr interpreted as CSC foot-dragging for the purposes of building enrollment in the state colleges.

The state colleges' history of freshman admissions made implementation of standards of any kind difficult. For all practical purposes, there never had been general admissions standards among the campuses, as the colleges had been founded independently, and each had set its own standards. From time to time there had been agreements among the colleges about standards, but these did not last long. Even after 1921, when the State Board of Education was clearly the governing board for all colleges, common standards were never actually followed. With the years after World War II and the implementation of the Strayer report, as well as the clear emergence of the presidents group as a de facto governing board, agreed-upon and adopted admissions standards were followed only when campuses wished to do so. So practices varied widely. Some campuses did adhere to published standards. This was the situation going into the implementation of the Master Plan.

As the chancellor's staff was being built initially by Chancellor Gallagher, the first administrator charged with some responsibility, even if only to think about admissions, was the state college dean for institutional research, Arthur Hall. When Dumke became chancellor in April 1962, implementation of admissions requirements moved up on the priority ladder. As president of San Francisco State, Dumke had paid attention to admissions. Among the few administrative appointments he had been able to make, due to personnel rules at that time, was a young individual from a major Midwest private university, just out of a PhD program and with admissions experience, to the position of associate dean of students for admissions and records—essentially, director of admissions. Dumke and his new staff member were strong proponents of a college preparatory curriculum. The state college admissions standards of the day, however, were based upon almost the entire high school curriculum. To be automatically eligible for admission as a freshman, a student had to have achieved, in the last three years of high school, fourteen or more As and Bs, in subjects other than physical education and ROTC, or ten to thirteen As and Bs, with a score above the twentieth percentile on a standardized national test. The state colleges had said that these standards, adopted in the 1950s, provided a pool with 45 percent of high school graduates eligible; there was no hard data to support this, and some disputed the percentage. Admissions directors, of course, had the authority to make exceptions.

In 1963, serious attention moved to the admissions matter. The state colleges made a minor adjustment in the existing admissions standards, designed to reduce the eligible pool of high school graduates to about 40 percent. Dumke brought to his staff the admissions director from the San Francisco campus for one year. Policy discussions involving administrators and faculty ensued. Simultaneously, a study was initiated of the 16,775 first-time freshmen admitted to the fifteen state colleges for the fall of 1963. The study reviewed the performance of these students during their first year of college. The major issue under examination was college preparation, due to the emphasis of the Master Plan recommendation upon college preparatory work and to Chancellor Dumke's strong desire to move to a required college preparatory curriculum. The study, which was conducted by individuals in institutional research, not the policy arm of the chancellor's office, concluded that there was "no significant difference in the predictive power of college preparatory high school achievement indices and those for total high school achievement less physical education and military science; it is recommended that other relevant considerations, such as administrative feasibility, enter into the choice between them." The advisory committee for the study was composed mostly of individuals not likely to favor a college preparatory curriculum.

The conclusion of the study disappointed some, but satisfied many within the state colleges. The junior college function of some of the campuses had only recently been phased out, and was still very much a factor at the Chico and Humboldt campuses. The more senior presidents were to a person in favor of liberal admissions standards. The more recently appointed presidents, but not all, generally tended to favor the concept of a college preparatory curriculum. To an extent, faculty divided this way. The trustees, certainly the leadership of the board, were disappointed. Louis Heilbron, Charles Luckman (the chair at that time) and Ted Meriam had strongly supported a college preparatory curriculum for admission.

The argument eventually went to administrative cost. Using the college preparatory concept can be more expensive than simply doing a calculation based upon almost all course grades on a transcript. The discussion of the report was extensive. The ultimate conclusion of presidents, faculties, the Academic Senate, and the chancellor was to go with the major recommendations of the report, and base freshman admissions upon a combination of the grade point average (GPA) in all courses taken in the last three years of high school, with the exceptions of physical education and military science, and a score either from the Scholastic Aptitude Test (SAT) of the College Board, or the then relatively new

13. President John F. Kennedy receiving the first California State Colleges honorary doctorate; from left, Governor "Pat" Brown, Chancellor Glenn Dumke, Kennedy.

American College Test (ACT). A lower GPA necessitated a higher test score. In the original implementation, a high school GPA of 3.2 or better qualified an applicant regardless of test score. Admissions directors maintained the capacity to make exceptions. Sometimes, upon close review of an applicant's record, it was recommended that the applicant otherwise eligible begin studies in a junior college in order to ensure the student's success later in the state college system; this approach was determined by the style of the individual campus admissions office.

The board acted in late 1964 and new admission requirements were implemented for the fall term of 1965, placing the California State Colleges in compliance with the Master Plan.[42]

* * *

In the autumn of 1963, the United States had a strong and vigorous president, John Fitzgerald Kennedy, who was interested in higher education. He was often found visiting and speaking on campuses. As a California visit was being planned, including visits to naval stations in the San Diego and Long Beach areas, the possibility of a visit to San Diego State emerged, and the idea of awarding an honorary degree, perhaps the LLD, was proposed.

Dumke took the idea to the trustees for their approval and acceptance. The board agreed, and San Diego State was selected for the event. President Kennedy was notified of the intent to award him the honorary degree, and he proposed to give a public address during the ceremony. When it became known that President Kennedy was to receive an honorary doctorate at San Diego State, the University of California leadership objected on the grounds that the state colleges could not award independently an earned doctorate, and thus could not award an honorary doctorate. Finally Dumke and Heilbron went to the attorney general to get clarification. The attorney general agreed with the trustees and supported their authority. The degree was conferred, and the students, faculty, and community of San Diego were treated to a superb address from the president of the United States.[43]

* * *

The Chancellor's Council of State College Presidents was fully functional, met monthly, and, on the surface, it was productive. But it was different than the Council of Presidents prior to 1960. The presidents were now no longer solely in charge of their campuses. There were limitations and regulations. There was a framework and a determined effort to define an overarching mission; and there was a restlessness, not only among some of the older presidents, but among some of the newer ones. The monthly meetings were held in a windowless interior conference room at the temporary "imperial headquarters," not at all in attractive or even comfortable facilities.

In February 1964, one of the presidents phoned Chancellor Dumke to tell him that a number of presidents were calling an informal meeting of all fifteen presidents, to have a general discussion about the work of the system. The meeting was to be held on the Chico campus. Only presidents would participate. The purpose of the call was to extend an invitation to the meeting, only to the chancellor, or to one individual he might select to represent him. It is not known with whom the chancellor consulted, the chair of the board of trustees (at this date Charles Luckman), other trustees, or the vice-chancellors. Dumke's decision was to send a junior member of his staff, a deputy state college dean (who reported to a dean who reported to a vice-chancellor who reported to the chancellor) who had worked closely with Dumke on a variety of matters.

On a beautiful spring day the deputy dean flew to Sacramento and drove through the central valley north to the Chico campus. This was the dean's first visit to Chico, so a walk around a beautiful campus with brick buildings, ivy-covered walls, and a creek running through the middle, seemed like a pleasant idea. Early the next morning the presidents convened. There was really no chair for the meeting; they simply conversed. The tenor of the conversations was on the whole complaining, and it gradually shifted to complaints about the chancellor, the chancellor's staff, more guarded complaints about the board of trustees, and change; the conversation became hostile to the chancellor and the system. Finally the most senior president, Julian McPhee, who had begun his leadership of Cal Poly in 1933, took the floor. He was a commanding figure, physically and in his speech. He advanced a forthright set of arguments: the world has changed; we are in a new era that requires us to rebuild relationships with state government; we are in a new organizational structure with new leadership, and we need to support the leadership. The tone of the meeting changed, and, substantially, it was over. Two additional speakers, Arnold Joyal of Fresno and Glenn Kendall of Chico (the host for the meeting, both presidents strongly committed to the teacher education role, and both on the brink of the mandatory retirement age, sixty-five), both senior presidents like McPhee, spoke out to support McPhee's position on the new organization. The message became one about building the new California State Colleges, and much was said about the importance of serving and educating the people of California.

While the meeting had been intended to have a quite different result, McPhee led the group in favor of support and leadership for the good of the people of California. In reality, this change was inevitable. Campus presidents had been accustomed to leading their individual campuses; now the campuses were each a part of a system. The meeting ended, the presidents returned to their campuses, the young dean reported to the chancellor the next day in Los Angeles, and that was the end of an incident in the development of the California State Colleges. Restlessness among the presidents did not disappear, but rebellion did for that time. There was work to be done by all. Surely the trustees were informed of the meeting and the outcome. However there was no further discussion, and the incident disappeared.[44]

* * *

Building a budget in the public sector requires technical skill. It also requires artistry. Building a budget for a public university and a system of public universities may require special artistry, especially when the details of the budget are locked into discreet line items and funds cannot be moved. The preparation of the budget for July 1, 1964, to June 30, 1965, necessarily began in the late spring of 1963, and each campus prepared an initial proposal, submitting a budget based on agreed-upon projected enrollment and other variables. Systemwide matters such as salaries were addressed by the chancellor's staff. The chancellor's office had a deadline of early November to present the budget, first to the trustees and then to the Department of Finance. A total budget was presented to the Department of Finance in November 1963. Finance worked with the governor and his staff, and the governor's budget went to the legislature in mid-January 1964.

Final action on the budget was in June. The legislature included a faculty salary increase for an eighteen-month period, six months in one fiscal year and twelve months in the succeeding fiscal year. When the chancellor's office received the budget, the salary increase funds were divided into three equal parts as funds were transmitted to campus accounts. This calculation did not take into consideration that faculty, and in fact all employees, were classified in positions with five salary steps, 5 percent each. Growth in the early 1960s had been extensive, and many faculty and others were new and still progressing through salary steps. The five-step salary model was the norm in the 1960s and continued for some time. The increases were not automatic, in theory, but the overwhelming percentage of faculty and employees received them (the five-step model applied to presidents until 1984, and to others until the 1990s, and the assumption was that everybody starts at step one and moves to step five within five years; exceptions were very rare).

In late 1964, someone discovered that the state colleges had insufficient funds in faculty salary appropriations to cover salaries to the end of the fiscal year on June 30, 1965. An error had been made; the step increases had not been included in the calculations.

The funds were at that time specified in line items in the legislative appropriation. The state colleges in 1964–65 were simply another state agency. Funds could not be moved from one budget category to another. Campus budgets were analyzed after the discovery. Every campus had sufficient funds to cover the salaries, but not in the designated or proper categories. (The University of California received a single lump-sum amount in the budget each year. The same had been promised to the state colleges in the Master Plan, but the legislature simply repeated the promise each year in the budget act, while not fulfilling the promise in the detail of the budget.)

There were procedures to handle an issue like this. The first step was through the director of finance, who had some limited authority to make changes. The state college administration appealed to the director of finance for an internal transfer of funds, but the director declined to act. He had recently been severely criticized for overusing his authority. The next stop was the Joint Legislative Budget Committee, which at that time had the authority to approve budget transfers.

The chair of the committee was Senator George Miller, still chair of the Senate Finance Committee. Miller had participated decisively in the meeting in Governor Brown's office in March 1960, when the decision was made to go ahead with the Master Plan in the legislature, despite Clark Kerr's desire to place the state colleges in the constitution, and the ambitions of many in the state colleges to be in the constitution. While most others were willing, Miller was absolutely firm: there would be no transfer. (The common wisdom of the time is that he sought Dumke's resignation or removal by the trustees.)

The trustees and Governor Brown rallied behind the state colleges and the administration. The only avenue remaining open was to reduce salary expenditures. The staff and the board settled on an exceedingly controversial path—a salary reduction of 1.8 percent for the balance of the academic year (four months), of all faculties at and above the rank of associate professor, including all deans, vice presidents, presidents, chancellor's office academic staff, the chancellor, and nonacademic comparable staff. The total dollar amount was not large, $281,000, but its symbolic value was huge. The fact that the presidents and chancellor participated in the reduction did not help in any significant way.

John Richardson, the vice-chancellor for business affairs, took the fall and resigned, even though it was clear at the time to those who knew the circumstance, that the budget and finance staff were guilty not of committing the error, but of not checking on the personnel staff who did the calculation. There was significant turmoil within the system, and various groups took advantage of it. Dumke and the trustees were resolute. They simply pushed on. Harry Brakebill, now vice president for administration at San Francisco State, was asked to become vice-chancellor for business affairs, a position he could have had in 1961. His personal circumstance had changed; his only daughter had graduated from high school, and he now could accept the position. Brakebill, of course, was well known to Dumke, and he had earned the respect of the trustees when he worked in the administrative office of the new state colleges in the 1960–61 transition year, and during the first several months of the Gallagher administration. His return as vice-chancellor was welcomed by all, including the often critical faculty organizations, the presidents, and, more importantly, the Sacramento state agency establishment.

Brakebill, Dumke, and key trustees devised a strategy to take advantage of a bad situation. In May 1965, the chancellor announced the formation of a committee for fiscal responsibility. "The basic objective of the committee and its task forces is to devise fiscal machinery that will permit the California State Colleges to achieve greater effectiveness in their educational programs and in personnel, facilities, and auxiliary activities."[45] Eight task forces were established, each with a specific assignment to study and report to the committee. Appointments to the committee and the task forces included presidents, leaders of the statewide Academic Senate, vice presidents, two deans, and one student. The task force chairs were chosen carefully; the expectations were high.

The task forces covered the total range of state colleges financial activities of that time and were asked to address, in a sense, the unrealized promise of the Master Plan for fiscal flexibility. The agenda was to move the state colleges from state agency status to that of a system of colleges, with a gubernatorially appointed board responsible for the governance and administration and integrity of the colleges. The task forces addressed statewide relationships and responsibilities, level of support, budget formulation, budget administration, and accounting and reporting. Three task forces addressed self-supporting activities, noninstructional activities, foundations, and summer session and extension. The work of the task forces and the committee was completed in time for the legislative session that began in January 1966. The committee's approach was to send proposals to the legislature that implemented, piece by piece, the Master Plan. The committee and the board were successful, and over the next several years, the state colleges acquired substantial flexibility. In an oral history interview some years later, Harry Brakebill was able to state that every one of the committee and board proposals and strategies were implemented over a several-year period.[46]

Two Campuses

The mid-1960s saw the opening of two new campuses, the establishment of a third campus, and the separation of a large branch campus from the parent institution, four new state colleges. In 1960, San Bernardino County's senator, Stanford Shaw, introduced legislation to create San Bernardino–Riverside State College. Both counties are geographically sizeable and both were at the beginning of the substantial growth that continues to this day. The legislation specified that the campus would be in San Bernardino County; Riverside County had the University of California, Riverside, established as a general campus of the university only a few years earlier and based upon the university's Riverside Agricultural Experimental Station. The legislation passed easily and was signed by the governor.

The newly established board of trustees decided in 1961 that the establishment of new state colleges would follow a different pattern from the past. Heretofore, colleges had been created by the legislature and the governor, then presidents were appointed and, within months, classes began. The new approach included the appointment of a president after some deliberation about the mission of a new college, then the choice of a site, appointment of a planning staff, and a three-year period to plan the curriculum, the building program, and other aspects of a new campus.

In January 1962, in the midst of the Gallagher controversy, the trustees appointed Dr. John Pfau to the presidency of San Bernardino State College. Pfau had several degrees from the University of Chicago. He had experienced as an undergraduate the Hutchins-prescribed general education program for the baccalaureate degree, and had gone on to receive a doctorate in history. After a few years at Chicago Teachers College (which evolved to Northeastern Illinois State University), he came to California and Chico State College as chair of the Division of the Social Sciences. In 1960, he moved to the new Sonoma State College as the founding chair of the Division of the Social Sciences.

Pfau's first tasks as the newly appointed president of San Bernardino State College were to work with the chancellor's staff to select a site for the college and to build a planning staff. The responsibilities for site selection and the building program had moved from the various state government agencies in Sacramento to the board of trustees. Once the legislature and the governor had appropriated funds, the only Sacramento involvement was a final approval of the site selection by the State Public Works Board. There was competition among a number of cities in the San Bernardino area for the campus site, but the process was not long, and a site in the northern part of the city of San Bernardino was selected. The board made the formal choice on February 8, 1963, and changed the official name of the college to California State College San Bernardino.

Almost from the day of his appointment, Pfau encountered difficulty with the well-established San Bernardino Valley Community College, which was respected in the community and statewide. Its leadership feared loss of enrollment, especially what it called "quality students," and proposed to the trustees that the new campus be limited to upper-division students. The trustees rejected the proposal after some discussion.

Pfau's vision for the campus was embodied in a mission statement he and his planning staff presented to the trustees in January 1964: "It is the purpose of the California State College at San Bernardino to provide opportunities for education in the finest tradition of the liberal arts and sciences. The College is committed to the proposition that while education may have many valuable purposes, it should be fundamentally an intellectual enterprise. Thus, the academic program of the College is designed to encourage intellectual growth, excellence in the basic skills of educated men, and ample exposure to the liberal arts and sciences."[47] Pfau had pulled a planning staff together beginning in mid-1963. He wanted to build a staff with individuals who shared his academic values, and he succeeded. The mission statement reflects that. A cornerstone of the academic plan was the concept of intellectual community. General education would comprise half of the undergraduate program. Each student would be required, apart from classes, to read two of three selected books, common to all students, each academic year, and would be examined about these books. A foreign language was required of all undergraduates for the award of the baccalaureate degree, and comprehensive examinations were required in the major.

The building program was tailored to the academic program, and the concept of intellectual community was central to this. Classrooms were built to hold twenty students, but in order to pay for this, 22 percent of classes would be held in large lecture halls. The planning staff built a tight model, which, among other characteristics, was designed to control proliferation of courses. The staff also chose the quarter system for the calendar, easy to do at the time because of the trustee-chancellor's office stance. Much emphasis was placed on student-faculty contact outside of the classroom, and the staff prevailed in its request for the construction of single-occupancy faculty offices, uncommon at that time. The college would be void of any intercollegiate athletic program.

The college opened its doors to students in September 1965 with an enrollment of 293 students. By the end of the 1965–66 year, students began rebelling, initially against the tightly structured general education program and its relative size (half of the undergraduate program). President Pfau and his administration were firm in their support of the structure and content of undergraduate pro-

14. Governor "Pat" Brown signing legislation to establish CSU Dominguez Hills; from left, Senators Joseph Kennick and Stephen Teale, Brown, and Les Cohen, Director of Governmental Affairs.

grams. Student restlessness continued, and there was some attrition. One of the important issues was general education, and the linking of general education to junior college programs, and this took some years to resolve. The campus closed out the decade with an enrollment of 2,234 students in 1970–71.[48] Pfau remained as president until his retirement in 1982.

* * *

California State University, Dominguez Hills was originally named South Bay State College in the legislation that created it. In 1960, Los Angeles County Senator Richard Richards (prior to the establishment of "one person, one vote," each of the larger counties had one senator) introduced legislation to establish a state college near the Los Angeles International Airport, to be called South Bay State College. Sponsorship of the legislation was bipartisan, with two assembly members, Charles Chapel (Republican) and Vincent Thomas (Democrat) cosponsoring the legislation. It passed easily and the governor approved it. The population in southwest Los Angeles County had exploded in the 1950s, in some measure due to the growth of the aerospace industry. A local newspaper, in writing about the legislation to create the college, described the legislature at the time as "passing out colleges."

Like the San Bernardino campus, the actual establishment of South Bay State College was caught up in the transition of the state colleges to the newly established board of trustees and the chancellor's office. In January 1962, at the San Luis Obispo meeting, the trustees appointed Dr. Leo F. Cain as president of South Bay State College. Cain was a graduate from Chico State in the 1930s and had taught for a time in the public schools. Cain had also been a faculty member at San Francisco State College since the late 1940s and vice president on that campus since 1957, including the years during Dumke's tenure as president. He was a nationally known scholar and leader in the field of special education. He had been the dean responsible for extended education and a variety of other matters. Under his leadership, San Francisco State developed three extension centers; one, formally established as a center in 1956, would become Sonoma State College, and the other two would also become state colleges over time as well (Hayward–East Bay and Stanislaus). Cain proceeded to build an administration, drawing heavily upon colleagues from San Francisco State with whom he had worked for many years. Like the new college at San Bernardino, the initial headquarters were in the offices of the trustees and the chancellor on Imperial Highway near the Los Angeles Airport.

Soon after the authorizing legislation had passed in 1960, communities in the South Bay area began to compete for the location of the campus. In 1961, Charles Luckman, then chair of the board committee on campus planning, buildings, and grounds, was responsible for the appointment of internationally known architect A. Quincy Jones as the campus master plan architect.

One of the early communities entering the competition, as it turned out to be, was the Palos Verdes Peninsula. Essentially residential at that time, the peninsula is among those communities with the greatest concentration of wealth in the country. Rolling Hills Estates, one of the several cities on the peninsula, formed a South Bay State College committee. The leader of this effort was Paul Gilmore, the mayor who later became a longtime member and chair of the Dominguez Hills Advisory Board and a strong supporter of the state colleges over the years. Other cities and areas entered the competition. Perhaps most notable was the city of Torrance, claiming to be (and with some accuracy) the geographic center of the South Bay. In late 1962, after considerable trustee involvement and review of sites (the campus staff and master plan architect had reviewed about twenty locations) the board settled on a site on the peninsula. However, it did not take formal action, due to political pressure from other communities and some dissatisfaction expressed by Palos Verdes residents about students and traffic.

Early in 1963, Jesse Unruh, the Speaker of the assembly, who had been influential in locating the chancellor's office in his district, entered the deliberations about the location of the new college. Howard Ahmanson of the California Federal Home Savings and Loan Corporation (the owner of the building in which the chancellor's office was located and, again, to be the landlord of the chancellor's office when it moved to Wilshire Boulevard in 1965, where it remained until 1976) proposed a one-hundred-acre site in an area known as Fox Hills, some distance north of what would be commonly understood as the South Bay. Unruh supported the Fox Hills site, and a number of others, including trustee Luckman, joined him. At approximately one hundred acres, the site would have necessitated a high-rise campus as the college was being planned for twenty thousand FTE.

Quincy Jones, the campus architect, weighed in, asking the trustees to proceed with the Palos Verdes site. The trustees followed Jones's recommendation, and in July 1963, it changed the name of the college to California State College at Palos Verdes.

Planning for the new campus proceeded. Cain brought in several senior academics to join Dr. Joseph Axelrod, a renowned humanities scholar and educational leader who had come from San Francisco State.[49] The academic group planned for a baccalaureate degree curriculum that would require two majors of each student, one in a conventional discipline or applied field, and one in an interdisciplinary program. General education would be 40 percent of the undergraduate degree requirements. A small college would be established within the college, and would provide an integrated interdisciplinary program. At the same time, Quincy Jones and the college staff began planning for the campus physical master plan and subsequently secured board approval for a campus physical master plan on May 1964.

The college staff had moved to rented quarters in a Palos Verdes bank building in 1963. Negotiations to purchase the site the trustees had selected on the Palos Verdes Peninsula moved slowly. During this period of almost two years, the value of land on the Palos Verdes Peninsula escalated. Additional funds were requested for the site purchase. Hale Champion, the director of finance (earlier in the Brown administration, he had been press secretary and subsequently chief of staff to the governor) refused to include additional funds in the 1965–66 budget. Champion had in fact been urging the governor and the trustees to move the site from the hills of the Palos Verdes Peninsula to the flatland, to the communities of the South Bay and southwestern Los Angeles County. There was a strong element of social policy in Champion's position, for this section of Los Angeles County included areas with heavy black, Latino, and Asian populations, as well as affluent middle-class areas.

In July 1965, assistant vice-chancellor Harry Harmon told the trustees that the Palos Verdes site could not be purchased because of cost. Three other sites were identified, two of them near the peninsula: Friendship Park in San Pedro and a landfill in Torrance. The third was at what was then called Dominguez Hills, better described as a rise in the ground. At the July board meeting a presentation about the Dominguez Hills site was made by advocates, both community and corporate.

Dominguez Hills had been named for Juan Jose Dominguez, a Spanish soldier who received, when he retired in 1784, a land grant of seventy-five thousand acres from the governor of the Spanish province of California. Dominguez named the land Rancho San Pedro; it was the southwestern quadrant of what would become Los Angeles County. He established a home on "Dominguez Hill." Over the years, the land had been divided among heirs, but large pieces had been kept intact.

At the close of the July board meeting, the trustees announced that they would soon make a site selection. Were the trustees to select the Dominguez Hills site, they would have to expand the service area of the campus both north and east, and that would move the campus into newly emerging ethnic minority communities. Some legislative resistance to that emerged. Hale Champion, however, was already urging the Dominguez Hills site selection.

In August 1965, the Watts Riots occurred. Watts was an area in Los Angeles some distance south of downtown. Five days of rioting finally ended when the California National Guard appeared in South Central Los Angeles. Governor Brown was on vacation in Greece when the rioting began, and returned quickly. In the aftermath of the riots, Brown and his staff concluded that the Dominguez Hill site should be urged upon the trustees. Dr. James Gregg, a faculty member from Chico State, had just become Brown's education secretary (Gregg was on leave for one year from his professorship in political science and journalism); one of Gregg's first assignments from Brown was to work with board members individually to urge the selection of the Dominguez Hill site. Brown wanted the Dominguez Hill site to be selected. He wanted the campus to be with the people. To his death, Brown regarded the Dominguez Hills campus as his special creation.

California State College at Palos Verdes opened in September 1965, again in a California Federal Savings and Loan building. Classes were on several floors of the bank building in the center of the peninsula. Enrollment was modest, fifty students for the autumn quarter and an average of forty-four for the 1965–66 year. Shortly after the first classes began in the rented quarters on the peninsula, the trustees met. Quincy Jones and the campus staff recommended the Dominguez Hill site. The trustees approved the recommendation, set in motion the purchase of the property, and five months later, in March 1966, changed the name of the campus to California State College Dominguez Hills. A local builder named Watt offered to construct quickly a temporary campus complex near the newly selected campus site; thus it was called the Watt campus. The faculty and staff moved from the Palos Verdes bank building to the Watt campus near the Dominguez Hills site in August 1966, and classes opened in September, with one hundred and twenty-five students; exceeding the enrollment in 1965–66 of forty-four students.

The area was unincorporated land in Los Angeles County. A few years later, as the area developed, the city of Carson was born. Three generations after Juan Jose Dominguez, his great-grandson, who was heir to the ranch, had five daughters and no sons. Three daughters married men named Carson, Del Amo, and Watson; two daughters did not marry. The names Carson, Del Amo, and Watson still figure importantly in the life of Southwest Los Angeles County.

The physical move had happened; the academic plan for the campus remained the same; the circumstance of the campus had changed dramatically, and it is not clear how widely this was understood at the time. The Palos Verdes site had encouraged a pattern of thinking about building a college on a classical liberal arts model. The Dominguez Hills site was a setting to encourage thinking about a more conventional state college model with many applied programs. A stage was set for change over time. Unlike the other new campus at San Bernardino (they had developed at the same time), the students at Dominguez Hills did not urge substantial curricular change, and the early years were years of accomplishment. The curriculum did not change significantly until the 1970s. In 1970–71 the enrollment was 2,652.[50] Cain remained in the presidency until 1976, when he retired, returning to San Francisco State as a very active emeritus faculty member.

* * *

Cal Poly Pomona has been born twice.

Founded in 1901, from 1901 to 1966, the California State Polytechnic College was a single institution. In 1938, a small branch of the college was established at San Dimas, and this became known as the Voorhis campus. In the latter 1940s the Kellogg unit near the Voorhis campus was added. For years Cal Poly was administered as an institution on three sites; San Luis Obispo, San Dimas (the Voorhis Campus), and Pomona (the Kellogg Campus). Over time the San Dimas and Pomona sites became a single campus with Julian McPhee as president of both the San Luis Obispo and the Kellogg-Voorhis campuses.

The Kellogg-Voorhis campus acquired some of the features of a separate institution in the 1950s with separate administrators for a variety of functions, all reporting to McPhee or his representative. In 1959 Robert Kennedy became vice-president of Cal Poly—all of Cal Poly, at least in theory. One of the first assignments McPhee gave to Kennedy was the preparation of a confidential report on the relationships of the Kellogg-Voorhis and San Luis Obispo campuses. Kennedy did as requested. His report essentially said the problems were with an absentee president, whom he compared to George III, and he anticipated throwing tea into the harbor. McPhee read and listened, instructed Kennedy never to share or mention the existence of the report, and promised to implement it with variations. Kennedy had recommended that McPhee proclaim a five-year plan with steps leading to the separation of the campuses in 1966, the year when McPhee would retire. Retirement of presidents at that time, though mandatory at age sixty-five, could be extended to age sixty-seven; McPhee received a special extension to age seventy, with some help from members of the legislature. The extension was justified to secure the polytechnic role of the campuses in the new structure.

15. *President Julian McPhee, Mrs. Dorothy Dumke, Mrs. Alma McPhee, and Chancellor Glenn Dumke.*

McPhee implemented Kennedy's plan. The first thing he did was to send Kennedy to Kellogg-Voorhis to be a resident vice president in charge. Among other things, this gave Kennedy the opportunity to complete the PhD at the Claremont Graduate School, with a rather brilliant dissertation about the organizational dynamics of Cal Poly.

The legislature would have to act to separate the San Luis Obispo and Kellogg-Voorhis campuses. McPhee wrote the legislation. It passed without a murmur. He worked closely and easily with Chancellor Dumke and his staff toward the separation. McPhee and Dumke did not agree on educational policy and philosophy, but there was a mutual respect, and they did agree about the necessity to maintain the integrity of the California State Colleges. In fact, McPhee had been a strong supporter behind the scenes of the Master Plan and the move of the state colleges from the State Board of Education to a separate board of trustees.

In 1965, McPhee moved Kennedy back to the San Luis Obispo campus as vice president, and in a sense, his deputy. He recruited Dr. Robert Kramer, a faculty member and head of a center on agricultural marketing and utilization at Michigan State University, to be vice president in charge at the Kellogg-Voorhis campus. Essentially, McPhee picked his two presidential successors; with strong faculty support, both were subsequently appointed by the trustees to the presidencies of the two campuses.

Julian McPhee retired in 1966 after thirty-three years as the president of Cal Poly. Two weeks before his final commencement and retirement, McPhee learned he had cancer; he was dead within a year, but his legend lives on. The trustees implemented the authorizing legislation to divide Cal Poly into two campuses. The San Luis Obispo campus kept the name California Polytechnic State College, San Luis Obispo. The Kellogg-Voorhis campus was named California State Polytechnic College, Pomona, and Robert Kramer was inaugurated as its first president.

Cal Poly—then only San Luis Obispo—had 117 students in 1933. In 1947, when the Kellogg campus was joined with the Voorhis unit (and the practice of keeping numbers separate from San Luis Obispo began), the Kellogg-Voorhis campus had 386 students. In 1966–67, Cal Poly Pomona began with 5,668 students.[51]

* * *

California State College Bakersfield was the first state college to be established from the beginning by the board of trustees of the California State Colleges (the next campus would be established in 1989). Fresno State had long offered extension courses in Bakersfield and other communities to the south of Fresno. In the mid-1950s, Fresno president Arnold Joyal and his colleagues received approval to open a formal center in Bakersfield. The Bakersfield Residence Center opened in September of 1956 with an enrollment of 342 students. The Fresno campus would continue to operate the Bakersfield center through the 1969–70 academic year; the enrollment in the last year of the Fresno operation was 790 students.

In the meantime, community leaders in the southern San Joaquin Valley began a campaign to create a state college campus of their own in the region. The chairman of the Greater Bakersfield Chamber of Commerce, Ernest Stahlburg, who was also the mayor of Delano, was a key figure in pulling together a group. Rather easily, the group settled on Bakersfield as a site. Donald Hart, an influential businessman in the region, was one of Governor Brown's original appointees to the board of trustees in 1960; Hart would become chair of the board in 1966. In 1962, the Kern County Land Company donated 370 acres in southwest Bakersfield, then rural, to the state for the specific purpose of establishing a state college.

The senator from Bakersfield was Walter Stiern. He had been a close ally of Dorothy Donahoe in working the Master Plan through the legislature, and he had an interest in higher education. With the land now available to the state, he had no difficulty in securing the passage of a bill to create a new state college in

Kern County. The governor signed the bill without hesitation. Subsequently, Senator Stiern secured the necessary appropriation to begin a planning process.

Paul Romberg was appointed by the trustees in the spring of 1967 to be the founding president. A biologist who had completed his doctorate at the University of Nebraska and subsequently held faculty positions at Wabash College in Indiana and Iowa State University, Romberg had been the chief academic officer at the Chico State campus since 1960. Romberg had a reputation as a conservative administrator, about both academic programs and social issues. The trustees set a three-year planning period. Romberg was able to recruit an initial planning staff immediately in the summer of 1967, and brought with him one of his two deputies at Chico, Dr. Kenneth Secor, who would play the major role in building the physical campus, and become a source of stability for the campus over many years.

The three planning years for the new campus were relatively uneventful. The site had already been selected. On the academic side, the administrative leadership was conventional for its time, and built a conventional set of programs in the arts and sciences based upon the trustee requirement that about one-third of the undergraduate degree program would be in general education. Programs in business and public administration were planned as were programs in education.

At Chico State College, Romberg had learned from Glenn Kendall, a very wise and shrewd president, the many uses of a foundation or auxiliary corporation in building a campus. Foundations could be used in securing outside support and, especially, in managing funds that would be used for flexibility in academic program development. One of Romberg's first steps was to create a foundation with fourteen citizens from the several-county area of the campus, and he used this productively to develop a strong community relations program and to gain financial support for the new campus.

California State College Bakersfield opened on schedule in September 1970, in their first new building, in addition to some temporary facilities, with an enrollment of 971 students. President Romberg remained at the Bakersfield campus until 1973, when the trustees moved him to the presidency of San Francisco State to succeed S. I. Hayakawa, when Hayakawa was elected to the U.S. Senate.[52]

* * *

The chancellor's office, located in Inglewood in December 1961, grew steadily in numbers of staff, as the number of campuses and enrollment grew and as the system succeeded in securing additional authority and responsibility for the administration of the system from state agencies in Sacramento. The process of securing authority was to be long and slow (it continues at the time of this writing), but it had begun. By 1965, the staff had outgrown the available space at the Imperial Highway facility. The office moved to Wilshire Boulevard in Los Angeles, some distance west of the downtown. The new headquarters and conference facilities were again in a building owned and operated by the California Federal Savings and Loan Corporation. The chancellor's office and the board would remain at the Wilshire site until 1976. The quarters were far more adequate for the system's needs, including the meetings of the trustees. Prior to this move, many meetings had been held on individual campuses. The cost of campus meetings was always considerably higher than the cost of meeting at the "headquarters," and, as the campus unrest of the 1960s grew, campus meetings became more difficult.

* * *

As the state colleges grew in number after World War II, the concept of service areas developed. Each campus had a defined geographic area, the region each college served. The campus responsibility was several-fold. The campus admissions office was responsible for maintaining contact with the schools and junior colleges of the service area. Extension programs were the responsibility of the regional campus. Presidents were responsible for working with legislators from their region, a responsibility that remains today. This was a natural outgrowth of the origins and development of the campuses. They more or less belonged to the people of their region.

Service areas were the outgrowth of the regional campuses. The concept was alive and well in the 1960s, though it was becoming less useful, as the number of campuses increased. From 1945 to 1965, the number of campuses in Los Angeles County went from zero to four; the number of campuses in the San Francisco Bay Area (including San Jose) expanded from two to four. Many campuses, particularly those outside of the two major metropolitan areas, guarded their service areas. This was particularly true for extension programs. The unwritten rule with extension and admissions remained: create a program or visit a school in another service area only with consent of the other campus.

Politics, Policy, and Revolution

The 1966 gubernatorial campaign had a substantial focus on higher education. The University of California was far more in the spotlight than the California State Colleges. The first major student demonstrations occurred on the Berkeley campus in September 1964. The unrest and activity spread to other campuses of the University of California and eventually to the California State Colleges and private universities and colleges. In November 1966, Ronald Reagan defeated Pat Brown's bid for a third term. Campus "unrest" was a major campaign issue.

Soon after the election, Chancellor Dumke sought a meeting with the governor-elect. They met quietly at the Ambassador Hotel in Los Angeles, not far from the chancellor's office. Prior to the meeting, Dumke had sent a seven-page letter to Reagan. The letter focused on the budget for 1967–68. Reagan would take office January 1, 1967, and the new governor was expected to present a budget to the legislature in mid-January. Reagan already had staff in Sacramento formulating the initial budget presentation. Dumke began his letter to Reagan by stating that he had learned informally that the proposed budget would include the trustee-proposed enrollment increase with no accompanying budget increase, a difference in funding that could be measured as 12,600 FTE—the enrollment of a large university.

The letter went into some detail about the condition of the state colleges prior to the Master Plan and the Donahoe Act of 1960. Dumke carefully contrasted the difference in funding between the University of California and the state colleges. He specifically addressed faculty salaries, noting the trustee request for an 18.5 percent salary increase and his willingness to settle for the CCHE-recommended 10.4 percent increase. He acknowledged for the record faculty activity: "Admittedly some of the claims of our faculty pressure groups have been extreme, but we have not permitted these to influence our position.... Extremists . . . exist in any large organization. . . ." He offered a compromise position—no budget increase, no enrollment increase, and hold enrollments at the 1966–67 year levels. An underlying theme of the letter was parity with the University of California, not in function, but in funding for the functions performed.

The meeting on December 21 was cordial. Participants included Reagan, Dumke, newly elected Lieutenant Governor Robert Finch (a classmate of Dumke's at Occidental College), and Les Cohen, director of governmental affairs for the California State Colleges. Dumke did not secure any budget commitment, nor could he have expected one. What he did secure was a working relationship; the two men had not known each other before this meeting.

The early months of 1967, when Reagan was actually in office, were difficult. The campuses were soon considering 15 percent across the board cuts, then a backup position of 10 percent. The days of simply maintaining the 1966–67 budget levels were gone. The end result was a renegotiated budget for 1967–68; the actual enrollment increased by more than 19,000 individuals and the FTE by about 15,500.[53]

The change in the governorship from Brown to Reagan ushered in more than a renegotiated budget. For more than a year in office Reagan did not have a senior staff member focusing on higher education. His advisors were a mixture of conservative individuals focusing on finances and budget reductions and ideologues, and they were committed to an interpretation of history and politics that was more than simply conservative. For the chancellor's office, this was a time for careful negotiation and the development of new working relationships. A number of senior staff in the Department of Finance and other state agencies continued into the new administration, as was the custom at that time, and this was helpful to the state colleges. But customs and practices that had been taken for granted for years were often no longer followed. This was both a positive and negative. The negative side was budget reductions; the positive side was administrative flexibility. In fact, many within the system, both on the campuses and in the chancellor's office, had difficulty accepting the new unintended accidental flexibility.

Reagan's appointments to the board of trustees in the first two years were in some measure a product of ideological advice, and the impact on the orderly governance of the state colleges was substantial. There was a political overlay to the relationship with the state colleges in this first period. Dumke was a rather conservative Republican, and he used that, and the fact that the California State Colleges were not the University of California, to build relationships in the new administration. Not all of the presidents were on that team, and some pandered to Reagan's supposed points of view. The then president at Chico State, Robert E. Hill, for example, invited his student body president and the dean of students to accompany him to Sacramento to a meeting in the capitol without telling them the purpose of the meeting. In Sacramento, they went to the governor's office, were ushered in, and the president explained to the governor that he was doing his best to protect students and the campus from the left-wing faculty. Later that same day, Hill attended an Academic Senate meeting on his campus and told the assembled faculty that he had gone to Sacramento to defend them against an arch-conservative governor.

It was a complex time, and tensions surrounded the University of California and California State College campuses. The governor had an abiding distrust of the University of California. He had orchestrated the dismissal of Clark Kerr as president of the university at the first regents' meeting after he assumed office. Reagan and Dumke at least had some relationship, but disturbances and unrest were on state colleges campuses also.

The situation on state colleges campuses was an admixture: the university of California free speech movement; the Vietnam War; the nationwide racial revolution; internal issues attendant to the transition to a new state college structure; unrest among some about a seemingly major change in function, as well as governance, almost overnight; and the continuing quest of some faculty organizations for power all were factors. The statewide Academic Senate was still in the process of maturing, the presidents were hardly a settled group, and the California State College Student Presidents Association, which had been founded in 1963, was a long way from being a factor in the governance and politics of the state colleges.

* * *

In the California State Colleges, student unrest in the second half of the 1960s was generally synonymous for most with San Francisco State College; that was an oversimplification. Los Angeles State College had major demonstrations, although contained and not long lasting. With the exception of the Cal

Poly San Luis Obispo campus, every institution, even those in small town settings, experienced some unrest.

San Francisco State was different, however. Unrest there was major, and it persisted for a number of years. Its causes were complex, and in no way were they only the Vietnam War or civil rights issues. The causes rather were intermingled with the creation of the California State Colleges by the Master Plan and, subsequently, the implementation of the Master Plan. The San Francisco State story enhances the understanding of the growth and development of the state colleges in this important first decade. As the activities at San Francisco State unfolded, the system for many purposes went on automatic pilot for several years.

From the late 1940s into the 1960s, San Francisco State was an activist campus. It had an activist president, J. Paul Leonard, from 1945 to 1957. It was during Leonard's presidency that the fight for a sufficient amount of land to site a new campus occurred. The large number of students, mostly military veterans, who demonstrated at San Francisco City Hall in 1947 for a larger campus site, was not an accident. This activism was characteristic of the campus, with Leonard's encouragement. Leonard's administration was autocratic in many ways, but he encouraged bold academic creativity, and the faculty was characteristically dynamic in its engagement of social, civic, and educational issues.

Leonard moved to the presidency of the American University in Lebanon in 1957, and was succeeded by Glenn Dumke. Dumke's personal style was the opposite of Leonard's, and he set about making change. In just two years he became, for all practical purposes, the opposite number to the university's Clark Kerr in the Master Plan negotiations. The faculty at San Francisco State believed itself to be at the center of the Master Plan process, and in many ways it was, certainly more intensely so as the issues developed. The Master Plan became reality, and Dumke left and became chancellor, albeit with considerable opposition from the faculties statewide, catalyzed by the San Francisco State faculty.

Dumke's successor, an interim appointee who was clearly chosen by Dumke, was Frank Fenton, a genial bachelor and senior English professor whom Dumke had brought in to his administration shortly before he left the campus. Fenton was from the educationally conservative wing of the English faculty, and was respected on the campus. The search for a new president became inevitably mixed in time with several events, from Gallagher's resignation to the appointment of Dumke as chancellor. The search process was complex, but it did yield a new president, Paul Dodd.

Dodd was a longtime dean of letters and science at UCLA, an economist who had a substantial following on and off campus among academics. Not long after Clark Kerr became president of the University of California on July 1, 1958, the UCLA chancellorship became vacant. Dodd was the favorite choice of many, and it was assumed he would be named the new chancellor. Kerr surprised many and recommended an outsider to the regents. Dodd resigned the deanship, and there was some public bitterness, prompting him to leave the university. When the search for a San Francisco State president was underway,

Dodd was on an extended stay in Australia. He became a candidate, was interviewed by phone and appointed to the San Francisco State presidency. Faculty activists at San Francisco immediately claimed insufficient consultation, although the senate had been fully involved; among most there was a positive sense of anticipation.

Dodd's arrival on the San Francisco campus created shock waves. He was brought to the campus by Dumke and trustee chair Heilbron. No one involved in the appointment process had known that Dodd had suffered a serious accident while in Australia. The accident had affected him in terms of his quickness in meetings and in conversation. Dodd assumed office, leading a campus with substantial disaffection among many faculty and other leaders about the direction and leadership of the state colleges.

In the 1963–64 academic year, many of the more politically active faculty of San Francisco State expressed their disappointment with the Master Plan results and the leadership of the state colleges. Many faculty leaders not only at San Francisco but at most if not all CSC campuses, had convinced themselves that the Master Plan would enable state colleges to become like the University of California in funding, doctoral programs, and the like, and the implementation of the Master Plan for these faculty was a continuing source of irritation.

Disappointment was only a part of the story. The trustees and the chancellor and staff were building an integrated system; there was leadership and coordination. Two examples make the point. In the past, each campus's president and leadership brought proposals for new buildings to Sacramento and argued them through state agencies and the legislation (typically with the active involvement of local legislators); this process now changed to one in which proposals were submitted, with academic justification, to a central office and a public board; Sacramento came later and the board forwarded a single multi-campus proposal to Sacramento. Similarly, campuses had, for all practical purposes, set their own admissions practices. Now a central office performed studies, and a public board considered the results and set standards within a comprehensive public policy framework enacted by the legislature and the governor.

There was an overlay to this growing disenchantment. It was the issue of the shifting of teacher education from being the explicit central focus of the campuses to becoming a professional program on par with other professional programs, a role diminished in importance for some. For the teacher education faculty, the activity of the legislature, governor, and State Board of Education was a major factor in this. The Fisher Bill, named for Senator Hugo Fisher of San Diego, was the first of a number of actions changing the orientation of teacher education from departments of education to subject matter departments. In the early 1960s, the legislature had addressed teacher education "reform" and substituted a bachelor's degree in the arts and sciences for a bachelor's degree in education. This was the first of many legislative acts changing the education structure for teachers, and, of course, this legislative action heavily affected the state colleges. The faculty at San Francisco State believed itself to be more aggrieved than others; certainly, they behaved as if this were so. San Francisco

State had achieved national attention under its first president, Frederic Burk, for the character and quality of its teacher education program, and it continued to be a nationally known center for teacher education.

President Dodd was in many ways still nursing the wound of being passed over for the chancellorship at UCLA. He was not a strong president, doubtless due to his accident, but he developed a growing sympathy for the grievances of some of the faculty leadership on the campus. Dodd had delegated authority over many matters to the faculty, to an extent unusual for any college or university. He was also clearly not supportive on campus of the development of the new governance structure with the board of trustees.

In March of 1964, the dean of the School of Education, Robert Smith, resigned. Bob Smith was an enormously respected faculty member. Dumke had appointed him chair of the Division of Education in 1960 (under the pre–Master Plan implementation structure). Smith was everyone's only choice for dean when the new academic organization with schools was implemented in 1963. He wrote a letter of resignation to President Dodd, and he went public with the letter. The letter was essentially aimed at the new CSC structure and the incumbent chancellor and board.

> Major efforts of this college's administrative officers to assist in shaping the policies under which we work have come to naught, and many of the plans we have developed in good faith have been ignored or summarily rejected by the chancellor or trustees.... The drive for centralized control over the individual colleges poses a major threat to [their] uniqueness and their capacity to respond to the needs of the state and the nation.... It appears that strong college presidents with a penchant for independent thinking are under increasing pressures to conform to an imposed orthodoxy lest they be picked off quietly behind the scenes.... The system does not need a chancellor running scared before an aggressive and misguided Board of Trustees.[54]

Smith recited a number of what he perceived to be intrusions. A major issue was the Master Plan provision that rolled back admissions eligibility from 45 percent to the top third of high school graduates. Smith's letter was circulated not only on the San Francisco State campus but on all of the campuses and in the media. The San Francisco newspapers carried the full text. Shortly thereafter a petition was circulated among the campus faculty and signed by 450 faculty members. Addressed to the governor and the legislature, the petition asked for "a thorough public investigation of the administration of the state colleges before irreparable harm is done to the students that we, and you, are charged to serve." Dodd was clear in his support of Smith.

The trustees acted quickly. On April 1, 1964, they created the Ad Hoc Committee on Development of Policies and Administrative Procedures. The charge to the committee was consonant with its name: "to study the functional involvement of faculty and administrative staff in relation to the development of policies and administrative procedures affecting the several Colleges, and the

California State Colleges." The membership categories were defined by the trustee resolution, "two Trustees (non-voting) selected by the board; two members of the Chancellor's Office, selected by the Chancellor; two college presidents selected by the Council of Presidents; two chairmen of local faculty senates, and two members of the Statewide Academic Senate, all selected by the members of the Executive Committee of the Academic Senate." The trustees chose Charles Luckman, chair, and Louis Heilbron, the founding chair; the chancellor chose himself and the vice-chancellor for academic affairs, Raymond Rydell; the presidents chose Julian McPhee of Cal Poly and Malcolm Love of San Diego; the statewide senate chose its founding chair, Leonard Mathy of Los Angeles, and its 1964–65 chair, Samuel Wiley of Long Beach, and two campus senate chairs, G. W. McCallum of San Jose and Leo McClatchy of San Francisco. McClatchy, a professor in business law, was a central figure among the active faculty at San Francisco from the time of the many faculty meetings about the development of the Master Plan in the 1950s until the late 1960s.

The committee proceeded swiftly but carefully. Each campus was asked to prepare a written statement of specific problems the president or faculty wished the committee to consider, including supportive facts and suggested solutions. After two months, the members of the committee received written responses from all but one of the campuses. The committee then held three days of meetings open to the public, and participation from the campuses was encouraged and welcomed. Representatives from the Department of Finance and the Coordinating Council for Higher Education were invited and came to participate. The committee members held many working meetings; these were lengthy and full with debate.

The result, almost one year later, was a forty-five page report that was widely circulated on the campuses and in the capitol. The report was to the trustees and to the statewide Academic Senate and the Council of Presidents. The trustees would not act on the report until they received recommendations from the senate and the Council of Presidents.

The report could be characterized as well informed and realistic. Recommendations were made about policy formulation, communication, centralization, delegation and administration, educational planning, and fiscal and personnel planning. The report was carefully drawn to provide for a maximum amount of respectful and thoughtful interaction among faculty, students (although relatively little was addressed about students—this was 1965), administrators, presidents, the chancellor, and the trustees. The report did make clear that the trustees retained final authority on all matters, though it also identified carefully the role of the trustees as a board. The roles of the chancellor and presidents were affirmed, and these were defined as nonauthoritarian, though this specific word was not used. Similarly, the roles of the two primary consultative bodies (as they were understood to be at the time), the statewide Academic Senate and the Council of Presidents, were defined in such a way that the groups were parallel, and both were to communicate formally with the board through the chancellor, though provision was made for additional consultation with the senate when there was disagreement either by the chancellor or by the board.

The report was unanimous in the committee, save for three points of dissent, which were made explicit. Mathy and McClatchy recommended that the Council of Presidents not be a policy-recommending group, and that there be only one such group, the senate. The Council of Presidents' purpose would be "exploring problems associated with the administration of system-wide policies," and some representation might be provided for the presidents in the senate. Mathy and McClatchy were joined on this matter by McCallum, though his recommendation was separate and provided for a joint statewide body of presidents and faculty. The other two matters of dissent addressed appointments of vice-presidents and deans and a recently discussed issue, year-round operation.

After hearing from the senate and the presidents, the board adopted a modified report. The committee and its report—and the disturbance created at San Francisco State—had served an important and useful purpose. In the early years of the California State Colleges, it was important to spell out roles and procedures carefully. This had been done, but separately, by the faculty, the presidents, the chancellor, and the board; now it was done coherently, for the entire system.[55]

The San Francisco campus continued to be unsettled. President Dodd's health deteriorated, and he resigned early in the 1965–66 academic year. An interim president, Dr. Stanley Paulson, was appointed by the trustees after consultation. Paulson had been a faculty member in speech since the mid-1950s, and his original appointment had been in the more liberal Division of Language Arts (as contrasted with the conventional Division of Humanities). He had successfully steered an ad hoc committee consisting of three faculty and two administrators through a highly controversial issue in the last year of Dumke's presidency there, the establishment of a "literacy examination" for students to move to upper-division status, whether from an on-campus resident sophomore status, or as an incoming transfer student. The exam, called the Upper Division Written English Test (UDWET), was controversial among many faculty members and in the junior colleges. Paulson's efforts had earned the respect of the campus, and he quickly became a leader. His personal style was toward the quiet pipe-smoking side, and his interim presidency had a calming effect on the campus. He turned away many suggestions that he become president, though he was nominated, with the comment that he would not seek the position, as he thought the college had become ungovernable. Paulson left the college at the end of his interim year for Pennsylvania State University, where he became chair of the speech department and then provost of the university.

The faculty and the trustees and chancellor concluded that an outsider would serve the campus well. John Summerskill, a young Cornell University professor of psychology and former vice president for student affairs on the Cornell campus, was selected. Summerskill assumed the presidency as the academic year began in September 1966. He was the faculty's choice, and he had strong support. His background as a chief student affairs officer at Cornell was expected to equip him well to deal with the student unrest that, by 1966, was present at most college and university campuses. Berkeley was just across the San Francisco Bay. The fall semester was a positive one until shortly before, Christmas when a student boycott of the campus food service was initiated by a relatively small group of students, the campus Students for a Democratic Society. The college staff handled the boycott well and prevented a major confrontation. But the boycott drew support, ostensibly because of an increase in food prices. The boycott caught on with the usually politically active group of student leaders in such activities as the Experimental College. The holiday recess brought relief, but not for long.

The new year and a new semester brought about continued activity. There were blocs of students, each with some measure of faculty support, that came together. The catalyst was the cafeteria boycott. The anti-Vietnam War group, a group of black students and their allies, the student newspaper staff, and others became an informal coalition with the Students for a Democratic Society. The rules of the time required that colleges forward student class standings to draft boards. In the spring of 1966, the campus Academic Senate had recommended that the college stop sending class standing information to draft boards. Paulson, then acting president, declined to accept the proposal. The senate leadership let the issue go; this was despite the fact that President Paul Dodd earlier had delegated to the senate final authority in all academic matters, including this kind of policy. In the spring of 1967, the senate made the same recommendation, quite possibly with the anticipation that it would be accepted by Summerskill. Summerskill had marched with his two-year-old son on his shoulders in antiwar demonstrations. Summerskill consulted the chancellor's office, and was advised to deny the recommendation, and follow the Selective Service rules. He did that; it became a fuse that would ignite further campus activity.

Summerskill's inauguration was planned for May 1967. It was to be held in the stadium. The day before the inauguration, a demonstration about the Vietnam War developed. Students and others involved in many causes and issues joined. The president's office was occupied; Summerskill went home to work on his inaugural address. The occupiers left. On the day of the inauguration, about thirty picketers with signs assembled at the front of the academic procession and marched into the stadium, leading the procession. They placed themselves between the platform and the audience and shouted off and on while the convocation proceeded. At the end, the demonstrators marched out with the platform party, taunting them. The trustees were not impressed.

The second year of the Summerskill administration opened on a more somber note than the first. The campus quickly became involved in demonstrations and, ultimately, in internal conflict within the faculty and the student body. The conflict shifted from Vietnam to issues of race. The Black Student Union became involved. The offices of the campus student paper, the *Golden Gater*, were trashed by members of the Black Student Union; the editor, the faculty advisor, and others were beaten. Summerskill's actions were erratic. He suspended students involved in some of the activity; he later apologized and reinstated them.

All of this was followed in the media. Conservative students were reporting to members of the legislature. The Academic Senate, which had supported particularly the anti-Vietnam activity, began to lose faculty support. A large number of faculty coalesced and called for the restoration of order on the campus. The situation was enormously complex. Summerskill tried to be conciliatory, and he lost support from all sides. A final major demonstration and occupation of the campus administration building occurred on December 6, 1967. The campus partially closed. Some damage was done as demonstrators marched through the campus.

The board of trustees called an emergency meeting for the following Saturday. The public hue and cry was substantial, all calling for order on the campus. It was not supportive of Summerskill. The Assembly Education Committee held a special meeting, without public notice, on the San Francisco campus the night before the scheduled emergency trustee meeting. Students who were interviewed, none from the demonstrating group, and San Francisco's chief of police supported Summerskill's decision to not call out the police. (California State Colleges did not have their own police until the very late 1960s, and were dependent on local police.) The trustees were not so generous. They passed three resolutions. One specified that local police would make the decision about calling out police. Another created a special committee to examine the stewardship of President John Summerskill.

In the midst of the San Francisco State situation, and similar but far less dramatic circumstances on most other campuses, the American Federation of Teachers became involved. The national AFT invested two hundred and fifty thousand dollars to support a collective bargaining effort on California State College campuses. The leader of this effort was Arthur Bierman, of the San Francisco State philosophy department. Bierman had been involved in every significant campus political issue at San Francisco State since he joined the faculty in the mid 1950s. Three writers in a volume published in 1970 characterized Bierman as the "grey eminence" of the AFT in California.[56] A strategy was developed to take over the Academic Senate at the campus. The AFT wanted an immediate faculty strike. The AFT effort failed as more faculty became determined to restore some order to the campus. The holiday recess allowed for a reprieve.

The year 1968 opened with a disillusioned and demoralized student body, faculty, staff, administration, and community. The spring term was one long series of demonstrations, sit-ins, threats, and inaction by an often divided Academic Senate. The senate was more a key player than many would expect because of the amount of authority the previous president, Paul Dodd, had delegated to them. Summerskill seemed stunned by all of this, and repeatedly turned to others for advice. He attempted to be conciliatory with the activist forces, which included faculty and students as well as people from off campus. He attempted, on occasion, to be firm. The chancellor's office almost continuously had at least one and sometimes two fairly high-level administrators on-site to monitor decisions. A troika of campus administrators, all experienced, tried to hold the campus together: Donald Garrity, vice president for academic affairs, was new to that role but was an experienced San Francisco State faculty member; Ferd Reddell had been on campus over twenty years and dean of students for twelve years; and Glenn Smith, the vice president for administration, had come with Dumke in 1958 as assistant to the president, and was a veteran of many complex situations and developments. Summerskill could not have asked for a better team. As the spring wore on, additional factions developed. A group calling itself the Third World Liberation Front became a major actor. The presence of ROTC on the campus became a focal point of conflict. One clash after another occurred. Summerskill offered his resignation to the board in February 1967, began job hunting, but did not leave. His vacillation continued.

By mid-May students were having sleep-ins on the floor of the administration building. Two major issues were up in the air. The first was the admission of four hundred ethnic students who did not meet the defined admission standards and the further establishment of ethnic studies programs, with faculty already chosen by students and others. The second was the immediate termination of the air force ROTC program. Vacillation from the president continued. The team of three senior administrators, Garrity, Reddell, and Smith phoned the chancellor at his home one evening, as students and faculty milled about the administration building and elsewhere on campus. The three urged Dumke to remove Summerskill. The Council of Academic Deans renounced Summerskill's agreements which, unfortunately, the chair and vice-chair of the senate had subscribed to. Summerskill agreed in writing to both demands, then backed away on ethnic studies, and then once again agreed to it. The next morning confusion reigned. Summerskill did not come to the campus for work. He was at the San Francisco airport, awaiting a flight to Ethiopia to look at a new position. Only two of his staff knew that, and they finally revealed it. The press had learned of his imminent departure and, just before boarding a plane in San Francisco, Summerskill was interviewed; he told the press that he had solved the institution's problems and could leave. Dumke removed Summerskill that day and asked Don Garrity to assume responsibility.

Simultaneously, the statewide Academic Senate was meeting. Opposition to Dumke had been growing, given the campus unrest and increasing pressure from union activists about collective bargaining. The senate members heard reports about San Francisco State. Previously, an item had been placed on the agenda for consideration, a proposal to vote "no confidence" in the chancellor. Individual members of the senate, especially those advocating for formal trustee delegation of authority to campus senates, were frustrated in their hopes for achieving formal faculty authority as a result of the Master Plan. Almost every member of the statewide senate had experienced the 1965 1.8 percent salary cut. These issues were not forgotten. The San Francisco situation was a trigger. As Summerskill was at the airport, the statewide senate voted no confidence in Dumke, by a substantial margin. Dumke met with the senate before the vote, mostly about San Francisco State, and was simultaneously arranging a meeting of the board of trustees for that evening at the San Francisco airport.

On the evening Dumke heard from the three senior administrators and the Council of Academic Deans at San Francisco, he made the decision to remove Summerskill. He consulted with key trustees, and he asked Mansel Keene, the assistant vice-chancellor who was handling presidential searches, to talk with faculty and other leaders at San Francisco State. The result was a call from Keene to Robert Smith, asking him to assume the acting presidency. Smith demurred, but finally agreed to consider it. Keene kept up the pressure. There ensued five days of back-and-forth conversations involving Robert Smith, his wife, campus administrative and faculty leadership, the chair of the board, and others. Smith was not eager for the role, and his wife was absolutely opposed. Smith met with a trustee committee, but not the full board. The committee voted to recommend his appointment to the board. After that meeting, Smith finally agreed to accept the position. Smith was approached by two liberal trustees who informed him that they had voted against his appointment because they hoped for a black candidate.

The next day the full board met to confirm Smith's appointment. After the meeting, a recently appointed very conservative trustee, Dudley Swim, approached Smith and told him that he had voted against Smith's appointment in the trustees' committee two days earlier and then simply abstained in the final vote. In his own words, Smith returned to the campus knowing that "neither the most liberal, nor the most conservative among the trustees supported my appointment."[57]

The fall semester at San Francisco State opened with an exhausted administration and a divided campus. The divisions were not only among faculty and students, but in the administration. It also opened for all of the campuses with a divided board of trustees, a chancellor trying to bridge the divisions, and a governor now actively hostile to the situation at San Francisco State and other campuses. At the San Fernando Valley campus in Northridge, a black student group occupied the administration building and held administrators hostage. Part of the building was burned. There were sizeable demonstrations at a trustees' meeting on the Fresno campus.

At San Francisco State, the core issue was race. A part-time black instructor, George Murray, who was also a graduate student, was at the center. He had been involved the previous year in the sacking of the student newspaper office. He was convicted for this, but he was also reemployed by the English department on a part-time basis to instruct the students being admitted for the fall semester in the Educational Opportunity Program. In the previous spring semester Murray had given a number of incendiary and threatening speeches on the campus.

As the academic year opened, President Smith was pressured at trustee meetings in September and October (at the October meeting in Fresno, Murray was on campus and gave yet another incendiary speech) to suspend or dismiss Murray. The Murray issue became celebrated in the media—a great story to follow. Accompanying this was an upcoming national election in early November, and a threatened campus strike by the Black Student Union. At their Fresno meeting, the trustees rejected the architectural plans for a student union at San Francisco State, a building financed by student fees, which the students had earlier voted to assess themselves. This added to student anger on the campus.

Smith resisted action on Murray. His position was that due process must be followed to avoid a campus blow up. The mayor of San Francisco, Joseph Alioto supported Smith; his stated concerns were about public safety and police issues. Murray kept the pressure up by continuing his inflammatory behavior. The trustees and chancellor continued the pressure, as did the governor and many political figures. For the most part, this was not a partisan issue.

On November 6, 1968, a day after the presidential election, strike activity began. The Black Student Union and the Third World Liberation Front systematically visited classes. Their message was: "Why are you here—are you with us or not? Strike!" In some classes where faculty and students resisted, harsh arguments broke out; in a few there was physical intimidation. President Smith closed the campus. His fears—the cause of his continued attempts to keep due process on course—were realized. The Black Student Union held an off-campus press conference and announced a list of ten demands.

The campus reopened the next day, if reopening is defined as many classes meeting, but the strike continued. The faculty were divided. The AFT and a group of other faculty supported the strike, and the strike continued, even while classes continued. Wandering groups would occasionally invade an office or a classroom, create a disturbance, perhaps destroy equipment. This behavior continued for days, but seemed to be subsiding, and San Francisco was not the only campus with problems. Then, on Wednesday November 13, a riot broke out. A reporter had been roughed up and asked for police help. (There had been a police presence on campus for months.) The police moved to help the reporter and that was the trigger. The rioting was bloody. A group of faculty who were carrying signs supporting the strikers came between the rioters and the police, and in time calmed things to an extent. A member of the faculty William Stanton, went to the outdoor speakers' platform, took the microphone, and addressed students and faculty. His speech was filmed, and eventually widely circulated in the media.

> There are no more classes at San Francisco State! And we're not taking any more horseshit from the fucking trustees! The conduct of Dumke and the trustees has been absolutely criminal.... That man (Smith) is a dammed fool for trying to work within the system. The trustees must act to restore Murray, guarantee adequate funds for black studies and the Third World People, and make a clear declaration that the faculty will be free to run this college. They must tell us what they intend to do to restore justice on this campus.[58]

There ensued days of faculty convocations, Academic Senate meetings, administrative meetings, and a continuing uproar on the campus.

The trustees held a special meeting on November 18; the governor attended. Both Dumke and trustee chair Meriam tried to express support for Smith's efforts to bring about some consensus on the campus. Smith held absolutely firm on reopening and continuing classes despite enormous pressure to close the campus. Clearly the trustees as a group did not support Smith. The same two liberal trustees and the conservative trustee, who had all told Smith they did not support his appointment, came out in open session opposed to his continuing leadership of the campus. In spite of this, the trustees took no action beyond making it clear that classes must continue. The next day, the faculty met in convocation, often leaving to teach their classes and then returning. The faculty finally concluded that no classes would be held until the administration and striking student coalition met in an auditorium where the faculty could hear both sides and come to a conclusion about next steps. In turn, Smith decided to go to the whole faculty with paper balloting. The result was a 612 to 277 endorsement of Smith's policy to continue classes.

The coalition of students and others regrouped and decided to take action—to close down classes by force. Violence erupted; people were hurt, including law enforcement personnel. The mayor of San Francisco stepped in and attempted to take charge. Alioto was a democrat, and a perceived candidate for governor in 1970. Alioto announced that he would create a statewide arbitration process to address the problems of the California State University as a whole. It later became clear that the campus AFT group had come to Alioto with this proposal. In the midst of all of this, the AFT leadership moved in and simply took over leadership of the faculty protest, pushing the senate aside. After a meeting with a large number of faculty, many of whom he respected, Smith closed the campus for a three-day convocation of the entire campus community.

The trustees again convened for a two-day closed session. The governor attended but both he and Dumke sat silently through the first day. Much of it was consumed by a presentation made by three senior San Francisco State administrators in the absence of the president. The deputy president, DeVere Pentony, a ten-year veteran of the faculty who had assumed office with Smith, made a detailed presentation. Pentony's field was international relations, and he had experience doing complex briefings. His presentation brought some of the trustees into better understanding, or so it seemed. The afternoon of the first day turned to a discussion, but no conclusions. The trustees decided to continue the next morning and asked for President Smith to be at the meeting on the second day. He had stayed home on the first day to manage the campus, along with the dean of students and, in reality, the police. Smith came to the November 25 meeting, and after some exchanges, resigned.

The trustees were caught off balance. While many believed that Smith must go, no one, including the chancellor, had a backup plan. A San Francisco faculty group calling itself the Faculty Renaissance had formed, and had been active in a quiet way from the latter days of the Dodd administration. The group did not include notable faculty, leaders or otherwise, except for S. I. Hayakawa. Hayakawa was a part-time faculty member, an internationally known semanticist and successful author, among the best-known faculty of the college. He had been at San Francisco State for ten years, but not active in campus life until this point.

As the situation deteriorated, the Faculty Renaissance became more visible, and Hayakawa was its most visible and outspoken individual. They were in some communication with Dumke, who knew all of them from his years at San Francisco State. In fact, the group had tried to see Smith on the day before he resigned, but he had no time. They gave him a paper with a plan of action. Smith read the paper on his way to the trustee meeting. On Tuesday morning when Smith met with the trustees, the plan of action proposed by the chair of the board, Ted Meriam, was virtually identical.

After the meeting of the trustees with Smith and staff ended, the trustees reconvened. The accounts of what happened next vary. Someone proposed Hayakawa. Dumke was under considerable pressure for an appointment to be made immediately, and he knew Hayakawa. Dumke phoned Hayakawa and asked him to consider the presidency. Hayakawa asked for time to consider the idea before meeting with the trustees. Dumke explained that there was no time. Hayakawa met with the trustees in Los Angeles, and was appointed acting president.

The campus was closed for the long Thanksgiving weekend. On Monday the strikers resumed their activity. They positioned a sound truck about one hundred yards from the administration building and Hayakawa's office. After a few minutes of speeches, Hayakawa left his office, walked to the sound truck, climbed onto the truck, and the sound wires were removed. There are two versions about how this happened. Legend is that Hayakawa climbed onto the back of the truck and simply pulled the wires, cutting off the sound. That account was carried around the world. Hayakawa became an instant folk hero, and he became untouchable by any political or educational leader. A second account is quite different. The second account is that as Hayakawa climbed on the back of the truck, he tripped on the wires, disconnecting them and cutting off the sound; realizing what he had done, he held up the wires. The legend of pulling the wires was born.[59]

Strike activities continued on campus. Hayakawa worked with the deans and the senate. Early he made it clear to the senate that he would not be bound by the final delegations of authority that President Dodd had made to the senate. He made it equally clear to members of the administration that his mission was to restore order, peace, and the functioning of classes on the campuses. Other administrators would attend to the ongoing work of the college.

In the midst of Hayakawa's work and the continuing disorder, only some classes were being held; the AFT Chapter asked the San Francisco Labor Council to sanction the strike. San Francisco in the 1960s was a labor city politically. Mayor Joseph Alioto immediately stepped up his involvement at San Francisco State, but he was careful, given his gubernatorial ambitions. The labor council did not want to become involved, as many union members would likely not want to support the Third World Liberation Front, Students for a Democratic Society, and dissident faculty; but the council did not want to turn away a member union. Alioto and the council's executive secretary worked together to create a mediation process. The leader of the citizens' committee they created was Bishop Mark Hurley, an auxiliary bishop of the San Francisco Roman Catholic archdiocese. The secretary of the San Francisco Labor Council, George Johns, was competent and respected by civic groups. He began the process of assembling the citizens' committee and, with Bishop Hurley, took initial steps toward a mediation process. He engaged one of the top mediators in the country, Ronald Haughton of Wayne State University, to work with the parties. The AFT was not looking for mediation; they wanted a strike sanction. To bring the AFT along, the labor council granted the AFT request, but only if the board of trustees would enter into the mediation process.

Governor Reagan made a quick move. Almost simultaneously with the labor council move, his office issued a "report to the people of California" about college campus disturbances and interruption of classes. He was clear: there would be no compromise. He requested the trustee chair, Theodore Meriam, to reject the labor council–sponsored mediation. Meriam did so with a firm public statement. "It is the responsibility of the trustees, the representatives of the people of California, to address the San Francisco State situation."

At the same time, Meriam appointed a trustee liaison committee to work with the San Francisco State situation. Its members were the five Bay Area trustees, Louis Heilbron, George Hart, Albert Ruffo, James Thatcher, and Karl Wente. Reagan did not approve of this move, and asked Wente, whom he had only recently appointed, to not serve. Wente complied. Heilbron, the board's elder statesman at this point, chaired the group.

The student strike continued into December, and the AFT faculty strike proposal compounded the situation. Hayakawa was clearly in charge, but the situation was not improving. A major demonstration was planned by the student groups for December 16, Monday of the last week of classes prior to the holiday recess. On the previous Friday, Hayakawa simply closed the college for the holiday recess one week early. There would be no classes the week of December 16.

The college reopened in January. There was full student, and now faculty, strike activity. The AFT membership approached 20 percent of the faculty; the AFT members were on strike, though there was confusion about what a strike meant. Many striking faculty were unwilling to cross the faculty picket lines, some were unwilling to cross the student picket lines, and more classes were taught off campus, some in faculty homes, at churches, some in various community centers, and the like. For the most part, the action had moved from the inside of the campus to the perimeter; occasional demonstrations would be held on campus. Hayakawa had prohibited all demonstrations and comparable activity. Damage to the campus was visible—externally, with broken windows and the evidence of minor explosions, and internally, with some broken furniture, offices, and classrooms that had been trashed. Faculty who were not on strike, the greatest number, students, and staff made the best of the situation. Then the student strikers announced a mass rally to be on the campus on January 23, at the speakers' platform. More than five hundred individuals came for the rally, students, strikers, and faculty. A mass of police appeared from all directions. The police arrested 453 individuals including a dozen faculty. All were booked, held, and later tried; many were fined; and some were sentenced.

The San Francisco strike had really become two strikes. The AFT had in a sense moved in on the various student groups. The trustees' liaison committee, which Meriam had appointed in December, came into action. The AFT attempted to organize a one-day strike on all CSC campuses. This attempt failed. As the Bay Area trustees began conversations with the student and faculty groups, Reagan and some of the trustees objected. The issue was negotiating, the creation of precedents and a backdoor move into bargaining. This was exactly what AFT wanted. Reagan succeeded in early January in convincing a sufficient number of trustees to stop the Heilbron group from "negotiating."

As the end of January of 1969 approached, all but the most militant in the two striking groups were tiring of their efforts. San Francisco State had been in an uproar since the autumn of 1966, and before that, for four years had had inadequate leadership. Governor Reagan and Mayor Alioto had to calculate the political costs. The trustees wanted the educational process for students to resume; most students wanted their classes and ultimately their degrees; most faculty wanted to teach; and Dumke and Hayakawa needed an end to all of the disturbances. Reagan and the trustees who had agreed with him about calling off the negotiations had a change of heart. The Heilbron group went back to work.

The three trustees in the group who carried the effort were all prominent attorneys: Heilbron; James Thatcher, a senior partner in a major San Francisco law firm; and Albert Ruffo, recently mayor of San Jose. George Hart, the fourth remaining trustee, a wealthy San Francisco banker, attended most of the meetings and took copious notes, but did not participate in the give and take of the discussions. The other trustees believed he was reporting to Reagan. The group worked initially with both the student-based strikers and the faculty/AFT. Their principal efforts soon shifted to the faculty. Negotiations were not easy. Many individuals were locked in either to support for the students or support for the union, with the ultimate goal of formal union representation and collective bargaining.

The final AFT faculty agreement was fourfold. There would be amnesty for the faculty protesters; recognition of the Black Studies program and the requirement that it operate within college rules and conventions; an agreement that faculty absent for five or more days (which under state statutes constituted automatic resignation and termination) would be expected to file with the state personnel board an application for reinstatement. The fourth point had to do with a faculty grievance procedure. The statewide Academic Senate had been working on this for five years, since its first year in existence. The senate rose to the occasion, and in intense negotiations with the chancellor's staff reached an agreement that all parties believed they could live with. This was to go to the trustees at their February meeting. The governor had to be convinced, but Hayakawa had agreed to this settlement. Hayakawa publicly urged the governor to accept the agreement. The board did accept it on a fifteen to two vote, and Reagan voted with the majority. The final step was to secure a favorable AFT vote. After much contentious and bitter debate, the AFT faculty members voted 112 to 104 to accept the agreement, and the faculty strike ended.

The key players in ending the strike were the three Bay Area trustees, Heilbron, Ruffo, and Thatcher, and the union leadership in the San Francisco Labor Council, especially George Johns. Hayakawa supported the agreement; he knew that an end must come. Heilbron was lauded by many, including a number of trustees and Dumke, for his leadership. Reagan did not laud Hayakawa, and not long after, declined to reappoint Heilbron as a trustee, despite widespread bipartisan support. The AFT had gained nothing other than visibility, some of it positive, but mostly negative.

There remained the student strike. In the mix of the Third World Liberation Front, Students for a Democratic Society, and the Black Student Union, many had no interest in ending the strike. The faculty did. The citizens' committee chaired by Bishop Hurley reemerged. The campus Academic Senate withdrew in favor of a select committee established by the Council of Academic Deans. Hayakawa was convinced to delegate his authority to the select committee, which was chaired by Curtis Aller, a distinguished labor economist who had recently returned to the faculty from a three-year leave in Washington. A settlement was near, but Hayakawa from day to day would change about the agreement the select committee had negotiated. He was very much in the public eye. At one point he announced he had to leave a meeting to fly to Washington to meet with newly inaugurated President Nixon. He challenged the student leadership to produce a month of peace on the campus. The select committee and the leaders of the factions did reach an agreement. Hayakawa declined to sign it personally, but he did accept it. In April 1969 the student strike ended; the strikers really had gained nothing.[60]

The End of the Beginning

The first decade of the California State Colleges was complex beyond any reasonable expectation. The trustees had begun a planning year in the summer of 1960. The first meeting of the new board was August 12, 1960. Nothing like bringing together the separate state colleges had ever been attempted in the history of American higher education.

The '60s turned out to be a drama. New leadership was a constant theme of the era. First, and only briefly, there had been Buell Gallagher. His sudden departure worked for the best interests of the state colleges and to his best interests. His behavior in the months he was chancellor, both with respect to his political and social values and with the presidents and campuses, suggested a difficult tenure. Dumke's assumption of the chancellorship was rocky, and would remain so, in a roller-coaster kind of way, for the twenty years he would hold the office.

It fell to Dumke to build and maintain the senior leadership of the system. Only one of Gallagher's senior appointees, Mansel Keene, who became the vice-chancellor for faculty and staff affairs, remained with Dumke over the long run. Keene played a key role in recruiting presidents until he retired in 1976. Dumke personally recruited many of the initial senior staff, the vice chancellors and some other key positions, and he turned to experienced faculty and administrators. By the middle of the decade, consultative procedures with faculty and others were in place. Mansel Keene traveled the country looking for presidential candidates, and the results of his recruitment and the initial use of consultative procedures were uneven at best.

Presidential selection was important. From 1960 through 1970, thirty presidents, including several interims, were appointed. San Francisco State experienced seven presidents in the 1960s. With the exception of the Hayakawa appointment in 1968, faculty, students, staff, and others were involved in the screening and selection processes. A few appointees were clearly not a match or fit for their campuses, and a number were not ready to work in a new and untried multicampus system with a strong participatory orientation. Several presidents were removed, including one who had been appointed in the late 1950s. Many reached retirement age. It is arguable that the recruitment process was not a careful one with respect to a match of the values of candidates with the then emerging values of the California State Colleges and the strong participatory orientation, especially of faculty but also of students and staffs on the campuses. New and old presidents alike were being asked to lead campuses through a major reorientation from regional colleges into a new kind of governance.

Dumke, on a number of occasions, described the years as comparable to the early years of the United States prior to the Constitution, years when the Articles of Confederation held the states somewhat together. The system weathered major issues: the creation of academic planning and plans, the creation of a statewide academic senate and faculty involvement in governance at every level, and the 1.8 percent salary debacle, which was totally avoidable, simply by moving money already in state college and campus accounts, but totally unacceptable to faculty and others.

The biggest issue of all was San Francisco State. The last half of the decade saw the San Francisco State situation test every dimension and aspect of the newly created California State Colleges. The work of bringing together the disparate state colleges was difficult. The players and factors involved in the San Francisco State situation included two unwise presidential appointments, the Students for a Democratic Society, the Third World Liberation Front, the Black Student Union, issues of race beyond the agenda of the BSU, and the drive of some faculty to unionization. Added to the mix was a new governor with an ideological agenda entering his initial years in office, and several ideologically committed trustees.

While this work is not the history of any single campus, the San Francisco State story importantly reveals a kind of ultimate test—could the new structure hold together and maintain its integrity? San Francisco was not the only California State College campus with troubles in the last half of the 1960s. Los Angeles, San Jose, Northridge, Sacramento, and even rural Chico all went through difficult periods. But San Francisco State was the ultimate test. In some ways the system did go on automatic pilot in 1967. The San Francisco campus's unfolding drama, exacerbated by unrest and serious disturbances on some of the other campuses, was the focus of attention of the trustees and chancellor, and often faculty and staff and student groups as well as state government. In the meantime others, faculty, administrators, and state government agency staff went about the work of building the California State Colleges in a new structure.

Perhaps the two key figures, in addition to Glenn Dumke and several trustees, who gave leadership to this steady building were Raymond Rydell, who served as executive vice-chancellor to 1969, and Harry Brakebill who was vice-chancellor for business affairs from 1965 to 1969, and then executive vice-chancellor until 1975. It is clear that many unwise decisions were made on the campuses and by the state college system, the trustees, and the chancellor and his staff. The entrance of Governor Reagan did not help the situation. The important point is that the center held, and at that center were faculty and others on the San Francisco campus, the chancellor and his staff, and the trustees.

It would take twenty years, but San Francisco State would make a complete comeback. In 1973, Dumke sent a team of three experienced academic vice presidents to San Francisco State for a week. They were asked to prepare a report for the trustees, chancellor, and the college's new president, Paul Romberg, who had been moved from the presidency at Bakersfield to San Francisco. The report was prepared in conventional academic language; the three vice presidents in presenting the report to the chancellor, used language comparing the campus to a graveyard. Two presidencies were involved in a slow climb, and the creative presidency and strong leadership of Robert Corregan, beginning in 1989, brought the San Francisco campus once again to a leadership position in higher education.[61]

When the decade began in 1960–61, the total enrollment on twelve campuses was 94,837 students. When the full and often tumultuous decade ended in 1970–71, the total enrollment on nineteen campuses was 251,434 students.

The close of the decade was perhaps the close of the "Articles of Confederation" period. In fall 1970, chancellor Dumke redesigned the role of vice-chancellor for academic affairs. The board appointed as the vice-chancellor President William Langsdorf, the founder of the Fullerton campus, who was respected for his intellectual leadership, his style, and his thoughtfulness for others throughout the system. Dumke then proceeded to address groups over the state. His title and theme was the same, "The New Approaches of the California State Colleges." The subtext was the same wherever he gave his speech. The California State Colleges have gone through ten years of creating a system and coming together. Now we need to address programs, quality, meaningful access, and the higher education needs of all of the people of California. He proposed a radical restructuring of undergraduate education and student progress toward the baccalaureate. He seemed to have borrowed, to some extent, the ideas of Robert Maynard Hutchins of the University of Chicago about the baccalaureate. He went on to describe the California State Colleges as the "1,000 Mile Campus."

All of the state college campuses would participate in external degree programs. Higher education would be available everywhere in the state. Campuses would remain open six days a week. Classes would be available in the evenings. He ended by acknowledging that these ideas were not original with him, but that the "package" could work for the state colleges and the people of California.

The time to move on had come.

Notes

[1] California Education Code, sec. 1, div. 16.5, Higher Education, chap. 3, The State College System.

[2] *Ibid.*

[3] The correspondence referred to in this chapter and other documents, are without exception, in the CSU Archives; Donald Leiffer, oral history, November 24, 1980, and March 26, 1987.

[4] Minutes of the Board of Trustees of the California State Colleges (hereafter cited as the board of trustees), August 12, 1961, CSU Archives.

[5] Donald Leiffer, oral history, November 20, 1980, and March 26, 1987, CSU Archives.

[6] *Ibid.*, 8.

[7] Louis H. Heilbron, statement to a subcommittee of the Assembly Ways and Means Committee, California State Legislature, September 30, 1960, CSU Archives.

[8] Memorandum to Dr. Roy E. Simpson, untitled, the State College Presidents, August 3, 1960.

[9] Glenn S. Dumke to Donald B. Leiffer, October 18, 1960, CSU Archives.

[10] Leiffer, oral history, 10, 22–23, November 24, 1980.

[11] *Report on California State Colleges Conference*, March 4, 1961 (writer unknown), CSU Archives.

[12] Minutes of the board of trustees, April 6, 1961.

[13] Donald B. Leiffer, letter to Governor Edmund G. Brown, May 1, 1961, CSU Archives.

[14] Association of California State College Professors, letter to chair Richard T. Hanna, Assembly Committee on Higher Education, CSU Archives.

[15] There is no formal history for California State University, Stanislaus. This section is based upon papers assembled by colleagues in the president's office at Stanislaus, notably Julia Fahrenbruch and Kenneth Potts, and upon my papers and personal knowledge.

[16] There is no formal history for Sonoma State University. This section is based upon papers assembled by colleagues in the president's office at Sonoma State and upon my papers and personal knowledge.

[17] Louis H. Heilbron, oral history interview by Judson A. Grenier, August 18–19, 1986, and January 5, 1987, 20–22, CSU Archives.

[18] Editorial, *New York Times*, April 8, 1961.

[19] Minutes, board of trustees, July 6–7, 1961.

[20] I was field representative for World University Service in Southeast Asia during a portion of the time Gallagher served as U.S. chair.

[21] Glenn S. Dumke, letter to Chancellor Buell A. Gallagher, July 11, 1961, CSU Archives.

[22] Minutes, board August 4, 1961.

[23] Both the Dumke experience with Oregon and the "chief" position matters are based on my papers.

[24] John Connor, retired senior California state government executive, interview by Donald Gerth, November 2006.

[25] Mrs. Dorothy Dumke Elliott, interview by Donald Gerth, November 24, 2003.

[26] There are two oral histories with Heilbron; one by Professor Judson Grenier in 1986–87, to be found at the CSU Archives; and one by Ms. Carole Hicke of the Regional Oral History Office at UC Berkeley in 1991–92, for the CSU Archives. I also did two extensive recorded and transcribed interviews with Heilbron in 2003 and 2005, and these are in the CSU Archives.

[27] The Heilbron report is in the minutes of the board of trustees, April 5–6, 1962. The events in this saga, of the give and take of Gallagher's departure and the activity leading up to the board appointment of Dumke, are found in the Heilbron oral histories and interviews previously noted; in the oral history of trustee Theodore Meriam, June 11, 1987; and in an extensive collection of newspaper clippings, the greater number from the *San Francisco Chronicle* and the *San Francisco Examiner* of 1961–62. All of these sources are to be found in the CSU Archives.

[28] Glenn S. Dumke, letter addressed to the "Faculty and Staff of the California State Colleges," April 7, 1961.

[29] Minutes, Council of State College Presidents, May 21, 1962. A more detailed story of governmental relationships is told in a subsequent chapter in this work.

[30] Leiffer, oral history. November 24, 1980.

[31] Minutes of the Chancellor's Council of State College Presidents, May 21, 1962. An expanded story of governmental relationships is told in a subsequent chapter in this work.

[32] Raymond Rydell, oral history interview by Lawrence de Graaf August 27, 1987.

[33] Minutes, board of trustees, March 7–8, 1963.

[34] Rydell, oral history, August 27, 1987.

[35] Minutes, board of trustees, March 7–8, 1963.

[36] Raymond A. Rydell, memorandum to the college presidents, April 6, 1963, CSU Archives.

[37] Ellis McCune, oral history interview by Lawrence de Graaf, May 5–6, 1995; McCune oral history interview by Donald Gerth, June 23, 2005.

[38] Minutes, board of trustees, April 6, 1961.

[39] McCune, oral history; John W. Francis, oral history, June 22, 2004; G. A. McCallum, *Progress Report, Faculty Participation in Statewide Policy Formulation, Board of Trustees of the California State Colleges*, August, 1962. The more complete story of the development of faculty governance from the beginning of the present organization (1960) to the time of this writing, is told in a subsequent chapter.

[40] Norman Epstein, oral history interview by Judson Grenier, June 1, 1995; author's notes.

[41] Epstein, oral history. Epstein ultimately became vice-chancellor and general counsel, serving through December 1974. He was named to the bench and is a justice of the state appellate court in Los Angeles.

[42] The California State Colleges, "1963 Admissions Study: Technical Summary, Discussion, and Recommendations Based Upon the First Term Analyses," Office of the Chancellor; Hall, oral history; admissions focus group (Robert Bess, Kathleen Kaiser, Charles Lindahl, Sara Lundquist, Nancy Sprotte, Donald Gerth), October 27, 2004. All sources cited here are in the CSU Archives. The more complete story of the development

of admission standards and issues, from the beginning of the present organization (1960) to the time of writing, is told in a subsequent chapter.

[43] Louis Heilbron, oral history interview by Grenier, 41; various papers in the CSU Archives.

[44] The young deputy dean in question is the author, who has kept records and notes over the course of a forty-five-year CSU career.

[45] Glenn S. Dumke, memorandum to members of the task forces and the committee on fiscal responsibility, June 22, 1965, CSU Archives.

[46] Office of the Chancellor, *Report of the Committee on Fiscal Responsibility*, January 1961; records, Committee on Fiscal Responsibility; Epstein, oral history; Harry E. Brakebill, oral history interview by Lawrence de Graaf, July 9, 1987; CSU Archives. The more complete story of the development of financial support and programs is told in a subsequent chapter of this work.

[47] Minutes, board of trustees, January 23, 1964.

[48] The most authoritative document about the history of California State University San Bernardino is *In Search of Community: A History of California State University San Bernardino* by Ward M. McAfee, California State University, San Bernardino, 1989.

[49] Axelrod had been responsible for the San Francisco State general education program, which, for its time, was the most integrated GE program in any public university or college in the state. Prior to San Francisco State, he had been an important faculty member in the College of the University of Chicago. He would return to the San Francisco campus in 1965.

[50] The detail about the selection of the Dominguez Hill site comes from an email exchange among Grenier, a professor emeritus of history at Dominguez Hills; Donald MacPhee, a founding faculty member and dean, and later provost at Dominguez Hills; James Gregg, professor emeritus of political science at CSU Chico, and the author (email exchange of March and April 2008 are in the CSU Archives).

[51] Donald H. Pflueger, *California State University Pomona, A Legacy and a Mission, 1938–1989* (Pomona, Calif., 1999); Robert A. Kennedy, *op. cit.*; Kennedy interview by the author, *op. cit.*

[52] There is no written history of California State University, Bakersfield. I used materials provided by the public affairs office of the Bakersfield campus.

[53] Glenn S. Dumke to Ronald Reagan, December 12, 1966, CSU Archives; Les Cohen, director of governmental affairs, California State Colleges, 1962–1970, interview by author, January 24, 2006.

[54] Robert Smith, letter to President Paul Dodd of San Francisco State College, March 12, 1964.

[55] California State Colleges, *Report of the Ad Hoc Committee on Development of Policies and Administrative Procedures*, March 1965, CSU Archives.

[56] Robert Smith, Richard Axen, and Devere Pentony, *By Any Means Necessary* (San Francisco: Jossey-Bass, 1970).

[57] *Ibid.*, 81. In this volume, Smith authored a chapter describing all of the events leading up to his appointment.

[58] Smith, Axen, and Pentony, *By Any Means Necessary*, 165.

[59] Focus group on governmental relations (Kehoe, Les Cohen, Scott Plotkin, Karen Y. Zamarippa, Dorena Knepper), January 24, 2006; John Kehoe, interview by the author, February 8, 2008.

[60] The section about San Francisco State is heavily dependent on Smith, Axen, and Pentony, *By Any Means Necessary*; Heilbron, oral history interview by Carol Hicke of

the Regional Oral History Office at UC Berkeley and the CSU Archives; Heilbron, oral history interview by Judson Grenier at the CSU Archives; Heilbron, interviews by the author, December 14, 2003, and November 7, 2005; papers of Glenn S. Dumke, CSU Archives; Glenn P. Smith, interview, April 1, 2004; and my personal files; CSU Archives.

[61] Milton Dobkin, Harold Haak, and Donald Gerth, *Report About the San Francisco Campus*, 1973, CSU Archives.

Part Two
The Work of the California State University

Chapter 4

Academic Planning: Purpose and Direction

Academic planning as a concept in the California State University is the creation of the founding board of trustees, the chancellor, and the chancellor's staff. Over the years it has become an accepted way of organizing the curriculum on the campuses and with the board and state government. It did not, however, begin that way.

As a systematic and recurring means of authorizing and revising courses of study and degree programs, academic planning simply did not exist prior to the trustees. Campus presidents and faculty identified program needs and opportunities and advocated for these as they negotiated with the Department of Finance for budget support and for building programs. This was done campus by campus. One campus had developed a formal document in the late 1940s, an academic plan, to use in Sacramento negotiations. Julian McPhee, the president of Cal Poly, had used it to convince the governor and the legislature, about the funding of programs and buildings that focused on the Cal Poly mission of agriculture and technology. Programs were rationed, especially high-cost programs, by Finance and in negotiations with the Division of State Colleges and Teacher Education.[1]

When the trustees first called for formal campus academic plans, this call produced a general campus uproar. Their action was described variously as interference, micromanagement, and a breach of academic freedom. Campus leadership and faculties had not experienced a board action asking to relate the funding of new facilities to academic plans. The trustees and their staff in the chancellor's office imposed the discipline of academic planning not only upon campuses but upon the system, the chancellor's office, and themselves.

In the 1960s, guidance for academic planning came both from faculty and administration. Ellis McCune was a political science professor at the San Fernando

Valley campus, the president of the campus's early faculty senate, the chair of the committee that created the statewide Academic Senate, and then the first system dean of academic planning in 1963. He began his years as dean by inviting experienced campus faculty to join his staff in the chancellor's office, and together they assembled a process that served as the base for academic program development and maintenance to the early 1990s.

McCune and his colleagues had had a point from which to start, the careful work done by Vice-Chancellor Raymond Rydell and Dean James Enochs in 1962–63. These first steps are described in the earlier chapter on the 1960s, the years of forming the system. In March 1963, trustees had adopted as a policy statement "A Master Curricular Plan for the California State Colleges." This set the stage for the last of a three-part plan. Phase I had been "the identification of the basic complement of arts and sciences as the foundation program of the colleges"; Phase II the "review, evaluation, and recommendations concerning specialized programs"; Phase III, to begin with the arrival of the new dean of academic planning, was to be the "development of master curricular plans for each campus, to include review and evaluation of current programs, plus a tentative projection of programs for the future."[2]

McCune and his colleagues began the systematic work with the campuses to develop campus academic master plans one by one. One of McCune's first acts was to delegate to the campuses the responsibility for developing a plan. McCune defined the role of his office as one of integration. It was not to be simple, as some presidents and academic administrators and faculty were still smarting from what they perceived as trustee or chancellor's office imposition and interference with campus autonomy. McCune and his colleagues were careful to work with campus faculty and administrative leadership, the statewide Academic Senate, and the Council of Presidents. Finally, in 1964, the trustees received the first set of campus academic plans. The essential core for each was to be the liberal arts and sciences.

Chancellor Glenn Dumke had a background of involvement in accreditation. Even in these early years of developing the system, with the full support of the trustees he urged forcefully that all degree programs on campus academic plans be accredited where program accreditation was available. This was especially important for the array of professional programs emerging in many fields, including business, engineering, and nursing. That position has remained with subsequent chancellors and the board.

In the very early years, trustees discussed the concept of campus specializations. Members of the board, in this instance urged by trustee Louis Heilbron, asked particular campuses to develop and emphasize special programs related to a campus location, existing strengths, and perceived long-term needs. Extra resources were offered. Some campuses responded; others declined. The Humboldt campus, already with some strengths in forestry and other natural resource areas, responded positively. The Sacramento campus was offered funding to build an academic program focusing on state government and public policy, but it declined the offer.[3]

The academic planning process established in the early years of the system has remained constant. Each campus updates its academic plan annually, adding new programs and, occasionally, dropping some. The complete set of programs is presented by the chancellor to the trustees for review and recommended action. This is not just a formality. In the earlier years of the 1960s, the trustees paid attention to a change in orientation toward the arts and sciences, a change they sought. There was an emphasis on the consolidation of programs. The trustees were not, however, attentive to the needs of place-bound students and the distribution of programs around the state. The trustees participated actively when they reviewed the academic plans of the individual campuses. They viewed themselves as builders of programs in the new California State Colleges. It was a time when it seemed that every campus wanted everything that every other campus had, plus some unique things. The trustees held the line, particularly on high-cost programs such as engineering, architecture, agriculture, and specialized graduate degrees. The frequency of trustee discussions regarding the academic core of the CSU mission has declined over the years, although presentation to the trustees continues to be employed as an occasion for a campus to give a program elevated visibility.[4]

What has changed in the academic planning process is the tone, the sense of working relationships between the campuses and the chancellor's staff. McCune left the chancellor's office to assume the presidency of the Hayward campus in 1967. The academic planning office was fully established at that point, and provided both assistance to the campuses and orderly growth for the system as a whole. The orientation of the office subsequently changed.

The student and faculty turmoil of the '60s was most visible on the San Francisco campus, but some level of unrest was evident on almost all campuses. This was where trustee attention was now focused, not on academic planning, which for a time was taken for granted by the system and many campus leaders. A clear shift in orientation set in, in the largest measure due to personnel changes, and the academic planning office became considerably more regulatory and directive. This pattern of behavior would continue, with variations on the theme, down to the very early 1990s. The role of the dean of academic planning became a regulatory one, the gatekeeper for academic program development, from the campus viewpoint. Understood in a larger context, this was not always definitive for the campuses, but it did influence campus development. Campus leaders had to become adept in working with the staff in the chancellor's office. Much of the focus in academic planning shifted over time to budgetary issues.[5]

What did happen with academic planning from about 1965 onward was a shift to the allocation of resources, dollar support related to the specific characteristics of the academic programs. At the macro or system/Sacramento level, the dean of academic planning became a member of a three-person budget team: the vice-chancellor for business affairs, the head of the budget office, and the dean. This team spent specific time in Sacramento negotiating the annual budget and appropriations with the Department of Finance, the legislative analyst, and the legislature. The dean's role was to provide the academic program base for budget requests. This team concept continued over the years until the 1990s.

At the micro or campus/system level, a key deputy to the dean of academic planning was recruited from a campus to shape and coordinate new faculty positions and budget needs to specific academic programs and their support. David Benson, later to become president of the Sonoma campus, described the formulaic approaches to building an academic budget as "program faculty staffing . . . [was] a brilliant scheme for planning academic programs . . . [it was also] troublesome, [and] people fought it, but it worked for the system amazingly well in terms of letting growth happen."[6] Essentially this was program budgeting, although as it evolved over the years, the advantages were to some extent lost in the rigid application of formulas; all programs in any given discipline or field were assumed to be identical on all campuses.

The deputy dean brought in to accomplish this was William Mason from the San Francisco campus. Mason replaced McCune as a member of the budget team that would commute to Sacramento, while, at the same time, being the interface between academic planning and academic leadership on the campuses. This role contributed greatly to the redefinition of the academic planning office, and this redefinition was fully accomplished by 1970.[7] Part of this redefinition was the emergence of a brokering role, often, played by the academic planning staff between the campuses and state government.

The academic planning function remained relatively stable for twenty years. McCune was succeeded by Gerhard Friedrich, a faculty member from the Fullerton campus who had joined the academic planning staff shortly before McCune's departure. In fact the role of vice-chancellor for academic affairs had been vacant since 1965, when Ray Rydell became executive vice-chancellor and McCune was the de facto vice-chancellor. The search committee that recommended candidates to the chancellor had included McCune on the list but he was blocked by a few presidents led by Robert Hill, the new president of the Chico campus, who did not want a strong vice-chancellor. They got what they wanted. McCune left shortly for the presidency of the Hayward campus.

Friedrich began the shift of the office toward a more regulatory posture. He died suddenly in 1973, and was succeeded by his deputy, Anthony Moye, who remained in the office (while Moye held the office, it was retitled assistant vice-chancellor) until it was eliminated due to reorganization, shortly after the arrival of Barry Munitz in 1991. Moye continued the regulatory posture, the central issue, as always, being resources and control of the spread of high-cost and low-enrollment programs, some for which there was questionable state need. This approach made the development of the newer campuses difficult and often held them back.[8] In its almost fifty years of existence, the system has not addressed the developmental aspects of growing a new campus. On the other hand, it makes no financial or program sense to permit uncontrolled program development.

The academic planning function as a major activity was essentially on a maintenance pattern through the remaining years of the Dumke chancellorship. The initiative for academic program development moved elsewhere in the chancellor's office. The most important dimension of the academic planning office was in relating program needs and resources to the budget process in Sacramento. The team of Dale Hanner, the vice-chancellor for business affairs; Louis Messner, the assistant vice-chancellor responsible for budgeting; and Tony Moye, as assistant vice-chancellor from the academic side, was the system interface with Sacramento for many issues from 1973 until the early 1990s.

Ann Reynolds became chancellor September 1, 1982. Her eight-year administration had two academic focal points. One was teacher education. It was present on all campuses and in the trustees' Master Curricular Plan. On some campuses it was one among many programs; on a few campuses it suffered from neglect, depending on the campus history and campus leadership. Reynolds made clear soon after her arrival that teacher education was a priority. One move she was singly responsible for was to convince both the trustees and the campuses that students wishing to enter a credential program must be in the upper half of their class, major, or overall grade-point average, however measured.

In her first few months in office, Reynolds also focused on the arts. Her initial move was to breathe back life into admissions issues, and the most unexpected component of that had to do with the arts. (Admissions issues are addressed more extensively elsewhere in this work.) She instituted summer arts programs, which for a time moved among campuses and other sites. She also met regularly with the arts deans. While this special interest did not result in a rush of more performing arts program proposals, it did result in more support for the arts on the campuses.[9]

Similarly, she pushed programs to attract women to science and technology. Her academic agendas were hers alone. She worked with faculty, deans, and presidents. She did not lean heavily, or much at all, on the academic planning staff. That staff continued its customary work with campuses on new degree programs and program reviews.

In the early 1990s, academic planning went through a sea change. The arrival of Barry Munitz as chancellor—and Molly Broad as executive vice-chancellor, and effectively the CSU chief operating officer—brought a redefinition of the board of trustees and the chancellor's office, the system's center, and of the campuses, which circle around the center. Munitz and Broad reorganized the chancellor's office. The emphasis, however, was not on structure. The chancellor's office would focus on policy, strategy, and the state budget; on building campus capacities for fundraising and grant acquisition; and on governmental and public affairs. Lee Kerschner, a veteran of the California State Colleges from the 1960s and '70s, had left California for a major post in Colorado in the late '70s. He returned to California in 1986 to head a review of the Master Plan, and then joined the CSU as vice-chancellor for academic affairs for the final Reynolds years. He worked with acting chancellor Ellis McCune through the 1990–91 transition to Munitz, and he worked with Munitz through a first year, as Munitz assessed the academic role and work of the chancellor's office. He then moved to the Stanislaus campus as interim president. Munitz brought in as an interim vice-chancellor the recently retired president of Fresno State, Harold Haak. Haak had been in the CSU for most of the past thirty years, first as a faculty member at San Diego State, and leader in the statewide Academic Senate, then as a dean and academic vice president, except for an interruption for a few years as chancellor of the University of Colorado campus in Denver. The 1980s had set a stage for a change in the role of the chancellor's office. Munitz wanted to move academic program initiative and building—decision making, for the most part—to the campuses. With his campus experience, Haak helped accomplish that.

Control became a gentle art, as long as campus leadership was fundamentally reasonable. Jolayne Service, a longtime member of the academic planning staff, became the dean; her role was "to nudge campuses to do the sensible thing." Certainly, this shift was urged on by a significant state budget crisis in the early 1990s. The "orange book," the long-standing collection of funding formulas, disappeared, a decision made by Munitz almost as he assumed office, led by the work of his predecessor Ellis McCune and the presidents, who had laid a careful foundation for this move. Campuses had to manage reduced resources and mandated reduced enrollments as best they could. The presidents and others on the campuses wanted flexibility. It was a good move for both good and bad reasons, and would provide for an increase in creativity on campuses that encouraged and facilitated creativity in their cultures. Molly Broad encouraged the academic planning staff to help the campuses develop their programs, polish them, and secure them.[10]

The core of the Munitz-Broad academic interest was strategic. For a time, the budget focused on strategic issues, but an opportunity presented itself, and Munitz and Broad seized the opportunity. Cornerstones, a comprehensive strategic planning work effectively engaging all of the many groups and constituencies of the California State University, was initiated. (This project will be discussed later in this chapter.) This was the first encompassing strategic planning effort of the CSU since the 1960s. The activities of the 1960s had been strategic, but disparate; they were to be woven together by experience.

The academic planning activity in the chancellor's office became essentially a campus support activity. The process had not changed over the years, and it was both careful and time consuming. Lead time to implement a new program was measured not in months, but in years. The annual master plan submitted by each campus listed current and projected programs; the projected programs were two or more years in the future. In early 1997, which would be Munitz's last year as chancellor (he left December 31), the chancellor's staff proposed to the presidents a "fast track" plan for programs for which implementation within a short time was important. The campuses were delighted, the board approved it, the campuses continue to use it.

Charles Reed, the chancellor of the Florida State University System, was appointed to succeed Munitz in late 1997 and assumed the chancellorship on March 1, 1998. While he quickly understood that Cornerstones could be a major academic planning instrument, he did have a number of academic initiatives apart from Cornerstones. In the process of moving into the chancellorship, Reed had spent time with Governor Pete Wilson. Wilson talked with Reed about his initiative having to do with class size in elementary schools, and Wilson asked for help, offering financial support to increase the output of teachers from the California State University. Reed agreed. Teacher education became a priority for the Reed administration, and serious, productive time was given to systemwide efforts to strengthen teacher education.

The academic vice-chancellorship position had been filled for three years by Charles Lindahl, a longtime California State University administrator. Lindahl had come to the California State Colleges and the San Fernando Valley Northridge campus in 1964 as director of admissions on that campus, and then was invited to join the chancellor's office staff in the 1970s. Lindahl was highly regarded on campuses, in Sacramento, and certainly in the chancellor's office as an able and straightforward administrator. When Peter Hoff, Munitz's first appointee to the role of vice-chancellor for academic affairs, had left California in 1995 for the presidency of the University of Maine campus, Lindahl had been asked to take his responsibilities.

Charlie Reed, when he was appointed, quickly concluded that he wanted to give major attention to the academic side of the house. Reed had a very able vice-chancellor for academic affairs in Florida, David Spence, with whom he worked well, and who had previously been executive vice-chancellor of Georgia public higher education. Spence was a candidate, and was supported by the search committee. He arrived at the chancellor's office in June of 1998 and rather quickly gained the confidence of the statewide Academic Senate. Like his predecessor Bill Langsdorf, Spence worked easily and well with the faculty leadership; Lindahl continued as associate vice chancellor for academic affairs.

Spence redefined the role of the vice-chancellor. Reed and the board of trustees had named the role executive vice-chancellor and chief academic officer. Spence's focus was on system issues, not campus issues; he was a strategic planner. He effectively removed himself and the academic affairs staff from campus management, but not from the work of providing help and useful coordination. Reed was continuing what Munitz had initiated conceptually but had not yet fully implemented, or so it seemed to chancellor's office observers.

Spence would leave the California State University in 2005 to assume the presidency of the Southern Regional Education Board. He would have a major positive impact on the system and the campuses, not only in identifying the vice-chancellor role as a strategic one, but on resolving long standing important matters. His deputy Keith Boyum, a political science professor from the Fullerton campus, would assume an interim role for a year. In 2006, Gary Reichard, the provost of the Long Beach campus, would be appointed by the trustees as executive vice-chancellor and chief academic officer.

One of the first issues drawing Spence's attention was the relationship of the California State University and the California Community Colleges. A very significant percentage of California State University baccalaureate graduates begin their undergraduate higher education in California's Community Colleges. The percentage of community college transfers in a graduating class varies from campus to campus. See Table 4.1. In 2006–07, 54.8 percent of all students receiving baccalaureate degrees from a California State University were community college transfers. Setting aside the Maritime Academy at the low end, and the new Channel Islands campus at the high end, the percentage of community college transfers

Table 4.1. Community College Transfer Percentages among Baccalaureate Graduates

	Baccalaureate Graduate 2006–07	Community College Transfers in Graduating Groups	Percentage
Bakersfield	1,291	726	56.2
Channel Islands	402	339	84.3
Chico	2,900	1,356	46.8
Dominguez Hills	1,819	1,297	71.3
East Bay	2,407	1,554	64.6
Fresno	3,384	1,655	48.9
Fullerton	6,295	3,917	62.2
Humboldt	1,374	691	50.3
Long Beach	6,110	3,176	52.0
Los Angeles	3,097	1,923	62.1
Maritime Academy	148	19	12.8
Monterey Bay	598	268	44.8
Northridge	5,682	3,313	58.3
Pomona	3,768	1,666	44.2
Sacramento	4,953	3,052	61.6
San Bernardino	2,595	1,507	58.1
San Diego	6,433	3,146	48.9
San Francisco	5,230	3,273	62.6
San Jose	4,043	2,206	54.6
San Luis Obispo	3,613	949	26.3
San Marcos	1,598	1,084	67.8
Sonoma	1,688	818	48.5
Stanislaus	1,459	892	61.1

Division of Analytic Studies, Office of the Chancellor, California State University, April 2008.

ranges from 26.3 percent, at San Luis Obispo, to 71.3 percent, at Dominguez Hills. The issue of transfer from the community colleges to a state university campus, and the transferability of lower-division courses, either in general education or in majors, had never been resolved. It was a matter needing attention in 1960, and it still needed attention nearly forty years later.

Spence and Reed shared the Florida experience. Florida's network of community colleges and the public universities in the state (which Reed and Spence had administered) had long ago articulated lower-division and upper-division curriculum in both general education and majors. This was not at all the situation in California. Each CSU campus had its own discrete set of general education requirements, set by the faculty, and each academic program faculty set the lower-division requirements. Some progress had been made in the 1990s with securing a common transfer pattern for a major portion of general education. This was not easily done. Faculty had to come together, and community college and state university faculty had to reach agreement. The 1993 institution of an agreed-upon process of community college courses for general education eventually reduced general education (GE) as an issue at the public policy table.

When Reed and Spence came to California in 1998, they discovered that the average community college transfer student who receives a CSU degree takes 156 units. This was different from their Florida experience. Spence made an issue of this surplus equal to one year of course work that community college transfers accrued. This had not been on the California agenda. The solution to articulating requirements for the major in a baccalaureate degree program had to be with the faculty. Spence took the matter to the statewide Academic Senate. They agreed to a trial. For over a year, faculty from the campuses in a selected number of majors would work together to build a common lower-division set of courses for the major. This effort was successful. Once agreement was reached among the CSU campuses, the next step was to review the comparable courses on community college campuses. This is a very substantial achievement.[11]

Trustee concerns about the need for remedial programs are as old as the system. A variety of initiatives have been attempted over time. None has succeeded, short of simply curtailing access. The admission standards adopted by the trustees in the mid-1980s were based on a college preparatory curriculum that included four years of college preparatory English and three years of mathematics. Yet the large percentage of student requiring remedial attention, despite efforts to work with the secondary schools, did not significantly diminish. No one—neither the board, the faculty, the presidents, nor the chancellors—has been willing to limit access.

In 1996, the board adopted an initiative that originated with a trustee. Ralph Pesqueira, who served two full trustee terms from 1988 to 2004, proposed a gradual phase-down of the percentage of entering freshmen who would need remedial work. He visited every campus and met with faculty and students as well as administrators. On some campuses, opposition, especially faculty opposition, was fierce. Much of the opposition focused on whether CSU faculty would offer remedial work or whether that work would be done in the community colleges. The board adopted a modified version of the Pesqueira proposal in 1996, and called for annual progress reports. The 1996 policy did not deny admission to otherwise eligible students, but mandated prompt remedial action and placed the burden on both students and campuses.

The annual reports were not encouraging. David Spence, in conversations with members of the State Board of Education, made a proposal that might be described as in the category of "why didn't we start doing this a long time ago?" He proposed to the statewide Academic Senate, the board and presidents, and then the State Board of Education that a test comparable to the English placement test given to entering university freshmen be given to high school students during the junior year. Members of the legislature scoffed, protesting "not another test," given the burdens of testing programs nationally and in California already. In cooperation with the state board and others, a solution was developed. An existing test that all high school juniors are required to take would be used, and students would have the option of adding a brief supplement, a small number of questions. Thus, the Early Assessment Program (EAP) was born.

In the first year, with 390,000 juniors enrolled in 940 participating high schools, well over 150,000 students opted to do the English test; of the 150,000 students eligible (because of coursework) to take the math test, 115,000 opted to do the test. The test indicated to students, their families, and teachers whether remedial work would be necessary. The high school senior year could be used. This example is important, as it is illustrative of the chancellor's office repositioning in order to deal with academic strategy rather than detail. Spence made the point that it is essential to align CSU and secondary school standards and produce results.[12] EAP, first generally available in 2005, is still in its early stages of existence. The results to date are positive, and educators and policy makers beyond California have taken notice.

New Approaches

The 1960s was a decade of history making and of tumult in the California State Colleges. At the same time, it was also a decade of great accomplishment. The system was built. It was hardly mature, but it was established and had a place in California, and a promising place nationally as well as internationally for its time. By 1970 Chancellor Glenn Dumke thought it was time to pursue additional academic goals, to reach beyond the conventional strong state college model. The 1970–71 academic year was one he would use to call for rethinking both curriculum and instruction.

At the January 1971 meeting of the board of trustees, Dumke presented a major paper. The agenda of the meeting titled Dumke's presentation "A New Approach to Higher Education … for the California State Colleges." He and a number of close colleagues, William Langsdorf, the newly appointed vice-chancellor for academic affairs and founding president of the Fullerton campus, and John Smart and David Leveille, staff members in academic affairs, had extensive conversations. Alden Dunham, a senior individual with the Carnegie Corporation of New York, and Dumke were in close touch; in 1969, Dunham had authored *Colleges of the Forgotten Americans: A Profile of State Colleges and Regional Universities*, a volume in the Carnegie Commission series.

Dumke's proposals, which he acknowledged did not originate with him, were on the whole remarkable for their time in public higher education. They are remarkable today. Two principle ideas lay behind a number of proposals. The first was awarding baccalaureate degrees based upon large blocs of curriculum—essentially, a common general education program and defined majors, with student performance evaluated by means of comprehensive examinations in the areas of general education and the majors. This approach would lead to time-shortened degrees for many. Degrees would be awarded not on time serving, but on achievement measured by the faculty. Dumke estimated that the time to earn a degree would be shortened by a semester, or possibly an academic year, for many students, and perhaps a year and a half for some.

Dumke characterized the conventional awarding of degrees as being based on "bits and pieces, credits, units, grades, etc." He asserted that academic bureaucracy had overcome student achievement in measuring progress toward the baccalaureate. He was looking for "learning breadth, the development of perspectives, problem-solving skills, communication competence, and the appreciation of the liberal arts." He defined learning depth as "high competence in a specific major area." Faculty would identify the contents of the curriculum, and then develop comprehensive evaluation or examination instruments. All of this would necessitate a new way to measure faculty workload; twelve weighted teaching units would not do.

The second big idea was about taking the campuses to the people, over the state, and this will be addressed later in this chapter. Later in the year, in a major speech at an education conference, Dumke would propose funding of faculty positions on a student-faculty ratio, something that a number of the newer academic vice presidents had been pressing for. On this, he was headed off by his own staff, which had an investment in the established faculty staffing formula. Advanced placement, comprehensive entrance examinations, challenge examinations were proposed. General education (a term he never actually used) was defined in four broad categories: humanities, social sciences, natural sciences and mathematics, and communication skills. There would be comprehensive examinations in each of these four areas, and a comprehensive examination in the student's major field. All of this would lead to a change in the tasks and functioning of the faculty.

These ideas were to be pilot-tested at two or three campuses, a few at a time. This was not to be a massive shift, but rather carefully considered by the faculties. Dumke described two task forces. The first, called Innovation in the Educational Process, would address the broad range of ideas Dumke had presented, specifically the development of pilot programs. Vice-Chancellor William Langsdorf would chair the group, composed of three faculty and two presidents. The second task force, Improving Efficiency in the Use of Resources, would address ideas and efforts already in motion, to gain more effective uses of campuses and, at the same time, provide more convenient access for many students via evening and Saturday classes, year-round state-supported open campuses, off-campus programs leading to degrees offered off campus, and the like. This group would also conduct an in-depth evaluation of the idea of ceilings on the number of units for degrees and majors. The latter task force, also composed of faculty and academic administrators, would be chaired by President Ellis McCune of the Hayward campus, the system's first dean of academic planning.

Not long after the January 1971 trustee's meeting, a major conference was held at the then new Kellogg Center at Cal Poly Pomona; it was supported by outside funding. The gathering was the largest since the trustees had come into being in 1960 (more likely, it was the largest in state college history to that time); trustees, statewide Academic Senate members, students, campus senate leaders and faculty, presidents and academic vice presidents, and chancellor's office staff members all gathered for three days of intense discussion on this range of new ideas. The purpose of the conference was to examine the propositions in the "New Approaches" address, to probe what might work and then generate interest on campuses in exploring some of these ideas. For most of the participants, the conference opened thinking to the exploration of new approaches to the work of the colleges and the work of the faculty, individually and in groups.

Dumke took his ideas to the streets. He sought and accepted invitations to speak to civic, cultural, and educational groups and meetings around the state. He was seeking to build support for the California State Colleges from groups and communities over the state. This was a clear move into the next phase of life for the state colleges. Dumke's "New Approaches" project had both an inside constituency and an outside audience. In the public arena, a major effort to change the name to the California State University was underway. A Master Plan review committee, chaired by then Assembly Member John Vasconcellos, was beginning its work. Within the system, the objective was a new beginning and some transformation.

A first step within the chancellor's office was the creation of an informal unit that would bypass the normal review and approval procedures for academic planning and development, and have funding available to support faculty and campus proposals within the broad framework of "New Approaches." Langsdorf was careful to work closely with the statewide Academic Senate. The 1971–72 senate chair, David Provost, was heavily involved. Dr. John Smart, a relatively new member of the chancellor's staff, shepherded the implementation of New Approaches in his work with the campuses, from the first projects in 1971. Smart came to the chancellor's office with Sacramento experience, initially as a legislative intern and then as a staff member with the Coordinating Council for Higher Education. He would remain with the chancellor's office for a full career, retiring as a vice-chancellor. Smart was assisted by Dr. David Leveille of the student affairs staff in the chancellor's office, another individual who would remain with the chancellor's office until the mid-1990s in a variety of roles, many of them dealing with matters on the cutting edge. Leveille eventually became associate director and acting director of the California Postsecondary Education Commission.

The March 1971 meeting of the board of trustees brought trustee endorsement of Dumke's proposals. Shortly thereafter, a call went to the campuses. Individual faculty, as well as whole units, such as departments, were invited to submit proposals to implement New Approaches. The response was significant; seventy-two proposals were received. These were reviewed by the task force on innovation. Funds for the first year, 1971–72, were scraped together in the chancellor's office, until outside funding could be secured. Smart and Leveille, the two-person team that gave leadership to what was still not a formal program, worked with individuals on the campuses. A fund for innovation and improvement was established. Many of the proposals were funded with sufficient monies to begin the project but not to complete it. Some initial funding was received from the Carnegie Corporation to get the effort started.

Three campuses, Bakersfield, Dominguez Hills, and San Francisco, were invited to participate in a collaborative effort that the Carnegie Corporation funded for $451,428 in December 1971 for 1972–74. This project addressed a range of Dumke's ideas. From Carnegie's perspective, it was the opportunity for students to receive credit and place out of courses at the time of admission and, subsequently, all through the undergraduate years. The Dominguez Hills campus, for example, developed what was called a Small College, a college within the larger one, where students could move along at a different pace.

As the state support budget for 1972–73 was being prepared, a process that began in June 1971, the system, with the full concurrence of the statewide Academic Senate, requested the support of $1,418,720 for the program for innovation and improvement. In the budget discussions in Sacramento, additional faculty positions were added to support a substantial number of the campus proposals. The final appropriation for New Approaches projects for 1972–73 was in excess of $1.75 million. The chancellor's office was able to fund fifty-one projects on the campuses with those funds, including the establishment of twenty-one new faculty positions. A few examples of funded projects were ones focusing on student self-reliance, including credit by examination in various forms; a mentorship model for teaching at Sonoma; competency programming in special education, including a technology element, at San Jose; and the use of self-learning modules at four campuses with Los Angeles faculty playing the lead role.

The projects in the 1972–73 year were successful, and for the most part, there were enthusiastic supporters among the participating faculty and their students. Again a request was made for budget support; the 1973–74 budget included $1,308,040. A total of 219 proposals were submitted for this cycle, and five consultants reviewed the proposals: a dean for a school of humanities; a dean for a school of professional studies; a professor of engineering; and two students, one an undergraduate, and one a graduate student. The task force on innovation then met for three days and selected forty-five projects to be funded, twenty-three of which were continuing projects, and twenty-two new ones.

In the summer of 1972, Vice-Chancellor Langsdorf and Chancellor Dumke formally established a new unit, New Program Development and Evaluation, and named Dr. David Provost, the 1971–72 chair of the statewide Academic Senate, as dean. Provost was then a political science faculty member at the Fresno campus.

Opposition to this Dumke-Langsdorf initiative to New Approaches was strong among some of the chancellor's staff. The New Program Development and Evaluation office provided an alternative to conventional program and curriculum

16. Statewide Academic Senate Advisory Committee on Consortium.

development. It was to do exactly what Dumke and Langsdorf wanted, to open up avenues for faculty and student creativity. As a formal entity the New Program Development and Evaluation was not to be institutionalized; rather, its purpose was to change what was already institutionalized. The New Program Development had an additional function assigned to it when it was created: the uses of technology in instruction. Prior to this time, a division of information systems unit in the chancellor's office had focused on administrative uses of technology.

The federal government at this time was looking at establishing a unit in the US Office of Education to address innovation. A request came from the commissioner of education (this was prior to the establishment of the position of secretary of education) for information about the California State University and Colleges initiatives. Conversations followed. The Fund for the Improvement of Postsecondary Education (FIPSE) was established at this point.[13]

The accomplishments of New Approaches were subtle. Room for experimentation with curriculum and the delivery of academic programs emerged. The campuses and faculties took varying advantage of this. Much depended on a campus's leadership, on the president, academic vice president, campus Academic Senate chair, and other key faculty. In the chancellor's office there was a continuing tension, fed by budget stringencies and the roles played by the three-person team that worked the budget through the Department of Finance and the legislature, by the election of a governor in 1974 not significantly friendly to higher education, and by the constant pressures related to pulling the system together.

The projects that were supported and funded for the most part became institutionalized. The uses of technology, then in its early stages in higher education, remained supported, and were able to develop. New Approaches formally opened technology for the academic side of the institution, and individual campus efforts underway in this area were affirmed.

The 1,000 Mile Campus was a significant result of New Approaches, and would not have happened, at least at that time, were it not for the leadership of the chancellor's office.

The 1,000 Mile Campus

In Dumke's New Approaches presentation to the board of trustees in January 1971, he had talked and written about extension. This was the presentation's other important concept referred to earlier. Dumke urged the merger of extension and regular academic programs conventionally offered on a campus. He wanted extension programs to be thought of and used like conventional on-campus or residence programs; essentially he wanted to end the long-standing academic custom of treating extension as something different; off-campus programs would be a part of what the California State Colleges did. Dumke addressed providing "degree opportunities for substantial numbers of students other than through an on-campus program as students in-residence, students who, under our present rigid systems, we cannot hope to serve. Our extension operations should provide a degree aspirant with an alternative to the on-campus program."[14] He talked about adapting the then new British Open University to the California context; the uses of technology; self-study combined with intensive short-course on-campus programs. He recommended giving degrees through extension, and urged the involvement of regularly appointed faculty and of academic departments. And he suggested regional centers, operated either by one campus or a consortium. For its time and place, these were extraordinary proposals for California about a traditional state-funded college or university.

Dumke considered extension synonymous with continuing education, and encompassing summer sessions, external degree programs, special sessions (these are what the category suggests, sessions outside of conventional practices), off-campus instruction and centers, and uses of technology. In a sense, the San Francisco Normal School of 1857 was an extension operation. Held on Monday nights during the school year, it was a required program for "in-service" teachers. It was only in 1862, with its growth into the San Francisco State Normal School, that a full-time program for those who wished to become teachers was established. Programs under the broad rubric of "extension" were operated by all of the normal schools and state teachers colleges. These were programs for teachers and, in the instance of summer sessions, for regularly enrolled students as well. Not all of the programs were in conventional classrooms. The first travel study program was offered by the San Jose campus in 1909. The president and others took a group of elementary and secondary teachers to Europe in a summer program. The Humboldt campus offered field-study programs. The Fresno campus had an off-campus summer session, essentially a camp in the mountains away from the summer heat in the San Joaquin Valley. From 1910 to 1935, some campuses began to offer regular classes at sites off campus, sometimes in distant communities. Campuses established extension divisions. Generally courses would count for degree (certificate prior to 1923) credit.

The financing of these early extension activities was generally within the regular institutional budgets. As the activities expanded in the early 1920s, summer sessions moved to self-support. Not long after, extension also became a self-supporting activity, although the line between conventional and extension programming was sometimes fuzzy.

The transition from teachers colleges to state colleges greatly increased the range of courses that could be offered in extension and summer session programs. Only modest change occurred in the years leading up to World War II, and the war years saw little program development. The years after the war were years of growth. Some of the campuses developed the concept of "limited students," individuals who could register for courses up to six units in late afternoon, evening, or Saturday classes, pay a reduced fee, and be in the state-supported program. These students would not need to go through the formal admission process, and thus their academic records were not reviewed. They simply registered. The San Francisco campus developed "contract courses," courses that could be from the regular on-campus curriculum, or they could be specially developed to be offered on-site and could be for short, intensive periods, or longer.

In 1949, the Council of Presidents established a committee to study extension programs. The programs varied so much among the campuses, and were growing, that the presidents concluded some order and policy framework would be necessary. The most important policy to come immediately from this effort, in early 1950, would be to provide that up to twelve units in extension could be applied to a degree. Later, in November of the same year, this policy was revised to provide that "as a contribution to the present military effort, credit earned in regularly organized and established centers operated on the extension course basis be accepted as residence credit for purposes of meeting graduation requirements."[15]

San Francisco was the most active campus in the 1950s. The first position of dean of educational services and summer session was created on the San Francisco campus in 1951; Leo Cain, later to be the founding president of the Dominguez Hills campus, was the first dean. Other campuses followed in later years. The position was funded from multiple sources, extension and summer session revenues and funds generated by income from late-afternoon and evening students. In 1955, the then president of San Francisco State, J. Paul Leonard, made another move and asked for state funding for an off-campus center that would have the capacity to award degrees. The proposal went from the Council of Presidents to the state superintendent of public instruction and the board of education. In reality, the decision lay with the Department of Finance and the governor. The governor included funding in the budget proposal and the legislature voted to support it. The Santa Rosa Center became the first state-supported center. Fresno soon followed with a proposal for a center in Bakersfield; at the same time, San Francisco began extension courses through television. In 1958, San Francisco State made another move and established the Downtown Center, with both state-supported courses and self-supporting extension courses and programs. Today the CSU delivers some forms of instruction through multiple locations in the state.

The Master Plan had little to say about any aspect of continuing education. One immediate impact was the elimination of the late-afternoon and evening on-campus students who were not matriculated. All on-campus students and students in state-supported programs had to be formally admitted. At that time, competition, mostly with the University of California, was growing. The University of California had long put state support into extension programs. The legislature cut this back, but did not eliminate it.

The 1965 state college internal fiscal crisis, associated with the 1.8 percent salary reduction for many, caused the creation of a Committee on Fiscal Responsibility, which is addressed elsewhere in this work. One of the task forces created by this committee addressed extension and summer sessions. The task force recommended the adoption of the concept of continuing education, encompassing activities in extension, summer session, and related programs, and the creation of the Continuing Education Revenue Fund for the financial administration of these activities. The recommendation survived the review of the statewide Academic Senate and the chancellor's Council of Presidents and was adopted by the board of trustees. The legislature and the governor supported the concept, and it was adopted in two stages, in 1967 and 1970.

Programs encompassed by the concept of continuing education had increased in numbers and variety in the 1960s. By 1970, all of the campuses were involved. There was a looseness about continuing eduation administration and policy at the chancellor's office level. That was both a plus and a minus: there was moving room for creative people and programming on the campuses, which some campuses took advantage of and some did not. Regulation of financial detail could and did sometimes occur at a micro-level in the chancellor's office and on some campuses. At the system level, though, no one was paying attention to overall policy. This provided a circumstance in which those whose academic values were thoroughly conventional could interfere with creative program building.

New Approaches came at a good time for some campuses. The uses of technology were developing on campuses. The Chico campus was offering a degree program in public administration on two sites in northeastern California, using some very creative interpretations about what counted for residence credit. Dumke called for a great expansion of off-campus degree programs and a redefinition of residence credit—essentially giving credit for "sound academic classes." Thus the second big idea of New Approaches was born.

> Related to this proposal is the possibility of providing degree opportunities for substantial numbers of students other than through an on-campus program as students-in-residence, students who, under our present rigid systems, we cannot hope to serve. Our extension operations should provide a degree aspirant with an alternative to the on-campus program.... They would also provide for the giving of degrees through extension and the consequent upgrading of current extension offerings.... This proposal suggests the need to view the regular and extension

programs as much more closely interrelated than is now the case. Extension courses, under these proposals, must be made equivalent to the regular academic offerings. This is the means, however, by which the door of educational opportunity would be opened to thousands and thousands of additional students, especially those who for economic or personal reasons cannot afford to take four years out of life to attend college.[16]

A first move, in April 1971, was to create a commission on external degree programs. Membership in the commission included two faculty members selected by the executive committee of the statewide Academic Senate, two chancellor's office staff members, two campus administrators, and two presidents. President Thomas McGrath from the Sonoma campus was invited to chair the commission and would do so until his retirement in 1974. McGrath was succeeded by Leo Cain, the president of Dominguez Hills, who had been both the spirit behind the many San Francisco State programs in the 1950s and the person that made them happen. Cain served as chair until his retirement in 1976. The commission was funded sufficiently to create the position of executive secretary, someone to work with the campuses and the chancellor's staff. Dr. George McCabe, the Sonoma faculty member who had been director of the Santa Rosa Center from 1956 to 1961, was named to the position. McCabe had demonstrated his rather extraordinary talent for both working constructively with others and using superb judgment with the Santa Rosa Center.

The commission held a statewide conference in the fall of 1971. The conference was titled "The 1,000 Mile Campus." Many campuses responded enthusiastically with delegations. The academic vice presidents and senate chairs were invited, along with deans of educational services and summer sessions (a title then being changed on many campuses to continuing education). Campuses could pick their own participants. The conference was well attended.

The commission invited proposals for external degree programs. Their definition of external degree programs focused on off-campus instruction, uses of technology, and included the possibility of programs with mixed modes of instruction. The programs were to be self-supporting. The commission had the authority and responsibility to approve proposals for these degree programs, not unlike the task force on innovation, which was also considering the many proposals submitted within the set of expectations Dumke had set out. Thus, the customary machinery and procedures that had been developed since 1961 could be bypassed to allow for building creativity on the campuses.

The commission concluded its work with a final report in 1976. It was a summary of creating opportunities for the campuses and their faculties and students. A recommendation in its final report was to create a standing Commission on Extended Education. The Commission on External Degree Programs became the new commission. The new commission would address "all of extended education in the CSUC, including such activities as late afternoon, evening, and weekend study, extension and summer session classes, and external degree programs." The chancellor accepted the recommendation, and the commission is alive to this day. In a sense, its task is not an easy one, as it is a principal vehicle to deal with the change in the CSU that impacts extended education over time.

In the fall of 1972, nine external degree programs were in operation. Faculty interest remained strong. By 1975, forty-one external degree programs were functioning throughout the state.

The 1,000 Mile Campus conference in the fall of 1971 produced a line of thinking that a number of individuals, George McCabe principal among them, wanted to explore: Could a number of campuses join together to offer an external degree program? McCabe drafted a proposal that was circulated on the campuses. This resulted in a proposal to the Commission on External Degree Programs for the creation of "the Consortium." The Consortium was to provide a mechanism for campuses to work together and offer degree programs, including interdisciplinary degree programs, as faculty could cross departmental lines in making proposals. There was strong presidential and faculty opposition. The deans responsible for campus continuing education programs were, almost to a person, vociferously opposed. In part, to gain faculty support, a Consortium advisory committee was proposed; it was to be a standing committee of the statewide Academic Senate. The Commission on External Degree Programs approved the proposal and recommended it to the chancellor. Despite the opposition, the chancellor approved the establishment of the Consortium; indeed, he was genuinely enthusiastic.

The operation of the Consortium was not easily understood. In 1972, the chancellor, at the suggestion of the commission, established the position of state university dean for continuing education. Dr. Ralph Mills, the Chico faculty member who had become associate vice president for regional and continuing education and had worked with the development of Chico's homegrown external degree programs since 1969, was appointed dean. When the Consortium was established, George McCabe was appointed director; he was housed in Mills' office, was responsible to an advisory committee for program purposes, and to the Commission on External Degree Programs for policy and financial purposes. Opposition to the Consortium remained strong, and McCabe was in the crossfire. Some members of the commission were skeptical. The Consortium had no faculty of its own; it would integrate faculty and resources from the campuses. It had a modest appropriation from the state general fund, and it used support from the Continuing Education Revenue Fund (CERF). The CERF money was, of course, generated by the campuses from their operations. By the spring semester of 1976, the Consortium had seven intercampus programs operating from eleven of the nineteen campuses. The Consortium director helped individual campuses with program development.

The Consortium survived for thirteen years. McCabe returned to the Sonoma faculty in 1978, and Dr. Helen Gilde, an active leader in the statewide Academic Senate and faculty member from the Long Beach campus, became acting director. In 1979, Dr. David Elliott, a faculty member from San Jose and chair of the statewide Academic Senate, became director and he remained with the Consortium until 1986, when it was discontinued, in part due to state budgets, and in part due to a loss of vision in the CSU.

Several points are relevant. The Consortium was strongly opposed by campus administrations from the beginning, and that did not change. After the passage of Proposition 13 in 1978, money became tight. The Department of Finance had initiated the practice, some years earlier, of assessing a small percentage of CERF money (and other self-support programs), essentially charging for chancellor's office and state government services. After a state audit, Finance began the practice of charging indirect costs (light, space, telephones, heating, etc.) to self-support programs.

Experience of the California State University system over the course of almost fifty years, teaches a fundamental fact of life. Presidents especially, and other campus administrators when affected, do not want any entity that appears to be like another campus. For the most part, new conventional campuses are accepted; there is no choice; the trustees and the state create them. But the wagons circle around something that has some of the attributes of a campus, a capacity to offer courses and confer degrees. With only a few exceptions, there was no support for the Consortium; rather, it brought hostility. The number of presidents, over the life of the system, who support the system as such and understand that the whole is more than the sum of the parts, is modest. Dumke remained supportive to the end, until his retirement in 1982.

The Consortium did not have a lasting impact. Campuses within the CSU are free to cooperate and do joint programs. Few do. The impact of the Consortium, limited as it was, had most to do with setting a tone among faculty and others about what could be done with some creativity.

New Approaches was successful. What it did was enable faculty and supportive administrators to think about and act on new ways to operate. The environment was changed, more on some campuses, less on others. The projects supported by the task force on innovation and the administrative unit, New Program Development and Evaluation, were in many instances institutionalized. More to the point, it became clear that there was room for innovation. The 1,000 Mile Campus became a reality. Changes were made in administrative procedures to support the development of degree programs throughout the state. In the late 1970s, legislation authorizing special sessions was enacted, and campuses had the ability to categorize programs as self-supported or state supported. For the most part, programs and activities initiated under New Approaches, including the activities of the 1,000 Mile Campus, became simply a normal way of operating in the California State University.

The impact of a program like New Approaches does not last forever. Again the experience of almost fifty years suggests that an effort to affect the environment and the culture of the California State University can be productive. It is not an approach to academic planning that can be used often, but it can be successfully used.[17]

Cornerstones

Cornerstones was a systemwide strategic planning work. It employed the talents of all of the many groups and constituencies of the California State University. The Cornerstones project originated in a 1995 conversation between Chancellor Barry Munitz and Thomas Ehrlich. Ehrlich was a nationally known leader in higher education; he had been dean of the law school at Stanford University, provost at the University of Pennsylvania, and president of Indiana University from 1987 to 1994. As he left the Indiana presidency, he was asked by the Pew Charitable Trust to assist in identifying a few promising higher education strategic planning innovations, which Pew would then fund. Ehrlich proposed to Munitz that the California State University be the multicampus system among the several projects Pew would fund. Munitz said yes.

The Pew leadership agreed, and set few conditions. The major condition was that all of the constituencies within the California State University must participate. The timing of the Pew proposal was good for the CSU. It was coming out of "dramatic budget problems and into a period of growth in California's economy and enormous growth in university enrollment." Cornerstones would "take a long hard and careful look at how well we were prepared to meet the opportunities and all the forces of global change."[18]

Munitz took the idea to the presidents in the executive council, the statewide Academic Senate and the board of trustees. All supported the proposal. He also invited Ehrlich to become a "CSU Distinguished Scholar" and assume a leadership role. As senior advisors to the chancellor, he brought in Jane Wellman, a former deputy director of the California Postsecondary Education Commission and nationally known personality in a Washington think tank about higher education, and Brian Murphy, a legislative staff member with Senator John Vasconcellos, known as a creative critic of higher education, and later to become a community college president.

Cornerstones was launched in May 1996. Appointments to the task force were from across the spectrum of the CSU; all had some experience systemwide. Their number included six faculty members from the statewide, Academic Senate including the chair; seven trustees, including the chair; the faculty trustee and the student trustee; three additional students; six presidents; the chancellor and three vice-chancellors. Tom Ehrlich was the convener or de facto chair, and he was ably assisted by Wellman and Murphy. Jill Murphy, a chancellor's office staff member who was a recent Sacramento State graduate and former executive vice president of the Associated Students of Sacramento State, was added to the staff group. The group met immediately, and continued to meet frequently in working meetings for the next eighteen months. Ehrlich, Wellman, and Brian Murphy gave initial direction and started the process.

At the start, it was made explicit that Cornerstones would not be "a comprehensive institutional planning process. The essential goals, mission, and policies that frame the university have been established by the California State Master Plan for Higher Education. The Master Plan remains a sound blueprint for the university and for the state of California. The issue is how best to reach our goals."[19] The theme that the Master Plan continues to provide the policy framework for California public higher education is a consistent one in the Munitz years, both implicit and explicit. The report noted other planning efforts underway, including teacher education reform and technology.

The process followed in the Cornerstones effort was to involve the task force in intensive working meetings, use staff to pull together the results, and encourage task force members to discuss widely goals for the CSU at the turn of the century. The work lasted from May 1996 to the issuance of the final report in December 1997. A major systemwide meeting addressing issues and themes in the work of the task force was convened in Monterey about two-thirds of the way through this period. More than six hundred faculty, students, trustees, and administrators gathered for two and a half days of intense discussion. There was much give and take among the participants, and the final report reflected this.

The substance of the report was organized around four policy goals: educational results, access, financial stability, and accountability. Within each of the policy goals, principles were defined and each principle was followed by specific actionable recommendations. Ten principles were submitted. Operational changes having to do with student services and admissions were proposed; the report was specific about covering programs supported both by state funds and those supported by fees. Organizational changes were proposed, including year-round operations (YRO), the scheduling of programs and courses, community college relationships, and, especially, increased integration of continuing and extended learning with the overall work of the campuses. Finally, program change and moving into new academic fields, especially applied and interdisciplinary programs, were proposed. While the report focused on students, both with respect to curriculum and support, attention was given to faculty development and to support for research and other scholarly and creative activity.

Access issues focused on relationships with K-12 and adequate preparation for university work as well as outreach to underrepresented communities. Joint and shared degree programs, preparation of students for credentials and careers in education received attention. The recommendation about collaboration with community colleges became very important, as this was effectively addressed. Access was understood in terms of entering freshmen and transfer students, but Cornerstones also addressed access to graduate programs and to continuing education. Emerging needs for professional education and the need for graduate education in applied fields were identified. The identification of access to continuing education was a reminder of the continuing importance of the 1,000 Mile Campus identified in the Dumke years.

In addressing financial stability, both for purposes of institutional support and for individual students and their families in planning for higher education, Cornerstones focused on one of the two significant shortcomings of the 1960 Master Plan: the lack of any agreed-upon public policy for the financing of public higher education in California. The findings on this issue included calls for public policy about state funding, the continuing development of what were called compacts for public financial support (the first compact had been negotiated three years earlier, in 1994, and was an agreement between the governor, Pete Wilson, and the heads of the University of California, the California State University, and the Community Colleges for state funding and its growth in relation to enrollments and other program considerations), and a call for a policy framework for generating private revenues. Accountability would be a part of the policy framework. This section was explicit about the public and private benefits resulting from investment in higher education and, consequently, student and family responsibility for a portion of higher education costs. This was an important statement for the California State University and a departure from past policy—the "pricing" of education fees. This section of the report used strong language: "The CSU must continue relentlessly to pursue state general funding to meet the core needs. . . ."[20]

A final major section of the report addressed accountability. The report called for the use of mechanisms to assess institutional performance. Student achievement and satisfaction as well as other factors would be assessed, and accountability would be open and public. Within this context, Cornerstones called for "significant campus autonomy" to develop missions and programs, and the flexibility for campuses to meet "clearly defined system policy goals." This was consistent with the Munitz-Broad approach to decentralization.

Following the major meeting in 1997, the task force members and staff put together the report. The twenty-five-page document was adopted unanimously by the members. Cornerstones was formally adopted by a unanimous board of trustees on January 28, 1998.

Molly Broad had resigned as executive vice-chancellor in spring 1997, and left at the end of June to assume the presidency of the University of North Carolina. To the surprise of all, Barry Munitz announced in July 1997 that he had accepted the presidency of the J. Paul Getty Trust and would be leaving at the end of the calendar year. The members of the Cornerstones task force, as they prepared their final report in the fall of 1997, knew they were putting together a document for new leadership in the chancellor's office. In the fall of 1997, Munitz informally commented on his role as a planner, the importance of looking ahead, and the role of the next chancellor as an implementer. Charles Reed was appointed chancellor in November 1997, and assumed office March 1, 1998.

Reed had learned of Cornerstones as he was being recruited to the chancellorship. As he characterized it, "[R]eally outstanding work had been done on the Cornerstones strategic planning, and I really appreciated it. In fact, the best thing that happened to me was being able to go to the Board at the very first meeting after I became Chancellor and recommend that they approve a ten year strategic plan called Cornerstones. It had taken two years to build it, there was a lot of involvement, and I had read and reread, and there was a lot of time on those airplanes going back and forth between California and Florida, but I said, '[H]ere's a road map.'"[21]

Patrick Callan, the president of the National Center for Public Policy and Higher Education, characterized Charlie Reed's response to Cornerstones as "this is like somebody handed me the Christmas tree already decorated."[22] Callan knew

Reed well and has been strongly supportive of the Reed agenda. His comment reinforces Reed's sense of being given a road map.

The executive council of the CSU (presidents, vice-chancellors, the chancellor who chairs the group, and a few key staff, depending on the agenda) meets in a retreat each June for two-plus days. The June 1998 retreat included a discussion about the implementation of Cornerstones. As David Spence, then the new executive vice-chancellor and chief academic officer put it, "this meeting with the presidents only reinforced that we had some work to do before we made it clear that we were going to implement it."[23] It is fair to assert that the California State University has a long history, not unlike many other higher education institutions, of doing complex and thorough and important studies that then gather dust on shelves. It is not at all apparent that the presidents believed at the conclusion of the retreat that Cornerstones would be the framework for a systemwide CSU academic strategy and actions over the next years. Nor is it clear that any other group within the system, save perhaps the trustees, thought about implementation.

Reed and Spence worked together to develop an implementation plan. This was not a work delegated to the staff. Reed and Spence did it. After three months' work, they unveiled an implementation plan draft. Spence involved the campus provosts. When Spence told the provosts that Cornerstones was to be implemented, only some seemed to believe it. The provosts and Spence, and then Reed, refined the plan. Many of the recommendations were made explicit in detail, and some points were reinforced. For example, the community college relationship and transfer students received added attention, as did attention to graduation rates, the substantial number of excess units accumulated by many students, and state-supported summer sessions.

In the fall of 1998, Reed and Spence presented a draft implementation plan to the statewide Academic Senate, the California State Student Association, the alumni council, and the presidents. Many or most presidents did not take the matter seriously. The students and the alumni made comments and were supportive. In the Academic Senate, many members were in disbelief. Senate members were not accustomed to being asked about implementation, nor were they accustomed to being asked to react to something within a one- or two-month timeline, which Reed and Spence had asked of them. The Senate's immediate reaction was that a longer time, perhaps a year, would be needed. With some difficulty, this was worked out, and, ultimately, the trustees received the Cornerstones Implementation Plan, and adopted it at the March 1999 meeting.[24]

The fourteen-page plan addressed actions, some of which all universities would be expected to address with substantial flexibility, as well as a small number of actions that would be commonly implemented across all campuses. The plan was explicit about where responsibility would reside for each action. In addition to Cornerstones, the plan addressed the implementation of a study about the baccalaureate degree, which had been completed and then adopted by the statewide Academic Senate in November 1997. This too was a first.

Spence's restructuring of the role of academic vice-chancellor and of the academic affairs staff was essential to Cornerstones. The Munitz group had made the first step, removing the micromanagement and regulatory functions. Spence replaced these with addressing educational policy matters that are essentially systemwide. Much of the agenda for academic affairs became the Cornerstones agenda; while academic affairs continued to do the routine things, reviewing new program proposals, working on student financial aid, and the implementation of new admissions standards, the "action" was to be Cornerstones.

Leadership of Cornerstones implementation was shared among Chancellor Reed, Vice-Chancellor Spence, and Vice-Chancellor Richard West. West had come to the California State University in 1994 from the University of California, where he had been associate vice president for administration. The spirit of the Munitz decentralization was in the chancellor's office. West over time, would implement sweeping and far-reaching changes in a variety of CSU administrative operations; the first he would tackle was capital outlay and the building program (addressed elsewhere in this work).

The principles relating to students and their academic programs encompassed a variety of areas. Faculty developed outcome and assessment measures on all campuses. This became a way of life at the departmental level. There is a substantial interface between this internally generated assessment activity and the work of the regional accrediting commission, the Senior Commission of the Western Association of Schools and Colleges (WASC), which accredits more than 140 colleges and universities. In 1993, the commission (whose chair then was a CSU president) began to experiment with a then new approach to accreditation, the assessment of outcomes rather than inputs, to consider what changes the years of study in colleges and universities had accomplished in individual students. The first two campuses to participate in this outcome-oriented approach, were the California State University campuses at Sacramento and Fresno.

The trustees reduced baccalaureate degree unit requirements from the long standing 124 units to 120; the 124-unit requirement was a holdover from a bygone time when students were required to take a one-half-unit physical education course each semester. The campuses responded, and most degree programs were shortened to 120 units, save those where professional licensing required a greater number of units, most often engineering.

With the full involvement and the leadership of the statewide Academic Senate, the trustees enacted the Lower Division Transfer Patterns program in 2004. This addressed a problem that had persisted since the founding of the first community (junior) colleges in California in the early twentieth century. By the fall of 2006, common lower-division curricula had been defined for forty-six majors. Students in any community college could follow these course patterns and be assured that the lower-division requirements for these majors would be satisfied on any of the CSU campuses. Given the evolution of public higher education in California, this was an enormous step. Academic support services for students were reinvigorated. Student progress to the baccalaureate was addressed, and programs were put in place in campuses to assist students in making efficient progress without wasting time.

Not all of the Cornerstones recommendations were successfully accomplished. After a surprisingly difficult startup with state-supported summer programs, the lack of financial support for the extra summer term caused a decline in state-supported summer programs. Greater use of Fridays for classes was not accomplished. Light scheduling of Friday classes, something that had gradually evolved over years, was not changed. This was not a matter of money, but rather of campus student and faculty cultures. The emergence of technology—mediated instruction was slow, a condition also related to student and faculty cultures.

The principle that urged students to become active partners with faculty in the learning process and in the university was partially successful. "Learning communities," the grouping of undergraduates, most often freshmen or sophomores, in a set of common courses, have spread to a number of campuses from their modest beginning in the late 1990s. Internships related to majors have been started and have grown. Perhaps the greatest success has been with community service learning. The system has made funding available to the campuses for program development. The CSU campuses are national leaders, with students in communities with programs addressing civic engagement, national and community service, and the like. The system has reinforced the annual student research competition, initiated in 1985. Undergraduates, graduates, and recent alumni participate in a competition, on a different campus each year, with varied presentations.

One of the Cornerstone principles addressed faculty and the primary mission of the CSU as a teaching-centered comprehensive university. Faculty development programs spread from initially just a few campuses to all of the campuses. On most campuses, it takes the form of providing assistance to faculty in preparing new styles of teaching, beginning research and scholarly and creative projects, and other assistance for the myriad activities in which they engage. For a time, there was a substantial emphasis on the uses of technology; most recently, the number of faculty with this competence has increased. Support for faculty research and creative activity comes from a modest fund, two and a half million dollars, available since the late 1980s, and from campus-based activities. As far back as the 1970s, some campuses have developed positions for directors of research to assist faculty in securing grants, contracts, and other like funding. All campuses were urged to give support to these activities.

An important principle in Cornerstones addressed the need for undergraduate education in California and, therefore, the need to increase outreach efforts and transfer, retention, and graduation rates. This effort is central to the future of California. Bluntly, the college-going rates of the diverse minority populations of California needed to increase. The college-going rates of all of California's population needed attention. Cornerstones provided a framework for this to be addressed on an almost massive scale. New outreach programs were developed. Programs already in existence were reinforced with more support. Posters for schools and homes, youth programs and the like were developed; one striking example is Super Sunday. In the Los Angeles area on one Sunday, and the San Francisco Bay and Sacramento areas on another Sunday, CSU leaders, trustees, presidents, the chancellor, and others visit predominantly African American churches. This bold important move was one that began in the context of Cornerstones.

The CSU has struggled with the issue of offering remedial programs for years. In the mid-1990s, trustee Ralph Pesqueira brought the issue to policy discussion and board action. But the needs of a large number of entering students for remedial work did not decrease. The Cornerstones report addressed this. David Spence took this issue to the State Board of Education and proposed that, in their junior year, high school students be given the equivalent of the freshman English and mathematics tests. That examination was built into the existing junior-year examination structure, and the Early Assessment Program was born. Hundreds of thousands of participating students so far have been able to repair deficiencies in their senior high school year. This is among the most notable accomplishments of Cornerstones, an idea so simple and natural, yet previously nonexistent.

Graduate and continuing education received attention. A funding level for graduate education that was different from the level for undergraduate education was achieved, and, after years, the CSU acquired the capacity to offer the independent doctorate. (The doctorate is addressed in Chapter 5.) Extended or continuing education continued to be a cutting edge for both development and delivery of programs. The Cornerstones objectives for graduate and continuing education were plans for growth, and these were actively pursued.

The Cornerstones report had been unequivocal about the need to establish a policy framework for financing public higher education. The trustees had adopted a student fee policy in 1993 and had entered into the Higher Education Compact in 1994 and 1995. What was needed was a policy framework that went beyond the Compact; the Compact for the most part funded the status quo and gradual enrollment growth. A broader policy is yet to come. The importance of private fund raising was reinforced by Cornerstones, and great progress was made in staffing and other provisions for fundraising. Faculty salaries and other salaries had been addressed by Cornerstones in 1997, and by the board's action in 1998. The 2006 evaluation of the achievements under Cornerstones made clear that much remained to be done.

Principle 9 of Cornerstones addressed accountability. In more recent years, accountability has become a federal government initiative. The Cornerstones report and its implementation predated this. This theme was persistent through most, if not all, of the report, beginning with defining expected student outcomes and assessing the achievement of these. Accountability was addressed immediately after the adoption of the Cornerstones Implementation Plan in March 1999. In November 1999, after widespread consultation, which produced some discomfort, the board approved the CSU Accountability Process. Campuses would be asked to report on eight areas: quality of baccalaureate degree programs; access to baccalaureate degree programs; progression to degree; persistence and graduation; relations with K-12 and college readiness; college readiness after one year; faculty utilization; and university advancement. Biennial reports were called for, and these began to be done in November of 2000. The reports are made by each campus. The data are aggregated by the chancellor and chancellor's staff, and a single consolidated report is presented by the chancellor to the board, to the governor and legislature, and to the public. The campuses are not identified in the report, though each campus knows its own position in the report, and can compare itself with others.[25]

The accountability process is one element among others in addressing accountability. There are also periodic economic impact studies and CSU Teacher Preparation Annual Evaluation and Accountability Reports. It is arguable that the principle addressing accountability is a key to Cornerstones.

In 2006, the Cornerstones process was ten years from the starting point in 1996. At the July 2006 meeting of the board of trustees, trustee chair Roberta Achtenberg and recently appointed executive vice-chancellor and chief academic officer Gary Reichard proposed to the trustees that the board receive, at its next meeting in September, a report on the CSU's accomplishments with Cornerstones and a proposal for "a forward systemwide consideration of the future of the California State University."[26]

At the September 2006 meeting, the "Evaluation of Achievements Under Cornerstones" was presented.[27] The thirty-five page document was both candid and detailed. It certainly affirmed what Charlie Reed and David Spence had said in 1999, that Cornerstones was the basic planning document they would use. There was disbelief in 1999. There could not be disbelief in 2006. Cornerstones had been the basic blueprint from 1999 to 2006.

> Achievements across the system have been especially noteworthy in areas related to learning outcomes and assessment of student achievement of those outcomes (Principle 1); sharpening of the focus on support for student success and active learning (Principles 2 and 3); outreach efforts to P-12 (Principle 5); efforts to improve progress to degree, retention, and graduation rates (Principle 5); and accountability and reporting of campus outcomes (Principle 9). Moreover, the CSU has developed funding strategies for such purposes as integrated technology initiatives, P-12 outreach, applied research and joint doctoral programs (Principle 8), and has adhered to *Cornerstones* Principle 10, which affirmed that "campuses shall have significant autonomy in developing their own missions, identity, and programs, with institutional flexibility in meeting clearly defined system policy goals.[28]

The all-important balance between the systemwide strategic plan and priorities, on the one hand, and the unique nature and strengths of individual campuses, on the other, had been carefully maintained.

Access to Excellence

The September 2006 board meeting saw not only the evaluative summary of Cornerstones. One document that went to the board used the phrase "choosing our future." Once again the trustees created a process to choose the future. Prior to the September meeting there had been broad consultation within the system involving all of the constituencies, faculty, students, alumni, administrators and the executive council, and community stakeholders. This latter group included both educators and individuals representing the broader community. The themes that were used to develop this new strategic plan were characterized as "the two fundamental and ingrained commitments of the CSU that have deepened under Cornerstones." The first of these was Access/Outreach, the second commitment was Excellence. Access/Outreach was defined to include "improvement of college-going rates in P-12, strengthened academic preparation of P-12 students, and ensuring of levels of financial aid sufficient to assume genuine access to the CSU for all qualified students." Trustees had been emphasizing for several years that access or entrance was not the ultimate goal; rather, the goal was completion. This became a theme of the new document. Excellence was defined as "providing adequate salaries and professional support for CSU faculty and staff, as well as elements identified by campuses as essential to high-quality academic programs for students."[29]

The trustees acted at this meeting to set in motion Access to Excellence. The process was comparable to Cornerstones, with two major additions. The campuses were each called upon to have a conversation, broadly based in nature, addressing the issues and themes developed by a steering committee. Access to Excellence was to include an initial implementation plan. The trustee action spelled out the membership of a steering committee. It would be composed of trustees, including the one faculty and two student trustees; provosts and a student affairs vice president; faculty, including the executive committee of the statewide Academic Senate, and three faculty members from campus senates, each with less than fifteen years of experience; two students, one undergraduate, and one graduate; one alumnus or alumna; the chancellor and vice-chancellors; community stakeholders, three from P-12 education, three from business and industry; and presidents. The group was large, forty-four in number, larger than Cornerstones, but it was also more broadly representative. It would be staffed by Jane Wellman, a veteran of Cornerstones, and by the vice-chancellors.

A specific timetable, with blocks of time for thirteen sets of activities, was included in the trustee action. Trustee adoption was enthusiastic, in significant measure because so much had been accomplished with Cornerstones, including the resolution of some matters that had been widely perceived over the years as not susceptible to resolution. The steering committee would be chaired by trustee Roberta Achtenberg, then the newly elected chair and a veteran and forceful chair of the Educational Policies Committee. Access to Excellence was to come to the board in May 2008.

The report came to the board on schedule. It was emphasized that this was a strategic rather than a comprehensive plan, and that it would define the general direction of the CSU for approximately the next ten years. It was explicit that the Cornerstones goals were "embraced ... and have become part of the CSU's essential sense of self and mission." Three "major domains" were named: "student access and success; meeting State needs for economic and civic development through continued investment in applied research and meeting workforce and other societal needs; and sustaining institutional excellence through investment in faculty, innovation in teaching, and better access to student research and service."[30]

The report included ten goals, eight of them internal to the CSU and measurable, or at least "traceable," in the accountability process. Two additional goals included influencing public understanding and expectations and strengthening working relationships and meaningful collaboration among all sectors of education.

The body of the report included an analysis of the relationship of the California State University to California and the people of California. In addition to all of the specific goals, it called for a new approach to master planning. Reed, since becoming chancellor in 1998, had often been critical of the shortcomings of the Master Plan. The report noted two major deficiencies of the 1960 Master Plan, the failure to address financing higher education, and the lack of any mechanism to provide for change over time. But it stated, accurately, the work of the CSU, "[A]s goes the CSU, so goes California."[31]

The report resurrected, whether the committee knew it or not, an issue dating to the earliest years of the California State University. It addressed in a routine way the matter of naming of the campuses, perhaps inadvertently using the language "the twenty-three universities that comprise the California State University." In one sense this suggested a throwback to the origins of the original state colleges, regional in nature. There was recognition that each CSU serves in some measure specific constituencies. These constituencies, however, are beyond regional in nature, and they have to do with academic programs, applied research, and the like. Some are statewide, some are national, and some are international. The fundamental issue is whether the California State University is an overarching identity including twenty-three campuses, each with its own identity, while at the same time part of a whole.

The steering committee had deferred a total implementation plan until after trustee action. A first step, after that by the trustees, would be preparation of a comprehensive implementation plan and the identification of outcomes for each of the eight measurable goals.

* * *

A thread of realistic organizational growth and development runs through the years of academic planning in the California State University. In the years immediately prior to the Master Plan, there was no academic planning, only a loose framework associated with the teachers college history. In the developmental years of the 1960s, the concept of academic planning was introduced. This was and is essential to the definition of the California State Colleges as an entity. In the late 1960s, arguably it became more rigid and top-down than it needed to be. In 1970–71, alternatives to this structure were introduced deliberately, to open room for academic program development. The rigid bureaucratic structure remained in place until the early 1990s, but the alternatives of 1970–71 were parallel and became institutionalized.

In the early 1990s, the bureaucratic structure was more than modified. In the largest measure decentralization set in, within only a sense of the Master Plan mission framework. This provided a setting for a shift of the system activities—the work of the chancellor's office and the board of trustees—to systemwide strategic issues. Cornerstones was the vehicle for this. Academic planning in the focused sense of review of specific proposed degree programs continued, but it was a technical review within an understood mission framework, a framework that was nondirective. Ten years of Cornerstones, in turn, provided a stage for Access to Excellence, which moved to a new level of addressing fundamental goals not only for the California State University, but for California and the society more broadly: "As goes the CSU, so goes California."

Notes

[1] Dr. Dorothy Knoell, interview by the author, March 14, 2005.

[2] Raymond R. Rydell, memorandum to the college presidents, April 6, 1963, CSU Archives.

[3] Louis Heilbron, interview by the author, December 2003.

[4] In this chapter, these titles are used. The California State Colleges existed to 1972; the system was titled the California State University and Colleges from 1972 to 1982; thereafter the system is the California State University.

[5] Focus group on academic programs (David Benson, James Cobble, Anthony Moye, Jolayne Service, John Smart, David Spence), March 30, 2005. The transcription and recording are in the CSU Archives. This chapter uses the discussions of this group extensively.

[6] Focus group on academic programs, 36.

[7] William Mason, interview by the author, February 13, 2007.

[8] The writer was president of a newer campus, Dominguez Hills, from 1976 to 1984, and would contrast that experience with before-and-after years at well-developed, long-standing campuses.

[9] Focus group on academic programs, 53 ff.; Ann Reynolds, interview by John Fowler, June 14, 2001; Ann Reynolds, interview by the author, August 20, 2004.

[10] Focus group on academic programs, 59–66; Molly Corbett Broad, interview by the author, November 4, 2005; Barry Munitz, interview by the author, November 18, 2005.

[11] Focus group on academic programs, 72–76, 82; Spence, interview by the author, March 17, 2005; Charles Reed, interview by the author, December 20, 2006.

[12] Spence, interview, 19–22; focus group on academic programs, 74–75.

[13] This section uses material from the focus group on academic programs; Mason, interview; John Smart, interview by the author, March 6, 2007; David Leveille, interview by the author, December 12, 2006; Ellis McCune, interview by the author, June 23, 2005; William B. Langsdorf, interview by Lawrence B. de Graaf, January 12 and 18, 1984, August 27, 1987; William B. Langsdorf, "The California State University and Colleges Program for Innovation," November 1973, Office of the Chancellor; Glenn S. Dumke, "A New Approach to Higher Education for the California State Colleges," minutes, board of trustees, January 1971.

[14] Dumke, "A New Approach," 4.

[15] Minutes of the Council of State College Presidents, November 28, 1950, CSU Archives; quoted in Marcia Salner, "Continuing Education in the California State University—A History," Long Beach, California State University, 1988.

[16] Glenn S. Dumke, "A New Approach," 8.

[17] The section on the 1,000 mile campus uses material from the focus group; Marcia Salner, *Continuing Education*; Leveille and Smart interviews; and two extensive interviews with Ralph Mills by the author, May 19, 2005 and June 6, 2005.

[18] Molly C. Broad, interview by the author, November 4, 2005, 6.

[19] California State University, Long Beach, *The Cornerstones Report*, December 1997.

[20] *Cornerstones Report*, 14.

[21] Reed, interview, 4.

[22] Patrick Callan, interview by the author, October 2, 2006.

[23] Spence, interview, 5. The writer was a member of the Cornerstones task force and involved, as a president, with its implementation.

[24] Minutes, board of trustees, March 1999.

[25] Spence interview, 20–23.

[26] Minutes, board of trustees, July 18–19, 2006.

[27] Board of Trustees of the California State University, "Evaluation of Achievements Under Cornerstones," September 2006.

[28] Minutes, board of trustees, September 19–20, 2006.

[29] *Ibid.*

[30] Minutes, board of trustees, Committee of the Whole, May 13, 2008.

[31] *Ibid.*, 21.

Chapter 5

Graduate Programs and the Doctorate

Graduate Programs and the Doctorate

Graduate programs leading to a master's degree were introduced in the state colleges in the years immediately after World War II. They were linked to teacher education without exception. Postbaccalaureate programs not leading to a degree had been offered for many prior years, as baccalaureate degree holders would attend a state teachers college (a state college, after 1935) to secure a credential. In 1958, the State Board of Education uncoupled master's degree programs from the necessity to link to a credential or other education-based segment.

As noted earlier in this work, graduate programs, together with research, were at the center of the Master Plan development. Most state college faculty and many of the presidents, if not all, were intent on acquiring the capacity to award the doctorate. The University of California was just as intent, if not more so, that the state colleges not acquire this capacity. Others, notably private university leaders, agreed with the University of California position, as did a fair number of civic and public figures; the UC carried the political educational position.

In the Master Plan negotiations, graduate education remained unresolved until the very end of the negotiations. In a summit session overnight at the final three-day meeting of the Master Plan survey team in December 1959, the concept of a joint doctorate was developed. This was clearly a compromise, and was reluctantly accepted by faculty in the CSC. It called for degrees to be awarded jointly by a California State College campus and a University of California campus. The joint doctoral program would be developed by a joint graduate board composed of five representatives each from the California State Colleges and the University of California.

The reaction to the compromise within the California State Colleges, among faculty and presidents alike, was mostly disappointment and anger. The primary purpose of the Master Plan proposal, characterized thirty years later by Dr. Dorothy Knoell in a report to the California Postsecondary Education Commission, was "to remove the last remaining barrier to the Survey Team's completion of its work. Beyond that goal, the Survey Team offered no formal statement of the purposes or goals that this expanded Mission of the State University was to achieve."[1] Both Knoell and Arthur Coons, the chair of the Master Plan survey team, noted that the University of California faculty had little incentive for sharing the doctorate; the joint doctorate was a concession.

As the trustees assumed responsibility for the state colleges, the campuses were awarding about twenty-five hundred master's degrees each year. Graduate education had expanded quickly from master's degrees in education and graduate teaching credentials to master of science degrees in business, master of arts degrees in the liberal arts and sciences, and professional degrees. An early professional degree, initiated only after serious combat with the University of California, was the Master of Social Work, limited to three campuses.

In an appearance before a legislative committee in September 1960, trustee Louis Heilbron had included graduate education in his text. He mentioned the joint doctorate, but gave more attention to the master's degree. Heilbron accurately characterized the degree as having become lost in most American universities between the baccalaureate and the doctorate, and observed that the state colleges, renewed with the Master Plan, would be in a position to give needed attention to the master's degree. He used an image that became familiar, as he visited campuses and talked with various groups: "we will cultivate our garden."[2] His point was that the newly restructured state colleges had full plates before them given the mission spelled out in the Master Plan.

When Glenn Dumke was appointed vice-chancellor for academic affairs in October 1961, one of his first efforts was to work with Clark Kerr's office in Berkeley to establish the Joint Graduate Board. He named to it President Malcolm Love of San Diego State, the most ardent of the state college presidents to pursue authority for the freestanding doctorate (and for support for faculty research), George Feliz, the widely respected and strong dean of graduate studies at San Francisco State; and two faculty members with substantial graduate teaching and research experience, Brant Clark, a psychologist at the San Jose campus and Frances Lord, a professor of education at Los Angeles State. Dumke would personally chair the state college team. The University of California appointees included faculty from the statewide Academic Senate, a Berkeley campus graduate studies administrator, and Dean McHenry, the university's dean of academic planning (statewide). McHenry had been the UC member of the Master Plan survey team, and was a widely respected political science faculty member at the UCLA campus and a confidant of Clark Kerr. The board had no mandate beyond the agreement reached in December 1959, to provide for joint doctorates between campuses of the two systems. When Dumke assumed the chancellorship in April 1962, he stepped aside from the board and designated Malcolm Love as the chair.

The work of the board did not proceed easily. A principle arrived at early was that all of the academic work in all joint doctoral programs would be absolutely equally shared. This was difficult to maintain, as the playing field was not level. University faculty at that time had an average teaching schedule of seven to eight units per semester; state college faculty schedules were set at twelve units, and there was little flexibility. University faculty and graduate students had access to substantial support funds; state college faculty had little or no funds, and funds for graduate students did not exist. One young state college faculty member who was also an assistant dean started a doctoral program (not a joint doctorate) at the Santa Barbara campus of the University of California in the mid-1960s, and noted that he had more support as a graduate student at Santa Barbara than any faculty member had at the state college campus he had left.

Rules and procedures were developed for joint degree programs. The fundamental rule that guided all of the development was that each university and state college campus in any given program would be equal in decision making and in all other aspects of the programs. An early state college move was to ask for a "graduate differential" in funding faculty workload. Faculty positions were budgeted by the state based on twelve-unit workload. Within the system agreement was reached upon a ten-unit workload for graduate degree programs (not including postbaccalaureate enrollments). The trustees' budget requested this graduate differential workload for four years, and finally it was funded. It was lost in 1970 in budget cuts, and not regained until thirty years later.[3]

The first joint doctoral proposal came from San Diego State and the University of California, San Diego. It was for a PhD in chemistry. The proposal went through an approval process involving both campuses and, ultimately, the Joint Graduate Board. The San Francisco and Los Angeles campuses followed in 1967 and 1968 with joint doctoral programs with Berkeley and UCLA, respectively, in special education, an area of strength at both state college campuses. The San Diego campus initiated two more joint doctorates before the end of the decade, in genetics, with UC Berkeley, in 1968 (the program was closed in 1986) and in ecology, with UC Davis, in 1970.

From a student's point of view, the concept of a joint doctorate had both favorable and unfavorable aspects. For some students, the program provided access; this was true if the student was not required to move to meet residence requirements on two campuses. Access includes pursuing a degree at lower cost and with minimal disruption of personal and professional life. Over the years of the joint doctorate, state college fees have generally been lower than fees at the UC and independent universities. Pursuing a doctorate is, of its nature, complex, and requires a measure of determination on the part of a student. A clear minus was the necessity for students to go through two faculty committees and campus bureaucracies.

The benefits to campuses favored the state colleges—prestige, for those faculty and administrators who saw the world that way, and some help in recruiting

17. Dedication of the Archives of the CSU, Dominguez Hills; from left, Donald Gerth, "Pat" Brown, Glenn Dumke, Helene Whitson, John O'Connell, and Louis Heilbron

faculty. There was a downside to that also, in terms of state college mission, as, in some ways, the joint doctorate was a distraction from that mission.

During the 1960s, pressure to achieve the independent or freestanding doctorate was consistent but modest. Trustees would occasionally address the matter, as would some faculty and presidents. Trustee Donald Hart, the chair of the board in 1967–68, urged the establishment of a teaching doctorate, as he was arguing for a name change to California State University. Chancellor Dumke remained supportive of the independent doctorate, while it was not a high priority for him. As a young system with a growing student population and new campuses, there were many other issues to address. In 1969, the legislature and the governor authorized the state colleges to offer joint doctorates with independent colleges and universities.

In the 1970s, serious opposition to the joint doctorate arose from the Legislative Analyst's Office, and this opposition remained consistent over the years and through three individuals occupying the position of legislative analyst. The analyst's report recommended in 1972 that no funding be provided for joint doctoral programs, and that these be phased out as students completed degrees. There was a moratorium on admissions for a short time, but this was soon dropped. The legislature was not prepared to address the issue, especially given the coincidence in time with the name transition from California State Colleges to California State University and Colleges. The San Diego campus began a joint doctorate in education with the Claremont Graduate School, the first program to use the 1969 authorization to develop joint doctorates with independent colleges and universities.[4] The California State University and Colleges campuses awarded fifty-eight joint doctorates from 1970–71 through the 1979–80 academic year.

The arrival of a new chancellor in 1982, Ann Reynolds, brought a revival of interest in the issue of the independent doctorate. This became a priority for the Reynolds administration. Reynolds proposed, with general CSU internal support, that the system's mission be expanded to include awarding the doctorate in education as a freestanding degree. The trustees acted at the November 1985 meeting to support this.[5] At the same time, a review of the Master Plan authorized by the legislature was initiated. The Master Plan Review Commission did consider and debate the idea of a CSU freestanding doctorate in education. The University of California strenuously opposed it. The commission staff prepared pro and con position papers. The staff director, Lee Kerschner, had been a vice-chancellor in the CSU, although he had come to the commission directly from a position in Colorado as head of that state's higher education coordinating body. Possibly because of Kerschner's role, the University of California lobbied commission members heavily. The commission's conclusion on the doctorate was that joint doctoral programs and intersegmental cooperation should be strengthened, thus negating the CSU request for an independent doctorate.[6]

The statewide Academic Senate was involved with the doctoral issue through the 1980s. When the trustees addressed the issue in 1985 at Reynolds' request, the senate asked the chancellor and trustees to address the matter of the substance of doctoral degrees, and the need for separate and adequate funding for graduate work. The senate's concern was that there was no evidence of any willingness on the part of the state to provide funding. The graduate differential funding had been dropped in 1971, and had not been restored for students in master's and joint doctoral degree programs.[7]

Reynolds was persistent about the issue of the independent doctorate, and it arrived in the legislative arena in 1989. At about the same time, she had revived the issue of constitutional status for the CSU, to be made parallel to that of the University of California. That issue did not have any support beyond a single friendly legislator who introduced a bill for her. Meetings in Sacramento and legislative hearings were not productive for the independent doctorate. The University of California leadership continued to be opposed. Leaders from the K-12 education sector had been involved, and were for the most part supportive to the California State University. For whatever reason, when the time came for support in Sacramento, K-12 leaders were not there. In 1988, Proposition 98, guaranteeing a level of support for K-12 and, eventually, the community colleges, was on the ballot. In the Education Round Table, Bill Honig, then state superintendent of public instruction, sought support for 98. Neither Reynolds nor UC President David Gardner gave support. Relations with K-12 were cool for a time.

Chancellor Emeritus Glenn Dumke was invited to speak in one of the legislative committee hearings. Reynolds asked a president whom she perceived to be close to Dumke, to speak with him to ask for his support. In the resulting conversation, Dumke declined his support, stating that he had committed himself to the joint doctorate in 1960 and would not back away from that commitment. In the committee hearing Dumke did not back the proposal for an independent doctorate.

At the January 1990 board meeting, the chancellor's staff prepared a detailed analysis about California's shortage of doctorates in educational administration and other educational positions. The thrust of the report was about joint doctorates in education. The statement was titled, "The Doctorate in Education: California State University Participation in California Educational Reform."[8] The agenda item noted that "[t]he Executive Committee of the Academic Senate may request that the Board of Trustees not take action on this issue until May. The delay would be to provide time for the Statewide Academic Senate to consult campus senates." At the conclusion of a substantial trustee discussion, the trustees adopted a resolution titled "Development of Joint Doctoral Programs in Education." The actual resolution did not mention joint doctorates but, rather, independent doctorates, and asked for consultation with the statewide Academic Senate and the preparation of an action item for the March board meeting, "[T]o alleviate the process to achieve that goal [the independent doctorate]."[9] The board did discuss the matter at the March 1990 meeting. Action was deferred to the following meeting in May.

The May meeting of the board was focused on the internal governance of the California State University. Chancellor Ann Reynolds, under fire, resigned. CSU Hayward President, Ellis McCune, was appointed acting chancellor through the 1990–91 academic year. The issue of the doctorate was deferred.

By the close of the 1980s, eleven joint doctoral programs were in operation on four campuses: Long Beach, Los Angeles, San Diego, and San Francisco. Eight of these programs were at San Diego. From 1980 to 1990, 129 joint doctorates were awarded.

The year 1990 was a year of change in the CSU, and was followed by some regrouping. Barry Munitz became chancellor in the summer of 1991. Both McCune and Munitz supported the joint doctoral programs, and additional ones were established in the 1990s. As he assumed office, Munitz assured UC President David Gardner that he would not press on the independent doctorate; he was clear that there were more important issues for the CSU.[10] The financial stringencies of the early 1990s took precedence over many issues.

Statewide Academic Senate interest in graduate education remained strong, as it had been over the years. In 1991, senate chair Sandra Wilcox, a psychology faculty member from Dominguez Hills, addressed a set of questions to Paul Spear, a psychology faculty member from Chico and then chair of the Senate Academic Policies Committee, about graduate education and, specifically, joint doctorates. Wilcox was probing fundamental questions not really addressed about joint doctorates—the relationship of the joint doctorate to the mission of the CSU, standards of quality, and funding requirements relevant to quality. She used as a starting point a December 1989 report from an advisory committee to study graduate education in the CSU.[11] The senate had paid attention to graduate education over the years and continued to do so. Spear's committee prepared a report that was circulated among faculty on the campuses. The report helped keep the issue of the doctorate alive, though not central.

The focus of the Munitz administration from 1991 through 1997 was initially, and necessarily, the critical financial situation of the early 1990s; after that it was the development of a longer-range mechanism to address stability of financial support. The compact about higher-education finances (addressed in Chapter 12) is a product of that work. The Munitz administration made clear in the design of Cornerstones support both for the Master Plan and for the ability for the California State University to change to meet new needs of the state and its people, consistent with the values of the Master Plan. Governor Pat Brown's admonition to Clark Kerr, in March 1960, that the details of the mission of the California State Colleges should not be fixed in the state's constitution remained relevant.

In the 1990s, the number of joint doctoral degrees earned increased substantially, from 129 to 363. San Diego remained the principal campus working with the joint doctorate.

With Chancellor Charles Reed, new leadership arrived at the California State University in early 1998. Cornerstones provided the context for the development of the next steps about the doctorate. The Cornerstones implementation plan went to the trustees in the spring of 1999. One of the principles it articulated addressed both graduate and continuing education as essential components of the California State University. While Cornerstones was silent about the independent doctorate, it provided a framework that included questions of access, public need, expansion of opportunities, and increased investment in graduate education.

Chancellor Reed was adept at building relationships with members of the legislature and others in Sacramento, including Governors Pete Wilson and Arnold Schwarzenegger. The independent doctorate was high on his list of goals. The first priority was a doctorate in education, the EdD.

In 2000, the California Postsecondary Education Commission published a study, "The Production and Utilization of Education Doctorates for Administrators in California Public Schools." The report was inconclusive, but did not support the CSU position regarding the specific doctorate in education. Rather, while sidestepping the question of need for the doctorate, it addressed the question of access and called upon the state to "address directly the question of access to the education doctoral (EdD) preparation in terms of affordability, time, and distance."[12]

The CSU used the report as the occasion to prepare and publish a forty-one page paper, "Meeting California's Educational Needs: Why California Needs More Holders—and Suppliers—of Education Doctorates."[13] The CSU paper addressed what it called "the artificial suppression of doctoral production." California was significantly short of doctorally educated leaders compared to national averages. Moreover, the demand for community college leaders to be doctorally educated was being overlooked, as was the need for faculty in higher education. The heart of the issue was the lack of programs and the lack of faculty interest in the University of California. Private institutions in California were not sufficiently sizeable or numerous to make up the difference, and costs for students in the private institutions were significantly higher.

The CSU paper provided a rationale for the move in the legislature. Reed marshaled forces within the CSU, the statewide Academic Senate, the presidents, trustees, and others. He did the same in Sacramento. The independent doctorate issue came to a head in 2001–02. Reed was certain he had the votes in both houses of the legislature. Senator Jack Scott, a former president of Pasadena City College and a lifelong educator, with a PhD from the Claremont Graduate Center, had been key to generating support. Scott was in the assembly from 1994 to 2000, and elected to the senate in 2000. Reed worked closely with Scott to gain legislative support. Reed went to Governor Gray Davis to tell him he had the votes and ask for support. Davis' response was that he had just had a letter from Clark Kerr asking for a veto, and Davis simply said he agreed with Kerr's position and the UC, and he would veto the legislation.

Kerr had also written to Senator Dede Alpert, opposing a CSU capacity to grant the doctorate in education. Alpert chaired the Joint Legislative Committee to Develop a Master Plan for Education, the group that was addressing a master plan for all of public education in California. In his letter to Alpert, Kerr acknowledged his disappointment that less use had been made of the joint doctorate than he had anticipated in 1960. He reinforced President Richard Atkinson's position that the UC would address whatever problem existed in the availability of doctoral programs and any insufficiency in the number of individuals completing degrees. Kerr reserved his strongest argument for last—that granting the CSU the capacity to do one doctorate in a field would breach the concept of differentiation of missions, the basic principle of the 1960 Master Plan.[14] Reed backed away from the legislation and dropped it.

President Atkinson proposed a major UC effort for joint doctorates in education and the creation of a UC Institute for Educational Leadership. He asked each UC chancellor to explore with CSU campuses in its region both in education and in all other disciplines. The results were poor. The curriculum in the University of California is controlled by the faculty. For the most part, faculties were simply not interested in joint doctoral programs. On one campus, Berkeley, the faculty committee with responsibility for graduate programs rejected a completed proposal from both their own departmental faculty and the CSU departmental faculty, with the assertion that any proposal must require three years of residence on that UC campus, just as their own doctoral candidates did.[15]

In November 2003, Gray Davis was recalled and Arnold Schwarzenegger became governor. Reed was asked by the Sargent Shriver family, the family of Schwarzenegger's wife, to help Schwarzenegger in his new role. Reed had come to know the Shrivers when he was chief of staff for Florida governor Robert Graham in the early 1980s. He quickly came to know the Schwarzeneggers and was able to be helpful in briefing the new governor about California's educational issues. Schwarzenegger's own higher education background was at a University of Wisconsin campus that was very much like some of the CSU campuses.

While all of this was underway, the CSU statewide Academic Senate was preparing a major report, "Rethinking Graduate Education in the CSU: Meeting the Needs of the People of California for Graduate Education in the 21st Century."

The task force brought together to accomplish this included some of the most able and knowledgeable faculty about graduate education in the CSU. The task force was chaired by Dr. Cristy Jensen, a professor at the Sacramento campus and the first chair of that campus's Department of Public Policy and Administration, a department granting only graduate degrees. The thirteen-member task force prepared a succinct forty-one page report that was widely circulated on campuses, among higher education groups, and in Sacramento. The report noted that "[t]he most recent review of the California Master Plan for Higher Education moved away from the historic emphasis on differentiating the state's public postsecondary institutions to an emphasis on an integrated system of education in California that links preschool through K-12 and higher education. It promotes partnerships with other segments (e.g., joint doctoral programs, efforts to smooth transfer from the community colleges to the CSU) and with business and private industry."[16]

The report observed that the commitment to joint doctoral programs had been uncertain, approval processes cumbersome, and funding not adequate. It asked for further study with a special focus on faculty. The disparity between the UC and the CSU in workload and support had grown substantially since the first joint doctoral programs in the 1960s. The report went on to note that "*If* the need for publicly supported doctoral programs in one or more selected fields is well established, if the UC does not respond by developing its own doctoral programs or joint doctoral programs with the CSU, if the faculty at one or more CSU campuses has the expertise to offer the programs and is interested in doing so, if adequate funding is made available, the CSU should seek authority to offer doctoral programs in those fields independent of other universities. A focus on applied fields and the education of advanced-level practitioners is encouraged."[17]

After the November 2004 elections, as the legislature convened for a new term, the CSU initiated a new campaign for the doctorate. Senator Jack Scott, now chair of the Senate Education Committee, introduced legislation that would authorize the CSU "to independently award professional/clinical doctoral degrees . . . awarded as part of a post–master's degree program that prepares students for entry to professional practice other than university faculty research and teaching."[18] Senate Bill 724 was introduced on February 22, 2005. In addition to education, the bill was intended to authorize degrees in audiology (which would require a doctorate for licensure beginning in 2008), physical therapy, nursing, and perhaps social work.[19] The combat level was fierce. Two briefs strongly supporting the bill were circulated in the legislature by Karen Zamarripa, the assistant vice-chancellor responsible for the CSU's Sacramento office; one was authored by Keith Boyum, the associate vice-chancellor for academic affairs. The second, by Thomas La Belle, a former provost and vice president for academic affairs at San Francisco State University, was a paper La Belle had done for the Center for Studies in Higher Education at UC Berkeley.

In the course of legislative deliberation, it became likely that the bill would be passed in the Senate Education Committee. The Assembly Education Committee was less likely. The chair of the committee, Assemblywoman Carol Liu, was a loyal and active UC Berkeley alumna and was considerably involved in

Berkeley affairs. She was opposed to any independent CSU doctorate, and remained opposed. Chancellor Reed and Vice-Chancellor Spence, with the active support of the presidents and the statewide Academic Senate leadership, worked their way through Sacramento and the legislature.

As the lobbying went on, the independent colleges and universities aligned with the University of California, but not strongly so. School administrators and community college leaders generally aligned with the CSU. It became apparent that the CSU quite likely would prevail, and the governor would sign the legislation. UC and CSU leaders talked compromise.

The CSU, UC, and Senator Scott agreed that the bill would only authorize the doctorate in "educational leadership"—educational administration. The agreement was styled as "an exception to the state's Master Plan for Higher Education."[20] SB 724 was amended; the EdD "shall be based on partnerships through which the California public schools and the California Community Colleges shall participate substantively in program design, candidate recruitment and admissions, teaching, and program assessment and evaluation. The degree shall enable professionals to earn the degree while working full time."[21] The amended bill passed in the full assembly and returned to the senate where it secured final passage. Governor Schwarzenegger signed the bill on September 22, 2005. It was to be effective on January 1, 2006, and the first students in EdD programs on selected campuses would begin their studies in the fall of 2007. Chancellor Reed issued a statement: "The legislation marks perhaps the most significant change in the California State University's role in the last four decades. We are extremely grateful to Senator Scott and to all of the supporters of this bill who understand the importance of creating access to high-quality programs that prepare leaders for California's schools."[22] As Scott approached the point of being term-limited out at the end of 2008, he was named chancellor of the California Community Colleges.

In February 2006, the selection of seven campuses to begin the independent EdD in the fall of 2007 was announced. The campuses selected were Fresno, Fullerton, Long Beach, Sacramento, San Bernardino, San Diego, and San Francisco. Six additional campuses were named for 2008, and other campuses would be added over the following two years. The programs were to be self-supporting, by adding fees to the base funding for all graduate students.[23]

At the July 2006 meeting of the board of trustees, a policy framework was adopted for implementation of the doctoral programs. President Emeritus Robert Maxson, of the Long Beach campus, had previously been asked to take on a one-year assignment to coordinate the development of the new programs. The presentation to the board acknowledged the collaborative efforts of the statewide Academic Senate, the campus provosts and graduate deans, campus faculty, and the chancellor's staff.[24]

The campus provosts and vice presidents for academic affairs undertook a study in 2006 that was in part a background piece for what would become "Access to Excellence." "The Place of Graduate Education in the California State University" was a summary of the status of graduate education at that point, but, more importantly, it was a document that looked to the future for the development of graduate programs, both at the master's and doctoral levels. The newly appointed executive vice-chancellor and chief academic officer, Gary Reichard, and associate vice-chancellor Keith Boyum worked closely with the group. An emphasis in the paper was on "addressing a wide array of contemporary issues through cross disciplinary collaborative efforts at the graduate level." The paper also celebrated the historic CSU development and emphasis on the master's degree. The financing of graduate programs, particularly the option of imposing professional fees on selected graduate programs, was proposed.[25]

Funding for graduate programs had been a problem for years, since the graduate differential had been removed from the state support budget in 1971. In 1999, the trustees had introduced a graduate fee differential; the fees were paid by students. A graduate differential was reestablished in the CSU general fund budget for 2006–07; graduate students would be counted, for purposes of creating the instructional budget, just as they were in the University of California. However, the graduate differential would only apply to program growth and new programs. Senate Bill 724 addressed state funding for the doctorate in education and specified that state funding would be provided on the same basis as funding for other graduate programs. The bill also stipulated that students should be charged fees no higher than those charged for doctoral candidates in the UC. The legislation was clear—the CSU "should not return to the Department of Finance and the Legislature requesting more state funds to support these doctoral programs."[26] at the November 2006 meeting, the trustees approved a fee policy that was consistent with the legislation in providing that fees for doctoral candidates would not exceed those of the UC; the board set the student fee for 2007–08, the first year when students would be enrolled in independent doctorate programs, at $6,897, or an amount equal to the UC fee for 2007–08 should the UC fee be changed.

The first seven campuses to offer the independent doctorate enrolled students in the fall of 2007. Executive Vice-Chancellor Gary Reichard reported to the trustees that the programs "reflect the commitment in Senate Bill 724 to substantive collaboration with practitioners in program design, candidate selection, delivery of instruction, and program evaluation. They include candidate preparation of a research-based dissertation, but they differ significantly from the traditional doctoral dissertation in that their emphasis is on applying educational research—on analyzing, piloting, and evaluation strategies for significantly improving outcomes in the regions P-12 schools and community colleges."[27]

When Senator Scott was interviewed in April 2007 about his central role in the development of CSU graduate programs and the doctorate, he speculated about the addition of doctoral degrees in allied health and other applied fields, and volunteered that this would surely happen, but most likely not before he left the legislature at the end of 2008. In February 2008, Scott introduced Senate Bill 1288, which would authorize the Doctor of Nursing Practice degree. The bill was designed to provide doctorates for CSU, community college, and UC faculty, and for those in advanced nursing practice. Unlike in 2005, regarding the doctorate in education, the University of California supported the bill. In April, the bill was killed in the Senate Appropriations Committee; the issue was not the doctorate, but the state's deficit of seventeen to twenty billion dollars for the coming fiscal year.

Graduate programs in the California State University have moved in substance, in kind, and in numbers in the years from 1960. In 1960–61, 2,062 master's degrees were conferred, mostly in the field of education. In 2006–07, 18,095 were conferred. From the 1960–61year through 2006–07, at total of 452,179 master's degrees were conferred, in all of the arts and sciences and diverse professional fields. Similarly, from the spring of 1967 through the 2006–07 academic year, 902 joint doctoral degrees were conferred. Trustee Heilbron's 1961 admonition that "we should tend our garden" and pay attention to the master's degree, so widely taken for granted and unattended in American higher education, was heard and followed.[28]

Research

Research had been a contentious matter in the Master Plan deliberations. Research and the doctorate were paired by the University of California to be protected and preserved as functions solely under the auspices of the University of California. Research here is meant to include creative and scholarly activity.

Prior to the Master Plan, research had been present on normal school/state college campuses in varying degrees, depending on the interests of faculty and administrators. Early in the twentieth century and with the strong support of founding president Frederic Burk, San Francisco State Normal School faculty had prepared texts and other teaching materials for public schools in northern California. Similarly, faculty at San Diego State Normal School had written and published materials for the schools. In the years after World War II, faculty in disciplines and fields including teacher education and beyond, had been active in publishing and research. Research in the sciences was modest, and on many campuses, the sciences were present only as support for general and teacher education. But in the humanities and social sciences, the arts, education, and business scholarly and creative activity was alive and well. The Master Plan language about research was specific:

> The primary function of the state colleges is the provision of instruction for undergraduate students and graduate students, through the master's degree, in the liberal arts and sciences, in applied fields and in the professions. . . . Faculty research is authorized to the extent that it is consistent with the primary function of the state colleges and the facilities provided for that function.[29]

This language was a disappointment to many faculty. The situation was parallel to the granting of the doctorate; the alternative for granting the doctorate was the joint doctorate; the alternative for research was "consistent with the primary function of the state colleges and the facilities provided for that function."

Faculty cultures on campuses vary widely, both generally and with regard to specific matters. Such has been the case with research. In the 1960s, only some campuses saw research embedded in the faculty culture. San Diego was clearly one such campus where research was valued, and these values resulted in the first and, subsequently, the most joint doctorates in the CSU. San Francisco shared these values, although the turmoil on that campus in the '60s interfered with development of much research activity. Each year the Los Angeles campus published a consolidated report for all faculties on all research activities and information about support to secure grants and do research.

In these early years, research per se did not receive direct support, though the trustees would request it. In February of 1962, then Lieutenant Governor Glenn Anderson, an ex-officio trustee (also a regent), and a strong supporter of the CSU through a long subsequent career as a congressman, wrote to George Miller, the chair of the Joint Legislative Budget Committee, in support of a modest appropriation of $645,000 for research. Portions of the letter described the thinking of the times on this issue:

> While I would agree that the state colleges should be regarded primarily as teaching, not research, institutions, and that the University of California is, and should continue to be the prime instrument of research, I do feel that a modest program of faculty research is essential if the state colleges are to fulfill the mission allocated to them under the Master Plan for Higher Education. Faculty research, along with adequate library facilities, is one of the traditional hallmarks of a fine college. To eliminate this entirely from the range of state college activities is to take a long step backward toward the teachers' college concept, and away from the idea of a true liberal arts program.[30]

Three decades would pass before explicit funding would become available. Indirect support for research took many forms, and much was dependent on campus administrations and faculty leadership. The most significant factor was the twelve weighted teaching units faculty load. Some campus administrations waived three or six units, to give faculty time for research. The chancellor's office supported this for the most part. The 1960 legislation had been specific about space; no space for research per se was to be provided. Campuses found creative ways to make space available. Campus foundations were used to provide for rented space. As campuses acquired property for expansion, buildings that were eventually to be removed would become available, sometimes for a substantial number of years. The Chico campus acquired a block-long strip of old houses that were used for years for faculty and student research and grant/contract activities. These research activities were often questioned, but tolerated and not endorsed by the Department of Finance and the Legislative Analyst's Office.

By the 1970s, most campuses had organized offices to support research, grants, contracts, all forms of scholarly activity. These offices provided assistance to faculty in securing support. All of the campuses were members of the American Association of State Colleges and Universities (AASCU). AASCU established an office to assist member institutions in the pursuit of grant support in Washington. For many years the CSU campuses were staffed by an AASCU staff member, Chris Bitting (she would later become the organization's vice president). This was important and useful help. Many campuses received support from campus auxiliary organizations or foundations. This support often took the form of seed money to start research or other projects that would, it was hoped, become self-supporting. The campus cultures were changing gradually.

In 1977, Ralph Mills, the state university dean of continuing education, gathered a small group of presidents to meet with a few members of the governor's cabinet. Mills had discovered that a great number of state contracts for research projects that were with universities were with a relatively small private university in Pennsylvania; no one knew why. Speculation was that some long previous senior administrator, perhaps a director of finance, was an alumnus of that university. The meeting with Mills, the presidents, and a few cabinet members was productive. An agreement was reached in which the California State University and Colleges would establish a small office in Sacramento, and an entity to be known as the University Services Program. State executive offices were invited to send requests for proposals for research on specific projects, and campuses, in turn, would respond with plans to carry out the research or activity that was called for.

The University Services Program (USP) was successful. A few presidents and campus administrators were critical; the culture of the CSU includes almost an automatic suspicion any time the chancellor's office becomes operationally involved in anything. The USP office remained small. The program lasted for almost twenty-five years. A result of the program was that state agencies became familiar with the campuses and their individual strengths. State departments and agencies became accustomed to working with CSU faculty and campuses without the need for an intermediary. The volume of activity became substantial, hundreds of millions of dollars in a year. The campus most involved with state-funded projects was Sacramento, doubtless due to its location in the capital.

The ultimate test of the relationship of research and related activities to campus faculty and administrative cultures was to be the faculty position on the use of research as a variable for retention, tenure, and promotion actions. The San Diego campus led the way in the 1960s. Others followed. Fullerton was notable in applying criteria that were demanding upon individual faculty members. There was from time to time concern that some campuses were becoming too research oriented, to the detriment of teaching, while other campuses formally ignored research, even though many faculty were actively involved.

On most campuses, uses of research-related criteria for retention, tenure, and promotion decisions varied from department to department. The chancellor's office, statewide Academic Senate, and the presidents essentially ignored the issue and its relevance to the mission of the CSU, as did state authorities. Clearly, it was relevant. The issue was too fraught with the potential of controversy for these bodies and individuals to tackle it. Open discussion of research was to some extent absent in the CSU. It was simply not on the agenda for the system, while it was at the same time alive and well, and often thriving from campus to campus.

In the mid-1980s, momentum built for support for research from the state budget. The legislature and the governor created a commission to review the Master Plan once again, the third such review. One of the appointed members, William D. Campbell, had some experience as a school board member and considerable interest in educational policy. Campbell became vice-chair and then acting chair for most of the working time of the commission, a two-year period. The commission's principal focus was the community colleges, their governance and finance, transfer issues, and the like. Campbell gave substantial time to the work of the commission. He was a law school graduate who had become a successful businessman and the president of a furniture company with a chain of stores. He spent a good amount of time learning about the CSU. When Governor Deukmejian asked Campbell for his choice of an appointment to a state board, he chose the board of trustees, and was appointed in 1987.

The Master Plan Commission recommended a change in the education code language adopted in 1960 about research. In its 1989 final report, a joint legislative Commission for Review of the Master Plan for Higher Education subsequently recommended that the state "support research, scholarly and creative activities in the CSU that serve the university's instructional mission and study issues or problems relevant to the changing social, environmental, economic, or cultural life of California's many regions. . . . Central to the role of any decent teaching institution is the research, scholarly and creative activity essential to the development of good teaching, and essential as a part of the education of students. The state should acknowledge this in the mission of the California State University and endeavor to support it."[31] Assemblyman John Vasconcellos and his assistant, Brian Murphy, played key roles in the shaping of this document.

William Campbell came to the board of trustees with both knowledge and thoughts about an agenda of things he wanted to address. He worked well with the then chair of the statewide Academic Senate, Bernard Goldstein, a faculty member from San Francisco State who would later become the faculty trustee. From his own agenda and conversations with Goldstein, Campbell determined that he would personally go to Sacramento to secure funding for three academic goals, one of which was funding for research. He consulted the CSU General Counsel about his capacity to do so. Campbell had been active in the 1986 gubernatorial campaign, and had come to know Peter Mehas, a Fresno-based educator who was then Deukmejian's education secretary. In 2007, Mehas was appointed to membership on the board of trustees. Campbell went to Mehas with the three goals and a request for five million dollars. Mehas was sympathetic to the research idea. Campbell in some measure laid the groundwork for the recognition and funding of research.[32]

The education code section that included the Master Plan statutory definitions for the three segments of higher education was amended in 1990. The mission of the California State University was broadened to include "research, scholarship, and creative activity in support of its undergraduate and graduate instructional mission."[33] At the same time trustee Campbell's efforts and those of others were successful and a two and a half million dollar appropriation for faculty research was accomplished, and that annual appropriation has remained over the years.

The Cornerstones report of 1997 reaffirmed and reinforced research in the work of faculty and in the instructional mission of the CSU. The 2004 Academic Senate report on graduate education further emphasized research. The 2007 Access to Excellence project, affirmed by the trustees in 2006, addressed the importance of research and created the opportunity for thoughtful consideration about research, scholarly, and creative activity.[34]

The research and scholarship accomplishments of CSU faculty, often including the involvement of students, have been remarkable over the years. CSU faculty have a primary responsibility for the quality and effectiveness of their teaching. They are not generously supported for research and scholarly and creative activity. Often they have no support. The character of their activity varies widely. Much of the research is of an applied character, yet it can inform basic issues. In recent years, faculty members have been active in disparate research projects ranging from a National Science Foundation project on bioethics to an electrical engineer's project having to do with leg muscle spasticity in children with cerebral palsy; the latter project was funded by the Shriners Hospitals for children. The State Department funded a project to develop an internal capacity within the Ghanaian judiciary and community for conflict management and resolution.[35]

The most important measures of research in the CSU are the existing or emerging faculty cultures on the campuses, and a possible emerging faculty culture among the campuses. Clearly the campuses cultures have changed. Few, if any, campuses have absolutely demanding and stringent cultures about research production like those found in research universities and would-be research universities. All of the CSU campuses are supportive of research and in varying degrees give organizational support. Most give support to student involvement in research. A systemwide student research competition, from a quiet beginning in the 1980s, is thriving, with students from all campuses participating.

CSU faculties are well along in building a distinct research culture that addresses applied research, that often relates research to students and teaching, and that often addresses real issues and questions in the life of the state of California or in other parts of the nation and world. This is a piece of the emerging maturity of the mission of the California State University.

* * *

Graduate studies, the doctorate, and research are inseparably linked. In the California State University, the linkage is more than educational. It has been a political and public policy linkage from the time of the Master Plan in 1960. Both in graduate programs including the doctorate, and in research, the impact on California's economy and social and cultural structures has been great.

Pressure for the independent doctorate and a clear field for research with support was very great in the 1960s. The pressure was strong enough to be destabilizing, and it was a destabilizing factor in the 1960s; in some ways that memory lingered on until the transition in the chancellorship in 1982. Some faculty and administrators ascribed the fact that the CSU did not achieve the independent doctorate in 1960 to Glenn Dumke and his negotiation of the Master Plan opposite Clark Kerr.

It is at least arguable that both the California State University and higher education policy and programs in California benefited from the CSU's "failure" to acquire the independent doctorate and an unlimited open field for research as a result of the Master Plan. It is arguable that the California State Colleges were not ready for such responsibilities in 1960. The California State Colleges instead secured time to grow and mature, as the California State University and Colleges in the 1970s and the California State University since 1982, to become a system and institutions of great strength and quality, a system unlike the University of California and other research universities, a system of first-rate institutions with a mission essential to the people and well-being of California and beyond.

The test of the California State University's ability to maintain a unique mission in California is likely to be found with graduate programs, the doctorate, and research over the next several years. The need to develop and grow continues, both in policy, for which the trustees are ultimately responsible; and in practice for which faculty, administrators, staff, and even students are responsible. That mission will take the form of doctorates that are applied in nature, and these need not be only in the professions. That mission will take the form of research programs that are both insightful and useful in communities, regions, and cultures in California, nationally, and internationally. Research, most especially the applied research done by numbers of faculty, has become respected within and without the CSU. A supportive infrastructure remains to be built; an early step in that direction was taken in 2006 with the appointment of an assistant vice-chancellor for research initiative and partnerships. Individual campuses do have supportive infrastructures, and these vary. This is an extension of the CSU mission if the matter is viewed narrowly, and a logical step if the evolution of higher education and its relationship to the greater society is fully understood.

There has been no thoughtful guiding hand addressing the character of and expectations for graduate programs, doctorates, and research. The statewide Academic Senate has produced over the years some very thoughtful studies and recommendations. In more recent years, perhaps the last dozen or so, strategic planning has been useful and productive, most notably in Cornerstones, in its creation and implementation, and now in the promise of Access to Excellence. More recently the group of campus chief academic officers has prepared a thoughtful report about research.

It is arguable that now is the time for a thoughtful guiding hand to work with faculties and leaders in the CSU; not to micromanage, but to move together, with the understanding and involvement and support of the board, to a sense of mission and framework for graduate programs, doctorates, and research that develop the opportunities afforded now in the CSU and further advance its overarching values. One of the significant tasks for both the campuses and the system is the building of graduate and research cultures among faculty and students, cultures that reach into the activities and sense of identity of graduate students and faculty as they work with graduate students. These will be cultures compatible and that fit with the overall mission of the CSU—access and excellence.

Notes

[1] Dorothy M. Knoell, "California's Joint Doctorate Programs," California Postsecondary Education Commission, January 1992

[2] Louis H. Heilbron, statement to subcommittee of the Assembly Ways and Means Committee, California State Legislature, September 30, 1960.

[3] Minutes, board of trustees, July 14, 1970.

[4] Dorothy M. Knoell, op. cit.

[5] Minutes, board of trustees, October 31–November 1, 1985.

[6] Lee Kerschner, interview by the author, June 9, 2006.

[7] Minutes, board of trustees, October 31–November 1, 1985.

[8] Minutes, board of trustees, January 9–10, 1990.

[9] Ibid.; papers and memoranda from statewide senate chair Ray Geigle relevant to this early 1990 period (and the 1985 senate discussion) are in the CSU Archives.

[10] Barry Munitz, interview by the author, November 18, 2005.

[11] *Graduate Education in the California State University: Meeting Public Needs Consistent with Educational Priorities*, report of the Advisory Committee to Study Graduate Education in the CSU, December 1989.

[12] California Postsecondary Education Commission, "The Production and Utilization of Education Doctorates for Administrators in California Public Schools," 2000.

[13] The California State University, "Meeting California's Educational Needs: Why California Needs More Holders—and Suppliers—of Education Doctorates," Long Beach, February 2001.

[14] Clark Kerr, letter to California State Senator Dede Alpert, April 4, 2001.

[15] Focus group on academic programs (David Benson, James Cobble, Anthony Moye, Jolayne Service, John Smart, David Spence), March 30, 2005.

[16] Academic Senate of the California State University, *Rethinking Graduate Education in the CSU: Meeting the Needs of the People of California for Graduate Education for the 21st Century*, report of the Task Force on Graduate and Post-Baccalaureate Education in the CSU, September 2004, 13.

[17] Ibid., 8.

[18] California Legislature, SB 724, February 22, 2005.

[19] Michael J. Fitzgerald, "Education Beat," January 28, 2005.

[20] CSU Leader, "CSU, UC Reach Agreement are EdD Bill," July 5, 2005; "Education Beat," (a newsletter covering the nexus of California education and politics), Sacramento, July 22, 2005.

[21] California Assembly, Committee on Higher Education, Amendment to SB724, July 5, 2004.

[22] CSU Leader, "Governor Signs Bill Authorizing CSU Education Doctorates, September 22, 2005.

[23] Fitzgerald, "Education Beat," March 10, 2006.

[24] Minutes, board of trustees, July 18-19, 2006.

[25] California State University Academic Council, "The Place of Graduate Education in the CSU," Office of the Chancellor, 2006; Gary Reichard, interview by the author, February 19, 2007.

[26] Minutes, board of trustees, Committee on Finance, November 14–15, 2006.

[27] Minutes, board of trustees, Committee on Educational Policy, September 18–19, 2007.

[28] The paragraphs on the events attendant to the move to the independent doctorate are based on the author's papers and, particularly, on the author's interviews of the following people: Chancellor Charles Reed, December 20, 2006; Vice-Chancellor David Spence, March 17, 2005; Senator Jack Scott, April 18, 2007; Vice-Chancellor Emeritus John Smart, March 6, 2007; Professor Cristy Jensen, May 27, 2005; the focus group on academic programs, March 30, 2005.

[29] California Education Code, div. 16.5, Higher Education: chap. 3, The State College System, para. 22606.

[30] Glenn M. Anderson, letter to George Miller, Jr., chairman, joint legislative budget committee, Sacramento, February 21, 1962.

[31] The California State University Academic Council, "On the Role of Scholarly Research and Creative Activities in the CSU," Long Beach, January 2007.

[32] William D. Campbell interview by the author, May 18, 2006.

[33] Education Code, chap.1587 (SB 1570), "On the Role of Scholarly Research . . . ," Scott Plotkin, phone interview by the author, June 7, 2008.

[34] Interview with Gary Reichard, *op. cit.*

[35] J. Terence Manns, memorandum to the author, June 30, 2008.

Chapter 6

Teacher Education: The Origins

For one hundred years, teacher education was the mission of the California State Colleges. From the 1857 establishment of Minns' Evening Normal School and San Francisco Normal School, to the 1960 Master Plan for Higher Education in California, teacher education was the core of the normal schools, the state teachers colleges, and the state colleges.[1]

The California State University has also played a played major role in the continuing development of quality teacher education in California, and in the nation. In 1875, the principal and faculty of the California State Normal School in San Jose invited teachers from throughout the state to a conference. The California Teachers Association (CTA) was founded at this conference, to address the professional growth and development of teachers, including the teachers of teachers. The CTA has had a major impact on policy and practice in California education, and has played a strong role in support for education in the state.[2]

Frederic Burk, the founding president of San Francisco State Normal School, led his faculty in the development of new approaches to pedagogy, and the preparation of materials and texts for practicing teachers, until the State Department of Education ordered this to be discontinued. Nevertheless, Burk and his faculty affected the character of teaching in the elementary schools of California and beyond.[3]

California was a frontier society in the 1850s, and the beginning of teacher education reflected that.

The author is indebted to Steven Gregorich, emeritus Dean of the College of Education at California State University Sacramento, for commenting on this chapter.

* * *

Teacher education and the licensing and credentialing of teachers are inextricably mixed. The story of teacher credentialing is a story of the efforts of educators, on the one hand, and political players, on the other, as both competed to control access to teaching positions. In 1851, the legislature required that a teacher "must have a certificate of qualification from the Superintending Committee of the School in which services were rendered."[4] The story of teacher education and the substance of that education is one of shared responsibility among several parties: the state, cities, counties, school districts, and teacher education institutions.[5]

The first public schools in California were governed by cities or counties that instituted examinations or interviews for teachers. In 1863, State Superintendent John Swett, who had been instrumental in convincing the city (and county) of San Francisco to establish a normal school, prepared legislation that, when adopted, made the State Board of Education responsible for examinations of teachers at all levels. However, there was no provision in the legislation that required school boards to hire only individuals who had taken those tests, and local school boards continued to employ teachers who had taken the local examinations. Each county had a school board, and county school boards hired primary school teachers into the twentieth century. The California Constitution of 1879 added to the county boards' authority the ability to issue certificates for high school teachers, and it eliminated those state examinations entirely.

This rather loose system made relationships important between the early normal school principals and local school boards and administrators that hired teachers. It also created opportunities for favoritism and corruption. The press reported on this at the time. In 1889, the legislature made it a misdemeanor for a school board member to coach candidates for teaching positions.[6]

In the 1890s, the state, in an environment of concern about corruption and poor leadership in the local school boards, began to reassert control. Control over the licensure of teachers coming from out of state was asserted by the State Board of Education, and the explicit justification for this was "acting on behalf of the normal schools." In 1897, a case regarding state authority went to the California Supreme Court (Mitchell v. Winnek), and the court ruled that the legislature could define the requirements for teacher certification.[7] A nearly immediate consequence of this ruling was the requirement that new teachers must be graduates of approved programs in a normal school or university. A partnership, sometimes easy, often uneasy, was born between the State Board of Education and the state superintendent (the Department of Education was yet to come). The stage was set for legislative involvement in teaching certification, which continues to this day.

The University of California bore the brunt of the State Board of Education actions in the years following the Supreme Court decision. The state board used the authority given to it by the legislature to prescribe the number of courses and units needed for licensure to teach in a secondary school. A next move was to require a fifth, or graduate, year. In 1914 the state board required prospective teachers to take at least one graduate course in the subject they would teach. From 1905 to 1921, the number of semester units in professional teacher education courses required for secondary school licensure was increased from twelve to twenty-one and then reduced to eighteen. In 1914, the state board forced the university to undertake internal reorganization and move all courses related to pedagogy to a new academic department the board designated, a Department of Education. The UC faculty had been reluctant to be involved in teacher education, leaving a vacuum that the legislature and the State Board of Education filled, either willingly or out of necessity.

Normal school principals and presidents had been meeting with the state board and superintendent for years. The legislature gradually gave the state board authority over the normal schools, and by 1917, this control was firm. With the 1921 legislation changing the normal schools to state teachers colleges, state board and superintendent control was complete.

The normal schools had gradually and quietly assumed a role in the preparation of secondary teachers. The key breakthrough was at the new Fresno campus, where secondary school teachers for so-called nonacademic subjects such as agriculture and home economics and vocational education were educated and subsequently employed by the schools. With the change to teachers' colleges and the authority to grant degrees, and the full support of the State Board of Education, preparation of secondary teachers became a part of the state teachers college mission. The education of secondary teachers was now to be made different from the standard preparation of students for a degree. There now was an institutional recognition of pedagogical skills required for good teaching in addition to knowledge of subject matter. That distinction was destined to be the ideological battleground between subject-matter specialties far into the future of education in California, each group tending to make impassioned charges about the limitations of the other to educate properly future teachers.

The 1931 Carnegie Foundation for the Advancement of Teaching report focused primarily on the University of California and its relationships to the state teachers colleges. The report recommended that the teachers colleges be subsumed under the University of California regents; that recommendation went nowhere. The state teachers colleges each enjoyed a strong regional base, and these together created a widespread level of support in the legislature. On the subject of teacher education, the Carnegie group recommended that all secondary school teacher education be done by the University of California, and that the university cede any role in the preparation of elementary school teachers to the state teachers colleges. The net effect of the Carnegie report was to identify the preparation of secondary school teachers as an issue, and subsequently the 1935 legislation changing the name of the State Teachers Colleges to State Colleges confirmed the role of State Colleges in the preparation of teachers for the secondary schools.

In the years before and during World War II, the State Department of Education, year by year, assumed or took more responsibility for prescribing the education of both elementary and secondary school teachers. The teacher education programs of the state colleges, the University of California, and the independent colleges and universities were defined by the State Department of Education staff. The State Board of Education supported the department, but did not become involved. The years after World War II saw the explosive growth of higher education, including teacher education programs, to meet the great expansion of elementary, and then secondary enrollment beginning in the early 1950s. To that point legislative involvement had been modest. In the 1950s, the focus in teacher education was on the need for many more teachers in the state. The education faculties on the ground, in the University of California, the state colleges, and the independent institutions, were in charge, and considerable flexibility had developed for the campus faculties as existing programs grew, and new programs were developed.

In the state colleges, the administration and governance of teacher education was centered in the Division of State Colleges and Teacher Education, a small unit within the State Department of Education. Teacher education issues were addressed in the same manner as all other state college matters, by presidents and deans and division chairs of education for the state colleges, and, mostly, by education department faculty for the University of California and the independents. The structure was defined by the cumulative actions of the legislature over the years; the content of the curriculum was largely defined by the faculties in departments and schools of education.

In the 1950s, coincident with the rise of pressure to change the governance structure of the state colleges, a rising concern developed in California and in the nation about the quality of elementary and secondary schools and reform. This was reinforced by the Soviet Union's launch of the spacecraft Sputnik, in 1957. A rising level of concern developed across the country about the adequacy of elementary and secondary education, and the concern was especially high in California where much of it focused on teacher education. A Committee for Improving Teacher Education (CITE), was formed. Members included the presidents of Claremont and Occidental Colleges (Arthur Coons of Occidental later became chair of the Master Plan Survey Team), two Nobel Prize winners (Edward Teller and Harold Urey), and the editor-in-chief (Harry Ashmore) of the *Encyclopaedia Britannica*. A statewide movement was underway. With the election of Edmund G. (Pat) Brown to the governorship in 1958, education reform became a priority in Sacramento. One of Brown's early appointments to the State Board of Education was Louis Heilbron, soon elected chair of the board. Heilbron and others, all Brown appointees, would remain on the state board until 1961 when they had to make a choice between it and the new California State Colleges board of trustees.[8]

Brown appointed Dr. Donald Leiffer of San Diego State College to a key position on his staff. In the aftermath of this appointment, the University of California asked for an appointment to Brown's staff also, and Dr. Harry Girvetz, a philosophy professor on leave from the UC Santa Barbara campus, was selected. While Girvirtz had no background in education or administration, he quickly developed a point of view. It had to do with teacher education, the substance of it; it also had to do with the leadership of the state colleges. He counted almost sixty leading state college administrators and found that more than fifty had graduate degrees in teacher education. He wrote incessantly to those involved in the Master Plan, demanding change. Girvetz wanted new leadership on the state college campuses, leadership from the traditional arts and sciences; he wanted the arts and sciences to be the core of the preparation of teachers.[9]

The focal point for teacher education reform was the substance of teacher preparation programs and whether these programs would continue to be under the control of education departments and schools, or be shifted to come under the control of academic and subject matter departments. A second issue was leadership in the schools. A statewide survey had revealed that the overwhelming number of administrators in the schools, principals, vice principals, and others, were from physical education. The call was for "leadership roles in the public schools . . . to be limited to those trained in one of the traditional liberal arts."[10] This issue was soon joined in the legislature. In 1961, State Senator Hugo Fisher of San Diego authored a bill, Senate Bill 57, to secure these modifications.

In late 1954, the president of the California Council on Teacher Education and the state superintendent of public instruction had together appointed the Committee for the Revision of the Credential System in California. This group had worked, rather quietly, for five years and, in late 1959, presented to the State Board of Education a report that could serve as a basis for legislative action to streamline the credential structure. The recommendations addressed structure, not substance. The state board approved these in February 1960.

At the same time, *The Sacramento Bee* began a public campaign to get the legislature into the picture. The *Bee* proposed a legislative-citizen commission on education, to look at all aspects of elementary and secondary education. The legislature responded by creating the Joint Interim Committee on Education, which, in turn, appointed the Citizens Advisory Committee on Education. This group held hearings throughout the state, and, after two years and some pressure to produce a result, it presented a report to the legislature and the public in 1960.

By 1960, the mix of interest groups related to teacher education was complex. In this mix were a set of interest groups focused on what they saw as a need for school reform, the teacher education establishment, a relatively new governor, a weak state superintendent with a small staff, and the State Board of Education in transition, not only in membership, but in its role with respect to the state's principal teacher training institutions. Added to this was a state legislature preparing to reassert its authority over teacher education through the credentialing and licensure process.

A young, ambitious senator from San Diego named Hugo Fisher introduced a teacher education reform bill, Senate Bill 57, in early 1961. It became the center of one of the hardest fought battles of the legislative session. The bill moved the locus of preparation of teachers from departments of education to subject matter departments. It set the stage for conflict about teacher education for years to come. Governor Pat Brown was supportive, and teacher education reform became a major element in his legislative program for the year. Various statewide study groups that had been formed took positions, generally in strong support of the bill. Professional education groups associated with teacher education and particular fields of teaching, especially those beyond the liberal arts and sciences, took positions, generally against the bill. The State Board of Education and its chair, Louis Heilbron, already chair of the board of trustees, were in strong support. Thomas Braden, the Southern California publisher who would succeed Heilbron as chair of the State Board of Education, then also a trustee, was among the most vocal supporters. There were conflicting points of view in the legislature, not about reform and change, but about the nature and content of reform.

In the end, SB 57 passed, narrowly in the assembly and with a good margin in the senate. The Licensing and Certificated Personnel Act of 1961 (also known as the Fisher bill) became law. The implications for the California State Colleges were major, but were, in the short term, lost to some extent in the activity surrounding the implementation of the Master Plan.

The matter was far from settled. Anticipating the passage of the Fisher bill, the president of the California Council on Teacher Education, Father Darrell Finnegan, and State Superintendent Simpson had appointed the ten-member Central Coordinating Committee on Credential Revision. The group, in turn, had appointed a number of subcommittees. The State Board of Education, given its very strong support for the Fisher changes, surprisingly went along with this action and appointed one of its members to serve on the ten-member steering committee.

As the subcommittees worked, it became apparent that the intent of the Fisher bill was in question. William Norris, a state board member later to be a trustee and then a federal appellate justice, reported to the state board that of the seventy individuals involved, six were faculty from subject-matter areas, three were classroom teachers, and the remainder were teacher educators.[11] The governor became concerned about the direction of the committee and asked an aid to alert the state board. Clyde Enroth, a Sacramento State faculty member and president of the English Council of the California State Colleges, contacted Senator Fisher about implementation of his legislation.

Superintendent Simpson presented the report to the State Board of Education in June 1962. This was an election year, and Simpson had already announced that he would not be a candidate for reelection. The report was lengthy. The state board scheduled hearings in September 1962 in Sacramento about the regulations that the State Department of Education would prepare based upon the report. The hearings were packed with various interest groups ranging from supporters of the Fisher bill and its academic orientation and intent to those who wanted inclusion in the academic subject matter lists and those who simply opposed the Fisher legislation. By way of example, the California State Dental

Hygienists Association made their case to the board about the training of dental hygienists, and, thus, the need to be classified as academic.

Senator Fisher appeared at the second day of the hearing and argued forcefully for the academic intent of the bill, the requirement for students to have academic majors outside of education. Fisher proposed that the board appoint an advisory committee reporting to the board, not the State Department of Education. In an interview with Sidney Inglis, the author of a history of this period regarding teacher education, Fisher shared that he had learned that a first draft of the proposed regulations had been prepared by Manfred Schrupp, the dean of the School of Education at San Diego State College. He also stated that the proposal had not been made available until the day of its presentation. Someone had shared a copy with him the night before the hearings; he changed his plans for a series of political campaign speeches (he was running for reelection in November 1962), and flew to Sacramento for the hearing. Fisher was followed by twenty-four other speakers on that day. Fisher was defeated for reelection in November 1962, in a campaign heavily financed by teacher education interests.

The next day the board decided to follow Fisher's recommendation and essentially rejected the report and implementing regulations prepared as a result of the Finnegan-Simpson–appointed committee. The president of the board, Tom Braden, appointed himself, Raymond Daba, and Margaret Bates, all former transitional trustees, Norris, soon to be a trustee, and Dorman Commons, a quiet and firm member with serious interests in education, to a five-person committee to draft regulations for the implementation of the Fisher Bill.[12]

While this committee of the board worked, public debate continued. Braden and Norris made many public presentations. Teacher educators and, especially, most state college deans of Schools of Education, were active in the public and political arenas. The State Board of Education Committee held eleven meetings from October 1962 to April 1963, and then proposed a set of implementing regulations. The State Board of Education met in April 1963 to hear the formal report of its committee and to take action. President Glenn Kendall of the Chico campus was the first to speak on behalf of the California Council for the Education of Teachers. Kendall opposed the implementation regulations and essentially argued against the Fisher Bill. He was speaking for state college education faculties and deans, though he did not have to say so. Kendall was followed by others, either for or against the proposed regulations. The board postponed action to its May meeting. At that meeting, the State Board of Education voted unanimously to implement the Fisher bill regulations, its version of the Fisher bill rather than that of the teacher education establishment. Implementation was to be effective on January 1, 1964. Media support for the board action was strong.

Implementation was not to be easy. School administrators, sometimes local district boards, and teacher educators initiated an onslaught of requests for clarification of details, requests for exceptions, and the like. The State Department of Education official responsible for teacher credentialing, a career civil servant, Dr. Carl Larson, had endured the give and take of the cries for change, the opposition to change, and all the activity in the legislature for years. Larson was the man in the middle. He attempted to stay friendly and in communication with both sides in the state colleges through all of the debate and disagreements. In January 1963, Dr. Max Rafferty, a new superintendent of public instruction, assumed office. Rafferty had emerged as a public figure almost solely on the basis of addresses, articles, and public activity, all of which claimed that the schools were failing. Among the issues he campaigned on was a stated need to change and make academic teacher education programs. After the election and taking office, he changed his position and supported the teacher education group in their opposition to implementation of the Fisher bill. Rafferty was, by virtue of office, the administrative officer for the State Board of Education and a trustee of the California State Colleges.

The credentialing of teachers was always a political issue, even in the nineteenth century. Rafferty attempted to turn it into a partisan issue, if only for a brief period of time, while he was ascendant in California politics. Governor Pat Brown had included improvement in the schools among his 1958 campaign issues, and he had given strong support to the changes in teacher credentialing. Sometimes forcefully, he had urged members of the legislature to support the Fisher bill. By the time of the 1963 state board action, every member of that board had been appointed by him. In his 1962 campaign for reelection he had pointed proudly not only to the Master Plan for Higher Education but to changes in K-12 education including the forthcoming implementation of the Fisher bill. Rafferty seemingly felt compelled, given his conservative Republican position, to take on Brown and his people on education issues, even though he left the mainstream of the Republican party over the issue.

The chancellor and the trustees had not been active in all of the events leading up to the implementation of the new credential programs. In the initial staffing of the chancellor's office there was no one with a teacher education background. Dr. James Enochs, the principal academic in the Division of State Colleges and Teacher Education, was in the transition staff for over a year before moving to the Sonoma campus, but he did not at all focus on teacher education in the transition. Indeed, there would be no one until 1978, when Dr. Ann Morey was appointed to the academic planning staff. An associate dean on the academic planning staff with a background as a biology professor was assigned to track the activities of the state board regarding teacher education, but essentially teacher education was treated like any other program.

The trustees' posture changed in February 1964. At the board meeting that month the trustees passed a resolution supporting the State Board of Education action and interpreting the board's action narrowly.[13] Essentially, the trustees asked the campuses to interpret the minimal number of education credit hours in the state board action of the previous May as near maxima: "[U]nits required in programs of teacher education should be at or reasonably near the minima established by the State Board of Education."

Robert Smith, the San Francisco State dean of the School of Education, who then President Glenn Dumke had appointed to the position (when it was titled chair of the Division of Education) was widely regarded by teacher education faculty throughout the state colleges and by many others as a principal spokesperson for the education of teachers and public education. Smith wrote a lengthy article in the May 1964 issue of the *CTA Journal* about the implementation of the Fisher bill. The article was not only lengthy but angry. Smith saw a coalition of the chancellor of the state colleges, the trustees, and members of the State Board of Education working "at odds with the Fisher act," as he interpreted it. Smith asserted that the trustees' February 26 action "was in its own words designed to ensure uniformity of application and to adhere to the requirements and enforce the spirit of the legislation. In effect, it translated the minima in the May 1963 State Board regulations into maxima in general education including student teaching."[14] The departments and schools of education on the state college campuses were not consulted, and Smith's anger was in part directed at this lack of consultation. "During the past three years, the transition from the old California credential requirements to the new regulations effective last January 1 has been poorly managed. Implementation of the new law has ignored the massive problems posed for the colleges. . . ." Smith predicted "a certification shambles." The Smith article appeared in the same time frame as did his very public resignation as dean of the School of Education at San Francisco State College.

An analysis of causal factors of the unrest and turbulence in the California State Colleges in the 1960s without doubt leads to the observation that a major cause was the disappointment, and subsequent anger, of teacher education faculties over the failure of the Master Plan to deliver the doctorate in education, and the convergence of this with public pressure that resulted in significant changes in teacher education. The substantive leadership of this disappointment and anger, which turned into action in faculty senates on some state college campuses and the statewide Academic Senate, came from the San Francisco campus.

As the implementation process went on, in 1964 and over the next years, so did the debate. Bills were introduced in the legislature to modify Fisher. One key bill, which both modified and reinforced the state board implementation, passed; the author was Senator Albert Rodda of Sacramento, a former faculty member at Sacramento City College and the holder of a PhD in economics from Stanford. State Superintendent Rafferty continued his vocal opposition; Governor Brown continued his strong support. The chair of the State Board of Education, Tom Braden, spoke at programs around the state that addressed K-12 education. By 1965, the implementation of the Fisher bill was in disarray on the campuses. The State Board of Education took control from the faculties. The state superintendent disagreed with the state board. The permanent staff in the State Department of Education was in the middle, trying to satisfy two masters. The college teacher education programs were in turmoil. Many colleges placed in their catalogs statements that catalog requirements were not firm and were subject to change as the result of new regulations.

Quite apart from the ongoing legislative debate about modifications and administrative interpretation of the Fisher bill, a new pattern of policy making and administration for teacher education was developing. The participants at the time were largely unaware of the consequences of their actions with the State Department of Education. Stone was an individual highly regarded by all parties in the credential controversy. "Regardless of the cause—and doubtless there are many indigenous to the [state] college faculties' resentment over the Fisher bill dictating college curricula—the panic button had been pushed. Imagine the problem of the school district personnel officer recruiting out-of-state teachers. Imagine the predicament of a college counselor trying to help a student who wishes to teach, when the requirements change each semester. On the one hand is a carefully cultivated image of the highest academic standards, which often dampens the enthusiasm of possible California migrants prepared in four-year programs. On the other hand, there is a series of escape hatches too numerous to be conversant with, while new ones are being added."[15] The pattern that emerged in the 1960s, a pattern of frequent legislative and state board (and later, Credential Commission) actions, persists to this writing.

Assemblyman Leo Ryan came on the scene in the mid-1960s. Ryan had been a high school civics teacher in northern San Mateo County. He captured an assembly seat in 1964 and remained in the assembly until his election to Congress in the early 1970s. (He was later killed in Guyana, while leading a congressional team to investigate a US religious cult group there). Ryan set out to remedy the deficiencies, as he saw them, of the Fisher bill, and he declared a purpose to make the credentialing of teachers both stable and more understandable. He promised not to reduce the academic standards specified in the Fisher bill.

In early 1967, a subcommittee of the Assembly Education Committee, chaired by Ryan, issued a report, *Restoration of Teaching*. In it, Ryan also addressed California's teacher shortage and enrollment declines in state college teacher education programs. Ryan caused the creation of a legislative joint committee on teacher credentialing practices, and secured a staff position for the committee. Members of the joint committee included a number of individuals who would be heard from for years to come on education subjects. The list included Assemblyman Ryan, who would chair the group, Assemblymembers Victor Veysey, and James Dent, and Senators Mervyn Dymally, John Harmer, and Albert Rodda. The staff position had been made possible by the Jess Unruh legislative reforms passed by the voters in 1966, creating a full-time legislature and legislative staff. The first hearing of the new joint committee was at San Francisco State College in April 1968.

An early proposal made to the committee was to introduce teacher examinations in place of the complex credentialing process. This was really a proposal to reintroduce examinations, as these had been used, beginning with the founding of the first normal school, until the normal schools and their faculties and the state board took control of the certification of teachers. A second hearing by the committee was held at the San Diego State College campus in May 1968. The consultant to the joint committee, Denis Doyle, was selected by Ryan. Doyle was a young and energetic public policy individual, and a noneducator. Doyle and Ryan would work closely together, and Doyle's influence on education legislation would become pervasive.

Doyle and the members of the joint committee set about educating themselves about the schools and, especially, about teacher licensing. Doyle established contact with legislators and policy people in a number of states, most notably in Massachusetts, where significant policy developments about both teacher education and the administration of teacher licensing were also under consideration. Doyle, and the entire joint committee made three separate trips to Massachusetts, Washington state, and Wisconsin, to look at other models. Doyle then drafted legislation and circulated a draft on a confidential basis to a Massachusetts policy person, a former MIT professor of engineering, selected professors in conventional academic fields (the arts and sciences and traditional professions), and a few others that were considered trustworthy. The document was confidential, and individuals in the educational establishment were consciously and carefully not told about it.[16] Events had come full circle, as subject-matter specialists attempted to undo what the legislature had done in 1921.

After much careful political groundwork was laid, Assembly Bill 740 was introduced in 1969 by Ryan and other members of the joint committee. AB 740 was sweeping in its proposed changes. Proposals included removing the governance and administration of teacher licensing from the State Board of Education and the State Department of Education, and the establishment of a semi-independent state agency, the Commission on Teacher Preparation and Licensing, to assume these functions; the establishment of new credential structures; elimination of the Fisher bill distinction between academic and nonacademic teaching areas; the declaration of undergraduate education majors as not acceptable (same as Fisher); the allowance of credential applicants to have a choice of a subject matter examination or completion of a subject matter program approved by the proposed commission; and, finally, a limit of nine semester units of coursework in education which could be required for a teaching credential. This was the central issue for teacher education faculty.[17]

Despite efforts to keep them confidential, the contents of the bill had leaked out as the final bill was drafted. The professional education communities and allied groups and organizations were in an uproar. Teacher educators in the state colleges expressed outrage. Perhaps most importantly, they sensed little support from faculty colleagues and no support from administrators, the chancellor, or the trustees. The California Teachers Association had long sought professional control of licensure for its members, not unlike the traditional professions, and, thus, was ambivalent about the bill. Despite all of the controversy and opposition and amendments, AB 740 passed in both houses of the legislature. Governor Ronald Reagan vetoed it, perhaps on advice of the legislative counsel, who had prepared a usual analysis and identified a number of inconsistencies. However, in his veto message, Reagan invited the members of the legislature to redraft the bill, retain its basic elements, and send a new version to him.

Leo Ryan did not surrender easily. He accepted the governor's invitation, redrafted the bill, and introduced AB 122 in January 1970. Many organizations, previously opposed, began to seek compromise. The most formidable and vocal opponent, Manfred Schrupp, still the dean of the School of Education at San Diego State, sought no compromise but only defeat of the bill. He focused particularly on the nine-unit limit on courses in education, and he testified that faculty and deans in all of the state college schools of education agreed with his position. The faculty at San Francisco State was successful in persuading President S. I. Hayakawa to oppose the bill. Ryan accepted a number of amendments, including defining nine units in education as a floor, not a ceiling. The amended bill passed in both houses. Governor Reagan signed it. What was really accomplished by the Ryan Act, as it is still known at the time of this writing, was twofold: the creation of an independent commission to license teachers, and a firm insistence that teachers must have either a subject-matter major or an interdisciplinary major approved by the new commission or passage of an examination. The provision for an interdisciplinary major (although the word *interdisciplinary* is nowhere to be found in the legislation) eventually resulted in the liberal studies major on state college campuses. This was to be an outcome of significant consequence for decades thereafter.

The Ryan legislation created a new playing field for teacher educators and provided a departure point for rebuilding relationships. New leadership was emerging on the state college campuses in teacher education programs.

The Commission on Teacher Preparation and Licensing held its first meeting March 17–18, 1971. It could be a new beginning. The newly elected state superintendent of public instruction, Wilson Riles, had just taken office. Thirteen members were appointed by the governor: four teachers, two school administrators, four college and university faculty members, and three public members. Five ex-officio members represented the Coordinating Council for Higher Education, the superintendent of public instruction, the board of governors of the community colleges, the regents of the University of California, and the trustees of the California State Colleges (soon to become the California State University and Colleges). The state colleges' representative for the first year of the new commission continued to be an associate dean from the chancellor's staff, not a top-level representative. Four of the newly named commissioners had worked together as members of a Commission on Education Reform, which Governor Reagan had appointed in June 1969 to be involved with the legislative process initiated by Assemblyman Ryan. These four had worked together well and provided a healthy nucleus from which to begin. The governor's education advisor, Dr. Alex Sherriffs, organized the first meeting; Sherriffs had been vice-chancellor for student affairs at Berkeley in the early 1960s, and in 1973 became the California State University and Colleges vice-chancellor for academic affairs. The meeting began with presentations from Governor Reagan, State Superintendent Riles, and Assemblyman Ryan. The meeting was harmonious and constructive.[18]

The relationship of the commission to the State Board of Education and the State Department of Education was ambiguous at best. The statute used the word "independent" to describe the commission. The president of the State

Board of Education, Henry Gunderson, was also present. He asserted a strong role for the state board, and used as his starting point wording also included in the statute that provided for a relationship with the state board. Gunderson told the new commissioners that they would receive goals and objectives from the board.[19]

The second meeting of the commission in April 1971 was still a developmental one. Three individuals who had been deeply involved in the Ryan legislation were invited to discuss the work of the commission. Dr. James Koerner, the MIT professor of engineering whose thinking had greatly affected Ryan, urged the commission to rely on three groups to guide their work: elementary and secondary classroom teachers, academic scholars, and citizens not in the field of education. Denis Doyle, chief of staff to Leo Ryan, focused on the independence of the commission, on examinations, and on commission responsibility for approving institutional programs in the subject matter areas of credential candidates. He was questioned about the statement of the president of the state board concerning policy and objectives coming from the board. Doyle responded that the commission was to be autonomous. The third guest, Lee Lowery, an aide to State Senator Albert Rodda, observed that opposition to AB 122 had been strong, but with its passage, the new commission "became everybody's." Rodda was now chair of the Senate Education Committee. Lowery made it clear he spoke for Rodda; legislative intent was clear: "The Board cannot tell you anything. They cannot say you shall do thus or so."[20]

From the time of the Sputnik launch in 1957, to the time of the beginning of the Commission on Teacher Preparation and Licensing, fourteen years had passed. There had been a sustained public preoccupation with teacher education. This would not soon abate.

At a subsequent meeting in late April 1971, Superintendent Wilson Riles joined the commission members. When asked about commission independence, he responded that no one is independent. The State Board of Education, in an attempt to capture the commission, had found an assembly member to introduce a bill, AB 1800, on its behalf to make the commission a creature of the state board; the board would appoint members of the commission; and the state superintendent would be the executive secretary to the commission. The bill was destined to go nowhere; should it have passed, there was a certain veto waiting. Riles' meeting with the commission was cordial.

There is no evidence other than anecdotal, but Sherriffs was likely a figure in all of this. He and Riles worked well together on many issues and were close. Riles was, from the standpoint of Reagan and Sherriffs, a great improvement over his predecessor. They wanted Riles to be successful, and they wanted the commission to work. AB 1800 disappeared. In May 1971, the commission appointed an executive secretary. The commission and its new executive secretary, George Gustafson, began the process of implementing the Ryan legislation. Gustafson, a controversial figure in terms of his style more than his policy positions, remained as executive secretary for two years. In 1973, the commission selected a new executive secretary, Dr. Peter LoPresti. LoPresti was a firm administrator; he was also a diplomat.

The California State University and Colleges made an important move in 1972. President Leo Cain of the Dominguez Hills campus went to Chancellor Glenn Dumke and urged the active involvement of the system in the work of the commission. The California State University and Colleges representative to the commission, a biologist with no experience in education who was a member of the chancellor's academic planning staff, was not a player. Cain proposed that he himself become the member. Dumke agreed and appointed Cain early in 1972. Cain was a nationally known figure in the field of special education. He could not be ignored as the CSU&C representative, and he was determined to be an active commissioner. Cain remained on the commission until 1977, one year after his retirement from the presidency of the Dominguez Hills campus. He was replaced by another president, John Greenlee of California State University Los Angeles.

The creation of the commission was the beginning of a ten-year period of tension and conflict and some efforts toward accommodation. The desire embodied in the Ryan Act was clear, a desire to regulate teacher education. The teacher education faculty wanted to resist; the gulf between teacher education faculty and subject-matter faculty was such that there was no united effort. The degree of this division varied from campus to campus. On the older and larger campuses, tensions were strong; on the younger campuses, with many new faculty, many, if not most, simply were anxious to continue their work. The commission was an outgrowth of the education politics of the 1960s. Essentially every college and university teacher education program had to rewrite their curriculum and submit it to the commission for review and approval. Both Governors Reagan and Edmond (Jerry) Brown tended to appoint individuals who were critical of teacher education. The appointees were individuals whose thinking was grounded in the Fisher and Ryan legislation, and they were seen to be opposed to established teacher education programs that were outside the direct control of academic disciplines.

On the CSU&C campuses, there was a turnover among the deans of education. One by one, the campuses responded to the need to rethink teacher education programs. The elimination of the elementary education major and the requirement of a subject-matter major had brought teacher education faculties together with faculties in the arts and sciences and some professional fields. There emerged a diversified major, the liberal studies major, and, ultimately, the multiple studies major for students whose goal was teaching in the elementary schools, and single-subject majors for those preparing to teach in secondary schools. A process of accommodation was underway. Two faculty cultures, teacher education and the arts and sciences, had to come together on the CSU&C campuses.

The first formal critical comments of this new approval process came in May 1973 from Sonoma State College and the academic assembly of its School of Arts and Sciences. The Sonoma faculty wrote:

> [T]he Teachers Licensing and Credentialing Law of 1970, as interpreted by the Commission and/or staff and provisionally implemented by the proposed professional programs, places severe restrictions upon the development of academic single subject and multiple subject majors which must be designed to further implement provisions of the Ryan Act, and . . . these restrictions create serious reservations about the quality of training, both academic and professional.

Perhaps unusual for an arts and sciences faculty at that time, the Sonoma faculty was concerned about an interpretation that there would be a nine-unit limit on professional or education courses.[21]

One of the early issues the commission was called upon to address was the instruction of students who did not speak English. In 1972, Dr. Tom Carter, the dean of the School of Education at California State University, Sacramento, proposed to the commission the establishment of what he termed a "bilingual/cross-cultural specialist instruction credential." The commission addressed letters to a wide range of individuals and entities asking the question: "Is there a need for a bilingual credential?" The responses were for the most part positive. In May 1973, the commission established the first bilingual credential in the nation.[22]

An external assessment process was initiated by the commission in 1975. Previously, the State Board of Education had ceded to the commission the responsibility for accreditation of teacher education programs. Teacher education bears an unusual responsibility among university programs that must be accredited. There are three processes for accrediting teacher education programs and, in the instance of some highly specialized education programs, additional professional accreditations. Institutional accreditation involves all programs on the campus; the regional accrediting body in California is the Senior Commission of the Western Association of Schools and Colleges (WASC). State licensure is necessary in teacher education and the granting of a credential; this review had been done by the Department of Education and would now be done by the commission. Professional accreditation is accomplished by the National Council for the Accreditation of Teacher Education (NCATE). The commission had neither the resources nor the capacity to undertake accreditations immediately, and rolled forward all existing accreditations.

In 1975, a new process, including team visits was initiated by the commission with four programs, at California State University Long Beach, Sonoma State College, the University of California Irvine, and Point Loma College. These visits employed teams of competent and knowledgeable outsiders. The visits for the first two years were spotty in their successes. The third set of visits saw a positive turning point. Given that the CSU&C campuses educated well over half of California's teachers, the faculties and deans were heavily involved, which helped to develop positive working relationships.

In 1978, the chancellor's office brought to its staff Dr. Ann Morey. Morey was the first education professional on the staff since the early 1960s, when staff that had been with the Division of State Colleges and Teacher Education, most notably the able Dr. James Enochs, had assisted briefly in the transition to a new governance structure. Morey brought a rich background of research and practical experience to the system. She was appointed to the academic planning staff, which, for the most part by that time, functioned as a regulatory unit and a gatekeeper for program development. Morey was energetic, and she had a sense of what the academic field of education was all about. She joined the meetings of the deans of education and became a regular participant. She later became dean of the College of Education at San Diego State University and an influential leader in the state and nationally in the field of education.

Growth of enrollment on the campuses slowed in the 1970s, and in the field of education, due to the history of the older campuses, there were many faculty retirements. The newer campuses had recruited faculty heavily in the late 1960s, and continued to recruit as they grew. Between the retirements on the older campuses and the young faculty (if not in age, in CSU&C experience) on new campuses, there was a new generation coming to teach at the California State University and Colleges. Many of these newer faculty had serious experience teaching and holding other responsibilities in the schools. Many of the deans were new. Thus, a new era was rising in the field of education in the CSU&C. This was reinforced by the nationwide emergence of a serious research base for the field of education in the 1960s and 1970s.

The culture of teacher education in the 1960s, not only in the California State Colleges, was a guild culture; teacher education faculty helped teachers, showing them what to do using their own experiences. Education as a field of study changed in the late 1950s and 1960s and became research based in significant ways. By the 1980s, education faculties in the California State University system were bifurcated, some from the guild culture, some from the research-based culture. Both cultures were important to the quality of programs.

In 1980, Morey, in her own account, read an article in *Time* magazine while on an airplane. The article noted that one out of every ten teachers in the United States was produced by the California State University. Morey talked with the vice-chancellor responsible for academic affairs, Alex Sherriffs, about the CSU taking an initiative to review education programs. Sherriffs gave Morey the assignment to prepare a major report to address education as a field of study. The chancellor created the Advisory Committee for the Study of Programs in Education, a group of eighteen individuals including two trustees, faculty and campus deans of education, representatives from the Commission on Teacher Preparation and Licensing and the State Department of Education, a campus president and an academic vice president, and three members of the chancellor's staff, including Morey and Sherriffs. The committee was asked to address four questions:

1. How has the California State University fulfilled its responsibility for the preparation of school personnel in the State of California?
2. What are the probable future conditions that will significantly affect the training of educators in the next two decades?

3. To what extent are CSU programs in Education in a position to respond to the changing needs of educators and demands for educational services?
4. Based on the answers to the above questions, what recommendations can be made for the continued improvement and responsiveness of CSU programs in Education?[23]

Morey was asked to chair the committee and assume responsibility for the preparation of a report. The committee visited six CSU campuses, and met many times with lively discussions, before turning to Morey to analyze the information and create a report. The report was massive, not in volume, but in the scope of its recommendations. It met some early resistance on the chancellor's staff as it went beyond an approach embedded in the administrative policies that had become routine in the functioning of the CSU. Sherriffs broke the logjam.

Excellence in Professional Education was a shrewdly developed document. It opened with three and a half pages addressing "Education as a Field of Study: Questions of Status." In a sense, it did for the field of education what Glenn Dumke's "New Approaches" had done for academic program development generally in the early 1970s. The report simply laid bare the tensions that existed between education faculties and arts and sciences faculties. It then went way beyond existing programs and addressed needs for change and for new programs. One of its recommendations concerned admission to professional education programs. The proposal was that "students admitted to the program shall represent the upper half of the undergraduate population on each campus."[24] The trustees later enacted this. It recommended the establishment on each campus of a credential advising office for students. Some campuses already had these; now all of them would.

The dramatic change in the diversity of California's population was well underway by the early 1980s. The report addressed multicultural and bilingual education, and the activity that followed the report in the schools and colleges of education on the campuses placed California at the leadership of these programs nationally.

For most, the transition from being a student to becoming a teacher is not easy. The report proposed an internship year for new teachers. In their first year of teaching, they received modest monetary support for supplies and the like, and active mentoring. This was partially implemented in 1985 as the Inner City Teacher Retention and Support Program; it went through a number of conflicts and struggles to the present-day Beginning Teacher Support and Assistance Program.

Finally, the report concluded with a proposed trustee policy for programs in education. This was a set of broad policy recommendations beyond the many specific recommendations in the body of the report. While never implemented as such, the proposal set a clear and positive tone.

The committee and Ann Morey completed their work in 1982. The report was dated February 1983. The report accomplished several things. It urged a renewal of the linkage between the schools (K-12) and the CSU; for the most part, the faculty understood the message and responded to the need. The leftover tension between faculties of education and faculties in the arts and sciences needed to be laid to rest. For the most part, this was accomplished in the 1980s. Of greatest importance, the rules of the game changed: For twenty years teacher education and the field of education had been driven for the most part by external forces—the Fisher bill, the Ryan Act, the Commission on Teacher Preparation and Licensing (its name was changed January 1, 1983, to the Commission on Teacher Credentials), and, to a lesser extent, the State Department of Education. Now, the balance changed. The programs in education continued to be affected, sometimes very significantly, by external forces, but education programs gained integrity of their own.

* * *

The early 1980s saw other changes. In the 1981 and 1982 legislative sessions, a new legislator arose to prominence, Assemblyman Gary Hart. Hart was well known in education circles. A Santa Barbara–based member, Hart held a master's degree from Stanford University and was a former high school teacher. He was elected to the assembly in 1974, and moved to the senate in 1983. Hart was a positive spokesperson for those concerned about the quality of teachers. He was the author of a 1976 statute requiring students to meet standards prescribed by local districts in reading, writing, and mathematics in order to receive a secondary school diploma. In the later 1970s, several school districts implemented a comparable testing program for prospective teachers. The results were poor. About one-third of the applicants in several districts, including Los Angeles, failed to pass one or more of the tests. Standards in Los Angeles were set at the eighth-grade level for reading and writing, and the seventh-grade level for mathematics. A national study by Professor James Coleman of the University of Chicago, using the Scholastic Aptitude Test and the Graduate Record Examination, compared college admissions applicants declaring a K-12 teaching as their objective with the general admissions population. The results were very negative about the prospective teacher applicants.

Hart introduced a bill, AB 757, that would require credential candidates and practicing teachers to pass an examination, the California Basic Educational Skills Test, (CBEST). The California Teachers Association opposed the bill, until Hart amended out the requirement that sitting teachers complete the test as well. AB 757 became law with Governor Jerry Brown's signature, and became effective on March 1, 1982.

CBEST (pronounced "seabest") was administered during the 1982–83 academic year on college and university campuses throughout the state. The scores were released by the State Department of Education in a single news release, and institutions could be compared. In the nineteen-campus state university system, three campuses scored poorly and were "at the bottom." This should have surprised no one, for the nineteen campuses varied widely in terms of the socioeconomic backgrounds of students and the strength of the schools from which students were drawn. A long-term view reflects significant shifts in student bodies among campuses. The variations were a product of the location of the campuses.

A furor arose within the CSU and in the communities principally associated with these three campuses. The media treated the issue, as one senior campus administrator put it, like athletic scores. Pressure on the "offending campuses" was substantial, and it was largely directed at the deans and faculties in education. This was a genuine misunderstanding of what CBEST was about. CBEST was about the quality of education in elementary and secondary schools and lower-division college work. It was not about schools and colleges of education. It was an entry-level examination for teacher education. Some did not grasp that. The CBEST examination became institutionalized and a routine part of the entrance procedures for teacher education programs.[25]

For the field of education, the 1982–83 academic year saw many changes. The California State University had a new chancellor, W. Ann Reynolds, on September 1, 1982. In November of that year, California voters elected a new governor, George Deukmejian, and a new state superintendent of public instruction, Bill Honig. Both would assume office on January 1, 1983, both would be trustees, and both would be generally supportive of the California State University and of teacher education programs.

One of Chancellor Reynolds's early actions was to bring the report *Excellence in Professional Education* to the trustees for their review. The trustees endorsed the report, as Reynolds recommended. Reynolds subsequently asked the board to act on the recommendation that individuals applying for admission to the credential programs be in the upper half of their class, however this was to be determined; the trustees approved this.

The report also recommended that each campus establish a university-wide committee on teacher education with representatives from the arts and sciences and professional education, so that there would be a means for obtaining cross-campus cooperation for all aspects of teacher education rather than competition and backbiting; some campuses already had such groups. The establishment of these committees was very important because it directly addressed one of the outstanding sources of contention in the state regarding teacher education, the ongoing battle between content specialists and professional teacher education faculty, a matter clearly dating back to the 1921 establishment of teachers colleges.

For Chancellor Ann Reynolds, teacher education was a major priority. In an interview, she commented that when she first came into the role of chancellor she observed that "people were almost ashamed of teacher education."[26] She wanted education faculty and deans to "sit high in the saddle." Reynolds used the report *Excellence in Professional Education* and the work of Ann Morey extensively. In her early years as chancellor, she found a supportive Republican governor in George Deukmejian. One of Reynolds's priorities was to expand teacher education programs. In the early to mid-1980s, California once again experienced a teacher shortage and was recruiting teachers from out of state. The CSU asked for funding to support enhanced education programs, and Reynolds took the proposal to the governor and, in turn, to the Democratic leadership in both the assembly and the senate; the funding was secured.[27]

One of the many significant sections of *Excellence in Professional Education* addressed bilingual and multicultural education. In 1983, in the early days of Reynolds's tenure, she established a Commission on Hispanic Underrepresentation; Tomas Arciniega, the newly appointed president of the Bakersfield campus, was designated as chair, and Robert Bess, the associate vice-chancellor for academic affairs, was both a member and staff director; Bess soon became executive vice president of California State University, Sacramento. Ann Morey was staff coordinator, with assistance from chancellor's staff members. The membership was unusual; it totaled eighteen individuals. In addition to the CSU members, there were two members from the business community, two individuals from major Hispanic organizations, two from out-of-state land grant universities, and two from community colleges. The commission was a working one, and seven symposia were held around the state in early 1984. The issues the commission addressed had budget implications. The first of two reports, both under the title *Hispanics and Higher Education: A CSU Imperative*, addressed Hispanic underrepresentation. The report had an impact on teacher education, as it addressed CSU relationships with the schools in an increasingly diverse student population. The report also served as a catalyst for the CSU to work with an increasingly diverse student population in the schools. Between *Excellence in Professional Education* and the work of the Commission on Hispanic Underrepresentation, strong stimulus was given to bilingual and multicultural education as a field of study and as a major dimension of the work of teacher preparation.[28]

In the final years of the Reynolds administration a major priority for the CSU in Sacramento was securing the authority to award the independent doctorate. The doctorate in education was the centerpiece of this effort, which was not successful. Nevertheless, the 1980s saw the reemergence of education as a field of study with substantial vitality in the life of the California State University.

There was serious trustee interest in education. Trustee Claudia Hampton, an educator and the most senior of the trustees during Reynolds's chancellorship (and the most senior member until her death in 1994), chaired a subcommittee of the Educational Policies Committee. As Barry Munitz assumed the office of chancellor in 1991, the committee published a report, *Programs in the California State University that Support Public School Improvement*, that had been prepared by Jan Mendelsohn, an associate dean in academic affairs. The report set forth what was essentially a policy statement about the place and importance of education programs, and it addressed the variety of education programs in which more than twenty-five thousand students were enrolled.[29]

Munitz changed the role of chancellor's office in academic matters and emphasized the responsibility of campuses to develop academic programs and plans. The role he saw for the chancellor's office and the board was a strategic one. In early discussions, Munitz remarked on the CSU education programs and observed that the fact that the majority of California's teachers were educated in the CSU, and not the University of California, gave the CSU an important and responsible role to play in strengthening the K-12 public schools.

Munitz called several meetings of the deans of education. He invited nationally known figures in education to come to the CSU to meet with the deans. These were not meetings in which strategy was planned for the campuses; consistent with his approach, he presumed that to be done by the campuses. The meetings were not received well by some of the deans, while they were seen to be helpful by others. The deans were feeling their strength.

Dr. Henrietta Schwartz, the dean of the College of Education at San Francisco State University, was appointed state university dean for education in December 1994. Schwartz was a strong dean, with major leadership experience in the Midwest prior to coming to the deanship at San Francisco State in the mid-1980s. She was a key figure in the reemergence of the field of education in the CSU. She had been a member of the Commission on Teacher Credentialing and had brought to the commission a publication about promising practices in the CSU. Schwartz maintained her office at San Francisco State while working with the deans on the campuses, the chancellor's staff, the commission in Sacramento, and others. She became a strong and vigorous presence for education in the state. An early project was a 1995 publication, *A Vision for the California State University's Schools of Education*.[30] It was the product of the deans of education from all of the campuses except the Maritime Academy. In some measure it was a restatement of the 1983 report. More important, the deans had come together, with a leader in a substantive position with the chancellor's staff. Schwartz made teacher education in the CSU more visible.

At the same time as the Schwartz appointment, Munitz recruited State Senator Gary Hart as director of the Institute for Education Reform. Hart brought to the CSU a reputation as a political leader with substantial integrity and knowledge of education. He and Senator Marian Bergeson had been the two major figures addressing education issues in the legislature for more than a decade. Hart declined to run for reelection to the senate in 1994 in a district where he was certain to be reelected. Munitz persuaded him to join the California State University. Hart's office was on the campus of California State University, Sacramento. For four years he brought together groups of individuals from over the nation and from within the CSU. His purpose was to explore new ideas and work with the deans and faculties as the California State University was emerging nationally as a leader in teacher education and in education as a field of study. Hart was a significant figure in the Munitz strategy to give education visibility as a major academic area within the CSU, and focus responsibility for program development on the campuses. In November 1998, Gray Davis was elected governor, and he named Hart to the post of secretary of education.

Pete Wilson had been California's governor from 1991 through 1998. His first years had been consumed by major revenue shortfalls, the need to balance impossible budgets, tax increases, major fires over the state, and other emergencies. He had been consistently friendly and supportive to the California State University. During Wilson's last two years, the CSU had been able to secure supplemental funding to address the economic impact of education programs over the state, nine million dollars for the first year, and an additional five million dollars for the second year.

Wilson had made a key move affecting education as he was midway through his second term. He proposed classroom size reduction for elementary schools, and an appropriation to support it. The legislature funded the proposal. Early elementary grades were to be reduced in size. This created a substantial need for additional teachers, and they were needed almost overnight. In the words of a dean of education at the time, class size reduction "hit us probably with a greater impact than any single event in the sixteen years I was dean...."[31]

School districts were authorized and funded by the legislation to hire thousands of additional teachers throughout the state. Credentialed teachers were not available. Districts hired teachers on a provisional basis. Would-be credential candidates would show up on campuses saying they had just been hired. They presented themselves in numbers. The urban CSU campuses were hit hardest. The dean at the Los Angeles campus estimated years later that the size of the teacher education program increased fivefold in one year.

An additional shift in teacher programs—the basic elementary program especially—was toward alternative scheduling. The basic credential programs had been, over the years, primarily traditional full-time programs. The new students were already teaching and needed evening and weekend programs. Schools and colleges of education have long had evening and weekend programs for advanced credentials, but not for basic credentials. The year before class size reduction, California employed fewer than five thousand emergency teachers; two-thirds of these were in Los Angeles County. Within five years of class size reduction, the public schools of California employed almost forty thousand emergency teachers; two-thirds of these were in Los Angeles County. Special appropriations eventually went to the Los Angeles County campuses.[32] The campuses most heavily hit by the class size reduction essentially lost control of admission to credential programs. The districts in question assumed control by hiring individuals. The impact of this well-intentional move to reduce class size was a serious short-term negative move on some of the campuses.

When Charles Reed was appointed chancellor in November 1997, one of his early moves was to meet with Wilson. In Chapter 14 "In Sacramento and Washington," Reed describes the first meeting with Wilson, and Wilson's interest in supporting teacher education. Reed secured additional funding for education in that first meeting, even before he assumed office.

Reed reorganized the group in his office dealing with education. Henrietta Schwartz had already announced her retirement. She had been instrumental in hiring two very able individuals from the CSU campuses, William Wilson and Beverly Young. Wilson was dean of the School of Education at Dominguez Hills. He had, prior to that position, been chair of special education at San Francisco State. Wilson was appointed first. Then Schwartz brought in Beverly Young, the faculty member from Fullerton who had been the CSU representative during the building of two key pieces of teacher education legislation. When Schwartz left, Wilson was assigned responsibility for teacher education, with Young as his deputy.

As Reed assumed the chancellorship, he made it clear that teacher education was among his top interests. In part, this was a result of the urging of Governor Pete Wilson. Reed was a teacher educator. His doctorate was in education, and his first five years after the doctorate were on the education faculty of the institution where he had earned the doctorate, George Washington University. Reed brought a teacher education agenda with him when he came to California.

Shortly before Reed's arrival, a group of campus presidents was formed to address teacher education. John Welty, the president of the Fresno campus, chaired the group. The purpose of the group was to raise the sights of faculty and others about the importance of teacher education. Reed used the Welty group and eventually established a successor group of presidents chaired by Robert Maxson, the president at Long Beach. This group brought in individuals from the schools, county offices of education, and the like. Reed began a practice of attending meetings of the statewide group of school administrators and then the California School Board Association.

A first initiative was to create an alternative path to the teaching credential, Cal State TEACH. Reed secured five million dollars to undertake the program. Beverly Young of the chancellor's staff directed the program (in addition to her other responsibilities). This program was directed at recruiting students to the teaching profession, students who could not come to a campus in the conventional way for classes. Materials prepared for the program were on a site-based model. It started slowly, with only one hundred–plus students statewide. Faculty on all of the campuses worked with the students. Nine years after its 1999 inception, 2,762 students had completed the program and been credentialed, and another 625 were expected for the fall term of 2008.[33]

The assessment and evaluation of teacher education programs has been a standing unresolved issue. In 2000, after discussion with presidents, deans, and the statewide Academic Senate, Reed took to the trustees a proposal for an annual evaluation of every CSU teacher education graduate employed as a teacher. This was prompted by a 1998 report to the trustees, *CSU's Commitment to Prepare High Quality Teachers*. The deans of education initiated work on the concept in 1999. Every teacher who is a CSU graduate is asked to respond to questions, which vary each year, relating preparation to their individual assessment of their performance.

The evaluation process is designed "to assess the extent to which CSU graduates have entry-level skills and understandings that are adequate or more than adequate for them to function as beginning teachers. . . ."[34] A report goes to the trustees each year. The report summarizes the responses from all participants and charts the information year by year, to show gains and losses. The assessment instrument is different each year, but comparisons are made and gains and losses can be identified. The findings that go to the trustees and the media (which curiously pay little attention) are aggregated. On each campus, more detailed findings are presented to the deans and faculties as well as to presidents and vice presidents. Administrators in the schools who supervise the teachers also participate in the evaluation process; they are asked to assess the individual CSU graduates. The graduates who participate do so not only for the first year but on a continuing basis. The faculties on the CSU campuses have heightened capacities to make sound academic decisions about teacher education programs. The accumulated experience and data generated in this process also sheds light on teacher retention.

This assessment and evaluation process is unique among colleges and universities in the country. It allows for the identification of pluses and minuses ("warts" and all) and provides a solid basis for change and improvement. It is administered by a small staff located on the Sacramento campus. The office originally established for the Gary Hart operation in 1995 was maintained by Dr. William Wilson and, more recently, by Dr. David Wright. Wright is the director of the California State University Center for Teacher Quality.[35]

In 2001, Chancellor Reed and the trustees redefined the two offices having to do with teacher education. Bill Wilson in Sacramento became an assistant vice-chancellor. Wilson retired in early 2007. Beverly Young in the chancellor's office in Long Beach became assistant vice-chancellor for teacher education and public school programs.

A next project Reed originated addressed reading. As David Spence, in his role as executive vice-chancellor and chief academic officer, explored the teaching of reading with educational leaders and teachers, it became increasingly clear that reading ability needed attention in the teacher education curriculum. Beverly Young's task to put together a report, *Preparing Teachers to Teach Reading Effectively*; this was published in 2002; a revised version was published in 2007. The Center for the Advancement of Reading was established in the 2002–03 academic year, and programs in reading were established on the campuses. This has had a direct impact on campus teacher education programs.

The governor and legislature established a "Math-Science Initiative" in 2004. This was funded both in the University of California, which received one million dollars, and the CSU, which received two hundred and fifty thousand dollars. The goal was to increase the graduation of mathematics and science teachers for secondary schools by the year 2010. As of this writing (June 2008), the CSU has increased the graduation of the teachers from 750 by 68 percent toward a goal of 1,500 graduates by 2010, a goal certain to be met with the classes of 2008-09-10. The program has been successful in the CSU, which is now solely responsible for it and continues to receive funding.

In 2003, when the Early Assessment Program (EAP) was implemented in the high schools, there was a role for teacher education. (See Chapter 9 for a full discussion of the Early Assessment Program.) EAP comes in three parts. High school juniors take the test (which is actually in the context of the conventional testing program for all students, with a few questions added). The second part addresses twelfth grade intervention programs in English and mathematics, to prepare students for university placement examinations, the purpose of EAP for students. The third part is the responsibility of teacher education faculties to work with the teachers who, in turn, work with students in their senior year efforts to address English and mathematics and thus avoid remedial work in a university freshman year. The chancellor's staff and the deans have instituted a program to do just that. EAP has received significant attention nationally, and is an important cooperative effort between the schools and higher education, with considerable national potential.

Many would believe that the most important achievement in the years since the turn of the century is the independent doctorate in education. From the standpoint of the organization and the mission of the California State University, that is doubtless true. It is a mission change that needed to happen, but it has happened only in part. The independent doctorate is limited to educational "leadership" in the language of the authorizing legislation—administration. The very existence of the joint doctorates in special education suggests that this limitation is foolish because the special education competence in the joint doctoral programs for the most part has come over the years from the CSU faculty. But this will be resolved in time. The independent doctorate in education is discussed in greater detail in Chapter 5.

* * *

The story of teacher education and education as a field of study is more like a saga. It is important to an understanding of the development and mission of the California State University, not only up to 1960 and the Master Plan, but to this day.

The twenty years after the implementation of the Master Plan were difficult ones for teacher education, made so in part by education faculty themselves, in fighting change, and in part by faculty in other fields unable or unwilling to understand the role of teacher education in a healthy college or university. The lack of attention to teacher education by the chancellor's staff and many campus administrators was certainly a factor. Teacher education was used as a political weapon especially in the first decade, the 1960s, again both by faculty inside and outside the field, and by others. The issue of teacher education and how it was addressed or not addressed in the implementation of the Master Plan, the creation and operation of the board of trustees and the new state college system in the 1960s were underlying conflict with the board and chancellor, and conflict in the statewide Academic Senate and on some of the campuses. In the judgment of many, it was not well handled by the trustees and chancellor, by some of the presidents, and by many faculty on all sides.

The story has, however, a happier ending. Beginning in the 1980s, many contributed to a rebirth of teacher education and education as a field of study and research. The California State University is now among the most significant institutions in the country in teacher education. Just a few of the many leadership positions held by faculty and deans in education in recent years is illustrative of the point: the American Association of Colleges for Teacher Education, the Association for Teacher Educators, the National Reading Conference, the Association for the Study of Higher Education, the American Education Research Association, the Association of Mathematics Teacher Educators, and the National Council on Rehabilitation Educators.

* * *

As I have gathered material, interviewed people, and then written this chapter, I have been impressed by a factor I had not really internalized over years, as a vice president for academic affairs and then a president. The average faculty member lives life in a department that for the most part determines its program and curriculum; there are curriculum committees and academic senates and administrators beyond the department, and there are the professional constraints and expectations of peers in the discipline or applied field as well as accreditation bodies. Faculty members and deans in education face all of these same variables. In addition, however, education faculty and deans in California face a state legislature that continually, almost annually, addresses curriculum and overall program and admissions standards. They face state agencies and commissions, some merely regulatory, some with the power to make substantive changes. They face a constant searching inquiry from a public and media concerned with education but often unwilling to start with the premise that professional education faculty and leaders, like chemistry and business faculty, likely understand what they are doing. It is not clear that all in the higher education community understand this.

There are lessons to be learned from the story of teacher education. The most important one is about faculty working together, or not working together. The gulf between teacher education faculty and faculty in the arts and sciences and other subject matter fields is not recent, and it is most certainly not unique to the California State University. When powerful interest groups fail to resolve their issues over time, a recycling of these issues can occur, as groups compete rather than cooperate. Often a vacuum of policy invites others in.

The faculties of the California State University have a unique opportunity, and evidence of this can be seen on some campuses. The mission of the California State University embraces the application of knowledge. Teacher education is about the application of knowledge. This common bond that faculty members can enjoy, and many do enjoy, can lead to an extraordinary strength in teacher education, and this point is relevant to the many applied fields within the programs of the California State University. The strength in these applied fields, joined by the faculty with the traditional disciplines, can move CSU programs in exceptional ways. There is some evidence that this is happening in recent years in the California State University.

Notes

[1] This chapter benefits from the shared wisdom of six individuals who participated in a daylong group discussion on August 11, 2006: Dr. Phillip Fitch, a longtime educator, dean, and leader in state commissions and other groups; Dr. Ann Morey, the first professional educator on the chancellor's staff in 1978, and later the dean of the College of Education at San Diego State University; Dr. Allan Mori, longtime dean of the College of Education at California State University, Los Angeles, and subsequently provost and vice president for academic affairs at California State University, Dominguez Hills; Dr. Henrietta Schwartz, who was dean of the College of Education at San Francisco State University and then state university dean for education; Dr. David Wright, thoughtful veteran leader in the Commission on Teacher Credentialing and, subsequently, director of the California State University Center for Teacher Quality; and Dr. Beverly Young, California State University, Fullerton faculty member and assistant vice-chancellor for teacher education and public school programs.

[2] Benjamin Franklin Gilbert, *Pioneers for One Hundred Years: San Jose State College 1857–1957* (San Jose, Calif.: San Jose State University, 1957), 67–68.

[3] Arthur Chandler, *The Biography of San Francisco State University* (San Francisco: Lexikes Press, 1986), 47–53.

[4] California Statutes, 1851, chap. 126, art. IV.

[5] This chapter uses the work of the California Commission on Teacher Credentialing, "History of Credentialing" (edited by Linda Bond, Sacramento, Calif., 2006; available on CTC web site. The years 1850–1952 are addressed in the first monograph, "Establishing State Responsibility for the Quality of Teachers (1850–1952)," Irving G. Hendrick.

[6] Hendrick, "Establishing State Responsibility," 4.

[7] *Ibid.*

[8] The second and third monographs in the above series are "The Fisher Reformation 1953–1961" and "Specialized Interests Challenge California Fisher bill 1961–1965," both by Sidney A. Inglis.

[9] Inglis, "The Fisher Reformation," 3.

[10] *Ibid.*

[11] Inglis, "Specialized Interests," 3.

[12] *Ibid.*, 3.

[13] Minutes, board of trustees, February 26, 1964; Inglis, "Specialized Interests," 14–20.

[14] Robert R. Smith, "Teacher Preparation Curbed and Confused"; California Teachers Association, *The CTA Journal,* Burlingame, California, May 1964.

[15] James Stone, quoted in Inglis, "Specialized Interests," 39.

[16] This section about the impact of Assemblyman Leo Ryan's work draws upon another paper in the California Commission on Teacher Credentialing series: Sidney A. Inglis, "California Develops the Ryan Reforms, 1966–1970."

[17] *Ibid.*, 29–30.

[18] Richard K. Mastain, "California Establishes a New State Educational Agency: 1970s," California Commission on Teacher Credentialing series.

[19] *Ibid.*, 3.

[20] *Ibid.*, 5–6.
[21] Mastain, "California Establishes," 15.
[22] *Ibid.*, 76.
[23] Ann I. Morey, *Excellence in Professional Education: A Report of the Advisory Committee to Study Programs in Education in the California State University*, Office of the Chancellor, The California State University, February 1983.
[24] Morey, *Excellence*, 78.
[25] Ralph Brodt, with Linda Bond as editor and contributor, "Senators Bergeson and Hart Lead the Way to Reform in the 1980s," California Commission on Teacher Credentialing series; the author was president of the CSU, Dominguez Hills campus at the time of the first administration and report of CBEST. The three CSU campuses were Dominguez Hills, Hayward (now East Bay), and Los Angeles.
[26] W. Ann Reynolds, interview by the author, August 19, 2004, 7–9.
[27] *Ibid.*
[28] *Hispanics and Higher Education: A CSU Imperative*, part 1 of the report of the Commission on Hispanic Under-representation, the California State University, Long Beach, September 1984; W. Ann Reynolds, interview by John Fowler, June 14, 2001.
[29] Mendelsohn, Jan, *Programs in the California State University That Support Public School Improvement*, Institute for Teaching and Learning, the California State University, Long Beach, 1991.
[30] Diane Cordero de Noriego and Henrietta Schwartz, *A Vision for the California State University's Schools of Education*, California State University, Long Beach, 1995.
[31] Allen Mori, teacher education group, August 11, 2006, 49–50.
[32] David Wright, teacher education group, August 11, 2006, 50–51.
[33] Beverly Young, phone interview by the author, June 23, 2008; Crystal Gips, memorandum, August 6, 2008.
[34] California State University Board of Trustees, Committee on Educational Policy reports, March 16, 2004, March 15, 2005, March 14, 2006.
[35] Interviews by the author: David Wright, December 18, 2006; Chancellor Charles Reed, December 20, 2006; William Wilson, August 9, 2006; David Spence, March 17, 2005.

Chapter 7

International Programs

From the day he took office as president of San Francisco State College in 1957, Glenn Dumke was determined that opportunities for study in other countries should be made practically accessible to undergraduate students. Dumke saw this as an important part of a liberal education, an important part of a baccalaureate degree.

While collected under the umbrella of the State Department of Education, the state colleges in 1957 did not constitute a system and, from an academic program point of view, were loosely tied together. Some campuses over the years had made available summer programs for study abroad or educational tours. Lew Oliver, a professor of history and a classicist at Chico State, guided tours through Italy, focusing on classical sites and history. Oliver was the leader of the only California State College academic year abroad program in the 1950s. One of the two smallest campuses at that time, though the second oldest campus among the California State Colleges, Chico State was the most active of the campuses in offering study abroad programs in summers, and was the home of the one full academic year program offered in 1959–60. Five faculty members were involved. Evaluations of the program were strong.[1]

The Master Plan was silent on the subject of study abroad and, generally, about international programs. Early after the implementation of the Master Plan, however, both the California State Colleges and the University of California began to address international matters at the state or system level. The University of California assigned a faculty member at the Santa Barbara campus, William Allaway, to prepare a program for undergraduate students from all of its then six campuses to study in France in the 1962–63 academic year. The chancellor's office of the

California State Colleges commissioned a study of international education for review by the board of trustees in 1962.

An early effort of the newly established chancellor's office was this first report about foreign study. The body of the report, presented to the board in March 1962, was very general. The recommendations included some very specific, detailed rules and provided for decentralized academic year study abroad programs with some level of coordination in the chancellor's office and a part-time director of foreign study. The board was not presented with a formal action. The report stated that two campuses and their presidents were moving ahead; Los Angeles in the fall of 1962 in Barcelona, and San Diego in the spring of 1963 in Rouen.[2] The trustees took no formal action. At the time that Buell Gallagher, the chancellor, had resigned to return to New York, and the attention of the board members was directed to the politics and processes of finding a new chancellor.

Glenn Dumke was appointed chancellor in April 1962. On the long list of matters to be addressed was the development of a coherent policy to guide the establishment and management of study abroad programs. Trustees had made it clear that a policy was needed, and that it should be a systemwide policy. At the July 1962 meeting of the board of trustees held on the Cal Poly Pomona campus, the chancellor and his staff described several reports underway about study abroad programs. The Chico State activities of the 1950s and the San Diego and Los Angeles efforts were reviewed and discussed. Out of this emerged a trustee resolution requesting the chancellor "to study the problem of overseas programs and to present a plan for development of a unified state college program in this field." The chancellor had not recommended the concept of a unified program in the language that had been prepared in the trustees' agenda, although the issue had been raised, along with questions of financing and the content of programs.[3]

Dumke turned for assistance to Thomas Lantos, a San Francisco State associate professor of economics who had been a strong supporter of Dumke's sometimes controversial presidency. Lantos had come to the United States from Hungary in the years immediately after World War II; as a young teenager, he had been conscripted into labor and building groups by German occupying forces during the war. Lantos had completed a doctorate in economics at the University of Washington and subsequently joined the faculty at San Francisco State in 1956. At the December 1962 meeting of the board of trustees, held on the Fresno State campus, Chancellor Dumke and Raymond Rydell, the newly appointed vice-chancellor for academic affairs, introduced the proposed overseas program: "carefully put together . . . not constituting an addition to the support budget . . . tailored to emphasize academic excellence . . . limited in scope . . . a pilot program." Tom Lantos walked the trustees through the development of the program, which had included consultation with all California State College campuses (all campuses were "prepared to support the program") and was restricted in size for the first two years.

The proposal that was presented to the board was comprehensive. It addressed curriculum, selection of students by committees of faculty from the student candidate's home campus, the role of host universities in other countries, and a clear commitment that the program would work through established host universities, academic standards, total insulation from commercial tours, and the like. Proposed student and program budgets were presented. Each program center, at a host university abroad, would be directed by a California State College campus faculty member. It was clear from the outset that the cost to the state would "be in an amount not in excess of the average system-wide support expenditure per full-time equivalent student enrolled." The members of the board of trustees were unanimous in their vote for "a joint offering of all of the California State Colleges, acting in concert."[4]

This initial action is important not only in itself, but for establishing a framework that, for the most part, persists to this writing. At the March 1963 meeting of the board, a comprehensive publication titled The *California State Colleges Overseas Programs* was distributed. An office of overseas programs was established in these early months; it was part of the chancellor's office but was physically located at the San Francisco State College campus, with Tom Lantos as the first director. A strategy to help students finance their costs for participating in the program was developed, using various forms of financial aid available at that time, notably the National Defense Student Loan Program. An advisory committee to the office of overseas programs was created, made up of one faculty or academic administrative member from each campus.

In the spring of 1963, two members of the board of trustees visited potential host universities, at their own expense. Paul Spencer visited a number of universities in Europe. With his wife, Delphine, board chair Louis Heilbron embarked on a nearly seven-week expedition around the world. Governor Edmund G. (Pat) Brown wrote United States ambassadors in the many countries the Heilbrons would visit, requesting assistance with university contacts. Appointments were made at selected universities. The Heilbrons visited universities in Germany, France, Switzerland, Italy, Egypt, India, Thailand, Hong Kong, Taiwan, and Japan.[5] The trustees were enthusiastic as they heard reports from Heilbron and Spencer at the May 10, 1963, meetings. The trustees were on board.[6]

The international programs of the California State Colleges began in the fall of the 1963–64 academic year, in five countries, France, Germany, Spain, Sweden, and Taiwan. The host universities were the Free University of Berlin, the University of Heidelberg, the University of Aix-Marseille, the University of Madrid, the University of Stockholm, and the National University of Taiwan. This first year was watched closely by the chancellor's staff and the campuses, and detailed reports were made. The trustees monitored the program and asked for full reports. This was a pioneering venture for the campuses and for the system. In 1964–65 the program expanded to the University of Granada in Spain, the University of Uppsala in Sweden, and Waseda University in Japan.

At the April 1, 1964, board meeting Governor Brown, who did not usually attend meetings of the board, asked if the California State Colleges planned to open a State College campus in another country. Louis Heilbron, who was at that time chair of the Committee on Educational Policy, responded that the California State Colleges considered it "preferable for the student to attend regular classes in the foreign university in order to attain the greatest benefit from overseas study. The program gives our students the experience of participating in the student life of the country. . . ."[7]

The trustees also took an important step at this time, removing the prohibition on campus institution of a foreign language requirement for the award of a baccalaureate degree. This prohibition had been yet another throwback to the pre–Master Plan and teachers college era.[8]

As the international programs operation grew in numbers, strength, and reputation, the Academic Senate of the California State Colleges began to pay attention. In April of 1966, the CSC senate established an ad hoc committee to do a complete evaluation. Three members of the statewide senate and one former faculty resident director (of the center at Waseda University in Japan) were named to the committee. The committee conducted a comprehensive review of the academic, financial, and administrative aspects of the operation, and reviewed in some detail arrangements for students, including student selection, language competence, housing, and fees. In addition, it reviewed two audits performed by the State Department of Finance in 1964 and 1967 (the latter covering the program from its beginning through March 31, 1967).

The report, given to the Academic Senate in May 1967, after a year of study, was a detailed and positive one.[9] The findings were clear and were accompanied by recommendations. The report made reference to the Department of Finance audits and noted that the committee was informed that there were no questions raised. The recommendations in the report were largely directed toward building and improving the program. The report was also very positive about the director. This report was important, given the developments in the program several years later.

As the 1960s were coming to a close, it was clear to everyone that the California State Colleges international program was an established fact. The program had been in operation for six years. The Academic Senate, the International Programs office, the statewide advisory board of International Programs, and the Division of Academic Planning in the chancellor's office together formed a joint ad hoc committee to review the program and prepare a policy to move the program from its experimental phase to a regular function. A revised policy was presented to the board of trustees. The material given to the trustees indicated that 350 students were in twelve locations worldwide. The revised policy did not include any major changes. The several trustees taking part in the board discussion each reflected satisfaction and considerable pride in the program. The revised policy reaffirmed the financial base of the program—that per-student costs not exceed that of on-campus programs. The major organizational change was the formal establishment of the Academic Council on International Programs to take the place of the advisory committee, a group that has continued to exist in its original form to this writing.[10]

At the close of the decade, the International Programs of the California State University operated in Africa, at the University of Ghana; in India, at the University of Delhi and Andhra University; in Japan, at Waseda University in Tokyo; in

Taiwan, at National Cheng-chi University in Taipei; in Denmark, at the University of Copenhagen; in France, at the University of Aix-Marseille; in Germany, at the Free University of Berlin and the University of Heidelberg; in Greece, at the University of Athens; in Italy, at the University of Florence; in Hungary, at the National Academy of Music; in the Netherlands, at the Netherlands School of Business, the Institute of Social Studies (the Hague), and the University of Amsterdam; in Portugal, at the University of Coimbra and the University of Lisbon; in Spain, at the University of Granada and the University of Madrid; in Sweden, at the University of Stockholm and the University of Uppsala; in the United Kingdom, at Oxford and the universities of Bristol, Dundee, Exeter, Leicester, Liverpool, London, Nottingham, Sheffield, Southampton, Surrey, and Wales; in the Soviet Union, at the University of Leningrad; in Columbia, at Javeriana University, the National University of Colombia, and the University of the Andes; in Peru, at the Pontifical Catholic University; in Israel, at Hebrew University and Tel Aviv University; and in Lebanon, at the American University of Beirut. A number of these sites were in cooperation with other US institutions. Operational units with larger numbers of students in residence were referred to as study centers; those with smaller numbers of students were referred to as specialized placements. From 1964–65 to 1970–71, enrollments increased from 212 to 474 individuals.[11]

Beginning in 1969, the State Department of Finance conducted a series of audits of the California State College International Programs. The California State Colleges were still only recently beginning to be free from highly restrictive financial controls, when they were essentially viewed like other state agencies by the Department of Finance. Flexibility and the capacity to operate like conventional colleges and universities is a continuing story, from the time of the creation of the board of trustees in 1960 and 1961 to the time of this writing. A state agency with international operations was a novelty. Thus a routine audit performed in 1969 by the Department of Finance led to additional audits over a two-year period. Irregularities were found, such as bank accounts in other countries that were separate from the conventional state accounts, and unusual procedures handling student funds for travel and housing at the various sites, different from conventional student housing on campuses. One of the issues was the location of the system office for International Programs at a campus, San Francisco State College, distant from the Los Angeles based system offices other than the governmental affairs offices in Sacramento and Washington.

In the report, the chief of the audits division of the State Department of Finance wrote to Chancellor Dumke in July 1972 about these many audits. The final report contained five recommendations, preceded by the statement: "This study has disclosed numerous practices and transactions which were either irregular or highly questionable. . . . We are pleased to state that the Chancellor's Office took prompt and positive action on the major problems as they were disclosed by this study."[12] The audits division chief noted "lack of controls over foreign bank accounts, irregularly established accounts, apparent gifts of public funds, extravagant, inadequately documented, and misclassified expenditures, and services rendered to persons not students of California State Colleges."[13]

The five final recommendations from this two-year-long audit process included:
1. review of programs in countries where students study in institutes or extension study centers;
2. critical review of all noninstructional services rendered students including, but not limited to, transportation arrangements, room and board arrangements, conduct of orientation, payment of vacation and holiday allowances, and financial aids;
3. a study to determine if there are measurable benefits that should accrue to students participating;
4. the California State Colleges actively seek the establishment of programs of overseas study in cooperation with the University of California;
5. the California State Colleges visualize the International Programs as a system-wide extension program with two funding sources, the General Fund, and a student special tuition fee.[14]

The International Programs office had been audited annually and consistently approved. The 1971–72 audit received attention within the California State Colleges and in the state government, including a hearing in the legislature. The underlying issues in these audits were several. The International Programs operation was necessarily very different from conventional state college activities, and it was large enough to be noticed. The earlier state college single-campus programs had been operated by individual campuses through self-supporting extension and summer session accounts. The program established by the board in 1962 was a part of the regular state college operations, and thus operated through the state general fund just like any other instructional program.

This was in some measure a bold program, the kind of program the University of California might develop—and did develop, at the same time that the state college program emerged. Still to this day, on more than one occasion the question is asked about a CSU program that some think should be operated by the University of California. The idea that the state colleges would initiate bold projects was still new to many in the 1970s. The location of the program away from the chancellor's office was controversial for a variety of reasons. The fact that the chancellor's office was not in Sacramento was still an issue with some, and efforts were still going on to force the office to locate in Sacramento. One immediate result of the audit was the move of the International Programs office to the chancellor's office in Los Angeles.

Tom Lantos resigned as the director of International Programs in the fall of 1971, and returned to the faculty and the economics department at San Francisco State. He remained at the San Francisco campus until 1980, when he was elected to a seat in the House of Representatives; he remained in the House until his death on February 9, 2008. He served for years as the ranking member, and later chair of the House Committee on Foreign Affairs. In an interview at the time of the November 2006 election, Lantos stated that the biggest obstacle to establishing International Programs was that the California State Colleges were "totally unknown." He cited as the biggest achievement of International Programs the impact on the lives of student participants and placing the California State Colleges in new international arenas.[15]

By the time that all of this occurred, the International Programs were institutionalized in the California State Colleges. The first decade had been founding time, not only for International Programs but for the California State Colleges. Indeed, the end of that decade was marked by the change in the name of the system from the California State Colleges to the California State University and Colleges. To create a totally new program in a new institution, there must be a willingness to take risks, a willingness to push limitations, and a corresponding self-confidence. Lantos embodied these characteristics, and he had had the support of an international, albeit conservative chancellor. One must be able to inspire confidence in an initiative and get others to believe in the importance of that initiative. In the formative years, without that confidence, the program would have collapsed.

The International Programs encountered resistance as the end of the 1960s approached, some from administrators, some from faculty and senates, as this new phenomenon emerged. The program had hit against internal structures and conventions of the California State Colleges. Issues came to a head, not only financial management, but the role of faculty. (One such question was would International Programs be a twentieth campus?) These matters were resolved when the Advisory Committee for International Programs was created. Financial management was integrated into the chancellor's office administrative structure, and the International Programs office was moved from a campus to headquarters, as one might call it. In a private university or, indeed, in the California State University of thirty-five years later, many of the problems of the late 1960s and early 1970s would, to a great extent, simply not be issues. The state university had acquired the flexibility to operate unconventional programs, operate with foreign currencies, and administer programs in other countries. One condition has not changed. Any entity in the state university that appears to be like an emerging campus or have the characteristics of a campus is quickly targeted.

On July 1, 1972, a new director, Kibbey Horne, took office. A retired army colonel, Horne had been commandant of the Defense Language School at Monterey, California. He was an experienced administrator and certainly no stranger to working with large and complex organizations, nor was the academic world foreign to him, as he had an earned doctorate. He brought with him as an assistant director Richard Sutter, another army officer just then completing the doctorate at the Claremont Graduate School. The era of consolidation of the California State University and Colleges International Programs had begun.

Horne set about reinforcing the more successful programs. Success was, for the most part, defined by enrollments. The 1960s had been a developmental time, with an emphasis on new sites and opportunities. Academic and administrative procedures were solidified. The new leadership benefited from a review, essentially an accreditation review, by the Federation of Regional Accrediting Commission for Higher Education, (FRACHE). An accreditation review at the time of institutional leadership transition is inevitably a positive action, most often for both departing leadership and new leadership. The past, on which building inevitably must occur, is defined. Questions about future decisions and paths that might be followed are informed. The FRACHE review was positive and constructive.

The early years of consolidation were not without problems. One of the early resident directors of an International Program site, Gustav Matheu of the Fullerton campus, initiated a series of complaints, filed over several years, against many aspects of the program. These were followed by voluminous correspondence with the chancellor, vice-chancellors, Kibbey Horne, and others.[16] Finally the Advisory Committee on International Programs convened a three-person panel from its members to hear and review the many—twenty-two in number—complaints, which ranged from student selection to academic standards to matters of budget and administration. The members of the panel found that the staff in the office of International Programs was without exception proper in their actions, including a willingness to hear complaints, to investigate, and, when necessary, to take appropriate action. The members of the panel concluded, "Further replies from the Office of International Programs, the Academic Council on International Programs, or the Chancellor's Office to charges or inquiries . . . about the operation of the International Programs cannot be justified."[17]

A more serious threat came in 1975. Jerry Brown, newly elected as governor in November 1974, deleted the International Programs operation entirely from the budget. The leadership of the California State Universities and Colleges fought back, Chancellor Glenn Dumke most of all. Dumke was backed by most trustees; the most conservative of the Reagan appointees agreed with Brown. Dumke went on a statewide campaign, concentrating on key individuals who might influence the budget. On one occasion he brought Kibby Horne with him to see the members of the Bohemian Club, an assemblage of key political influence and wealth not only of California, but, at its annual encampment at the Bohemian Grove north of San Francisco, of the country as a whole. On his own, Horne, with the aid of the California State University and Colleges Sacramento office, worked on the legislature.

Support for the International Programs came from many quarters. The legislative analyst, Alan Post, one of the state's most respected public servants in Sacramento, was often a supporter of the University of California over the California State University and Colleges. He took a sweeping view of the program's importance and came to its strong support. Students who had participated in the program came to the legislature, and some testified.[18] The budget was restored and has not been threatened since.

Chancellor Dumke continued his strong support of International Programs and of the international role and responsibility of the California State University and Colleges. In an address delivered in 1976 at a conference of the American Association of State Colleges and Universities, he noted that the board of trustees made "its commitment to International Programs fourteen years ago, just one year after the founding of the California State University and Colleges as a separate system."[19] The board had defined and maintained the purposes of this program as threefold: "(1) to contribute to the liberal-cultural education of the students who participate; (2) to provide opportunity for better development of knowledge and competencies in certain fields of study than can be provided on the local campus; and (3) to develop on a broad scale better international understandings and relations."[20] No California State University and Colleges faculty would go to an International Programs Center to teach, only to advise and administer; students would enroll in established universities; students would live among the people of the community. "No 'little Americas' representing California campuses would be established within the walls of overseas campuses."[21] Dumke went on to note that thirty-eight hundred students had participated in programs in twenty-two countries.

Dumke also discussed positively campus-based programs typically operated by continuing education programs and the need, as he saw it, for much greater emphasis on foreign language instruction. Rather whimsically, he noted the difficulties of convincing legislators that students are not on a Grand Tour; of convincing students that they could come to know the people in an International Programs environment while pursuing a rigorous course of study; and of convincing faculty that sending students abroad would not take full-time equivalent enrollment (FTE) from their departments. He observed that some have said, "If Goethe were to come alive tomorrow and give a course in Faust to our international students in Germany, only half of our German departments would give credit for it."[22] The importance of Dumke's address is that it was a firm restatement of the structure and character of International Programs. Essentially, it has retained this structure and this character to the time of this writing.

These years of the International Programs were years productive for students. The programs were strengthened, new sites were added on occasion, and other sites were dropped as interest on the part of students waned. In 1981, the American Council on Education (ACE) published a study of international programs on campuses over the country. The California State University and Colleges International Programs was identified on a list of outstanding international academic programs and publicly given recognition by ACE.[23]

By 1982, International Programs centers were in fourteen countries.[24] In connection with an accreditation visit to California State University, Long Beach, the Senior Commission of the Western Association of Schools and Colleges (WASC) caused a "self-study" of International Programs be done. The evaluation team selected six sites, all in Europe, for site visitation. The report of the visiting team was positive (a very strong report even to this writer, a veteran of accreditation teams and a former WASC chair). The major findings and observations were all positive; there were no negatives. Recommendations focused on matters that the evaluation team thought could be improved, the most substantive of which had to do with additional library resources. Another WASC review occurred in 1988, with similar positive findings.

Over a long period, enrollment remained constant, four to five hundred students in each academic year. The sites remained relatively stable. Peru, always with a small enrollment, dropped off the list in 1990; Zimbabwe was added in 1991, and Korea in 1997.

In 1978, the office of International Programs was asked to assume responsibility for oversight of foreign student programs on the campuses. These programs operated independently of each other, and still do today. The period of greatest significance for foreign student programs, arguably, was years earlier in the 1950s and '60s, when new nations were emerging. A substantial number of leaders in these new nations were former students of the California State Colleges. This was true for a variety of reasons; major among them was the very low fees paid by foreign students, the same low fees that California residents paid. This changed in 1968 when the legislature and governor mandated that foreign students would pay out-of-state fees, as other students from outside the state did. Foreign student programs have continued to be important on many of the campuses; the heaviest concentrations of students in more recent years have come from the Middle East and Asia.

In the chancellor's office a proposal was made to create a position of a state university dean of international education. The mid- to late-1980s was a time of some unrest regarding International Programs, but only in the chancellor's office. The top leadership, the chancellor and provost/vice-chancellor for academic affairs, wanted to have more personal involvement. There was no support for growth; the status quo was the order of the day. The operation was stable, but not growing. The Academic Council on International Programs functioned smoothly and was supportive. The presidents were content, perhaps too content, as the topic of International Programs was seldom—perhaps never—discussed at the executive council meetings of that time. Campus administrators and faculty, particularly faculty who had been resident directors, were supportive of the program. In the midst of this Kibbey Horne retired and his deputy, Dr. Richard Sutter, who had been with International Programs since 1972, was named to succeed him.

Before Horne retired, the then vice-chancellor for academic affairs, Lee Kerschner, asked Horne to prepare a set of five papers. Together, these would be a thorough review of the status of International Programs. They included a very general and comprehensive paper—essentially a proposal—to organize and fund a function in the chancellor's office to provide leadership for campus study abroad programs. Other, more specific papers addressed staff functions, foreign or international students, and the future of International Programs.

Horne was a firm and strong administrator, and he joined issues such as the possible return of the office of International Programs to a campus; oversight, or even leadership, for campus-based study abroad programs; representation and participation of the California State University at national and international levels; and his concerns for adequate support (not only financial), of the existing operation. He joined the issue of foreign and international students. He made the point that one student in thirty-six is a foreigner on a student visa, but that one student in eight is not a citizen. He argued that both groups have many of the same issues to confront, particularly cultural and linguistic differences.[25] The Horne papers addressed fundamental matters. Other than being used to support the addition of a position of state university dean, which Chancellor Reynolds and the then new vice chancellor for academic affairs, Lee Kerschnew wanted, they had no or little impact, however.

Seemingly, the chancellor wanted something more in the international arena. This could have been caused by the OECD study of the California Master Plan discussed in Chapter 15 in this work. The position of state university dean of international education was created, and an individual with only limited experience, none of it in a complex organization, was appointed early in 1990. Many people were interested in encouraging more international activity within the California State University. There was conversation in the statewide Academic Senate about "internationalizing the curriculum." When the new dean arrived, the director of International Programs was assigned to report to the dean. The dean attempted to exert influence over campus programs; for the most part this was ignored at the campus level. There were some serious eruptions at the chancellor's office level—a problem with the program in Florence, the temporary discontinuation of the program in Taiwan, conflict with the Academic Council on International Programs. Eventually, the dean's position was eliminated, and the incumbent was moved to another position on a campus. Things settled down.

When Barry Munitz assumed the chancellorship, the function of the office of academic affairs and the vice-chancellor for academic affairs changed. This was discussed at some length in Chapter 4. The locus of leadership of academic programs moved to the campuses; the role of the academic affairs vice-chancellor and staff was to give leadership to systemwide policy matters. In this context a new vice-chancellor, Peter Hoff, commissioned a study of International Programs throughout the CSU. Hoff indicated that this would be a first phase of a larger study of all international aspects of the California State University.

The International Programs study was done by Dr. Henry Weaver, then the deputy director of international programs for the University of California. The University of California Office for Education Abroad Program was (and still is) located at the Santa Barbara campus. Weaver chose a metaphor to label the study: "IP is a Tree"; and he carried this metaphor through the entire twenty-four page report. By way of example, the recommendations in the report, considerable in number, were grouped under extensions of the metaphor: I. "The Tree is Beautiful. The Maintenance Team Is Doing an Excellent Job"; II. "Although Beautiful, the Tree Is Dying [sic]"; III. "The Forest Visitors Need Help"; IV. "There Really Is No Forest"; V. "There Are Other Forests in the State. All Forests Should Be Open to All Citizens"; VI. "The Whole Park System Needs to Be Examined."[26]

The report was substantive. The program itself received high marks. The report noted that recruitment of students on the campuses was weak, and that there existed an imbalance between students in centers in Europe and in the rest of the world. Without question the report stated that International Programs is "a first-class academic and student program." But the thrust of the report was to urge a rethinking and reshaping of international study opportunities for the students of the California State University, to "vastly increase the numbers of students, reshape the division of labor between the Chancellor's Office and the campuses . . . start with a clean slate. The goal is clear: get more California State University students to study abroad." The report recommended that campuses be enabled and encouraged to operate programs of varying lengths; short term, semester, yearlong. Campuses singly could operate programs, or in consortia with other CSU campuses. The role of the chancellor's office and the International Programs office would be to assist and encourage international efforts of the campuses, and to act "as an agent for the campuses or consortia of campuses when it is financially or operationally advantageous to them [campuses] for it to do so."[27]

Another important recommendation was that the California State University operate international academic programs in concert with other universities, specifically, the Education Abroad Program of the University of California. (As mentioned earlier, Weaver was the deputy director of the UC Education Abroad Program.) The report noted that both the CSU and the UC had difficulty in operating programs in less-developed countries and that a joint operation would help the UC system.[28]

The Weaver report can be characterized as important in the sense that it called forth matters that needed attention. For example, it went into some detail about the financial needs of students and the importance of scholarship support for students. But the report was received with a dull thud. There may be several reasons for this. The metaphor "IP is a Tree" did not help. As I interviewed individuals knowledgeable about International Programs over the years, the reaction to the report was to recite the metaphor, smile, and dismiss the report. Moreover, the report recommended overthrowing the established order. The roles of the International Programs office and the Academic Council on International Programs were greatly modified, and in the sense of direct program control, reduced significantly. The campuses then operating with virtual total freedom for anything but academic yearlong programs, could be compromised by a new coordinating leadership function within the International Programs office and its academic council. For all practical purposes the report had no effect. It was not given to the presidents or executive council or to the statewide Academic Senate for review, the expected steps for any systemwide matter of even modest consequence.

Another change of leadership took place in the mid-1990s. Richard Sutter had succeeded Kibbey Horne as director in the late 1980s. Sutter had joined the International Programs office in 1972, shortly after Horne, and he and Horne had been a team. As director, Sutter employed an assistant, Leo Van Cleve in 1994, and a short time later Sutter retired (in fact, he went to the Sonoma campus for a period). Van Cleve then became the regularly appointed director in 1997.

When the 1994 report was commissioned, it had been made clear that it would be a prelude to a comprehensive report addressing all aspects of international activities of the CSU. Thus, in early 1997, a California State University Task Force on Globalization was created. Peter Hoff was gone from the CSU by that time. Both then Chancellor Munitz and Executive Vice-Chancellor Molly Broad were involved in this action, along with Associate Vice-Chancellor Charles Lindahl, who at that time acted as the vice-chancellor for several years. The charge to this task force was broad, and deliberately so. "The primary responsibility of the Task Force will be to review the existing state of affairs in international education, determine met and unmet needs, and develop a strategic plan for improving and—as appropriate—expanding international activities."[29] This task force was a piece of an overall effort to address the substance of the work of the California State University. The Cornerstones project, designed to develop a medium-range strategy for the CSU is addressed elsewhere in Chapter 4. The statewide Academic Senate was addressing the baccalaureate degree and issued a report "Baccalaureate Education in the California State University," where there was crossover with the Task Force on Globalization.

The task force addressed the existing International Programs operation among other matters. It did not meet head-on the issue of the essential monopoly by the International Programs office on conventional academic year programs and the campus virtual freedom to do academic programs in other formats and time frames. The task force report formally recommended:

> That Study Abroad be recognized by an integral part of the globalization strategy of the CSU and that efforts be made to increase the diversity of the programs in duration, content, and opportunities, and to maximize access as well as cost effectiveness.... That for purpose of balance and diversity, the gradual development of additional opportunities for study abroad be explored in the Pacific Basin countries as well as in the developing countries.... That system-wide study abroad programs be funded at the level equivalent to the campus average general fund support per full time equivalent student FTES.[30]

Perhaps the most important practical recommendation was that "an Office of Global Education be created at the Chancellor's Office reporting to the senior California State University officer in charge of academic affairs and that this office be dedicated to serving the CSU campuses in their globalization efforts and plans in providing a set of valuable system-wide services."[31]

The task force report was far broader than the now traditional International Programs of the CSU. It addressed mission and the fact that the CSU was a major presence in higher education in the United States and in the world. It addressed the potential of telecommunications and Internet-related technologies, internationalization of the curriculum, international students, faculty development, and, perhaps before its time, even accountability for global/international programs. The membership of the task force was broadly drawn, with some fifteen individuals, including two from the business sector.

The task force report was widely circulated. It had the disadvantage of emerging in the midst of a transition in the chancellorship. One of its practical results was that controversy over the locus of International Programs in the chancellor's office disappeared (perhaps declined is a better word; some things never disappear). For whatever reason, as a statement of the importance of international and global programs, the report became a part of the culture of the CSU. And so the office of International Programs was important. When the report was presented to the presidents in executive council, reactions and discussion were modest. The report did not receive further formal consideration.

Trustee Stanley Wang was appointed to the board in 1994. A businessman from the San Francisco East Bay area, he had been born in China and had spent some years there. He was somewhat unusual as a trustee, for he established and funded two programs during his tenure. One of these was in the international arena. Since the beginning of International Programs, the focus of the CSU, with respect to China, was on Taiwan. In large measure this was due to the preference of Chancellor Glenn Dumke. A limited number of presidents began to establish relationships and then exchanges with universities in the People's Republic of China in the late 1970s. No major push was made by the CSU with respect to mainland China, though the campuses began to enroll many international students from China in the 1980s, and some campuses established functioning institutional relationships. Trustee Wang approached Chancellor Reed about supporting a major initiative with China, at least major with respect to what had been done up to that time. He proposed a ten-year program, ten CSU students for the People's Republic of China and ten for Taiwan, each student to receive four thousand dollars for the year. In addition, he funded four faculty positions, at ten thousand dollars each for ten years, to be resident in Chinese universities. He identified the four institutions, and all are of international standing.[32]

In 2003, International Programs celebrated forty years of offering study in other countries and cultures to the students of the CSU. Over these forty years, students had studied in more than fifty universities in eighteen countries. The numbers per year had begun to stabilize at around six hundred. The Academic Council on International Programs decided to create a long-range planning group. The group was asked to address "vision for the CSU International Programs as projected to be in ten years, and a year by year implementation plan."[33] The planning group set for itself a goal, "[T]o make education abroad accessible to a greater number and wider variety of CSU students."[34]

The planning group tackled some important questions. The International Programs for forty years had included only academic yearlong programs. The planning group paid attention to trustees' resolutions, beginning back in 1962, and to other actions of the board, and concluded that yearlong programs were not a mandate but a tradition. But the members of the planning group were also sensitive to the fact that campuses had had for years had free rein in semester and shorter programs. The conclusion of the planning group was that International Programs should experiment with duration of programs, subjects, and location of programs.

The planning group also addressed topics such as program development, review of existing programs, resident director roles, and the relationship of the Office of International Programs to the Academic Council on International Programs. The members recommended the development of a mission statement—there was none, though early actions of the trustees certainly established a mission framework. What the group did not address was its own stated goal "to make education abroad accessible to a greater number and wider variety of CSU students."[35]

The International Programs operation has evolved into a stable and institutionalized part of the richness and variety of CSU programs. In the 2006–07 academic year, 607 students participated. These students were in eighteen countries.[36] The total enrollment of the CSU in the fall 2006 semester was 417,000 students.

The International Programs have an interesting characteristic given the history of the CSU since the Master Plan. International Programs is a systemwide program operated from a center; in early years, this was on a campus. That did not work for a number of reasons, so for the last thirty-five years the center is within the chancellor's office. And it has been successful on its own terms; it has survived organizationally. Only two other systemwide programs (if the definition of a systemwide program is one operated from a central point) have been attempted. The first was the Consortium, a mechanism to link campus continuing education programs in offering external degrees, with faculty drawn from various CSU campuses, while it operated from a central point. The second was the California State University Institute, a structure to create a capacity for financing and operating programs at a system level, outside of the state budget and financial operations of the CSU, and governed by a body including trustees, prominent citizens, presidents, the chancellor and two vice-chancellors. Neither of these other two programs succeeded. There were proximate and detailed reasons, but there was one fundamental reason: a majority of the presidents did not want them to succeed—the wagons were circled. The CSU still has to address the matter of defining capacities for systemwide educational programs that are not to be like a new campus.

Why then did International Programs succeed, even if only at a modest level? The answer may not be a satisfactory one for those interested in internationalization and globalization of the CSU. The International Programs operation is small, occupies a very specific niche, and is not a threat to campus interests. This is in contrast with the early years of International Programs, when faculties and presidents were threatened by it, in part because of its newness (for that matter, the newness of anything). The program's enrollment is modest and is not seen as taking away from campus budgets or departmental enrollments. But this begs the question of the CSU addressing the goal "to make education abroad accessible to a greater number and wider variety of CSU students," and the role of the CSU as a citizen in the national and international higher education communities. Perhaps the recommendations of the 1998 task force report, which were essentially strategic rather than tactical, should be revisited.

* * *

The California State University was not a major player in American higher education when the California State College system took its present form in 1961. The impact of the institutions from 1857 to 1961 upon the people and culture and economy and institutions of California had been enormous, but were little understood or appreciated until sheer numbers brought the existence of the state colleges to greater attention. As the California State Colleges, they emerged on the national scene in the 1960s, and over the years the system became a significant player on the national higher education scene. With the

OECD study as a milestone, the California State University emerged on the international stage in the 1980s.

The International Programs operation had put in place a framework from the beginning in the 1960s. The campuses selected as sites for International Program centers around the world were major institutions. The fact that the California State University is the largest system of higher education in the United States, and among the largest (if not the largest) in the world, certainly is important.

While individual campuses and faculty have emerged in active roles in the international arena, the California State University has not done so as a whole, beyond International Programs. It has certainly emerged nationally. Chancellor Barry Munitz and his successor, Chancellor Charles Reed, have been major figures in American higher education. Munitz chaired the board of the American Council on Education; Reed serves in most if not all major national higher education entities and enjoys widespread respect among both Republicans and Democrats on Capitol Hill and in governmental agencies. Many campus presidents have served on boards and as presidents or chairs of national organizations such as the National Science Foundation, American Association for State Colleges and Universities (AASCU), the American Council on Education (ACE), the National Association of State Universities and Land Grant Colleges (NASULGC), and the International Association of University Presidents (IAUP),[37] to mention a few.

Similarly, individual campuses and their presidents have been active and a presence on the international scene. Yet the California State University as a whole has not played a compelling role in international higher education. However, just as it is true that the whole is more than the sum of the parts with respect to the life of the campuses and the California State University, so it is true in the international arena. The CSU is a citizen of the global higher education community, a major citizen. Exercising the responsibilities of that citizenship is an agenda yet to be developed.

Notes

[1] Office of the Chancellor, College and University Programs of Foreign Study: Their Status and Prospects, a report prepared for the trustees of the California State Colleges, March 1962 meeting of the board, CSU Archives.

[2] *Ibid.*, 4.

[3] Minutes of the California State Colleges board of trustees (hereafter cited as "board of trustees"), July 13, 1962.

[4] Minutes, board of trustees, December 6–7, 1962.

[5] Board of trustees' file, 1963, CSU Archives.

[6] Minutes, board of trustees, May 9–10, 19, 1963.

[7] Minutes, board of trustees, April 1, 1964.

[8] Minutes, board of trustees, December 2, 1965.

[9] Report of the Ad Hoc Committee on International Programs, May 17, 1967, CSU Archives, statewide academic senate records.

[10] Minutes, board of trustees, July 8–9, 1969.

[11] Academic Master Plan for International Programs 1971–76, August 20, 1970; CSU Archives.

[12] "Review of the California State Colleges International Programs for the Period July 1, 1969, to June 30, 1971," 2, CSU Archives.

[13] Some of the centers had individuals enrolled that were students of other colleges and universities.

[14] Review of the California State Colleges," 5–9. The University of California, given its constitutional independence, operated outside the controls of state agencies, and thus has a capacity to function like conventional higher education institutions, a capacity the CSC has been building carefully and gradually since 1961.

[15] Thomas P. Lantos, interview, October 26, 2006, Donald R. Gerth.

[16] The individual referred to in this instance actually served as a resident director at two sites in Europe.

[17] Final Report of the Ad Hoc Committee to Examine Complaints Expressed . . . Concerning the International Programs, May 1975, CSU Archives.

[18] Group interview with past and present international program directors, June 1, 2006, CSU Archives. Participants included Kibbey Horne, Richard Shek, Richard Sutter, Leo Van Cleve, and the writer.

[19] Glenn S. Dumke, "The International Role and Responsibility of U.S. Higher Education," American Association of State Colleges and Universities conference, February 1976, CSU Archives.

[20] *Ibid.*

[21] *Ibid.*

[22] *Ibid.*

[23] Group interview with past and present international program directors.

[24] Brazil, Canada (Quebec), Denmark, France, Germany, Israel, Italy, Japan, Mexico, New Zealand, Peru, Spain, Sweden, and the Republic of China.

[25] International Programs Collection, CSU Archives.

[26] Henry D. Weaver, IP Is a Tree: Review of CSU Statewide International Programs, June 29, 1994, CSU Archives.

[27] Weaver, IP Is a Tree, 11–12–13.

[28] *Ibid.*, 14.

[29] Report of the Task Force on Globalization, May 1998, CSU Archives. The author chaired the task force and wrote a seven-page substantive cover letter for the report.

[30] Report of the Task Force, 13–14.

[31] *Ibid.*, 14–15.

[32] Minutes, board of trustees, CSU Archives. The four universities Wang selected are Peking University, Shanghai Jiaotung University, National Taiwan University, and Ching Hua University in Xinchu.

[33] Report of the Long Range Strategic Planning Group to the ACIP, April 2005, 1, CSU Archives.

[34] *Ibid.*, 2.

[35] *Ibid.*

[36] Office of the Chancellor, CSU Statistical Abstract, July 2007. Australia (25), Canada (6), Chile (16), China (20), Denmark (40), France (97), Germany (46), Ghana (9), Italy (96), Japan (24), Korea (8),Mexico (24), New Zealand (8), South Africa (10), Spain (88), Sweden (18), Taiwan (9), the United Kingdom (63).

[37] The author of this work is the individual who served with the IAUP.

Chapter 8

Information Technology

Electronic data processing (EDP) and the California State Colleges began together in the early 1960s, around the time that audiovisual technology began to extend beyond the enthusiasts. Many CSC campuses were producing programming, slide presentations, film and filmstrips, and video. Campus-based radio and television programming was beginning to flourish. All this involved the construction of studio facilities and engaging in partnerships with educational and commercial outlets. Several campuses produced more local programming in the 1960s than has been produced since the year 2000.

As a result of individual faculty and administrator entrepreneurial activity, the California State College campuses have increased their computing and other technical capability. In addition, individual departments and deans, along with the special interests of many committed faculty members, provided the impetus to foster technological capabilities. In 1963, the board of trustees adopted a brief statement about data processing. "Data processing equipment now installed in the colleges, together with that added in the future must be adequate to meet the dual needs of instructional and administrative programs. To the extent practical, such equipment shall be used for both purposes."[1] Data processing in the chancellor's office was

---

The author is indebted to Spencer Freund, Vice President for Information Resources and Technology and Chief Information Officer, California State University, San Bernardino, for reviewing and commenting on this chapter. The author convened a focus group to address the development of technology in the California State University on January 19, 2006. Those participating were David Ernst, Spencer Freund, James Rosser, Richard West, and Thomas West.

among the responsibilities of the business affairs staff. The campus presidents assigned data processing to an office or individual, sometimes the business office, sometimes a faculty member in engineering or another field, with released time from one or two courses. On one campus in 1964, a new and relatively young administrator was greeted by an engineering professor who inquired whether the administrator had any knowledge about computers, or was like all the other campus administrators, who had no experience. Receiving the latter answer, the engineering professor, whose responsibilities included a nascent computer operation, responded good-naturedly that he would undertake the education.[2]

In the spring of 1968, Alan Post, the legislative analyst, joined the issue of computing in all of California state government. He was concerned that substantial sums of money were being spent for computing equipment, facilities were being constructed, positions created, and there was no plan. "Suddenly we had these big computers and big budgets for them. They didn't speak to each other. You had individual plans, different institutions within different institutions. . . ."[3] Post was explicitly concerned with the California State Colleges. He observed that within the University of California, with its budget flexibility, each campus went its own way with computing; likewise, within campuses individual units went their own way.

In March 1968, Post issued a report that contained two major thrusts: within the California State Colleges, a hierarchy of computing resources should be established supporting both instructional and administrative computing; and central coordination for computing should be maintained through the chancellor's office. The California Legislature then mandated the establishment of an administrative unit within the chancellor's office; no formal campus computing organization was called for.[4]

The chancellor's office established a Division of Information Systems (DIS) later in 1968. The division was not in Academic Affairs but in Business Affairs. The budget for 1968–69 funded the establishment of a California State Colleges distribution computer network and central timesharing for academic activity and campus timesharing for administrative activity.[5] By the end of the 1960s data processing centers had been created for the northern and southern campuses at San Jose and Los Angeles. The state financial systems were used for financial administration and the campuses were beginning to establish student systems, each campus separately. Sixteen of the nineteen campuses at that time had computer capability of some kind. In 1969–70 the budget provided for the acquisition of a modest computer capability on all campuses. The chancellor's office had an account to provide for the rental of equipment.

The 1970s saw the evolution of computing systems on two different levels. The Division of Information Systems in the chancellor's office addressed the development of computing systems ostensibly for both systemwide administrative and academic uses. The emphasis was on administration. The presidents of the campuses, or at least a substantial majority of the presidents, had a very different viewpoint. Certainly they were aware of the legislative analyst's 1968 report and the following legislation mandating the DIS and the development of systemwide approaches to technology and especially computing. But the presidents, in the Council of Presidents, resisted the development of any and all systemwide approaches to technology and computing. The head of DIS, Lawrence Baker, though not a member of the Council of Presidents, was an invited participant when technology and computing were on the agenda. He was not able to secure agreement for the most part on his plans. Technology and computing were not among the chancellor's office priorities. The result was that no systemwide strategy for the uses of technology and computing developed.[6]

In the early 1970s, DIS staff, working with the business management group on the campuses and in the chancellor's office, initiated the development of CSU-wide accounting systems. Embryonic computing organizations were developing on most campuses. In the area of academic planning, an instrument known as the "academic planning database" was developed and this remained in use for years. A routine audit done by the trustees' audit unit led to a trustee policy statement in 1974 that reaffirmed the role and responsibilities of DIS in developing "uniform administrative systems which will allow for individual campus flexibility." The trustees asked for "an EDP Master Plan to be completed immediately and presented to the Trustees."[7]

The legislature, consistent with Alan Post's continuing concern about computer costs, included language in the 1975 Budget Act essentially directing consolidation and uniformity in equipment and procedures within the California State University and Colleges. This was pivotal in refining the mission of DIS. The Budget Act also required Department of Finance approval for all state agencies of technology expenditures over twenty-five thousand dollars; approval could be sought expenditure by expenditure, or with the submission of a plan for the year. Finance used the language to institute a requirement for submission and review of annual processing plans. The California State University and Colleges (CSUC) used this to begin to make the case for more support for technology. The 1977 report included information about professional undergraduate and graduate degree programs in which students must acquire computing skills in order for the programs to be accredited and for the graduates to find employment. "The determination of systemwide standards for the allocation of instructional computing resources among computing issues rests on the answers to two questions: (1) What demands for competing knowledge does the economy make upon graduates of the CSUC as a prerequisite to entry into gainful employment; and (2) What computing skills should students acquire in various academic disciplines?"[8]

The campuses varied greatly in their start-up activities for technology and computing. Campus libraries, for the most part, initiated efforts in the early 1970s. Initially proceeding independently, the library deans and directors on the campuses met with some frequency, and they achieved a measure of coordination. By the end of the decade, library automation efforts were underway. Instructional computing use varied widely among the campuses, and among the disciplines and fields of study. Engineering programs were the most avid users, followed by business and management programs. Several art departments on campuses developed courses in the use of computers for art. Two faculty members on two of the campuses, Grace Hertlein at Chico and Maria Winkler at Sacramento, became nationally known for computer art. Some campuses established media and audiovisual centers.

The chancellor's office added a staff member in 1976 to give some leadership to instructional technology. Gene Geisler was a faculty member in the government department at San Francisco State. He had used computers both in teaching and research. Geisler remained in the chancellor's office for four years before returning to the San Francisco faculty. Geisler was a recognized excellent teacher and scholar; some faculty members worked with him For the most part, however, campuses were resistant to his efforts. Academic administrations resisted; the academic affairs staff in the chancellor's office did not involve him. Eventually conflict developed over the relationship of academic computing to the administrative functions of DIS. At that point Geisler departed.[9]

The one academic area that was able to pursue the use of technology relatively freely was continuing education. In a sense, this was consistent with the cutting-edge role that continuing education began to pursue after the Dumke New Approaches initiative of 1971. Continuing education had independence, its own money, and the support of the chancellor. A major thrust in continuing education was the use of Instructional Television Fixed Service (ITFS). A number of campuses were using television to distribute courses. The Chico campus had been the first, in 1975, to develop ITFS as a mechanism to bring academic courses and programs to learning centers and corporate sites throughout the region. In 1980, a proposal was made by Royd Weintraub, of the Chico campus, to implement a concept proposed in 1979: "a telecommunications network for the California State University and Colleges." Television instruction had not until that time been a major activity at CSU, having been somewhat overshadowed by computer technology developments, but it became an established teaching method and has continued with considerable strength and substantial enrollments on some campuses.[10]

As the decade ended, computer development and usage was underway. DIS and campus staffs worked together, often in teams or task forces, and computing as an instructional tool was beginning to gain momentum. There was little or no presidential involvement, no collaboration by the Council of Presidents, and only occasional vice-presidential participation. The campuses were proceeding more or less independently with respect to program development and equipment acquisition. Department of Finance efforts to coordinate and control were not productive; there was too much to coordinate and control.

The end of the 1970s saw two major changes. With presidential retirements, newly appointed presidents with technological competence and knowledge joined the leadership. In two years, three new presidents with substantial technical knowledge and experience came to the CSU: Thomas Day, a physicist, to San Diego State; James Rosser, a biologist and health scientist, to the Los Angeles campus; and Warren Baker, an engineer, to Cal Poly at San Luis Obispo. In 1981, the DIS leadership changed. Dr. Thomas West came to the California State University from a senior position at Indiana University and was named the director of

DIS, a position that was changed, during his eighteen-year tenure, to assistant vice-chancellor for information technology services.

West found, in his own words, "an insulation between the campuses and the chancellor's office about technology." He found "no sense of system." The technology program was adrift. The rift between the chancellor's office and the campuses was, at least in part, a product of a perception on the campuses that the DIS represented the state and state government, not the campuses and students, faculty, and staff. The campuses saw the heavy hand of government. But West also saw a new generation of presidents forming. In 1984, San Diego State President Thomas Day played a leadership role, with the support of some other presidents, in getting the CSU technology operations away from the second-guessing and micromanagement of the Department of Finance.[11]

Tom West's counterpart in the University of California was an associate vice president named Richard West. West became vice-chancellor for business affairs on January 1, 1994. Years later, they would joke about allegations that the "West twins" were taking over educational technology in California. They soon forged a productive working relationship that was unusual for that time among senior administrators in the CSU and UC systems.

Personal computers came into play as a major factor. This technological achievement inevitably changed the rules for the development and management of technology. It created opportunities for new uses of technology in teaching and learning, and research and scholarship. It changed decision making. It changed the potential for management of computer systems. In a sense, personal computers created an independent environment for users.

In 1983, DIS proposed a comprehensive technology resource plan. The plan profiled "the development of computing and telecommunications in the CSU against the evolution of information technology generally."[12] The paper proposed a five-year plan to bring campus and system technological capacity to a level consistent with (1) the administrative needs of the CSU, and (2) ways that its academic programs could reasonably be applied. The five-year plan closed with a statement: "It is clear that telecommunications and computing will significantly impact the academic missions of the campuses. This will require additional resources in the form of professional people, facilities, and funding if the CSU is to remain effective and to maintain and enhance its high quality educational delivery system."[13]

The work of DIS shifted to a style of collaboration with the campuses, replacing an ongoing battle of campuses and DIS to gain resources. California state government, to an unusual degree, was suspicious of technology in state agencies generally. This may be traced to some early efforts in various areas of state government in the 1960s that did not work well, and the legislative analyst's 1968 report about controlling the costs of technology.

The growth of telecommunications was rapid in the 1980s. The campuses moved to create integrated telecommunications and media centers. Campus Information Resource Plans (CIRP) were developed. Each campus developed a full-scale computing organization. The Library Automation Project was initiated. The campus librarians became important advocates of technology as it touched them. The systemwide Council of Library Directors (COLD) was an important group in moving technology forward. Students and faculty achieved access to library resources on their own and other campuses, the Library of Congress, and elsewhere.[14]

In the fall of 1987, Chancellor Ann Reynolds established a Commission on Instructional Technology (CIT). The purpose of the Commission was in part to share and encourage the substantial impact that the availability of technology was having on academic programs and students and faculty. The commission also was a vehicle to advocate funding as the demands for access to instructional technology far exceeded financial capacities.

The Commission on Extended Education, which had been created in 1972, remained a strong advocate for technology and a source of financial support for new ideas about the uses of technology. The use of ITFS expanded.

The objectives of the 1983–88 CIRP plan were systematically addressed. These included the development on each campus of a comprehensive voice, video, data, and computing capacity with access by students, faculty, and staff members; an integrated network among the campuses and the chancellor's office; acquisition of hardware and software; and adequate staffing and facilities. These objectives were substantial. They were achieved only in part, limited by funding and the varying levels of support among presidents and senior administrators on the chancellor's staff. The statewide Academic Senate did not play a significant role in technology in part due to the pace of other events. There was an uneasiness about technology and the senate did become constructively involved with the Commission on Instructional Technology (CIT). The CIT report in 1990 was strongly supportive of the uses of information technology in undergraduate and graduate programs and urged a variety of student and faculty targeted recommendations. The report included an analysis of additional instructional computing needs at an elementary level of about fifty-five million dollars per year. The absence of "comprehensive technology infrastructure and a coherent management approach to achieve and operate it" was emphasized. The report included a set of recommendations. Without change and with executive council support, the trustees adopted the recommendations at their March 1990 meeting. This policy framework was comprehensive.

- Infuse technology when deemed academically appropriate by the faculty into the curriculum of all CSU academic disciplines on all CSU campuses to enforce the teaching/learning process on and off campus.
- Strengthen the CSU faculty, as knowledge professionals, by providing them: (1) basic technology tools; (2) ongoing technology training; (3) access to essential knowledge bases on and off campus; and (4) adequate personnel support services and operating expenses.
- Engage all CSU students, as learners, by providing them access to the essential technology tools and knowledge bases that will improve their educational experience and enhance their involvement in their education.

- Provide an integrated technology infrastructure on each campus and across the CSU system and state which will link all CSU students and faculty to the knowledge bases and technology tools needed in the teaching/learning process, regardless of where they might be physically located.
- Support and encourage individual campus initiatives to utilize telecommunications technology to extend the educational and student services of the CSU to distance learners.
- Provide the system-wide and campus management structure, policies, and procedures to ensure effective planning, development, deployment, and utilization of the technology infrastructure resources and support services of the CSU.
- Utilize technological capabilities to serve more effectively the State of California through academic programs, especially those for which the CSU has a special role in providing instruction in technical and professional fields.
- Encourage and support research to evaluate the impact of technology on the programs and mission of the CSU, especially teaching/learning, and to identify future needs.[15]

This remained the CSU policy about information technology planning until 1996. The trustees' policy provided substantial moving room for campus faculty and administrators, including presidents, to develop technology in its many uses, if they could fund it.

In the 1980s, funding for technology had been difficult with the state government. A major project, Administrative Information Management Systems (AIMS), had been developed using outside consultants and campus faculty and staff. The purpose of AIMS was to initiate coordination of work and procedures among campuses and with the chancellor's office. The state denied funding for it in several iterations. This was the situation for many of the proposed initiatives of the CSU with respect to technology. State government in California has had a long-standing suspicion of technology, not only in higher education but also across the board. In fact, state government technology projects that have gone bad, some with the expenditure of hundreds of millions of dollars, are not found in higher education.

The year 1990–91 was a transitional year. The new chancellor, Barry Munitz, arrived in the late spring of 1991. One of his first appointees, after consulting with faculty and others, was Molly Broad, then the executive director of the Arizona Higher Education Board, essentially the head of higher education in Arizona. She was recruited to replace Dale Hanner, who was completing twenty-three years as vice-chancellor for business affairs. He had stayed through the transition of chancellors to be helpful, but wished to retire. At the same time, Executive Vice-Chancellor Herbert Carter was offered the post of president for United Way of the Los Angeles region, and he accepted. Molly Broad was appointed by the trustees to the position of executive vice-chancellor. She and Munitz became a two-person team, Munitz as CEO, and Broad as COO.

An early outcome from the trustee action of 1990 was the establishment of a Commission on Learning Resources and Instructional Technology (CLRIT) to address further implementation of the AIMS work and to bring the work of the CSU Library Advisory Committee together with other academic technology initiatives. A sign of things to come was the appointment of two presidents (as chair and vice-chair) of CLRIT. Munitz initiated the practice of a retreat at the end of each academic year for the presidents, vice-chancellors, and a very small number of immediate staff. At the close of the second retreat in June 1993 in the Napa Valley, Vice-Chancellor Broad asked a small number of presidents, five or six, to remain for a conversation about technology. She and Munitz had initiated earlier the practice of bringing outside people who had something to contribute to meet with various administrative groups. Information technology was one of the subjects that had received attention. The Broad meeting was informal and focused. She reviewed the state of technology in the CSU, invited others to add to her comments (and they did), and then made it clear that she and Munitz thought it was time for presidential leadership to focus on information technology. The conversation concluded with a suggestion, perhaps a request, that this same group of presidents meet again to plan an approach that would bring all of the presidents into a leadership role in the CSU. The group of presidents met again.

The president of the Sacramento campus was asked to host a meeting of all the presidents, the chancellor, and the executive vice-chancellor. That meeting occurred on December 1, 1993, in a large conference room in Sacramento State's computing and telecommunications facility. The meeting was a closed-door event. The chancellor did not attend. The executive vice-chancellor, the presidents, Tom West (whose role was soon retitled to assistant vice-chancellor for information resources and technology), and one invited consultant were the participants. Spencer Freund, the associate vice president for technology at Sacramento State, was asked to listen and contribute ideas to benefit the students and faculty and the success of the process. The thrust of the meeting was that the time for serious presidential leadership had come. Vice-Chancellor Broad played a leading role. The result of the meeting was the creation of four task forces composed only of presidents. These addressed intracampus infrastructure, intercampus networking, administrative applications and funding alternatives, and priorities for implementation. The majority of the presidents, those with technical competence and those without, were energized. The task forces went to work and were productive.

Broad initiated a series of dinners at her Long Beach home. She selectively invited a number of presidents at most executive council meetings to join for a discussion about technology. The council met at that time about eight times each year—always prior to each trustee meeting, and these were bimonthly. The presidents were, for the most part, those who had met at the Napa meeting in the summer of 1993.

An Academic Communications Network Committee had been created within the Academic Information Resources Council chaired by Fred Dorer, the academic vice president at Bakersfield, not long after the December 1991 publication of "The Plan for Telecommunications in the CSU; 1992–1995." The network group published a report in January 1994, immediately after the presidents' meeting at Sacramento State; the chair of the subgroup that put the report together was

Raymond Clark, a longtime chancellor's office senior IT staff member. Clark was not an academic; his higher education work had been in history. He joined the chancellor's staff in 1968 and grew up with technology in the CSU. The network subgroup included individuals with substantial competencies from the CSU campuses. The report laid out a plan and presented recommendations for action.[16] This was followed shortly by a proposal from the system's Council of Library Directors, "CSU Libraries for the 21st Century: A Strategic Plan for the CSU."[17] These two reports were a foundation for the next steps.

The presidents' four committees reported simultaneously to the executive council in August of 1994. The result was a clear definition of presidential leadership for technology. To complement the work of the Commission on Learning Resources and Instructional Technology created in 1991, two new commissions were established by the chancellor. The Commission on Institutional Management and Institutional Technology (CIMIT) would serve as an administrative counterpart to CLRIT. The work of CIMIT was to address increasing levels of institutional productivity and accountability. The Commission on Telecommunications Infrastructure (CTI) was to oversee the construction of an electronic highway to support both academic and administrative activities, in essence to provide the necessary infrastructure to make possible the activities and programs of the other two commissions. The two new commissions would follow the CLRIT model and the chairs and vice-chairs would be presidents. The membership of all three commissions was created to be broadly representative of the campuses and the internal constituencies of the CSU.

A build-up process had begun in 1991, first with CLRIT, then presidential discussions, and then the December 1993 meeting and the following activities of the presidential working groups. Barry Munitz had addressed the trustees at their regular meeting in January 1992 about the importance of engaging technology for the future of the CSU, its students, and its faculty. He returned to the board in November 1994 to announce the Integrated Technology Strategy (ITS), "a comprehensive planning framework and process of the California State University. It is meant to be system-wide in scope, encompassing all campuses. It is centered around a series of programmatic initiatives designed to improve student learning and the quality of the student experience generally, and to increase levels of personal and administrative productivity. The Integrated Technology Strategy is a means for leveraging resources through the use of information technology, and is a force for transforming the institution."[18]

At the same time, Munitz created the "Technology Steering Committee" (TSC) to provide leadership to all technology activities. The TSC included six presidents who were chairs and vice-chairs of the three commissions, the executive vice-chancellor, and two senior vice-chancellors (later on, the two executive vice-chancellors) and the assistant vice-chancellor for information resources and technology. Later another president was added. Not all commission members were necessarily experienced with technology, but they did understand the need for technology in the twentieth century. The TSC oversaw the work of the three commissions and quickly moved to a leadership position for all technology. The

TSC also provided a model, followed in subsequent years, to engage the presidents as a group in systemwide leadership. The TSC has been a successful vehicle for leadership and for bringing together most, not all, technological activities that support academic and administrative programs. The TSC still exists and is healthy to the time of this writing.[19]

As 1995 began, a consulting firm was chosen to begin the planning for ITS. Subsequently, David Ernst, an experienced and diplomatic professional, was appointed to the chancellor's staff as the ITS executive director. Ernst worked with the TSC. Over the next several months, a variety of campus and stakeholder meetings were held. These planning activities emphasized feedback, broad participation, and input. In the late months of 1995, the Technology Infrastructure Initiative (TII) emerged. This was a prioritized plan for implementing the ITS. Each campus was then invited to prepare and submit a Telecommunications Infrastructure Master Plan. In March 1996, the ITS was presented to the board of trustees; the trustees approved the plan and, at a subsequent meeting, formed an Ad Hoc Subcommittee on Technology Utilization.

As these events were underway, the chancellor's senior staff was addressing the financing of technology. The vice-chancellor for business affairs by this time was Richard West, the former UC associate vice president who had been Tom West's counterpart in the University of California in the 1980s. Richard West observed that the UC had concluded in the 1980s that the state, the Department of Finance, and the legislature were unwilling to support the development of technology beyond a token level. Repeated requests for funding for technology equipment were denied, as were requests for staffing technology. Campus staffs were most often "bootlegged" from other activities. Munitz and the other leaders of the CSU, including the presidents on the TSC, agreed that the state would not support the development of a sufficient technology capacity within the CSU. This was not a small amount of money; it was unlikely to be raised in the context of the then new CSU fundraising and development programs. Quiet exploration of alternative funding was underway.[20]

In the summer months of 1996, this conversation continued. A System-wide Internal Partnership (SIP) was created, with members from each campus and the chancellor's office. SIP was to have responsibility for implementation of the TII; essentially, this meant it was to find funding. In October 1996, a team was created with members from each campus, the chancellor's office, and faculty from the Academic Senate. At the same time, funding was made available to campuses so that engineering and other consultants could be engaged to develop preliminary plans. A new program was initiated, Baseline Access, Training and Support (BATS). The trustees requested a modest augmentation of eighteen million dollars to the general fund budget for this training, and this was eventually secured.

With the arrival of 1997, a program of briefing members and staff of the legislature and other officials in state government was initiated. The system position was straight forward. There was no expectation that the state would fund the approximate cost, three hundred million dollars, to implement a basic technology program in the CSU. Thus, the CSU would necessarily have to pursue some form of public/private partnership to secure adequate technological capability. In February 1997, the same team members and others conducted an extensive environmental scan and contacted nearly a hundred corporations about their interest and their capability to partner with the CSU in the implementation and operation of the TII. Subsequently, the SIP leadership invited fourteen potential corporate partners to Long Beach to discuss ITS-TII. Ten of the fourteen responded positively and came to Long Beach. Subsequently, six corporate teams submitted proposals; these were then narrowed to three.

While all of this activity was underway, Vice-Chancellor Molly Broad was appointed to the presidency of the University of North Carolina system. She departed in late June 1997. Vice-Chancellor Richard West took the leadership of the project. In early July, Chancellor Barry Munitz convened a telephone conference meeting of the presidents, announcing that he would be leaving at the end of the calendar year to assume the presidency of the Getty Trust. Richard West, Tom West, and Maynard Robinson, former vice president for administration at CSU Stanislaus, became the individuals to carry this project forward.

In the late summer, the SIP group received three finished proposals. These were from Ericsson, Oracle, MCI, and Hewlett-Packard; IBM and Pacific Bell; and CETI, the California Education Technology Initiative including GTE, Fujitsu Business Communication Systems, Hughes Communications, and Microsoft. A careful analytical process ensued; each campus president was asked to have the proposals reviewed by a group that included individuals competent in technology and in finance.

On September 15, 1997, the chancellor announced the selection of the California Education Technology Initiative (CETI) group. CETI (pronounced sety) was to enter the vocabularies of faculty, students, staffs, and administrators in the CSU, and not long after, it would be a major topic in Sacramento.[21]

The board of trustees held a scheduled meeting immediately after Chancellor Munitz's announcement of CETI. President James Rosser of the Los Angeles campus, a member of the TSC, was on the agenda to update the trustees about the ITS and TII. Rosser went into some detail about the state's lack of willingness to fund technology, and the state's budget situation in the 1990s. He reported to the board of trustees and executive council that the consensus of October 1996 was not to seek funding for the technology infrastructure through capital outlay. He reminded the board that the executive council had estimated in 1996 a capital outlay gap of $200 million, and a funding gap of $70 million to $120 million annually. He described briefly the next steps, the creation of a System-wide Internal Partnership (SIP) of all twenty-two campuses and the chancellor's office to pursue a public/private partnership, and the intent of the presidents and the chancellor "to have a signed partnership agreement in December 1997."[22]

President John Welty of the Fresno campus then went into some detail about CETI, and the CETI team was introduced to the board of trustees. The elements of the CETI project included the creation of a for-profit limited liability corporation with five partners, a CSU nonprofit auxiliary corporation, and an advisory commission internal to the CSU. The CSU would hold a majority position on the board of the for-profit corporation. CETI would implement the CSU ITS-technology component. The four business partners would fund approximately three hundred million dollars of capital outlay. The CETI partnership would generate revenue in order to be self-sustaining. These revenues would be used to support the technology initiative and build a reserve to expand and replace capital equipment. The four business corporations would gain access to a huge market, profits from the operation (the CSU would share in the profits), and access to the people of the CSU—students, who would graduate and become employees, faculty and staff, which would be available for consultation—and a marketplace position in a major university alliance; they would have exclusive rights to provide technology services to the CSU.

The CETI plan had supporters and opponents. It was vetted in the media time after time. Opponents included the California Faculty Association, which worked very hard to create a coalition; other unions; the California State Student Association (though some individual campus Associated Student organizations supported CETI); some faculty; corporate interests beyond the CETI partners; and the California State Employees Association, among others. The CETI proposal raised fundamental questions about relationships between the public and private sectors.

The CSU leadership, including the presidents, mounted a massive campaign after the September trustees' meeting. The CETI team, including the corporate representatives, visited all of the campuses, some multiple times. Meetings were held with every conceivable group, from vice presidents to library directors to the CFA and other unions, groups of deans and faculty, and student representatives. Two major concerns emerged. The first had to do with jobs: Would CSU employees be secure in the short and long term? Would growth over time, as enrollment increased, be accomplished with additional CSU employees, or with corporate employees? The second set of concerns had to do with the fundamental character of the academy: Would academic freedom and intellectual property rights be assured, and if so, how? Would faculty control of the curriculum be compromised? Underlying these concerns was an uneasiness shared by many about the unknown.

James Wood, the chair of the sociology department at San Diego State and an active CFA member, wrote a lengthy article for the *Chronicle of Higher Education*, raising legal, financial, and educational policy questions. His fundamental argument was that CETI "would commercialize higher education, allowing profit motives, rather than pedagogical ones, to drive university policies regarding curriculum and employment."[23] On the other side, Michele Buttelman, the opinion editor of the CSU Northridge student newspaper wrote for the *Daily Sundial* under the headline "Doomed to a second-rate future without CETI." She used a quote from Barry Munitz, now the former chancellor, "[N]o academic institution is going to be competitive if it is not on the cutting edge of technology." She argued that "if the state is not going to pay for it . . . what are the choices . . . does anybody have a better idea?"[24]

The lobbying in Sacramento for and against CETI was intense. A coalition of the CFA (the faculty union), the California State Employees Association, and some other CSU-related unions, were joined by the California State Student Association. In November of 1997, Karen Yelverton, the chief professional officer of the CSU office in Sacramento, wrote to every member of the legislature as well as to others, including legislative staff. She outlined the steps that led up to CETI, the need for technology in higher education, and then she made the case for CETI. "We need to prepare for the information age now, not later. We also need to be realistic about the availability of state resources for CSU and all of higher education given current budget restraints and growing needs. It is clear to us that we cannot, and probably should not, rely on the State to fund the total capital and operational costs of building and supporting the baseline infrastructure that is needed to achieve the ITS goals in a timely fashion. Therefore, the CSU is pursuing a new and creative public/private partnership to secure funding outside of traditional state resources."[25] She addressed the two major concerns that were being raised by opponents of CETI, (1) CSU staff losing positions, and (2) faculty control of curriculum, intellectual property rights, and academic freedom.

On January 6, 1998, the Assembly Higher Education Committee, the Assembly Appropriations Subcommittee #2 on Education Finance, and the Senate Budget and Fiscal Review Committee held a joint informational hearing. President James Rosser and Senior Vice-Chancellor Richard West presented the CETI proposal. Eighteen other individuals presented a variety of positions about CETI. Rosser and West, after outlining CETI, indicated that the trustees and the chancellor planned to take formal action to create the CETI partnership to the board meeting later in January. The speakers that followed were largely negative. The CFA presenter, Rolland Hauser, a distinguished scientist from the Chico campus, raised questions about both the process of forming CETI and the substance of the proposal. Hauser made it clear that CFA had wanted to be included in the development of CETI, from the beginning through to "signing" and implementation. Faculty and faculty senates were on both or all sides. Five campus faculty senates had opposed the CETI proposal formally (Fresno, Hayward, San Diego, San Jose, and Sonoma). Individual faculty were present and outspoken on both sides, for and against. The Academic Senate, represented by its chair, James Highsmith of the Fresno campus, did not take a substantive position, but urged the board not to take action in the final two months of the chancellorship of Barry Munitz, but defer the decision until the arrival of the incoming chancellor, Charles Reed, on March 1, 1998. While Reed's appointment was to begin March 1, 1998, he had become a presence soon after his selection in November of the previous year.

Student opinions, too, were varied. One campus Associated Students board, Los Angeles, took a formal position in support of CETI. "The proposed CETI partnership grants students access to an infrastructure that will provide them with high speed and reliable network access to invaluable educational resources worldwide." The statewide organization of student presidents expressed concern about private corporations influencing the mission of CSU campuses, and all of the student groups opposed any technology related fees.

Business interests were represented at the hearings and were active in the attendant lobbying. The issue essentially was privatization and a perceived "lock" that the four corporations in the CETI proposal might secure for present and future services and equipment acquisitions. At stake, critics said, were competition and the potential for long-term profit by the four corporations. The selection process had been open, but business interests not selected had found allies.

The hearing was inconclusive. Richard West stated that the board would delay a decision until March and the arrival of Charles Reed.[26] The trustees had appointed Reed to the chancellorship at their November 1997 meeting, and he had almost immediately become involved with CSU matters. He had spent a portion of the December recess over the holidays in Los Angeles at meetings he had scheduled. Reed had become convinced early on, as he read reports from various units in the chancellor's office, about the state of the CSU, and that the system was some years behind in technology. He had not been able to get the information he wanted on any number of topics—finances, audits, human resources, students and progression to graduation. "I was kind of taken aback that the CSU was a decade behind with it's technology; I asked for a whole lot of information when I prepared to come, but, you know, I found out that there was no human resource system. There was not a comprehensive financial information system; there were pieces. I got the very first audit, a financial audit of the system, and it probably had a hundred and seventy-five footnotes in that audit. You couldn't audit this place the way it was."[27]

In January, on one of his many commutes from Florida to Los Angeles, Reed spent Super Bowl Sunday in a meeting at the Long Beach Hilton on the subject of technology, and much of the discussion focused on CETI. The four business partners were already reduced to three. Microsoft was in the midst of critical audits and charges and countercharges about its relations with the federal and some state governments; a minor partner, it dropped away. Reed was not impressed with the presentation and raised many questions. He particularly questioned the willingness of the business partners to invest the funds needed to bring the CSU infrastructure to the level required to implement the ITS, as he did not see what certainty they would have about recouping their investments. He had a high-level contact in Fujitsu, through a vice-chancellor in his Florida administration, and he arranged for a meeting with the leadership of Fujitsu at a golf tournament. At that meeting, he found that the multimillion dollar investment was not firm. Reed came away from that meeting knowing that he must rework the CETI project.[28]

CETI was in the public media domain, and it was a major topic of discussion at all levels of the CSU in the months after the January legislative hearing. Reed took office as chancellor on March 1, 1998. At the March board meeting, for which advocates and opponents of CETI were much in evidence, Reed told the trustees that two of the four partners, Hughes and Microsoft, were out of the picture, and indicated that it would be necessary to renegotiate CETI. Reed said that, in his judgment, there was "a fifty-fifty chance that CETI would be implemented." The situation was a sensitive one. Some of the most active members of the board of trustees had become convinced that CETI was a practical and useful solution to a major need of the CSU—instructional and academic information systems and administrative management systems that would work and inform policy decision making.

In mid-April, Reed issued a statement that he had not changed his mind about the fifty-fifty prospects for the negotiations. He confirmed that negotiations were continuing with GTE and Fujitsu. "Let me also reiterate, there is little doubt in my mind that the state is unable to provide the three hundred million dollars needed to build this technology infrastructure." He was supportive of CETI, but at the same time he made it clear that it must be financially sound and produce the needed technology capacity.[29]

In mid-June, Chancellor Reed and GTE Government System President Thomas Muldoon issued separate statements that negotiations over CETI had ended. Both expressed regret that the negotiations had not been successful. Muldoon observed that "we have been unable to arrive at a financial plan that is both responsive to the CSU and responsive to our shareholders. . . ." Reed expressed regret and went on to say, "The CSU will now review all of its options. No university can maintain its academic quality and remain competitive if it is not on the cutting edge of technology. The CSU will spend the next several weeks assessing new funding sources."[30]

The events of the first six months of 1998 and Reed's own recollections, along with those of Executive Vice-Chancellor David Spence, make clear that Reed was carefully laying the groundwork from January on to move on from CETI, if necessary, and achieve the implementation of the ITS and more.

The issue returned to the agenda of the executive council. The CETI process had enlivened the interest of the presidents and many others—certainly including trustees, students, faculty, and staff—in the importance of and the extent to which the CSU must invest in technology. CETI had fallen apart due to a number of factors: union opposition, an inability to bring together the financial bottom lines of both the business partners and the CSU, and opposition from vendors that were not in the mix.

The executive council was ready to take on the issue. Unlike in the autumn of 1996, when the presidents had rejected the idea of using capital outlay funds for technology acquisition, the presidents now almost unanimously agreed that using a major portion of the annual capital outlay budget made sense. A bond issue for capital outlay and higher education had passed in the 1998 election. Almost to a person, the presidents had been personally involved with CETI. They were ready for a next step, and they wanted to achieve the ITS and TII. Moving to use a major portion of capital outlay money was not painless: virtually every president lost a project immediately and the impact continued. The decision was made by the chancellor to fund technology from capital outlay. What had not been possible in 1996 had now been made possible by CETI—and a strong and assertive chancellor.

While all of the CETI and related activity was underway, there was a movement undertaken to bring together management systems. Historically, management systems of all kinds had been, for the most part, unique to campuses and, sometimes, to units within campuses. For systemwide integration of reports and systemwide operations, the chancellor's office would have to accomplish integration. Translation would be necessary, and similarly translation to campuses from the system office would be necessary. This was a long-standing issue; earlier in this chapter, it was noted that the resistance of the campuses and presidents to any uniform technology had been very strong in the 1970s. In the mid-1990s, campus and system staffs had begun cooperative efforts to bring some management systems together. Reed picked up on this, and "Collaborative Management Systems" emerged as a theme.

From it, the concept of "Common Management Systems" emerged. This was a systemwide massive effort, focusing on management, not the academic side of the house, to create systems in financial administration, personnel administration, student services administration, and all related areas. Once again, campus chief information officers, vice presidents, and others were mobilized. In many ways the development of CMS, a segment of the ITS, was more sensitive than the overall ITS and the following initiative had been. Systems had to be developed that reached far down into the ranks of campus staffs.

The advent of CMS reignited the conflict in Sacramento about CSU technology, and this would remain alive for several years. Repeated efforts were made, often by the 1998 opponents—especially the California Faculty Association—to halt CMS. The issue was money that the CFA proposed go to salaries. An underlying issue was organizational maintenance for the union. CFA had been successful in demonizing administrative leadership, especially the chancellor, for a time. Hearings which reasonably could be called brutal were held. The chancellor and vice-chancellor West were the ones castigated. Some legislative members became aggressively hostile to CMS.

The CMS project went ahead. The turmoil about it made implementation more difficult than it might otherwise have been. CMS called for a great measure of change, not just at the top of the CSU structure, but at all levels. The amount of change varied among campuses and within campuses, but it was sizeable everywhere.

In 1999, Tom West, by then assistant vice-chancellor for information technology, moved to the presidency of the Corporation for Education Networking Initiatives in California. This new entity, CENIC, was to leverage network resources among the various segments of education to build a high-band network within reasonable costs. David Ernst, who came to the CSU in 1995 as executive director of the integrated technology strategy, became the new assistant vice-chancellor for information technology and would remain in that position until 2008.

The role of student services received significant attention in the CSU in the late 1990s, and the attention level continued to increase. No previous chancellor had paid attention to student services beyond admissions and student financial aid; the assumption had been that student services were in the hands of competent professionals and that all was well. Then, the trustees began to ask about retention and graduation rates, the numbers of units students would take toward degree, and the time to degree: Did transfer students receive timely evaluations? Did candidates for graduation receive graduation evaluations? Did they received these evaluations in a timely way, so they were useful and allowed graduates to plan for themselves?

Was individualized financial aid information available to students? Technology became central to student services.

CMS, as it developed, was not the heart of the ITS. It was a means to an end, and the end was students and their progress, and programs of learning and research. In a sense, the library projects are illustrative of the heart or the core of the Integrated Technology Strategy. The library and other projects have quietly been productive for students and faculty as have the always costly campus programs to provide access for students and faculty to the world of knowledge, and the capacity for linkage among student scholars and faculty scholars across universities and even countries. Distance learning and online Web-based education undertaken by a number of the campuses has become a growing activity.

By the midpoint of the decade, two campuses were still resisting some CMS and other technological implementation. CMS implementation had been hard for campuses that had invested large sums in systems different than those selected. The TSC and, ultimately, the executive council and the chancellor had made decisions along the way about particular systems, operations, and providers. The system ultimately selected PeopleSoft as the major provider for CMS. The presidents in the TSC and the groups of faculty and others chaired by these presidents were the major figures in these activities.

In February 2002, the presidents decided to have another retreat on information technology. Once again, the president of the Sacramento campus invited all of the presidents. President James Rosser of Los Angeles opened the day with a wide-ranging summary of the CSU's evolution in the uses of technology. He began with the challenge that Chancellor Barry Munitz had given in a January 1993 report to the board of trustees, "[T]o do things differently." Rosser characterized this as a challenge to move "away from a culture of every campus on its own to one of capitalizing on the size and strength of the system."[31]

The presidents went on to assess the state of information technology in the CSU and its future. Technology was playing a major role in the implementation of Cornerstones. One of the early products of Cornerstones was the system of annual accountability reports to the trustees and the world, which was only possible with some of the early implementation of ITS initiatives.

In March 2006, the trustees did a major review of technology. The evaluation of the ITS focused on infrastructure development, academic technology, and administrative systems. Beginning in 1999, the CSU had made formal reports to the legislature and these were, and are, widely available. Essentially, the status report made clear that ITS had been a success, and that with strong faculty support, student usage, and a well-recruited staff and strong continuing leadership, ITS would serve well the people of the CSU.

"Technology has mirrored the organizational growth of the CSU."[32] The Early Assessment Program, initiated in 2004, would have been practically impossible without technology, and this assertion can be repeated many times over, about other matters and programs. The infrastructure, for the most part, is in place and at a level of some maturity. Assuming a continuing adequacy and cutting-edge character of the infrastructure, what are the upcoming challenges? These lie largely in the area of interinstitutional collaboration, within the CSU and beyond, and in a new conceptualization of distance education and teaching/learning across geographic distances. But the challenges also lie with the uses technology can afford in addressing the quality of education in urban and isolated schools; essentially all schools.

The nineties and first years of the new century also brought home a lesson to the CSU about the uses of presidential leadership. The models developed around technology, the TSC, the closed retreat, and about presidential collaboration with others, are not lost, and have been emulated in a few other circumstances. In the instance of information technology, one factor that helped to drive the utility of the model was the amount of money involved, and a second factor was the purposeful behavior of the participants. No one did not want to be there.

Technology has grown with and parallel to the CSU. That will continue, and much depends on strong and innovative leadership.

List of Acronyms
AIMS   Administrative Information Management System
BATS   Baseline Access Training and Support
CENIC Corporation for Education Networking Initiative in California
CETI   California Education Technology Initiative
CIMIT Commission on Institutional Management and Institutional Technology
CIRP   Campus Information Resource Plans
CIT   Commission on Instructional Technology
CMS   Common Management Systems
CLRIT Commission on Learning Resources and Instructional Technology
COLD   Council of Library Directors
CTI   Commission on Telecommunication Infrastructure
EDP   Electronic Data Processing
DIS   Division of Information Systems
ITFS   Instructional Television Fixed Service
IT   Instructional Technology
ITS   Integrated Technology Strategy
SIP   Systemwide Internal Partnership
TII   Technology Infrastructure Initiative
TSC   Technology Steering Committee

Notes
[1] Minutes, board of trustees, December 1963.
[2] The author's papers.
[3] A. Alan Post, interview by the author, February 28, 2006.
[4] State of California Legislative Analyst, "Computing in the California State Colleges," March 1968; Raymond Clark, interview by the author, January 18, 2006.

[5] Patricia Cuocco, "Integrated Technology Strategy—Technology Infrastructure Initiative Background," Appendix A, unpublished manuscript, Office of the Chancellor, "Matrix of Major CSU Technology Initiatives," 1998.

[6] In August 1976, I moved to the presidency of the Dominguez Hills campus and was a direct participant in the events at the system level that are chronicled in this chapter.

[7] Office of the Chancellor, "Planning for Electronic Data Processing in the CSUC," 1975; Patricia Cuocco and Stephen Daigle, "Information Technology Matrix of Major CSU Technology Initiatives," Chancellor's office document, January 11, 2005.

[8] The California State University and Colleges, "Planning for Electronic Data Processing in the CSUC," spring 1977.

[9] Clark, interview, 6–7.

[10] Royd Weintraub, memorandum to Ralph Mills and David Leveille, April 10, 1980; Marcia Salner, "Continuing Education in the California State University—A History," Long Beach, California State University, 1988,128–29.

[11] Focus group on technology, January 19, 2006, 6.

[12] Cuocco, "Integrated Technology Strategy," 36.

[13] Cuocco, "Integrated Technology Strategy," 37. (The formal title of the report is *The CSU Information Resources Plan: 1983–88*.)

[14] Cuocco, "Information Technology Matrix."

[15] Commission on Instructional Technology, "The Student, the Faculty, and the Information Age: The Power of Technology," The California State University, January 1990; minutes, board of trustees, March 1990.

[16] The California State University, "Leveraging the Future: The Telecommunications Plan for the CSU," January 1994.

[17] The California State University, "CSU Libraries for the 21st Century: A Strategic Plan for the CSU," January 1994.

[18] The California State University, "Integrated Technology Strategy, Planning and Implementation Process," 1997.

[19] I was a nonchair member of the technology steering committee, for several years, until my retirement in 2003.

[20] Focus group on technology, 13.

[21] I am indebted to Dorena Knepper, a longtime director of governmental relations, and now *emerita*, at California State University, Northridge, for making available a large file on CETI; the file is in the CSU Archives. Details of many actions from the Chancellor's office are in an email dated November 5, 1997, from Karen Young of the Information Resources and Technology office.

[22] Minutes, board of trustees, September 17, 1997.

[23] James L. Wood, "In California, A Dangerous Deal with Technology Companies" (*The Chronicle of Higher Education*), February 20, 1998.

[24] Michele Buthelman, "Doomed to a second-rate future without CETI," (*Daily Sundial*, California State University, Northridge), February 4, 1998.

[25] Karen L. Yelverton, letter to Senator Tim Leslie, November 6, 1997, CSU Archives.

[26] Dorena Knepper, notes and papers from the hearing, Assembly Appropriations Subcommittee #2, Educational Finance, and Senate Budget and Fiscal Review Committee, January 6, 1998.

[27] Charles Reed, interview by the author, December 20, 2006, 4, 5, 18.

[28] *Ibid.*

[29] The California State University Media Advisory, "CETI Update," April 16, 1968.

[30] *The Chronicle of Higher Education*, "California State University Ends Disputed Technology Partnership Negotiations," June 29, 1998.

[31] James M. Rosser, opening remarks, CSU information technology retreat, February 19, 2002, transcript, CSU Archives.

[32] I would be happy to claim the authorship of this phrase, but it belongs to Executive Vice Chancellor and Chief Financial Officer Richard West, in the January 19, 2006 focus group on technology.

Part Three
The People of the California State University

Chapter 9

Who Attends the California State University—Students and Alumni

The student experience at the California State University is timeless. What the CSU has to offer a student does not change based upon the date on the calendar. It does not change based on having world-class athletics, premier facilities, or global recognition. These things are important, but they are a by-product of something else. These things come about when there is a strong emphasis on the student experience. This experience is about any student coming to a campus of the CSU and being able to become whoever they want, engage however they want, and learn whatever they want—regardless [of] their race, creed, or economic background. The CSU has done a remarkable job ensuring [the] protection of this experience. Ensuring its future means that the other elements of an outstanding university, world-class athletics, premier facilities, and global recognition will naturally come about because they are a result of a focus on the core responsibility of the CSU: to provide access to quality education. . . . The CSU experience is basic and fundamental. It's about students coming in as one person and leaving as another person. It's about what happens between those two events . . . , the core of the student experience.

Shaun Lumachi and David Sommers[1]

The author is grateful to Dr. Charles Lindahl, Emeritus Associate Vice-Chancellor for Academic Affairs, who critiqued this chapter, especially the material on admissions. Lindahl's service of more than thirty years with the California State University and his leadership roles, including interim senior vice-chancellor for academic affairs for three years, give him a sweeping perspective about academic policy issues.

Who are the students of the California State University? Why should the CSU be labeled "the people's university?" History tells that the majority of the students of the CSU, up to and perhaps through the 1930s, were individuals from families of modest means. They either wanted to be teachers or wanted further education and the only option available to them was a normal school or a state teachers college. In a 1970 conversation I had with a prominent northern California lawyer, he told his story: a high school graduate from a small town, he attended Chico State Teachers College, where he was one of the first graduates with a degree in the mid-1920s, so that he could apply for law school at the UC Berkeley campus, which led him to forty years of a highly successful practice and civic leadership in the state.

The 1935 change from state teachers colleges to state colleges was a modest beginning of a change in the student population. The newly named state colleges enrolled students with various career goals until the years immediately following World War II, which brought not only the beginning of the great expansion of the number of students in the state colleges, but students in virtually every undergraduate major. To the extent that enrollment defines the character of an institution, students redefined the state colleges from those postwar years up to the Master Plan of 1960.

Prior to 1935, the overwhelming percentage of students had been women. This is not surprising, given the fact that the sole mission of the normal schools/state teachers colleges had been the education of teachers. A modest increase in the number of men enrolled began in 1935, and went up to the start of World War II. After the war, and the entry of many veterans to the campuses, there was both an explosion of total enrollment—from 5,034 in 1944–45 to 30,502 in 1949–50—and in the enrollment of men.

The changes underway in the state colleges were not always understood in the public arena, or even in other sectors of education. In 1959, a new director of admissions at San Francisco State visited high schools in the San Francisco service area. In one high school he had scheduled meetings with several groups of students. After meeting the second group of juniors and seniors, he commented to the high school counselor that he was surprised that there were only young women in the two groups. The counselor's response was that since San Francisco State was a teachers college, and really only for elementary school teachers, she had only invited girls to the admission meetings. The admissions officer shortly instituted a quiet and hopefully subtle program to address this matter in high schools.[2] Records about student gender prior to 1960 have not been preserved. In 1960 enrollment of men was exactly 60 percent, and the other 40 percent of the students were women. The ratio has changed over the years, slowly and steadily. In 2005, women made up 59 percent (166,873 men, 237,121 women, for a total of 403,994). The change is not unique to the California State University, but is reflective of a national trend.[3]

In the 1960s, the level of student unrest related to the Vietnam War, the draft, race relations and issues of ethnic studies and curriculum, and the cold war generally, varied among the campuses. The most extensive and prolonged student activism of the 1960s was on the San Francisco campus. San Francisco State's turmoil, which began in 1963 with issues essentially about the new California State College structure and was almost exclusively faculty and administration driven, was ripe for serious student activism on virtually any topic. At the other extreme was the Cal Poly campus at San Luis Obispo. Both student and faculty cultures there had been affected by the leadership discipline of its long-serving president, Julian McPhee; indeed one could argue that the ethic of McPhee affects that campus to this day. The San Luis Obispo campus had effective and skilled leadership through this period, and student activism was very modest. The other campuses fell someplace in between.

Campus by campus, the extent of the impact was dependent on presidential and faculty leadership, student leadership, community involvement, and factors unique to each campus. The significant question is the impact of this period on student life and student culture, and the resulting impacts on the educational programs and cultures of the campuses. For the most part, faculty leaders and administrators went out of their way to be accommodating to what they perceived to be student desires. This was particularly the case with the regulation of student behavior and the provision of structure in the curriculum, particularly general education. To the extent that parietal rules had survived to this point on state college campuses, they simply disappeared. The regulation of most aspects of student life diminished greatly. One of the most significant impacts was on curriculum. The interests and desires of many students and faculty coincided in the scaling back of structured curriculum, particularly in general education.

It is arguable that the activism of this period set in motion in the California State Colleges an irreversible change in the place of students and the importance of considering their interests in the life of the campuses, and, ultimately, their place in the entire California State University. The unrest of the 1960s and early 1970s foreshadowed a new climate in student life on the campuses. In some measure this was associated with generational change. The "greatest generation" of the late 1940s and early 1950s, was followed by the "silent generation" of the later 1950s, and then the "baby boomer generation" of the 1960s. It was this generation that set in motion a change in campus climate. There were few things so sacrosanct that students could not question them. Campus administrations and student affairs staffs—and faculty senates—had to pay attention to student interests and be open to substantial give and take with students in order to maintain a healthy campus.

As the years went on, other movements affected campus cultures and inevitably student roles on the campuses. The feminist movement caused campuses to take seriously issues ranging from safety on campus to women's studies. Information technology has also had an extraordinary impact on student life. Technology in many instances has brought students together, working with partners or in groups, and, where students are capable of using technology, it has increased their independence from faculty. In the 1990s, students on some campuses became involved with issues about homosexuality and the gay community, within the context of then President Clinton's "don't ask, don't tell" policy, which did not work, and the impact of this issue on the ROTC. In fact, this began as a faculty issue for the most part, but, as is often the case, faculty issues cross over to some part, or sometimes all, of the student community.

In the 1980s and 1990s, the frequency of Friday classes diminished greatly. Many students became accustomed to long weekends. The CSU and some of the presidents joined the issue and built up the frequency of Friday classes. On one campus the Associated Students president led a sit-in in the campus president's office. It attracted little support, but was a measure of the times.

* * *

The state colleges first began to pay serious attention to the enrollment of minority students in the 1960s. Varying from one campus to another, the attention began in some instances in the early 1960s, and on other campuses stemming from student and faculty unrest in the mid-1960s or later. The chancellor's office initiated the Educational Opportunity Program (EOP) on the campuses in 1968. The admissions standards initiated in 1965 provided for a minimum of two percent of students whose grades and scores did not meet these standards to be admitted as exceptions. In 1968 another two percent was added, explicitly for EOP students. Campus actions in adopting EOP as a major component of institutional mission varied, from enthusiastic and aggressive, to something less than that. Much depended on campus leadership. In the early 1970s, the chancellor appointed the first system director of affirmative action, Herbert Carter. Carter's focus was on faculty and staff recruitment, but his work reinforced the importance of student affirmative action.[4] On three of the campuses, the increase in enrollment of nonwhite ethnicity groups was at the core of the growth and development of the institutions, Dominguez Hills, Los Angeles, and Hayward.

Minority enrollment gradually emerged as a major concern of public higher education in California, indeed, of all education segments. In 1974, the State Department of Education reported an increase of minority enrollment in the public schools, from 23 percent in 1967–68 to over 30 percent in 1973–74. The legislature asked the three segments of public higher education to submit "a plan that will provide for addressing and overcoming by 1980, ethnic, economic, and social under-representation in the make-up of the student bodies in institutions of public higher education as compared to the general ethnic, economic, and sexual representation of recent high school graduates."

What came to be known as "student affirmative action" was not a new matter to the California State University. In the early to mid-1960s, faculty and administrative voices were raised on some campuses about the underrepresentation of ethnic groups and economic classes in student bodies. The Great Society programs of President Lyndon Johnson brought Upward Bound and other federal programs to some campuses. The advent of EOP systemwide in 1968 focused on underrepresentation.

In 1977, the system created a thirteen-member Task Force on Student Affirmative Action including students, faculty, and administrators from campuses, two members from the chancellor's office, and representation from the State Department of Education and the California Postsecondary Education Commission. Chancellor Dumke, in his appointment letter, asked the task force members to "inventory and assess existing programs and system activities designed to address under-representation of historically under-represented groups," requesting proposals for new programs. Dumke noted the legislative resolution of 1974 which called for "overcoming by 1980 under-representation . . . in the makeup of student bodies."

The task force turned first attention to the recruitment and admission of students, and called for extensive outreach programs not only to schools, but also in communities. It emphasized the importance of financial aid, and a community's need to know that this could be available, to make college attendance a real possibility. "Traditional CSUC outreach activities have not been effective in reaching minorities in large numbers. . . . Such efforts have been too narrow in focus, and have been primarily oriented to the middle-class Anglo student."[5] On the subject of admissions, the task force asked campuses to prepare alternative admission criteria proposals emphasizing factors other than test scores—specifically, autobiographies, recommendations, and interviews.

The task force's report went well beyond admissions policies and recruitment procedures and addressed academic programs, faculty and staff awareness and development, and other factors. The impact of the report, which was supported by the chancellor and advocated at the campus level by most presidents was a systemwide cultural change. Student affirmative action was coming of age in the CSU.

The early 1980s saw a renewed and open emphasis on student affirmative action. The phrase became a part of the California State University vocabulary. Among the important legacies of Chancellor Ann Reynolds' tenure in this decade, two stand out in particular: student affirmative action and new freshman admissions standards requiring college preparatory curriculum. Great emphasis was placed on student affirmative action recruitment, minority enrollment figures were monitored closely, and a sense of campus accountability emerged to that end. Every campus had staff dealing with student affirmative action. As Chapter 10 notes, the emphasis on student and faculty/staff affirmative action grew side by side. Most campuses developed student affirmative action recruitment plans. Student affirmative action became a part of campus cultures, perhaps more so for students than for many faculty and staff; student newspapers reported numbers and successes. When it became known in the late 1970s that a department on one urban campus with a substantial nonwhite enrollment had not one nonwhite major, a modest storm developed.

The momentum of the 1980s carried into the 1990s. Affirmative action was an important part of the California State University culture. Inevitably, occasional resistance developed; a campus issue where there is not resistance is rare. A new gubernatorial appointee to the regents of the University of California and an alumnus of California State University, Sacramento, Ward Connerly soon took issue with affirmative action programs within the UC, and he initiated a campaign among the regents to curtail them. Connerly's position was that the culture needed to become race neutral and thus programs of any kind directed at ethnic groups or ethnicity should be ended. Connerly's proposals became enormously controversial among the regents and within the UC as a whole. The regents developed and adopted a policy that in effect was a precursor to Proposition 209, an initiative to ban all public sector activity directed toward specific ethnic groups. Connerly, along with others, moved the matter beyond the UC into the public arena.

The then president of the University of California, Jack Peltason, shared with chancellor Barry Munitz his concern for the regents' action. Peltason was hopeful that the Education Round Table would temper the impact of the regents' action. Munitz brought all of the presidents together at a special closed-door meeting in a Sacramento hotel. Only the general counsel of the California State University, Christine Helwick, and the executive vice-chancellor, Molly Broad, were present with Munitz and the campus presidents. The purpose of the meeting was to talk through approaches to be used on campuses to continue the recruitment of a diverse student body. Munitz made it absolutely clear that all campuses would follow a single strategy. A major discussion was scheduled for the May 1995 trustees' meeting. Charles Lindahl, newly named interim senior vice-chancellor for academic affairs, worked with Munitz in preparing for the trustees' meeting.

With a full trustee discussion, in which Delaine Eastin, the new state superintendent of public instruction, was an important and positive participant, the state university approach to student diversity became based on student economic and educational background. Student recruitment on the campuses became defined in this context. This meeting happened well before the emergence of Proposition 209 on the November 1996 ballot. The meeting was productive, and the social purpose of affirmative action was maintained in a redefined approach. It was the means that were changed, not the end; the redefined approach was realistic toward achieving a diverse student body.

The voters enacted Proposition 209 in November 1996. There was considerable campus student and faculty political activity leading up to the election. Only two presidents were publicly opposed to Prop. 209.[6] Munitz hoped to keep the California State University away from the political activity in order to ensure the success of the redefined approach to diversity. The impact of Prop. 209 on actual enrollment on California State University campuses was modest, if any. Subsequent to the election, Assembly Member Bernard Richter of Chico, who had authored Prop. 209, scheduled an Assembly Ad Hoc Committee hearing about state university political activity in the public debate leading up to Prop 209. He sought evidence of inappropriate political activity on the part of state university administrators. Munitz and the president of the Sacramento campus were called. The hearing did not produce any further activity. Subsequently, Munitz made clear to the presidents what one commentator called "a rule of expectation": "I know you will act in an informed way; you will do what you always do—act in the highest interests of students." He expressed his expectations.

Efforts to recruit a diverse student body, to reach out to eligible students from all sectors in the state continued, and indeed were strengthened. The best evidence of this is to be found in degrees awarded by the CSU campuses. Starting from the 1985–86 academic year to the 2005–06 academic year, baccalaureate degrees awarded to nonwhite students increased by nearly 210 percent in a steady climb. Growth in baccalaureate degree awards for underrepresented minorities varied among groups. The percentage of Latino students receiving degrees increased by more than 350 percent; Asian, Pacific Islander, and Filipino students (a grouping within which percentage increases are uneven) by approximately 160 percent; American Indian students by just over 100 percent; and African American students remained around the zero point, that is, no increase or decrease in percentages, with a slight decrease by 2005–06. These figures are to be understood in the context of California's growing and changing population. The numbers tell the story clearly. See Table 9.1.

The commitment of the California State University leadership (trustees, chancellors, faculty, student leaders, and presidents) to diversity in the student bodies on the campuses is strong. This has become embedded in the culture of the CSU.

* * *

Student financial aid programs in the California State University have grown substantially in the years since the Master Plan, as they have in all of higher education in the United States. In the years prior to the Master Plan, financial aid was modest. The campuses had scholarship programs, mostly based on merit or geared to a specific group. These scholarships were the result of individual gifts. Only the Cal Poly campus systematically sought these gifts. Individuals, families, community groups, and businesses would establish funds for scholarships. Some of the older campuses actually had reasonably substantial amounts of money, often unused, as the result of gifts earmarked for very specific categories of students. One campus administrator at the time of the Master Plan wrote about a mythical fund, unused for years, for the "daughters and sons of Scandinavian sea skippers." In 1965, the Chico campus secured a legal ruling permitting the aggregation of unused designated funds into a more general scholarship program. This was a different time in American higher education. Many deans of students or other student affairs staff had small amounts of private discretionary money they could give or loan to students to see them through a difficult situation.

The federal government entered the financial aid picture in 1957, the year of the Soviet launch of Sputnik. This would quickly have an impact and be a stimulus to the development of student financial aid programs. Initially, given the

Table 9.1. Undergraduate Degrees Granted in Selected Years

Ethnic Group	Number of Undergraduate Degrees Granted		
	1975–76	1985–86	2005–06
African American	1,764	1,569	3,317
American Indian	510	546	509
Asian American	1,862	3,775	8,701
Filipino	67	607	2,837
Mexican American	1,742	1,953	10,028
Other Latino	321	1,061	3,849
Pacific Islander	244	169	395
White	28,958	29,614	27,387
Unknown	8.054	3,607	9,482
Nonresident aliens	1,076	1,391	2,845
TOTAL	44,598	44,292	69,350

Note: Graduate degrees granted in 1999–2000 numbered 13,584; 10,359 graduates identified themselves by ethnicity, and of these, 3,764 were from underrepresented groups. In 2005–06, 18,330 graduate degrees were granted; 13,379 graduates identified themselves by ethnicity, and 6,049 were from underrepresented groups.

Office of the Chancellor, "The California State University Statistical Abstract to July 2006," CSU Long Beach, 2007, 248–51.

rigid State Department of Finance formulas for administrative positions, there were no individuals to administer the newly developing federal programs or the modest scholarships. In 1959, Glenn Dumke, then the president of San Francisco State, converted half of a faculty position to a position to administer scholarships and the new federal programs; this was a bold move for the time, almost a defiance of the Sacramento bureaucracy. Dumke made it clear that he wanted fundraising to begin. Staffing for financial aid operations soon became a priority of the newly established chancellor's office and was secured by the mid-1960s.

The cost of attending a California State College at the time of the Master Plan was principally forgone income, and for students of typical college age, the expense of living away from home or of living at home if they elected to do so. The fees were small—a leap from ten to fifteen dollars per semester occurred in 1959—and the publishing industry's price-setting practices for college textbooks were, on the whole, modest (see chapter twelve, which is on finance). The surge in professorial authorship and a publishing industry with a major focus on the higher education market were yet to come.

One of the by-products of the Master Plan was making California State Scholarship Commission awards accessible to students in private colleges and universities. This expanded the scope of Scholarship Commission activities and helped to pave the way for the California Student Aid Commission and the expansion of its substantial range of activities over the years.

18. Trustee Herbert Carter and Chancellor Reed at Super Sunday.

The system, essentially the chancellor's office, paid attention to student financial aid programs. In addition to supporting campus programs with adequate staff and consistent attention to policy, the CSU placed a priority, perhaps not consciously, on student financial aid. In the late 1960s, Sumner Gambee became the senior chancellor's office staff member responsible for student financial aid. In addition to giving strong and credible leadership to the programs on the campuses, Gambee became a nationally respected leader and spokesperson for higher education student financial aid programs. Gambee retired in 1987, and was replaced by Allison Jones, the director of financial aid programs at the Fullerton campus. Jones built from Gambee's work, providing leadership to the campuses and credible representation in Washington and, in the 1990s, he became assistant vice-chancellor for academic affairs responsible for all student support services. Jones is frequently called upon to testify in Congress, and is a member and vice-chair of the Federal Advisory Committee on Student Financial Assistance. In fact, student financial aid of all kinds is vital to the mission of the California State University, even more so with the steadily increasing student fees of the last two decades.

With a recession in the background, the early 1990s brought pressure for increased student fees. In 1994, Chancellor Barry Munitz brought to the trustees a proposal for a substantial increase in fees, which included the provision that one-third of all the new student fee income would be used exclusively to ensure continual access of low-income students. Munitz had secured support from the

California State Student Association and the Sacramento government establishment, and the proposal was adopted.

The importance of student financial aid programs to the students of the California State University is underscored by the numbers of students receiving aid. In 1983–84, approximately 18 percent of all undergraduates received some form of financial aid, including 21 percent of all entering freshmen; 7 percent of all graduate students received aid as well. In 2005–06, the figures were 53 percent of all undergraduates, 54 percent of all entering freshmen, and 41 percent of all graduate students. Almost 223,600 students (of a total enrollment of 432,816 students) received financial aid in 2005–06, a total dollar amount of $1,755,998,077.[7]

* * *

The CSU campuses have not lost their regionally based character, although some changes have occurred over the years. The urban-based campuses, with the exceptions of San Diego and San Francisco, draw the great number of their students from the cities and surrounding regions in which they are based. San Diego draws undergraduates from over the state based upon its location and the attractions of San Diego. San Francisco draws students, in part because of the city, and in part because of distinctive programs in several areas such as the creative arts, language arts and creative writing, and international relations. The more rural campuses, such as Chico, Sonoma, and Stanislaus, draw students seeking a more residential campus. San Luis Obispo historically attracts students to its areas of specialization, engineering and agriculture. Like San Luis Obispo, Fresno, Chico, and Pomona have agriculture programs.

Each campus has a distinctive culture, the result of history, programs, people, and, to an extent, location, and this culture affects the draw of the campus, the ability either to recruit students (and faculty) or to in some instances consistently attract more students than the campus can accommodate. Some students are also drawn by the campus's geographic location, its nearness to the ocean and its climate, or by the size of the student body. Campus cultures have changed over time. A major cause of this can be a change in the demographics, the socioeconomic characteristics of a regional population. Certainly the advent of a substantial diverse population in the state is a cause of change. In the years since the Master Plan, the increase in California's immigrant population has brought about an ever-increasing diversity in the student populations of all campuses, though the percentages vary widely, largely a function of geography.

Patterns of student choices of a particular campus are useful in understanding campuses. In the late 1970s, addressing the building of a new campus, an institutional research study was done at the Dominguez Hills campus. Student migration patterns were studied among five Los Angeles Basin CSU campuses. Taking into account the network of freeways in the Los Angeles Basin, the study revealed that students would drive by one or another campus in significant num-

19. Graduating and celebrating.

bers to enroll in a different CSU campus, and undertake a specific major. Even in a state as large and populated as California, the student and alumni network about programs and campuses is significant. Not surprisingly, students choose campuses at least in part using information gained from other students.

Educators experienced in addressing the quality of undergraduate education know that the environment and culture of a campus and the institution is a potent instrument that can be used to educate students. Each of the CSU campuses places great emphasis on the quality of undergraduate education and uses that environment and culture to build among graduates "the marks of an educated person." Residential campuses have an advantage using the campus culture, but the urban campus, with large numbers of commuting students can, and many do, address the environment and culture of the campus. I have worked at four CSU campuses over forty-five years, and each had a different culture. Three of these campuses are urban, San Francisco, Dominguez Hills, and Sacramento. The nonurban campus, Chico, is a residential campus.

Using the culture of a campus as an educational instrument is not a well-developed faculty or administrative skill. It is a part of educational programming to be developed. Students and their programs are clearly a major determinant of campus culture. A strong and educationally oriented campus culture can benefit students, although individual students themselves have to be willing to participate, for the culture to be a major educational factor.

The San Francisco campus has undergraduate programs in the creative arts and writing, the richness of a major city, and the strength of the first program in the United States to offer an undergraduate degree in international relations. Dominguez Hills is located in an extraordinary multicultural community and this has strengthened the capacity of the campus and its students and faculty to engage and learn from, and in, the greater community. Chico is a classic residential campus. To understand the residential character of a California State University campus, you need to answer the question, how many undergraduates move away from home to be at the campus (not only those living on or off campus in student housing)? The Chico campus, located in a city of 50,000, generally has used its residential character in a smaller community to its advantage for student recruitment. Sacramento is California's capital city. That fact does not suggest that only government majors should do undergraduate or graduate work at the Sacramento State campus. It does suggest the many opportunities for students in all fields to think about the public policy issues relevant to their interests and goals.

In the almost fifty years since the California Master Plan and the drawing together of the campuses with the board of trustees, an extraordinary complex of external variables and forces have reshaped the student experience. Student roles in developing curriculum have changed from virtually no role to substantial and very often practical ones. Student influence in this area amounts far more than the addition of ethnic studies and women's studies programs on campuses in the 1960s. The college or university experience is no longer one for only a narrow segment of society. Despite socioeconomic forces that remain strong and even fierce, higher education generally, and most certainly at the California State University, is reaching into every corner of society. In turn, one might observe that many, if not all, of the events of the greater society impact higher education. This has been true from the events of the 1960s and the war in Vietnam through the turmoil of presidential administrations (and gubernatorial administrations in California), and national and state legislatures, to the impact of changing economies and national and state budgets on student fees, student financial aid, and the level of support necessary to maintain student access to public higher education. Groups such as animal rights activists and both extreme right and extreme left activists bring themselves on the campuses.

In the 1990s, the issue of gender orientation was a significant one on some campuses. On the campus at Sacramento, the actions of a senior officer in the ROTC program forced the issue of gender orientation and homosexuality to the point that the president announced the termination of ROTC. This happened during President Clinton's first term, at the time of the failed "don't ask, don't tell" federal policy. The Sacramento State president had a sense of how issues like this were handled by the military. He had five years of active military duty and was familiar with the Uniform Code of Military Justice, and he had sat on a general court at the major military command level. During the George H. W. Bush presidency, he also had been a member of a small group (seven or eight individuals) of university and college presidents negotiating under the auspices of the American Council on Education with the office of the secretary of defense (then Dick Cheney) toward some reasonable solution.

After the November 1992 presidential election, negotiations ended, and "don't ask, don't tell" emerged. When the Sacramento president finally announced the termination of ROTC on the campus, a public furor broke out. A member of the legislature, purporting to represent many others, went to the chair of the board of trustees and demanded the dismissal of the president. The chair, Martha Fallgatter, informed the president of this and made clear that she would support the president, and told him he should do what he thought to be right. The congressional passage of a rider on the student financial aid appropriation bill later that year, removing all federal financial aid funds from any campus terminating ROTC, brought an end to the controversy. The Sacramento State president backed down; there was no choice. When the president retired seven years later, he was quietly told by some that this was the most serious crisis of his nineteen-year presidency, in terms of public support.

The U.S. invasion of Iraq in 2003 once again brought a national agenda on to campuses. Demonstrations, and in a few instances disruptions occurred. But there was almost an acceptance on many campuses that government was in some measure dysfunctional, accompanied by a resigned, "what can we do about it?" attitude. Life went on.

As this manuscript is being completed and reviewed, the most serious financial crisis since the depression of the 1930s has emerged. It too has an impact, not only on the ability of campuses to provide access and a good and useful education, but on the lives of the half million people of the California State University, students, staff, and faculty.

College and university campuses once lived in relative isolation from the main currents of society. The students of the California State University are clearly in the main currents of American and global society in the twenty-first century. The spirit of the California State University would have it no other way.

* * *

The campuses have built student recruitment strategies over the years. At the time of the Master Plan and in the formative years of the system, at least in theory, campuses were not only responsible for working with the high schools and community colleges within their service areas, but also limited to recruiting within those areas. The entire state was divided into service areas, with each campus having a defined responsibility. Unique among these, the Cal Poly at San Luis Obispo campus had not only a geographically contiguous service area, but a statewide responsibility because of its programs.

The limitations of service areas quickly dissolved in the first decade of the newly defined California State Colleges, with the advent of additional campuses. Regions remained important in the building of a student body and would continue to be important, but campuses with their individual character and programs attracted students statewide and beyond. For example, the Chico campus continues to have a strong identification with northeastern California and is that region's campus; but beginning in the 1960s, the growth on the Chico campus has been from the San Francisco Bay Area, and then from the state as a whole; it is a residential campus. Inevitably, economic factors, family and student income, play a role in building the student body, even with the advent of student financial aid. Similarly, the San Francisco campus acquired early, largely through the informal networks of student and alumni communication, a reputation as a campus more than usually hospitable to students from other countries; doubtless, the aura of San Francisco, the city and the campus, attracted potential student interest. By the early 1960s, some San Francisco State faculty members asserted that San Francisco State had played a significant role in the higher education of leaders in a number of the newly emerging states in Africa.

The campuses defined their own student recruitment strategies. The chancellor's office and the trustees gave leadership only in a general sense. The administrations of Chancellors Dumke and Reynolds gave increasing emphasis to building ethnically and economically diverse student populations. Programs that were initiated in the context of the Great Society strategies of the Lyndon Johnson administration, such as Upward Bound, were encouraged. There was a gradual buildup of expectations about campus-based recruitment of students. Reynolds added to the mix an emphasis on recruiting women into science and technology careers. Munitz found himself leading the effort to reposition student recruitment and admissions in the context of Proposition 209. Chancellor Reed, after his 1998 arrival, became dissatisfied with the recruitment of students and, particularly, the lack of black students. Reed initiated Super Sunday, a day when he, campus presidents, trustees, and others would speak in predominantly black churches in the major metropolitan areas of the state. He and others would speak to typically large congregations, while campus admissions staff would be present to meet with potential students and their families. Reed was addressing a dangerous imbalance among Californians enrolling (and completing) university education.

The selection of a student body is a direct expression of the purposes of a college or university. Colleges and universities typically pay great attention to the selection of faculty members. They do not always seek a match between those selected and the culture of the institution; but the selection of a student body is a different matter. Students select themselves, sometimes with serious attention to making a fit with an institution, but often more influenced by practical matters such as distance to or away from home and workplace. Institutions inevitably define a target population, consciously or unconsciously. They also help (or neglect to help) potential students to prepare themselves for college and university study.

The story of admitting freshmen to the California State Colleges begins with the normal schools. Initially, each of the several normal schools set its own admissions standards. These tended to focus more on character and personal references than on academic preparation or career goals. By the late nineteenth and early twentieth centuries, common standards were developed among the several campuses, but they were used as guidelines, rather than criteria, for selecting individual applicants. For all practical purposes, each normal school and, later, state teachers college selected its own student body. From an educational standpoint, the more important decision was the level of placement of new students in the normal school curriculum, and this was heavily dependent on the previous educational attainment of each newly admitted student.

In the early 1930s, the State Board of Education adopted admissions requirements for what were then the state teachers colleges. These included formal recommendations from high school principals and school performance. The requirements were not absolute, and campuses had discretion to choose applicants. In 1937, the state board eliminated common requirements, and each campus became responsible for its requirements and procedures. The Strayer report of 1948 identified the development of admissions standards as an important issue, noting that the regulations in effect at that time addressed "fitness to profit from college instruction, such fitness to be shown by previous scholastic records, by evidence of good moral character and personal qualifications and by a satisfactory score on a standard college aptitude test." The report recommended that "admissions requirements should be reviewed and revised."[8]

The campuses and presidents did address admissions and the State Board of Education adopted admissions standards in 1951. Freshmen were to be admitted when they completed ten semester courses with grades of A or B in the last three years of high school, or when they attained a score above the 20th percentile on a college entrance examination; at the time it was estimated that approximately 60 percent of high school graduates would meet these standards. The board also adopted standards for transfer students, a C average or a test score above the 20th percentile. The board gave substantial discretion to the campuses for admitting graduate students, specifying only that applicants have an "acceptable" baccalaureate degree and "other qualifications as determined by each college."

In 1954, in the context of the restudy, another review of admissions for freshmen was proposed and the Committee on State College Entrance Requirements was formed. In December 1954, the state board adopted new standards for freshmen. Applicants would be admitted when they had fourteen semester grades of A or B in the last three years of high school in subjects other than physical education and military science, or more than ten semester grades of A and B, as above, with a test score above the 20th percentile. This modification resulted in the shrinking of the pool of eligible high school graduates to approximately 45 percent. Both the 1951 and 1954 state board actions gave to the "appropriate campus authorities" the capacity to admit on probation students who did not meet the standards.

In the Master Plan deliberations, three factors were major in addressing admissions: finances and a desire to limit state college and UC enrollments by diverting students to the community colleges; the establishment of educationally sound admissions criteria; and the desire of the UC leadership to contain the growth of the state colleges. Some state college leaders, presidents, deans, and faculty worked to protect existing or desirable new programs or educational policy positions, and other state college leaders wanted to establish new educational standards. The Master Plan Survey Team established a Committee on Selection and Retention of Students. Its chair was Herman Spindt, the UC Berkeley and UC system director of admissions, a nationally known and respected figure in admissions near the end of his career. The state college member of the committee was Ralph Prator, the newly appointed founding president of San Fernando Valley State College, and a former director of admissions at the University of Colorado.

While the admissions committee deliberated, the survey team made the first decision, to divert at least fifty thousand students each year from the UC and state college campuses to the junior colleges, essentially a financial decision to shift the cost of lower division instruction for a significant number of students from the state to local junior college and school districts. The survey team asked a Department of Finance advisor about the mathematics of this policy. This is the origin of the top 12½ percent and top 33⅓ percent figures for UC and CSU admissions. This was a financial decision, not an educational decision.

In the Master Plan admissions discussions, Glenn Dumke, who had an interest in the topic, presented a paper about state college admissions.[9] He argued several points. He opposed arbitrary enrollment ceilings in programs; the argument was based on the fact that the state colleges were public institutions, and must admit students who meet minimal standards. He assumed that the top one-third concept was a reasonable one within which to set sound admissions standards. He acknowledged that it might be desirable to be selective among applicants, as private colleges and universities are, but rejected that as public policy. He also rejected limiting enrollment by selecting students in the order of application, on the grounds that some of the best students apply only shortly before the beginning of a term. To the point of this paper, he argued that graduate standards were reasonable, as these were standards for institutional admission, not admission to candidacy for a degree; and that the transfer standard of a C average for upper-division undergraduates was reasonable within the national context of that time. The main point of his argument had to do with the admission of students to programs in the sciences, nursing, and engineering. "There are compelling reasons, both of educational and financial policy, which would suggest that we begin to explore the matter of selective admission to particular programs on a statewide level." Dumke was opening the issue of college preparatory curriculum.

Dumke addressed the issue of freshman standards. He acknowledged that fourteen As and Bs in the last three years of high school can be adequate. But "we would probably all agree that an applicant who, in his high school career, has studied subjects less related to college work is less well prepared." He argued for a subject-matter pattern or "at least a general one requiring that the . . . units be in academic or 'solid' subjects." He acknowledged that an alternative could be a sound college entrance examination. Finally, he argued that "this problem *must* be solved" to get the state colleges out of remedial education and to address the not uncommon practice of the time of high school counselors advising students who planned to attend a state college to "stay away from 'solids' and to take 'easy' or 'snap' courses."

In the Committee on Selection and Retention of Students, Herman Spindt joined the Dumke argument and took it one step further, urging that the state colleges use the University of California's A–F pattern of high school curriculum for the primary route to admission. The A–F pattern included English, mathematics, foreign languages, social science, and the natural sciences. Dumke's position quickly became controversial within the state colleges. Some of the fiercest opposition came from his own campus, San Francisco State, where the teacher education faculty and the campus chief academic officer were in strong opposition. Ralph Prator, the state college member of the Committee on Selection and Retention, did not support a college preparatory curriculum for the state colleges.

The final Master Plan recommendation about state college freshman admission standards was simply that they be raised to the top one-third of all California public high school graduates, and that graduates of private and out-of-state secondary schools be held to the same levels. The survey team did note that it favored requiring that all or almost all of the recommending grades be in college preparatory courses, and that this be carefully studied in 1960, leading to implementation for students admitted for the fall of 1962. The Master Plan also recommended that transfer students ineligible for freshman admission complete a minimum of fifty-six transferable units before being considered for admission, that applicants who are legal residents of other states be held to a standard of the upper half of the top one-third, that serious attention be paid immediately in 1960 to transfer procedures, and that a continuing committee on selection, admission, and retention of students be created by the proposed Coordinating Council for Higher Education. Finally, the recommendations addressed the admission of students as exceptions to established standards and required that these be held to 2 percent of all freshmen admissions. With the exception of the recommendation that the UC campuses admit students from the top 12½ percent of high school graduates, the recommendations for freshmen and lower-division transfer admissions were identical for the state colleges and the UC.[10]

Implementation of the admissions standards was more complex for the state colleges than for the University of California. With the passage of the Master Plan, a first priority for state colleges was creating a new entity and an organizational structure. In the 1960–61 transition year, admissions was not addressed. When Chancellor Gallagher arrived in 1961, he did not identify implementing the Master Plan admission standard of the top 33 1/3 percent as a priority. When Glenn Dumke was appointed vice-chancellor in October 1961, he attempted to begin the necessary study and procedures, but Gallagher deferred action. The political turmoil about Gallagher's background became a higher priority. In August 1961, UC President Clark Kerr wrote to Gallagher about implementation. Kerr's letter was firm in reminding Gallagher that the Master Plan called for implementation of new standards for students being admitted for the 1962 fall term. The University of California would meet that schedule. Within the state colleges, there was little pressure or enthusiasm to implement the 33 1/3 percent goal. With a few notable exceptions, most of the presidents and other administrators and faculty leaders were focused instead on the new structure and on building enrollments.

Gallagher's sudden departure and the appointment of Glenn Dumke as chancellor in April 1962 brought a change to the state college approach to admissions standards. Dumke set in motion a serious conversation about implementation, including the studies and processes necessary to accomplish this. For the most part, to appease the University of California and to demonstrate good faith, minor modifications were made in admitting students for the fall of 1963. Dumke initiated a massive admissions study under the direction of a competently staffed institutional research function headed by a state college dean (a title used in the first decade and longer to denote a senior system administrator), Arthur Hall, a veteran mathematics professor from the San Francisco campus who had been in the comparable role there. In 1963, Dumke brought to his staff the director of admissions from San Francisco State, who had staffed him, along with Hall, in the Master Plan deliberations about admissions.[11]

Dumke remained convinced of the desirability of freshman admission standards based on a secondary school college preparatory curriculum. His immediate staff was split on this matter. An advisory group was appointed for the study, and members leaned toward not emphasizing a college preparatory curriculum. The report of the admissions study did not support the importance of a college preparatory curriculum. Dumke had little support on the campuses for this position; even the newer and more academically oriented presidents went along with tradition. The key variable was the assurance of enrollment. After widespread consultation on the campuses, Dumke recommended to the trustees the implementation of freshmen standards employing a mixture of the high school grade point average and a test score (the tests subsequently selected were the the College Entrance Examination Board's Scholastic Aptitude Test [SAT] and the American College Test [ACT], then a new arrival on the college and university scene). The standards became effective for the fall term of 1965.

These standards were used until the late 1970s. The Master Plan had called for the continuing review of all admissions standards within the context of the Coordinating Council for Higher Education (CCHE). In the late 1960s, the first eligibility study was done by the CCHE staff. Using the existing standards of the time, these studies assess the percentage of graduating high school students eligible for UC and CSU admission. The need for such studies was created by changing secondary school grading practices. Continued by the California Postsecondary Education Commission (CPEC), the studies are conventionally done every five years. The most recent study reported by CPEC, in 2008, showed that 13.4 percent of 2007 California public high school graduates were eligible for UC admission (against the 12½ percent standard), and 32.7 percent were eligible for CSU admission (against the 33⅓ percent standard). The comparable figures for the previous eligibility study in 2004, which reviewed the 2003 graduates, were 14.4 percent and 28.8 percent. Researchers reviewed 72,000 transcripts of the 350,700 graduates from the class of 2007. The CSU eligibility rates for blacks, whites, and Latinos all increased from 2004 to 2008, black students from 18.4 percent to 24 percent, Latinos from 16 percent to 22.5 percent, and white students from 34.3 percent to 37.1 percent.[12]

With the election of Ronald Reagan in 1966, budgets in the state colleges tightened. In March 1967, all admissions deans were called to the chancellor's office to discuss curtailment of admissions for the fall term of 1967. For the coming 1967–68 year, campuses in some instances would have to cope with an overflow of students, as admissions applications had already been processed prior to the March meeting. Campus responses varied. By the 1968–69 year, as admissions applications for the fall 1969 term were being processed, it became clear that some campuses would not be able to admit all eligible applicants. This quickly became publicly known. Lines appeared outside admissions offices on some campuses. On a few campuses, applicants brought sleeping bags to join lines formed the night before the opening of an admissions application period.

Admissions professionals from campuses and in the chancellor's office developed procedures for a university-wide common admissions program. Heretofore, each campus had designed its own application and procedures. Computers were coming into some administrative use. The chancellor's office brought in an administrator from UCLA, and he gave leadership to a new common admissions program. A single application form for all campuses was designed. All undergraduate applicants would send their applications to a central location where data could be entered and tracked. The applications were then sent to the appropriate campuses. If a campus could not accommodate all of the eligible applicants, applicants would be advised to apply to a campus where space was available. A common application period was defined, initially the month of November; eligible applicants were promised admission to a California State College campus, though not necessarily their first-choice campus. All applicants were asked to identify five campuses, in order of preference, on their forms. If the first choice campus was not available, the applicant would be diverted to the second choice campus. The "diversion" of applicants became a part of the state college admissions vocabulary. The common admissions program was ended by 1972; essentially, it fell of its own complexity and weight.

A new concept emerged, that of "impaction." An impacted campus or an impacted program was one in which all of the fully eligible applicants who apply during the systemwide defined application period cannot be accommodated. Campuses then had to develop additional criteria beyond the systemwide admissions standards, for the selection of applicants. Essentially, the criteria developed aimed to identify the potential students most likely to complete their academic programs successfully and in a timely period. Campus impaction criteria were subject to system review.

The campus that was the original focal point of the impaction problem was San Luis Obispo, and the campus has remained impacted over the years. Programs that have been impacted over the years on other campuses are principally in the health science areas, notably nursing. The issue came to the fore again in the late 1990s when the San Diego campus became substantially overcrowded. The campus developed impaction procedures and the central issue of accommodating local applicants rose to the trustees. The trustees called for a task force to reexamine impaction; this was accomplished and procedures were updated. In the spring of 2000, the trustees received a report from a special task force, which essentially reaffirmed the earlier procedures in a new and emerging context. This became important as the first decade of the new century brought increasing disparities between the numbers seeking a CSU education and specific CSU programs and resources made available in state budgets.

"The Master Plan is for recent high school graduates," so asserted a number of individuals within and without the CSU. In the early 1970s, the CSU established a committee to address alternative admission criteria. This committee was to address the development of admission criteria for older students, defined as age twenty-six and above. The Committee on Alternative Admissions Criteria invited proposals from the campuses to experiment with new criteria. About one-third of the campuses responded quickly. Obviously, there was an audience for the idea. The proposals were carefully constructed and evaluated. The approach was embraced by many faculty. In October 1976, Chancellor Dumke signed a memorandum to the presidents, encouraging additional proposals from the campuses and extending the life of the committee. While the alternative admissions approach was designed to address older adults, one campus, Chico, used it to conduct a three-year experiment, "accelerated college admissions" for students who have completed the tenth or eleventh grade and rank in the top 10 percent of the class. The experiment was successful, but the program was not continued as a result of personnel changes. The net result of the alternative admission concept has been to provide for the admission of older students without using the admission by exception limited numbers. The approach has been successful over time.[13]

* * *

The student and faculty unrest of the late 1960s had many impacts. One of these was on curricular structure. Many colleges and universities abandoned serious structure in their general education programs, or at least tempered it. With only two notable exceptions among the campuses, the California State University was part of this loosening of structure in curriculum. Secondary school faculty and administrators inevitably became aware of this, and structure in secondary school curriculum similarly diminished. This, in turn, had an impact on preparatory curriculum for college and university study. The erosion was substantial in the 1970s. The research leading to the freshman admissions standards of 1965, based on no differentiation of secondary school curriculum, was supported at the time by two factors. The first was the rigor of the time generally found in many secondary schools, and the second was that all of the students in the study group had self-selected to be in a state college. In the 1970s, the rising percentage of ill-prepared freshmen and the need for more provision of remedial work revived the conversation about a college preparatory curriculum. In 1979, the trustees made a first step on the strong recommendation of Chancellor Dumke to address the college preparatory curriculum issue, with a requirement that applicants for freshman admission complete three years of college preparatory English and two years of college preparatory mathematics.

The chancellorship changed in 1982 with the retirement of Glenn Dumke, and the arrival of his successor, Ann Reynolds. Reynolds had been chancellor no more than two to three months when she scheduled a meeting with me. In the fall of 1982, I was president of the Dominguez Hills campus. I had been involved with admissions issues since coming to California in 1958, in the post commonly known as a director of admissions at San Francisco State. In the 1970s, I was the chair of the Committee on Alternative Admissions, until I relinquished that position to assume the role of chair of the Commission on External Degree Programs at the request of then Chancellor Dumke.

Chancellor Reynolds also invited to the meeting Robert Bess, then the associate vice-chancellor for academic affairs. Bess also had a background in admissions; he also arrived in the state colleges in 1958 as the registrar at the Chico campus. Since 1965, he had been a member of the chancellor's staff, and by 1982, he was the go-to person in academic affairs to create and move important academic ventures. Bess later became executive vice president at the Sacramento campus and then moved on to become president of the Minnesota State University campus at St. Cloud.

Reynolds was clear and to the point. She wanted the California State University to require a college preparatory curriculum for freshman admission. She wanted me to resume the chair of the admissions committee (renamed the Admissions Advisory Council), and she wanted Bess to lead the necessary work within the chancellor's office to accomplish this. Reynolds's definition of college preparatory work included college preparatory English, mathematics, US history and government, science (which included biology, chemistry, and physics), foreign languages, and the visual and performing arts. The first five subject matter areas were not unusual in any college preparatory curriculum; all were included in the long-standing University of California A–F admission requirements. Including visual and performing arts would be another matter, as they were not in the UC pattern and uncommon across the country. Reynolds was firm and clear about the visual and performing arts (VPA) requirements. Looking at the impact of Reynolds's eight-year chancellorship, her stand on admissions is not a surprise. She gave leadership to the visual and performing arts in a variety of ways.

I accepted the assignment (and continued in it to my retirement in 2003). Bess took on the project within the chancellor's office and with the Admissions Advisory Council, and we worked as a team. The first task was to strengthen the council. Another president was added, Jewel Plummer Cobb, a distinguished biologist known for her work with cancer cells and recently appointed to the presidency of the Fullerton campus (the third black president and third female president in the history of the CSU). Bess talked with the leadership of the statewide Academic Senate about the importance of the charge from the chancellor, and the opportunity for the faculty to play a significant role with knowledgeable appointees to the council. Similarly, the California State Student Association (CSSA) leadership was urged to appoint a student who would be active. Campus administrators, a director of admissions and an academic vice president were carefully selected and appointed. One important by-product of the council over the next twenty years was that it functioned almost as a model of collegiality.

The issues before the council were not only important to the academic life of the CSU, but laden with political content. Admissions policy is a central and defining matter for any college or university. The council functioned productively over the years, moving the CSU in an academic direction with undergraduate curriculum and redefining the curricular relationship of the CSU to California's secondary schools. It was a forum for varying points of view, but it always found reasonable solutions. The actions of the council were in the form of recommendations to the chancellor, and consultation requested by the chancellor would follow. In fact, that consultation was not complex because the members of the council had kept their varying constituencies informed as the council deliberated. Perhaps the most important consultation was with the secondary schools, which required consultations also with State Department of Education officials and professional groups related to the schools. Eight hundred individuals outside the CSU were involved, including high school teachers and principals, superintendents, school board members, professional association representatives, and community leaders. Public meetings along the style of hearings were held in San Diego, Pasadena, Ontario, Ventura, Oakland, Fresno, Chico, and Sacramento.

The conclusions of the council deliberations were widely discussed before the chancellor submitted them to the trustees for formal action. The council recommended four years of college preparatory English; three years of mathematics, including algebra, geometry, and advanced algebra; one year of US history, or history and government (later increased to two years of social science, including one year of US history); one year of laboratory science (later increased to two years, including one year of laboratory life science and one year of laboratory physical science); two years of foreign language study (which could be waived for applicants demonstrating equivalent competence); one year of visual and performing arts (including art, dance, drama, or music), and three years of electives from any of the college preparatory areas on the list (later reduced to one year, and agriculture added).

A new eligibility index was to be defined. The eligibility index is a weighted combination of a grade point average and a test score. At the time of initial implementation of these new standards, a high school grade point average of 3.2 or above in the courses used to meet the admission requirement would qualify an applicant for admission.[14]

A first issue was to determine which high school courses fulfilled the college preparatory requirement. The chancellor's office staff reached an agreement with the University of California to use the UC lists of college preparatory courses. This also initiated a discussion with the UC about defining a common list of college preparatory subjects. The University of California had used for years the same list that the council had developed, with the exception of the visual and performing arts. This had commonly become known in all of California education as the A–F list, the set of required courses for regular freshman admission to UC.

The new standards were adopted by the board of trustees on November 13, 1985. They would become effective with students admitted for the fall term of 1988. Negotiations over the visual and performing arts went on for ten years. As chair of the Admissions Advisory Council, I initiated a discussion with the Board of Admissions and Relations with Schools (BOARS) of the UC. BOARS was one of the outcomes of what is sometimes known as a faculty revolution in the UC, which occurred in 1919 at the end of the presidential administration of Benjamin Ide Wheeler and the transition to the presidency of David Prescott Barrows. The regents delegated a number of matters to the faculty, including admissions; BOARS was chaired by a faculty member.

The members of the Admissions Advisory Council first discussed among ourselves the idea of working with the University of California not only on certification of courses, but also to recast the A–F pattern into A–G, which would include the year of visual and performing arts that the trustees had already adopted. I subsequently secured the agreement of the chancellor for this. The negotiations with BOARS were long and arduous. At first, in a sense, there were no negotiations. The chair of BOARS simply dismissed the idea that the arts could be related to college preparation. The conversation continued, as the chair and members of BOARS changed.

With the 1990 departure of Ann Reynolds, the champion of the arts, and the 1991 arrival of Barry Munitz as chancellor, the question of whether to maintain the arts in the CSU A–G pattern was raised by one of the presidents. Munitz was willing to back away if the council was willing. I finally concluded that the CSU had so much invested in the issue that we would be unwise to back down. Finally, as the mid-1990s brought substantial change to the BOARS group, a council member, Gary Hammerstrom, a statewide Academic Senate appointee, brought about an understanding with a new chair of BOARS, and BOARS did accept a change: A–F became A–G, and the CSU and UC were sending the same message to high schools, students, parents, and the public. There were minor variations, but these were not of consequence.

The California State University, with its massive size, inevitably has an impact on the structure and substance of secondary school curriculum. The University of California had had an impact for years, with the A–F pattern, but the numbers of students preparing for UC in many schools was comparatively small, and some high schools developed a set of classes for those aiming to UC enrollment or other comparable institutions. The CSU's move to A–G had an impact on the total high school curriculum. It is not an exaggeration to state that Chancellor Ann Reynolds's insistence on the visual and performing arts saved secondary school programs in the arts in many school districts over the state, at least for that period in time.

* * *

In 1983, the trustees appointed Tomas Arciniega to the presidency of the Bakersfield campus. Arciniega was the first Hispanic president in the history of the California State University. At the same time, Chancellor Reynolds created the Task Force on Hispanic Students and Issues. Arciniega was appointed to chair the task force, and Associate Vice-Chancellor Bess was the principal staff person. Bess directed as well as coordinated the work of the task force, and continued to do this after he moved to the vice-presidency of the Sacramento campus in 1984. The task force completed its work in late 1984 with recommendations that included outreach to the schools and the selection and admission of students. The impact of this task force was to underscore the work of the earlier Task Force on Student Affirmative Action and the continuing efforts to build minority enrollment in the California State University.

By the late 1990s, a number of campuses were using the impaction process developed in the early 1970s to cope with receiving more eligible applicants for admission than resources or space could accommodate. Impacted program procedures were in use on most (and some years all) campuses for nursing programs. There was a shortage of nurses in California, and, at the same time, nursing salaries, which had long been modest, began to increase substantially.

San Luis Obispo had long been an impacted campus—in some measure, the impaction procedures had been originally invented for San Luis Obispo. The San Diego campus became impacted in the mid- to late 1990s. Criteria for acceptance of eligible applicants were developed by the campus and approved by the chancellor's staff. The criteria did not consider local students and the need of some to attend a campus within commuting distance. This had not been an issue for San Luis Obispo since the campus was located in a relatively rural area, in contrast to the densely populated San Diego metropolitan area, and in specific instances in which students needed to attend San Luis Obispo for its proximity to home, the campus simply addressed each individual situation to work out a practical resolution. San Diego was a different situation, however, with a rapidly growing new population. Many local applicants to San Diego could not easily attend another CSU campus. Not only were the city and adjacent communities growing rapidly, but freeways gave fairly quick access to the campus; San Diego had become over time a destination campus for many students in and out of California.

Early in 1999, trustee William Campbell raised the policy question about preference for local applicants. Campbell lived in southern Orange County and had been drawn into the issue by families of affected applicants. The issue had an ethnic content, as many of the San Diego applicants for whom commuting from home was the only economically viable option were Hispanic. Campbell discussed the matter at a presidential inauguration on the San Marcos campus with Vice-Chancellor David Spence and the chair of the CSU Admissions Advisory Council; he ultimately asked for a special task force to be appointed. The task force reviewed the immediate issue of place-bound commuting students and impacted campuses. It then went beyond its initial charge and reviewed all aspects of the system policy on impacted campuses.

The task force was chaired by the chair of the Admissions Advisory Council, and included another president, the chair of the statewide Academic Senate, two trustees, and others. The trustees viewed the issue as a serious policy question. The comprehensive review that ultimately resulted in board action in May of 2000 was fortuitous, as the next decade and the budget cuts in the year 2007, 2008, and 2009 required extensive use of the impaction policy. The board action of May 2000 did provide for consideration of local applicants, essentially those who were place bound.

The development and systemwide administration of admissions in the California State University has received careful oversight since the time of the Master Plan. In part, this is due to the interest of the first two chancellors, Glenn Dumke and Ann Reynolds, in admissions. That interest has been carried on by their successors. Munitz saw admissions and student enrollment, and especially student affirmative action, as central to the CSU mission. Charles Reed has a major interest in the relationship of the CSU to the schools.

The Early Assessment Program (EAP), which was developed in partnership with the State Board of Education and the schools, is an important move in building these relationships, as well as strengthening the quality and capacities of entering students. Admission matters have had the careful oversight and leadership of a number of very able career CSU administrators who have each made a difference. Robert Bess was that key person from 1965 to 1984. Charles Lindahl, a Northridge administrator from 1964 to 1974, and then a key chancellor's office staff member, gave leadership to admissions to his retirement in 2001; he had been named associate vice-chancellor for academic affairs, and in 1995 became interim senior vice-chancellor, until June of 1998; some of his work was handled by Gary Hammerstrom, a San Francisco State faculty member and statewide Academic Senate leader for a number of years, who joined the chancellor's staff in the mid-1990s. Allison Jones had been the key staff member for student financial aid since the mid-1980s, and he became the central figure for admissions with the retirements of Lindahl and Hammerstrom.

* * *

The adoption of the A–G standards did not include career or vocational technical subjects. High school faculty and others protested this almost immediately upon learning of the Admissions Advisory Council proposal. Their protests were heard, but the council and the CSU remained firm about college preparatory curriculum. As the issue came before the Admissions Advisory Council, the Council would advise faculty and occasionally others to make the case for particular courses. This eventually happened for specific courses in agriculture. The decision to include a course is based on the course's content. Not every high school course in biology is included. Similarly, a course in agriculture, based upon its content in the sciences, can be included. The issue was broadened in 2001–02 and succeeding years. Instead of meetings with the Admissions Advisory Council, representatives of teacher groups in areas of vocational education went to legislators and conferences. A campaign was mounted. The support of California's newly elected governor, Arnold Schwarzenegger was secured. The CSU held firm to the A–G pattern, but the issue is not dead.

In 2008, the Sacramento campus-based LegiSchool program probed the issue. Created in the early 1990s, LegiSchool is a program of the Center for California Studies. Periodically, high school students from over the state meet for a daylong town hall debate about an issue currently before the legislature. The issue is always one of immediate interest to high school students (for example, legislation permitting school districts to require high school students to wear uniforms). A senior member of the legislature suggested career technical education in high school curriculum, and a town hall meeting was held. Student reactions to career technical education were mixed. Those who thought of themselves as college bound were generally not supportive, and expressed particular concern about costs; these students were aware of budget stringencies in the schools. Students who saw themselves as moving from high school to the workforce were more interested and supportive. Panelists from both the State Department of Education and the business-industry sector presented versions of career technical education, one emphasizing the development of curriculum that would meet A–G standards, as had been done for agriculture, another emphasizing a vocational curriculum from which a high school graduate would directly enter the workforce. Students were reported as not swept away either by the arguments or the issue.

The issue of career technical education in high schools and its relationship to higher education admissions is not resolved and needs leadership. It could be an opportunity for the CSU to assert leadership in thinking through technical high school curriculum that is realistic in today's world, and based on the sciences and mathematics.

In 2008, there were two pressing admission issues. The first was the state budget, and the continuing lack of adequate funding for fully eligible students. Most recently, the trustees dropped enrollment for the 2009–10 year by 10,000 students because of budget limitations. The second issue was in the secondary schools—encouraging a sufficient number of students to make themselves eligible to move from high school to higher education, whether it be through a community college or directly to a four-year college or university with the completion of a degree as a goal.

One of the by-products of the 1960 Master Plan has been the loss of many linkages between colleges and universities and the elementary and secondary schools. This is arguably more the situation for California State University campuses than the UC and community colleges. The causes are understandable, and include the pendulum swing away from teacher education and the emphasis on university status. The California State University campuses each have multiple missions. One of these missions, a defining mission, is that the CSU campuses are "the people's university" campuses, and relationships to the people of a region and the state are just as important in the twenty-first century as they were when the regional campuses were established in the nineteenth century. It is in that context that the time has come to rethink working relationships with the schools, for the schools too have changed. Ann Reynolds as chancellor did place emphasis on teacher education. Charles Reed has led a broad reengagement with the schools and dimensions of that range from curriculum and the Early Assessment Program to the personal engagement of presidents and the chancellor with the schools.

The high school curriculum of 1960 is not the curriculum of 2008. The substance of college preparatory courses has in many instances drifted downward in content and rigor. Advanced Placement courses have contributed to this; they are often the real college preparatory courses. Thus, the meaning of the concept of the top one-third of high school graduates has changed. Anyone who has taught college freshmen over the years has experienced this. It is arguable that the real standards for admission to CSU campuses are the placement examinations in English and mathematics.

It is time for the California State University to reassert itself with respect not only to college preparatory curriculum, but a working relationship with the schools. Clearly, this is happening in teacher education. It needs to happen on other fronts. Students and teachers need signals. The Early Assessment Program is a strong signal and tool. The reassertion of the role of presidents as educational leaders for a region would be a strong step. The assumption by the CSU of a strong role in determining what is and is not college preparation in secondary school curriculum, a process now dominated by the University of California, would be a step. Leadership on the matter of career technical education would be a step. The admissions story of the California State University is hardly ended.[15]

* * *

> The alumni experience is about never losing sight of how the student experience changed your life, and continues to shape your life in the present day. It's about never losing sight, whether for professional or personal decisions, and how you interact with people. As an alumnus or alumna of the California State University,

all aspects of the rest of your life can be directly tied to aspects of the student experience both on professional and personal levels.

David Sommers and Shaun Lumachi[16]

In 1935–36, the first year in which records were maintained, 1,417 students received degrees from the seven newly named California State Colleges. In June 2007, the number of degrees awarded since that beginning year totaled 2,671,780. Master's degrees have been awarded to 215,677 individuals since 1949–50, and 703 students have earned the doctorate (PhD or EdD) in joint doctoral programs since1967. Governor Edmund "Pat" Brown signed the Master Plan for Higher Education in California in 1960; the trustees first met on August 12, 1960. Since that day 2,558,647 of these degrees have been awarded.

The impact of alumni of the normal schools, teachers colleges, state colleges, and, for the last twenty-six years, the California State University has been and continues to be pervasive in the state and nation and, in more recent years, the world arena. From the beginning in 1857, alumni taught California's students. From the early years of the twentieth century, alumni have staffed California's economy. In the years of extraordinary growth of the state colleges and the state university, no sector of the state's economy, the cultural life, or politics has not felt the presence and leadership by alumni. The presence of alumni in the 120-member state legislature has grown from the three members in 1960. After the November 2008 elections, thirty-eight members in assembly and senate were alumni. Nationally, for a number of years beginning in 2001, a look at the US paper currency revealed two signatures: on the left was that of Paul O'Neill, secretary of the treasury and an alumnus of the Fresno campus, and on the right was Rosario Marin, an alumna of California State University Los Angeles, then Treasurer of the United States and presently (2008) secretary of California State and Consumer Services Agency and a member of the governor's cabinet.

During the commencement ceremonies on some campuses, presidents have followed the custom of asking graduating students who are the first in their families to graduate from a college or university to stand. The patterns vary among the campuses, for the campuses themselves vary in the socioeconomic makeup of their student populations. In my experience on four campuses, the percentages responding positively to this question have varied from perhaps 25 percent to well over 50 percent. Clearly, the California State University is a vehicle for socioeconomic mobility. No formal records are maintained on this data, but experience speaks for itself. This is one measure of "the people's university."

In the alumni focus group and in numerous conversations with alumni, one comment commonly arose, though it was not on the prepared list of questions to be asked. Many alumni expressed emphatically an appreciation of general education and its value. Over many years, beginning in 1970–71, my first year as an academic vice president, I have interviewed the graduating seniors in one or two departments each semester; I continued this practice through the spring term of

2003, when I retired from the presidency of the Sacramento campus. In these conversations, most often in small groups, students about to graduate expressed with frequency a low priority and value on their general education experience. Students often prefer classes in their major rather than experiencing a rounded education. But as they mature and face the real world, they come to appreciate the value of their general education.

The discussion in the alumni focus group was remarkable. All of the participants had read the CSU mission statement adopted in 1985 by the board of trustees; they were more familiar with it than I. All agreed that the mission statement was too long and wordy (450 words) and too abstract and detached from the real world. They wanted a mission statement of a few words, a mission statement understandable by entering freshmen, as well as affluent donors. The CSU offers affordable quality, and it offers options. The group finally settled on the line, "Enter to become, go forth to be."

The early campuses organized alumni groups, and often alumni organized themselves. By the 1960s, the then nine more mature campuses each had some form of alumni organization. The newer campuses would form organizations in the 1960s and 1970s. As the campuses secured greater budget freedom, many began to staff alumni organizations. In 1971, a group of public affairs and alumni staff gathered to form an alumni network and to encourage linkage between the campus-based alumni organizations and the development activities beginning to emerge on some campuses. They formed a systemwide Alumni Council and secured agreement from the chancellor's office about the use of the California State Colleges name.

An early activity of the Alumni Council was support for the proposed name change to the California State University; the first step of this change occurred in 1972, with the name change to the California State University and Colleges. The council's programs included the coordination of legislative activity among the existing campus groups, increasing alumni involvement with what was still a new system, and simply providing a forum or gathering point to share common interests.

With the success of the name-change legislation and the achievement of a student trustee position, the Alumni Council sought to establish an alumni trustee position. They were successful, but it took time. The council wanted the authority to appoint the alumni trustee, not submit a panel of names from which a governor would select one individual. To accomplish this required legislation beyond establishing the trustee position and statutory recognition of the Alumni Council. This was achieved, and John O'Connell was appointed the first alumni trustee in 1977. He served until shortly before his death in 1984. He was chair of the board for three years.

The Alumni Council has emerged as a major factor in the life of the California State University. Trustees listen, as do legislators and leaders in the state. The council's work in Sacramento is a significant factor giving support to the CSU. Early in the life of the council, it succeeded in legitimizing campus and chancellor's office funding of alumni organizations. Now, active alumni organizations exist on all of the campuses. On the larger campuses, alumni houses have been established, with active involvement in university programs and with students and faculty. The impact and meaning of the California State University is nowhere more clear than its well over two million alumni and their activities in the greater community.

Notes

[1] Shaun Lumachi and David Sommers are alumni of California State University, Sacramento. This quote is from an email sent to me on December 4, 2006, in the context of the invitation extended to Lumachi and Sommers to participate in a small focus group of alumni on March 1, 2007. The participants in the March 1 focus group, in addition to Lumachi and Sommers, were Robert Linscheid, Chico alumnus, businessman, and the alumni member of the board of trustees; Rosario Marin, Los Angeles alumna, former treasurer of the United States, and secretary of the California State and Consumer Services Agency; and Christine Rubin, San Diego State alumna and a senior administrator in California state government. Lumachi, who majored in government, is former vice president of the Long Beach Chamber of Commerce and owner-president of Chamber Advocacy; as a student, he was chair of the board of the California State Student Association. Sommers a government-journalism major, was the 1999–2000 editor-in-chief of the *State Hornet*, the university newspaper, during which time he endured the wrath of a superior court judge who had ordered him to surrender interview notes basic to a news story that had been used as evidence in a trial. Sommers refused to surrender the notes and was about to go to jail, when a local television station mistakenly broadcast the information, which put it in the public domain. Sommers subsequently became the first student to chair the board of the university union. After graduation, Sommers became news director-producer for a network television station in Boise, Idaho, then assumed the same role in Portland, Oregon, and is presently press secretary for a member of the Los Angeles County Board of Supervisors.

[2] The "new director of admissions" was the author, then associate dean of students for admissions and records (every state college had one, and they were all white males) at San Francisco State College.

[3] The specific numbers for the paragraphs about students are from the "Statistical Abstract of the California State University to July 2006," Long Beach, Office of the Chancellor; the abstract is published annually, approximately eighteen months after the close each July. The references to early numbers, prior to the 1960 Master Plan, come from the histories of the individual campuses.

[4] Carter would go on to have an extraordinary career in the California State University. After being appointed as director of affirmative action, he enrolled in a doctoral program at the University of Southern California and completed work for the degree. In the 1980s, he became assistant executive vice-chancellor, and later executive vice-chancellor. At the time of the 1990 change in the chancellorship, he was offered the presidency of United Way in greater Los Angeles. Charles Reed, the new chancellor, persuaded him to return to the CSU in 1998 as interim president at Dominguez Hills for one year. Governor Arnold Schwarzenegger appointed Carter to the board of trustees in 2004.

[5] Office of the Chancellor, *Report of the Task Force on Student Affirmative Action*, November 1977, CSU Archives.

[6] The presidents were Corrigan, of San Francisco State, and myself, of CSU Sacramento. I publicly debated Bernard Richter, the assemblyman who authored the bill, per Richter's request.

[7] Office of the Chancellor, "The California State University Statistical Abstract," 151–56.

[8] The paragraphs on admissions in the early years up to the Master Plan, the Master Plan negotiations, and the implementation of the Master Plan provision for admission are based on a number of reports and other sources. These include Glenn S. Dumke, "Admissions Standards in the State Colleges," working paper, 1959; Dorothy M. Knoell, interview by the author, March 14, 2005; Arthur Hall, interview by the author, March 1, 2005; Arthur Hall, miscellaneous papers; *State College Report for Master Plan Survey Subcommittee on Selection and Retention of Students*, November 4, 1959; and the papers of the author, who was a researcher on the topic for President Dumke and subsequently served briefly on the chancellor's staff, with some responsibility for admissions matters. All of these items are in the CSU Archives.

[9] Dumke, "Admissions Standards."

[10] California State Department of Education, *A Master Plan*, 4–5, 45–81.

[11] I was the individual. I stayed only one year, due to a variety of circumstances, notably the amount of travel in the context of having a young family, and an invitation to become dean of students on the Chico campus.

[12] California Postsecondary Education Commission, press release, December 9, 2008.

[13] Lyle D. Edmison, interview by the author, December 30, 2005; Glenn S. Dumke, "Committee on Alternative Admissions Criteria," memorandum to the presidents, October 8, 1976.

[14] California State University, "Stateline" November 25, 1985. The records, minutes, studies of the admissions advisory council from 1982 to 2003, along with the records of predecessor groups and essentially all admissions issues and policy matters are in the CSU Archives.

[15] Charles B. Reed, interview by the author, December 20, 2006, CSU Archives. The section on admissions is based on the materials described in the previous footnote; on the Judson Grenier interviews with Glenn Dumke, July 18, 1984, and March 27, 1987; and on a focus group on admissions, October 27, 2004, that included Robert O. Bess, Katherine Kaiser, Charles Lindahl, Sara Lundquist, and Nancy Sprotte. The following interviews were conducted by the author: Senator Dede Alpert, April 18, 2007; Gary Hammerstrom, March 4, 2004; Allison Jones, April 17, 2007; Michael Kirst, November 7, 2005; Barry Munitz, November 18, 2005; and Ann Reynolds, August 19, 2004. The author is particularly grateful to Michal Kirst, of Stanford University, for a rich conversation about CSU relations with the schools. It is proper for the author to note that he has consistently been supportive of and an advocate for the use of college preparatory curriculum in the standards for admission, since his arrival to the San Francisco State College in 1958.

[16] Lumachi and Sommers, email communication.

Chapter 10

Faculty and Staff—Collective Bargaining

When the board of trustees assumed responsibility for the California State Colleges on July 1, 1961, responsibility for several thousand employees—faculty, staff, and administrators—came with the campuses. The Master Plan was silent about faculty and staff, other than addressing the need for many additional faculty in the years immediately ahead. The Liaison Committee of the Regents and the State Board of Education had completed an in-depth study of faculty demand and supply in 1958.[1]

The state college employees, faculty, staff, and administrators, all save the presidents, were in a modified version of civil service. From 1921 to 1961, employees of the state teachers colleges (from 1935, the state colleges) were managed by the Division of State Colleges in the State Department of Education. State employees generally were placed into a civil service system by a Constitutional amendment in 1934. Employees of the state colleges were exempted from civil service, but their salaries mirrored those of the civil service. In 1953, legislation was enacted to place state college employees under the jurisdiction of the State

---

The author is indebted to Dr. David Wagner, Vice President for Human Resources at California State University, Sacramento, who critiqued this chapter. Dr. Wagner is a thirty-four-year veteran of the faculty at California State University, Sacramento, a professor of communication studies, and an attorney (though he does not practice, as he devotes his full efforts to his university work). He is a former associate dean of the School of Arts and Sciences, and for the past twenty-one years has been the dean for faculty and staff affairs and vice president for human resources. He is the senior campus human resources officer in the California State University.

Personnel Board, California's civil service agency, both for setting salaries and for disciplinary and appellate purposes.[2] Provision for faculty probation periods, the award of tenure, and faculty promotions had been made in the years of growth following World War II. These were in place. Similarly, definitions of administrative positions and rules for these were in place; the State Department of Finance played a major role in the definition of campus administration.[3] The State Personnel Board was the ultimate authority, short of the legislature, regarding state college personnel.

One of Buell Gallagher's early appointments after he assumed the chancellorship on July 1, 1961, was that of an acquaintance of his, C. Mansel Keene, to the position of chief of personnel on Gallagher's staff. He would report directly to Gallagher. Keene was a career federal civil servant with an academic background. He had earned a PhD in psychology at Stanford University before beginning his career, and during the years of World War II had headed a branch personnel office for the federal government in Los Angeles.

The personnel activities of the Gallagher months were largely housekeeping. Two presidencies needed to be filled immediately on the new campuses at San Bernardino and the South Bay area of Los Angeles County, Dominguez Hills. Glenn Dumke, in his role as vice-chancellor for academic affairs, was largely responsible for these appointments, both made from inside the state colleges. Revisions had to be made in the California Administrative Code. The State Board of Education had been responsible for Title 5 of the code; this was the portion of California's administrative code that addressed education and still does to this date. In the transitional 1960–61 year, Don Leiffer directed a staff member to identify all of the sections of Title 5 pertaining to the state colleges. The board of trustees assumed legal responsibility on July 1, 1961. In this context, Keene identified personnel policies that could be candidates for modification as the state colleges moved into a new era. Changes or additions in the California Administrative Code can only be made with formal public notice and a formal open hearing. The process was long and cumbersome. Many portions of the code pertaining to personnel matters were amended in February 1962.[4]

Accomplishing the revisions of Title 5 was more than a routine task. Some trustees favored centralizing personnel authority for the campuses with the board—board approval would be required for all appointments, promotions, and tenure actions of faculty and administrators. This had been the custom in both the University of California and the state colleges. While the regents still took this seriously in some instances, the State Board of Education had treated this responsibility as a routine formality; not since 1926, at the insistence of the then governor, had the board declined to confirm an appointment.[5]

Chancellor Gallagher, whose actions in his brief months in California were strongly centralizing, insisted on a review and approval by the chancellor of all faculty and administrative personnel actions. One of the early trustees, William Coblentz (who a few years later became a regent) was chair of the Trustee Committee on Faculty and Staff Affairs, and he prevented Gallagher and the small number of trustees who wanted centralization from achieving it.[6] Coblentz, an attorney, had a sense of how organizations work well or do not work, and he was a key figure in the first years of the trustees. He was also close to Governor Pat Brown, and had been a member of the governor's staff.

As Gallagher resigned, he invited Keene to join him to return to the City College of New York. Keene declined and remained with the California State Colleges. He soon invited a longtime associate in the federal government, Lois Feldheym, to join his office staff. Feldheym had initially been contacted by Don Leiffer in late 1961 to come to California for an interview. She received a verbal offer from Leiffer after Gallagher's resignation, but did not accept it, pending some resolution of the chancellorship. In June 1962, Feldheym joined the California State Colleges. She was a Stanford graduate with a baccalaureate degree in drama. Her job title was faculty and staff affairs specialist; in reality, she was Keene's deputy. She did not acquire an academic title. In a 1987 interview she observed, "I don't have a doctorate, so I didn't have the trappings for any title like 'dean,' and I didn't think I deserved it. It wasn't a problem with me. But one of the things we had said later on was that the campuses should not call people 'dean' unless they were truly academically respectable. So I had that odd title. I guess I'm the only one that's had that title in the system."[7]

Feldheym immersed herself in the literature of higher education, and quickly became more knowledgeable than many academic administrators about the organization and administration of higher education. She had been attracted to the position, in part, because it addressed both faculty and staff, a combination then unusual, if not rare, in American higher education. It would be 1976 before the first campus in the system would follow this model. Faculty personnel administration was conventionally done only by academics. Feldheym would, in her eighteen years as the deputy in faculty and staff affairs, have a great impact on building both personnel structures and fundamental principles of organization within the system. Feldheym did her homework and gained great respect. She was an individual who was easy to work with and easy to like.

* * *

Among the early issues that the board encountered was that of administrative tenure—not academic tenure for administrators, but for administrators in their administrative positions. The tenure regulations for the state colleges, as they had been written in the years of growth before the Master Plan, provided for tenure in all academic and administrative positions, save that of president; civil service permanent status was accorded to nonacademic and nonadministrative position holders under conventional state employee rules. All of this was administered by the State Personnel Board. The rules for those in full-time academic and administrative positions were clear. Tenure was conferred on the first day of the fourth year of service; it could not be conferred earlier. Thus, the third year was the time for a decision. In the absence of a decision, tenure was automatic. Moreover, once tenured, in a move to a new position, the individual carried tenure to the new position immediately. As an example, a tenured faculty member appointed as an associate dean or dean became tenured in that new position on the first day in the position. Thus, presidents had tenured-in administrations. This could be especially problematic for new presidents, as it was for Glenn Dumke when he arrived at San Francisco State as president in 1957. The Master Plan called for change. Resistance to that change ranged from modest to major in all of the state college campus administrations other than the newest of the campuses in 1960—Fullerton, Sonoma, and, to some extent, Stanislaus. In the 1961 legislative session, Don Leiffer, acting for the trustees, shepherded a bill (SB 157) taking a first step to address this issue, giving trustees the right to transfer administrative employees commensurate with their qualifications.

The direction that Glenn Dumke wanted for the campuses was away from the Department of Finance–dictated models and the traditions of teachers colleges, and toward that of liberal arts colleges. Lois Feldheym drew as her first assignment the review of organization and structure and personnel administration on the campuses. The organization and structures were uniform, at least in theory, with the exception of the two smallest campuses, Chico and Humboldt, and Cal Poly because of the evolution of its agricultural and technical programs. Each campus had, in addition to a president, four deans (dean of instruction, dean of students, dean of educational services and summer sessions, executive dean [responsible for the building program]), one vice president on the larger campuses (a position first made possible in 1957), and a business manager. The instructional program was organized in divisions with chairs (faculty positions paid on a twelve-month schedule) and the student affairs programs had three associate deans responsible for defined areas (admissions and records, counseling and testing, and student activities and housing), a placement officer, and a director for student health. The structures were archaic, but there were substantial interests vested in maintaining them; the interest included not only many of the incumbents, but those who felt well served by or a kinship with the structures and the orientation of their programs. This was especially true for teacher education faculties and their leaders.

Feldheym's proposals included the establishment of a vice presidential–level chief academic officer, a vice presidential chief financial officer on the larger campuses (and soon on all campuses), the establishment of schools with deans and departments and department chairs (there were no departments in the previous divisional structure, though often faculties in disciplines and applied fields established their own departments within whatever moving room a president would allow), and great flexibility in the definition and titles for all administrative positions. The proposals provided for presidential delegation of authority and responsibility to vice presidents and deans, not a practice to that time. Her proposals assumed the termination of tenure in administrative positions. On the surface, these proposals could have been costly. For the most part they were not, as existing positions were used. There was little formal resistance to these proposals. Even the most senior presidents accepted them and worked with them, although roughly three years would pass before full implementation. The trustees took the necessary steps, including removing tenure in administration positions; administrators could earn tenure or be accorded tenure as faculty, according to the rules of each campus. The policies for awarding tenure were modified slightly to make it possible for tenure to be conferred at the end of a first year of employment.

There was resistance and anger among some incumbent administrators and a few others, but in most instances this quickly disappeared with retirements and changes of assignments. The campuses were growing, and growth afforded flexibility and moving room. There was one celebrated case: the vice president for academic affairs at San Jose State College sued, upon reassignment, to retain a position at least comparable to a vice presidency, but his suit did not prevail.

This set of early moves by the new leadership and the trustees of the state colleges provided a framework for the orderly evolution of campus organization over the years. It was definitive.

* * *

When the legislature and the governor placed the Donahoe Act (the implementation of the Master Plan) into statute, they were attentive to faculty salaries. Part of the act placed into the Education Code addressed faculty salaries directly:

> In establishing and adjusting such [academic] salaries, consideration shall be given to the maintenance of the state colleges in a competitive position in the recruitment and retention of qualified personnel in relation to other educational institutions, private industry, or public jurisdictions which are employing personnel with similar duties and responsibilities.[8]

In 1963, the legislature initiated the practice of requiring an annual report from the Coordinating Council for Higher Education about faculty salaries in both the University of California and the California State Colleges. In conjunction with the Coordinating Council staff, each system selected a set of comparison institutions. This approach was reaffirmed by the legislature in 1964 in a resolution adopted by both houses asking the Joint Legislative Budget Committee to "study the subject of salaries and the general economic welfare, including fringe benefits of faculty members of the California institutions of higher education, and ways and means of improving such salaries and benefits…." In the 1960s, California public higher education institutions were estimated to be hiring approximately 10 percent of all new faculty members in the nation.[9] The annual comparison study became institutionalized and remains so to this date.

Mansel Keene addressed faculty salaries early. Glenn Dumke, on assuming the chancellorship in April 1962, asked for a review in the context of the budget for the coming year. Keene used the salary scales of the American Association of University Professors (AAUP). He discovered a significant disparity in faculty salaries among the ranks. The two lower ranks, instructor and assistant professor, were consistently at the A or B levels of the annual AAUP ratings, but the senior ranks, associate professor and professor, were at the C level or lower. Keene argued for a larger increase for the upper ranks and encountered significant faculty objection, which was on behalf of those in the lower ranks, and related to unrest on some campuses (in a sense, early pro-union activity). Nonetheless, Keene prevailed in the 1964–65 budget. The lower ranks received 2.5 percent and the upper ranks 7.5 percent salary increases. Unfortunately, 1964–65 was the year when a calculation error was alleged by the Department of Finance, and the upper ranks, along with comparable and higher positions up through the chancellorship, had a salary reduction of 1.8 percent for the last months of the fiscal year; the reduction was restored in the next fiscal year.[10]

The comparison institution studies were not always well received by faculty and faculty leaders. In the mid-1970s, when many matters were in flux and the major issue was collective bargaining, there was faculty resistance to the continued use of the comparison studies. However, the studies continued. Presidential and other administrative salaries were added to the annual studies. Both faculty and presidential salaries have consistently lagged those of the comparison institutions since the late 1970s. Initially, the state college comparison institutions were twelve in number. By 1972, when the University of California used eight comparison institutions, all major research universities, the California State University and Colleges used 102 institutions. The then executive director of the Coordinating Council urged a reduction in number to a figure comparable to the UC's, and the number settled to twenty in 1974. The system responded positively.

The comparison study process was modified slightly in 1981–82. The parties to the agreement for the comparison studies, as these have been formalized over the years, include the California Postsecondary Education Commission (CPEC), the Department of Finance, the Legislative Analyst's Office, the University of California, and the California State University. Since 1995, an outside group has conducted the studies for CPEC. For the California State University, twenty institutions from four geographic regions of the United States are in the study; the institutions are changed from time to time by agreement.

In the 1980s, the salary lag for faculty in the California State University was a single digit; by 1991–92, it was 4.1 percent, and by 2006–07, it was 15.21 percent.[11] California State University faculty salaries have not kept pace with salary increases for the University of California faculty over the years.

Keene's early observation about the balance of salaries by rank were important, but not widely discussed. A careful analysis done unofficially in the state colleges in 1963 suggested that an average faculty member who experienced a full career in the state colleges, contrasted with the University of California, might well have lifetime earnings higher than her or his UC colleague. A UC budget analyst, Robert Johnson, wrote a concerned memo to Angus Taylor, then the UC vice president for academic affairs, about the trustees' budget request of November 1970 for faculty salaries in contrast with the regents' request. Johnson identified what Keene had learned years earlier, that lifetime earnings for an average faculty member were very close, and for some individuals, could be greater in the state colleges. Johnson's report set aside medical and law school

Table 10.1. California State University Comparison Salary Institutions

1984	2007
Northeast Region	
State University of New York College, Albany	Bucknell University*
State University of New York, Buffalo	Rutgers, State University of New Jersey, Newark
Syracuse University*	State University of New York, Albany
	Tufts University*
	University of Connecticut
North Central Region	
Bowling Green State University (Ohio)	Cleveland State University
Illinois State University	Illinois State University
Indiana State University	Loyola University, Chicago*
Iowa State University	Wayne State University (Michigan)
Miami University (Ohio)	University of Wisconsin, Milwaukee
Northern Illinois University	
Southern Illinois University	
University of Wisconsin, Milwaukee	
Wayne State University (Michigan)	
Western Michigan University	
Southern Region	
Virginia Polytechnic Institute and State University	Georgia State University
	George Mason University
	North Carolina State University
	University of Maryland, Baltimore County
	University of Texas Arlington
Western Region	
Portland State University	Arizona State University
University of Colorado	Reed College*
University of Hawaii	University of Colorado, Denver
University of Nevada	University of Colorado, Denver
University of Oregon	University of Nevada, Reno
University of Southern California*	University of Southern California*

* Independent institution

Note: California Postsecondary Education Commission, *Fifth Annual Report on Faculty and Administrative Salaries in California Public Higher Education, 1984–85*; minutes of the board of trustees, the California State University, September 18–19, 2007.

faculty, or faculty in advanced salary steps at the rank of professor—the salaries that most often drew attention—and addressed the salaries of the typical faculty member. The analysis was based on faculty salary structures and conventions of the time in the state colleges and the university, especially promotion practices. This "imbalance" from the vantage point of the University of California would prevail for an additional number of years, but substantially change after the early 1980s.[12]

A long-standing rule within the state colleges imposed by the State Department of Finance and agreed to by the presidents in 1953, was the 60/40 balance for faculty ranks. The rule provided that no more than 60 percent of the faculty could be at the ranks of associate professor and professor. The rule was enforced by the Department of Finance. It did not have to monitor the rule closely; the veteran presidents did it for them. In the mid-1960s the rapid expansion of the state colleges and the need to hire numbers of new faculty, often at advanced steps in the assistant professor rank and, with some frequency a need to bring in senior faculty for program development, was bumping up against the 60/40 rule. In 1964, for example, the president of San Jose State, John Wahlquist, retired. Wahlquist was like almost all of his colleagues from the "old school teacher education" mold of presidents. He was replaced by Robert Clark, a veteran faculty member and administrator from the University of Oregon. Clark saw a rebuilding task ahead of him, and he almost immediately encountered the 60/40 rule as he sought to bring in faculty leadership in the arts and sciences and newly emerging professional programs.

President Clark appealed to the chancellor's office for help. Dumke had experienced his own difficulties with the 60/40 rule when he assumed the presidency of San Francisco State; he did not have to be convinced. Some relaxation of the rule was secured in the 1965–66 year; the Department of Finance agreed not to count administrative time (individuals in class and rank faculty positions with administrative assignments, a throwback to the 1951 Department of Finance study of administrative organization and staffing) or administrators with faculty appointments in the computation. Finance also agreed to count lecturers in the base; in the 1960s, most lecturers were paid on the scale for instructors or assistant professors. Some relief was secured in 1968, but only for San Jose State as an exception; the San Jose campus was permitted to go to 65 percent.[13] The San Francisco campus experienced a loss of faculty positions in the early 1970s, and its percentage exceeded the 60 percent limit. The strike and other activity of the late 1960s had impacted student enrollment. The legislative analyst challenged this; the only answer was to let time and growth in faculty positions resolve the matter. The 60/40 rule disappeared in the context of collective bargaining.

Faculty demand and supply studies and reports were initiated in the 1950s, prior to the Master Plan, for both the state colleges and the University of California. The subject was under continuing review in the 1960s, as the growth of the campuses was substantial. In 1969–70, the trustees, chancellor, and the leadership of the statewide Academic Senate moved from faculty supply to an approach they labeled "the procurement and retention of a quality faculty." This shift in focus now provided the setting for discussions not only about recruiting faculty, but, equally important, keeping quality faculty once they committed to the state college campuses. A study group was created that included trustees, faculty, presidents, chancellor's staff, and a student. The report of the group was a positive one, and addressed matters ranging from standards and procedures for faculty appointments, retention, tenure, promotion, merit salary increases, the use of evaluative criteria, post-tenure review, and the creation of additional salary steps for professors beyond the traditional five-step salary schedule, and extending to department chairs and their work.

The report was accepted formally by the trustees and was supported by all parties to its preparation. The report specifically addressed tenure and the four-year probationary period for the award of tenure. The length of the probationary period had been questioned by a few trustees. The committee concluded that "the problems inherent in the current tenure system were not amenable to solution by an extension of the probationary period." The report was blunt about the need for adequate procedures to address "faculty members who have been accorded tenure, become incompetent as teachers, or who engage in unprofessional conduct." These were identified as matters not addressed by extending the probationary period. The report was adopted in two board actions on September 23, 1970, and January 27, 1971.

The campuses worked variously in the years after the 1971 report to address the recommendations. Several recommendations were not taken up in any meaningful way. The recommendation on merit salary increases fell victim to inaction. By contrast, the practice of advancing faculty one step each year, on the five-step salary schedule for each rank, was deeply embedded in the culture of the state colleges and, in fact, in the culture of all California civil service and state units, save only the University of California, which had developed its own customs within the context of its constitutional independence. The recommendation for the creation of advanced steps for professors in the salary schedule was not seriously considered for funding, despite the fact that it was a direct parallel to the University of California practice.

In September 1974, the board of trustees responded to a request from the statewide Academic Senate and the chancellor and presidents for the establishment of a new ad hoc committee to review the 1970–71 reports, and "study all matters relating to the procurement and retention of a quality faculty." The ad hoc committee, structured like the earlier group, met over a period of a year, and prepared a detailed report that was widely circulated within the California State University and Colleges, supported by most leaders in all categories, and adopted by the trustees in November 1975. Three points need to be made about the process and the report. Both the earlier report and the 1975 document explicitly recognized research as part of what at least some faculty do, and thus a part of faculty evaluation. The 1975 report was prepared in the context of "steady state," the unplanned for shift in the early 1970s from enrollment growth on virtually every campus each year to stable and, in some instances, declining enrollment. The years from 1970 through 1975 were years of turbulence—one issue after another, leading up to the serious consideration of collective bargaining. The 1960s and the tumultuous years at the end of that decade provided the setting. The actions of the board of trustees, the governor and others from state government, and the administration of the state colleges, accompanied by faculty activism and some genuine faculty enthusiasm, in a limited but energetic number of individuals, reinforced interest in collective bargaining.

* * *

In the 1960s and early 1970s, the focus of much of the activity in the faculty and staff affairs unit in the chancellor's office and the board committee on faculty and staff affairs was on the faculty. This would continue to be the situation in many ways over the years. The chancellor's office simply adopted State Personnel Board rules for the nonacademic employees of the state colleges. These would be modified about specific matters unique to higher education; the State Personnel Board rules and procedures had applied to all of the state employees in the executive branch, save those employed by the other three constitutional branches of government, the legislature, the judiciary and court system, and the University of California. While the board of trustees was certainly not another branch of government, personnel authority was transferred to the trustees after the adoption of the Master Plan. The State Personnel Board continued to be used for many appellate procedures until the implementation of collective bargaining in the early 1980s.

The personnel function was developed in the chancellor's office and on each of the campuses. Campuses secured over time the delegated capacity to classify positions and essentially deal with the whole range of personnel responsibilities. This would change, in some measure, with the coming of collective bargaining. The educational and political/educational conflicts of the faculty were avoided on the staff side of the house in the '60s and '70s.

The senior personnel officer for the system since his appointment by Buell Gallagher in 1961 had been Mansel Keene. Keene's deputy, Lois Feldheym, arrived in June 1962. Keene built the first classification structure and faculty personnel systems, and he necessarily did this hurriedly, as the trustees assumed full responsibility for the California State Colleges. Keene was involved in policy matters and the recruitment of presidents through his years as chief of personnel, assistant chancellor, and then vice-chancellor for faculty and staff affairs. In many ways, the heart of the personnel operation was Lois Feldheym. She was not an academic, but she instinctively had the values of an academic. In the late 1960s, an additional senior position was created, dean of faculty affairs, and this was occupied over the years by a series of academics drawn from the campuses; Lee Kerschner from the Fullerton campus; Milton Dobkin from the Humboldt campus, who would return to Humboldt and serve as the academic vice president for many years and one year as acting president; Clay Sommers, who would move to the presidency of one of the Pennsylvania State Colleges; Robert Tyndall, a longtime music professor and dean from the Long Beach campus, and finally Judith Hunt, an active faculty member from the Hayward campus who would later be associate vice president for faculty affairs at Sonoma.

Keene retired in 1976, Lois Feldheym filled the role for a time, and then the chancellor, with the advice of a search committee, recommended Marjorie Downing Wagner, the president of Sonoma State, to the trustees for appointment as vice-chancellor. Downing Wagner had been the president at Sonoma for two years; prior to her appointment at Sonoma, she had been dean of faculty and professor of English, the chief academic officer at Scripps College, one of the several private colleges in the Claremont complex. She was the first woman regularly appointed (there had been two interim appointees in the 1920s) to a presidency in the system. She was soon followed, in 1978, by the appointment of Gail Fullerton at San Jose, and then by Jewel Plummer Cobb at Fullerton in 1981. Downing Wagner remained in the vice-chancellorship for only four years before retiring. Unlike Mansel Keene, she worked easily and candidly with the union leadership groups. She was characterized by one major union leader at the time as "a practical, pragmatic administrator." As implementation of bargaining approached, she did develop what might be called training programs for presidents and, subsequently, other campus administrators. She recruited Robert Tyndall to the position of dean of faculty affairs in 1978, and he played a transitional role after her retirement. Lois Feldheym gave leadership to the personnel function and continued to work constructively with campus leaders until 1980, when she retired.

Historically, the student affairs area on the state college campuses had not been integrated with academic affairs and the faculty. This had been made clear by the Department of Finance study, completed in 1951, addressing a prescribed organizational structure for all campuses. Some deans of students (the title for all chief student affairs officers until the 1980s) held professorial appointments earned prior to their appointments to a deanship, but they were, in a legal sense, honorary. When I was appointed to the position legally defined as an associate dean of students (every campus was budgeted for three associate deans) at San Francisco State in 1958, I made it clear that I wanted an appointment in the government department, and I wanted to teach one class each term. The government department accepted me within their ranks as a colleague. However, I could not have a conventional faculty appointment because I was in a student affairs classification; I settled for a designation as "member of the government department," and taught my class most semesters.

Lois Feldheym's first major task was to study and recommend changes in administrative structures and personnel practices, as the trustees and, particularly, the chancellor, moved the campuses from an administrative model built around teacher education. When Feldheym came to San Francisco State I became, for whatever reason, one of the individuals to work closely with her in her study and development of recommendations to the chancellor. I pushed very hard to develop a new professional personnel structure in student affairs that would, at a minimum, allow for joint academic appointments, and would define key student affairs positions as faculty. Out of this, the parallel concepts of conventional faculty appointments for administrators and the definition of student affairs professional positions as faculty with faculty qualifications emerged. This did bring about change on some campuses, though there was also resistance among some student affairs staff, who saw themselves in work apart from the faculty with graduate degrees in disciplines and defined professional fields. The 1950s and 1960s were also the time of the emergence of graduate programs in student personnel work, and many in those programs wanted to be seen as distinct from instructional faculty.

The advent and implementation of collective bargaining revived the issue. As the Public Employee Relations Board worked with the unions and the individuals involved with collective bargaining, the issue of student affairs employees simply was lost. The counselors were a tight group, and professional issues were involved; they managed to establish themselves, over time, as integral members of the faculty bargaining unit. Many in student affairs saw themselves as and were understood by others to be administrators, and were placed in the management category. Student affairs staffs, more often than not, were fragmented. The student affairs classifications, precisely parallel to conventional faculty ranks with comparable career patterns, were dropped. Student affairs positions, apart from counselors and those placed in management, returned to the position-by-position classification mode. There was simply no discussion of the matter; it just happened. At the time, I was the only president with any student affairs experience, and the issue simply did not get on the table.

* * *

The board of trustees, with the appointment of the early Reagan trustees in 1967 and 1968, underwent a change of tone with respect to faculty. This was the time of serious social upheaval on many campuses, and state college campuses were not immune, particularly the San Francisco campus. Relationships among the Academic Senate, the several faculty organizations, the chancellor's office, and board were at a low point. Campus administrations were swept into this. Only a few campuses, with skillful faculty and administrative leadership, leadership in which cooperation between faculty and administration, however achieved, was absolutely essential, avoided the growth of tension and continuing conflict. At a May 1969 meeting of the board of trustees, Governor Reagan proposed that the trustees take back the power to appoint, tenure, and promote faculty on all of the state college campuses. The presidents unanimously opposed Reagan's proposal. The chancellor supported the presidents. The governor made the same proposal at a meeting of the regents six weeks earlier, and he prevailed. He did not prevail with the trustees.[14]

In 1970 the trustees examined faculty disciplinary procedures. Some of the trustees, presidents, and faculty did not believe that a capacity to discipline faculty was sufficiently strong. The trustees asked the chancellor to assemble an ad hoc committee to address faculty discipline. This committee consisted of four presidents (including S. I. Hayakawa), three trustees, two members of the chancellor's staff, and four faculty. The committee's report recommended removing faculty discipline from the conventional faculty committee/president format to a hearing format presided over by a lawyer with the responsibility to determine the facts. This was to be followed by a faculty committee to consider the case with no new evidence. The committee would forward a recommendation to the campus president, who would forward his or her action to the chancellor; the chancellor had the authority to change the decision. The four faculty on the ad hoc committee wrote a minority report and presented it to the board of trustees. Only one trustee, William Norris (who would later become a federal judge), supported the faculty position. The board adopted the report and then went on to adopt a similar set of procedures for addressing faculty grievances.[15]

In February 1969, the trustees considered a proposal to require each faculty member to certify monthly that he or she had met all responsibilities; this certification was to be under penalty of perjury. The proposal was a product of its time. The trustees did not adopt the proposal but simply gave presidents the authority to require an individual certification in any instance in which they thought this to be necessary. In March 1971, a trustee brought the idea back to the board. This time the proposal was for individual certification by each academic employee, again under the penalty of perjury. The chancellor's staff was directed to bring an action item to the board at the May 1971 meeting. The staff brought four alternative resolutions to the board. A trustee committee adopted a resolution directing each president to require certification from each academic employee for each pay period, and made certification optional with the president for administrative and nonacademic employees; the penalty of perjury clause was dropped.

In the full board discussion, the motion was changed and the thrust of the action redirected; each president was required to verify that all employees of his or her institution had met their responsibilities, except as noted on the monthly attendance reports beginning with the September 1971 pay period. Further, each president was asked to report, at the November 1971 board meeting, about the procedure he or she had implemented. The presidents were on their own. Presidential responses varied from no change, to the existing monthly attendance report completed by administrative units, to actually implementing individual faculty certification. Presidents who did the latter were fearful of board intrusion on campus administration. At the scheduled November meeting, the presidents urged the board to drop the certification issue. The discussion became heated. Presidents accused trustees of causing deterioration in faculty morale. Some trustees accused presidents of being "over-zealous" in their implementation of a benign procedure. The conclusion of the board discussion was to leave the board resolution in place; in effect, this was no change from long-standing procedures of attendance reporting and payroll verification. The impact of this adventure of several trustees, poorly handled by the chancellor's staff and some of the presidents, was a negative one, impacting faculty relationships and perceived support from the trustees and system leadership.[16]

* * *

Faculty workload had been a continuing concern of faculty leadership since the time of the Master Plan. The normal faculty workload had been twelve weighted teaching units each semester for many years. For conventional lecture and discussion classes, this translates to four three-unit classes. For classes involving laboratories or other activities, equivalents had been developed over the years. In 1954, the deans of instruction from the state college campuses achieved agreement among themselves and then secured the concurrence of the State Department of Finance for the adoption of a "faculty staffing formula." In one sense, this was an accomplishment. The faculty staffing formula was like a program budget. Thus, faculty positions were secured on a regular and predictable basis each year, based upon careful and detailed microprojections for enrollment in each course; these were done on the campuses. While perhaps useful as a budgeting tool, this approach created the risk, and often the reality, of program inflexibility, locking in modes of instruction and the details of curriculum. Implementation of the staffing formula was done each year on the campuses, course by course, and then forwarded to the chancellor's staff for review; the chancellor's staff, with some frequency, raised questions about projected enrollment in courses, and sometimes challenged the course classifications and more often enrollment projections. When the chancellor's staff and the campuses reached agreement, the projected implementation was forwarded to the Department of Finance, where the same review would take place. Budget analysts, most often junior staff in Finance, would on occasion challenge course classifications and projected course enrollments, and a process of reconciliation would follow.

By the 1960s and the years of Master Plan implementation, the conventional teaching load on many, if not most campuses nationally, comparable to the state colleges, had become nine units. One of the early accomplishments of the new chancellor's staff was to secure agreement from the Department of Finance that the normal load for teaching graduate students would be ten units, resulting in generation of additional faculty positions. (This "graduate differential" would disappear in the early 1970s and, after years of asking, reappear after the year 2000, as the independent doctorate was implemented.) Faculty pressure to reduce the normal course load from twelve to nine units was a developing cause in the 1960s. The president of San Diego State became a leader in this effort; San Diego was the first campus to implement the joint doctorate and an early campus to define research within the context of the state college mission. In a 1968 legal opinion, Norman Epstein, the vice-chancellor and general counsel, outlined a range of flexibility in the use of the faculty staffing formula. The ultimate test was teaching the number of students and generating the number of full-time equivalent enrollments that the staffing funded. "The formulas and guidelines which make up the faculty formula are for each college to administer according to their terms. . . . They include a considerable degree of flexibility when translated into practical application at the campus. . . . There is no doubt but that the college president and his designees are empowered to do this."[17] Epstein's view was far more benign than actual implementation.

The Epstein memo was not widely circulated among the campuses. However, the Dumke initiative of 1970 and 1971, New Approaches, engendered a spirit of experimentation on some of the campuses, largely dependent upon the style of leadership of presidents and academic vice presidents. The academic vice presidents for a time in the 1970s played an important leadership role as a group. In 1973, they proposed as a group the replacement of the faculty staffing formula with a structure of student faculty ratios, while maintaining the same basic budget generation factors. This was rejected by the academic planning staff. The end result was that on some campuses, creative faculty members, department chairs, deans, and/or academic vice presidents were able to work around the faculty staffing formula and achieve some level of flexibility. The formula was maintained in theory for a number of years, but the impact of "unallocated budget reductions" after Proposition 13 and, subsequently, the impact of collective bargaining provided the circumstances for the faculty staffing formula simply to expire of its own weight.[18]

* * *

Faculty grievances had been an issue on some campuses, and for some faculty, since the time of the Master Plan. As Master Plan discussions were underway, and in the months of early 1960 when the two houses in the legislature were considering the Master Plan recommendations, members of the legislature were lobbied on both the topics of collective bargaining and grievances. The lobbying principally came from San Francisco State and an active faculty member in philosophy, Arthur Bierman was key to it. The lobbying did not produce any results, but it did contribute to setting the stage for events in the later 1960s. Bierman remained as an active participant in many faculty political activities through the 1960s and into the early 1970s.

Grievance procedures developed soon after the 1961 assumption of responsibility by the board of trustees was implemented. Grievances are always the source of some tension. In 1970, new grievance procedures were adopted by the trustees, following a review of existing procedures that focused largely on faculty disciplinary matters. The ad hoc committee that drafted the proposed new grievance procedures was the same group that drafted the faculty disciplinary procedures (four presidents, three trustees, four faculty and two chancellor's staff members). The report of the committee on grievance procedures, just as in the disciplinary procedures report, had four negative faculty votes.

The newly adopted grievance procedures were identical to the disciplinary procedures, and included an outside hearing officer selected by the campus president, a final campus decision by the president, and ultimately a final decision made by the chancellor, with the possibility of a board review and action. An early grievance case that became celebrated was on the San Jose campus. Jack Kurzweil, an engineering professor and liberal political activist, was denied tenure after a positive faculty committee recommendation. Kurzweil filed a grievance seeking the award of tenure. He was successful at the campus level. The chancellor overturned the campus decision. A political storm erupted, not only on the San Jose campus, but on other campuses, bringing some unity to a number of the faculty organizations seeking wider faculty support and, ultimately, collective bargaining. One tactic used on some campuses was the filing of many grievance actions, in effect, flooding the system. Kurzweil ultimately prevailed in court, and had a full career at San Jose State.

The statewide Academic Senate pressed for changes. Some progress toward reconsideration seemed possible, and serious discussions were underway in early 1974. The chancellor and some members of his staff met with the executive committees of both the Academic Senate and the Council of Presidents. Shortly thereafter, Chancellor Dumke proclaimed he was giving up temporarily any total revision of the executive order governing grievances; the issue was simply too intense within the board of trustees. He did want to secure some revisions, and he specifically wanted to remove his office from the process. The meeting resulted in a set of principles that would replace the appeals process beyond the campus with outside arbitration. The Academic Senate accepted the principles. The Council of Presidents declined to approve them. The chancellor, however, went ahead with some of the revisions. The statewide Academic Senate had hoped for more. The presidents were split. In formal meetings, the prevailing tone was that of being "firm" with faculty. However, a substantial block of presidents hoped for the emergence of a spirit of comity with the faculty.[19]

The November 1974 election brought California a new governor, Edmund (Jerry) Brown. Brown had committed himself during the campaign to the support of collective bargaining in public higher education. A young member of the legislature, Assembly Member Howard Berman from Los Angeles, had been the attorney for one of the faculty groups urging collective bargaining and hoping to be the agent to represent the faculty. Berman responded to the interest of the statewide Academic Senate and the faculty organizations; he introduced Assembly Bill 804 on February 17, 1975. The bill was brief. It provided for the inclusion of temporary and part-time faculty in grievances, optional (for the grievant) faculty hearing committees, open hearings, the right to counsel or an advisor, and, "[I]f there is disagreement between the faculty hearing committee's decision and the university or college president's decision, the matter shall go before an arbitrator whose decision shall be final."[20] Most legislators, on both sides of the aisle, were familiar with the faculty issues; the Academic Senate and faculty organizations were in members' offices regularly with their concerns. The chancellor's office and the trustees strongly opposed the bill, and some efforts were made to seek a compromise with the Academic Senate leadership; these went nowhere, and the bill was enacted with bipartisan support in September. New procedures complying with the legislation became effective on January 1, 1976.

* * *

In 1973–74 and 1974–75, a new phenomenon emerged on most, though not all of the campuses, "steady state," stable enrollment with no growth. The campuses, for the most part, had experienced growth year after year beginning in the early 1960s, and program development and the management of academic programs had become dependent on growth. This was not true for all campuses, as some had, for whatever reason, deliberately held back growth and had developed budgeting assumptions and processes not based on growth. In a sense, the sudden emergence of the issue was surprising because the demographic information was available and known prior to the concern about steady state. All of the potential students had been born eighteen years earlier. Individual campuses addressed the matter in different ways, and some campuses did not address the issue at all. The Chico campus made a first move, developing within the context of established meetings of academic deans and department chairs what it called the "75/25 policy." The focal point of concern was not program development per se, but faculty positions. The 75/25 policy at Chico required that departments or other defined "teaching service areas" (a concept that then had legal meaning. as faculty appointments and tenure were on a campus and within one or more teaching service areas) have no more that 75 percent of their faculty in tenured or tenure track positions. The rationale for the policy was that student interests and enrollments change over time, as do program needs, and thus a margin of useful flexibility would not only serve individual faculty members, but the integrity of the concept of tenure. The policy was generally accepted on the campus, though not by all.

In January 1974, the chancellor created the Task Force on Steady State Staffing, to address the issue of faculty appointments in a time of steady state enrollments. The task force included five vice presidents for academic affairs, two members of the statewide Academic Senate, and three chancellor's office staff members.[21] The task force's report in November 1974 was descriptive, but not definitive; it was circulated widely within the system, but not addressed in any significant way. The report did not recommend changes in the existing system policies about layoff.

At the November 1975 meeting of the board of trustees, trustee Jeanette Ritchie, in a discussion about layoff of nonacademic employees, proposed that layoff of employees of the California State University and Colleges in all categories, including faculty, be based on competency and merit. The words were used interchangeably; the proposal was immediately understood by faculty and others as an attack on tenure. Ritchie knew the system reasonably well; she had been a part-time faculty member in nursing at San Francisco State. Her proposal caught all by surprise. Her motivation was not clear; the assumption was that her thinking was affected by her experience at San Francisco State. It would require board action to change the California Administrative Code, an action that legally requires advance notice. As her proposal was not germane to the immediate discussion, it was laid over to the January 1976 trustees' meeting, and the chancellor's staff was instructed to bring to the board agenda implementing language. Heretofore, layoff had been sequenced from temporary employees to probationary employees to tenured employees (or those with permanent status in the nonacademic ranks) in order of seniority and by classification. The Ritchie amendment, as it was immediately labeled throughout the state, became the focal point of great controversy.

The trustees received an enormous amount of correspondence and phone calls. The pressure became great, so great that a special interim meeting of the Trustee Committee on Faculty and Staff Affairs was called for January 15 in the new year, 1976. Attendance at the meeting was unusual and included the entire statewide Academic Senate. The senate was scheduled for the opening of its periodic meeting on that morning in Los Angeles; the entire senate membership came to the trustee committee meeting. Testimony was heard from Dr. Gerald Marley, Academic Senate chair, and presidents or representatives of the American Association of University Professors, the United Professors of California, the Association of California State University Professors, the California College and University Faculty Association, the Congress of Faculty Associations, the Clerical and Allied Services Employees, the California State Employees Association, and the California Teachers Association, and representative faculty and staff from the Los Angeles, San Jose, and Fresno campuses. Clearly the proposal had brought together faculty interests and traditional civil service interests.

Mansel Keene brought a proposal to the trustees at the January 1976 board meeting, the week after the special board committee meeting. Keene's proposal was, in the eyes of the affected groups of faculty and other employees, more narrowly drawn that Ritchie's statements had been. He proposed that layoffs be based only upon "relative competency," not competency as an additional factor. Discussion among the trustees was lengthy and strong. Two trustees, William Weissich, a Reagan appointee and at that time the district attorney of Marin County, and Mary Jean Pew, one of the two first Jerry Brown appointees and a former president of Immaculate Heart College in Los Angeles, strongly disagreed with the proposal. Trustee Roy Brophy was the chair of the board's Faculty and Staff Affairs Committee; he supported the proposal. Trustee Charles Luckman came late to the discussion. Luckman was by this time the senior member of the board, an original Pat Brown appointee; he was particularly negative toward the faculty in the give and take of the meeting. The presidents tried to stay clear, but could not completely do so, and the chair, L. Donald Shields of Fullerton, presented a written statement endorsing the concept of merit and calling for further work on a policy. The set of resolutions that Keene had brought to the meeting was adopted by the board with three negative votes; the action was not final, as this was a first reading.

In the wake of the board meeting, activity was furious. Commitments were received from ex-officio members of the board, Lieutenant Governor Mervyn Dymally, Speaker Leo McCarthy, and State Superintendent of Public Instruction Wilson Riles, to oppose the proposal. The governor publicly stated in late February, a full month before the March Board meeting, that the proposal was dead. Chancellor Dumke's concern rose, and he sent one of his infrequent memos: "To the Presidents, Faculties, Administrative and Support Staffs, and Students of the California State University and Colleges." He opened with a sentence revealing concern: "The ferment within our system over the Trustees' January 28 resolution concerning layoff has been stronger and more unsettling than that over any other recent issue. It has confounded those who saw the issue as simply the furtherance of the concept of merit. . . ."[22] Dumke asserted strongly that this was not an attack on tenure or permanent status for staff who had earned it through a probationary period.

In early March, Dumke met with of the statewide Academic Senate's executive committee. It became clear that he was looking for a way out of the controversy. Not long after, President Robert Kennedy of the San Luis Obispo campus wrote to the governor (who is ex-officio president of the board) and copied all of the trustees, presidents, senior chancellor's staff, and the chairs of the Student Presidents' Association and the Academic Senate. His message was that it was possible to respect both tenure and merit. He urged the adoption of a practice that had existed at Cal Poly at San Luis Obispo since 1971 that addressed merit in a context of improvement and growth. His was an effort to end an extraordinarily divisive discussion and issue. The March meeting of the board produced a surprise. The chair of the board, Robert Hornby, asked that a statement on his behalf be read to the members of the board and all those present. Lee Kerschner, then a senior member of the chancellor's staff, read the statement and made clear that Hornby wanted to address competency and merit. In part, the brief statement read, "[T]o delineate a procedure on layoffs if and when they should be required . . . involves matters other than seniority and program balance, affirmative action, and merit. Merit is always difficult to define, although it may be recognized in reviewing the performance of individuals. . . . Further effort requiring more time must be devoted to attempting to resolve these complex matters. At present, there is no immediate need to define a layoff procedure."[23] Hornby then called upon Ritchie, who withdrew her earlier motion and called for a study over the coming year. The issue died.

* * *

These events of the late sixties and early 1970s help in the understanding of the advent of collective bargaining, a complex narrative. Collective bargaining had been on some agendas since the days of Master Plan discussions. A small number of faculty and a few union officials had raised the matter with members of the legislature in 1959 and 1960. There was no serious consideration of collective bargaining in the Master Plan discussions, and no legislative pressure developed.

In the early to mid-1960s, the possibility of collective bargaining was a consistent undertone in the state colleges. The interest and pressure, which was not strong, was, for the greater part, from faculty. There was little organized staff interest, although an attempt was made at San Francisco State to organize food service employees. In March 1961, Glenn Dumke, then president of the San Francisco campus, wrote to Assembly Member Phillip Burton that "the official policy of the administration of San Francisco State College, which has been made very clear to all employees, is that we are not opposed to their joining a legitimate union. We will work with any legally recognized employee organization in connection with working conditions or other problems."[24] Dumke's letter, conciliatory in tone, did not address the meaning of "work with any legally recognized employee organization," nor could it, realistically. This was in the middle of the transition year from the State Board of Education to the board of trustees. There was no public policy framework.

Bargaining continued to be in and out of discussions on the campuses, among the trustees and chancellor's office, and in Sacramento. Potential faculty union leaders on two campuses, San Fernando Valley and San Jose, in early 1966 wrote to Chancellor Dumke, asking him to "join in conducting a collective bargaining election among the academic employees. . . ." Similar letters were sent to all of the trustees. Dumke responded in a letter to John Sperling, the president of the American Federation of Teachers local at San Jose State; the letter, in which Dumke declined to join in conducting the election, was widely circulated on the campuses.[25] Trustee Louis Heilbron, no longer chair of the board, also wrote to Sperling. "I am obliged to decline your invitation. As I am sure you know, the Board of Trustees has not met to take action on this proposal—and, indeed, your letters do not ask that it do so, nor do they follow the appropriate procedures for making such a request; they ask, instead, that each individual Trustee join in the proposed election. Consequently, my denial of your request is as an individual member of the Trustees." Heilbron went on to state that all trustees with whom he had discussed the matter agreed with Dumke's response. "[I]t is our view that the substitution of a labor-management collective bargaining approach to faculty relations, in place of faculty senates and councils would not only exceed our legal authority, but will introduce an employer-employee relationship into a highly professional field. . . . [B]y forcing the Board into an adversary position on questions of faculty benefits, your proposal would impair the effective efforts and leadership of the Board in striving to extend and expand these benefits and damage the professional relationship. . . . This would not only be inconsistent with our primary charge as Trustees, but an abrogation of the responsibility which that charge connotes." Heilbron went on to write that there had been no "subject which has engaged more of our attention since 1961 than support for the faculty." In a sense, Heilbron's letter was an eloquent summary statement of a continuing position held by many members of the board.[26]

In April 1966, the statewide Academic Senate established the Ad Hoc Committee on Collective Bargaining. In the fall of 1966, this committee recommended to the Academic Senate that it "should serve as an information source and election agent for the faculty."[27] The committee went ahead with its plan. An issues list was prepared by the committee, with the cooperation of the then existing faculty organizations, the American Association of University Professors (AAUP), the Association of California State College Professors (ACSCP), the American Federation of Teachers (AFT), the California College and University Faculty Association (CCUFA), and the California State Employees Association (CSEA). This was published in booklet form and circulated to all faculty members. The wording on the ballot was "Collective Bargaining—The faculty should elect an exclusive bargaining agent from those faculty organizations which are prepared to recommend and apply sanctions in efforts to secure adequate economic support for the goals of the faculties and which are willing to place their names on an election ballot." The voting boxes were labeled "for" and "against." Four of the five organizations supported a "for" vote. The CSEA was "against."

The balloting was held on all of the campuses in the week of May 22, 1967. A total of 8,496 ballots were distributed and 5,757 were returned, a return rate of almost 68 percent. The results doubtless surprised some individuals, disappointed some, and satisfied others: 2,741 ballots were cast "for," 47 percent, and 3,016 ballots cast "against," 52 percent. A majority of the voting faculty on six campuses, Hayward, Los Angeles, San Bernardino, San Fernando Valley, San Francisco, and San Jose supported collective bargaining at rates ranging from 54.7 percent (San Jose) to 71.0 percent (San Bernardino). On the remaining twelve campuses, a majority of the voting faculty opposed at rates ranging from 50.7 percent (Sonoma) to around 70 percent (San Luis Obispo, 72 percent; Chico, 69.8 percent; and Humboldt, 71 percent). The votes "for" were in an absolute majority on the San Bernardino campus, and just a few short of an absolute majority at Los Angeles.[28]

At the same time the faculty poll campaign was underway on the campuses, the Association of California State College Professors was selected by the faculty at San Francisco State College as their bargaining agent. In the summer of 1967, a legislative hearing was held about the status of faculty senates on the campus and statewide. The California State Employees Association, in testimony before the state Senate, gave strong support to placing the faculty senates in statute, beyond the recognition already accorded by the board of trustees. That did not happen; the votes were not there. They did, however, secure the commitment of Senator George Miller, still one of the most powerful members of the legislature, that collective bargaining in the California State Colleges was not legal, and he would oppose it on that basis. This position was disputed by many groups maintaining that a prior legislative action, the George Brown Act of 1961, authorized in a general way meeting and conferring with employee organizations about employment conditions—in fact, authorized collective bargaining. The Brown Act did not establish a process for determining bargaining units or for establishing exclusive representatives.[29]

The trustees scheduled a major discussion with a joint meeting of the Committee on Educational Policy and Committee on Faculty and Staff Affairs for the September 1967 board meeting. As he so often did, trustee Heilbron prepared a lengthy (twenty-four page) paper for members of the two committees. The audience was really a wider one, not only trustees, but the state college community. Heilbron observed early in the paper that the adoption of collective bargaining would fundamentally change administration and faculty professional relationships. He examined in some detail the legal and professional implications of collective bargaining. He concluded that the people of the state colleges and of California would best be served by the already classic model of governance set forth by the

American Association of University Professors in 1966. "As applied to the system of State Colleges, these principles support the continued growth, strengthening, and development of the statewide and local senates." He observed that bargaining had not been authorized by the legislature, and his set of draft resolutions stated unambiguously that "[t]he Trustees will not advocate such legislation."[30] Not without controversy, Heilbron's position prevailed and, in one form or another, continued to be the position of the trustees into the 1970s, and the drive toward collective bargaining attendant to the 1974 gubernatorial election campaign and the election of Jerry Brown to the governorship.

Faculty interest in collective bargaining did not subside, but it was consumed by the events of the later 1960s, the continuing conflict at San Francisco State, and the spread of that conflict, in one form or another, to many campuses, along with the Vietnam War and the emergence of major racial and ethnic activism. Statewide Academic Senate agendas continued to include the topic. The faculty membership organizations continued to strengthen themselves, and ultimately to sort themselves. In reality, the Academic Senate, and particularly its Committee on Faculty Affairs, handled many of the matters that a membership organization, a faculty union, would address. This was simply by default. Often the Academic Senate leadership would reach out to the several faculty membership organizations for help in the legislature.

In 1971, Governor Ronald Reagan signed Executive Order 71-3, which provided for employee-employer—actually meet and confer—meetings about wages, hours, and other terms and conditions of employment. Signed memoranda of understanding (MOU) could be the result if the representatives achieved a mutual understanding. The executive order had little or no impact in the state colleges. The parties were focused and intent on collective bargaining, for and against.

A shakeout occurred among the faculty organizations in the early 1970s. Five organizations soon reduced to two. The process was complex and accompanied by much organizational infighting. The Academic Senate leadership was not directly involved, in part, due to several major issues in which the Academic Senate took leadership—tenure procedures, grievance procedures, faculty disciplinary procedures, payroll certification, steady state, and the Ritchie amendment. The senate leadership would make common cause with faculty organizations, but it was issue oriented. The American Federation of Teachers units on the campuses became the United Professors of California (UPC). The California College and University Faculty Association, the California State Employees Association, the American Association of University Professors, and the California Teachers Association, which had worked with CCUFA and was the California affiliate of the National Education Association, came together and became the Congress of Faculty Associations, and then the California Faculty Association.

The faculty grievance issue, discussed earlier, became woven into the ongoing collective bargaining discussion. Howard Berman's bill, AB 804, brought together UPC and CFA leadership. Both organizations worked for the bill. Warren Kessler, a faculty member from the Fresno campus and the president of UPC, and June Pollak, a faculty member from the Fullerton campus and a new leader in the formation of CFA, became familiar figures on the campuses and in Sacramento. Pollak was followed by William Crist, an economist at Stanislaus, who emerged as a major leader in the give and take with the legislature in 1977–78, and in the implementation process after 1978. Crist, as president of CFA, remained a major player in faculty union activities and a respected figure for years.[31]

With the assumption of the governor's office by Jerry Brown, the activity around Berman's grievance bill, and the apparent cumulative impact of the trustee initiatives of the past five years, two senior members of the chancellor's staff came to the same conclusion: there was an inevitability about collective bargaining. James Jensen, the director of the Sacramento office and the principal lobbyist in Sacramento, and Lee Kerschner, by then assistant executive vice-chancellor, were convinced that a collective bargaining bill would pass in the legislature. Governor Jerry Brown had already committed himself to supporting legislation and signing a collective bargaining bill. Kerschner and Jensen went to Glenn Dumke and urged that the staff undertake the writing of collective bargaining legislation. They told Dumke that they were certain union legislation could successfully work through the legislature—which faculty group, UPC (originally the AFT) or CFA (an amalgam of several faculty organizations),would be the lead was not clear. What was clear was legislative ultimate support. Dumke refused, a decision of extraordinary consequence. His reasoning was that Governor Ronald Reagan's appointees made the board very conservative, and he feared the consequences of opening the issue with the board.

With the 1976 midterm election concluded, CFA leaders went to work on drafting legislation. Lawyers from the American Association of University Professors and the National Education Association, along with a small number of faculty, drafted collective bargaining legislation. Bargaining legislation had recently been enacted for K-14 school faculty; the Rodda Act was named for its principle author, Senator Albert Rodda. Rodda was an economist and a former faculty member at Sacramento City College. William Crist, Robert Phelps (then the chief staff member of CFA), and others went to Rodda to ask that he carry the bill they had prepared. Rodda declined; his explanation was that he thought it unwise, as he had so recently carried the K-14 legislation. He suggested Howard Berman. The CFA leadership of course knew Berman from AB 804, the successful legislation about grievances; the UPC leadership had worked with Berman and knew him well. CFA and UPC joined forces. Berman agreed to carry the legislation.

Berman's staff, UPC and CFA leadership, and the Academic Senate, all participated in a series of meetings. Representatives of the University of California Academic Senate participated, as did a senior UC administrator. The regents had passed a formal resolution directing the president of the UC to participate in deliberations about collective bargaining legislation. Archie Kleingartner, the UC vice president who worked with personnel matters, and the UC Academic Senate were there to see that the bill did not upset the satisfactory governance situation for faculty in the University of California. They had a second objective, to keep graduate student assistants out of any proposed legislation. They succeeded in both objectives. The California State Employees Association (CSEA) became heavily involved at this point; their initial involvement in the 1960s had focused on faculty. They were now involved on behalf of nonacademic employees, half of the California State University and Colleges workforce. CSEA had a strong higher education group and it was well staffed. The coalition was large and, in fact, reached beyond California. The UPC and the American Federation of Teachers had to support the ultimate bill; the CFA and the National Education Association had to support the bill; the California State Employees Association had to support it. The drafting was carefully done to avoid the use of the words "collective bargaining." William Crist, who played a major role working the bill through the legislature, later commented that he would always describe the bill as a "meet and confer" bill in meetings with legislators and staff.

The product of all the staff work became Assembly Bill 1091, introduced by Assembly Member Berman. It was a two-year bill. It did not pass during the 1977 session; in large measure, this had little to do with the California State University and Colleges, and was related to struggles among various state employee groups.

With the introduction of AB 1091, the issue of collective bargaining was joined for all within the California State University and Colleges. Trustee Roy Brophy, chair of the board's Committee on Faculty and Staff Affairs, was active in his opposition and, in a practical sense, took charge of the issue for the trustees and for the chancellor's staff. The presidents, who were not involved as a practical matter, were mostly opposed. Those presidents who thought there might be some reasonable and practical way out of a conventional labor-management model effectively silenced themselves, although a small number did try to work with statewide Academic Senate leaders. Brophy undertook visits to campuses and proposed alternative models to collective bargaining. The Sacramento lobbyists for the system, Jim Jensen and Scott Plotkin, simply had instructions to oppose 1091, but had no authority to engage in any of the give and take of the legislative deliberations.

The collective bargaining bill was about both the California State University and Colleges and the University of California. In fact, the impetus and the driving force behind the bill were the CSUC, the faculty organizations, and the Academic Senate. However, the regents and the senior administration of the University of California deliberately became involved. The chair of the regents at the time, William French Smith (later to be US attorney general during Reagan's first presidential term), made clear to Assembly Member Berman that while he was not an advocate for AB 1091, he and the regents were not opposed, as long as legislation would address specific concerns and not abrogate the role of the UC Academic Senate. Vice President Kleingartner of the University of California attempted to work with CSUC individuals about the legislation, but was not successful. He later said that the UC and the CSUC were "on two different tracks." Kleingartner told Berman and his legislative colleagues that the University of California agreed that employees should have the right to unionize; the regents adopted a resolution to that effect. With respect to the faculty, a union would have to be subordinate to the Academic Senate, and the Academic Senate would have to vote and grant authority. Kleingartner and Berman worked out language for 1091. The UC's potential union groups agreed.[32]

The contrast between the CSUC and the UC was not lost on legislators. The senior administration of the CSUC simply was not part of the process. The CSUC had only one position—opposition to any proposed legislation authorizing collective bargaining. For all practical purposes, the CSUC was represented by a single trustee, who appointed himself to the role. As the UC was developing its position, trustee Roy Brophy phoned Kleingartner and urged that the UC "get on board" with the CSUC. This did not happen. Brophy, whose membership on the board was unique, was appointed by two governors at two different times, was three times chair, became the CSUC primary advocate against 1091; he later became a UC Regent. Others involved in the process believed that his opposition was genuine, and that he firmly believed the bill would not pass.

The statewide Academic Senate played an active and, ultimately, a critical role in the adoption of AB 1091. In many ways, the focus of the Academic Senate in the early 1970s had been on a combination of the Dumke New Approaches initiative and, as the years wore on, the initiatives of the trustees that were often perceived as negative from a faculty point of view. In 1975, Gerald Marley from the Fullerton campus was elected Academic Senate chair; his competition for the position, David Elliott of San Jose, was elected vice-chair. Events moved the senate toward a more active concern with issues relevant to collective bargaining. It voted to support collective bargaining, and had a firm position during Marley's 1975–77 chairmanship. The Academic Senate became involved in the discussions leading up to the introduction of AB 1091 in early 1977. Not long after the introduction of the collective bargaining bill, trustee Roy Brophy invited John O'Connell, the newly appointed alumni trustee (and then the president of the Bechtel Corporation, substantially experienced in employee and labor relations), Marley and Elliott to his townhouse in Sacramento for lunch. Brophy, who was also an alumnus (he had studied at San Luis Obispo and, after World War II, received the baccalaureate from San Jose State), personally prepared lunch. The conversation turned to collective bargaining. Brophy made it clear that he opposed collective bargaining; he believed it would erode quality and destroy collegiality. He sought another model. Brophy had proposed a model of "internal bargaining." This model was not essentially different from existing procedures, but did represent a significant commitment from the trustees to make very broad and inclusive consultation actually work. He was determined to hold on to the final responsibility of the board of trustees. Marley, about to leave the role of Academic Senate chair, was firm in his response that the senate was clear in its support of collective bargaining and that the faculty was supportive systemwide. Marley was in effect asserting that much had changed since the faculty poll in 1967.

Brophy did follow through with his concept of internal bargaining; he visited campuses, he spent time at the capital in Sacramento (Sacramento was his home; he was a successful builder and community leader there), and he was ever present for trustee discussions about collective bargaining. He made a major effort at the

20. Campus protest.

September 1977 board meeting to have the trustees develop a new model; he did not give up on the concept of internal bargaining or negotiations.

From the standpoint of the statewide Academic Senate, the major issue was the scope of bargaining and the role of faculty senates should bargaining be adopted. The Academic Senate agreed to the conventional National Labor Relations Board language, "wages, hours, and working conditions." Thus, the Academic Senate was walking a path between the trustees and administration and the potential faculty unions—the advocates of the legislation. This became the major work of David Elliott in the first of his two years as chair of the statewide Academic Senate. Members of the legislature were not disinterested in the language of the bill and how it would work. Senator Rodda, an experienced academic, was insistent that the role of the statewide Academic Senate and campus academic senates be maintained and that a collegial governance process would prevail. Elliott was out of action, due to surgery, for more than a month in late 1977. While he was hospitalized and recovering, he drafted a proposal to define the scope of bargaining as wages, hours, and terms and conditions; the proposal provided for instances when management refuses to consult "in good faith" with academic senates, both statewide and campus, on other matters outside the scope of bargaining.

These matters could become the subject of bargai...ng. Subsequently, Elliott drafted a paper that began the discussion on the role of academic senates in an era of collective bargaining. This became a critical discussion in the spring of 1978. The turning point was convincing Senator Rodda of the continuation of the roles of academic senates—that the senates would have an appropriate and substantive role in decision making. Rodda's focus was on the system level. The Elliott proposal, in his words, was that "on the employee side of the faculty member, there be a collective bargaining process that could secure and maintain fundamental rights to which people are entitled as employees. But for the other side, the academic side . . . [to] develop a collegial decision-making process that allows us to exercise responsibility and authority. . . ."[33] Elliott's work was not over; he had to convince the leadership of the two key faculty organizations, William Crist of the CFA and Warren Kessler of the UPC, and he did so. The several staff associations were supportive; they simply wanted the collective bargaining proposal enacted. Howard Berman agreed, and Senator Rodda became convinced of the continuity of academic senates.

The final legislation was modified to include provision for criteria and standards for retention, tenure, and promotion to be the joint responsibility of the trustees and the statewide Academic Senate, and it stopped short of giving the senate unilateral authority to place matters into bargaining; it simply stated that *when* management fails to consult, the issue shall be subject to bargaining.[34]

Howard Berman had worked with his colleagues in the assembly; AB 1091 passed with a substantial margin. The senate was a different matter; the Education Committee and the Finance Committee were both unpredictable as to the outcome. Trustee Roy Brophy was certain, to the time of the last vote, that he would succeed in defeating the proposed legislation. In both committees, the proposal passed by one vote. With passage of the bill in the Finance Committee, its passage in the senate was assured. Elliott, after the Finance Committee vote, returned to Long Beach and the statewide Academic Senate office; he asked for an appointment with Chancellor Dumke. Dumke, who generally was available to meet people, invited him to meet immediately. When Elliott conveyed the news of the Finance Committee vote, both knew that this meant collective bargaining would soon be a fact. Dumke's reaction to Elliott, as Elliott paraphrased it, was to shake hands and say, "Dave, you did it fair and square; congratulations."[35] Governor Jerry Brown signed the collective bargaining legislation in September 1978.

It is reasonable to ask the question about the inevitability of collective bargaining. The most important factor in the changing governance of the California State University was the maturing of the system. It is at least arguable that the most important decision made about governance was the 1978 decision to enter into collective bargaining. The history of the years leading up to the 1978 decision suggests several factors. The very beginning of the system, 1959–61, was a time laden with anger. The faculty at San Francisco State (a sufficient number to cause others to generalize about "the faculty," as if it were a whole) were angry with their new president, Glenn Dumke, who was in many ways very traditional and determined to change the character of the institution to align with his philosophy of a strong academic college. Glenn Dumke was many things; he was a quiet, pipe-smoking academic who seldom, if ever, raised his voice, and his leadership in the creation of what is now the California State University was extraordinary. He was not a skilled politician, inside or outside of the academy, although he certainly prevailed with his most basic goals. His faculty's anger, even though from a small group in number, contaminated other campuses and the life of the system for years beyond Dumke's presidency and subsequent chancellorship. It was a major factor in the events of the later 1960s. The trustees were, without exception, new to their roles, yet remarkable productive leadership emerged on the board. The gubernatorial pendulum swung from the always supportive Pat Brown, to the initially negative Ronald Reagan, and then to Jerry Brown. One of the early Reagan appointees, Dudley Swim, was open about his opinion that the California State Colleges should not exist; when asked why he would want to be a trustee, his response was that he was there to keep the campuses under control while they existed.

The presidents were not united. During most of the 1960s, the strongest presidential supporters of the system included those who had been the most critical during the Master Plan negotiations; some of the newer presidents waivered about support for the system. The chancellor's staff, not unlike the trustees and for the same basic reasons, were new to their roles. Some were constructive and quick to respond to their roles and opportunities, and some simply did not have the skills to build new roles. All, certainly including faculty leadership, were feeling their way.

In the late 1960s and the first half of the 1970s, the board and the administration made a series of unfortunate moves that were essentially negative to the great majority of the faculty. Ambient faculty anger was the most significant causal factor in the collective bargaining story. The stage was set for the introduction of collective bargaining for good or ill. The decision of Chancellor Dumke to absent the system from the conversation and negotiations in the legislature and elsewhere in Sacramento, and the acquiescence of the trustees to permit one member to be the only player, were significant errors in the development of the California State University. The interests of students and faculty, and all others involved with the CSU, were in the hands of statewide Academic Senate leaders, most notably, David Elliott, and Senator Albert Rodda, and Assembly Member Howard Berman.

* * *

With the signing of the collective bargaining bill, the early moves were initiated. The state created the Public Employee Relations Board (PERB). The PERB had the ultimate responsibility of defining bargaining units. If the California State University and Colleges and the proposed union in question were in agreement, they could resolve the creation of a bargaining unit short of going to PERB. The criteria for the creation of a bargaining unit are established in statute, and essentially can be understood as based on a community of interest. Initially, nine bargaining units were established systemwide. The original nine bargaining units included the following:

1. Physicians and dentists;
2. Healthcare support positions, including nurses, pharmacists, clinical lab techs, physical therapists, x-ray techs, speech pathologists, and health educators working in student health centers;
3. Faculty, including professors, lecturers, librarians, coaches, and psychological counselors;
4. Academic support, including professional student services employees such as counselors and advisors in areas such as career development, financial aid, disabled student services, equal opportunity programs, residential life, student development, credential analysts, and transcript evaluators;
5. Operations support, including custodians, groundskeepers, gardeners, equipment operators, bus drivers, laborers, and food service workers;
6. Crafts and maintenance and the skilled trades, including carpenters, plumbers, mechanics, and electricians;
7. Clerical and administrative support, including administrative support personnel, buyers, library assistants, payroll techs, account clerks, public safety dispatchers, and many other classifications;
8. Public safety, including police officers, corporals, and sergeants;
9. Technical support, including information technology, instructional support techs, public affairs assistants, research techs and others working in performing arts, agriculture, athletic departments.

In subsequent years, four additional units were formed: one small unit for the skilled trades at the California Maritime Academy, when CMA was integrated into the California State University in the 1990s, and two units for specific groups of employees at the Los Angeles and San Francisco campuses. One very large unit, currently in excess of five thousand members, is for "academic student employees, teaching associates, graduate assistants, and instructional student assistants."[36]

The process of defining the bargaining units went well, as did the identification of relevant unions to represent the units. But the biggest prize was the faculty—which union would represent faculty, then as now approximately half of the employees in the system. The two contenders were the United Professors of California, UPC, related on the national scene to the American Federation of Teachers, and the Congress of Faculty Associations, soon to be the California Faculty Association (CFA), related to the National Educational Association. The matter could only be settled by a systemwide election, as both potential unions had petitioned PERB to be the exclusive representative. Both the AFT and the NEA regarded the California State Colleges and University (which would become the California State University in 1982, in the midst of all the activity implementing collective bargaining) as a prime catch. Both invested significant sums of money and staff time in the selection of the bargaining unit. The competition was intense. The two leaders were William Crist of CFA and Warren Kessler of UPC, both of whom had been deeply involved in the legislative activity leading up to the adoption of collective bargaining. Faculty leaders in both UPC and CFA were on the campuses speaking, and the great majority of faculty on most campuses were attentive.

There were significant differences between the two groups. Faculty perceptions were generally that UPC was in the mainstream of unions in the country, and its relationship to the American Federation of Teachers made it likely the more militant of the two organizations. The CFA, on the other hand, with its relationship to the National Education Association, was seen by some faculty as the more professional of the two groups. Both CFA and UPC were seriously considered.

The outcome of the competition was close. More than 80 percent of the faculty voted. The statewide election among all faculty resulted in a close victory for the CFA, by less than a one-hundred-vote margin. Once the election was over, Warren Kessler, the leader of UPC, joined in support of the CFA. The next step would be to bargain for an initial contract. Much work remained. William Crist was the president of a union representing more than twenty thousand faculty members.

* * *

Collective bargaining legislation did not address administrators and managers. Prior to collective bargaining, there had been no need to develop provisions and rules for campus administrators and managers. Now a clear line must be drawn. The chancellor's staff prepared a proposal to define four levels of management, with increasing levels of responsibility. This proposal resulted in the Management Personnel Plan (MPP). While its instigation was collective bargaining, some kind of plan, with flexibility as a key feature, was long overdue. AB1091 and the subsequent definition of bargaining units left management and supervisory employees in the middle, between executive employees (presidents, vice-chancellors, the chancellor) and the many thousands of employees in the units. These management and supervisory employees were still in a quasi–civil service status. The groups were labeled MPP I, II, III, and IV, with four being the highest level of responsibility. The plan that was brought to the then relatively new executive council (vice-chancellors, presidents, and a few others, and chaired by the chancellor) and, subsequently the trustees, was a flexible one. Previously, management or administrative positions had been defined or classified position by position, each with a specific salary schedule. Those included would range from night-shift supervisors in plant operations to vice presidents on campuses and associate vice-chancellors. The new MPP system provided for a rather extensive salary range within each of the four levels, and did not define which level any given position should be in. For example, deans of schools or colleges were found in levels III and IV; deans could be paid different salaries. In effect, this introduced concepts of payment including market conditions, merit or performance, and the value placed on a role by a president or whoever sets salaries. Initially perceived by many as a step forward and sensible, the MPP met fierce resistance. The resistance did not come from academic administrators or those in comparable positions. Their status, at least in terms of permanency in their positions, though not salaries, had been defined by the trustees in the early 1960s. Rather, the major resistance came from those in staff supervisory and management positions, who had enjoyed the status and protection of the quasi–civil service rules that had been shifted from the State Personnel Board to the trustees in 1961–62. The California State Employees Association (CSEA), to which many of those affected belonged, took up the cause.

California statutes provide that when the trustees (or other bodies that can make administrative law) create or amend a section of the administrative law code, they must secure the approval of the Office of Administrative Law (OAL). The vice-chancellor and general counsel had advised the chancellor and board that the MPP proposal was exempt from the statutory Administrative Practices Act. The trustees adopted the MPP in November 1983, to be effective on January 1, 1984. It might be noted that this action was at the same board meeting where the trustees abolished five-step salary schedules for presidents and vice-chancellors, and instituted an experience/merit–based evaluative approach to salary setting for these positions. When a copy of the proposed Title 5 provision was sent without any substantive detail to the Office of Administrative Law, the OAL refused to approve the change, making it ineffective; the basis of their action was not on substance (the OAL had not received the substance) but rather procedural matters and "clarity." The CSU declined to accept the OAL decision, and formally requested a gubernatorial review. The matter finally reached a point at which Rusty Areias, a former Associated Students President at the Chico campus and the chair of the Joint Legislative Oversight Committee for the Administrative Procedures Act, intervened on behalf of CSEA. The governor at the time, George Deukmejian, supported the Office of Administrative Law.

The substantive issue for CSEA was the accumulated rights of the individuals affected by the Management Personnel Plan, as well as the role of CSEA and their capacity to represent nonunion members. The CSEA position prevailed, and the MPP was implemented with all of the changes CSEA sought. Importantly, those in the MPP were at-will employees and gained no permanent status in their management positions. This was also a test of will between a new senior group in the chancellor's office and state government, and it doubtless was of some significance in the change in the chancellorship in 1990.[37]

* * *

With the departure of Marjorie Downing-Wagner in late 1980, Robert Tyndall assumed interim responsibility for the faculty and staff affairs unit. He was the architect, or at least the visible architect, in bringing the Management Personnel Plan to the executive council. He would lead faculty and staff affairs through the implementation of collective bargaining, and a transition in the chancellorship from Glenn Dumke to Ann Reynolds. The chancellor's staff had no member experienced in collective bargaining. The appointment of Thomas Lambre in the faculty and staff affairs area to implement collective bargaining was made. Lambre was an unknown to many in the system, certainly to the presidents, others in the administration, and to the union leadership as well. He worked quietly and alone, and he was not communicative with the presidents, even when pressed. Lambre had no collective bargaining experience in education at any level.

In 1982, the first two contracts negotiated were for units 5 and 7, the operations support group and clerical and administrative support. The next year, contracts were negotiated for unit 2, health care support, and unit 9, technical support. These were done by the California State Employees Association, now the California State University Employees Union. Units 9 and 7, technical support and clerical and administrative support, were and are consistently the second largest units in the CSU, second only to the faculty. Contract negotiations were completed with the other units.

Negotiations with the faculty unit, CFA, were the most complex. These were underway as the chancellorship changed. Ann Reynolds had to recruit a new leadership group. The vice-chancellorship for faculty and staff affairs was occupied by Tyndall, an interim appointee. This position was central to collective bargaining, and the negotiations with the units were underway. Two were signed in 1982 as Reynolds was arriving. Negotiations with CFA and the faculty were proceeding in a context conditioned by the experience of the state colleges in the 1960s and 1970s. In the early years of the system, faculty groups, particularly groups discontented with the progress of the system, found that going to the legislature to get some very specific legislation would be productive. California in the 1960s, 1970s, and 1980s, could be characterized as having a prounion legislature. Negotiations with the CFA proved to be difficult, and in many ways, Lambre was beyond his depth.

These negotiations were underway as recruitment for the vice-chancellorship was ongoing. Two of the individuals invited to be candidates, both nationally known figures in higher education collective bargaining, were subsequently invited for interviews. Both urged Chancellor Ann Reynolds to put the faculty collective bargaining on hold until new staff experienced in higher education negotiations were in position in the chancellor's staff. For whatever reason, bargaining was not stopped.[38]

The board of trustees appointed Caesar Naples as vice-chancellor for faculty and staff affairs. Naples was nationally known in higher education collective bargaining. Naples had discussed the faculty negotiations with Chancellor Reynolds, and believed the bargaining negotiations were on hold. However, the day before Naples's arrival on the job, Lambre signed a tentative agreement with CFA. From Naples's point of view, the agreement was unfortunate, and gave away items that should have been part of ongoing negotiations, some with the legislature, as bargaining was implemented. From the CFA point of view, working with Lambre was a satisfactory experience.[39]

Two issues remained major points of contention with the faculty contract. The librarians' group wanted to be included in the faculty unit with the same salary and benefits as the professorial faculty. This was not a new issue, but a long-standing one. The custom in the state colleges had long been for librarians to be considered as full faculty. In the early years of the campuses, librarians had simply been conventional faculty with library responsibilities in place of a class or two. In the 1930s, when civil service classification systems took hold in the state colleges, librarians became classified and paid separately from the conventional faculty. The librarians' quest for conventional faculty salaries enjoyed the support of most faculty, and the union took up the cause. The presidents were not unified, and the chancellor's staff was not prepared to take a strong position. The librarians prevailed, and librarians became appointed identically with faculty; four ranks were created, parallel to faculty rank, and library faculty were appointed, secured tenure, and advanced through the ranks. Salaries were identical with the four faculty ranks, although most librarians were paid on a twelve-month basis rather than a nine-month one.

Department chairs and their place in the collective bargaining scheme were and continue to be a matter of deep division. From a management perspective, many viewed department chairs as the first line of management. From a union point of view, department chairs are faculty in a department and belong in the union. This was a divisive issue as collective bargaining was being implemented. Perhaps to the surprise of some, the presidents were divided. Strong voices urged that chairs be in management. Other voices urged that chairs be in the unit and argued that chairs, for the most part, saw themselves as faculty; this was probably the view of a minority of presidents, though no one took a count. In the course of negotiations and initial implementation, chairs were first in the bargaining unit, then out of it, and then back in, where they remain to this day. In a sense, the argument is symptomatic of a division among the presidents that continues into the early years of the twenty-first century regarding the question, does collective bargaining with faculty confirm a fundamental relationship of employer and employee, or does a professional relationship continue to exist—can the two relationships coexist?

Collective bargaining changed the functions and roles of the faculty and staff unit in the chancellor's office and the comparable personnel functions on the campuses. It also changed how many individuals on all sides saw themselves. On campuses, presidents had a great deal to do with setting a tone. At the system level, the chancellor and staff, the trustees, the statewide Academic Senate, and the unions were all players.

The statewide Academic Senate worked diligently over the years at maintaining the traditional role of a senate and a set of collegial relationships. Not all members or all leaders on the Academic Senate placed the same great value on collegial relationships. The Academic Senate adopted two major documents addressing the role of senates in a time of collective bargaining, both documents prepared with presidential involvement and the support of Chancellors Dumke and Reynolds, successively. While one might not argue that the role of the Academic Senate has been strengthened by collective bargaining, in a sense, collective bargaining removed from its agenda issues that were time consuming and inevitably controversial, and afforded it the opportunity to focus on educational and professional matters.[40]

* * *

The emphasis that developed in the mid- to late 1960s on student affirmative action, the recruitment of students from minority populations and those in significant economic distress, was soon accompanied by the establishment of an affirmative action effort in the faculty and staff affairs office. The first systemwide affirmative action officer was Herbert Carter. He began to work with the campuses in 1973, and the campuses responded variously. Some campuses also created an affirmative action position to give leadership to the recruitment of women and minorities to the faculty and staff and in administrative positions. The real leadership for this effort had to come from presidents and vice presidents and deans, if campuses were to successfully diversify their faculty and staff and administrations. There was at least some initial resistance to this effort on all campuses, and on some of the campuses the resistance persisted.

In 1985, two presidents, James Rosser of Los Angeles and Stephen Horn of Long Beach, proposed a new program in the executive council: the Forgivable Loan/Doctoral Incentive program. It was designed to urge and support selected graduate students throughout the California State University to continue graduate study, complete a doctorate, and return to a CSU campus to join the faculty. The program's original emphasis was to encourage completion of doctoral programs in fields where women and minorities were most severely underrepresented at the time—the sciences, mathematics, engineering, and computer science. The presidents supported the program. Chancellor Ann Reynolds was very supportive; one of the major themes of her eight-year chancellorship was strong support for minority and women students, faculty and staff. Reynolds brought the program to the trustees, and they approved it as a pilot program for 1987–88. Participants were identified by faculty and advanced to a systemwide selection process. Those finally selected were supported financially by the CSU through a doctoral program. The program was and still is financed with lottery funds, and support given is in the form of a loan, to be forgiven when the individual is appointed as a faculty member at a CSU campus and remains for a number of years.

For the first year, 1987–88, 269 individuals applied, and 60 were selected. The program was a success from the beginning, if success is defined by the quality of the participants and their effectiveness as faculty upon return to a campus (not necessarily the campus from which they had come). In 1988, the new Task Force on the Recruitment and Retention of a High Quality Faculty endorsed the program, and it received strong support from virtually all groups within the CSU, the statewide Academic Senate, the presidents, and others. In 1990, persons with disabilities were added to the group. That year as well, the first white male was funded to pursue a doctorate in nursing. The published criteria for the program continued to refer to minorities and women until 1995–96. As students were selected for 1996, the same changes were made for this program that were made for student affirmative action programs in the context of Proposition 209, which made illegal the use of criteria based on ethnicity in personnel actions. While the impact of 209 in the CSU was principally on student admission and financial aid programs, it was equally significant for faculty and staff, as individuals of all ethnicities and both genders now apply and receive awards.[41]

Anticipation of Proposition 209 and the ongoing controversy within the University of California about student admissions and affirmative action caused the chancellor at the time, Barry Munitz, to initiate the same kind of review of faculty recruitment and appointments that was underway regarding student admissions. This resulted in substantial board discussion, just as it did for admissions. An extended review was undertaken at the May 1995 board meeting. This had the same productive results for faculty recruitment that were achieved for student admissions.[42]

In February 2009, the total number of individuals who had participated in the program was more than seventeen hundred; of those who have completed degrees, approximately 60 percent have returned to the California State University faculty. The greatest number of individuals completing this program have come to the Sacramento campus.[43]

The statewide Academic Senate and the chancellor's office initiated another of the studies addressing faculty recruitment. "The Recruitment and Retention of a High Quality Faculty" was completed in 1988. Again, the study focused on the importance of faculty salaries and support generally. The point was to create and maintain momentum about support for faculty. The report emphasized recruiting and retaining minority faculty. The trustees adopted the report, and made clear the importance of building a faculty with ethnic minority members.

* * *

Campuses were having increasing difficulty recruiting faculty in some areas. Bringing in business and engineering faculty on many of the campuses was becoming more difficult in the 1980s. Chancellor Reynolds and Vice-Chancellor Caesar Naples went to Governor George Deukmejian to ask for extra funding for a salary differential for business and engineering faculty. The conversation was candid—they did not believe they could get agreement for a salary differential in the collective bargaining process. Deukmejian agreed to funding a differential and identifying it in the budget, thus forcing the differential issue; CFA resisted, but backed down when they understood the political implications of standing in the way of an increase for some faculty. This was a key move, the first trustee-management breakthrough on the traditional ranked five-step salary schedule for faculty. It would be followed by other moves.

With the full backing and encouragement of the trustees and substantial support from the presidents, Barry Munitz addressed merit pay. This had been attempted earlier, but had not succeeded. The faculty culture was virtually universally negative about merit pay, though there were some who were quietly supportive. The significance of merit pay as it was initiated in the mid-1990s was in the principle, not the process used or the amount of money distributed and the number of faculty who received it. The number of awards made was very small, and this made decision making about merit pay difficult.

Beginning in the 1990s, the faculty salary structure moved away from the traditional civil service model toward a flexible and somewhat amorphous set of ranges. The concept of firm steps and movement from one step to another was lost. Each rank had a salary range; there was no ceiling on the salary of professor other than a practical one imposed by the availability of funds. This eventually resulted in unplanned, sometimes difficult anomalies. Presidents and campus administrations were sometimes placed in situations in which new faculty were appointed above the salaries for faculty recruited earlier.

Historically, the rank of lecturer had been used only in limited ways: part-time faculty teaching specialized courses, such as a member of a symphony orchestra coming to teach a class about the oboe, a business person teaching a particular, defined aspect of business. Lecturers were appointed to fill in for faculty on sabbatical or other absences. The use of lecturers was not widespread. Tenured and tenure-track faculty workload was computed as twelve weighted teaching units and three units for advising, scholarship, university service, and the like. However, lecturers were presumed to be responsible only for instruction, not for advising or university service. Workload was computed as fifteen weighted teaching units of instruction. Thus, for a dean or a department chair, the use of faculty positions as lecturers provided a means to stretch a faculty-position budget into additional classes and sometimes into lighter teaching responsibilities for tenured and tenure track faculty. As budgets became tighter, additional faculty positions were designated as lecturer. One result of Proposition 13 was the appropriation of state funds previously available for the general fund to local governments and special districts. A resulting byproduct of this, cut backs in state general fund budget allocations, resulted in increased use of lecturer positions. Those have become more widespread each year, varying from campus to campus and, within campuses, among departments and colleges.

Inevitably, the situation became both a collective bargaining issue and an educational policy issue. The educational policy issue was clear: what was the qualitative impact on instruction of the use of part-time faculty (in urban areas, some held part-time appointments on multiple campuses—the so-called freeway flyers)? From a collective bargaining standpoint, the CFA, the faculty union, was torn in two directions: the aggregation of part-time positions into tenure track appointments and positions, and serving the interests of the increasing number of part-time CFA union members. Instances began to emerge in the 1990s in which some part-timers had served ten (in some instances twenty) years on a campus. One president who tried to force the conversion of full-time lecturer positions to tenure track with the individuals in them was blocked because of rules in the union contract. Often, deans resisted efforts made to convert part-time or lecturer positions to tenure track.

Lecturers served from term to term as needed. With the number of lecturers growing in the mid-1990s, CFA mounted a campaign for some form of tenure or secure status for lecturers. The chancellor's office, with considerable presidential support, resisted this. However, over time, resistance wore down and provision was made for lecturers to gain increased salaries equivalent to promotion in rank after a specified number of years. Additionally, after a number of years of service, lecturers were granted modified job security—not tenure, but preference for available work and three-year appointments.

* * *

The unionization of California State University faculty was a major change for the system and has had an increasing impact each year on the life and work of the campuses. All of those in faculty positions on all campuses were in a single bargaining unit, numbering more than twenty thousand members. This was the largest faculty bargaining unit in the country. Relationships between the bargaining units and unions other than faculty most often draw less attention than do those with the faculty union, but they are just as important. Most faculty quickly learn that a student's contact, person to person contact, with the department secretary is key to a relationship with a major. The tone of a campus is greatly affected by all of the staff, not only the faculty.

A merit salary structure had been created by the legislature in 1945, and provision made for all employees to be on a five-step salary schedule. Most employees were appointed at step one in a classification. If judged by supervisors to be performing with merit (generally translated as "satisfactory performance") they would advance one step each year to step five, the top step in a given position. In 1953, the legislature added a provision to the education code, moving state college employees to the jurisdiction of the State Personnel Board, thus assuring that state college personnel would receive merit salary increases. With the implementation of collective bargaining in 1982, merit salary adjustments, or MSAs, were based upon collective bargaining agreements. In the late 1980s, the Deukmejian administration stopped funding MSAs. In 1988, the CSU suspended funding MSAs, but subsequently resumed the funding, as negotiated with each bargaining unit.

In 1995, an even more significant move was made, this time at the urging of Governor Pete Wilson, who proposed the elimination of merit salary adjustments for all state employees. A new classification system was proposed, along with performance pay. The chancellor's office staff member charged with accomplishing this was Sam Strafaci, who had joined the staff in 1984. Initially working with several of the campuses, by 1993 he rose in the ranks to be immediately in charge of collective bargaining. He was generally respected by the unions and had, on the whole, worked well with them. The proposal to end almost automatic salary adjustments and establish a performance pay system was not acceptable to any of the unions.

Merit salary adjustments had been a contentious issue for some years among the presidents. Some maintained that it was simply a five-step salary schedule—everyone received the annual merit salary adjustment. One president demanded that all presidents bring in a list of all those faculty and staff who were denied an

MSA in a given year. (Some clever person could have asked for a list of presidents *ever* to be denied an MSA; one actually had been, in 1973, essentially for political reasons, but it was restored one month later.) Every regular position in the CSU, including presidents to 1984, was on a five-step salary range, except the chancellor, who was appointed by the board of trustees on a fixed salary. The executive council discussion did not go anyplace.

The governor's proposal about performance pay was for all state employees under his jurisdiction; he did not back down. Most state employees, outside of management, were unionized by 1995. Many unions, including some inside the CSU, came to terms with performance pay; some went to mediation. Within the CSU, mediation did not produce agreement. The next and final step was to a fact-finding panel. The report of the fact-finding panel did not result in an agreement. Lacking an agreement, the employer, the California State University, could implement its last, best, and final proposal. The California State Employees Association, which represented the largest percentage of employees other than faculty, refused to agree to the elimination of merit salary adjustments. With the pressure of the governor upon them, the chancellor's office and the board of trustees did a unilateral imposition, effective on April 1, 1996, ending MSAs. In April 1996, performance pay was implemented, along with the elimination of merit salary adjustments and the implementation of an open-range salary system. For staff, a further step was taken in 2000: the Merit Salary Increase Program was implemented, a new program with built-in accountability points. The issue that was not resolved was the ability of individuals to move through a salary range, and the resulting salary stagnation that some individuals experienced.

The performance pay plan did not work well on most campuses. As a result, the chancellor's office and the California State Employees Association (CSEA) established in 1999 a Labor Management Committee to address the matter. The Federal Mediation and Conciliation Service was invited to participate, and did so. As a result of these discussions, a new merit salary increase program was established and minimum and maximum salaries—essentially, salary ranges—were created for staff positions represented by CSEA. Others of the staff units followed. The new Merit Salary Increase Program provided for all employees on a campus in the same classification with the same performance rating to receive the same salary increase, thus addressing the issue of favoritism.

In recent years, the staff union—management relationships, those other than units three and four, the CFA and the Academic Professionals of California, are reaching some level of stable relationships, and in the context of the general review of collective bargaining beginning in 2007, a further maturing can be anticipated.[44]

* * *

In early 1992, Barry Munitz brought new leadership to the personnel management group. June Cooper was appointed vice-chancellor for human resources and operations (the "operations" portion of the title referred to designating her as the chief internal administrative officer for the chancellor's office). Cooper was a longtime vice president at the Long Beach campus and was widely respected throughout the California State University. She steered the human resources function through nearly five difficult years, which included changes in both personnel administration and the first unilateral imposition in CSU collective bargaining. She selected Sam Strafaci as her deputy. Upon Cooper's retirement in 1996, Munitz, doubtless anticipating his own departure, appointed Strafaci as the interim senior director for human resources.

With the change in the chancellorship, Charles Reed brought in as vice-chancellor for human resources an experienced administrator, Jackie McClain, from the University of Michigan. For a time, McClain worked well with the nonacademic unions, although she had not been in the role long when she was caught up in the substantial conflict with the California Faculty Association.

In November 1998, California voters elected Gray Davis to the governorship. In his more than four years in office, Davis made key moves that affected the California State University. For sixteen years, Governors George Deukmejian and Pete Wilson had been generally supportive of the collective bargaining positions of the trustees and the chancellors. In the 1998 election campaign, Davis made it clear that he was supportive of the CSU unions, particularly the faculty union. Not long after the opening of the 1999 legislative session, a bill was introduced in the legislature to provide for "agency shop" for the collective bargaining units in the California State University. Agency shop requires all of those in a bargaining unit to support the union financially. Members of the union pay full dues. Those who are not members pay only for the services and benefits they receive as a result of union activities, an amount determined by the union. Normally this amount is about 90 percent of the full membership dues. The agency shop legislation passed easily and Gray Davis signed it.

Agency shop inevitably changed the relationships among the unions and with the trustees and CSU management. The capacity for union political activity with the legislature and elsewhere was greatly increased with additional funding. All of the unions had built strong relationships in the legislature over the years. In the instance of CFA, the increase in union political activity was substantial.

CFA membership on the campuses prior to agency shop varied. Some campuses were "CFA campuses" with heavy membership, and often CFA-control of the campus Academic Senate. Some campuses were the opposite, and faculty leadership over the years had worked to maintain that balance. Most campuses were somewhere in the middle. Agency shop did not change the political balance among faculty on the campuses, but it did increase the sense of union strength.

A major phenomenon that emerged in the 1990s was part-time faculty-lecturer membership in the CFA. In absolute numbers of individuals, tenure-track and tenured faculty, and lecturer numbers became approximately equal. Lecturers became active in the CFA in substantial numbers. The CFA agenda reflected this.

* * *

With the almost simultaneous arrival of Chancellor Charles Reed and the emergence of new leadership in the CFA, coupled with the resources made available by agency shop, the relationship between the CFA and the CSU leadership and the board changed. Charles Reed is an open and aggressive individual. No one leaves a meeting with Reed wondering where he stands on an issue. He is blunt, and his language can be colorful. The CFA leadership, particularly in the person of Susan Meisenhelder, a faculty member from the San Bernardino campus, became more aggressive and confrontational. An early issue in the Reed administration was the implementation of a long overdue technology strategy, the cost of which was estimated to be more than four hundred million dollars. The issue ended up in very tough legislative hearings. Reed prevailed by sheer determination and force. The CFA interest was the use of money, and a drive for more funds to be allocated to salaries. It was not alone in its opposition to the technology strategy. The California State University Employees Union (the renamed California State Employees Association unit only for the CSU employees previously represented by CSEA) was opposed and vigorous about their opposition. The combat between the CFA, the CSUEU, and the board and chancellor and the chancellor's staff became more intense by the year. Reed not only did not back down, but became personally involved for a time in negotiations with the CFA. In a very real sense, the CFA leadership and the chancellor bounced off of each other. The CFA set out on a strategy to demonize the chancellor in the eyes of faculty, and to some extent, they were successful early on.

The relationship between CFA and the leadership of the system quickly became dysfunctional. The ostensible basic issue was, for the most part, faculty salaries, which were lagging always against the California Postsecondary Education Commission (CPEC) comparison institutions. The underlying issue was power and control. Relationships with CFA and the role of this union had reached a point in which first the union and then management seemed to want a basic realignment. The board of trustees, with the clear exception of one member, a union official in Los Angeles, was solidly behind the chancellor. Presidential reactions varied. All were supportive of the chancellor. Some tried to temper the buildup of faculty hostility and concern about the chancellor's leadership; some unintentionally fed it. In 2003, Governor Gray Davis, after his successful 2002 campaign for election to a second term, appointed Susan Meisenhelder, then outgoing president of CFA, to the board of trustees. The board's reaction was intense and furious; the likelihood of Chancellor Reed tolerating such a move was nil, and the appointment could have caused his departure. The governor backed down. Davis had made this appointment and another controversial one on the eve of the election for his recall. Both appointments could be understood as efforts to gain support in the recall election, which Davis lost. The appointments were withdrawn.

The CFA had new leadership, and, around that time, the budget situation dramatically worsened for the CSU. For a time, the CSU management leadership and the union leadership, CFA and all of the units, made common cause. This prevailed for a few years, and then began to fragment. In 2008, the advent of a forty-two-billion-dollar deficit in California created the setting for a revival of a unity effort through the creation of the "Alliance for the California State University." In January 2008, a memorandum about the CSU budget situation and the need for a unified force in Sacramento was sent to all California State University employees, staff, and faculty, full-time and part-time. The memo was signed by Chancellor Charles Reed; Lillian Taiz, president of the California Faculty Association; Pat Gantt, president of the California State University Employees Union; Floyd Anscombe, president of the Union of American Physicians and Dentists; James Banks, president of the United Auto Workers (representing graduate student teaching assistants); Charles Goetzl, president of the Academic Professionals of California; and Jim Procida, president of the State University Police Association.

A fundamental error had been made as this controversial and combative environment had grown over six to eight years. The management side, at least at the state level and on the board of trustees, had identified the faculty union with the faculty in general. Unions have organizational lives of their own, and organization and tactics to achieve their goals. Hopefully, these include the goals of the membership, but in large unions these goals often go beyond those of the membership. The CFA is a large union. The number of faculty in the bargaining unit for the fall 2007 was slightly in excess of twenty-four thousand.

In 2006, the board and the chancellor concluded that a new start was needed for collective bargaining. A first step was to hire a nationally known and credible consultant to assess the state of bargaining. A second step was to change the top leadership of collective bargaining on the management side. Sam Strafaci, the veteran leader of the staff, an individual with both significant credibility on the campuses and with unions, but inevitably bruised by the CFA central conflict of the past several years, departed. Jackie McClain left the vice-chancellorship for an appointment on the Chico campus.

* * *

What has happened with collective bargaining in the California State University in the more than thirty years since AB 1091 became law? Arguably, the development of the legislation and the give and take in the legislative process was faulty. The ultimate responsibility for the health of collective bargaining necessarily rests with the board of trustees and the chancellor. The board was not unified regarding a position about collective bargaining in the mid-1970s, nor were the chancellor and his staff major figures in the give and take in Sacramento. The issue was taken over by a single board of trustee member, Roy Brophy, who was opposed to collective bargaining per se, but an advocate for another model or models that were not clear. The contrast with the role played by the University of California was substantial, but in fairness, the faculty and administration of the UC were more than content with the status quo. The collective bargaining legislation did afford nonacademic groups in the UC to unionize, and it did provide the framework for efforts to unionize graduate students years later.

The implementation of collective bargaining in the CSU was done at a time of transition. In the years from 1976 to 1983, three individuals occupied the vice-chancellorship for faculty and staff affairs, and the transition from Glenn Dumke to Ann Reynolds in the chancellorship occurred. Dumke was not really active with respect to collective bargaining, but simply was opposed to it. The reason Glenn Dumke did not engage in the give and take in legislative activity is not clear; it was caused by the board, or at least some members of the board. Whether Dumke's inaction, and his check on the CSUC Sacramento office staff from engagement, was a result of fear of board action on the issue, or, perhaps, of being trapped in a board situation that was particularly dysfunctional, is a mystery. What is not a mystery is that the CSUC did not play a hand. Dumke was supportive of the statewide Academic Senate efforts to maintain its role and keep educational policy and professional matters away from the bargaining process. In her turn, Ann Reynolds was not knowledgeable about bargaining and was simply thrust into it. The initial contracts were negotiated by Thomas Lambre, who had no background in higher education and was new to the California State University. He left the CSU shortly after the negotiations and the arrival of Caesar Naples, a new vice-chancellor. There was no firm hand at the tiller through this process of at least seven years, 1976–1983, and no generally agreed upon long-term strategy.

The actions of the chancellor and the board of trustees in 2006–07 could be promising. From the vantage point of this writer, a new beginning needs to happen. The exceedingly negative environment of recent years has been one in which the CFA, the major union central to the mission of the CSU, and management have each escalated tensions and exaggerated differences.

It is arguable that the single most important variable in collective bargaining is that of the relationships among the parties. Management frames the tone, and it initially does so not with a union as an organization, but with the employees. Universities are necessarily organizations with many highly educated professionals at the center of the organization. Their interests go beyond conventional union issues. The tone of labor relations needs to start at the top—campus presidents, the chancellor, the trustees. If the tone focuses on the people within the organization, the employees, the role of campus presidents and the organizational cultures they create become central. Presidents and chancellors and trustees cannot create a culture by themselves. Even though we all know that faculty and staff make up the backbone of the university, unions in this instance must cooperate where possible, and presidents, chancellors, and trustees need to listen, understand, and make cooperation possible.

* * *

The faculty and staff cultures of the California State University have changed in the almost fifty years since the first meeting of the trustees on August 12, 1960.

The staff has become more complex, as the work of the California State University has become more complex. Much of the increase in staff is the result of the imposition of government programs, some unique to higher education (various reporting requirements, for example), some more general (such as environmental safety). One of the determined efforts of a key leader in the chancellor's early staff, Lois Feldheym, was to provide career ladders for non-faculty employees. This has been reasonably successful on most campuses. Moreover, a spirit about the California State University and working with or around students has grown. This becomes clear in conversations and meetings with staff of all kinds, and at all levels of the organization.

The faculty culture has changed markedly. In the early to mid-1960s, the transition from the State Board of Education to the board of trustees, and a system of colleges emphasizing the arts and sciences and a variety of professional programs, many of them just being established, was dominant in the lives of faculty. The faculty cultures were a mixture. Some faculty were upset, if not hostile, with the shift away from the dominance of teacher education and related programs. Some were angry that the Master Plan had not resulted in PhD programs and major funding for research—"just like the University of California." Some faculty simply did not know what to expect from the change, and had something like a fear of the unknown. And some faculty anticipated the excitement of transforming an institution. As the 1960s evolved, there came to be an overlay of unrest, some of it the product of the student and faculty political and social activity of the 1960s and militant behavior and attitudes, some of it the product of the changes within the California State Colleges.

Time and the aging of the California State University faculty who had experienced the transition or its aftermath brought about change in the faculty culture (and cultures since each campus developed a faculty culture within the whole of the CSU). For the most part, faculty became committed to a new California State University, one that included an emphasis on teaching and research, mostly of an applied nature and, for many, if not all faculty, a level of professional involvement in the broader academic community.

Perhaps one dimension of the state of the faculty in the California State University is an organization called the California State University Emeritus and Retired Faculty Association (CSU-ERFA), which was founded in 1985. It was originally a political and economic interest group, established in response to perceived threats to reduce or eliminate CSU faculty retiree rights and benefits. The founding president was a Los Angeles campus faculty member, Sid Albert. As membership grew, now approaching three thousand, an office was established on the Northridge campus. Robert Kully, a former chair of the statewide Academic Senate and the first faculty trustee, became the first executive director. He was succeeded in more recent years by a retired Northridge faculty member and dean, Don Cameron. The organization as an interest group has explicit goals. A legislative affairs committee monitors legislation and government policies that affect retired faculty and staff. A health benefits committee works with members regarding problems with health-care benefits. Each campus has an organization of retirees, and CSU-

ERFA assists these campus groups with program development, communicating information about successful programs conducted on each of the twenty-three campuses.

CSU-ERFA makes an important contribution to the life of the campuses and the system, and to the lives of its members. Most faculty and many staff have given their professional or much of their working lives to the CSU. Working in a university is no ordinary job. The continuing relationship, at some level, of emeritus and retired individuals can add a certain richness and quality to the lives of the institutions.[45]

* * *

What evaluative template is appropriate to determine the actual results of the many personnel changes of the 1960s and 1970s, and the impact of collective bargaining? Did these changes make the California State University a better place for its students and the people of California, for faculty and scholarship and the impact of campuses upon communities and regions?

The cumulative impact of changed personnel practices, the movement away from rigid procedures and rules, and the adoption of contemporary reasonable and even good practices are, beyond question, positives for the mission and work of the California State University and for all the people of the CSU who are touched by it.

Collective bargaining is a work in progress. It is practical to divide the matter between the faculty and a number of professional categories, particularly those in student affairs, and the staffs. Collective bargaining has become customary for state employees and most local government employees in groups comparable to the staff groups in the CSU. There is no reason to believe that comparable employees in the CSU would be different.

Faculty and a limited number of professional categories are a different matter. Collective bargaining was not inevitable for them. But a combination of ineptness on the part of the administration at the system level, and on many of the campuses, and particularly the makeup of the Reagan appointments to the board of trustees from the late 1960s, and state government leadership in both the Reagan and Jerry Brown administrations (although the matter was really mostly settled before the Jerry Brown administration), as well as the absolute determination of a relatively small number of faculty, beginning at the time of the Master Plan negotiations, created an inevitability. The trustees in the mid-1970s were not really together. A single trustee, Roy Brophy ran with the ball. It is reasonably clear that at the time he did not think bargaining would be adopted by the legislature; he wanted to provide an alternative. The decision made by the chancellor, for whatever reason, to not actively participate in the legislative process was without question a major factor.

Collective bargaining over the years has been addressed as a matter of tactics, not strategy. There has not been any serious or unified discussion among presidents and the chancellor, at least prior to 2003, of long-term goals in working with faculty, and presidential styles have varied widely over the years. The 2007 actions of the board and chancellor in causing a total review of collective bargaining could be the occasion for the development of strategic goals.[46]

Notes

[1] T. C. Holy and H. H. Semans, "A Study of Faculty Demand and Supply in California Higher Education 1957–1970," Liaison Committee of the Regents of the University of California, Berkley, and the California State Board of Education, 1958. The study anticipated the need for additional faculty in the years immediately ahead and through the 1960s, given substantial projected growth in student numbers.

[2] Teven Laxer, "Who Took Away Our Steps?" email October 31, 2007, CSU Archives.

[3] See Chapters 1 through 3 of this work for more details.

[4] C. Mansel Keene and Lois Feldheym, oral history interviews by Laurence de Graaf, August 6, 1987, 15–21, CSU Archives.

[5] See Chapter 2 of this work.

[6] Keene, Feldeym, interviews, 23.

[7] *Ibid.*, 26.

[8] California Education Code, sec. 22601.

[9] Coordinating Council for Higher Education, *Annual Report on Faculty Salaries and Fringe Benefits, 1971–72*, November 9, 1972, CSU Archives.

[10] Keene, Feldeym, interviews, 16–17; see Chapter 12 for details on the 1.8 percent issue.

[11] Minutes, board of trustees, September 18–19, 2007.

[12] Angus E. Taylor, memorandum to Chester McCorkle, University of California, March 22, 1971, CSU Archives.

[13] C. Mansel Keene, memorandum to trustees, July 31, 1968, CSU Archives.

[14] Minutes, board of trustees, *San Francisco Chronicle*, May 28, 1969.

[15] Minutes, board of trustees, September 22, 1970; *San Francisco Chronicle*, September 23, 1970.

[16] Minutes, board of trustees, February 1969, March 1971, May 1971, November 1971; Academic Senate of the California State Colleges, "The Academic Senate," vol. 1, no. 1, January 1972 .

[17] Norman Epstein, memorandum to Executive Vice-Chancellor Raymond Rydell, March 11, 1968, CSU Archives.

[18] See Chapter 12.

[19] Charles Adams, chair, statewide Academic Senate, memorandum to members of the academic senate and local senate council chairs, June 12, 1974, CSU Archives.

[20] California Legislature, Reg. Sess., AB 804, February 17, 1975; California Education Code, sec. 24315, 1975.

[21] The author was one of the vice presidents.

[22] Glenn S. Dumke, "The Chancellor Comments: Trustees Resolution Concerning Layoff," February 24, 1976, CSU Archives.

[23] Minutes, board of trustees, March 24, 1976. Other sources used for this discussion of the Ritchie amendment include minutes of the board, November 23–24, 1975 and January 27–28, 1976; Glenn S. Dumke, memorandum to board of trustees, summary of January 15 hearing; Charles C. Adams, "The Ritchie Amendment: A Giant Step Back-

ward," Statewide Academic Senate, January 30, 1976. All sources here are in the CSU Archives.

[24] Glenn S. Dumke, letter to Phillip Burton, member of the California State Assembly, March 1, 1961, CSU Archives.

[25] Glenn S. Dumke, letter to John G. Sperling, dated May 2, 1966, CSU Archives. Sperling was an activist on several fronts. In the early 1970s, he led an effort at the San Jose campus to implement Dumke's "New Approaches" address, specifically with respect to external degrees. He did not succeed; he was blocked by the campus faculty senate, something that happened on several campuses. He resigned his faculty position and became the founder and first president of the University of Phoenix.

[26] Louis H. Heilbron to members of the board of trustees, "Memorandum Re Collective Bargaining for the Joint Meeting of the Committee on Faculty and Staff Affairs and Educational Policy," September 20, 1967, CSU Archives.

[27] Ad Hoc Committee on Collective Bargaining (undated, but clearly in late April or early May 1967), CSU Archives. Lee Kerschner, then associate professor of political science at Fullerton, chaired the committee; Kerschner would later join the chancellor's staff, in Faculty and Staff Affairs, and ultimately became a vice-chancellor.

[28] Academic Senate of the California State Colleges, collective bargaining vote summary, June 1967, CSU Archives.

[29] Teven Laxer, "History of Collective Bargaining Laws in California," paper for the California State University Employees Union, undated.

[30] Louis H. Heilbron, "Memorandum Re Collective Bargaining," September 1967.

[31] The author has used a variety of sources for this section about the activity in the legislature, beginning in 1975 through the adoption of legislation in 1978, and the period thereafter. Documents from the statewide Academic Senate and the chancellor's office as well as interviews are found in the CSU Archives. Interviews include: David Elliott, interview by Judson Grenier, May 24, 2001; and interviews by the author of William Crist, August 19, 2007; Lee Kerschner, June 9, 2006; Archie Kleingartner, March 19, 2007; and Howard Berman, April 3, 2007; Donald R. Gerth, focus group on collective bargaining with units other than faculty (Pat Gantt, J. W. Jiminez, Peter McClory, Virginia Watts, and Brian Young), November 2, 2007; Tevin Laxer, interview by the author, January 15, 2008.

[32] Congressman Howard Berman, phone interview by the author, April 8, 2008; Archie Kleingartner, phone interview by the author, April 14, 2008.

[33] Elliott, interview, 50–51.

[34] *Ibid*, 52.

[35] David Elliott, conversation with the author, February 2, 2009.

[36] California State University, HEERA Bargaining Unit Profiles, April 2006.

[37] Correspondence between the California State Employees Association, the Office of Administrative Law, Assembly Member Rusty Areias, and the author's notes; CSU Archives.

[38] Donald R. Gerth, focus group of chancellor's senior staff on collective bargaining (June Cooper, Jackie McClain, Caesar Naples, Jack Samit, Sam Strafaci), June 20, 2006.

[39] Caesar Naples, interview by the author, February 23, 2007; Crist, interview.

[40] See Chapter 11, The Academic Senate.

[41] See Chapter 9 of this work.

[42] Minutes, board of trustees, May 9–10, 1995. Also see Chapter 9 regarding student admissions.

[43] Margaret Merryfield, senior director, academic human resources, the California State University, email to the author, February 24, 2009.

[44] Teven Laxer, "Who Took Away Our Steps? The History of MSA Payments to CSU Employees," paper for the California State University Employees Union, April 20, 2006, CSU Archives.

[45] Don Cameron, email to the author, February 16, 2009, CSU Archives.

[46] For this chapter, as with others, I interviewed a number of individuals and did two focus groups on collective bargaining with leaders of the staff bargaining units and with key management individuals from the early 1980s to 2007. I tried repeatedly to do a focus group with the leadership of the California Faculty Association, but the leadership would not return my calls or emails. I was successful in talking on the phone with Professor Lillian Taiz, who became president of CFA in 2007. Professor Taiz told me she could not talk with me, as a conversation could only occur as a result of a collective decision. I regret that there was no group discussion with CFA leadership and other faculty about the important relationships of faculty and administrations and the trustees. I must also note that I was not able to interview Charles Goetzl, the longtime president of Unit 4, the Academic Professionals of California. He did talk with me by phone, and he initially agree to an interview, but subsequently declined, and was not able to reschedule due to a family illness.

Part Four
The Support of the California State University

Chapter 11

Organizing the Furniture of Governance

Governance and Relationships

Higher education institutions, both public and private, require structures of governance and networks of relationships that are complex, powerful, and not easy to maintain. Organizations populated by substantial numbers of highly professional and educated individuals are not susceptible to conventional hierarchical structures as the sole approach to their collective governance and the overall life of the organization.

The California State University has grown from a relatively simple formal organizational structure—albeit with extensive networks of relationships—at the time of the Master Plan in 1960. The California State University of the present is a complex formal organization, one that is extensive and necessarily involves thousands of individuals, that encompasses all aspects of the life of the campuses and the system, and that reaches not only throughout California but the nation and the world—networks of relationships that are national and increasingly global.

    The author is indebted to Dr. Cristy Jensen, Professor Emerita of Public Policy and Administration at California State University, Sacramento, who critiqued this chapter. She is an experienced, respected faculty leader on the campus as well as throughout the state. She has been a member of the statewide Academic Senate for several terms, a member of the executive committee, and chair of the Committee on Governmental Relations. She served as a member of the Joint Graduate Board with the UC, and two terms as chair of the faculty senate at the Sacramento campus.

Yet there is something unique about these relationships and their importance. California higher education generally, and the California State University and its campuses, are in many ways their own world. This has been historically so for a number of reasons. State government procedures have been and are different in California from other states. The procedures in California have not been constant and unchanging. California, in some ways, has never gotten over being a frontier society. It is still a state and a culture on the cutting edge. California's size, both geographically and with regard to population, together with the extraordinary mosaic of that population, makes California a place different, almost a nation-state. For decades California was isolated, largely by geography and size relative to other states, from the rest of the country. Only the University of California had relationships with universities throughout the country and world, and with other institutions. Since the Master Plan this has changed, but being from California in the national higher education environment was in some measure like having a permanent security blanket; the campuses were stable and the life of the campuses was largely predictable. The California State Colleges as they developed were unique in the nation. Some of this is related to support.

This chapter addresses both the formal structures of governance and the most often informal networks of people that make the California State University what it is today. This exploration cannot and will not be exhaustive, but it will attempt to present an understandable and historically useful evolution of governance structures and roles.

The Trustees of the California State University

The transition from the State Board of Education to the board of trustees was artfully designed. The Master Plan legislation, passed in the late spring of 1960, provided for the board of trustees to assume authority and responsibility for the California State Colleges on July 1, 1961. The State Board of Education, long the governing board, at least in theory, would remain responsible until then. However, a provision was made for a board of trustees to begin functioning and planning during the 1960–61 fiscal year. Governor Pat Brown appointed all of the ten members of the state board, along with six new individuals, to create the sixteen-member board of trustees. Brown had already made appointments for two years to the State Board of Education. The two boards were mostly synonymous, and the transition proceeded smoothly. Brown's administration made funding available to this new board for its planning work, including support for an administrative officer and a small staff.

Without question, one reason for the smooth transition was the appointment of Louis Heilbron to the State Board of Education in the spring of 1959. He was elected chair of the board of trustees at their first meeting on August 12, 1960, a meeting held in the governor's conference room. Heilbron would prove to be a superb chair of the trustees, not only for the transitional 1960–61 year but, subsequently, for the first two years of the board when it had governing responsibility for the state colleges. He remained on the board until 1969, and remained a leader, playing a central role in resolving the San Francisco State situation in the late 1960s (see chapter three). Even though Heilbron's appointment as a trustee ended in 1969, many quietly sought his advice until his death at the age of ninety-nine in 2006. He was a thoughtful, caring, and dedicated servant of public higher education.

The early work of the trustees was organizational and necessarily focused on the recruitment of top leadership for the system and presidents for the campuses. The original board members were faced with the responsibility to build not only structures of governance, but the character and mission of the state colleges. Thus, the board involved itself in the details of academic planning, site selection, and construction for new campuses, and the creation and operation of financial systems, and the like. The board was not, however, successful in gaining the financial independence promised by the Master Plan legislation, and it remained a task for administrations and chancellors over the next almost fifty years, always with the support of the trustees, to secure, step by step, delegated financial authority to operate a system of campuses.[1]

One of the early moves of the board was to promote specialization on the campuses. Campuses were urged to emphasize existing fields in which they had already built strengths, or to develop a field; special financial support was offered. Humboldt was offered and accepted support for forestry; Cal Poly accepted support for agriculture. Sacramento was offered support for public administration, but declined the offer. It took the Sacramento campus more than twenty years to seize the opportunities afforded by presence in the state's capital city.[2] Similarly, as the trustees acquired the responsibility to manage building programs, the board, while consulting with the campuses, proceeded to select campus master plan architects. Charles Luckman, a renowned architect who served on the board of trustees from 1960 to 1982, personally supervised the selection of architects and sought to have each campus build an architectural vocabulary.

Among the most important moves of the early board was to put in place policies and procedures for personnel matters. The trustees did not simply accept what was transferred from the state Department of Education, but rather created rules and procedures as well as policies for appointing faculty and tenure practices and policies. For the most part, the trustees initially used established state government policies and procedures for the staff. Both policies and procedures were rewritten, virtually completely, for administrators, both academic and nonacademic. In the instances of faculty and administrators, the board had the challenge and the need to bring policy and practice into the contemporary higher education world. The policies or practices of the UC were sometimes followed, but this was less about UC than it was about the conventions of the academic world.

The tone and work of the trustees has been in part affected by the practices of the appointing governors. Governor Pat Brown, on the whole, appointed indi-

21. Dr. Claudia Hampton.

viduals who were leaders in professions and communities, and those appointees together created a stable board that established a positive climate that has persisted. With only infrequent exceptions, board members have worked well together over the years, and have not divided into factions defined by which governor appointed them. In public universities this is not common.

Ronald Reagan, in his first two years as governor, made some appointments of conservative ideologues that were disruptive to the orderly work and progress of the board. With the 1968 selection of Alex Sherriffs as his education advisor, Reagan's appointments continued often to be conservative, but, at the same time, they were individuals who worked constructively with their colleagues from the previous administration and, in later years, with the succeeding one.

One of Reagan's appointees, Dr. Claudia Hampton, had an unusual career on the board. An educator and not a Republican, Claudia (a much-admired person who preferred being called by her first name by those who knew her) was a former elementary school teacher who had grown up in a segregated neighborhood on the south side of Chicago. At the time of her appointment, she was in charge of desegregation in the Los Angeles Unified School District. She had been in a number of meetings with Alex Sherriffs, the governor's education advisor. Sherriffs was impressed with her ideas and asked her to meet, one on one, with the governor. Shortly after their meeting, Claudia was appointed to the board of trustees, a position she had not sought. She served for more than twenty years, the longest serving trustee to date (2009), and was reappointed by Governors Jerry Brown, Deukmejian, and Wilson. She was the first woman to be elected chair of the board, and she served in that role from 1979 to 1981. Her interest was educational policy, and she was a major figure in that area. She was also, without question, a major figure in the maturing and growth of the board. On every campus, faculty, student leaders, presidents, and other administrators inevitably developed the idea that one or two trustees were "their" trustees; Claudia was considered "our trustee" on all of the campuses.

Jerry Brown's appointees included some single-issue trustees, some appointed as rewards for campaign support, and some who became positive leaders on the board. Blanche Bersch was a strong supporter of women as potential administrators and on the faculties; Juan Gomez Quinones was always there for issues regarding ethnicity. Wallace Albertson, simultaneously elected to the Los Angeles Community College District board, soon became chair of the trustees. It was during the Jerry Brown administration that new legislation created—and Brown supported and signed—the establishment of three new positions on the board of trustees. Kathleen Carlson, the first student trustee, was appointed for the term 1976–78. The legislation creating the student trustee position provided for the California State Student Association to nominate three currently enrolled students. The Governor was to select one of the three nominees, and appoint the candidate for a two-year term. Shortly thereafter, the statewide Alumni Association successfully lobbied for an alumni position on the board. John O'Connell was appointed in 1977 as the first alumni trustee. Unlike the student trustee position, the alumni trustee was selected by the California State University Alumni Council. John O'Connell was a Chico graduate from the 1930s. At the time of his appointment, he was president of the Bechtel Corporation, a worldwide construction firm. O'Connell served until shortly before his death in 1984. He was chair of the board from 1981 to 1984, and led the search that resulted in the appointment of Ann Reynolds as chancellor in 1982. In the final year of the Brown administration, the faculty were successful in gaining legislation, which the governor signed, establishing a faculty trustee position. The process of appointment was comparable to that for the student trustee; the statewide Academic Senate would nominate three individuals to the governor, who would then choose the appointee from among them. The first faculty trustee, Robert Kully, a former chair of the statewide Academic Senate, was appointed by Brown's successor, George Deukmejian, and served two successive terms, from 1983 to 1987.[3]

George Deukmejian made twenty-two appointments to the board of trustees. Not all trustees stay for a full term, and some are reappointed. The student seat was left vacant for a time when Jennifer Oropeza, an appointee, originally selected by Brown, left to pursue a political career that would culminate, at least for a time, with fourteen years of service in the state legislature.

The Wilson administration was a continuation of the Deukmejian years. The appointments, for the most part, were individuals seriously interested in higher education. Once again, an alumni trustee, R. James Considine, not selected by the governor, but by the CSU Alumni Council, became chair of the board. Considine chaired the board of trustees from 1994 to 1996.

Gray Davis became governor on January 1, 1999. His appointments to the board were mixed. Some were builders, but among them were a few purely political appointments, several of whom Davis withdrew at the time of the 2003 recall election. In 2000, the student trustee position was changed to provide for two student seats on the board. Each was to serve two years: one student would be appointed each year, and during the first year would be a nonvoting member, and then a voting member the second year. Davis was not quick to fill trustee vacancies. Early in the life of the system, trustees whose terms expired would continue to serve until a reappointment or a successor appointment was made. The statute was changed in the late 1970s and trustees could only remain for thirty days beyond the March 1 end of the term date. Davis left unfilled vacancies at the time of his recall.

Governor Arnold Schwarzenegger was able to make seven appointments to the board of trustees in 2004, his first full year after assuming office. In addition, he made a student appointment. Schwarzenegger returned to the Deukmejian/Wilson pattern of selecting for trustee positions individuals with substantial and serious interest in higher education.

As established by the Master Plan, the trustee positions included sixteen members conventionally appointed by the governor with the consent of the state senate, complemented by the governor, lieutenant governor, state superintendent of public instruction, the speaker of the assembly, and the chancellor, bringing the total to twenty-one. Four more positions were added over the years—a faculty member, an alumni member, and two student members—which expanded the board to twenty-five.

From 1960 through 2006, a total of 146 appointments have been made to the board. Four individuals have moved from the trustees to the regents; three, including Roy Brophy, moved directly from one position to the other, and another was appointed as a regent several years after concluding his term as a trustee. Arguably, in the earlier years of the CSU, some viewed movement from the trustees to the regents as a kind of step upward. The maturing of the California State University in the 1990s and the first decade of the twenty-first century has changed the perception of those knowledgeable about the work of universities. The California State University is seen as a distinct segment with unique needs requiring leadership by trustees. Brophy's appointment to the regents allowed him the distinction of serving on all three boards of higher education, the community colleges, the CSU board of trustees, and the UC regents.[4]

The board of trustees matured with the growing maturity of the system. Doubtless, the board and the system each influenced the other. The board gradually withdrew from being a quasi-managerial board, to one with a greater focus on policy, to one with almost a complete focus on policy. Two major developments from the mid-1970s to the mid-1990s greatly influenced the work and role of the board. The first was the legislation permitting collective bargaining, followed by the adoption and reality of collective bargaining. The story of collec-

22. Glenn S. Dumke Trustees Conference Center.

tive bargaining is covered in Chapter 10 of this work, but it is important to an understanding of the evolution of the trustees to mention here that the board did not handle well the legislative process and events leading to the passage of the collective bargaining statute. The members did not communicate and make decisions effectively. The implementation of collective bargaining in the 1980s did not go smoothly, and a trustee focus group conversation years later gives a clear picture of restlessness and significant dissatisfaction with the dynamic and the results. This is especially the case with the California Faculty Association (CFA), the group representing the faculty. Members of the board, for the most part, have not made the important distinction between the faculty and the union. This has been an unsettling factor as the board has matured over the past twenty-five years, and it is unfinished business.

Another factor influencing the board's development has been the policy role that the board has played, and the leadership of particular board members, in the establishment of a fundraising program beginning in the late 1980s and 1990s. The work of the board has been central to the development of a fundraising capacity.

Barry Munitz came to the chancellorship in 1991. He had in previous years served as an advisor to a national organization, the Association of Governing Boards, helping with board development on some campuses. He placed an emphasis on the policy role of the trustees and initiated the practice of board retreats. By law they were open, but no one ever attempted to sit in beyond the

23. Clark Kerr, Barry Munitz, Trustee Chair Anthony Vitti; joint meeting of trustees and regents, October 13, 1993, Assembly Chamber.

board members and senior Chancellor's staff. Munitz also urged the development of positive working relationships with the other segments of higher education. He proposed a joint meeting with the regents of the University of California and the trustees. This happened on October 13, 1993 in the Assembly Chamber of the state capitol; Clark Kerr delivered an address. This was the first joint meeting since the development of the Master Plan in 1959–60. Subsequently he invited the Board of Governors of the California Community Colleges to meet with the trustees. On October 31, 1995, the members of the two boards met on the Sacramento campus. The topic was of interest to both boards, precollegiate skills and remedial education.

In the mid-1990s, the Cornerstones project was developed. The concept did not originate with the board, but with Chancellor Barry Munitz. Individual trustees played a role in the rainbow group that developed Cornerstones (which is discussed more extensively in Chapter 4), but their real role came in the policy phase after the completion and adoption of the project's report. The trustees and the then new chancellor, Charles Reed, proceeded to address policy changes in the substantive work of the CSU, the educational programs and direct work with students. Cornerstones became a series of important educational policy initiatives. As the work with Cornerstones came to a close in 2005–06, the chair of the board's Educational Policy Committee initiated discussions about a sequel among trustees, the chancellor, faculty and student leaders, and presidents and other administrators. Access to Excellence became the next major educational policy vehicle for the board. The concept was adopted in 2006, and in 2008, the trustees adopted a detailed plan for policy issues to be addressed.

The integration of newly appointed trustees into the board is important. The chancellor's staff has developed a formal process over the years, essentially briefing new trustees about the work of the central office and the campuses and the issues of the moment, while providing an opportunity to know major administrators at the system level. Presidents variously work at building a relationship with board members. But almost from the beginning of the board, an informal process of integration for new appointees has been successfully employed. For the most part, continuing trustees work with new members on the issues and agenda items. "We have worked at keeping people [trustees] together."[5]

The initial board of trustees quickly developed a practice of involving faculty, students, presidents, and chancellor's staff in their deliberations. Provision was made for seating presidents and faculty and students in a pattern partially encircling the board tables. When the trustees moved from rented quarters to their own building in Long Beach in September 1976, the boardroom accommodated this, as did the new chancellor's office and the Glenn S. Dumke Auditorium in the new chancellor's office-trustee headquarters building occupied in 1998.[6] This was more than symbolic, and in a sense, the Dumke facility was aptly named.

At the beginning in the 1960s, the board of trustees was not necessarily a policy-initiating board, although it did take such initiative in that first decade, both in the context of creating the structure and functioning of the system and in the context of addressing the San Francisco State situation at the end of the 1960s. The chancellor and chancellor's staff often played the initiating role. By way of example, the board played an initiating role with respect to fundraising; the chancellor and staff were in the initiating role with respect to technology; a single trustee, Ralph Pesqueira, played a major initiating role in the 1990s about remedial programs. Clearly the board has emerged as a policy board.[7] The interaction of board members with leaders in the statewide Academic Senate, the California State Student Association, the CSU Alumni Council, and with presidents and other campus leaders and the chancellor and staff, has become extensive over the years.

The Academic Senate

Faculty participation in governance on the campuses of the California State Colleges prior to the Master Plan was modest. The form it took was entirely at the discretion of the individual campus president. Only a few of the campuses had formal structures (a senate or a faculty council) in 1960. By the end of the 1960s, every campus had a faculty governance structure. There was no common structure; each campus built its own. As new campuses were established, a first order of business was the establishment of a faculty body to be a formal part of the campus governance structure.

With the adoption of the Master Plan in the spring of 1960, the leadership of the State Board of Education—the transitional formal governing body—made clear an intent that faculty be involved in the governance of each campus and of the emerging state college system. As the initial trustees took office, there was a continuing reaffirmation of this principle. No one was more clear and persistent about this than Louis Heilbron, the newly elected chair of the State Board of Education and, then, of the trustees. The topic had not been addressed in the Master Plan. Such a practice was assumed traditionally in the University of California, and state college faculty wanted to adopt it as well, and attempted to involve members of the legislature in support of a faculty governance role. Heilbron, when elected the first chair of the board of trustees in August of 1960, remained consistent with and persistent about his support.

Dumke became chancellor in April 1962. One of his first acts was to convene a meeting of campus faculty chairs, and he invited them to proceed with the establishment of a statewide academic senate immediately. That happened, and faculty leaders from the campuses spent almost a full year developing its structure and functioning. Ellis McCune, then president of the faculty at the San Fernando Valley campus, and Jordan Churchill, a philosophy professor at San Francisco, drafted and redrafted a constitution, and travelled throughout the state visiting campuses advocating for the Academic Senate. There was some faculty resistance to a statewide senate. The point of resistance was campus autonomy, and a fear of any statewide body, administrative or faculty, interfering with that autonomy. Dumke, on the other hand, saw a statewide senate as an important vehicle to bring the campuses together on basic educational policy and governance issues. In January 1962, while still vice-chancellor for academic affairs and in a windowless office with a packing crate for a desk, at the new chancellor's office on Imperial Highway in Inglewood, Dumke had shared his views about a statewide senate with a young campus administrator.[8] Dumke was pushing for a senate, with some resistance or, perhaps more properly put, simply a lack of interest on the part of the chancellor at the time, Buell Gallagher. Dumke viewed the senate as essential to sound academic governance, and essential to giving the faculty a stake in building the new system of California State Colleges; he thought also that it was politically essential. A constitution was ratified by the faculties in campus-by-campus votes. Subsequently, the trustees approved the constitution, and the Academic Senate became a formal part of the governance structure of the California State Colleges.

The first meeting of the Academic Senate of the California State Colleges was held on May 14, 1963, in the newly established chancellor's office in Inglewood. Chancellor Dumke opened the meeting noting that "[t]he Assembling of the Senate constituted a major step in the achievement of a long-held personal objective."[9] He told the members that funding would be available in the fiscal year beginning July 1, to make the senate operable and effective. He affirmed a classic concept of representation: the members represented their campuses, but their overall responsibility was for the statewide system. More important was Dumke's ten-point list of specific matters he asked the senate to address. These tell a story: "(1) [e]stablishment of an annual State College conference; (2) . . . a framework for curriculum studies; (3) ways and means . . . to achieve a desirable academic climate; (4) [a] selection procedure for . . . awards to outstanding . . . professors; (5) philosophy and basic policies of general education; (6) uniformity and diversity of educational programs; (7) guidelines for activities of local senates; (8) evaluation of professional colleagues; (9) financial aspects of academic programs; (10) research policy."[10] This list says much about Dumke and his values and purposes as chancellor. It also defines his lack of understanding of the faculty politics of the time, and the agendas of most faculty leaders, at least of those who saw themselves as faculty leaders. Glenn Dumke as chancellor was like Glenn Dumke as a president, a dean, or a professor. He was essentially an academic. Many thought over the years that he was really his own vice-chancellor for academic affairs, and this was true on many issues; the exception was during the three years of William Langsdorf as the academic vice-chancellor, when Langsdorf and Dumke were partners. More importantly, Dumke's ten-point list overlooked what the faculty political and policy leaders wanted: clear authority for the faculty, massive changes in personnel practices, and changes in the way decisions were made. The faculty had wanted the independent doctorate and support for research.

Little of the structure of the Academic Senate has changed over time. As new campuses were established, the formula for determining the size of a campus delegation was altered, from time to time. The senate did secure a regular place in the system budget, and a secretariat was established. The quality of the principal staff member in the secretariat has remained high over the years.

The evolution of the Academic Senate is best understood in the context of the internal political and policy evolution of the California State University. A first test was a final two-day meeting to review the senate's proposed constitution. The chancellor invited all campus presidents and campus senate and council chairs to the meeting. Not all attended, but there were equal numbers of presidents and faculty chairs. The draft provided for the proposed senate to elect its chair. A motion was made to have the chancellor be chair of the senate. The Los Angeles campus faculty chair, Leonard Mathy, a professor of economics, was chairing the meeting. Chancellor Dumke was seated next to him. The fact that Dumke would see himself as a legitimate chair of the academic senate is illustrative of the argument that he saw himself first and foremost as an academic. After considerable discussion and a motion, there was a tie vote. (Later it was learned that there had been some crossover voting.) Mathy voted no to break the tie. On the second day, Fred Harcleroad, the founding president of the Hayward campus, arrived and asked for the opportunity to vote. The chair asked for a motion for reconsideration. There was no motion, only silence. The issue was decided. Dumke accepted the result graciously, as was his style.[11] Mathy went on to become the first and founding chair of the statewide Academic Senate and dean of Arts and Letters at California State College Los Angeles. He served for many years in the statewide Academic Senate, even while a dean, and for a number of years after retirement he was the senate's emeritus faculty representative.

After the constitution was adopted, members of the Academic Senate were dissatisfied with their perceived failure to gain a clear delegation of final authority from the board of trustees over academic matters. Their model was a 1919 delegation of responsibility, from the regents of the University of California to the UC Academic Senate. The UC delegation was most clear about admission standards and somewhat less clear on curriculum and personnel. The perception in the state colleges at the time of the Master Plan (and persisting as a myth to this day) is that the UC regents had delegated great powers to its Academic Senate. In fact, the alignment of power and responsibility within the University of California more nearly represented steps in the maturing of that institution. Senate chair Leonard Mathy and a colleague, Levern Graves of the Fullerton campus, met with trustee chair Louis Heilbron and another trustee, William Coblentz (the first of the aforementioned four trustees who would move to the board of regents). Heilbron and Coblentz, who were very supportive of faculty, declined to make any final delegation. This has remained an issue over the years. In fact, the regents act on issues when they believe that they need to do so, regardless of perceptions about delegation. The issue is one of trust and respect rather than formal delegation.[12]

The first year of the senate was not a good one. The biggest issue on the first substantive meeting agenda on September 26–28, 1963, was year-round operations (YRO) and the quarter system. In an October 4 memorandum to Chancellor Dumke, Mathy, the senate chair, wrote that the senate recommended that "favorable consideration be given to the quarter system." But the senate also recommended that "changes in college calendars should not necessarily be applied uniformly to all state colleges."[13] The YRO issue was an outgrowth of the Master Plan, which had addressed it as a means to save on costs of capital outlay. At about the same time that the Academic Senate acted, the president of the University of California said publicly that he was waiting for more faculty input. The recently appointed chancellor's staff member handling YRO was a longtime faculty member from Fresno State, Bruce Fisher; he had no administrative or campus governance experience. He made exactly the wrong move and interpreted the Mathy memorandum as a signal to forge ahead with YRO conversion. The result was not only fatal for YRO (other than on several new campuses, the Cal Polys, which had been on the quarter system, and one established campus with a new president who imposed it), but it also poisoned the well for faculty-administration relationships, particularly at the system level.

In a sense, the work of the senate in the 1960s was not unlike the work of the trustees. New procedures and policies were to be built in the new context of the Master Plan and the newly developing state college structure and mission. However, many of the policies the senate was attempting to create required the concurrence of the chancellor or a board of trustee action. The senate became involved, necessarily, with the adoption of new personnel rules. Relationships with the chancellor's staff about personnel issues were strained, at best, from the 1960s and 1970s to the time of the enactment of collective bargaining legislation. The issue of faculty grievance procedures was in dispute for a dozen years. The senate became embroiled in the 1964 San Francisco State dispute with the chancellor's office about governance, and then again, inevitably, in the faculty and student unrest and strikes of the later 1960s. Within the context of the San Francisco State student and faculty strike activity, the Academic Senate voted "no confidence" in Chancellor Dumke. The trustees took no action. Only two trustees wanted a total crackdown on the so-called dissident students and faculty at San Francisco State and other involved campuses.

An early action of the Academic Senate addresses a report of the Senate Faculty and Staff Affairs Committee, *Principles and Procedures for Academic Due Process*.[14] The report's subtitle, *Rights of Academic and Academic-Administrative Personnel*, introduced a document that in many ways was almost combative, given the context. To some extent, it paralleled the American Association of University Professors policy, but the context of the time was not receptive. Similarly, the administration—in particular, the system office headed by the assistant chancellor for faculty and staff affairs—was insensitive to faculty interests, and together these two positions set a tone that would lead, with a certain inevitability, to the collective bargaining legislation of 1978.

At the request of the trustees, the senate became involved in the work of the Ad Hoc Committee on Policies and Procedures, a committee whose existence was triggered by the resignation of Robert Smith as dean of the School of Education at San Francisco State College.[15] The dissents in this committee's report were those of the senate appointees.

The senate became active about educational policy matters early on, and relationships with the chancellor's staff and the presidents were positive, even when there was disagreement. The academic planning staff in the chancellor's office, with Ellis McCune as the dean of academic planning, was careful to work with campus faculty leadership as well as with campus administrations; similarly, McCune and the academic planning staff worked well and productively with the Statewide Senate, so well that some presidents complained about the relationship. McCune and his associates were without exception brought to the chancellor's office from the campuses. The vice-chancellor for academic affairs, Raymond Rydell, was one of the first faculty members at the Los Angeles campus, and moved to the San Fernando Valley campus in 1956 as a dean. Rydell was an historian and a quiet, thoughtful individual who worked constructively with faculty and did his best with presidents during the '60s, when roles were still being defined. Rydell became executive vice-chancellor in 1966 and served in that role until he retired in 1969. McCune was de facto academic vice-chancellor until 1968, when a group of presidents blocked his formal appointment to the position; they wanted a weak vice-chancellor who would neither interfere with the campuses nor work closely with the statewide Academic Senate. McCune then moved to the presidency at Hayward.

With the Dumke "New Approaches" speech and strategy, cooperation and involvement about academic matters between the senate and system leadership was reinforced. The 1971–72 statewide senate chair, David Provost, became the first dean of the new program development and evaluation unit in the chancellor's office. The Commission on External Degree Programs, created in 1971, included active membership from the statewide senate. The initiatives associated with New Approaches involved the senate throughout. In 1973, the chancellor initiated a new look at admissions, and asked for the development of criteria that would reach out to those beyond conventional college student ages. The Committee on Alternative Admissions Criteria drew substantial membership from the statewide Academic Senate. This committee became the Admissions Advisory Committee in the late 1970s and persists as of this writing in 2008. The committee has throughout its more than thirty years been one in which faculty and administrators work cooperatively and productively. Faculty have played a major role from the beginning.

In the 1970s the buildup to collective bargaining legislation was a central preoccupation of both senate leaders and membership. The election of Jerry Brown as governor in November 1974 brought the certain promise of collective bargaining. Brown had committed himself to collective bargaining in the election campaign. Faculty organizations were among the leaders of the campaign. The statewide Academic Senate was inevitably involved in a variety of ways. The 1975 legislative session began an open competition among faculty organizations for position as the bargaining group. The Academic Senate was drawn in, and some senate leaders inserted themselves. The issue was providing for and carefully defining the role and work of the statewide Academic Senate in a world in which it would coexist with a faculty collective bargaining unit. The trustees and chancellor attempted at times to use the promise of a strengthened senate as a counter in the politics leading up to legislation and in the legislative arena. Faculty organizations sought senate alliances. David Elliott, senate chair from 1977 to 1979, became directly involved with the legislative process. Elliott played a role in Sacramento, spending serious time with legislators, faculty organization leaders, system lobbyists, and trustees.

There was competition not only among the faculty organizations in the effort to become the bargaining unit, but between the organizations and the senate in the effort to define respective roles. Elliott had been successful in inserting into the legislation explicit and specified responsibilities for academic senates. "The Legislature recognizes that joint decision making and consultation between administration and faculty or academic employees is the long-accepted manner of governing institutions of higher learning. . . . Nothing contained in this law shall be construed to restrict, limit, or prohibit the full exercise of the functions of the faculty in any shared governance mechanisms or practices including . . . the Academic Senates of the California State University and Colleges . . . with respect to policies on academic and professional matters."[16] Legislative intent was clear and it encompassed the Statewide Senate and campus senates.

24. Statewide Academic Senate Leadership, 1978; David Elliott, chair; Helen Gilde, Judson Grenier.

Assembly Bill 1091, authored by Howard Berman, passed in 1978 and Governor Jerry Brown signed it. The long, multiyear process of selecting a faculty bargaining agent began. As the final debate over collective bargaining was underway, David Elliott penned first an outline and then a draft of a paper that would be discussed in the years to come. The paper addressed the coexistence of the statewide Academic Senate and collective bargaining.

Professor Robert Kully became chair of the Academic Senate in 1979 and served to 1982; later he was appointed as the first faculty trustee. A senate committee in 1979 addressed a first formal draft of "Responsibilities of Academic Senates Within a Collective Bargaining Context." After lengthy discussions in the statewide Senate, and considerable exchange with potential faculty bargaining agents, the board of trustees formally approved the document as CSU policy on May 8, 1981.[17] This was followed by correspondence between Chancellor Dumke and the senate chair, Robert Kully, spelling out the implementation of the document. Subsequently, the senate leadership, two presidents, and Academic Vice-Chancellor Alex Sherriffs prepared another paper on "Collegiality in the California State University," and this was adopted by the senate, the board of trustees, and some campus senates and presidents.[18]

The attention of the statewide Senate was necessarily focused heavily on the implementation of collective bargaining, in the early 1980s. Collective bargaining did have an unintended consequence for the statewide Academic Senate. It provided the circumstance for the senate to move away from a range of personnel matters, and thus to capture time to address educational policy and related matters. As the 1980s moved on, the senate prepared major reports about undergraduate education, baccalaureate level courses, faculty professional development, faculty scholarship, affirmative action, and the like. These reports were important to building the CSU and the campuses. William Campbell, a newly appointed trustee in 1987, developed first an interest and then a strategy, working with senate chair Bernard Goldstein (later, the faculty trustee) to secure funding for the first time for faculty research. In the early 1990s, senate leadership worked with then new Chancellor Barry Munitz on a range of issues. Senate chair Sandra Wilcox (1990–93), a CSU Dominguez Hills psychology professor and the first woman to chair the senate, described the three issues of her years as relationships with trustees, Sacramento, and the chancellor. Sacramento was particularly important, as the system was building and rebuilding new relationships in the state capital.

The trustees, the Chancellor, Barry Munitz, and Vice-Chancellor Molly Broad then surfaced with Cornerstones, a major undertaking to build a strategic agenda for the CSU. At the same time, the statewide Academic Senate had underway a major study, "Baccalaureate Education in the California State University," and this would influence Cornerstones.[19] Members of the Senate played a major role in the preparation of Cornerstones, and this became the CSU agenda from 1999 to 2006.

The statewide Academic Senate has matured, as has all of the California State University. The focus is on educational policy, on professional development, often on academic relationships with the California Community Colleges and the University of California. The senate sponsors and prepares reports. These are circulated widely to its members. They are not always adopted by the trustees as such, but they become a part of the continuing conversation concerning the California State University; they are setting the climate. The faculty in the senate meet and often agree with faculty in the University of California and the community colleges about significant educational matters. After years of discussion, the inclusion of the fine arts in the common curricular pattern of high school preparation, for both the University of California and the California State University, the A–G pattern for freshman admission, was the result of faculty members in the Admissions Advisory Council working with counterparts in the University of California. The major senate report, *The California State University at the Beginning of the 21st Century: Meeting the Needs of the People of California*, was a document that affected the thinking of many, inside and outside of the CSU, about the work of the CSU. The continuing pressure from the senate about the independent doctorate certainly was a factor in the achievement of the authority to award the independent doctorate in education, and that will be followed by other fields. The senate continues to address specific items that need attention. The Academic Senate is the faculty, in an important way, in the statewide mix within the California State University.

At the very beginning of the statewide Academic Senate, some were concerned about its role vis-à-vis campus senates. This was a matter of discussion, more on some campuses than on others. There was a small movement, at the time of the statewide faculty vote about the senate constitution in early 1963, to encourage faculty to vote "no" against a statewide senate of any kind. The "no" vote was very modest. The experience of almost a half a century of the statewide senate has been without meaningful conflict with any campus senate.

There is frequently some tension (as well as collaboration) between the statewide Academic Senate and the faculty union. Old scars, some on the part of faculty and some on the part of trustees and administrators, continue to influence relationships. Senate involvement could be far more effective if this underbrush would be cleared away, as it will in time.

Students

Students have been a significant presence in the governance of the California State University. They want to be involved, and they have a voice— sometimes a major voice—in policy issues and on specific higher education issues. Administrators and faculty groups want students on their side in issues before the board of trustees and in the capital. The trustees want students on their side about issues with faculty and others, especially in Sacramento. In Sacramento, everyone wants students on their side, for students learned in the early 1960s that they could walk into a legislator's office and say, "We represent 100,000 students," and in 2008, "We represent 450,000 students." Students vote. Whether they vote their interests as students is not clear, and perhaps not likely, but some do. On the campuses in smaller communities, such as Arcata and Chico, there are enough student votes to affect community election outcomes, and that does occur.

Students and their formal organizations have held a place in the organizational structure of California State University campuses for years. Prior to World War II, student corporations were formed as nonprofits on several of the campuses. In the years after the war and leading up to the 1960 Master Plan, a nonprofit corporation called Associated Students was established on all campuses as auxiliary organizations. Associated Students had as a common primary function, the operation of representative student governments. There were as many patterns of organizations and sets of responsibilities as there were campuses. Most often, the Associated Students organization included the coordination of recognized campus student organizations. On the Chico campus, the Associated Students corporation included the campus bookstore and food service, and the Associated Students general manager was a significant campus administrator, albeit employed by the AS board. Shortly after World War II, the general manager of the Chico Associated Students, Paul Byrne, became a candidate for the California State Senate. He won election and remained there until the end of his career. He was influential in promoting legislation that supported students and Associated Students organizations. The involvement of students in overall campus governance was widely varied, dependent on campus histories and cultures and campus president's administrative style. Campus Associated Students presidents were frequently included in the cabinets or other advisory bodies of campus presidents.

25. Trustee William Hauck.

In 1958, three years before the formal establishment of the California State Colleges and the board of trustees, a group of Associated Student presidents gathered and founded the Student Presidents Association. The organization was mostly a forum for student body presidents to share information and ideas. While it did not become involved with the Master Plan negotiations, it developed a relationship with the chancellor's office when that office was established. In the fall of 1963, the board of trustees formally recognized the California State Colleges Student Presidents Association (CSCSPA) as the organization officially representing students and their interests with the board. This brought the students to be seated, along with faculty from the statewide Academic Senate, at meetings of the board of trustees, and it brought students into regular contact with the chancellor and the staff. The students had a presence. The trustee resolution acknowledged "legitimate interest" of students in the work of the board, and invited the CSCSPA chair to attend board meetings and provide counsel on discussions and issues. Two students negotiated this new relationship. One was from Cal Poly, the other from San Jose State. The San Jose student, William Hauck, was president of the Associated Students on that campus, and in 1993 was appointed to the board of trustees and subsequently became chair of the board. Hauck would later become president of the California Business Roundtable and a major figure in Sacramento, with credibility on both sides of the aisle. He was reappointed to the board in 2001 and again in 2009.

Les Cohen, the director of governmental affairs in Sacramento, soon began to invite student representatives to join him in contacts with state government offices and in meetings and testimony with the legislature. Cohen found the student representatives to be exceedingly effective. He involved them in a variety of issues. Two of the early persistent student advocates who worked with Cohen were Hauck and Jud Clarke. The testimony and activity of students weighed heavily in the legislative action to change the name of the system to the California State University and Colleges.[20]

CSCSPA became organized and soon established a dues structure based on campus enrollment. Dues were used to establish a modest office in the CSU headquarters building. CSCSPA leaders also wanted to establish a lobbying presence in Sacramento. In 1970, Joe Hay, a Vietnam veteran and a student at Sacramento State, was appointed legislative advocate. CSCSPA sought and secured legislation authorizing the expenditure of student body fees to fund a lobbyist position in Sacramento. In 1975, Scott Plotkin, the Associated Students president at Cal Poly at San Luis Obispo, chair of what was now called the California State University and Colleges Student Presidents Association (CSUC-SPA), and successor to Hay, undertook a campaign to create a student position on the board of trustees. The campaign was successful and legislation was signed by Governor Jerry Brown. The legislation provided that the CSUCSPA board nominate three to five current students to the governor for his selection and appointment of a student trustee with full voting privileges. The first student trustee, Kathleen Carlson, took office in 1976. This legislation was modified in the year 2000 to create a second nonvoting student trustee position. Student trustees now serve two-year terms, the first year nonvoting, and the second year as a voting trustee. The student trustee legislation helped to pave the way for the 1977 creation of an alumni trustee position, and the later creation of a faculty trustee position.

By 1979, the level of activity in CSUCSPA was such that many campus Associated Students presidents felt they could no longer spend sufficient time with both their campus responsibilities and statewide activities. Some campuses elected or appointed separate representatives. CSUCSPA joined the issue and renamed itself the California State Student Association (CSSA), while providing for representatives other than student body presidents.

During the 1980s and early 1990s, CSSA's political strength and activity grew year by year. CSSA leaders had long since learned that legislators understood the representation of the hundreds of thousands of students enrolled in the California State University. Representation of the California State University became more complex in the 1980s and '90s, with the advent of collective bargaining. The collective bargaining legislation gave students a seat at the table, though they seldom used this. Three would-be major players became four; the CSU chancellor and Sacramento office, the statewide Academic Senate, the unions, most often the California Faculty Association (CFA), and CSSA. CSSA did not always play a hand.

Students have a natural interest in student fees. Student trustees over the years have consistently argued against fee increases, though, on occasion, ultimately voting for their approval. They have always faced an uphill battle, as proposals for student fee increases, by the time they reach the board, are set in the context of a total budget reality. (It should be noted that one-third of the

26. *Students outside the State Capitol "Protect the Future of California."*

amount of a fee increase is dedicated to student financial aid, as a result of student negotiations with Chancellor Barry Munitz in 1994.) The issue of student fee increases in the 1990s brought CSSA to the fore. By the mid-'90s, CSSA was advocating that students should play a dominant role in fee setting and in the use of student fees on the campuses. It was successful with the latter matter, and provision was made for student body voting, along the lines of the voting procedures on Associated Students and student union or other fees. Students would vote on instructionally related activities, fee allocations, and on-campus–based discrete fees for new student-oriented facilities and on athletic support allocations, for example. Students did not have final authority, but as a practical matter, most often campus presidents were reluctant to set aside student votes.

CSSA initiated an annual major conference, always held in Sacramento with students and student leaders from all of the campuses. The chancellor and some presidents also participate in two days of activities, which include substantive presentations and panels and legislative visits. The students are well organized and purposeful. In the most recent of these conferences, Chancellor Reed made a major presentation about the student interest in higher education policy. Shaun Lumachi, the 2001–02 CSSA chair (now a successful businessperson and activist), addressed the value of organizing students.

Students were involved in most of the key issues in the latter 1990s. The leadership of CSSA wanted to see student roles institutionalized and, in October 2000, adopted a proposal, "Shared Responsibility: Enhancing Institutional Effectiveness by Encouraging Student Participation in CSU Policymaking." The CSU Advisory Committee on Student Participation in Policy Development was formed, and in July 2001 the board of trustees adopted a policy addressing students:

> The California State Student Association, or its successor, is recognized as the official representative of the students of the California State University before the Board of Trustees and the Chancellor's Office. The Board of Trustees and the Chancellor will provide CSSA an opportunity to offer opinions and make recommendations to the Board of Trustees and the Chancellor and/or the campus President with regard to university policy and procedures that have or will have an effect on students at the systemwide level.[21]

The Trustees adopted parallel language about campuses and student input.

Student participation in the governance of the campuses varies widely. It is a function of the style and values of presidents and faculty, the history of the particular campus, and the interests and skills of students. From the very earliest years in the nineteenth century, and the years leading up to the transition of the early campuses to State Teachers Colleges and State Colleges, examples of student responsibility for projects and programs abound. Beginning in the 1930s, at the Chico campus, with the leadership of Hugh Bell, a remarkable twenty-five-year dean of students and internationally known psychology professor, student associations were able to incorporate and operate campus enterprises. Almost simultaneously, a new Cal Poly president, Julian McPhee, brought more student involvement to the actual operation of the campus and created a student-local bank partnership to operate some campus activities. Associated Students on all but the smallest campuses are multimillion dollar enterprises, and their leaders have some formal roles in campus governance.

Among representative student organizations in multicampus systems (public universities and colleges), and most private universities of any size across the country, the students of the California State University are in the top few effectively represented with trustees and state government. To the extent that there is any flaw, it is the flaw of democracies—the interest and participation of the electorate. Unlike campus Associated Students, CSSA is an unincorporated nonprofit association. Were it incorporated, it could not engage in advocacy before the state government and others until the board of trustees took a position. Financially, it is dependent upon campus Associated Students organizations (in 2008–09, member campuses contributed seventy cents per student per year), and modest fundraising; this yields almost 60 percent of the $436,000 CSSA budget (in 2008–09). The chancellor's office has consistently made available about 40 percent of the budget to stabilize the organization (this is in contrast with chancellor's office full funding of the statewide Academic Senate).

27. The California State Student Association.

Campus membership in CSSA fluctuates from 60 percent to almost 100 percent of the campus Associated Student organizations. This can be volatile, as student leaders react to fee increases with demands that CSSA stop them, or when students on large campuses seek more voting power in CSSA than small campuses. The CSSA constitution provides one vote for each member campus; nonmember campuses may participate, but not vote. CSSA has a regular place on each trustee meeting agenda, along with the statewide Academic Senate and the alumni council, as well as a seat in the "outer ring" of tables, along with senate, alumni, and campus presidents.

It is at least arguable that the relationship of the student representatives is the strongest and most effective of the groups seated at the outer ring of tables. Students can be and, in fact, have been of great assistance to the board on specific issues. In part, this is because in the early days of the board in the 1960s, faculty relationships with it were sometimes clumsy. Neither the faculty (the statewide Academic Senate or, subsequently, the faculty union) nor the chancellor's office and presidents handled relations well over the years, and that legacy lives on. Curiously, it is clear from correspondence that Glenn Dumke understood the matter. Students have moved cautiously, for the most part and, given their centrality to the mission of the CSU, are increasingly heard by the trustees and others on the selected matters where they choose to speak.

Presidents

Holding a college or university presidency is a rare privilege. Only a small number of academics have the opportunity to be a president, or a chancellor, rector, or vice-chancellor, whatever the title. This is not to say that academics necessarily desire to hold an administrative role. An even smaller number of individuals from outside academia share in the privilege. So what is the privilege? It is not about managing, though managing a complex institution with a high percentage of well-educated employees can be interesting. It is not about power, as power in a healthy university or college is widely distributed. It is not even necessarily about leadership, though leadership of a college or university, most often both within and without the institution, can be demanding and exhilarating. It is about the life of the mind and the intellectual and creative interpersonal skills that grow in students as they prepare for productive and useful and rewarding lives. The privilege of the job is in creating, developing, and re-creating an institution that is at the heart of a responsible learning society, and being responsible for the strength and quality and integrity of an academic community and its role in the greater society.[22]

The contemporary California State University presidency is a unique role in American higher education. The president is the leader of a campus, and often a leader in a region or the state, nationally, sometimes even internationally. The president is also an individual, albeit an important one, in a large and complex organization. The president's role is to maintain and grow the uniqueness and vitality of a campus and bring along not only students, faculties, and communities, but also the trustees, the chancellor, and others, all within the overarching mission of the large and complex organization.

The history of the presidency in the state colleges prior to the Master Plan is a mixed one. The nineteenth-century principals and, later, presidents needed to be strong individuals. They were on their own, for the most part, while they often enjoyed the support of a local board. Most served only a few years in the presidency. It was a very practical hands-on role, assuring support from the state, making do with whatever support was secured, while working with regional schools. In the early 1900s, the presidency changed. Presidents were recruited by local boards, but were culled, at least, from among candidates state-wide and outside the state. Several of the campuses benefited from long-term presidential leadership. Frederic Burk, the founding president of the San Francisco campus, stayed for twenty-five years, until his death, and he enjoyed a national reputation as a teacher educator. The presidency began to move to the intellectual and educational leadership on campuses, in some instances to leadership in campus regions.

Sacramento and state government rarely intruded. In the mid-1920s, the combination of a conservative governor and moderate to liberal state superintendent of public instruction held up two presidential appointments that resulted in interim presidencies. The power of appointment had moved to the state superintendent, who would recommend to the State Board of Education. The custom became the selection of a single individual by the superintendent and state board approval.

In the early 1930s, the presidents created a structure with periodic meetings, at which the superintendent, or his designee, would participate. The pattern of meetings and great attention to detail persisted into the 1950s. In the 1940s, as state college enrollments expanded dramatically, the meetings became more formal; with the creation of the position of associate superintendent of public instruction responsible for a division of state colleges and teacher education, the incumbent in that position (there were only two in the time from the mid-1940s until 1960 and the Master Plan implementation) became a regular participant. The first associate superintendent, Aubrey Douglass, played a major role, though not with an authoritarian style, in moving the state colleges through a period characterized by growth and program development in the liberal arts and sciences and some professions. The presidents began a schedule of meetings, almost monthly. (In Chapter 2, the point was made that the presidents became a de facto governing board.)

The transition caused by the Master Plan, from the State Board of Education to the board of trustees, created uncertainty about the role of the presidents as a group. With the advent of the appointees of Governor Pat Brown in 1959 and 1960, the State Board of Education began to assert the responsibilities of the board; this became clear with the transition board of trustees in 1960–61 and the assumption of legal responsibility by the new board on July 1, 1961. The presidents were not ignored in the transitions, but neither were they collectively involved.

Buell Gallagher assumed the chancellorship on July 1, 1961, and soon afterward met with presidents. Gallagher subsequently informed them that they would not need to meet frequently (they had been accustomed to almost monthly meetings, a schedule they maintained through 1960–61). He would inform them of policies and practices they would need to follow. Gallagher also informed the presidents that they did not necessarily need to attend trustee meetings, though they might wish to attend meetings in geographic proximity to their individual campuses. The significance of the regional base of campuses, most particularly the long-established campuses, was not understood by Gallagher. Gallagher's appointment of Glenn Dumke as vice-chancellor for academic affairs was welcomed by most, if not all, presidents, even those who had disagreed with Dumke in the Master Plan negotiations. He was one of their own, who would understand the presidential role, and would be in the small group at the center of the new structure of governance.

The role of president on individual campuses varied greatly. This has been true from the very beginning. Certainly the administrative style and values and interests of an incumbent president were major variables. The roles played by presidents in individual institution governance were the products of each campus. The rapid growth of the 1940s and 1950s, and the roles of state government agencies, notably the Department of Finance and the Legislative Analyst's Office, brought the presidents together, but each president remained close to absolute on his or her campus and an almost independent player in Sacramento. This was to change, but not without resistance from some presidents.

Glenn Dumke had the support of most presidents, even if begrudgingly in some instances, when he was appointed chancellor in April 1962, after the sudden departure of Buell Gallagher. The presidents did not want another "outsider," and most reasoned that they could work with Dumke, despite many instances in which there were rather basic disagreements about the mission of the state colleges. On Dumke's first full day in office he called for two statewide meetings, campus presidents and campus faculty senate or council chairs. Dumke defined for the presidents as a group a formal consultative role. He established the Council of Presidents, and initially chaired it. A schedule of meetings was prepared, and the presidents met every month or six weeks, almost invariably the week before a board of trustees meeting. As the system began to function, there were fifteen presidents responsible for sixteen operating campuses and two additional institutions in the planning stage and scheduled to open to students in 1965 (the president of Cal Poly was responsible for two campuses, San Luis Obispo and Pomona, and Dominguez Hills and San Bernardino were in planning stages). With the separate establishment of Cal Poly Pomona and the founding of Bakersfield in 1967, the number of presidents reached nineteen and remained so until 1989 and the founding of the twentieth campus, San Marcos.

In the 1960s, there was no single model for the presidential role. By the end of the 1960s, only two presidents remained who had been in office at the time of the Master Plan, Malcolm Love at San Diego and Cornelius Siemens at Humboldt, and they would both retire shortly. The two next most senior presidents were the founders of two campuses established in the 1960s, Leo Cain at Dominguez Hills, and John Pfau at San Bernardino. Seven of the campuses had experienced three or more presidents throughout the decade—San Francisco State had a total of five appointed presidents and two interim presidents. In part, the turnover was due to normal retirement. At that time, the mandatory retirement age in the state colleges was sixty-five. The trustees had the authority to extend the age to sixty-seven, but no longer. The legislature extended Julian McPhee's tenure as president to seventy, before he then retired in 1966 (McPhee was a great exception in many ways). A few presidents moved on to other interests. One, Fred Harcleroad at the Hayward campus, resigned after substantial faculty unrest. Harcleroad was a president with considerable administrative experience and out of the teacher-education style of administration, and he was unyielding in that style.

The role of a president was simply not a priority for the trustees or the chancellor, so the presidential role continued to evolve campus by campus, shaped by each individual filling the office. The chancellor and trustees were preoccupied with building a system and with the growing faculty unrest, much of it emanating from the San Francisco campus. The 1966 election and the Reagan budget reductions following it compounded the situation, along with the major unrest of the later 1960s at San Francisco State. Retired vice-chancellor Mansel Keene volunteered the observation, in an oral history interview, that presidents in the 1960s were often not selected with sufficient care.[23] Success in a presidency is measured in many ways; one important variable is who is doing the measuring.

For the 1960s, arguably the most significant development affecting the presidents was the establishment of the Council of Presidents. The group was renamed the Chancellor's Council of Presidents (CCOP); the Chancellor withdrew from the role of chair of the group, though he could, and did on occasion, take the chair for a specific discussion. The CCOP organized itself into a committee structure parallel to the trustees' major committee structure. The presidents elected a council chair and an executive committee; the executive committee appointed the working committees and their chairs. The particular interests of individual presidents were most often respected and considered, and presidents could become specialized in particular areas of system activity— educational policy, finances, etc. Many of them wanted to be on the committees addressing finances and capital outlay.

The process of presidential selection was important from the beginning. After the passage of the Master Plan legislation, State Superintendent Simpson became attentive to what he perceived as the desires of the trustees. During the year of Buell Gallagher's chancellorship, two presidents of newly established campuses were appointed, both individuals obviously selected by Glenn Dumke in his role as vice-chancellor for academic affairs. Gallagher made a small number of key staff appointments. The Gallagher appointment of C. Mansel Keene as chief of personnel would have the longest impact. Keene became assistant chancellor for faculty and staff affairs and, subsequently, vice-chancellor for faculty and staff affairs, which he remained until his retirement in 1976.

Keene was a volatile person with firm opinions about administrative style and operations. He acquired the responsibility of traveling the country in search of presidential candidates. He had an impact. In the 1960s, in this time of great presidential turnover, presidential appointments essentially came from two sources. The first included only a few individuals whom Dumke wanted to see in a presidential role, individuals from California State College campuses whom Dumke thought to be supportive to the mission change he sought. Examples include Leo Cain at Dominguez Hills, John Pfau at San Bernardino, Ellis McCune at Hayward, Robert Kennedy at San Luis Obispo. Dumke's choices worked well and remained for years in the presidential role. The second included individuals identified by Keene as potential candidates. The choices, recruited nationally by Keene, were more varied in their successes. The research into the background of the individuals identified as candidates was not extensive. A number of appointments were made that simply did not fit with the campus and with the mission and culture of the California State Colleges.

It is fair to be critical of the process of presidential selection. Dumke and the trustees were intent upon change in the mission and in the culture of the California State Colleges. In the 1960s, indeed, until perhaps the late 1980s, institutional culture was not widely understood as an important factor in the quality and productivity of a college or university. What Dumke and the trustees sought was in many ways a change in culture at least as important as a change in mission. Most simply understood, the move was to be from a set of campuses dominated by the concept of teacher education (with the exception of Cal Poly, due to its being dominated by vocational programs) to institutions dominated by the liberal arts and sciences and professional programs, including emerging professions. Certainly teacher education was to be important, but no longer the centerpiece. Thus, some appointments were made of individuals who had perhaps impressive backgrounds in the liberal arts or a professional area, without questioning how they fit with the values of the new California State Colleges, with the emerging new missions of the campuses, and with the overarching mission of the system.

The campuses had widely varying cultures among faculty, staff, and students, in significant measure the product of history. Some new presidents fit, some did not. At the San Jose campus, an authoritarian president, John Wahlquist, dating back to the teacher education focus, retired according to the maximum age requirement in 1964, and after a recruitment process was replaced by a respected professor and administrator from Oregon, Robert Clark. There was an instant fit. Clark steered the campus through a difficult time in the late 1960s, and left in 1969 to become president of the University of Oregon, much to the dismay of many at the San Jose campus. At the other extreme were a number of presidents recruited by Mansel Keene and sold to campus selection committees, the chancellor, and the board, who upon assuming office were recognized almost instantly as misfits with the campus and for the leadership role, but stayed long enough to do real damage to the fabric of relationships.

Governance of the individual campuses and of the system was a key variable for new presidents, especially those new to the California State Colleges. The campuses were moving, within a few years, from governance structures in which faculty roles varied from modest to nonexistent. For most presidents new to the California State Colleges, this was a new phenomenon, and even for some of the internal appointees, genuine and meaningful faculty involvement in governance was difficult to understand. Arguably, this was also true for faculty; many faculty, especially those active in governance, had unrealistic expectations in terms of governance, within the customs of American higher education and the customs and rules of the greater society, including governments and business.

The 1970s introduced new possibilities for presidents. Dumke's New Approaches programs created room for campuses to develop new programs and new instructional delivery systems. Some campuses, most often those with strong presidential or other leadership and support, moved to take advantage. The presidents as a group became closer, some of this stability due simply to the length of holding the office. Presidents' meetings were almost always for two days, as were board of trustee meetings. The presidents began a custom of cocktails and conversation at the end of the first day, followed by dinner, sometimes with all together, sometimes in smaller groups. An extraordinary amount of presidential collective business was accomplished at these social gatherings, and the opportunity for partnerships of varying sorts between and among presidents and campuses was created. The chancellor was always invited and would come once or twice in a year, have a social drink, engage in relatively brief conversations, and leave. He accepted the custom, and saw the benefits, and showed no evidence of being annoyed by it. The Chancellor's Council of Presidents invitation did not include the vice-chancellors, some of whom made no secret of their annoyance and tried to tease out details about the meetings from the presidents.

With the 1976 move of the chancellor's office from Wilshire Boulevard, in a very urban area in which individual presidents and trustees were scattered among hotels, to the smaller locale of the Long Beach waterfront, the presidents and trustees were brought together with much greater frequency, first at the Queen Mary Hotel, and later at hotels within easy walking distance from the newly constructed chancellor's office at 400 Golden Shore. A new custom emerged. Sometimes at board meetings presidents would invite a few trustees to the cocktail and conversation hour. More often, a small group of presidents would invite a few trustees to dinner with an unstated agenda; at some board meetings there would be several of these small dinners. Dumke was generally kept informed and seemed comfortable with this, while quietly keeping track of all that was going on.

The Chancellor's Council of Presidents functioned well on the whole, even where there were issues regarding which it took consistent positions protective of campuses. An early important example of this was the development of technology in the 1970s. The senior individual on the chancellor's staff responsible for technology was not comfortable working with presidents, and the relationship was awkward. No individual vice-chancellor would adopt technology as a cause—perhaps they did not know enough about what was at that time a new phenomenon. The great majority of the presidents were determined to have technology systems that were not integrated across campuses and with the chancellor's office—so that one computer could not communicate with another. There were some presidents who saw the need for computers to be able to communicate, but their number was small and their views not popular. In fairness to the presidents, their campus technology staffs for the most part were not enthusiastic or supportive of integrated computer development. It would take twenty years, the initial work of Barry Munitz and Molly Broad, and the strong leadership of Charles Reed, the skilled work of Vice-Chancellor Richard West, and the emergence of a presidential "Technology Steering Committee" to overcome this presidential resistance, with a resulting change in the role of presidents in system governance.

The presidents did not have fundamental positions as a group on many matters within the California State University and Colleges in the 1970s. With only some exceptions, the presidents were focused on their individual campuses, much like some legislators focus on their districts and interests. Essentially, thirty years would go by, until the chancellorship of Barry Munitz, in which the common interests and good of the system as a whole would be present only in the background of discussions. They could build a system by defining what it was not, but they did not get to the bottom of things. The CCOP was a management group, not a leadership group.

The CCOP had developed a committee structure in the 1960s. The committee paralleled those of the Board of Trustees and would both develop issues for board presentation and critique agenda items. The tension in the CCOP migrated to the committees. In one committee the relevant vice chancellor and his staff, by 1978, refused to attend meetings because of the level of what he perceived to be abuse by one of two presidents in the meetings.

A change in the CCOP, subtle at first, began to emerge in the latter half of the 1970s. It was exacerbated by the Sacramento debate about collective bargaining and the passage of the Berman Bill, the statute authorizing collective bargaining in 1978. Presidents generally did not favor collective bargaining, particularly faculty collective bargaining. Some presidents blamed Dumke for the passage of the legislation, and a few trustees encouraged this point of view. Three groups began to emerge among the presidents: those who supported the chancellorship, those who opposed the chancellorship and wanted to see the role greatly diminished, and those on the fence. As a place to accomplish anything, the CCOP began to degenerate rapidly. In some measure, this was due to the chair and a few others among the presidents who were in the anti-chancellorship faction. In the 1979–80 year, the factions became more set. As might be expected, the presidents talked among themselves, and the annoyance level among the presidents who supported the chancellorship increased.

Three of the presidents in this group, Cleary from Northridge, McCune from Hayward, and myself, then from Dominguez Hills, had begun the habit of having dinner together the night before a CCOP or board of trustees meeting. We developed a plan to meet with a respected trustee, Claudia Hampton, then the chair of the board, and with the executive vice-chancellor, Harry Harmon, for a quiet discussion to address restructuring the Chancellor's Council of Presidents.

This small group gathered at the trustee's home in Los Angeles. Everyone attending the meeting knew what the purpose was. After some discussion of governance in the system, the group agreed on a strategy to bring the issue before the entire group of presidents at the next scheduled CCOP meeting. It was agreed that Ellis McCune would raise a question about the efficiency of the CCOP and the possible restructuring of the group. Cleary and I would join the discussion with the assumption that a sufficient number of presidents would enter the conversation to get serious deliberation underway. The strategy went like this: once the matter was on the table, one of the presidents would propose changing the CCOP to an executive council. The body would function as a whole with no committee structure; the chancellor would be the chair. Neither the trustee (who would not be present) nor the executive vice-chancellor was to play a role at the CCOP meeting as the issue was discussed. The executive vice-chancellor would brief the chancellor in advance of the meeting and inform the group if the chancellor demurred.

The day of the next CCOP meeting, McCune followed through and opened the topic. Other presidential hands went up. Before the chair (Stephen Horn of Long Beach State, a president who was vocally in the opposition group) could recognize anyone, a relatively new president, Jack Frankel of Bakersfield, broke in and asserted that he had been concerned with the CCOP and whether it served a useful purpose. He proposed the dissolution of the CCOP, and the establishment of an executive council with the chancellor as chair. The conversation proceeded from that point, and the outcome became inevitable. That meeting was the last of the CCOP. The divisions in the group persisted quietly, but the presidents settled down. The executive council became functional quickly and remained so until the end of the Dumke chancellorship in the summer of 1982. The presidents' evening gatherings continued as did their informal relations with trustees.

* * *

Presidential search procedures began to be standardized in the mid-1970s. In each instance a search committee was appointed. The trustees were represented by a number of their members, usually five, appointed by the chair. The campus was represented by faculty selected by the local academic senate, one or two students, a staff member, an administrator usually selected by the chancellor, and a campus community advisory board member. The chancellor would appoint a president from another CSU campus, and the chancellor would be an ex officio member. This general approach has remained constant. Minor changes have occurred over the years. The only significant change occurred in the 1980s, when the membership was redefined with only the trustees as voting members of the search committee, or Presidential Advisory Selection Committee.

In 1972, in a Mansel Keene–led search, Dr. James Bond was appointed president of California State University, Sacramento. Bond, then vice president for student affairs at Miami University in Ohio, and an individual with a career in student affairs administration, was the California State University and Colleges first black president. Sacramento State was generally perceived at that time as among the most liberal in sociopolitical values, yet also one of the most aggressive in terms of faculty seeking control of institutional governance. Bond was in conflict with the faculty almost from the beginning, as he sought to gain, or regain, proper presidential control, as he saw it. Bond persisted in the presidency for six years until he virtually forced the hand of the chancellor and board to remove him. In an open board meeting, he complained that he was denied access to faculty files in the review process leading to tenure decisions.

Bond's appointment was a first step to the appointment of ethnic minorities to presidencies, just as the appointment of Marjorie Downing Wagner to the presidency of Sonoma State in 1974 would be for women. Downing Wagner was the first woman regularly appointed to a presidency in the 117-year history of the California State Colleges. Similarly, the appointment of Tomas Arciniega at the Bakersfield campus in 1983was the first Hispanic appointment, and Chia-Wei Woo a first perceived Asian appointment the same year, at San Francisco State. Arciniega was a long time CSU faculty member, formerly Dean of the College of Education at the San Diego campus and Vice President for Academic Affairs at Fresno; he would stay in the Bakersfield presidency for 21 years, to retirement. Chia-Wei Woo was a distinguished scientist and dean at the University of California San Diego campus; he would remain at San Francisco State for only five years and then he moved to the new University of Science and Technology in Hong Kong as president. (The appointment of S. I. Hayakawa to San Francisco State was understood as an appointment resulting from an admixture of politics and ideology.)

With the retirement of Mansel Keene as vice-chancellor for faculty and staff affairs, selection and appointment of presidents changed. The initial post-Keene appointment was made in 1976. The trustees selected a vice president from a California State University campus, the first presidential appointment from inside the system in a number of years. Presidential searches became conventional, with search committees that really worked, and national searches that were thorough. The matter of linking appointments to the values of an appointee and a fit with the campus, beyond the judgment of search committees after interviews and background reviews, was not joined, however.

In the 1978–79 year, a search was conducted for the Los Angeles campus presidency. The incumbent of fourteen years had announced his retirement. The conventional search committee was formed, made up of campus, trustee, and system representatives. It was no secret that the chancellor liked the candidacy of a faculty member from another CSU campus; that faculty member had no higher education administrative experience, but he had substantial experience in the public policy arena. A national search ensued. Marjorie Downing Wagner, the vice-chancellor for faculty and staff affairs, ran the search. As the search committee narrowed the field of candidates, Governor Jerry Brown weighed in, putting pressure on the trustees whom he had appointed and who were also on the search committee to recommend a specific candidate, Julian Nava, to the full board for appointment. Curiously, the individual the governor supported was also Dumke's choice, although the committee members, all but one, were not aware of this. Dumke and the governor had very different reasons for their choice; Dumke's had to do with the person's substantial academic credentials and his known public policy competence. The governor's reason for pressing the appointment of Nava was simply political. The trustees on the search committee rebelled against the governor's message, and Nava's candidacy effectively ended. The search reopened and produced a successful candidate, James Rosser, who was appointed and remains in office to the date of this writing, thirty years later.[24]

* * *

With the 1979 shift from the Chancellor's Council of Presidents to the executive council format, with the chancellor in the chair, the meetings became somewhat more useful for the presidents. Glenn Dumke's years in the chancellorship were waning. New blood had come into the presidents' group, and the presidents were feeling a level of freedom to give leadership to their individual campuses, at least those who chose to do so. The sense of the presidents at that time was that the chancellor did not want to interfere with presidential leadership. Dumke was comfortable with the presidents meeting as a group, and he was comfortable with the relationships they were developing with board members, and his annual reviews of presidents continued to be amazingly substantive.[25] (Dumke had his agenda. In significant measure it had to do with the advent of collective bargaining, for the legislation that had been enacted in 1978 had to be implemented in succeeding years.[26] It also concerned consolidating the system and the gains made since the Master Plan.) From the viewpoint of the presidents of the time, in the late 1970s and early 1980s, campus freedom to act was far more circumscribed by vice-chancellors and members of their staffs. This would lead to confrontations on some occasions, and often these would end in the chancellor's office. More often than not, Dumke would support the presidents.

The year 1982 brought a change in the chancellorship. Dr. W. Ann Reynolds, the Provost of Ohio State University, was appointed to the position. At the very beginning of Reynolds's chancellorship, both she and a number of presidents wanted a private meeting with only the chancellor and the presidents. This happened. At the conclusion of the first day of a July 1982 presidents' meeting, Reynolds and the presidents met for dinner and an extensive conversation at a downtown Long Beach hotel. A leader in arranging the meeting was Stephen Horn from Long Beach State, the last president to serve as chair of the defunct Chancellor's Council of Presidents. Essentially, the message of many presidents to the new chancellor was that they wanted a direct working relationship with her, and did not want to work through vice-chancellors and other staff. One president told his colleagues that he refused to take phone calls from vice-chancellors, including the executive vice-chancellor, and would only speak with the chancellor. The meeting was cordial on the surface, but an almost angry undertone from some presidents was present. Chancellor Reynolds listened carefully and assured the presidents that she wanted to work with them.

From the vantage point of 2008, it is clear that each chancellor has had a set of rules, and that these had to be learned by the presidents, not with the aid of an executive order or rule book, but through experience. Reynolds's rules about presidents soon became clear. At the private July dinner meeting, she had made reference to working with trustees. It soon became clear that she did not want presidents generally talking with and working with trustees. Then it became clear that she did not want presidents working independently in the capitol's halls in Sacramento. Presidential assistants sometimes received phone calls from the CSU office in Sacramento, saying that the president of their campus had been seen in the capital that day, and asking what the president had been doing there, and with whom had the president talked.

Among the presidents, tensions that had been just beneath the surface came to the fore. The divisions among the presidents about the governance of the system and relationships to the board of trustees became open. The three groups of presidents that had begun to form in the late 1970s became more firm and sometimes more open and clear. Some presidents thought they reported to and, in a sense, worked for the chancellor; some were neutral on the subject; and some subscribed to the dotted-line theory that emerged in the 1980s. This was explicit: presidents had a dotted-line relationship with the chancellor and a solid-line relationship with the board. The chancellor was a coordinator. The impact of all of this tension was substantial on the functioning of the executive council, and on relationships between presidents and some senior campus administrators, faculty leaders, and members of the chancellor's senior staff.

Reynolds began the practice of entertaining both trustees and presidents at the chancellor's home in Bel Air, some thirty-one miles via a congested Highway 405 from the chancellor's office in Long Beach. This new custom effectively brought to an end the informal Tuesday evening dinners of small groups of presidents and trustees at the time of board meetings. The impact of this change was eventually negative. The cocktail hours were lengthy and both presidents and trustees were present in full force, with the exception of Stephen Horn from Long Beach State. (He had not come to the presidents' informal gatherings over the years. He was a major leader of the presidential group advocating the dotted-line theory.) Some of the trustees appointed during the Jerry Brown governorship years were focused on a narrow range of issues. Some presidents questioned trustees about their reporting relationships. These conversations were not subtle. At times trustees quizzed presidents about possible dissatisfaction with the system. The presidents' evening gatherings did not end altogether; they simply happened after, after the dinner at the chancellor's home.

By the 1987–88 academic year, tensions had reached a point at which the presidential reporting relationship issue had to be settled, and the board did so. It made clear, without a formal resolution, that presidents reported to the chancellor, who reported to the board. These relationships were not defined in an authoritarian sense; clearly the board wanted positive relationships and open communication with presidents, just as members did with faculty and students, but the board confirmed the responsibility and authority of the chancellor, and thus of the presidents. The matter would remain below the surface into the early 1990s.

The year 1990 brought anther change in the chancellorship. The chancellorship of Ann Reynolds had become increasingly controversial with the board and in Sacramento with both the legislature and governor. Some of the issues were minor, some major; the latter included executive salary setting and forced presidential retirements, as well as the debacle of purchasing six Ford Taurus automobiles for systemwide administrators. Reynolds resigned, in the midst of great controversy. Her resignation was forced by the board. A number of factors contributed to the situation, ranging from major loss of support (but not all support) in Sacramento, to a controversy about presidential retirements at age sixty-five.

Ellis McCune, the twenty-three year president of the Hayward campus (now East Bay), became acting chancellor. The McCune year was not eventful, but a number of issues that had plagued the presidents in their relationship with the chancellor's office were addressed and resolved. The most significant of these had to do with fiscal administration. The stage was set in executive council discussions for major changes in budget procedures. McCune did not occupy the chancellor's residence in Bel Air. The presidents continued their working relationships with board members. McCune with his extraordinary experience as a sitting president devoted time to rebuilding the Sacramento office of the CSU; he was comfortable with presidential presence in Sacramento.

The fifth chancellor was appointed early in 1991. The arrival of Barry Munitz brought major changes for the roles of presidents, both as leaders of campuses and as a group. Munitz had rules, unstated but clear. It soon became apparent that he would not tolerate dissension among the presidents. During the transition year the chancellor's Bel Air residence had been sold and a home, State University House, was purchased in Long Beach, a short commute to the chancellor's office. Munitz resumed entertaining the trustees and presidents in the evening between the two board meeting days. It became clear that while he was not distressed with presidential-trustee conversations, he wanted to be informed about the discussions. He was a decentralizer, not a centralizer, with respect to the operation of the campuses. He wanted to build new relationships in Sacramento, and he welcomed presidential involvement as long as he and his staff were kept informed. Munitz's choice for executive vice-chancellor, Molly Broad, was equally committed to decentralization of operations to the campuses, and given the role that emerged for her, that of a kind of chief operating officer, this was important.

An early manifestation of this new order of things was in the academic affairs area. Munitz and Broad made it clear to staff in Academic Affairs that their job was to assist campuses in developing new programs and, when requested, in the refinement of existing programs. Presidents, provosts, and vice presidents for academic affairs, would discuss with vice-chancellors and other senior administrators and, on occasion, the chancellor, the desirability of developing or modifying academic programs. This soon led to a "fast track" process for approving and implementing new programs. Munitz brought in for a brief time a retired campus president to replace the departing vice-chancellor responsible for academic affairs in the previous Reynolds administration. That vice-chancellor, Lee Kerschner, moved to the interim presidency of the Stanislaus campus. Subsequently, a vice-chancellor was appointed, Peter Hoff, who came from a comparable post in Georgia and who would oversee the beginning of the transformation of academic affairs from a regulatory mode to an assistive mode.

Executive council discussions in the interim McCune year had set the stage for the abandonment of the "Orange Book," a set of standards and formulas for funding virtually all aspects of a campus, as a departure point for budget discussions. By the spring of 1992, at the close of the first Munitz year, this was accomplished, and it provided one more dimension for the assertion of a new level of presidential leadership in financial administration. The net effect of the need to cut budgets beginning after the passage of Proposition 13 in 1978 and the final disappearance of the Orange Book, was to empower presidents in the management and substantive leadership of their campuses.[27] The end of the Orange Book was a major cultural change for campuses and faculty. It had created a sense of entitlement, and both academic units (departments for example) and administrative units sought funding for what they saw as their entitlement, seemingly oblivious to the fact that the sum of the entitlements was not funded.

The trustees had given major attention to fundraising as a priority talent in their recruitment of a new chancellor in the 1990–91 year. Munitz, once appointed, and the trustees wasted little time in getting underway significant fundraising activity. The setting of a goal of 10 percent of the general fund appropriation for each campus would have a profound impact on the presidential role. For the first time, presidential performance could be measured by a number. All those involved—trustees, presidents, the chancellor, faculties, and system watchers—knew that campus capabilities for fundraising varied widely and were dependent to some extent on the characteristics of academic programs, the age and size of a campus, a campus's location, and the like. Surely campus performance in fundraising was also affected by the role played by the campus president, the allocation of resources to fundraising activities, and the professional talent of fundraising staff. Fundraising became a part of the evaluation of presidents, and for some presidents this caused an awkward situation. Only with the 1990s did fundraising ability become one of the criteria, both formal and informal, in the selection of presidents. It is not yet clear what the impact of fundraising ability has on the selection of presidents and on presidential evaluation. Presidents whose campuses raise sizeable percentages (measured against general fund budgets) clearly are applauded. As the years have gone by, the pressure to allocate substantial resources to fundraising at the campus level have built at the same time that budgets have been shrinking.[28]

The mid-1990s saw yet another emphasis emerge that would have a substantial impact on the presidential role, most especially on presidential leadership at the system level. Information and communication technology and its uses became a priority as never before. In the context of the executive council, presidents became major activists and leaders.[29] The technology thrust of the 1990s was initiated by Molly Broad in a meeting with a small presidential group, which became a task force. Several additional small presidential task forces were then formed, and finally a group, which became the Technology Steering Committee (TSC). Richard West became the leader and convener of the TSC. The technology thrust bridged the chancellorship of Barry Munitz with the following one of Charles Reed. Reed, who became chancellor on March 1, 1998, had to rebuild the technology strategy, as the initial effort did not come together. The use of small groups of presidents, individuals knowledgeable about the matter at hand or the policy issues involved, became a strategy of the Reed administration.

The ground rules for presidents in the Reed chancellorship have been similar in many ways to those in the Munitz years. Presidents have been encouraged to be active in Sacramento and Washington. Reed reinforced the annual day in Sacramento, where presidents and others from the campuses, including alumni, meet with members of the legislature and others. This was a tradition that went back to the Dumke chancellorship. In the Reed years, the importance of this has been emphasized. The day is structured and significant campus and chancellor's staff and trustee energy goes into preparation for the day.

The Washington scene has received new attention. The presidents as a group, together with key staff members selected by them, meet for two very full days in Washington. Each president meets with every member of his or her campus regional area congressional delegation. The annual Washington days are more than meetings and receptions. The California congressional delegation is the largest of any state, and the purpose of this activity is to bring them together around the California State University. The presidents are key to this, and those presidents who grasp this are important to the effort, and their work in this area strengthens their roles.

Just as the custom of trustee-presidential dinners at the chancellor's home in Long Beach continued, trustee-presidential openness has been strongly encouraged. The basic ground rule for both the Munitz and Reed years has been keeping the chancellor and staff informed. Just as the dinners at State University House continued, so do the late-evening hotel gatherings of the presidents.

Teacher education has been the subject of two successive presidential groups. A revitalized interest in teacher education was high on the agenda of the CSU in the late 1990—the strengthening and in many ways the revitalization of California's preschool, elementary, and secondary school programs, as well as the reaffirmation of the historic role of the California State University.

The use of groups of presidents, executive council members, typically including a vice-chancellor, and often one or two additional chancellor's staff, has become more common, and by 2007 there were five such groups functioning regularly. This strategy, as a practical matter, has strengthened both the executive council and the presidents individually, to the extent that the presidents took advantage of it.

California State University presidents have been active nationally and internationally in the years since the Master Plan. Indeed, some national presence predates the Master Plan. The presence of California State University presidents in national groups and organizations is now well established, and many of the presidents devote significant time to leadership positions. This has an impact, albeit subtle, on the role of presidents in the governance of the system.

* * *

Presidential compensation and support have changed substantially over the years since the Master Plan. When the trustees assumed responsibility for the state colleges, salaries and support were modest compared to like institutions. Presidential salaries were on a five-step ladder, like those of most state employees. Salaries of deans and vice presidents were a few salary steps (steps are at five percent intervals) above those of full professors (step five), with vice presidents one or two steps higher than deans, and presidents one or two steps higher than vice presidents. It was a civil service approach to compensation, and it remained in place until 1983.

A few of the older campuses (Chico, Humboldt, and San Luis Obispo) had presidential homes on their campuses, sometimes configured with family living quarters on the second floor, while the first floor and gardens were used for entertaining purposes. These presidents paid neither rent nor in lieu taxes. (In the 1970s, some county assessors began to levy an "in lieu" tax on campus housing, and this quickly became a statewide practice.) Living in a college home on campus had its pluses and minuses; definite advantages were that the on-campus staff were available for setting up and dismantling equipment, tables, chairs, entertainment and technical equipment and the like, and the campus caterers were in familiar and convenient territory to accomplish their duties.

An on-campus home was not regarded by some presidents as desirable. That became more apparent when the trustees, during the chancellorship of Ann Reynolds, established housing allowances for all of the CSU campuses without on-campus housing; subsequently, several presidents moved off campus and requested the housing allowance. Privacy and housing allowances were preferable to some.

Staff support for presidents was a secretary and, on most campuses, one other position chosen from the small number of top academic or professional positions in a campus budget, most often the budgeted position of public affairs officer provided to each campus. Discretionary funds were specified in the state budget for one reception per year for faculty and staff, although campuses with affluent auxiliary organizations were able to support additional presidential activity. Presidents had the use of one well-marked state-owned car, identified as such. In the 1950s and early 1960s, until the trustees were able to implement their own travel policies, the custom of the time was for each president to make one out-of-state trip each year to recruit faculty. Presidents personally, most often, appointed faculty. The permission of the governor's office was required for all out-of-state travel. Again, auxiliary organization support was available on some campuses. On those campuses lacking well-developed auxiliaries, presidents either funded activities and travel themselves, or would forego community relations and travel activity. Expenditures from auxiliary organization funds were monitored closely by legislative committees and the Department of Finance.

Chancellor Dumke would sometimes quietly assert a ground rule that he would use in his thinking about presidential salaries—they should be approximately twice the salary of a top full professor. In 1963, the legislature requested the newly established Coordinating Council for Higher Education (renamed the California Postsecondary Education Commission [CPEC] after 1974) to study the faculty salaries at comparison institutions for both the California State Colleges and the University of California; subsequently presidential salaries were included. Comparison institutions were defined as those comparable in mission and other characteristics. In 1964 and 1965, the assembly and then the senate directed that these studies be done annually, that they include salaries and "fringe benefits," and that they be reported to the legislature and the governor. Originally, in 1963, there were twelve comparison institutions for the California State Colleges. In 1974, the number was increased to twenty, where it has remained up to the present time. The institutions have changed over the years, as the California State University mission has evolved, and as other institutions have changed.

The comparison institution reports are used and they are credible. The studies initially focused on faculty salaries. Presidential and other administrative salaries were added. In 1977, a methodology was agreed upon. The California State University and Colleges, the University of California, the State Department of Finance, the Legislative Analyst's Office, and CPEC were parties to the this agreement.[30] Though CPEC is in most ways weak, this study is a useful product. In more recent years, the issue has been securing attention to it as California's state finances have declined over the years.

The Dumke administration did make consistent efforts to loosen the use of auxiliary organization funds, and they were successful in gaining significant (for that time) increases in travel and eliminating requirements for controls, permissions, and the like. These efforts were made not only for presidents, but for all faculty and staff. The growth of research and other activities operated through auxiliary organizations created more resources in auxiliary organizations. A very small appropriation was included in each campus state budget for discretionary money for entertaining: three hundred dollars per year. That amount remained constant to the early years of this century.

The 1982 change in the chancellorship was accompanied by new thinking about presidential compensation and support. Ann Reynolds proposed to the trustees early in her chancellorship that salaries of presidents be set individually, and she made a set of recommendations to the trustees. Presidential salaries were to be set by the board based upon a chancellor's evaluation of individual presidential performance. Size of a campus would not be a criterion; that was clear from the trustee action on salaries. The criteria were not made specific. Presidents were authorized to use state funds to purchase a car of their choice, but Reynolds admonished them: "no Cadillacs." Travel restrictions had been

28. *Proclamation by Governor George Deukmejian, February 1986.*

430   *Organizing the Future of Governance*

29. *Governor Deukmejian Proclaims March 9–15, 1986, "California State University Silver Jubilee Week," Governor George Deukmejian, Chancellor W. Ann Reynolds, Trustee Chair Roy Brophy.*

ended in the 1960s, and auxiliary organizations were sufficiently affluent (some more than others) to support presidential activity and that of others in the administration and faculty. On a number of campuses, "president's associates" groups emerged, with the avowed purpose of creating needed discretionary funding for presidents and others.

In 1984, Reynolds also brought to the board a proposal entitling the presidents, vice-chancellors, and the chancellor to earn the status of "trustee professor" (provision for the use of the title under specific circumstances had been established by the trustees in 1981). A president, vice-chancellor, or chancellor with an academic appointment on a campus and a minimum of five years of service could, upon leaving office, elect to become a trustee professor, with compensation somewhat above that of professor, and modest support. Some vice-chancellors had campus academic appointments. Dumke never relinquished his appointment as professor of history at San Francisco State, and Reynolds, a biologist of some accomplishment, was appointed professor of biology at Dominguez Hills in 1982.

In the 1980s, real estate prices in California increased dramatically, in comparison to other parts of the country. Recruiting new presidents was sometimes difficult because housing was often unaffordable, compared to the cost of housing where candidates already lived. Presidential housing had been a point of irritation for some presidents. Reynolds proposed housing allowances for those presidents not living in a university-owned residence; allowances were set related to the cost of housing in the varying campus communities. The trustees adopted Reynolds's proposal. Following out logic of in lieu taxes, the Internal Revenue Service insisted on presidents claiming the value of provided housing or the amount of a housing allowance as income subject to taxation.

Just as Dumke felt it important for the Chancellor to reside in a "University House," in 1988, Reynolds requested all of the presidents who did not have presidential homes on campus or housing furnished by an auxiliary organization to acquire such housing, with either the donation of a suitable home or the contribution of auxiliary organization funding. A number of CSU campus auxiliary organizations did acquire presidential homes within their communities, but other campus auxiliaries did not have the funding capability to respond to the request.

Reynolds was a very trim individual, with much determination. One weekend morning, as she and her husband were jogging in the general vicinity of the Bel Air "University House" in Los Angeles, they came across a sign advertising a home free for moving. Reynolds went to the door of the home to inquire. The current owner needed the building moved in order to build a new structure. Before the conversation ended, Reynolds had agreed to move the house to the Dominguez Hills campus, a young campus that, at that time, had neither a presidential residence nor a flourishing nonprofit foundation. Built in 1923, the free house had once belonged to Tom Mix, an early star in Western movies. Because there was a large tree on the lot, it would be necessary to split the house in half in order to move it. The cost to relocate the house would be thirty thousand dollars. The campus was notified of the chancellor's decision. The interim president, John Brownell, would soon retire and his response to the proposal to move the house to the Dominguez Hills campus was negative. The board of trustees had just appointed Robert Detweiler, the academic vice president at California State University San Bernardino, to the Dominguez Hills presidency. Detweiler and his wife had already purchased a home in Long Beach, and he declined the use of the house. The chancellor's office pressed the matter. The campus principle auxiliary organization refused to fund the cost to move the house. Finally, the chancellor's staff proposed that the system auxiliary corporation loan the campus auxiliary the money, with the understanding that there would be no expectation to pay back the loan. There were two individuals caught in the middle, David Karber, then vice president for administration at Dominguez Hills, and Herbert Carter, then executive vice-chancellor.

Karber had inspected the house. It was thirteen hundred square feet in size, with two bedrooms and one bath. And even though it was in serious disrepair, with termites and structural problems, it soon became a part of the Dominguez Hills campus. Reynolds wanted the structure to be called "the President's House"; Detweiler refused. Another impasse! As the house, sat in two sections on blocks on a site next to the campus corporation yard, Karber was summoned to the chancellor's office to meet with the executive vice-chancellor and the vice-chancellor/general counsel. Reynolds still insisted that the structure be named "the President's House," and Karber formed a committee on the campus to address the use and naming of the house. The committee settled upon using the structure for international program activities, and proposed naming it "Heritage House." The cost of readying the structure to be used was determined to be in excess of three hundred thousand dollars, far more than the campus could envision spending. Time passed, and with a change in the chancellorship, the Tom Mix house was removed free of charge by the same house moving firm that brought it from Los Angeles. As of 2008–09, ten of the twenty-three CSU campuses have presidential residences either on campus, or off campus within the community and provided by a campus auxiliary organization.

In 1986–87, Reynolds proposed a presidential salary increase, and the board accepted her recommendation; the board acted in closed session, which caused a legislative furor. The director of the Sacramento office at the time, James Jensen, wrote a letter to an assembly subcommittee, stating that it was simply an error and would not happen again. In early 1990, Reynolds proposed another increase, and once again, the board acted in closed session. (It should be noted that presidential salary increases are the occasion of salary increases for the vice-chancellors and chancellor.) The second increase set all presidential salaries at the same figure, one hundred and thirty thousand dollars per year, and thus returned to the old civil service approach. The second increase was rolled back in 1990 after Reynolds' departure. Legislative and other protests at the second round of raises being done in a closed board meeting forced the issue. Ellis McCune was acting chancellor when the rollback occurred, and this caused bitterness among some of the presidents, who did not let go of the issue.

Barry Munitz addressed the presidential salary issue early in his tenure as chancellor. He asserted correctly that presidential salaries had fallen behind the rest of the country, and he very deliberately and openly proposed salary increases. He maintained the individual evaluation and salary setting process initiated during the Reynolds years. When the trustees rolled back the 1990 increase, the action returned the process to individual salary settings.

In the 1990s, presidential salaries in some of the leading or high-status institutions across the country began to increase in sizeable amounts. For that small proportion of faculty in some professional schools and disciplines who were more highly compensated, this was reasonable. From the perspective of many faculty, presidential and other top-level salaries were becoming disproportionate.

At least in part, as a result of the 1990 presidential salary situation, the trustees adopted an "executive compensation" philosophy at the January 1991 board meeting (while recruitment for a chancellor was underway).

> The California State University is committed to establish and maintain an executive compensation program which is designed to attract and retain educational administrators who have experience and abilities to keep the CSU in the forefront of higher education. . . . The compensation program must be competitive with that of major comprehensive universities to advance the educational vision of the

CSU. The compensation program must recognize attainment of institutional goals. The compensation program should also foster professional growth and encourage individual achievement within the CSU educational setting.[31]

Not long after the board action, the legislature included in its 1992 budget bill language requiring the trustees and regents to report each year beginning January 1, 1993, about executive compensation.

Later in 1992, the trustees established an executive transition program for those appointed on or after November 18, 1992. This action replaced the trustee professor program and provided for compensation of departing executives either into retirement, away from the CSU, or, in some instances, into other CSU positions. This trustee action, which was modified over subsequent years but conceptually remained the same, would lead to significant negative publicity and manipulation of facts in the media fourteen years later, as the media and some union leaders attacked the CSU for paying departing executives for "doing nothing." Then in September 1993, the trustees addressed the detail of a presidential compensation policy:

> The CSU shall establish the target for the average total compensation of presidents as being approximately the mean for comparable positions in the twenty comparison universities with actual distribution based on mission, scope, size, complexity, and programs of each campus; the formal recognition of individual performance and experience, and recruitment and retention experience.

The policy also addressed the adequacy of housing allowances related to the markets in the areas of CSU campuses.[32]

From the time he assumed the chancellorship, Charles Reed paid attention to presidential salaries, and he sought to increase salaries toward those in the group of comparison institutions. In Chancellor Munitz's last year, in 1997, the trustees had underway an extensive review of executive compensation, and adopted a "three-year plan" for increasing salaries.[33] Administrative salaries generally and, especially, executive salaries (chancellor, vice-chancellors, presidents) were increased, in some years ahead of faculty and staff salary increases, which were in the often lengthy collective bargaining process.

At the September 2007 board meeting, the chancellor's staff brought a new approach, a comprehensive policy, to address compensation for all CSU employees. The executive salary issue was set in this context. The resolution proposed by the trustees addressed compensation for "faculty, staff, administrators, and executives whose knowledge, experience, and contributions advance the university's mission." The context for this proposed resolution was a complex one; conflict with the faculty union, the California Faculty Association (CFA), had been intense in preceding months. The trustees had recently approved a faculty salary increase of 6.2 percent effective for the 2006–07 year. The resolution was, in a sense, a reaffirmation of trustee practice—since the 1960s, for faculty, and the 1970s, for presidents—of the use of a comparison institution group as one basis for salary determination. The resolution affirmed the desire of the trustees to reach parity with the comparison institutions, noted that the faculty lag for the CSU was 15.2 percent, and the administrative lag had reached 46 percent by 2006. The agenda item noted that faculty salary adjustments are made in the collective bargaining process, and in subsequent individual decisions on campuses. It directed the chancellor to recommend "salary adjustments for CSU executives phased over the next four years, beginning in 2007–08." A companion proposed resolution on the agenda provided for increases in executive salaries and these averaged 11.8 percent. Both resolutions were adopted by the board of trustees, the policy resolution at the September 2007 meeting of the board, and the executive salary increase at the annual budget meeting of the board in October 2007.[34]

The real issue about salaries is balance, maintaining a reasonable balance between presidential salaries and faculty salaries. An often-used argument about presidential salaries is recruiting and the market place. It is arguable that California has had little difficulty recruiting able and talented top-level people over the years, in good times and bad times. Only a few California presidents have left for presidencies elsewhere.

The narrative supporting the September 2007 policy resolution noted the process of performance reviews or evaluations of executives. The evaluation of presidents began with the Dumke chancellorship. I will address this topic in the context of my experience with it. As a dean, and subsequently vice president at the Chico campus, I was not aware of any presidential evaluation process. At the end of my first year as president at Dominguez Hills (late spring/early summer 1977), I received a call from Chancellor Glenn Dumke's secretary to schedule an evaluation meeting; I had no idea what to expect. When I entered the chancellor's office, Dumke was at his desk, the executive vice-chancellor, Harry Harmon, was at the side of the room with a notepad and pen, and I was seated comfortably, yet a bit nervous. It was an astonishing experience. Dumke proceeded to raise a variety of issues. He was well informed about issues and activities both on campus and in the university's broader relationships. He made suggestions about issues, expressed satisfaction or concern about a matter, asked for an occasional explication of a matter, and asked for my opinion; it was an altogether cordial and supportive conversation, not without clear direction and judgment about some matters. These evaluations continued annually. The astonishing factor for me was how he could be so well informed about the life of a campus—and eighteen more campuses.

With the change in the chancellorship came a change in process. In addition to the informal give and take that is always underway, a formal process was established. Each president would be evaluated every three years. The three-year evaluation would be a paper one. The individual president would prepare a lengthy statement of achievements and issues, a form of self-evaluation. This would be followed by the preparation of a letter, tailored to the president and the campus, which would be sent to a wide distribution of students, faculty, staff, campus leaders of all categories, administrators, advisory board members, community leaders, and, eventually, education leaders beyond the campus; the president in question was to suggest a list of names. The recipients of the letters would be asked to reply to a senior chancellor's staff member, who would then write a detailed analysis for the chancellor. The chancellor would use the analysis as she/he wished, and send an evaluation letter to the president. There was not necessarily a conversation.

The six-year review was more extensive. It included the presidential self-assessment. A visiting team was assembled; one trustee, one former CSU president or vice president, one president from outside the CSU, a student recommended by the campus Associated Students president, and one or two faculty recommended by the chair of the statewide Academic Senate. The process was administered in the Reynolds years by a vice-chancellor, and in the Munitz and Reed years by the chancellor's chief of staff; these individuals accompanied the team. A three- or four-day visiting schedule was widely publicized on campus and in the community. Open meetings were held, and opportunities were made available for individual meetings. At the end of the visit the team chair (in my experience, either a retired CSU president or a non-CSU sitting president) would meet with the president being reviewed and go through a number of observations. The senior administrator from the chancellor's staff simply observed and kept some semblance of order and time in the process. A written report was prepared by the team chair and given to the chancellor, and the chancellor would send this report, along with a letter, to the president. Except for the exit interview with the chair, there was no conversation.

At the conclusion of each evaluation, the chancellor reviewed it with the board in closed session. The president was then invited to join the conversation with the board and respond to any unanswered questions. At the close of presidential evaluations, both three-year and six-year, the Chancellor would issue a letter to the campus community addressing the particular value of the evaluation. The letter would be supportive. When a chancellor removed a president, and all chancellors have done so, with the concurrence of the board, of course, it has always been in context of a particular issue or set of issues, and not in the context of an evaluation.

Candidly, I found the process that began in the 1980s often sterile. The Dumke reviews were stimulating and thought provoking. I do not recall that he gave me any directives. The meeting with him provided a sense of direction—sometimes affirmations, sometimes issues to which I needed to give serious thought. The more structured processes initiated in the 1980s were useful on some matters and did provide stimulation for thought, and some new matters would appear on the agenda.

As a president I have used established, regular, and open evaluation procedures for many years—indeed, I began to use them before they became fashionable within the California State University. Their most significant value is the understanding of an administration open to criticism, advice, and change. It is important, in my judgment, not to define an evaluation process as an occasion to attack someone. I made it a personal rule never to change an administrator at the conclusion of an evaluation process, but I was willing to change administrators and did, always as a result of experience working with and observing them. I found periodic evaluations useful as occasions to sharpen a style of administration or focus on particular issue or range of issues. Admittedly, the range of a president's span is much less than that of a chancellor with twenty-three campuses and presidents; the circumstance is different.

Are the California State University presidents essentially branch managers of a statewide franchise? I have heard this assertion for most of the past fifty years. Periodically this phrase is used in frustration; or is it reality? One fundamental characteristic of a California State University presidency is the individual's relationship to the board of trustees. Conventionally, in colleges and universities, the president is immediately responsible to a board, her or his board. When the board of a single campus meets, it is about the president's campus. It is inevitably about the president. When the state colleges' board of trustees first met in 1961, the subject was the fifteen institutions on sixteen campuses; when the board meets in 2009 it is twenty-three campuses, the California State University, and one chancellor. That is an oversimplification, but a useful one. Other than a campus-specific proposal, such as the funding and construction of a building or new academic program, the board's sights are on system policy. The freedom and room that a campus president has is substantial but not infinite. It is freedom within the parameters of the mission of the California State University and system policy.

In the early years of the California State Colleges as a system, in the 1960s and, to a lesser extent, the 1970s, the trustees, chancellor, and presidents, indeed all of the players, were feeling their way through the evolution of a system. There had been no California State College governance in any meaningful way prior to the Master Plan, short of the framework of state government. The trustees and chancellor were creating a system, and so were the presidents, but many presidents did not understand their respective roles in those terms.

The impact of the system upon a president is whatever the president allows it to be. That assertion too is an over-simplification, but a useful one. The California State University has an overarching mission, overarching with respect to all of the campuses. It has a unitary governance structure. That is by design, and in a state populated by thirty-six million people with a college and university student population growing to three million, there would seem to be no sensible alternative. The challenge to the system, the trustees, chancellors, and presidents, and, ultimately, to the faculties, is to maintain and grow the uniqueness of campuses and their vitality. The challenge to a president is to be the leader that can do that and bring the trustees, chancellors, and others along.

This is not to suggest that there have not been constraints and problems for presidents along the way. There are the best of times and the worst of times. The budget is always a constraint; inevitably, the best of organizations will on occasion include authoritarian or unreasonable individuals; policies and practices on occasion emerge which are simply foolish, and do not stand the test of time. But in the longer run, the presidency is a challenge and an opportunity.

The Chancellor

The chancellor's office has been in five locations since 1960. The transitional year of 1960–61 and almost the first half of the 1961–62 year were spent in Sacramento in a building across the street from the state capitol. The office and center of trustee activity moved to Los Angeles at the end of 1961, and was located for three and a half years near the Los Angeles Airport; a 1965 move brought the office to Wilshire Boulevard, still in rented quarters, but at least somewhat more suitable in the minds of some for the center of a major, but still emerging, higher education system. With help from Senator Joseph Kennick of Long Beach, the trustees secured a site and funding to build a headquarters on the Long Beach waterfront. The first meeting of the board of trustees in the new headquarters of the California State University and Colleges was in September 1976. The building had been dedicated the evening before in a cap and gown ceremony. The speaker had been Alden Dunham, of the Carnegie Corporation of New York. Dunham had authored a small but major volume in the Carnegie Commission series on higher education, *Colleges of the Forgotten Americans: A Profile of State Colleges and Regional Universities*.[35] The Carnegie Corporation had provided major funding for Dumke's New Approaches initiatives earlier in the decade, and Dunham had been important in that relationship.

By the early 1990s, the chancellor's staff had outgrown the building on the Long Beach waterfront. About two hundred staff members were working in rented quarters a number of miles from the headquarters building; among these were staff members working with technology, campus planning, and other functions. The then new Munitz team wanted to consolidate the staff in one location, and the first plan they pursued was to add a wing to the existing building.

Earthquake standards for construction in California are revised with each earthquake experience. In the 1980s and early 1990s, Southern California and the Los Angeles region experienced a number of earthquakes; the 1994 Northridge earthquake caused severe damage, particularly to the Northridge campus. With construction near a waterfront, earthquake issues must be explored. Core soil samples were drilled at the Long Beach headquarters, and the conclusion reached was that construction on the existing site was not possible. This caused there to be immediate reinforcement of the headquarters building while alternatives were explored, including purchasing an existing building elsewhere in Long Beach. Finally, a decision was made to locate a new building on a parking lot across the street with different soil conditions. The headquarters building and the parking lot exchanged locations. In the late spring of 1998, the address of the California State University changed from 400 to 401 Golden Shore. The staff was brought together into a single building.

The location of the chancellor's office outside of the capital, Sacramento, was not without controversy, but the action of the trustees was deliberate. Similarly, the choice to not locate the headquarters on a campus was deliberate. The trustees were influenced by what they saw as the negative impact of locating the University of California president's office adjacent to the Berkeley campus, an impact that they saw to be a negative for the Berkeley campus, for the other University of California campuses, and for the general health of the UC system.

The role and institution of the chancellor is one that has evolved over the years. There was no useful established model for the architecture of the role. In 1960–61 and the following decade, as the initial elements of the role were defined, the organizational model most often in the minds of those inside and outside of the California State Colleges, was the presidency of the University of California. This was particularly true for most, if not all of the faculty leadership that sought results from the Master Plan that would provide for an independent doctorate and public funding for research, solely within the sphere of the University of California at the time. They saw Robert Gordon Sproul, the UC president from 1929 to 1958, and Clark Kerr bringing fame and fortune to the University of California. There was not a widespread understanding of the fundamental difference in the organizational histories and structures between the University of California and the California State Colleges. The University of California as a system had emerged from a single campus and the culture of that campus, and the other campuses and their cultures were, for the most part, offshoots from that single starting point. Moreover, the organization and structure of the university had been influenced by its federal land grant status, and by the emergence of World War II–inspired research and medical schools and faculties. When the first state college chancellor, Buell Gallagher, assumed office on July 1, 1961, he became the leader of fifteen institutions, each separately founded, each with its own political base, each with its own culture.

Gallagher came to the chancellorship from the presidency of the City College of New York. The city colleges of New York were not a system in a single organization as they later became. Each campus had its own board, its own president, and each competed for resources from the city government and the state with all other institutions, a clear parallel to the structure—or lack of structure—from which the California State Colleges were emerging. Gallagher was a liberal president from a liberal campus, and his reputation as an administrator and public figure in New York was positive. His appointment was welcomed by most faculty, by the trustees, and generally received positively, with a major exception: when announced, the appointment was opposed by a number of conservative or right wing groups. Gallagher then made a fundamental political error. He fought back against the attackers, and that consumed much of his time and energy after his arrival. In a sense, he and those who attacked him fed off each other, and that served to enlarge the controversy.

Within the state colleges, Gallagher did not work to develop a relationship with presidents or faculty leaders. He did make a tour of the campuses and made a formal address to each campus community, complete with cap and gown. In his little more than seven months as chancellor, he met with the presidents once, beyond a first get-acquainted session. His preference was that he represent the campuses and his staff solely at meetings of the board of trustees. At one point, he privately complained to a trustee about the attendance of Vice-Chancellors Leiffer and Dumke. Less than six months into his role, the chancellor's office moved from small temporary quarters in Sacramento to a headquarters in a bank building near the Los Angeles Airport, clearly not Gallagher's choice of location. Gallagher pushed hard to locate the headquarters office in San Francisco, where he and his wife wished to live, a cosmopolitan city with characteristics similar to those of New York City. In the fall of 1961, Gallagher made three major appointments to three vice-chancellorships.

In the initial implementation of the Master Plan, two issues were important to developing a positive relationship with the University of California: the establishment of a structure for joint doctorates, and the redefinition of admissions standards in order to create the zones of student eligibility—top one-eighth of high school graduates to be eligible for admission to the University of California, top one-third to be eligible for admission to the state colleges. Clark Kerr was anxious to move on the redefinition of admissions standards, and pushed the University of California into action. When Glenn Dumke assumed office as vice-chancellor for academic affairs, he moved on the joint doctorate. A first action was to select and appoint the state college members of the new Joint Graduate Board to be responsible for UC/state college joint doctoral programs. He appointed himself as chair of the state college delegation, and he brought the San Diego faculty into the group. Dumke was unable to secure an appointment from Gallagher of a staff member to move the freshman admissions issue along, and that angered Kerr, who said so in correspondence.

The short period of the Gallagher chancellorship was lacking in accomplishment. Gallagher was preoccupied with the far-right political attacks on him, and his administrative style was too authoritarian for the California context. This surface contradiction is not a surprise, as the authoritarian right and the authoritarian left often meet each other as they come around a circle. In February 1962, he resigned. Actually, he phoned the board chair, Louis Heilbron, and Vice-Chancellors Leiffer and Dumke in the middle of the night from New York to tell them of his departure, as the news of his return to the presidency of the City College of New York would be published in the morning New York newspapers.

Gallagher's resignation threw the new system into great internal turmoil. He had been expected to begin the integration of existing and new campuses, and create a system of campuses within a shared mission while maintaining the distinctive character of each campus. This was to be a substantial task, a task for the years ahead. Clearly, that was not how he understood the role. Gallagher had wanted a formal installation as chancellor. The trustees had agreed to a March date, reserved facilities in downtown Los Angeles, and mailed invitations to a large number of individuals in the state, nationally, and internationally. He resigned less than one month before the scheduled event.

It was time to begin again to shape the role of chancellor. With Glenn Dumke's appointment to the chancellorship in April 1962, the building of the role began. It was to be not simply the role and institution of chancellor that needed to be conceived, but an entire administrative structure and set of relationships inside and outside of the California State Colleges—it was almost like beginning over again. In some measure, this new beginning was starting from a negative position, as a result of the failed Gallagher leadership. The task ahead was to change to fundamentally new and different organizational structures.

The major theme of the Dumke chancellorship was establishing the system. The early moves included establishing the statewide Academic Senate and Council of Presidents. These two structures were set in motion immediately in the Dumke administration. Faculty leaders worked for a full year to establish the senate, involving all the campuses and those representative faculty bodies existing on the campuses. The presidents' group was immediately convened, and a regular schedule of meetings, initially every four to six weeks, was established. Dumke observed later that the campuses were like medieval baronies, and the need for change was immediate and substantial.[36]

Student presidents soon sought recognition, and the trustees formally recognized their organization and brought them to the table, actually along with the faculty and presidents.[37]

The chancellor's office was to be built. Don Leiffer, who had played the key role in the transitional year and, for all practical purposes, continued to do so during the months of Gallagher's chancellorship and the two-month interim between Gallagher's sudden departure and Dumke's appointment, indicated that he wished to return to the San Diego campus. Leiffer left in place the beginnings—or, perhaps, departure points—for building an administrative structure. He had not touched upon those elements of a structure that would be inevitably political.

As he saw it, Dumke needed to put together a structure that looked two ways, to the campuses and to Sacramento. He and his most immediate colleagues would do so by creating counterparts—roles that matched roles in campus-wide administrations, and also roles in state government in Sacramento that were important to the new state college system. At the time, there were those who argued that the chancellor's office and campus roles should, for the most part, not be counterpart matched, and that this would encourage administrative creativity on the campuses.

Gallagher's initial move to create three vice-chancellorships was reinforced by Dumke, with the organization of the staff into clear areas of responsibility. With Leiffer's departure as executive vice-chancellor, that position was left vacant for a time before being filled for two years with an appointment that included a set of responsibilities essentially in governmental relations and public affairs. Offices and roles in Sacramento and Washington (although the chancellor personally attended to the Washington office) were created along with a public relations staff. In 1966, the position of executive vice-chancellor was restored, and the role of deputy to the chancellor was confirmed, though its focus changed over the years as incumbents and chancellors changed and vice-chancellorships for academic affairs and administrative business affairs became institutionalized. Several years passed before a vice-chancellorship for personnel matters emerged. Gallagher had made an appointment of a chief personnel officer, attached directly to the chancellorship. Dumke changed that and created a separate personnel office. After a battle with the attorney general, a position of general counsel was created, and this eventually became a vice-chancellorship (the vice-chancellor title was dropped in 1990, but the place of the role in the hierarchy remained).

Dumke was anxious to provide for staff movement between the campuses and the chancellor's office. A structure and procedures were created to make movement possible to the chancellor's office from a campus, and a subsequent return. Personnel rules made it easily possible for a faculty or staff member to move, especially faculty, who could keep an academic appointment essentially on a term leave, and then return to the campus. The opposite could occur. In the 1960s and 1970s, these procedures were used almost exclusively in academic affairs; the procedures gradually fell into disuse, and were dropped with the change in chancellors in 1982. For the most part, they were not used by staff, especially senior staff in the chancellor's office.

During the twenty years of the Dumke administration, key moves were made to build a system. Among these in the 1960s were the creation of the academic planning process, the establishment of building programs, and the move from budgets submitted from each campus to Sacramento to a single budget proposal. The implementation of the admissions policies called for by the Master Plan added to the momentum, as did an emphasis on accreditation of individual academic programs. The trustees adopted a policy, almost universally resisted on the campuses, requiring programs in fields in which accreditations existed to secure that accreditation.

A residence for the chancellor had been on the agenda of the trustees since the beginning of the board in 1960–61. The lack of a residence was a factor, though in reality a minor one, in the abrupt resignation of Chancellor Gallagher in early 1962. Glenn and Dorothy Dumke were active in the Los Angeles community while living in a Pasadena apartment; they worked consistently at building support for the California State University and Colleges.

In 1973 a wealthy Los Angeles businessman and friend of the Dumke's, John Brown Cook, mentioned to the chancellor that he and his wife were planning to move from their home in Bel Air and would be interested in donating their home as a chancellor's residence. Dumke approached the board to accept the gift. The process of acceptance was not easy. The vice-chancellor and general counsel, Norman Epstein, wanted to be certain that if the time came when the trustees did not want to use the residence as a chancellor's home, it could be sold and the funds retained by the board for a chancellor's residence elsewhere, rather than reverting to the state general fund. Epstein accomplished this, foresight that came to be important in 1991.[38]

Located at 620 Stone Canyon Road, the home became familiar to many in the California State University over the years. It was sufficiently large, not only for entertainment, but also for meetings. The grounds included a second structure adjacent to a pool. It was far more than a pool house; it contained, in addition to a suite that could accommodate guests, a common room large enough for meetings of the presidents or others, and a kitchen with capacity for preparing for numbers of guests. Meetings of the Council of Presidents were held there once or twice a year. The Dumkes also used the home for entertaining supporters of the California State University and Colleges, and it was convenient to what were then the system offices, only a short distance away in Los Angeles. When the headquarters moved to Long Beach, a move that was in motion at the time the home was acquired, the distance, in excess of thirty miles via two crowded freeways, was substantial.

The acquisition of the home was something that Dumke wanted to accomplish, another piece of building a system of universities and colleges. Glenn and Dorothy remained in the Bel Air chancellor's residence throughout the remainder of his chancellorship. Ann Reynolds continued to reside at the Bel Air address from 1982 to her departure in 1990. When Ann Reynolds left the chancellorship, James Gray, a Long Beach trustee and a bank president, arranged for the home to be sold and the funds used to purchase "state university house" in Long Beach near the system offices, where Barry Munitz and his wife Ann made their home during his chancellorship.

Dumke was a strong supporter of accreditation; he had been chair of the regional accrediting commission in the 1950s when he was a dean at Occidental College. He thought it important to use specialized accreditations (accreditations for particular fields, most often in the professions and applied fields) as a recurring means to address quality of programs. Dumke's interests as chancellor were academic. He was not always able to secure his academic objectives; the politics of the early years were often dysfunctional from an academic perspective. The system was reshaped academically during his twenty years of leadership. The structure of the California State University was built and the framework provided for the maturing of the system.

Dumke's academic agenda was based on several judgments he made as he assumed the chancellorship. The academic objectives of the Master Plan were to be achieved. Two explicit objectives were about admissions, the selection of the undergraduate student bodies, and graduate education and the implementation of the joint doctorate. The standards called for in the Master Plan were successfully implemented, though not in the precise form Dumke personally had hoped for. The joint doctorate was implemented, but it never was institutionalized as a significant component of the academic mission of the campuses, while it was successful in a number of programs at the San Diego campus.

Implicit in the Master Plan was a shift in the primary mission of the state colleges. While the campuses had become liberal arts colleges in their 1935 legislative renaming, from state teachers colleges to state colleges, the centerpiece of academic programs for the most part remained teacher education. Cal Poly was an exception for the focus on that campus was on vocational and professional education; Fullerton was the other major exception, for its founding president, in the late 1950s, was determined that it be oriented to the liberal arts and sciences and a number of professional fields. A major goal of Dumke's academic leadership was the diversification of academic programs and strengths to include the arts and sciences and a range of professional programs open to the state colleges. The Master Plan had assigned law, medicine, and veterinary medicine exclusively to the University of California. Professional programs in other fields were to be developed and strengthened in the state colleges.

One of the final accomplishments of the Dumke years in the chancellorship was to rename the system. Since 1972, the system had been the California State University and Colleges. Initially, fourteen campuses had been designated universities, and five had remained colleges. Two of these five had met the university criteria in the ensuing years. In 1982, through the persistent efforts of the Sacramento office and its able professional staff, the name of the system was changed to the California State University. The new chancellor would be chancellor of the California State University.

The year 1982 brought to a close what for all practical purposes had been the founding chancellorship. In September 1981, Glenn Dumke announced at the opening of the new academic year, that after twenty years he would retire in the summer of 1982. A nationwide search for a successor was set in motion. The chair of the board of trustees at the time, John O'Connell, was the alumni trustee. He was a graduate of Chico State College from the 1930s and the president of the Bechtel Corporation, a family-owned worldwide construction firm. He became chair of a search committee that was focused within the trustees but included faculty and students in the process. The entire system was in the midst of implementing collective bargaining; this was not an easy time in the California State University. O'Connell dominated the search process, and he was significantly influenced by a colleague at the Bechtel Corporation, Stephen Bechtel, who recommended that he look at the then provost of Ohio State University, Dr. W. Ann Reynolds. Stephen Bechtel had some familiarity with higher education; thirty years before, in the 1950s, he had played a constructive role in the loyalty oath controversy at the University of California. There were four strong internal candidates for the chancellorship, notably Presidents James Cleary of Northridge, President Warren Baker of San Luis Obispo, and President Lloyd Johns of the Sacramento campus. (The other strong internal candidate was removed by O'Connell just before the final interviews.) Lloyd John's identity as a candidate did not leak to the media, and he had surprising support. Reynolds was in a sense a stealth candidate. Someone leaked to the press that there was a woman among the finalists, and immediately search-watchers jumped to the conclusion that a chancellor of a major Midwestern state university would be chosen; she had been the June commencement speaker at one of the campuses.

Reynolds became chancellor on September 1, 1982. She brought with her only one person from Ohio State, a staff assistant, Joy Phillips, who would be important through the years of her chancellorship as well as after it, during Ellis McCune's interim year as chancellor, and subsequently, the chancellorship of Barry Munitz. Phillips was a talented intermediary between three chancellors and staff, presidents, and others. The executive vice-chancellor, Harry Harmon, was at retirement age, and he offered his resignation; Reynolds asked him to stay for a transitional year. The vice-chancellor for academic affairs, Alex Sherriffs, who had moved to the position from Governor Reagan's staff in 1973, stayed, as did the vice-chancellor for business affairs, Dale Hanner, and the vice-chancellor and general counsel, Mayer Chapman. The position of vice-chancellor for faculty and staff affairs was held by an interim appointee, Robert Tyndall, a former dean from Long Beach State.

Reynolds proceeded to rebuild the staff during her first year. She combined the positions of executive and academic vice-chancellor, retitled the position as provost, and brought to the appointment William Vandament, a Midwestern university administrator whom Reynolds had known earlier. She recommended to the trustees the appointment of an experienced and nationally known administrator in higher education collective bargaining, Caesar Naples, as vice-chancellor for faculty and staff affairs. Naples inherited the most difficult agenda of the new appointees, collective bargaining, which had become law in 1978. Implementation and the early steps were well underway, but there had been no firm hand at the tiller.

An academic agenda soon emerged. One of Reynolds's early moves was to ask the former chair of the Admissions Advisory Council to return to that role, and with the associate vice-chancellor for academic affairs, Robert Bess, undertake the restructuring of freshman admissions requirements.[39] Reynolds wanted significantly greater emphasis on high school preparatory requirements in traditional academic areas, and she included the arts among the academic areas, a first for California. This effort would be accomplished in her first years in the chancellorship, although the full accomplishment of the arts requirement would take years, well into the 1990s. An emphasis on the arts was soon followed by the development of a summer program for students in the arts. The program provided enriched experiences in all of the arts for students from throughout the California State University.

The state colleges had been among the early campuses in the country to adopt a variety of approaches, such as Educational Opportunity Programs (EOP) and curriculum, to address the enrollment of minority students. This had originated in the context of the San Francisco State and other state college campus movements of the latter 1960s. Affirmative Action, as a series of substantive programs and efforts on the campuses, emerged in the early 1970s. Early in her administration, Reynolds made it clear that admission of students, faculty and staff appointments, and curriculum addressing minority communities were important matters to her. She was persistent, and one of the characteristics of her eight-year administration was continuing pressure on the campuses and the presidents, and, for the most part, the campuses responded positively, though sometimes grudgingly.

Reynolds's emphasis on secondary school preparation for study on the state university campuses was evident. She was also very conscious of the fact that the state university campuses educated and prepared more than 70 percent of California teachers. She made a number of moves, including the creation of two trustee task forces. The impact of her concern on the campuses was largely in morale and support for teacher education faculties. The deans of education as a group gathered some strength; Reynolds personally built relationships with the leadership of the deans' group as well as relationships with the state's Commission on Teacher Credentialing.

When Ann Reynolds assumed the chancellorship, she worked with an incoming chair of the Academic Senate, John Bedell, who was new to statewide leadership. He remained chair for three years. The major issue with faculty governance in these years was the implementation of collective bargaining and building the distinction between the roles of the statewide Academic Senate and the California Faculty Association, the bargaining agent selected by the faculty. The groundwork for this had been laid mostly by the Academic Senate, with some involvement by the chancellor's staff in the late 1970s, and came to some conclusion with the 1985 statement on the role of senates in an era of collective bargaining.

Tensions between the presidents and chancellor had not been alleviated by the early meeting between Reynolds and the presidents in 1982. The division of the presidents into three groups subsided but did not disappear after the change of the Council of Presidents to an executive council. Ann Reynolds took part in the selection of fourteen presidents in her eight years as chancellor, albeit three successive presidents on one campus and two on a second campus. There was some stability among the leadership of the presidents, and new presidents were often bewildered by the divisions in the group.

The dotted-line/straight-line controversy among the presidents grew in the first five of the Reynolds years, and it became something that presidents and chancellor's staff had to work around. Perhaps a by-product of this was an impact on the role of vice-chancellor. The merging of the roles of executive vice-chancellor and academic vice-chancellor did not work well. The conflict among the presidents and with the chancellor certainly contributed to this. After William Vandament left the chancellor's office, Reynolds and the board looked to two familiar figures for fresh leadership. Herbert Carter, who had been with the system since 1973 when he became the first affirmative action officer, was appointed executive vice-chancellor. Lee Kerschner, who was initially on the faculty at California State University Fullerton, and subsequently in a number of roles in the chancellor's office, returned to the California State University from the executive directorship of the 1987 Master Plan Review and became vice-chancellor for academic affairs. A new phenomenon began to emerge, close working relationships between individual vice-chancellors and individual trustees. This situation had always existed between individual presidents and board members, and Dumke had taken it in stride. Reynolds did not feel comfortable with such an arrangement and intervened in some measure with the scheduling of the all-inclusive trustee-president staff dinners at the time of board meetings. The vice-chancellor–trustee relationships were a new and untested phenomenon, however, and included only some of the vice-chancellors, not all. It was a product of growing unrest about Reynolds among some board members, and the desire of these members for more involvement.

In 1987, the trustees joined the dotted-line/straight-line issue in the context of a periodic review of Chancellor Reynolds. There were other sources of restlessness within the system, and these inevitably came back to the chancellor. In 1986, there had been legislative concern about executive salary raises being done behind closed doors. The Sacramento advocate, James Jensen, had written the legislative leadership that this had been an error and would not be done again. But it was done again, and in a 1990 legislative hearing with the chancellor, the chair, and vice-chair of the board of trustees, the 1986 letter was produced. At about the same time it was revealed to the media that the system had purchased six cars for the six vice-chancellors, at a total figure of more than ninety-nine thousand dollars, only a few dollars under the hundred-thousand limit allowed without requiring Sacramento approval. This and reports about repaving the driveway in the chancellor's house became fodder for the media.

The personnel rules of the board, established in the 1960s, provided for "executives," including presidents, vice-chancellors, and the chancellor, who serve at the pleasure of the board. In 1981, the board had created the position of "trustee professor." In 1984, the board expanded the concept of trustee professor to provide for presidents, vice-chancellors, and chancellors holding tenured professorial appointments, after five or more years of "executive" service, the opportunity to move to a trustee professorship on the campus where they held tenure, and teach or engage in research or other scholarly activity. This provided a way out for both the individual concerned and for the board or chancellor, when a move was deemed desirable for whatever reason. Trustee professorships were funded by the system budget, and salaries, after a one-year paid leave, were set at the midpoint between the top professorial salary and the individual's executive salary; clerical and other support would be provided.

In 1990, Reynolds addressed retirement for presidents with the board in executive closed session. In closed sessions, the chancellor was usually accompanied by some or all of the vice-chancellors and a member of the legal staff to take rough notes. As the discussion ensued, all the staff (the chancellor is a trustee) were excused. Someone took rough notes. Reynolds proposed that presidents generally leave the presidency at age sixty-five and retire or move to a trustee professorship. The rough notes of the discussion reflect that it came to an end because of time; someone moved "the sense of the discussion." All agreed. The meeting adjourned. The meaning of the motion is ambiguous. Sometime after, Chancellor Reynolds, without an accompanying trustee, visited Presidents Jewell Plummer Cobb at Fullerton and Ellis McCune at Hayward, both over sixty-five, and informed them of the discussion, as if a decision had been agreed upon in the closed-door trustee meeting. Neither of the two presidents were prepared to retire, but both agreed and stepped aside. President Cobb went to a trustee professorship at the Los Angeles campus, and President McCune announced his retirement.

In the search for a replacement for McCune as president of Hayward, the chair of the board, who was a member of the search committee, subsequently learned of the reasons for the McCune and Cobb departures, during discussions about the age of one of the serious candidates, Norma Rees, who was sixty. The discussion went something like this: "She won't even have time to vest for retirement." This was the point at which it was learned that the board had not adopted a firm position. Norma Rees became President Norma Rees, and President Ellis McCune would soon become acting chancellor.

The combination of all of these events and the turmoil of the times with budgets and collective bargaining moved the board to request Ann Reynolds to resign, and she did. Her departure was more precipitous than she had wished, but before she left California and the chancellor's house, she was appointed to the chancellorship of the City University of New York.

The Reynolds years were not ones of good relationships in Sacramento. She was and is a very strong and authoritative person. Unlike Dumke, who had relied upon an ably administered Sacramento office, some presidential involvement, and his budget team (Vice-Chancellor Hanner and Assistant-Vice Chancellors Messner and Moye), Reynolds had wanted to play a role in Sacramento, and she did. Reynolds was not encouraging to presidents about developing Sacramento relationships, and she believed it important that the chancellor personally be involved in Sacramento. She did not work closely with the Sacramento office staff, nor was the staff always aware of important discussions with legislators and others. A certain partisan character developed. She had only limited Republican support but strong Democratic support, particularly in the person of Willie Brown, the powerful Speaker of the Assembly.

There was little change in the chancellor's role in governance in the period from 1982 to 1990. The tests that would result from collective bargaining were still in the years ahead. There was a change in the academic policy role of the chancellor. Dumke, for the most part, had worked quietly, and over time. Reynolds, by contrast, identified a number of issues where she was pushing for change. Her impact on this range of issues was substantial. She changed the position of the CSU irreversibly on affirmative action and outreach to minority groups, and through her insistence on the arts as a component of admissions and the support of the summer school for the arts, she had much of the responsibility and deserves much of the credit for saving the arts in the public K-12 school curriculum of that time. She also brought back teacher education as a priority. She did not change the basic operating mode of the chancellor's office.[40]

Reynolds' departure was surrounded by controversy and anger. Many campus senates joined the issue with resolutions addressed to the board, resolutions that were not supportive of the chancellor. She attempted, publicly, to designate Herbert Carter as the interim chancellor. The board did not appoint Carter, a move that had nothing to do with him but was a clear rejection of Reynolds. When Reynolds resigned, the trustees appointed Ellis McCune as acting chancellor and immediately initiated a national search. McCune's influence was a calming one. He knew Sacramento and had a sense of how to work there. He rebuilt relationships with the legislative and executive branches. One of McCune's actions angered some of the presidents: he rolled back the salary increases for presidents that had been awarded in the closed board session in the spring of 1990. He had no choice given legislative pressure; the board and he took the action and bore the brunt of the complaints. He met with the presidents by himself on occasion. The work that year in the executive council laid a foundation for one of the most important of the early decisions of the Munitz administration.

Barry Munitz came to the chancellorship in 1991. As a young academic (with a doctorate in comparative literature from Princeton) Munitz had worked with Clark Kerr in the Carnegie Foundation project. He subsequently became a vice president of the University of Illinois, president of the University of Houston, and president of the Maxxam Corporation. Among other holdings, Maxxam had redwood forests in northern California and had done some redwood cutting. Munitz's appointment to the chancellorship was criticized by some because of his recent corporate background, and by some environmentalists because of the Maxxam redwood forest cuttings. On his round of first-year campus visits at Sacramento State, a number of students dressed as trees, held themselves rigid, made sounds like a buzz saw, and fell to the ground. Munitz and his wife handled the situation well. A major factor in the search that resulted in the Munitz appointment was the clear desire of the trustees to initiate a strong fund-raising and development program. The appointment of Munitz promised this, and Munitz followed through (Chapter 12 addresses this at some length). Once appointed, he moved quickly to take charge—became familiar with issues and people, and laid groundwork for the coming year when he would assume formal responsibility.

Munitz had to rebuild the chancellor's staff. Herbert Carter was leaving the executive vice-chancellorship for the presidency of the United Way of Greater Los Angeles, and Dale Hanner retired, as he had earlier indicated, after staying for a brief time to assist with the transition. In some months, Caesar Naples moved from the vice-chancellorship for faculty and staff affairs to a trustee professorship at the Long Beach campus, and Lee Kerschner moved from the academic vice-chancellorship to the position of interim president of the Stanislaus campus. Mayer Chapman, the veteran vice-chancellor and general counsel during Dumke's later years as chancellor and then during Reynolds's time, was asked by the trustees to step aside; board members blamed Chapman for many of the problems in the last years of the Reynolds administration. He moved to a trustee professorship at Long Beach State as well.

Munitz restaffed via a number of searches, all done with committees mirroring the profile of the California State University and resulting in final appointment action by the board of trustees. Molly Corbett Broad, then executive director of higher education in the state of Arizona was appointed executive vice-chancellor, and became in essence the chief operating officer to Munitz's role as chief executive officer. Louis Messner, the veteran chief budget officer (since 1968), became vice-chancellor for business affairs for a brief year, and then retired for health reasons. Mernoy Harrison, then vice president for administration at the Sacramento campus became the acting vice-chancellor and also chaired a search committee, which resulted in Richard West's appointment as vice-chancellor for business affairs. West had been a senior statewide administrator in the University of California, and most recently associate vice president for information systems and administrative services. Harold Haak, the retired Fresno president, became the acting vice-chancellor for academic affairs for one year and was succeeded by Dr. Peter Hoff, a vice-chancellor from Georgia. Munitz and the trustees brought in a new general counsel, who stayed only briefly, followed by Christine Helwick, then the chief deputy to the general counsel of the University of California; the use of vice-chancellor in the title was dropped. Faculty and staff affairs was a critical area, given collective bargaining, and June Cooper, a highly respected veteran vice president from the Long Beach campus, was appointed to the position of vice-chancellor for human resources and operations.

Through this period of reorganization, Munitz worked with the presidents as a group in the executive council, and individually on various matters. The Munitz-Broad partnership arrived at a difficult time, with CSU budget curtailments and resulting enrollment controls and declines. Munitz personally became involved with a potential substantial faculty layoff at San Diego and mooted it. It became clear that Munitz was a take-charge chancellor, though highly skilled and diplomatic in his actions.

In a two-year period, Munitz effectively restaffed the system administration. He did not wait to set in motion major changes in administration. With the abolition of the Orange Book, he empowered campuses and presidents to begin to reframe budgets. He initiated decentralization of financial administration. He made it possible for presidents to initiate and shape academic and other programs. Each of the vice-chancellors whom he selected would make a difference in administrative style, and in the distribution of responsibility between the chancellor's office and the campuses. The campuses simply had the opportunity to shape and initiate programs and to order budget proposals and allocations addressing the substance of academic and other programs. Munitz observed some years later that he thought it important "to change the balance between the system and the campuses, and it's not at all by weakening the system, but by defining the system's role more clearly and more positively, and by allowing the campuses to really stretch out."[41]

The three factions among the presidents simply disappeared. It became clear that Munitz, while allowing the presidents very substantial moving room, would not countenance presidential insurrection or game-playing. The presidents, really for the first time in the years since the Master Plan, were all in support of the chancellor—their chancellor. There was no choice. Thus, another benchmark in the healthy maturing of the system was achieved.

The initiatives in the Munitz years as chancellor, in addition to the procedural ones in the chancellor's office toward decentralization, encompassed a broad range, from the academic side (Cornerstones) to the administrative (budget allocation authority on the campuses, massive decentralization of the building program) to public affairs and fundraising, with the focus on and the majority of the responsibility with the campuses.

One of the initiatives of the Munitz years was the establishment of the California State University Institute. An auxiliary organization tied to the chancellor's office, the institute was governed by a board of business people, a small number of faculty and presidents, and members of the chancellor's staff that included the chancellor and two vice-chancellors. The executive vice-chancellor chaired the board. The purpose of the institute was to create public (i.e., CSU)-private or public-public partnerships related substantively to CSU programs and to the CSU mission. The partnerships would be at a minimum self-supporting, and some would be profit-making. The institute had a small staff initially supported by the CSU Foundation and the chancellor's office and, subsequently, by its own operations. From its first activities in 1995–96 to the fall of 1997, the activity was modest. With the change in the chancellorship beginning in early 1997 with Molly Broad's resignation (she left for the presidency of the University of North Carolina, and she went on to become president of the American Council on Education), the institute went into a holding pattern, and with the arrival of a new chancellor, Charles Reed, early in 1998, it ceased activity. The corporate shell was maintained for use as a vehicle for chancellor's office projects.

Despite the institute's limited initial activity (which primarily amounted to simply getting organized), it was controversial among many of the presidents. Not unlike the Consortium of the 1970s, it was seen as a campus-like entity operating directly from the chancellor's office, and a long-term threat to campus programs, enrollment, finances, and fundraising. The system had yet to fashion a model for significant systemwide vehicles to connect programs to a particular audience or constituency.

There were no formal changes in the governance of the California State University or in the responsibilities of the chancellor in the Munitz years. The changes were in leadership, administrative style, and working relationships. The centralizing measures of the 1960s and 1970s that had been essential to the establishment of the state college system had persisted in the 1980s, resulting in a certain brittleness of relations between the chancellor's office and the campuses. Some presidents and others on the campuses understood this as a necessary part of the growth of the system; some did not and bridled at or fought the system. The decentralizing moves of the early and mid-1990s were important steps in the maturing of the California State University.

Munitz announced in July 1997, shortly after Molly Broad had departed, that he would leave at the end of the calendar year; he had accepted the presidency of the J. Paul Getty Trust. Charles Reed was appointed by the board of trustees as the sixth chancellor of the California State University in November 1997. The search that led to the Reed appointment was conducted by a trustee committee. Outgoing chancellor Barry Munitz was not a member of the committee, but he was strongly supportive of the Reed appointment. The chair of the board, Martha Fallgatter, was the chair of the search committee.[42] As members of the search committee talked with leaders throughout the nation, and sought advice from the Association of Governing Boards, Reed's name surfaced frequently. Fallgatter took Reed to breakfast when he had come to California to attend a Florida football game with the University of Southern California. By

30. Chancellor Charles Reed, Trustee Chair Martha Fallgatter, Chancellor Barry Munitz, November 1997.

the end of breakfast, Reed had agreed to meet with the full board. Board members were positively impressed, and he became their choice. Reed had been chancellor of the Florida university system for twelve years, and prior to that he had been chief of staff to the governor of Florida; he was both politically knowledgeable and astute. He was known as a strong and decisive administrator. He had earned a doctorate at George Washington University, had been on the faculty at GWU briefly, for five years, and then moved to the public policy arena, eventually in Florida.

In the interim between the departure of Munitz and the formal assumption of office by Reed, June Cooper became vice-chancellor in charge. Cooper had retired from the position of vice-chancellor for human resources and operations, where she had had a successful five-year run. Once he was designated as the incoming chancellor, Reed began frequent trips from Florida to California, acquainting himself with his expected role and with the players. One of his early meetings was with Governor Pete Wilson, which resulted in a budget augmentation for the next budget year (for more about this story, see Chapter 4 and 12).

It became clear to the presidents that Reed had come with a plan; the plan was not clear, but there was one. Soon after taking office, he met with the presidents for a working dinner and a long evening discussion. If it had not been clear to presidents before, as a result of their background research and experience with Reed in the interim since his appointment, it was clear from that meeting that he was in charge. Reed brought with him his assistant in Florida, Sandra George. Before working for Reed, George had been an assistant to the governor of Florida. She played and still plays a vital role in the Reed administration.

Two important interim vice-chancellor situations needed attention. The vice-chancellorships for academic affairs and faculty and staff affairs were vacant. Peter Hoff, whom Munitz brought to the position of vice-chancellor for academic affairs in 1993, left for the presidency of the University of Maine in 1995. Charles Lindahl, the associate vice-chancellor, filled the role for a period of several years until 1998. The traditional functions of academic affairs concerning degree programs and academic planning had been largely decentralized in 1993. Academic planning had been redefined to a function supporting the campuses and considering questions of broad strategy. Lindahl, as associate vice-chancellor, had been immediately responsible for the student support functions, admissions, financial aid, and the like, as well as general coordination of other areas, including institutional studies, extended education, and teacher education. Lindahl was vice-chancellor through a long interim, and his work had the practical consequence of redefining the academic affairs role at the system level. Lindahl earned a level of quiet and substantial support for the academic affairs function from the campuses and among the presidents.

Reed moved quickly after his March 1, 1998, arrival to initiate a search for the vice-chancellorship. Working with a search committee, Reed brought to the trustees a recommendation for the appointment of Dr. David Spence as vice-chancellor for academic affairs. Spence had been in the same role with Reed in Florida, and had worked closely with him. The statewide Academic Senate members were unsure of the appointment Reed had urged, but Spence soon earned great respect from the faculty as one they could strongly support.

Spence went to work immediately with Reed on the implementation of Cornerstones, which had been adopted by the board only a few months earlier. He worked easily with the presidents and constructively with the Academic Senate. Essentially, he rebuilt the role of vice-chancellor. Spence emphasized the thrust and style of the Lindahl interim period, a supportive relationship with the campuses and the effective functioning of the system offices in academic affairs. During his seven years as vice-chancellor, Spence built a new dimension into the role in academic affairs—system strategy and goals. This was a major change that moved away from efforts to manage academic affairs on the campuses from a distance. System strategies certainly involved the campuses, in building relationships with the community colleges around transfer programs, and in an initiative to test high school juniors in English and mathematics in order to provide time and courses in the senior year, to reduce the need for remedial work in the college freshman year. Spence worked with the leadership of the State Board of Education as well to accomplish this initiative; called the Early Assessment Program, it drew national attention.

Spence also played a key role in a major program step—legislative and gubernatorial authorization for the California State University to award the independent doctorate in education. This step was the result of years of systematic and constant work (see Chapter 5 for a detailed account of this development). Spence, along with Judson King, the provost of the University of California, cochaired a joint group to bring about a reinvigorated joint EdD. That effort was not productive, so the CSU turned its efforts once again to the independent doctorate, which came to fruition for the CSU in 2005.

Spence left the position of executive vice-chancellor in 2005 to assume the presidency of the Southern Regional Education Board. Upon Spence's departure, Keith Boyum, a political science professor from the Fullerton campus, filled the position as interim vice-chancellor for academic affairs for one year. Gary Reichard, the provost at the Long Beach campus, was appointed to the position of executive vice-chancellor and chief academic officer in 2006.

The chief academic officers on the campuses (by the time of Spence's arrival, given the title of provost and also, in some instances, vice president for academic affairs) have no formal role as a group in the life of the system. They can have substantial influence, and exercise considerable leadership. In the years 1970–1973, during the time that William Langsdorf was the academic vice-chancellor, the group had drawn together, elected a chair, and generally had been productive in building a positive tone on the academic side of the house. Working together, the vice presidents had become a positive force influencing the system, even at a time when enrollments had stabilized and growth was coming to a halt on many campuses, the time when "steady state" became a part of the academic vocabulary.

Subsequently, however, the vigor of the vice presidents as a group became dormant. Six of the members of the group moved on to presidencies, both in and beyond the system. When Barry Munitz arrived in 1991, he remarked on several occasions to the presidents that he was surprised by the weakness of the vice presidents. He was reacting not to the roles the vice presidents played on their campuses, but the role he saw in them as a group. Whether it was Spence's objective or not, the Spence style had the net effect of enlivening the work of the provosts as a group. Called the "academic council," this group met regularly, and worked significantly with the implementation of Cornerstones and other initiatives. Spence worked not only with but through both the statewide Academic Senate and the provosts to develop a CSU strategic agenda.

Not long after Spence's arrival, Reed reshuffled the chancellor's office organization. This would not be so major a change on the surface that a bystander would call it a reorganization, but it would have a serious and positive impact over time. When Reed arrived, there was no incumbent executive vice-chancellor; Molly Broad had departed in June 1997, and soon thereafter, Barry Munitz announced his departure. Munitz's decision to leave the executive vice-chancellorship open, even on an acting basis was a sensible one. Reed brought to the board a proposal to retitle the post of vice-chancellor for academic affairs to executive vice-chancellor and chief academic officer, and the post of vice-chancellor for business affairs to executive vice-chancellor and chief financial officer. This alteration was far more than symbolism. It was the signal for a style of leadership that would focus on policy and strategy for the California State University. The impact of this approach, a strong reinforcement of what Munitz had initiated, was twofold. Over the years, the trustees had changed the management style of the 1960s and 1970s, when the system was to be built, to a policy board. The campuses had been able to assume more responsibility in the 1990s, not only operationally but strategically, within the overarching mission of the CSU and trustee-chancellor policy direction. The net effect of this restructuring was to create a strong, policy oriented leadership team that would successfully reshape how the California State University would operate over the next years.

Reed asked the vice-chancellor for business affairs, Richard West, to assume the role of executive vice-chancellor and chief financial officer. West spent the next ten years reshaping not only how the financial, technological, and development functions of the CSU would operate, but opening up new paths for campuses. The redefined vice-chancellor role provided the stature and the support for initiatives of consequence. This vice-chancellorship has been occupied by six individuals, three for relatively short periods. Harry Brakebill, who occupied the role for three years, followed by seven years as executive vice-chancellor, built the initial role and significantly shaped the internal financial structure of the CSU. Dale Hanner was in the position for twenty-four years as the structure slowly evolved, but was still within the basic framework of centralization and decentralization defined in the late 1960s. Hanner worked credibly and effectively with the campuses, his counterparts in Sacramento, and the statewide Academic Senate. The transformation of this pattern began in the early 1990s. By the time Richard West left the role of executive vice-chancellor at the end of 2008, the responsibilities of the role had changed significantly, with the importance of the system development of an integrated technology strategy, the coordination of investment and bonding, the growing importance of fundraising and development, and the establishment of the treasury function.

At the time Reed arrived, the second vice-chancellorship in an interim state was held by Samuel Strafaci. June Cooper had retired in December 1996, and Strafaci had assumed the interim role. Strafaci had come to the California State University from the private sector in 1985. His work in the faculty and staff affairs area had been in collective bargaining and labor relations; he had worked closely and effectively with the campuses, and brought stable leadership to a difficult area. He continued in this interim role until 1999. Reed had placed a first priority on the academic and financial/technology areas. With the 1988–89 academic year, a national search was initiated. Jackie McClain, then executive director of human resources and affirmative action at the University of Michigan, was appointed as vice-chancellor for human resources. For this area, the central concern for the next years was collective bargaining (see Chapter 10). Personnel administration had settled over the years, both on the campuses and in the chancellor's office, to a well-managed operation. The campuses acquired more flexibility over time, as they had in other areas.

In the 1990s, fundraising and development had gradually acquired greater importance, and this growth would continue in the Reed administration. Douglas Patino, the vice-chancellor for university advancement, had spent seven years building a framework of policies and procedures to institutionalize "university advancement," essentially fundraising. He resigned in 2000. Once again a search ensued. The search led to the appointment of Louis Caldera as vice-chancellor. Caldera had been earlier a member of the California State Assembly from the Los Angeles area, and he had served as secretary of the army in the second Clinton term. Caldera came to the vice-chancellorship in 2001, and continued the role Patino had built, giving some measure of coordination to the many fundraising efforts on the campuses. He did not remain long; in 2003, he moved to the presidency of the University of New Mexico. The ten-year experience of great emphasis on fundraising had made it clear that the thrust of fundraising activity took place on the campuses. The building of the structure had been completed for the time. The vice-chancellorship for university advancement was left vacant, and the post of assistant vice-chancellor for systemwide advancement was created. The function became a part of the general responsibility of the executive vice-chancellor and chief financial officer.

The Sacramento and Washington offices of the CSU had reporting relationships to the chancellor directly over the years. Toward the latter years of the Munitz administration, the Sacramento relationship was shared with the executive vice-chancellor. In the restructuring of 1998–99, the Sacramento office became the responsibility of the executive vice-chancellor and chief financial officer, and the position of the administrator of the Sacramento office, then held by Karen Yelverton Zamarippa, was retitled as assistant vice-chancellor. This was done in part to recognize that a principal activity in Sacramento was the budget. The system also appointed a person experienced in Sacramento higher education matters, Patrick Lenz, to an assistant vice-chancellor position in financial administration, and Lenz spent a major part of his time in Sacramento.

The Reed administration has not been a time of structural change in the formal governance of the California State University. Rather it has been a time of major initiatives, with substantial trustee involvement and action at a policy level, initiatives that have changed roles and emphasized accomplishments. These have occurred in all areas. In some ways the system has become more unified in mission and sense of purpose. Roles have changed, some in a policy direction, some in the direction of implementation.[43]

The years of the California State University have seen six individuals occupy the role of chancellor: Gallagher, Dumke, Reynolds, McCune, Munitz, and Reed. Two individuals were for short periods, and four were and/or still are in office for periods ranging from almost seven to twenty years. In the transition year of 1960–61, Don Leiffer, the San Diego State professor of political science who was administrative officer through that year, had begun to define some attributes of the role of chancellor, though that was not his intent. For most purposes, Leiffer carried the role of chancellor during the brief seven months of Buell Gallagher.

When Glenn Dumke became Chancellor in April 1962, there was no model. The closest thing to a model for the chancellorship was the presidency of the University of California, though the history of the UC was so different that patterning the chancellorship on the presidency made little sense. Consequently, during those early years, Dumke, the trustees, and many others were the creators of the system. In 1962, Clark Kerr was still redefining the UC presidency, four years after succeeding to the almost twenty-nine year presidency of Robert Gordon Sproul. State college faculty and faculty leaders were then assuming the University of California to be the model—for everything, not only the chancellorship. The role of chancellor had to be built. It is fair to assert that in the twenty years of the Dumke chancellorship, the role was built pragmatically. Dumke, as chancellor, was not the only orchestrator. Board members, and particularly board chairs, legislators, the three governors who held office in the twenty-year period, politics, and many people inside and outside the California State Colleges, all contributed to shaping the role. Dumke was not prone to thinking about organizational theory; he thought about building a system and about academic matters.

Each of the subsequent chancellors built on the shoulders of the previous chancellors. Alex Sherriffs, in his nearly ten years as vice-chancellor for academic affairs (1973–83), would remind especially the presidents in the Chancellor's Council of Presidents/executive council meetings that universities are built on the shoulders of predecessors. The role of chancellor has been built by the incumbents to a great extent. Each chancellor has had the opportunity to make a difference; changes and opportunities in our society demand it, and the citizens of California expect it. Each chancellor has made a difference for his or her time, and then passed the baton.

* * *

The chancellor's staff has grown. Don Leiffer was the first employee in September 1960. For the first board of trustees meeting on August 12, 1960, the chair of the board had to borrow a secretary from the governor's office to take minutes. In 1961, as the California State Colleges began actual operation as a system, the staff numbered ten. In 1963–64, as the chancellor's office became settled in for a few years at the "imperial headquarters" (unfortunately located on Imperial Highway near the Los Angeles airport), the staff had increased to eighty-three, including Tim, the mail person. As the system grew, and the offices moved to Wilshire Boulevard in Los Angeles and then to Long Beach, and the size of the staff grew along with enrollments, faculty, and staff, and new program initiatives. For some time in the later 1970s and early 1980s, the staff stabilized in size to somewhere between 350 and 400 people. With the advent of technology, the resumption of enrollment growth, and the addition of four campuses, the staff grew in size. In 2008, the size of the staff of the chancellor was 628 individuals, including employees in the Washington, D.C. (three) and Sacramento offices (eleven). In addition to Long Beach, Washington, and Sacramento, the chancellor's office currently operates a Center for Distributed Learning (with eleven staff) on the Sonoma State campus, and a Center for Teacher Quality (with seven) on the Sacramento State campus. The major increases of the 1990s and 2000s have been in technology, auditing, reporting, fundraising, and workload growth.

The Coordinating Council for Higher Education/California Postsecondary Education Commission

The 1959–60 deliberations about the creation of a Master Plan for Higher Education in California included the development of a coordinating mechanism for public higher education. The 1945 creation of the Liaison Committee of the regents of the University of California and the State Board of Education had been a first step; the establishment of the Joint Staff of the Liaison Committee in 1953, with two senior and respected individuals, was an important move leading to the Master Plan. The final Master Plan was actually the proposal of the Master Plan Survey Team, "prepared for the Liaison Committee of the State Board of Education and the Regents of the University of California."[44]

The Master Plan proposed the creation of a Coordinating Council for Higher Education. It was to be in Article IX of the constitution, just as the California State Colleges would be. The council would have twelve members, three each from the California State Colleges, the University of California, the junior colleges, and the independent colleges and universities. The CSU and UC members would be designated by their respective governing boards and would include in each instance the system chief executive officer and two board members. The junior colleges would be represented by a State Board of Education member or the state superintendent of public instruction, a representative of the junior college district governing boards, and a representative of local junior college administrators. The independent college and university members would be selected jointly by the president of the University of California and the chief executive officer (chancellor) of the California State Colleges. "Effective voting and action" were defined. On matters affecting the University of California and the state colleges, only the university and state college member votes would be effective, and four of the six university and state college members must vote affirmatively; on junior college matters, the junior college representatives would also have effective votes. On the appointment and removal of the director of the council, all twelve members would have effective votes.

The functions of the Coordinating Council of Higher Education (CCHE) were defined as advisory to "appropriate state officials." These included review of operating and capital budgets of the university and state college systems; interpretations of the differentiation of functions and "advice to The Regents and The Trustees on programs appropriate to each system"; and planning the orderly growth of higher education and recommending to governing boards about the need for and location of "new facilities and programs." The council was given the power to require that the public institutions supply data about costs, enrollments, selection and retention of students—matters related to planning and coordination.[45] This initial proposal from the leaders and trustees of higher education tells the story of the work and the fate of coordination and the orderly growth and development of higher education in California through at least the beginning years of the twenty-first century.

The legislature and the governor, while they had not weighed in about the particulars of the proposed coordinating body, found neither the idea of a constitutional entity nor a group composed entirely of those who were to be governed, or at least advised, to be attractive. The legislation introduced in March 1960, Senate Bill 33, principally authored by Senator George Miller, expanded the CCHE to fifteen members by adding three public members to be appointed by the governor, and did not place the council in the constitution. The legislation also eliminated the concept of "effective voting and action," and simply provided that the council determine its own rules, that all members vote, and that "effective action shall require the affirmative vote of eight members." The functions in Senate Bill 33 were identical to those proposed in the Master Plan. Perhaps as a safety valve, the legislation provided that it would only become effective if the constitutional amendment creating the state college trustees, independent of the State Board of Education, were to be approved by the electorate later in 1960.[46]

Governor Pat Brown moved on the appointment of the public members in the summer of 1960 at about the same time as he did on the appointment of the state college trustees. One of his original appointees to the trustees, a young attorney, Warren Christopher, had been on Brown's staff. He participated in part of the first meeting of the trustees in August 1960, and then announced his resignation, in order to accept the appointment to the Coordinating Council.[47] He would play a key role for the governor in the creation of the Coordinating Council and its early years. At the council's first meeting, Governor Brown presided initially. He asked Keith Sexton, who had staffed Dorothy Donahoe in the development of the Master Plan and was sitting in the audience in the governor's conference room, to take minutes and make a record of the occasion. Sexton was known to the governor's staff for the role he had played in the Master Plan discussions. Shortly after the meeting, Warren Christopher asked Sexton to be the first member of the council staff. Sexton agreed to do it half time for the balance of the calendar year (1960), in order to complete responsibilities with the Assembly Education Committee. Subsequently, Robert Wert, the first chair of the council, brought Sexton to the council full time, with the title of assistant to the council. Sexton played a tempering role that was important to the California State Colleges through the 1960s. Wert was then vice-provost at Stanford University and later president of Mills College.

A first task for the council was to select a director. A national recruitment process led to the appointment of Dr. John Richards. Richards had held a comparable position in Oregon, and he had also been a candidate for chancellor of the California State Colleges when Buell Gallagher was appointed. Richards was not politically adept with the legislature or the executive branch. He wanted to move the council headquarters from Sacramento to San Francisco, as he and his wife wanted to live in San Francisco. There was great resistance in the legislature, and particularly in the Department of Finance. Richards prevailed, and a set of offices was acquired in a state building in San Francisco. Part of Richards's reasoning was to get away from state agencies. The council maintained its original small office in Sacramento, and Keith Sexton moved between the two offices. Richards was asked to resign by the council after eighteen months. He had brought from Oregon Willard Spalding, an experienced and senior administrator. Spalding became acting director for several years, and ultimately director. Spalding worked constructively with state college leaders, as he did with the leaders of all of the segments and the legislature. When Spalding first became acting director in 1962, one of his first actions had been to move the council offices back to Sacramento.[48]

Early in 1961, several resolutions were introduced in the legislature to study adult education. The president's cabinet in the University of California had been discussing the matter. The assembly resolution that was adopted requested the Coordinating Council to study extension programs of the three segments of public higher education. This drew attention at the highest level of the UC administration and the regents.[49] The issue was enrollment and the funding of extension programs.

For years the individual state colleges had enrolled part-time students at lower than regular fees, and had enabled part-time students to register without going through established admission procedures. In the early 1950s, the presidents had defined procedures and policies for part-time students. Individuals enrolling for six or fewer units could enroll as "limited students." A reduced fee schedule was set for these students. The larger campuses established the position of "late afternoon and evening coordinator." Limited students were not required to matriculate—that is, to meet established admission standards. Limited students on most campuses would register in the late afternoon and evening hours. Essentially, these limited students in the state colleges were almost totally state supported. In contrast, state college extension programs were totally self-supporting, at least in theory; on some campuses some overhead costs were doubtless absorbed.

In the Master Plan, discussions, Glenn Dumke, in his role as the state college representative, had agreed to the matriculation of limited students. Limited students were required to meet the established admissions standards. This was not received well by many state college administrators, who saw enrollment and money potentially disappearing. The heavy enrollments of limited students were on the urban campuses, and the process of matriculation, carried on within one admissions cycle, was rather massive. The impact on enrollment was small, despite the fears of administrators; most limited students were older than the conventional college age and were purposeful; they were not drop-ins, and most met conventional admissions standards.

From the standpoint of the University of California, the matriculation of limited students only addressed a part of the problem as they saw it. They understood the limited student to be a student like the students who enrolled in university extension programs. University extension programs were partially subsidized by the state, but not wholly. University extension courses often were not comparable to courses in degree programs. By the late summer of 1961, President Kerr had become critical of the state colleges and said so in Coordinating Council meetings and in correspondence. Kerr's two concerns were both focused on enrollment, the limited student programs and a need to restructure part-time and extension programs as he saw it; and the failure, as he defined it, to implement new freshman admissions standards cutting back the zone of eligibility from 45 percent to 33⅓ percent, as called for in the Master Plan.[50]

The study of adult and extension education was undertaken by CCHE staff and outside consultants. It generated a fair amount of stress within the University of California and the California State Colleges. In the UC, considerable discussions at successive monthly president's cabinet meetings ensued, followed by a policy discussion including all of the campus chancellors, with the Regents Committee on Educational Policy,. This resulted in an agreement about an expanded role for university extension and the definition of a new concept for on-campus regular enrollment, "extended day" students, who would parallel the California State Colleges limited-student category. The UC proposal urged that state college extension include graduate and upper-division instruction on campus for degree candidates, and selected lower-division instruction for degree candidates; programs and activities then existing on campuses would be folded in. The practical effect of this policy, were it to be implemented, would be to curtail conventional state college extension activities beyond campuses. The university argued that state college programs must operate only on campuses and approved centers, and must be limited to students who are admissible degree candidates.

University of California economist and dean, Frank Kidner, who was the president's cabinet member responsible for relations with the state colleges, junior colleges, and education in general, and who played a major role in the practical and operating relationships between the UC and CSC in the 1960s, advanced the proposition that "the University maintains the only true extension service."[51] At the next cabinet meeting Kidner expressed his concern that the state colleges had appointed a statewide director of extension. Kidner carried this concern to the Coordinating Council arena. Kerr asked Kidner to discuss the state college position on extension and extended day programs and their funding with the director of finance and the legislative analyst.

The University of California was prevailing in the Coordinating Council's drafts. All of this was not lost on the state college leadership. In late July 1962, Chancellor Dumke wrote to CCHE director Richards, the opening sentences of his letter setting the tone: "Reports reaching me regarding the study of education for adults in California now being conducted by a survey team working with you and your staff are somewhat disquieting…. The University of California, I am told, formally has recommended that state colleges close offering extension courses altogether."[52] Dumke argued that the main emphasis of state college extension should continue to be upper-division credit courses. He did not argue for a state subsidy for extension. He defended his designation of one of the campus deans of educational services as a staff coordinator to gather information about extension practices. Dumke had asked Dean Raymond Doyle of San Francisco State to take on this responsibility.

In a sense this story has no ending. The Coordinating Council did make a descriptive report to the legislature. The major recommendation was to establish a State Committee on Continuing Education. Neither the University of California nor the California State Colleges achieved any short-term significant goal. Dean Paul Sheats, the administrator at the University of California long responsible for extension, represented the UC; the state colleges were represented seriatim by several individuals, as the chancellor's staff was being built—the appointment of an administrator responsible for extension or continuing education did not happen until 1971, when the first dean for continuing education took office.[53] With the 1971 appointment Ralph Mills as state college dean for continuing education, state college extension and academic outreach programs developed substantially; they are now pervasive in the state. In the longer run, both the state colleges and the University of California maintained the status quo.

In the 1960s through 1974, the CCHE addressed a wide range of issues. The staff work in the council profited from the guidance of director Willard Spalding, who stayed with the council to 1969, when he elected to return to Oregon and a professorship at Portland State University. Council reports addressed faculty salaries in all of the segments, general education, transfer programs from the redefined community colleges to the UC and CSC, the establishment and financing of Educational Opportunity Programs—the wide range of issues and topics attendant to the functioning of the three public higher education segments.

The Master Plan called for the diversion of a substantial number of students from the UC and the CSC to the junior colleges. The senior segments were to maintain a 40 percent / 60 percent ratio in the undergraduate student bodies between lower division and upper division. In the state colleges, the chancellor personally monitored this balance, as he did a number of aspects of the Master Plan.[54] The actual Master Plan goal was to reach the 40/60 balance by 1975. Dumke saw the early attainment of the 40/60 goal as an important matter for state funding.

The Master Plan did not significantly affect the functioning of the junior colleges. This worried some members of the legislature, as they watched the state college campuses pull together as a system. Senator Walter Stiern, a veteran member from Bakersfield, was vocal about his concern. Stiern had been close to Assemblywoman Dorothy Donahoe, the chair of the Assembly Education Committee and author of the first call to create a statewide plan for higher education. In 1967, Keith Sexton, Donahoe's former chief of staff and by then assistant director of the Coordinating Council, met Stiern's principal assistant and, rather by happenstance, discussed the governance of the junior colleges.[55]

They did a rough draft of a proposal to create for the junior colleges a statewide board that would have a chief executive officer. Their proposal would not eliminate district boards but provide for a quasi-regulatory board that would give statewide leadership with an appointed statewide chief administrative officer. Senator Stiern liked the proposal, and Sexton passed it by the Coordinating Council leadership, who also were favorable. Stiern introduced legislation; the Coordinating Council unanimously endorsed it, and the board of governors and state chancellor of the renamed California Community Colleges were born.

In the early 1970s, the legislature created a Joint Committee on Higher Education to review the 1960 Master Plan. The chair of the Joint Committee was Assembly Member John Vasconcellos, a Democrat from San Jose who had been elected in 1966, and who quickly became heavily involved with higher education matters.[56] Vasconcellos, or "Vasco," as he soon became to those who worked with him, including those in higher education, had a principal aide for his work on higher education, Patrick Callan, who was then new to Sacramento. Dissatisfaction with the Coordinating Council had become pervasive in Sacramento. The council was viewed as dominated by the groups it was designed to coordinate, if not regulate, and not capable of resolving issues that needed attention. The matter of extension and adult education, recited earlier, is illustrative of the legislative and executive concern. Vasconcellos, never reluctant to join an issue, brought the structure of the council to the legislature. He introduced legislation to create a new body, the California Postsecondary Education Commission, with a new and different membership structure. The Coordinating Council for Higher Education was abolished.

The biggest change was in membership; the new commission would have a majority of public members. This change, which took place in 1973, was not welcomed by the leadership of the California State University and Colleges or by the University of California, but it was not contested. Neither the council nor the commission was perceived to be a threat, but rather a necessary part of a complex state structure created by the Master Plan. The commission was charged by the legislature to be the primary and independent planning and coordinating agency for higher education.

Membership on the California Postsecondary Education Commission (CPEC) includes nine members representing the general public—three each appointed by the governor, the Speaker of the Assembly, and the Senate Rules Committee; two students appointed by the governor from lists of three to five nominees submitted by the three statewide student organizations of the three public segments; one member from each of the four state public education boards, the State Board of Education, the Board of Governors of the California Community Colleges, the Board of Regents of the University of California, and the Board of Trustees of the California State University and Colleges; and one member appointed by the governor to represent the independent California colleges and universities selected from a list submitted by the Association of Independent Colleges and Universities (the organization of almost all accredited independent California institutions).

The legislation creating CPEC, Assembly Bill 770, also established a Statutory Advisory Committee, composed of the heads of each of the public segments (the state superintendent, the president of the University of California, the chancellor of the California State University and Colleges, and the chancellor of the California Community Colleges) and a representative of the independent colleges and universities.

The 1973 legislation was signed by the governor and became effective on January 1, 1974. The commission essentially picked up where the council had ended. Little of note happened. Some of the routine functions that had been developed were important to the segments and to the maintenance of the Master Plan. The zones of eligibility for freshman admissions to the CSU remained at the top one-third of high school graduates and at the University of California the top one-eighth of high school graduates. The actual admissions standards had to be reviewed periodically against high school grading practices, for these shifted with time. Thus, the eligibility studies completed approximately every five years were important, and these gave assurance to the legislature and the governor that the Master Plan was being followed.

Similarly, the commission staff had the responsibility of doing salary studies. Both the UC and the CSU had comparison institutions; in the instance of the CSU, twenty institutions over the country were used. On the basis of these salary studies and other considerations, faculty and administrative salary ranges were determined by the board of trustees. These salary ranges were often not funded by the legislature, and salary lags were common. This salary methodology remains in effect.

Similarly, over the years, space standards were developed and used. One of the most important functions of both the CCHE and the CPEC was—and is—the review of proposals to establish a new campus or center by a community college district, the University of California, or the California State University. A declaration of legislative intent, contained in statute, provides that the commission must recommend positively for a site acquisition to proceed. Additionally, the segments must forward proposals for new programs for review and comment within sixty days; these are returned to the systems or districts. In fact, unlike the establishment of new sites, the segments are not bound to follow the commission staff review, and often do not. Many of these initiatives have their roots in the 1960s.

Patrick Callan moved on from the legislative staff to become head of the Higher Education Coordinating Agency, first in Montana and then in the state of Washington, and then returned in 1978 to California as executive director of the commission, with a warm welcome both in Sacramento and in the higher education community. Callan's judgment was respected, and the reports and proposals he made received attention. He was credible with the system heads as well, and he had the full support of the commission members.

David Saxon, the president of the University of California from 1975 to 1983, proposed the creation of an Education Round Table. This would include both Saxon and Glenn Dumke, as well as the chancellor of the Community Colleges, the state superintendent, and the CPEC director. Dumke was not an enthusiastic participant. He had spent a career maintaining a distance between government and higher education, at least in his own behavior and activity. The years of Callan and the Round Table were, however, positive ones, and productive working relationships were established. Dumke later commented that Callan was by far the most effective and productive executive director. There were no great moves, only steady progress. Callan had returned to California and CPEC a few months before Proposition 13 passed in June 1978, and he was inevitably drawn into the issues attendant to the implementation of Proposition 13, and the resulting cutbacks on higher education funding.

Callan left CPEC for the Education Commission of the States in 1986. He was succeeded by his deputy, William Pickens. Pickens had a sharp mind and could be a critic as well as an advocate. He became director just as yet another review of the Master Plan was initiated by the legislature, and as relationships between the California State University and the University of California were becoming more tense, in the context of a renewed effort by the CSU to secure the independent doctorate. Pickens was not reticent in his comments about either the University of California or the California State University. One of the issues the commission and Pickens were called upon to address was the establishment of a center in Contra Costa County, to be a branch of the Hayward (now East Bay) campus. Pickens was adamant in his opposition, and the statute creating CPEC gave the commission a veto. The force behind the Contra Costa proposal was trustee Dean Lesher, a newspaper publisher. Lesher eventually prevailed, despite the objections of Pickens and the fact that the president of the Hayward campus had no enthusiasm for the creation of a center. Chancellor Ann Reynolds and President David Gardner made common cause, and Pickens moved to a senior administrative position at California State University, Sacramento, where he became a valued and respected member of the campus leadership.

With the departures of Callan and Pickens, CPEC settled into a routine of doing studies and reports that were important; they had to be done to keep the machinery of higher education functioning. The eligibility studies, to keep the Master Plan admissions standards for the CSU and the UC on track, were essential, as were the faculty salary studies and methodology that had been carefully developed. Neither the commission nor its staff played a vital role in the planning and coordination of higher education in California. The participation of the segments of higher education declined. In the early years of the Coordinating Council, the chief executive officers of the segments, more often than not, would attend council meetings. Over time, deputies participated in place of the chief executives; participation then devolved to other staff members and then, frequently the director of the Sacramento office. Gray Davis became governor on January 1, 1999. His administration cut the CPEC budget from forty-eight to twenty-two positions and it has remained slightly below that level since.

In a 1984 interview, former chancellor Glenn Dumke commented on the Coordinating Council and its successor commission. He characterized the body as having been political at times. The contrast in two decisions made at the turn

31. Seated left to right: Author Hughes, President, University of San Diego; Patrick Callan, Executive Director, California Postsecondary Education Commission; W. Ann Reynolds, Chancellor; standing: Gerald Hayward, Chancellor, California Community Colleges; Bill Honig, Superintendent of Public Instruction; David Gardner, President, University of California.

of the century is substantial. The commission staff, and then the commission, supported the establishment of a new University of California campus at Merced. In a sense, the discussion about a new UC campus for the San Joaquin Valley revived the Master Plan discussion about the number of research university campuses that the state would need beyond the nine planned at that time. Within the University of California, there was little support beyond the senior administration and regents for a tenth campus. There was substantial support from legislators and political and civic leaders in the San Joaquin Valley. On yet another issue, the doctorate in education, CPEC staff completed a study, which they designed, that demonstrated the lack of any need for the doctorate; this was despite substantial need argued by K-12 and, especially, community college educators. In the end, the political process drove both decisions.

At times, the University of California and the California State University would make common cause, sometimes joined by either or both the California Community Colleges and independent college and university leadership. One such issue has been accountability. In 2007, the members of the Statutory Advisory Committee, representing the principals of the segments, including the private sector and the state superintendent of public instruction, together signed a strong letter to the executive director of CPEC; their letter, in a sense, had less to do with accountability, although that was the subject, than it had to do with working relationships and their perceived absence. The letter addressed a conflict between the assumptions used in the staff study about accountability and legislative direction, and asked for better working relationships. "This latter example is but one of many examples where we could offer guidance to the Commission, and could share information about several initiatives that would achieve common goals more realistically and effectively than policy options outlined. Collectively, these recommendations seem out of context and ill-informed."[57]

* * *

Did the leadership of the University of California and the California State Colleges in 1960 want a strong coordinating body? Did the political leadership of California, the governor and lay figures in the legislature, understand what would be needed over time? To the latter question, one answer is clear: legislative leaders did not want a coordinating entity in the constitution, an entity that would interfere with legislative control. The University of California leadership wanted a coordinating body that could legitimize reasonable growth and maintain the status quo, especially regarding the distribution of functions among the segments. The California State Colleges' leadership needed a coordinating body to help move forward the building of a system and the development of a mission beyond the pre–Master Plan status quo, but clearly not with any capacity to interfere with the growth and development of the CSC. The Coordinating Council was an extension of the Liaison Committee, created in 1945. The early lay leadership in the council saw it as not exercising a strong role, but exercising a necessary function. In some measure, the council was for all of higher education a legitimizing institution—it had to exist. The early CSC perception was that the council would play a leading role toward orderly growth of higher education, to adjudicate differences among the segments and play a lead role in financial advocacy.[58] Neither the leadership of the California State Colleges or the University of California wanted a strong council.

All of the segments of California higher education have on the whole operated in their individual "silos" over the years.[59] Leaders of higher education, public and private, have more to unite around than to divide around. The substantial, if not steep, decline in public financial support over the almost 50 years since the Master Plan, is evidence of the failure of the segments to pull together. The Council and the Commission have been more for protection than advice.

The Community Colleges

California's 110 community colleges and the 23 campuses of the California State University have been intertwined and interdependent for almost one hundred years, since the opening days of the Fresno Junior College in 1910 and that of the Fresno State Normal School in 1911. These were legally two separate governing boards on one campus with one president, one faculty, a comingled curriculum, and a comingled student body.

In the years from 1910–1911, some state colleges established junior college functions on their sites and these were important—essential, might be a better word—to building curricula beyond teacher education. One state college, Sacramento, was founded on a junior college campus and was a tenant of Sacramento Junior College for six years. Relationships between faculties and administrators were for the most part informal, and a spirit of cooperation generally prevailed among them. The most difficult relationships, then as now, were about the transfer of students from junior colleges to state colleges. In the late 1950s, prior to the Master Plan, the presidents of the junior colleges, the state colleges, and the chancellors of the University of California campuses still met to decide upon course transferability issues. The meetings were chaired by the president of the university, Robert Gordon Sproul, and were staffed by a senior statewide aide and former junior college president, Grace Bird, responsible for UC relations with the other education leaders. There were at the time only thirty junior colleges, nine state colleges, and five general University of California campuses.

The meetings were well attended; the discussions were direct; the decisions were unambiguous. Sproul presided, and he would declare a consensus on each agenda item after discussion. With Sproul's retirement, Clark Kerr suggested that the meetings continue, but with other campus academic administrators or faculty; the result was a first step toward bureaucratization of the articulation process. Similarly, among the institutions, there were direct relationships, and these were most productive. In 1958, a new director of admissions at a large (for that time) urban state college campus soon knew on a first-name basis the junior college deans and many of the presidents in the six to eight nearby junior colleges from which many students transferred.

One veteran observer suggested chaos theory as a description of junior college–state college relationships—the more chaos, the better it worked for students and for relationships. Individual students with individual transfer problems found someone who solved their problem. This may have worked in the 1950s, but would it in the future?

Joint meetings of state college and junior college presidents became routine in the late 1940s. Subsequently, as the numbers of junior colleges grew, the executive committee of the California Junior College Association met with state college presidents. The agenda for a February 2, 1961, meeting of the presidents of junior colleges and the state colleges, held at the San Francisco State College downtown center, is illustrative of the issues at that time; this was at the beginning point of Master Plan implementation.

What will the new governance structure be—how will guidelines and procedures in relationship[s] . . . be established? . . . May we anticipate uniformity in general education requirements for the State Colleges? . . . What should be the ultimate goal of a relationship between upper and lower divisions? . . . Can a common experience be identified in the lower division which will make less formal the transfer into the upper division? . . . Will the State Colleges continue to move lower division courses to upper division? . . . Would it be helpful if the State Colleges, in implementing the Master Plan, would work toward agreement with the University of California on transfer credit from State Colleges?[60]

Clearly, this agenda was built by the presidents from the junior colleges. There were other questions asked in this two page document. None of these issues were new. The state college presidents could have built a similar list. The important point is that the leadership of the two segments were talking past each other. Every question in the previous paragraph had an answer at the time, and no accurate answer would really have been acceptable to the junior college presidents. There was no coordination among the state colleges; no mechanism existed, nor were there relevant and useful relationships across campuses, either administrative or among faculty in the disciplines and professions/applied fields, to address these issues. The same was true in the junior colleges.

New mechanisms were needed to address the issues common to the three public segments. By far, the largest number of students moving from the junior colleges to baccalaureate programs transferred to the state colleges. The junior college–state college relations were not only important, but affected large numbers of people. In the 1960s, the articulation meetings that had been the province of presidents moved first to presidential designees, and then to delegations from the campuses, junior colleges, the University of California, and the state colleges. The purpose of the articulation conferences was to reach agreements on what would transfer from one institution to another.

The transfer of courses continued to be an issue. In 1967, the legislature changed the statewide structure for the junior colleges, moving the statewide office from the Department of Education and the state superintendent of public instruction. The legislation created the board of governors of the California Community Colleges, with a chancellor as the chief administrative officer. The individual community college districts remained, with their taxing authority, budget setting, and personnel responsibilities. Some expressed the opinion—in reality a hope—that the new structure would quickly emerge as an almost identical parallel to the recently created trustees of the California State Colleges. This line of thought overlooked the fact that the state colleges historically were state supported, while the junior colleges, from the beginning in Fresno, were locally supported.

Legislative interest in the relationships among the segments of public higher education remained high. A primary interest was the transfer of courses from the newly named California Community Colleges to the California State Colleges and the University of California. In 1970, state college chancellor Glenn Dumke responded to a legislative inquiry from the Joint Committee on Higher Education. In his letter, Dumke explained. "[B]ecause of their early development as autonomous institutions with a regional focus, each State College had well developed, but independent, articulation agreements with their 'feeder' community colleges. These agreements were based upon the particular curricular emphasis of the individual State Colleges, as well as the strength and curricular emphasis in the area community colleges. They were typically the result of many hours of conferences between the respective deans and faculty."[61] Dumke noted a new board of trustees policy permitting any accredited college to certify the completion of up to forty units of general education, while acknowledging that for "remaining units a student may present ... there is no blanket uniformity." He concluded his three-page letter, saying, "I believe that the segments are currently working together in such a way as to resolve any significant problems, and we intend to continue to work closely with the community colleges to overcome their concerns."

The transfer of courses from the California Community Colleges to the campuses of the California State University has remained, in one form or another, the single greatest problem between the two segments over the years and to this day. The Articulation Conference structure continued through the 1970s and into the 1980s. The most important question about the articulation process—was anyone paying attention—was really not answered. In 1987, the Education Round Table created the Intersegmental Coordinating Council (later renamed the Intersegmental Coordinating Committee [ICC]) as a creature of the Round Table. It was, among others of its charges, the successor to the Articulation Conference. The ICC was an organization bringing together issues at a statewide level and, in the public sectors, working with the central offices of the three public segments. Over the years, the ICC has quietly done foundational work on a variety of topics, including standards for English and mathematics, leading to action by the State Board of Education and the research and years of conversation that would lead to the Early Assessment Programs. The CSU, with Vice-Chancellor David Spence's leadership, wove the research into a program, agreed to by the State Board of Education, for the testing of high school juniors to determine whether they would need remedial attention as freshmen on a CSU campus. This program has allowed students who have needed to repair their competency to do so in a secondary school.

The statewide academic senates of the three public segments created in 1989 the Intersegmental Committee of the Academic Senates of the California Community Colleges, the California State University, and the University of California (ICAS). In 1990, that group developed an Intersegmental General Education Transfer Curriculum (IGETC, and pronounced "I getsee"), designed to "permit a student to transfer from a community college to a campus in either the California State University or the University of California systems without the need, after transfer, to take additional lower-division general education courses."[62]

The review of the Master Plan in the mid-1980s focused significantly on the California Community Colleges. The review pointed to the multiple points of leadership in the community colleges, the boards and superintendents/chancellors/presidents of more than seventy districts, and the board of governors and state chancellor at the state level. The legislature addressed the issue, and Assembly Bill 1725 (AB 1725, as it is still known) was adopted and signed by Governor Deukmejian. Largely drafted by community college people, including the legal counsel to the board of governors (Thomas Nussbaum, who later became state chancellor), the legislation created a complex governance structure. It addressed four areas: access, quality, accountability, and the development of a system.[63] The statute created by the legislation empowered a statewide Academic Senate for the community colleges. This had the effect of making the Academic Senate responsible not to the chancellor or the board of governors, but to the legislature; recognized in statute, the Academic Senate, would receive money in the annual state budget. The state chancellor was placed in a position where he or she would have to negotiate with multiple groups to secure agreement on an issue.

The IGETC curriculum was followed by some state college campuses in the 1990s, and not followed by others. The Munitz administration of the CSU, consistent with its decentralized approach to academic matters, relied on the individual campuses and their regional and other relationships with the community colleges. Munitz did initiate one joint meeting of the board of trustees and the board of governors. The meeting was amicable; there were no policy results. The CSU had been working on the implementation of new freshmen admissions standards that emphasized a college preparatory high school curriculum, an idea dating back to the beginning of Chancellor Ann Reynolds's leadership in 1982. In the mid-1990s, after years of discussion, the University of California agreed to a common college preparatory curriculum.

The chair of the statewide CSU Admissions Advisory Council, after a discussion with Chancellor Munitz, invited the state chancellor of the community colleges to lunch for a thorough discussion of a proposal that the board of governors might endorse the college preparatory curriculum. This would encourage high school students planning to attend a community college and undertake a transfer curriculum to study a college preparatory program in high school. The college prep curriculum would not be a requirement for entrance to a community college but a recommendation, something for students to consider. The meeting was not productive. The state chancellor said there was no way he could bring along all or even most of the district boards and superintendents/ presidents/chancellors, or the community college statewide Academic Senate, given the history of the community colleges and the varying interpretations of their mission. The matter was dropped. In the 2000 Master Plan discussions, the idea was discussed and dropped once again, only to be brought back to the table by a faculty member from Diablo Valley College in an open meeting of the Master Plan committee addressing academic programs. The members of the committee agreed with the proposal and incorporated it in their set of recommendations, but it was deleted subsequently by a senior member of the California State Legislature.[64]

The change in the chancellorship in 1998 brought Chancellor Charles Reed from Florida. Florida had a developed community college system, separate from the state university system, with structured and defined relationships between the community colleges and the state universities. There was a transfer associate degree, and there were explicit definitions of courses in the first two years of collegiate work, the lower division, between the community colleges and the state universities. There was little slippage in transfer of courses. In contrast, in California, community college transfer students often would accumulate more than sixty community college units, even though only sixty units could transfer; frequently, courses intended to meet general education and lower-division requirements for a major would not match the specific requirements of a state college. This was simply the result of inadequate information in the hands of students and the widely varying lower-division requirements on the twenty-three CSU campuses, for both general education and majors.

David Spence, Reed's vice-chancellor for academic affairs in Florida, soon came to California as executive vice-chancellor and chief academic officer. While baccalaureate degree requirements were not the first priority for Spence or Reed, they did address them. In 2002, they questioned the 124-unit minimum for the bachelor's degree. After learning that the number 124 was a legacy from the days when students were required to take a half-unit physical education course each semester, they proposed a reduction to a required 120 units, and this was adopted by the trustees. Engineering and a few other faculty disciplinary groups argued for exceptions, and provision was made for these.

They next brought to the table, in 2003, in the executive council the number of units students were actually completing for the baccalaureate degree. The number was substantially in excess of 120 or 124 units. The average community college transfer student completed a total of 157 units, when only 120 were required for most baccalaureate degrees. Certainly, some students changed majors, but this was not a significant cause of the imbalance. It was the result of students simply taking more units than necessary, either at a community college or CSU campus and, more often, the need to meet CSU campus lower-division specific requirements in general education or a major. Reed and Spence argued that this was wasteful of students' time and the resources of both students and the state.

Spence and Reed argued that in states with numbers of community colleges, and where transfer has been handled well, "[T]here is a common curriculum in the lower division, a common curriculum through each major. . . . The test is that the student from community college A [who] transfers to any of the twenty-three CSU campuses ... will have taken the right courses and won't have to retake courses."[65] Spence asserted that faculty groups by subject matter or major fields should agree on common lower-division curriculum. The conversation moved to the CSU statewide Academic Senate, and that body, after considerable discussion, agreed to encourage and support faculty groups in the disciplines and applied fields to work together—community college faculty and CSU faculty across the two systems.

Spence took the discussion to the community college leadership, first to the presidents. The initial conversation was productive. But Spence also took the idea to Senator Jack Scott, the former Pasadena City College president and chair of the Senate Education Committee. Spence's motivation was to gain support for the concept among CSU people and the statewide Academic Senate immediately. The community college leadership did not see Spence's move in that context, but rather saw it as placing pressure on them. Scott introduced legislation mandating the process, and this blindsided the community college presidents as well as some others; they did not accept Spence's reasoning. The project proceeded, but there was anger in the community colleges. The goal was to make it possible for a community college transfer student to come with sixty transferable units, including a forty-unit common core across all campuses; potential transfer students were to apply to the CSU campus of their choice by the time they had reached forty-five units, declare a major, and, in turn, be informed of any specific courses they needed for their major at the campus of their choice, so that they might complete these within the sixty units.[66] All of this required community college faculty to go through massive reviews of potential transfer curriculum and courses. This was initiated, and in 2008 it is still underway.

The Lower Division Transfer Patterns project, while a massive undertaking, has not been as productive as was hoped for. Reed, Spence, and Spence's successor, Gary Reichard, maintain a key point: the curriculum leading to the baccalaureate degree belongs to the CSU, as it is the CSU that awards the degree. This point is not well accepted by community college leaders and faculty. To the point of this writing, the California Community Colleges and the California State University faculty have reached agreement on courses that satisfy requirements across institutional lines in about 50 percent of the reviews.[67]

Other matters have been examined over the years. In 1994, a trustee, Ralph Pesqueira, brought the issue of remedial education to the trustees and then to a general CSU discussion; Pesqueira conducted hearing-like meetings on every CSU campus. His objective was to reduce the need for freshmen remedial instruction on CSU campuses. At that time it exceeded 50 percent of entering freshmen in English and mathematics on almost all CSU campuses. There was fierce resistance to Pesqueira's thinking on most campuses. Again, the issues became autonomy and academic freedom. The trustees eventually adopted a policy mandating percentage reductions in remedial instruction beyond the turn of the century, and urging CSU campuses to work with community colleges to address the issue. Only one campus, San Francisco State, responded, developing a relationship in which the local community colleges would offer the remedial work, and the university would stop much remedial instruction. On the whole, community college faculty and administrative leadership were supportive of the idea; a few additional CSU campuses in ensuing years have joined San Francisco State's efforts.

The issue eventually became faculty control of the curriculum. A cynical point of view is that the real issue is budget and faculty positions. It is arguable that the community college mission more nearly addresses provision for remedial instruction than does the CSU mission. One of the interesting pieces of fallout was at the Sacramento campus. The Sacramento region has a quarter century history of effective working relationships among the three public higher education segments and the schools, the K-12 sector. The remedial conversation inevitably migrated to the group known as Colleagues in Conversation, the leadership of UC Davis, CSU Sacramento, the community college districts and campuses, and the K-12 districts in the region. While the Sacramento State faculty resistance centering in the English department was strong, the University of California Davis faculty and administration welcomed the Los Rios Community College District as a partner to offer remedial instruction for its students. This was a precursor to the later Los Rios district establishment of a quasi-branch on the University of California Davis campus to offer lower-division work, an achievement with significant long-term policy potential.

By 2007, the Early Assessment Program initiated by the CSU earlier in the decade was clearly productive. The CSU leadership had not sought UC or community college involvement in undertaking the program. Legislators became interested, and in the 2008 session, the ever-present Senator Jack Scott introduced legislation authorizing the California Community Colleges to use the Early Assessment Program. This was a positive and cooperative move.

* * *

The California Community Colleges and the California State University need each other. This is not an accident. It is by design. The Master Plan of 1960, and every succeeding act of the legislature since, has explicitly stated or assumed the partnership of the CSU and the CCC. Nowhere is this more clear than in the number of graduates of the twenty-three California State University campuses. In the 2006–07 year, 70,887 students received baccalaureate degrees from the CSU. Of these, 38,827 (54.8 percent) were transfer students from California Community Colleges.

One of California's well-known commentators on higher education, Michael Kirst, a distinguished professor at Stanford University, stated in an interview that a major problem with the structure of public higher education in California is that the segments live in "silos": there is not sufficient cooperation or joint anticipation of issues to come. The segments and their faculties, leaders, and board members are in a defensive mode with respect to each other. There is some validity for this point of view. Yet in a focus group of community college leaders, when there were critical comments about CSU understanding of the community colleges and their work, one of the prominent participants argued that "articulation is an issue we have made complex . . . it doesn't have to be as hard as we have made it." The same person later observed that "we could within six months get uniform transfer among all the systems in this state if we decided that was something we wanted to do, and we were all agreeing to do it."[68]

The California Community Colleges are in a difficult governance situation, and this makes working with the other segments of higher education complex. Governance of the California Community Colleges is in many ways anachronistic. The junior colleges in California were established by school districts, and they were supported to the greatest extent by the taxpayers of the districts. They "belonged" to the people of the district, and the governing boards were elected by the people of the district. The parallel with the normal schools and state colleges is not a useful one, although it does help to understand some CSU behavior even to this day. In 1978, Proposition 13 changed the base of community college financial support to the state, but it did not change a culture of almost seventy years regarding the sense of ownership of the district community colleges. That culture had in fact been reaffirmed by the legislature and governor, in the 1967 legislation creating the board of governors and the state chancellor's position. The legislation did not address the distribution or redistribution of governing authority. The same culture was again affirmed with AB 1725 in 1987. This is a situation not easily changed. Thus, extraordinary skills and personal characteristics are demanded of community college and CSU leaders who work with transfer issues.

I came to California in 1958, just fifty years ago, from the point of preparation of this manuscript. My work in my first role involved me heavily with colleagues and students in all categories of education—the schools, what were then the junior colleges, "the University," and both public and private institutions. We are all in the same business, or, perhaps more elegantly put, the same enterprise. We and our students have everything to gain, for our students and for our missions, by working together—and much to lose by not working collaboratively.

Working Together

Governance in the California State University was not easily resolved. The history of the development of the individual campuses, the desire of many, especially faculty, to parallel the University of California, and the turbulence of the times intersecting with a rapid rate of sociopolitical and economic change virtually guaranteed that the maturing of the California State University would only be able to occur over years. The very nature of governance in universities is people-dependent. The styles and skills of key administrators and faculty, and most certainly governing board members, affect governance, as do governments and political leaders. It is arguable that the CSU reached some point of maturity in the 1990s, though clearly the still unsettled and unresolved matter of collective bargaining remains.

In the 1990s a pattern of overall policy leadership and operational decentralization cognizant of the unique characteristics of the campuses emerged. Operations and the initial definition of the unique mission of each campus are largely at the campus level. At the center, the overall governance of the CSU, is policy in a broad sense and the evolution of the overarching mission of the California State University as a whole. Structures are in place for the people of the campuses to have a give and take relationship with the center. These are used, sometimes effectively, sometimes less than effective. An uneasy balance has been reached about centralization and decentralization.

The leaders in the governance of the CSU are driven by both internal and external pressures. Internal pressures are substantial, and they always will be. Just as in the broader political arena, interest groups are numerous. The faculty as a whole is an interest group, but so are many subsets of faculty, from disciplinary groups to full-time or part-time faculty; so are staff and administrators; and the interests of students must be significant. Interest groups in the community and the greater society are abundant; these often develop around specific issues, many external to higher education. The pressures on all of the leadership, not only presidents and the chancellor, are substantial, as individuals take their roles seriously. The most important pressure is to do "what is right," but for whom? The concept of the common good once was widely understood, as was the concept of following a moral compass. The world of universities is inevitably a political one, and the fact that there is always a well-educated faculty and group of administrators does not make life in a university any simpler than life generally.

The greatest point of external pressure on decision making in the California State University is financial. The Master Plan had two major shortcomings. One of these was an assumption, essentially a bipartisan assumption, that the state would adequately support public higher education to the end of the defined life of the Master Plan in 1975, and at least implicit was a promise of support indefinitely. The promise lasted six years beyond 1960, and then encountered ideology, a political point of view that minimized government and all that it does. The financing of public higher education in California has been, since 1966, an unending story of financial pressure, some the result of ideology about public funding, some of shortage of funds reasonably available. Without question, this has put pressure on the trustees and chancellor, often from two directions, as individuals on campuses express discontent with what they describe as the failure of the system to produce adequate resources.

The second shortcoming of the Master Plan has directly to do with governance. The Master Plan did not provide an adequate structure for coordinating and planning higher education in California. The Coordinating Council for Higher Education and the California Postsecondary Education Commission simply have not been adequate for a variety of reasons, beginning with the initially proposed membership exclusively representing the segments. Both CCHE and its successor agency, CPEC, have done useful things, and CPEC continues to accomplish tasks that are essential to the orderly functioning of higher education. Patrick Callan as executive director did probe far-reaching policy questions. The audience was not adequate to the speaker.

There are two sets of interests at play in support for higher education. The state interest is in the adequacy of colleges and universities to meet the public need for higher education, often understood by many in terms of the economic well-being of a society. The state interest is also in the social and cultural well-being of a society. But embedded in the good society is support for the well-being of individuals. The second set of interests at play are the institutional ones, and these are often not selfless. Institutions almost inevitably want to maximize what they see as self-interest. It takes courageous individuals and leaders to understand and advocate a mission that has less color or perhaps status in the eyes of some.

At the time of this writing, California, along with the country, is facing its most severe financial crisis since the depression of the 1930s. This must be a test of the leadership in higher education. Can it draw together in the face of the financial crisis? Out of this crisis, which is far more than financial, can the leadership fashion a coordinating and planning mechanism that will work? Does higher education want coordination and planning?

Higher education in California is in need of a core of leadership that speaks to higher education and the common good, to people and colleges and universities as the indispensable foundation of a healthy and viable society. That was the understanding and the promise of the Master Plan.

Notes

[1] This segment about the evolution of the role of the board of trustees uses material from a daylong trustee focus group discussion on April 28, 2006. Trustees present were Roberta Achtenberg, Wallace Albertson, James Considine, William Hauck, Louis Heilbron, all former board chairs; Considine was the alumni trustee for eight years. Additional sources are interviews conducted by the author: William D. Campbell, May 18, 2006; Martha Fallgatter-Walda, October 13, 2006; Louis Heilbron, December 10, 2003, November 7, 2005.

[2] Trustee focus group, 5, the CSU Archives.

[3] Office of the Chancellor, "The California State University Statistical Abstract to July 2006," Long Beach, September 2007.

[4] *Ibid.*, Governor Pat Brown appointed thirty-three trustees; eight became chairs of the board. Governor Reagan appointed nineteen trustees; five became chairs. Governor Jerry Brown appointed twenty-four trustees, including student and alumni faculty trustees; two became chairs. George Deukmejian appointed twenty-two trustees; five became chairs. Pete Wilson appointed eighteen; three became chairs. In his nearly five years, Gray Davis made fourteen appointments; three became chairs. In his first three years as governor, Arnold Schwarzenegger made fifteen appointments; one became chair in 2008. *Ibid.*

[5] Trustee William Hauck, trustee focus group, 14.

[6] The auditorium was named by the board of trustees for Glenn Dumke, after his death in 1989 at the age of seventy-one.

[7] Trustee focus group, 14–16, 39–40.

[8] The young campus administrator was the author.

[9] Minutes of organizational meeting, the Academic Senate of the California State Colleges, May 14, 1963, CSU Archives.

[10] *Ibid.*

[11] There were two focus groups of former statewide Academic Senate chairs and other leaders. The June 7, 2005, group included Theodore Anagnoson, David Elliott, Judson Grenier, and Lee Kerschner. The June 8, 2005, group included Robert Cherny, Harold Goldwhite, Jacqueline Ann K. Kegley, Robert Kully, Leonard Mathy, and Sandra Wilcox. This citation is from page five of the June 8 group record.

[12] *Ibid.*

[13] Leonard Mathy, memorandum to Chancellor Glenn Dumke, October 4, 1963, CSU Archives.

[14] Academic Senate of the California State Colleges, *Principles and Procedures for Academic Due Process: Rights of Academic and Academic-Administrative Personnel*, report, March 19, 1964, CSU Archives.

[15] The full story of the ad hoc committee can be found in Chapter 3 of this work, which addresses the 1960s.

[16] Papers of the Academic Senate of the California State University, "Principles and Policies," vol. 1, 1988, CSU Archives.

[17] *Ibid.*

[18] This section addressing the development of collective bargaining uses the discussions of the two focus groups of senate chairs (note 11 above) and Judson Grenier's interview of David Elliott, May 24, 2001, CSU Archives. President James Cleary of Northridge and the author were the two presidents involved.

[19] Academic Senate of the California State University, "Baccalaureate Education in the California State University," 1997.

[20] Focus group on governmental relations, Sacramento (Les Cohen, John Kehoe, Dorena Knepper, Scott Plotkin, Karen Zamarippa), January 24, 2006, 9ff.

[21] California State Student Association, "A Short History of Shared Governance in the CSU," (undated, but subsequent to 2001; probably 2005). This section also uses material from the California State Student Association web site of May, 2008, and a telephone interview by the author with Susana Gonzalez, executive director of CSSA, September 24, 2008.

[22] The author did a focus group with four senior CSU presidents: Warren Baker, Robert Corrigan, James Rosser, and John Welty, on October 23, 2006; this four-hour conversation informs the section about presidents. The values expressed in the first paragraph are those of the author. The author has benefited from twenty-seven years as a California State University president, and interaction with colleagues in the CSU from 1958 to the present.

[23] C. Mansel Keene and Lois Feldheym, oral history interviews by Lawrence de Graaf, August 6, and August 11, 1987, CSU Archives.

[24] The author was the president on the search committee.

[25] CSU presidents' focus group, 12ff.

[26] See Chapter 10.

[27] CSU presidents' focus group, 40.

[28] See Chapter 12.

[29] See Chapter 8 for the more detailed story of the emergence of technology in the 1990s and the 2000s.

[30] California Postsecondary Education Commission, *Final Annual Report on Faculty and Administrative Salaries in California Public Higher Education, 1984–85*, 1984. The comparison institutions for 1983–84 and for 2006–07 are identified in Chapter 10.

[31] Minutes of the Board of Trustees of the California State University (hereafter cited as "board of trustees"), January 1991.

[32] Minutes, board of trustees, September 1993.

[33] Minutes, board of trustees, September 1997.

[34] Minutes, board of trustees, September 2007, October 2007.

[35] E. Alden Dunham, *Colleges of the Forgotten Americans: A Profile of State Colleges and Regional Universities*, the Carnegie Commission on Higher Education (New York: McGraw Hill, 1969). The author was present at the dedication ceremony; the meeting of the board of trustees on the next day was his first as a president.

[36] Glenn S. Dumke, oral history interview by Judson Grenier, July 18, 1981–March 27, 1987.

[37] William Hauck, trustee focus group, 9.

[38] Honorable Norman Epstein, interview by Judson Grenier, June 1, 1995, 14, CSU Archives.

[39] The author is the former chair of the council; he returned to the role and remained in it until his retirement in 2003.

[40] The paragraphs about Chancellor Ann Reynolds draw from many interviews and focus groups, most especially from W. Ann Reynolds, Lee Kerschner, Caesar Naples, the presidents' group, the admissions group, and the author's papers and notes.

[41] Barry Munitz, interview by the author, November 18, 2005.

[42] Martha Fallgatter Walda, interview by the author, October 13, 2006.

[43] The following interviews were conducted by the author: Barry Munitz, November 18, 2005; David Spence, March 17, 2005; Richard West, August 14, 2006; Charles Reed, December 20, 2006; presidents' focus group, October 23, 2006.

[44] *A Master Plan for Higher Education in California, 1960–1975.*

[45] California State Department of Education, *A Master Plan*, 3.

[46] California Legislature, 1960, First Extraordinary Sess., SB no. 33, March 9, 1960.

[47] Christopher was deputy secretary of state in the Carter administration and probably received the most public notice in the role when he negotiated the release of the U.S. diplomats held in the U.S. Embassy in Tehran; he was secretary of state in President Clinton's first term.

[48] Keith Sexton, interview by the author, January 26, 2007; John M. Smart, interview by the author, March 6, 2007.

[49] Minutes, Committee on Finance, the University of California, June 23, 1961. The author has reviewed minutes of the presidents cabinet and regents for the period of the study on extension; copies of these are in the CSU Archives.

[50] Clark Kerr letter to Buell Gallagher, August 20, 1961, CSU Archives.

[51] Minutes of the president's cabinet, the University of California, June 13, 1962.

[52] Glenn Dumke, letter to John Richards, July 20, 1962, CSU Archives.

[53] In the mid-1960s, the author represented the state colleges on this committee for about two years.

[54] When I was dean of students at the Chico campus from 1964 to 1968, I received a personal phone call from the chancellor, probably in 1966, noting that the campus lower-division enrollment exceeded 40 percent. The chancellor wanted to know what the campus was doing to assure that this did not happen again.

[55] Sexton, interview, 13–14. Actually, Stiern's assistant and Sexton had been to Reno, and on the drive back to Sacramento they talked about the matter. By the time they reached Sacramento, as Sexton tells the story, they had a draft.

[56] In his first full month in office in January 1967, Vasconcellos, at his own request, met with all of the deans of students in the California State Colleges, to discuss student unrest.

[57] Statutory Advisory Committee, California Postsecondary Education Commission letter to Murray Haberman, Executive Director, CPEC, July 26, 2007. This section about the Coordinating Council for Higher Education and the Commission on Postsecondary Education has benefited from interviews by the author with the following: Glenn S. Dumke, July 18, 1981, and March 27, 1987; W. Ann Reynolds, August 19, 2004; Ellis McCune, June 23, 2005; Barry Munitz, November 18, 2005; Charles Reed, December 20, 2006; John Smart, March 6, 2007; Murray Haberman, January 24, 2007; Dorothy Knoell, March 14, 2005; Keith Sexton, January 26, 2007; and William Pickens, June 25, 2007.

[58] Glenn S. Dumke, interview, April 1984, Regional Oral History Project, the Bancroft Library, University of California Berkeley, 19; see also Dumke's letter to Jesse M. Unruh, August 5, 1969, in an appendix to the interview.

[59] The author is indebted to Professor Michael Kirst of Stanford University for the concept. See Michael Kirst, interview by the author, November 7, 2005.

[60] Agenda, Joint Conference, State College Presidents—California Junior College Association Executive Committee, February 2, 1961, CSU Archives.

[61] Glenn S. Dumke, letter to the Honorable William Campbell, Chair, Joint Committee on Higher Education, April 9, 1970, CSU Archives.

[62] "Intersegmental General Education Transfer Curriculum," March 28, 1990, CSU Archives.

[63] Chancellor David Mertes, Assembly Subcommittee on Higher Education Oversight Hearing on the Implementation of AB 1725, March 20, 1990.

[64] The author was a member of the Master Plan group that heard and recommended the Diablo Valley College faculty member's proposal.

[65] David Spence, interview by the author, March 17, 2005, 15.

[66] Spence, interview, 14–18.

[67] Focus group with senior community college administrators (Brice Harris, Gerald Hayward, Thomas Nussbaum, David Viar), interview by the author, November 8, 2006.

[68] In addition to the focus group and interview with David Spence, interviews by the author with the following were important to this discussion of California Community College relationships: Senator Dede Alpert, April 18, 2007; Dr. Penny Edgert (Intersegmental Coordinating Committee), November 20, 2008; Dr. Cristy Jensen (California State University Sacramento), May 27, 2005; Mr. Allison Jones (CSU assistant vice-chancellor for academic affairs), November 20, 2008; Dr. Dorothy Knoell (retired, California Postsecondary Education Commission), March 14, 2005; former Chancellor Barry Munitz, November 18, 2005; Dr. William Pickens (retired, California State University, Sacramento, California Postsecondary Education Commission), June 25, 2007; Chancellor Charles Reed, December 20, 2006; Senator Jack Scott, April 18, 2007; Dr. John Smart (the California State University), March 6, 2007.

Chapter 12

From Orange Book to Compact: Financing the California State University

The Master Plan set the stage for the board of trustees to take responsibility for the financial administration of the California State Colleges. The promise of the Master Plan was to provide, in statute, the structures and processes for flexible financial administration parallel to those of the constitutionally independent University of California. This was not to be. In the years immediately after the 1960 adoption of the Master Plan, each year the legislature would reaffirm the intent of the Master Plan about board responsibility for financial administration, but there was no follow-through. Thus, the story of financial administration of the California State University for almost fifty years is one of establishing credibility, putting in place structures and practices and customs that would simultaneously serve the CSU's mission, and provide a positive working relationship with state government. It's a story of building. Boyd Horne, then a young financial analyst and one of the few individuals to move from the State Department of

---

This chapter about the finances of the California State University was read in draft by two retired veterans of the CSU business affairs and finance staff, Boyd Horne, former Assistant Vice-Chancellor for Business Affairs, and John Richards, former Director of the Budget. The author appreciates their comments and corrections and remains responsible for the judgments expressed here and in the narrative. Horne reminded the author of his omission of a section about the lottery (doubtless due to the author's strong disapproval of the lottery as public policy); Horne drafted two paragraphs about the lottery, and sent them to the author, who has used them here.

Education to the chancellor's office, was able to assert years later, "[I]n 1961, everyone thought we had all the financial authority we would ever need."[1]

The 1950s had seen great growth in state college enrollments. The tradition of each campus preparing its own budget and defending it in Sacramento with the Department of Finance and ultimately the legislature, was well established. The Department of Education was only minimally involved; staff in the Department's Division of State Colleges prepared summaries and assisted the campus business managers. In their monthly Sacramento meetings, the presidents compared budget ideas and proposals. Growth led the presidents to ask the business managers to compare campus budgets and reach at least some measure of agreement about what would be needed to support various campus programs. The detail of budget discussions among presidents was great. One set of minutes reveals a discussion about travel budgets and an argument among presidents about the cost of travel relative to distance from Sacramento, San Francisco, and Los Angeles. The business managers made some progress in developing standards for budgeting, and thus they and the presidents were sometimes able to present a common front to the Department of Finance.

In the 1950s, the Department of Finance undertook a number of studies about various aspects of state college budgeting. The study that most affected campus operations was about campus administration structures and funding for these. This 1950 study, known more by its number, 828 (or as the Chandler report), than by the title "Administrative Staffing in the State Colleges," defined a common pattern of administration, roles, and positions. Variations for the sizes of campuses were provided. Each campus would have a president, four deans, and a business manager, and other positions. In practice, presidents used positions variously. This study defined campus administrations and programs for more than a dozen years, extending into the early years of the board of trustees and the newly created system of state colleges.

The campus chief academic officers, uniformly called deans of instruction, learned from the work of the Department of Finance. Heretofore, each campus faculty allocation had been based on the skill of a president or business manager negotiating a figure with the Department of Finance, and maintaining or increasing this in the legislature. Presidents would bring programs and proposals that had community support or legislative interest to the Sacramento bargaining process. The deans built what became known as the faculty staffing formula. The formula was complex and technical and subject to interpretation. The deans proposed to the presidents a detailed formula that projected every section of every course to be offered in the succeeding budget year. Enrollments were projected. Every course had a classification as lecture, laboratory, or supervision, and a mode and level of instruction. Courses were assigned to a lengthy list of categories. Distinctions were made; faculty time for a physics laboratory, faculty time for a physical education activity class, faculty time for a history professor in a lecture hall, all of the myriad instructional roles of faculty were addressed. The presidents agreed with the concept, and negotiations with the Department of Finance ensued. The faculty staffing formula was implemented in the 1957–58 year, and was used into the early 1970s. It remained a factor in budgeting until the early 1990s. In some ways, it was a sophisticated program budget for determining the number of faculty needed to serve the variety of academic programs, but it was a set structure built upon an assumption that one size fits all across all campus lines.[2]

With the implementation of the Master Plan, policy and administrative responsibility for the state colleges moved from the State Department of Education to the board of trustees and the newly established chancellor's office. The transition headquarters of the chancellor's office was for a time in Sacramento. The first chancellor, Buell Gallagher, was from New York and not familiar with either California politics or the operation of its state government. An early decision to move the chancellor's office and the state college headquarters to Los Angeles was not well received in many quarters of state government. The move took place on December 1, 1961. The political skills of Don Leiffer, the administrative officer in the transition year and later executive vice-chancellor, were positive, but Leiffer would remain in the chancellor's office only to May 1962; Leiffer was an advocate for keeping the chancellor's office in Sacramento. Gallagher simply did not devote time to the Sacramento scene, and the relative alienation of the new system headquarters, particularly from the Department of Finance, was substantial.[3]

An early issue in the 1960s was student fees. California had a historic policy opposing tuition in public higher education, but the practice of imposing fees was accepted and long standing. The theoretical basis for this policy was that tuition would pay for costs of instruction, whereas fees would pay for some things outside of the formal instructional program. Student fees were modest on state college campuses. In 1959, a proposal to raise the materials and service fee from twelve dollars per semester to fifteen met fierce student and faculty resistance. By 1963, the basic student fee was thirty-eight dollars per semester. Out of state students, who had for years paid an additional fee, were charged two hundred and fifty dollars each semester. Student fees were an issue early and remain a contentious subject to the present.

The establishment of the chancellor's office brought new individuals to the financial administration of the state colleges. During Buell Gallagher's brief tenure, he recommended to the board of trustees the appointment of John Richardson to the post of vice-chancellor for business affairs. Richardson was an experienced public administrator. He had been director of finance in the state of Oregon and subsequently vice president of the Asia Foundation in San Francisco. Richardson recruited three division chiefs, George Clucas, an experienced Cal Poly administrator, as chief of budget planning, George Merrill, a veteran administrator of nonprofits, as chief of auxiliary and business services, and Harry Harmon, a senior campus architect at UCLA, as chief of facilities planning.

Financial administration in the early 1960s focused on building a new set of working relationships. The chancellor's office staff in finance was for the most part new to the California State Colleges. George Clucas played a key role due to his experience on the Cal Poly campus. The Master Plan had specified that the state colleges would have a financial administrative structure parallel to the University of California. Under the Department and State Board of Education, decision making was centralized in the State Department of Finance. With the establishment of the state college system, the legislature did provide the trustees with full and independent authority over academic and personnel matters, but did not follow through on the Master Plan provision for financial administration. In the annual budget act, the legislature stated each year, for several years, that the board of trustees "should have such authority," but as a practical matter, the legislature was not willing to relinquish Department of Finance and, ultimately, legislative control. Thus, the cumbersome review by the Department of Finance staff and the line-item control of the legislature continued.[4]

The most eventful financial occurrence in the early years of the board was the miscalculation of the cost of a faculty salary increase for the 1964–65 year. When corrected, this miscalculation resulted in a cost that exceeded the state appropriation for this purpose. The cost was reduced by implementing a 1.8 percent salary cut for the last three months of the fiscal year, a cut that applied to all faculty at the rank of associate professor and above, and to staff at comparable pay levels. The political uproar in and out of the state colleges was loud. A shake-up on the chancellor's staff became inevitable, though it was not clear where the responsibility for the error in calculations occurred.[5] In this context, John Richardson resigned as vice-chancellor for business affairs; he was soon was appointed mayor of Washington, DC (then an appointed, not an elected position). Harry Brakebill, by then vice-president for business affairs at San Francisco State College, became vice-chancellor. Brakebill brought years of financial campus experience, his involvement as a senior administrator in the transition of 1960–62 from the State Department of Education to the board of trustees, great credibility in Sacramento and within the state colleges, and a solid working relationship and level of confidence with Chancellor Glenn Dumke, from Dumke's years as president of San Francisco State. Under Brakebill's leadership, a special assignment was made to Boyd Horne for the calculation and implementation of salary increase costs, which became a rigorous process. There was never a reoccurrence of the problem.

One of Brakebill's first responsibilities was to lead a newly created Committee on Fiscal Responsibility. This committee addressed relationships and responsibilities; budget formulation; levels of support; budget administration; accounting and reporting; three task forces on self-supporting activities; noninstructional activities; college foundations; and the financial administration of summer session and extension programs. Membership in the committee and in the task forces was drawn from faculty (the statewide Academic Senate) and campus and chancellor's office administrators, and included two students. Each task force was chaired by a campus president save two, one of which was chaired by an officer of the statewide Academic Senate, and the other by a campus dean of students. The work of each task force was openly circulated. In a sense, the best talent was drawn upon to complete a full review of financial administration within the new system. The committee consolidated the work of the task forces and assembled a report to the trustees. The report was without question a political document; it was designed to achieve from the legislative and executive branches fiscal authority that was politically attainable. The trustees approved the report, and a three-phase program was submitted to the legislature. Phase One addressed the authority of the trustees to move money within budgets and individual campus appropriations, the capacity to classify and control positions, and, finally, the capacity to administer the fiscal affairs of extension, summer-session, and other self-support programs. Phase Two gained further control for the trustees to transfer funds. Phase Three required five years to achieve. Historically, each college had its own appropriation. The proposal provided that the trustees should receive a single appropriation for all campuses and permitted the transfer of funds among the colleges.

The 1.8 percent salary cut, as the matter was commonly referred to at the time, was a political nightmare, most especially for the chancellor and his staff, and it doubtless contributed to the political disorder of the later years of the 1960s. Clearly however, it provided the circumstance for the California State Colleges to become free of line-item budget control and assume both authority and responsibility for programs and activities. The story of fiscal administration hardly concluded with these moves, but they were a major beginning. Brakebill was able to assert, in a 1987 oral history interview, that "at this time all the goals were achieved."[6]

* * *

The election of Ronald Reagan to the governorship in November 1966 ushered in a new era in the financing of public higher education in California. Reagan's first budget, transmitted to the legislature in January 1967, called for drastic cuts in state spending for higher education. For the state colleges, this proposed cut was 28 percent from the 1967–68 budget proposal, a proposal based upon existing understandings with Finance and the legislature, projected enrollment growth, and the Master Plan. The trustees' request was for $213 million; the governor's proposed budget was for $154 million. The 1966–67 budget was $175 million, so there would be an actual reduction from the current year levels. The proposed budget created controversy in higher education, in the media, and among civic and political leaders. The proposed budget recommended tuition for state college students at the level of $150 to $160 per year.

The Master Plan report, while inadequate to the issue of financing public higher education, had addressed the matter of tuition. The Master Plan noted that students "contribute directly to the financing of college programs by the payment of tuition or fees." The report went on to define tuition and fees: "[t]uition is defined generally as student charges for teaching expenses, whereas fees are charges to students either collectively or individually, for services not directly related to instruction, such as health, special clinical services, job placement, housing, recreation." The Master Plan emphasized the legislative action of the 1867–68 session, in creating the University of California. The legislature was specific that public higher education institutions in California would not charge tuition to "bonafide legal residents of the state."[7] Nonresident tuition was charged and covered a portion of the cost of instruction in both the California State Colleges and the University of California. In 1959, the legislature had authorized nonresident tuition for junior colleges.

The tuition issue was joined. On a 12–3 vote, the trustees opposed tuition; Chancellor Dumke strongly opposed tuition. The media reported that private colleges and universities favored tuition in the state colleges and the University of California.[8] Faculty senates on UC and CSC campuses passed resolutions and urged individual faculty members to lobby legislators. The Reagan administration proposals for tuition were not successful, but there was a modest increase in student fees (from $86 to $108 for an academic year). The issue may have been joined but it was hardly resolved. Fees can be substantial, when defined as the Master Plan had defined them—to include laboratory fees, health, athletics, student activities and services—and the definition can be a moving one. The Master Plan did not really develop a policy for the support of public higher education. The Reagan budget proposals were addressed in the legislature, and eventually compromises were reached. A new and reduced level of support for the state colleges was a result.

Harry Brakebill redirected the work of the business affairs staff in the chancellor's office. George Clucas, the first chief of the budget unit, was both a professional administrator and an academic; he elected to return to the San Luis Obispo campus as an academic dean and did so. Brakebill recruited as chief of the budget division Louis Messner, a young budget analyst who had been responsible for state college budgets in the Department of Finance for a number of years. He had developed a rapport with the campuses, unlike the business affairs administration in the chancellor's office. Brakebill, as the vice-chancellor, and Messner, as the chief of budget planning, were a credible team both in Sacramento and with the campuses. Messner became assistant vice-chancellor for business affairs in 1979, and vice-chancellor in 1991. He retired in 1993, and died not long thereafter.

Budget negotiations in Sacramento had been the responsibility principally of the vice-chancellor for business affairs and the chief of budget planning. Others would be involved as necessary. Brakebill instituted a budget team, consisting of himself, the chief of budget planning, and the dean of academic planning. This became Brakebill, Clucas and then Messner, and Ellis McCune, before he left to become president of the Hayward campus; McCune was followed by William Mason, a staff member in academic planning and an economist from the San Francisco faculty. The team worked well together and the concept became an institution that would survive until the early 1990s, though it was a bit frayed in the 1980s.[9]

One of Messner's first moves was to involve two young and able staff members who would add to the strength of the budget staff, Boyd Horne and Howard Hicks, who had moved from the Department of Education in the 1960 transition.

Messner wanted to build a computer-oriented staff, and their task was to work from existing formulas and budget understandings, address the responsibilities and work of the campuses, and generate a set of formulas which would address all of the work of a campus. This effort created the "Orange Book."[10] The Orange Book began as a loose-leaf computer readable compilation of previously determined formulas and standards for campus administrative and support staffing. Over the following years, studies of a variety of other campus operations were incorporated.

The Orange Book and the faculty staffing formula became the two principal documents for budgeting in the California State University for more than twenty years. There were both positive and negative aspects to this. Each would have only a limited full life. The faculty staffing formula was breached early in the 1970s, the Orange Book in the late 1970s. Yet each was used as a management tool way beyond its life as the basis for the state budget. The formulas were not secrets. Thus, whether in a department of any subject, or in an administrative unit responsible for a given set of activities, the cry would be, "generation equals allocation." From a management point of view, whether at the chancellor's staff or especially on a campus, the aphorism was, "generation does not equal allocation." The formulas in both documents, for the most part, did not recognize program differences among campuses. The faculty staffing formula had the potential to be sensitive to program differences, for it took into account both modes and levels of instruction. The administration of the formula, in the chancellor's office, was based on assumptions about what modes of instruction were appropriate in the various disciplines and applied fields. In the more traditional disciplines, understandings of what could be done were for the most part fixed in custom.

This situation led, quite naturally, to a premium on creativity among campus academic administrators and department chairs. Presidents wanting to establish new programs, or to move certain activities to a new level were called upon to be very creative. This situation was not unrecognized by the chancellor and his senior administration, especially Vice-Chancellors Harry Brakebill (who had become executive vice-chancellor in 1969) and William Langsdorf (who had moved from the Fullerton presidency to become vice-chancellor for academic affairs in 1970). In the 1970–71 academic year, Dumke went to the trustees and the campuses with his New Approaches strategy to give campus faculties and leadership flexibility and money to initiate new and often unconventional ideas. At the same time, the self-support programs, which had been freed from pervasive State Department of Finance control in the actions resulting from the 1966 report of the Committee on Fiscal Responsibility—essentially those traditionally called summer session and extension and now operating for the most part under the rubric of continuing education—became major vehicles for experimentation and change on some campuses. Much depended on the creative leadership of key campus figures.

The convention of salary savings had been in state government financial administration for years. Individuals leave positions for various reasons, such as retirement or a new position. More often than not, especially when they are senior and in a top-step position, they are replaced with individuals at a lower pay level.

This is made very clear by the common academic practice of replacing retiring professors with new appointees at the assistant or associate professor level. The resulting accumulation of reduced costs was known as salary savings.

During the Korean War years, A. Alan Post, the legislative analyst, introduced the concept of salary savings as a rationale for budget reductions in recognition of state employees leaving to serve in the military. At the beginning of the Pat Brown administration in 1959, Brown's first director of finance, Bert Levit, introduced the practice of using salary savings as a management device. Levit had the staff in Finance estimate salary savings accrued in various state operations in previous years and, with the governor's concurrence, set salary savings levels for each state government entity. Salary savings were budgeted and, in the practical world of budgeting, this meant a reduction from the published budgeted amount. By the mid-1960s, the state colleges' salary savings amounts levied by Finance had settled to 2 percent for budgeted faculty positions and 4 percent for all other budgeted positions. By the early 1970s, some of the more creative campus administrators, using another Committee on Fiscal Responsibility reform concerning transfer of funds among budget categories, had come to realize that salary savings could be a campus management tool used to move funds into and out of budget categories for the support of new campus ventures. By way of example, a campus administration could increase the salary savings requirement in a unit and decrease it elsewhere. This was used to move money into instruction and develop new academic ventures on some campuses. Three campus administrations, Chico State, Dominguez Hills, and Sonoma State took the lead to use a combination of salary savings, continuing education revenue fund money, and the funds resulting from the Dumke New Approaches initiatives. Campus administrations thus could set priorities in important ways; this breakthrough occurred in the administrative climate of the early 1970s and the New Approaches program. As a practical matter, money could be moved not only into instruction and academic affairs, but out from them as well. Thus, perhaps it was fortunate that this kind of creativity among campus administrators was not widely engaged in.

Leadership in the business affairs sector of the chancellor's office changed in 1968; Harry Brakebill became executive vice-chancellor. A recruitment process resulted in the appointment of D. Dale Hanner as vice-chancellor for business affairs. Hanner moved from the position of chief of the audits division of the Department of Finance. Louis Messner, who had worked for Hanner in Finance, played a role in recruiting Hanner. Hanner began as vice-chancellor for business affairs early in 1969. He remained as vice-chancellor until 1991. He was widely respected within and without the California State Colleges/California State University, and developed essentially good working relationships with Sacramento that included members of the legislature and Finance, with the statewide Academic Senate and other faculty leaders, and with most campus administrations and leadership groups. He was credible.

The years of the Reagan administration were in a sense difficult ones for state college budgeting. Dumke was successful in convincing Reagan to support the New Approaches initiatives for the final years of Reagan's governorship, beginning with the 1972–73 fiscal year. But there was a continuous tension with the Department of Finance. Some staffers and officials in Finance used the negative public opinion influenced by student and faculty activism of the 1960s as an instrument to support stringent budgeting.

In 1970, the Reagan administration began a series of management and budget reviews of various state agencies and operations. The state colleges were included. The report on the state colleges focused on the use of faculty positions. It quickly became known, by the name of its author, an engineer in the State Department of Water Resources, as the Teerink report. Teerink did not accept the validity of some of the faculty staffing formulas. In preparing his report, he examined the work of individual faculty members. He started from the assumption that the normal faculty workload of twelve weighted teaching units would translate to time in a classroom or laboratory. The faculty staffing formula, developed in 1957 when the teacher preparation function of the state colleges was still in ascendency, contained what was known as the "S factor," provision for supervision of students outside of a conventional classroom setting, and had been designed to provide for the supervision of student teaching. With the broadening of state college curricula and the diversification of student enrollments in the 1960s, instruction using the S, or supervision, factor broadened and increased beyond teacher education. The formula for teacher education remained more abundant or rich than most others, but faculty workload credit became used in fields like social work (graduate students doing practicums), biology (fieldwork for students in conservation/ecology programs), business and public administration (internships), and the like. Faculty workload credit was given for work with graduate students on theses. Teerink's position was that all of this should be beyond the conventional twelve-unit workload. The Department of Finance proposal, incorporated in the governor's budget for 1971–72, reduced the number of faculty positions by about one thousand. This was in the face of a 19,000 FTE projected enrollment increase from 1970–71 to 1971–72.[11]

In the budget negotiations, the Teerink position prevailed for the most part. Thus, the faculty staffing formula was, in a sense, set aside. Even so, the academic planning staff in the chancellor's office continued to use it both to generate budget requests (even though these were not fully funded) and to hold campuses accountable for faculty utilization.

The vice presidents for academic affairs on the campuses were a tight group. They met formally probably three or four times in an academic year, had a chair they elected (this was recognized by the chancellor's staff), an informal executive committee, and substantial communication lines. Almost to a person, they requested in 1973 the substitution of student-faculty ratios by campus and discipline or applied field. This could legitimize the many different approaches to teaching and experimenting with teaching on the campuses. This was at a time of some turmoil in the leadership of academic affairs in the chancellor's office; the highly respected vice-chancellor retired that year, rather unexpectedly for reasons of health, and the dean of academic planning died quite suddenly. The vice presidents did not prevail.

The 1971–72 budget, with the implementation of the Teerink report, spelled the effective end of the faculty staffing formula, but it remained for years as a factor to be called upon by campus department faculties and others. It was not until 1992 when the Munitz budget revolution occurred, that it would completely disappear. Beginning with the 1973–74 academic year, the faculty staffing formula became a point of departure for budget proposals from the campuses and the chancellor's office, a would-be regulatory device for the academic planning staff to use with the campus, and the occasion for many discussions, agreements, and disagreements about faculty position utilization over the next years.

The impact of the Reagan years, 1967–1974, on the finances of the then California State University and Colleges was mixed. The overall level of support by any measure declined. The student-faculty ratio increased, and that is a direct measure. At the same time, some budget flexibility was joined with the full implementation of the 1966 report of the Committee on Fiscal Responsibility and the modest support received for the New Approaches initiatives.

* * *

The year 1975 saw the inauguration of the son of Edmund Brown as governor. Jerry Brown was at least a skeptic about the work of institutional higher education. This became clear in his first year as governor and with his first budget. His proposed budget had a variety of cuts; among them, international programs were completely eliminated. This issue is described in more detail in Chapter 7 in this volume. After an almost yearlong campaign, international programs were restored. Brown came to be a consistent critic of higher education, and state appropriations for higher education were not exempt from his criticism. Some semblance of the status quo in state college budgeting was maintained through much of Brown's first term. The Teerink faculty cuts had the impact of throwing open the methodology for calculating faculty position budgets. The Orange Book formulas remained intact, though always subject to interpretations and debate. Brown's office itself took rigorous control of some aspects of travel.[12] The relationship between this Brown administration and the leadership of the California State University and Colleges was not a cordial one.

Proposition 13 emerged in the spring of 1978. The state had experienced good economic times for several years. No one in leadership was questioning overall taxation structures. The legislature failed to deal with the issue of property taxes or tax reform generally. Property values were increasing according to the sales prices of properties in immediate areas. Thus tax assessments were increasing according to the sales prices of one's neighbors, and property taxes were calculated upwards with no limits. Surpluses were accruing in cities, counties, and special districts. Individuals on fixed or modest incomes often could no longer afford to stay in their homes. Two little-known longtime tax critics, Howard Jarvis and Paul Gann, both active in a variety of antitax organizations, emerged with an idea: fix the base property taxes to the dollar value determined by the cost of the property at the time of construction or purchase of the property with a 2 percent limit on increase in any year thereafter. Howard Jarvis and Paul Gann became the leaders of the Jarvis-Gann Proposition 13 movement. The legislature remained inactive; the governor was at first negative, then ambivalent, and, finally, ten days before the election, supported Proposition 13. It passed in June 1978, and its language provided for immediate implementation.

Proposition 13 did not address state budget appropriations financed by income taxes but property taxes that supported cities, counties, schools, community colleges, and special districts for water, recreation, sewers, and so on. The legislature and the governor, however, moved virtually immediately to replace the funds that cities, counties, and special districts had lost from property tax reductions with money taken from the state general fund. This in turn impacted the California State University and Colleges, the University of California, welfare, health, prisons—the entire range of state activities supported by the general fund (it should be noted that this started the use of the ballot box and the propositions to come that would lock in various portions of the budget and greatly reduce the discretionary portion of the state budget from which the California State University and the University of California receive support).

One impact of Proposition 13 would be to reduce the appropriation for the California State University and Colleges (the name of the system from 1972–1982) by an amount in excess of fifteen million dollars. For state college administrations, both at the campus and system levels, and for many faculty senate chairs and others, the summer was full of serious challenges. Presidents and other senior administrators met in Sacramento on at least two occasions with state officials, to review strategies and in some measure to probe what could be done legally.

Campus budgets were reduced. Student fees were increased modestly (see Table 12.1 on page 498) For the longer term, two significant things occurred. Actions had to be taken quickly. Rather than going through the Orange Book or the battered faculty staffing formula, the State Department of Finance and the chancellor's office agreed to the concept of unallocated reductions. This moved the locus of decision making and priority setting from the state to the chancellor's office to the campuses. This would be the beginning of the system and the campuses gaining greater control. There was not, at this beginning, total freedom, and cuts were made carefully, to avoid interfering with things that were sacred to individual legislators or interest groups. The freedom to set priorities at the system, and particularly the campus levels, would evolve over time. The driver was the budget; as cuts were made and requests unfunded, campus leaders would be called upon to make the decisions about where the cuts would be made. To an observer, it would appear that there was a tradeoff—reduced overall budgets for more fiscal autonomy. In fact, the budget negotiating team understood the process as one of tradeoffs. This prevailed until the budget reforms of the Munitz administration in the early to mid-1990s.

The second significant and unexpected outcome had to do with flexibility on the campuses. This was particularly true with the work of faculty. Departmentalization had brought with it an increased specialization of faculty. Over time rules had developed about faculty tenure and the concept "teaching service area" had emerged. Faculty held tenure in primary and secondary teaching service areas. Particularly on smaller and younger campuses this approach to faculty staffing simply would not work, and faculty were encouraged to teach beyond their specialized fields. On one young campus in the fall term of 1978, 26 percent of the faculty would teach at least one course outside of his/her primary teaching service area (few faculty had secondary teaching service areas, as the concept was not widely utilized). Many would regard this as progress in the maturing of the campus. The explosion of knowledge and the growth of colleges and universities in the 1950s,'60s, and '70s had brought about increased specialization among faculties. Bureaucratization, in its negative sense, can set in among faculty, particularly when they are beset by regulators.[13]

The impact of Proposition 13 would be lasting. It simply reduced the base of the budget. The trustees did not accept this readily. In December 1978, the trustees rejected a request from the governor to cut the budget by 10 percent. The governor asked the system to identify low-priority programs and activities. Chancellor Dumke told the trustees that a 10 percent cut, amounting to sixty-nine million dollars, would cause the system to reduce enrollment by 3200 students, and cut 1300 faculty and 1800 other employees. The then chair of the board, Roy Brophy, blamed the governor for "creating a fiscal crisis "by dumping higher education in the same bag with governmental administrative agencies. The point is that this system doesn't have any lowest priority programs that will cost out at sixty-nine million dollars."[14] As usual, staff in the chancellor's office and in Finance would have to work out a compromise budget.

The year 1978 also saw passage of the Berman Bill, which authorized collective bargaining within the California State University and Colleges. A key decision in the legislation placed collective bargaining in the California State Universities and Colleges at the system level, whereas collective bargaining in the University of California was to be at the campus level. The impact was not immediate, and several years would pass before either the unions or the chancellor's staff would be sufficiently organized to utilize and accommodate the presence of collective bargaining. For the most part, the major union presence became the faculty union, the California Faculty Association (CFA). Over the years, the unions and collective bargaining have had only modest impact on CSU budgets. There have not been instances where budgets have been reduced. Often a union—most often CFA—will ask for special language on a budget item, language that would define or limit the expenditures. The unions, especially the CFA, sometimes have not supported CSU budget proposals. In the 1990s, union relationships became more adversarial, and this increased through 2000 to the time of this writing. This did create credibility issues as the CSU negotiated budgets. In the most difficult budget situations, where the CSU budget has been seriously threatened, unions, again with the CFA as the most prominent player, have made common cause with the trustees and chancellor. In 2008, a difficult budget year, there was a common front; unions and all other internal CSU groups were in support of the trustees' budget.

* * *

The 1980s were somewhat stable years for CSU finances. In 1982, Glenn Dumke retired after twenty years as chancellor, and the trustees appointed Ann Reynolds to the chancellorship. That same year George Deukmejian was elected governor of California. In the chancellor's staff the financial leadership remained constant. Dale Hanner continued as vice-chancellor and Louis Messner as assistant vice-chancellor and chief budget officer for the decade and through the entirety of the Reynolds administration. Deukmejian was a fiscally conservative governor, and appropriations did not come easily through him. However, Deukmejian was also genuinely supportive of higher education and did support both the overall CSU budget and some new initiatives that Reynolds promoted. Perhaps the most serious conflicts occurred around executive salaries, in 1986 and again in 1989–90, and chancellor/board action on these in executive session. Financial support for fundraising, in a very modest amount, was initially secured with Deukmejian.

In the early 1970s, state support for elementary "demonstration schools" on the older state college campuses was eliminated. Demonstration or laboratory schools are not uncommon in American higher education and have existed on campuses, from teachers colleges to the greatest of research universities. One of the initiatives of the 1980s was to bring back laboratory schools, and two secondary schools were established at campuses in the Los Angeles Basin, one at California State University, Dominguez Hills, focusing on science and mathematics, and the other at California State University, Los Angeles, focusing on the arts. State funding was secured for these.[15]

With Ann Reynolds's departure and the assumption of the role by Ellis McCune, the long-serving president of the Hayward campus, the focus of the presidents' group, the executive council, moved to a discussion about methods of budgeting and both securing and allocating resources. The Orange Book had ceased to have any practical meaning, once the practice of unallocated reductions of the budget took hold, the years immediately after the passage of Proposition 13. The Orange Book was still used to prepare budget requests and as a kind of benchmark for allocating the resources that were available, yet the presidents universally found this to be a nuisance or worse. The practice of continuing to use the Orange Book simply got in the way of flexible administration of a campus. It created a sense of entitlement in those whose allocations fell short of what they perceived to be their fair allocation based on their particular formula. McCune, a campus president for twenty-three years, not only understood this but shared the judgment of his former immediate colleagues. On the other hand, the chancellor's office staff defended the continued use of the Orange Book. Their argument, essentially, was that the formulas and theoretically accepted understandings about resource needs were better starting points for budget negotiations than nothing, or, alternatively, the base of current-year budget for the ensuing year negotiations. McCune did not bring the matter to final decision, but rather set the stage for the next chancellor.[16]

Barry Munitz became chancellor on July 1, 1991. He faced a changing staff situation in business affairs. Having served as vice-chancellor for business affairs for twenty-three years, Dale Hanner was on the brink of normal retirement age and had announced his retirement. Hanner's principal deputy, Assistant Vice-Chancellor Louis Messner, the long-time chief budget officer, became acting vice-chancellor in late 1991, then vice-chancellor; he retired soon after, for health reasons. Munitz recruited a campus vice-president for administration, Mernoy Harrison from Sacramento State, as interim vice-chancellor and chair of the search committee for the recruiting of a new vice-chancellor.

Munitz made an early decision to drop the Orange Book. When this was announced, the presidents were relieved, and the chancellor's office staff accepted the decision; despite the seriousness of the issue, both the presidents and the staff had carried on the argument with good will.

Executive Vice-Chancellor Herbert Carter, who had served the latter half of the Reynolds years and during McCune's interim year, left to become president of the United Way of Los Angeles. In a search for vice-chancellor, Munitz recruited to the position Molly Corbett Broad, the executive director for the Statewide Higher Education Board in Arizona. Broad had been educated as an economist and had held significant positions at Syracuse University prior to going to Arizona. She had earned a national reputation as a skilled and able administrative leader. Interestingly, as Munitz was being recruited into the CSU position, Broad was simultaneously attempting to recruit Munitz to the presidency of the University of Arizona.[17] Munitz and Broad quickly became partners in the leadership of the California State University. At the time, many characterized Munitz as the chief executive officer (CEO) and Broad as chief operating officer (COO). Munitz, from his experience, perhaps particularly with Clark Kerr, had firm ideas about the administration of a multicampus system. He and Broad, once she arrived, agreed that "on those things that were substantive and programmatic, the further down the decision was made, the better off we were; from the classroom to the laboratory and the studio, to the department, to the college, the last resort should be at the system."[18]

The objective was to decentralize program and centralize support. This reorientation of the chancellor's office role had a profound impact on the functioning of the staff. For Munitz and Broad, centralizing support had to do with encompassing policies at the level of the board of trustees, securing resources, and setting directions, but not controlling of the day-to-day campus administration of the these policies. For the chancellor's staff this meant reorientation. For the campus and particularly campus leadership, this was the creation of a new world.

Recruitment for a new vice-chancellor for business affairs was extraordinarily successful. The trustees appointed Richard West on the strong recommendation of Chancellor Munitz and the support of a rainbow search committee encompassing all segments of the CSU. West had been associate vice president for administration in the University of California systemwide administration. West had a background in the development of technology systems as well as business affairs, and he brought a set of skills resulting from working in a system office that involved relations with campus leadership and faculties. For fifteen years, West would have a major impact on the growth of the California State University, on growth in the quality of administration, on the creation of new programs, and on the support structures they would need.

The early 1990s were difficult budget years for the state. Revenues declined, and state budgets were tightened. The state budget situation was one of the contributing factors to the ease of securing Department of Finance acquiescence to the decision to end the use of the Orange Book. Over the years, the appetite of the staff and the political appointees in Finance to control the detail of allocations decreased remarkably, as decisions became necessary for cutbacks. Budgets for the campuses suffered, and the campuses were not able to take all eligible applicants. While admissions standards were not changed from the Master Plan top one-third, application deadlines and other procedural means were used to curtail and cut back enrollment.

With the demise of the Orange Book and the faculty staffing formula, the base for budgeting became simply moving from one year to the next. Both the California State University and the University of California were in this position. There had been some disagreement on budget strategy between the CSU and the UC. Munitz took the position that the CSU must go public about the negative impact of insufficient funding that had been induced by the 1990–92 recession; he went public in speeches around the state. "We had to find a way of demonstrating that we were being hurt, or else we'd have no credibility."[19] The UC budget team played the issue more cautiously; they did not want to risk the ire of the governor or legislature.

* * *

In 1994, at a dinner at the Il Fornaio restaurant in Sacramento, the idea of a public higher education compact for annual state funding was born. Chancellor Barry Munitz; trustee William Hauck, a 1993 gubernatorial appointee and a highly credible figure in Sacramento, Russell Gould, the director of finance, and William Baker, the UC vice president for governmental relations, developed an idea for a compact between California's public higher education systems and the governor and state. Shortly after the dinner, Baker, Gould, and Munitz spent the better part of a weekend at Baker's home in Calistoga amid the vineyards. It was on this occasion that "the Higher Education Compact" was developed. While it was developed at the executive level in both the CSU and the UC, it was accepted by the board of trustees and the regents.

The compact was to be a four-year plan. It principally addressed the CSU and the UC. It would provide for general fund increases of 2 percent for the first year, 1995–96, and an average of 4 percent each year in the following three years, the length of Governor Pete Wilson's second term. In turn, the CSU and the UC would grow enrollment by 1 percent each year to increase student access; increase transfer programs and student numbers with the community colleges; increase measurable productivity by ten million dollars each year; place a high priority on reducing time to graduation; and increase faculty salaries to competitive levels. An additional component provided for capital outlay funding each year at approximately one hundred and fifty million dollars for each segment, including the community colleges. The community colleges were not directly addressed in the Compact, as their support budgets were provided through the districts, but general provision was made to support them in a variety of indirect ways.[20]

Governor Wilson agreed to the compact. It was implemented for the 1995–96 budget year, and the following years. In addition, funds were appropriated for enrollment increases beyond the 1 percent provided for in the compact. There was some legislative resistance, particularly among staff. Staff argued that the compact was with the governor, not the legislature. The Compact not only prevailed, but the legislature increased the proposed budgets to avoid student fee increases included in the CSU and the UC budgets. An argument did develop about whether the Compact was a floor or a ceiling. The Compact was a floor, and both the legislature and the governor used it as a floor, at least in theory.

Resistance to the concept of the compact was principally in the legislature; legislative staff and some members remained critical over the years and the argument was always that the compact was with the governor. Within the California State University there would be strong pockets of resistance around the argument that the compact settled for too little, essentially, for inadequate support. A longer-term analysis of the compact suggests that it set the stage for student fee increases, another supporting leg of what Chancellor Munitz described as a three-legged stool. At a 1995 meeting of the board of trustees, Munitz characterized the total funding of the California State University as sitting on a three-legged stool. One leg was the state general fund support, one leg was student fee income, and one leg was external support. This notion became a recurring theme over the years.

At the same time, a significant budget redesign process was underway inside the CSU. With the end of the Orange Book, there came a shift from a needs-based budget to a revenue-based one. The Master Plan assumed a needs-based budget. The reality that set in in the early 1970s, with the overnight change in the faculty staffing formula, followed by the erosion and dilution of virtually all other agreed-upon formulas in the wake of Proposition 13, was complete by the early 1990s.

The leadership in the chancellor's office set about a redesign of the budget process. This would include the creation of a reserve fund, and the resulting establishment of some flexibility at the system level. Negotiations with the Department of Finance resulted in the establishment of a marginal cost per student to fund growth. Beginning in the 1980s, the system secured roll-forward authorization in some years. Year-end balances would be rolled into the succeeding year. This became institutionalized with the budget redesign and was passed on to the campuses. On some campuses, the funds available in year-end balances were passed on to academic and other major units or program centers. The redesign of the budget process was complete, for a time, by 1996.[21]

Student fees were modest at the time of the adoption of the Master Plan. For California residents it was possible to assert that the real cost of attending a California State College was foregone income and the cost of self-support. Even the cost of most books was modest. The Master Plan assumed this as enduring public policy. Pressure on student fees has, however, been a constant since the 1960s, and the rise in student fees, while sometimes sporadic, was significant. As additional student fees were considered during the Munitz administration in the mid-90s, Munitz proposed to the board of trustees that one-third of all additional student fee income be placed in student financial aid. The board agreed and this became policy.

The history of student fee increases is more a political one than an economic one. Fees were stable from the 1961 assumption of responsibility by the board of trustees until the Reagan administration. After a political battle, fees for California residents increased from $76 per year to $86 for the 1967–68 budget year, and each year thereafter by an average increase of a bit more than seven dollars, until 1974–75. They remained stable in the Jerry Brown administration until his last three years, the years after the passage of Proposition 13, when fees increased from $144 per year to $430. In Governor Deukmejian's first budget year, the fees were raised to $612, then decreased for the next three years to $573, only to be increased to $780 by his final year as governor.

The real tests on student fees were still to come. The cumulative impact of propositions approved by voters (Proposition 98, support for schools and community colleges, is a prime example) and fierce competition among interest groups to gain support for growing programs and effectively narrowed the portion of the general fund budget over which the governor and the legislature had control. In Governor Pete Wilson's first budget year, the annual student fee was $936. It rose in the next four years to $1,584, remained for the next three years at the same level, and was reduced in his last year in office to $1,506, all the result of legislative buyouts. Governor Gray Davis's first three budget years saw a further decrease to $1,428, in a time of general fund abundance, followed by a modest increase for 2002–03 to $1,507. After Davis's recall, when Governor Schwarzenegger assumed office in November 2003, the state of California was

Table 12.1. Full-Time Undergraduate Annual Student Fees

Year	California Residents	Nonresident
1960-61	$ 66	$ 250
1961-62	76	250
1962-63	76	250
1963-64	76	250
1964-65	76	250
1965-66	76	600
1966-67	76	600
1967-68	86	720
1968-69	108	780
1969-70	108	890
1970-71	118	1,100
1971-72	118	1,100
1972-73	118	1,100
1973-74	118	1,300
1974-75	144	1,300
1975-76	144	1,300
1976-77	144	1,440
1977-78	144	1,575
1978-79	146	1,710
1979-80	144	1,800
1980-81	160	2,160
1981-82	252	2,835
1982-83	430	3,150
1983-84	612	3,240
1984-85	573	3,510
1985-86	573	3,780
1986-87	573	4,230
1987-88	630	4,410
1988-89	684	4,680
1989-90	708	5,670
1990-91	780	6,170
1991-92	936	7,380
1991-93	1,308	7,380
1993-94	1,440	7,380
1994-95	1,584	7,380
1995-96	1,584	7,380
1996-97	1,584	7,380
1997-98	1,584	7,380
1998-99	1,506	7,380
1999-2000	1,428	7,380

2000-01	1,428	7,380
2001-02	1,428	7,380
2002-03	1,507	8,460
2003-04	2,046	8,460
2004-05	2,334	10,170
2005-06	2,520	10,170
2006-07	2,520	10,170
2007-08	2,772	10,170
2008-09	3,048	10,170

This information, compiled by Mary L. Robinson and Dean Kulju of the Chancellor's senior staff, is from Report of a Task Force on Student Service Fees, and a display on "calstate.edu."

in serious budget difficulty, and the basic fee for undergraduates was increased in 2003–04 to $2,046, and by 2008–09 it had risen to $3,048. See Table 12.1.

It is important to emphasize that there are additional campus-based fees, at every campus, for the campus Associated Students, the campus union, instructionally related activities, and other programs including student newspaper publications, wellness centers, athletics, and the like. These additional fees are voted upon by the campus student bodies and must be approved by the campus president and the chancellor. Almost without exception, campus presidents do not approve and send forward to the chancellor a campus-based fee proposal without a positive student vote.

In 2004–05, differential and higher fees were introduced for graduate credential candidates, other graduate students, and doctoral students. In 2008–09, these fees were respectively $3,540, $3,756, and $7,926 for the academic year.

In the 1970s, as the 1,000 Mile Campus concept was being initiated, the systemwide Commission on External Degree Programs asked the trustees to approve the concept of fees for special sessions and programs. These were originally intended for programs offered to specific groups in the private sector, such as businesses, or in the public sector. In ensuing years, the trustees made possible the award of degrees in continuing education/extension programs. These two policies have been used by some of the campuses to develop programs in continuing education for students in defined groups, mostly graduate, or simply students wanting the program in question, for example, an executive MBA program. Fees substantially in excess of regular fees are set for such programs, and students typically receive special attention and are often in small classes.

These fee increases did not happen peacefully. They were political to the core. California remained low among the states in student fee charges—but then it had a proud tradition of tuition-free public higher education. The Master Plan had reaffirmed this, and continued the story that California was tuition free, with modest fees not related to the actual cost of instruction. The statewide student association, the California State Student Association (CSSA) opposed fee increases and lobbied the legislature for buyouts. The student trustee would normally be in opposition, as would some other trustees. Trustees had acquired fee-setting authority long before these years. The trustees had in fact voted for a fee policy in 1993; one-third of the "total cost of attendance" was to be borne by students. All of this was lost in the events of subsequent years, and even many trustees were unaware of the fee policy. Fees were set by perceived necessity and a political process that centered on the board, but that involved Sacramento government, students, the unions, and other interest groups. It was a process of bargaining to keep the state university in reasonably good fiscal condition, supporting academic and other programs. Over the years, the common wisdom emerged that the state had a de facto policy that lowers fees in good economic times, and raises fees in bad economic times.[22] It was a process essentially addressing not what was necessary, but what was possible, as the entire budget process had become.[23]

* * *

Barry Munitz left the chancellorship in December 1997 to become CEO of the Getty Trust. Molly Broad had already departed, preceding Munitz by six months, to become president of the University of North Carolina system. Charles Reed assumed the chancellorship in March 1998. Even before his formal assumption of office, Reed had become acquainted with Governor Wilson through his years working as chief of staff for Governor Robert Graham of Florida. That acquaintance established a good relationship with Governor Wilson, leading to special support, beyond the regular budget, for teacher education programs.[24] Relations with the Wilson administration were good and his administration on the whole was supportive in his last year as governor and Reed's first year.

A new governor, Gray Davis, assumed office in January 1999. The state at the time was strong financially, and this was reflected in a modest measure in CSU budgets. Higher education was not a top priority for Davis, and he was more supportive of the University of California than of the California State University. An instance of this partiality was the funding of special programs for K-12 teachers in the University of California, in the face of the fact that the UC prepared only a modest number of teachers, whereas the CSU prepared the majority of California teachers. The compact, which had seen the CSU and the UC through four budget years, was to expire. A new compact was negotiated, based on the 1995–99 model and would be effective from the 1999–2000 budget year to the 2003–04 budget year.

In Reed's early years, an adversarial relationship developed between the chancellor's office and the board of trustees, on one side, and the California Faculty Association, on the other. This adversarial situation had a negative impact on the budget process. It did not cause budget increases or reductions, but it could cause the insertion of budget language in the legislative process, language designed to affect how funding is spent for a particular program. Unions other than CFA were generally less active in the budget process.

The administration of Governor Gray Davis came to an end in November 2003, when he was recalled. In January 2004, the governor's budget proposal to the legislature contained a substantial cut from the then current year, a cut explained by a multibillion-dollar state budget deficit. Since the budget compact was with the governor, a new compact had to be negotiated with Governor Arnold Schwarzenegger. This was accomplished in May when the governor, the president of the University of California, and the chancellor of the California State University announced a compact that accepted cuts for 2004–05, and then set in motion a new compact . . . for the budget years 2005–06 through 2010–11. The assumption was that Schwarzenegger would run for reelection in 2006 and serve through December 31, 2010. The community colleges were not part of the compact.

When the proposed compact was announced, opposition mounted quickly. The issues were twofold: the cuts in higher education appropriations for 2004–05, and the adequacy of the 2005–11 proposal. The legislative analyst joined in the opposition. At the end of the legislative session, the budget for 2004–05 had been increased modestly; the compact remained intact. It proposed a general fund increase of 3 percent to the prior year base for both 2005–06 and 2006–07, and a similar 4 percent increase for the next four fiscal years through 2010–11. It contained language urging both UC and CSU to seek outside funding and private resources. The compact added an extra 1 percent for the last three years for "core academic support needs," and promised support for capital outlay. In turn, the CSU and UC committed to enrollment increases and a variety of accountability measures. The CSU accountability measures were those developed in the late 1990s in Cornerstones. The compact contained a student fee policy. Increases in student fees would be based on the rise in California per capita personal income. The policy provided for trustees (CSU) and regents (UC) to go beyond an annual fee increase, when necessary, up to a 10 percent total increase, but only after consulting the governor and defining "compelling circumstances." The CSU compact assumed fee increases in 2004–05 of 14 percent for undergraduates, 25 percent for graduates, and 20 percent for graduate credential candidates.[25]

Richard West built a staff in finance that was strong by any measure. The individuals worked well with their counterparts and others on the campuses. Certainly, the decentralization of many operations helped relationships. Key members of the finance staff, led by West, built lines of communication with Sacramento, the Department of Finance, and other agencies and legislative staff. Trust was established, and this was reinforced by an essentially positive relationship between Governor Schwarzenegger and Chancellor Reed. Each year some progress was made in freeing the CSU from state agency management.

***

The year 2006 brought an important change in financial administration. The CSU acquired the "treasury function." Simply put this allowed the CSU to deposit student fee and other income into a university held trust fund rather than the State General Fund. The history of CSU management of funds dates to 1947 and in reality to the earliest campus operations in the nineteenth century. There are some parallels with auxiliary organizations.

The year 1947 saw the enactment of the State College Revenue Bond Act. This move provided for a "self-supporting financing vehicle independent of the appropriations of the state." The State Board of Education was authorized to issue bonds for programs such as student housing. With the passage of the Master Plan legislation and the assumption of authority by the board of trustees, the separate campus bond programs were consolidated into a single program. A gradual evolution of additional responsibility for trustee management of nonappropriated funds set in. The fallout from the 1.8 percent salary debacle of 1965, and the results from the work of the Committee on Fiscal Responsibility contributed to this evolution. In the early 1990s, a fundamental policy shift began linking campus management responsibility and authority. A decentralization process set in. Then, in 2000, the chancellor's staff initiated a study of debt capacity and, ultimately, debt management. The campus presidents and chief financial officers became involved and the trustees adopted a systemwide financing policy and debt management program in 2002.

This provided a context for a further step, the identification of a treasury function. In 2005, the trustees were asked to consider revenue management. The chancellor and the presidents proposed to the board that student fee revenue, a sum in excess of one billion dollars each year, be moved from the state general fund, where historically it had been deposited, into local trust funds. This, in turn, would provide the circumstance for a complete overhaul of financial management systems, procedures, and financial operations. The trustees incorporated this into the 2006–07 budget proposal. It was supported by the Department of Finance, included in the 2006–07 budget by the legislature, and signed by the governor. This was a major step for the CSU.[26]

One of the outcomes from the establishment of the treasury function was the creation of a systemwide investment fund in 2007. A centralized investment account was created. This moved investment operations from a cumbersome operation in which funds had to be withdrawn from varying campus and system accounts, to a simple process of "daily sweeping of available cash balances and pooling of cash into a centralized investment account."

The progress that has been made in financial administration in the almost fifty years since the Master Plan of 1960 was substantial. The pace was not even. There were years of progress, and years when there were setbacks. The gradual diminution of Department of Finance microcontrol over the use of state funds has cumulatively been substantial. The differences between the California State University and the University of California, with its constitutional independence, have lessened greatly. Both systems moved toward a moderate middle in terms of state government financial administration. The trend line of change is toward more flexibility for the CSU.

The financial challenges to the CSU are great. Higher education in California is no longer in a first-priority position. This is a result of social change in a variety of ways, particularly, the impact of special interest groups on state budgets. As this is being written, the state of California has a budget deficit of a minimum of $15.2 billion with no agreed upon budget for the 2008–09 budget year. Student fee levels have risen, by any measure, to a substantial level compared to 1960, yet these fees remain among the lowest in the country for public universities.

The financial administration of the CSU is a story of steady progress. The first ten years put a consolidated financial structure in place. The next twenty years were the years of firm financial leadership, at times in the face of great difficulties: the destabilizing impact of a governor who did not really support higher education; Proposition 13; the economic ups and downs of the 1980s; and the steady progress in orderly financial administration. The third period, beginning in 1992, has been a period of maturing for the CSU financial administration, while much remains to be done, and the open questions are many.

* * *

In 1984 the voters approved, with some controversy, the establishment of a state-run lottery program. The program began in 1985, and, initially, the use of revenue received from the purchase of lottery tickets was divided as follows: 16 percent for administration of the lottery program (purchasing online computers, paying retailers, etc.), 50 percent for payment of prizes, and 34 percent for contributions to all levels of public education. The funds provided to public education were restricted to pay costs directly related to classroom instruction.

The administration of the new lottery revenue program was assigned to the budget section of business affairs in the chancellor's office. However, care was taken to ensure that the lottery revenue budgeting was kept separate from the budgeting and allocation of state appropriated funds. A separate unit was given responsibility for lottery revenue financial administration and reported directly to Dale Hanner, the vice-chancellor of business affairs. The allocations and use of the lottery revenue program were not included in the annual state and special funds budget approved by the board of trustees, but instead was included in a separate budget document annually approved by the board of trustees and, in contrast with the normal budget process, was immediately implemented since it did not require the approval of the state. In that sense, the budget process was comparable to a campus auxiliary organization. The initial financial management goal of the CSU was to allocate 75 percent of the revenue received based on individual campus enrollments. The balance of 25 percent was conservatively invested in a system fund with the concept of creating a system endowment fund with the growing interest distributed to the campuses, also based on enrollment. In a few years this concept became a reality, with the system fund exceeding thirty million dollars. In the early 1990s, pursuant to a major priority of then Chancellor Barry Munitz to resolve a collective bargaining impasse with the California Faculty Association, the system lottery revenue investment fund was liquidated and the funds used for an extensive faculty early retirement program. Shortly thereafter, the lottery revenue budgeting and allocation program was decentralized, with lottery revenue automatically allocated to the campuses.

Controversy in the public arena about the establishment of the lottery at the time of the 1984 initiative was principally about the ethical propriety of a public lottery. However, inside public education concern was about a feared use of the 34 percent of lottery revenues as an excuse to reduce state general fund support. Over the years there has been little to support this fear, though some remain suspicious. In the initial year of lottery funding, 1985, the California State University received $31.16 million. In 2007–08, the lottery income was approximately $43.5 million. About five million of this was used for two special systemwide programs to encourage promising graduate students toward the doctorate and the CSU Summer Arts program; costs of program administration were taken from the total. The remaining almost forty million dollars was allocated to the campuses based upon enrollment. The actual performance of the lottery as a support for the California State University has been modest in the larger setting.

* * *

The early history of the normal schools was one in which financial administration was not spelled out in detailed statutes, and there were no central agencies ruling over the financial operations of the campuses. The individual campuses administered and operated within their accounts the programs financed by state appropriations and services, and activities financed by nonpublic funds. Thus, dormitories (as they were called well into the twentieth century), food services, scholarships, and whatever variety of activities and services might be necessary were administered by campus business officers.

The renaming and redefinition of normal schools to state teachers colleges in 1921 occurred at approximately the same time as the creation of more sophisticated public finance operations and the development of the State Department of Finance. In 1922, the first campus auxiliary organization was established on the Fresno campus. The Fresno State Teachers College Association began as an entity to make possible and practical the operation of a variety of functions and activities that were funded by students beyond the established student fee structure; these programs were essentially self-supporting. In 1931, the legislature established a ten-thousand-dollar revolving fund to back student agricultural projects at the San Luis Obispo campus, but this was declared unconstitutional by the attorney general. Subsequently, the campus created a special fund for students to use; this was financed with a ten-thousand-dollar loan from the local Citizens State Bank. In 1933, with the arrival of Julian McPhee as president at the San Luis Obispo campus, a revolving fund that was quasi-public was established by a committee of faculty and students and called the Special Cafeteria Fund. This operated until April 1940, when the California State Polytechnic College Foundation was organized under the California Education Code. In June 1940, the Chico campus followed with the incorporation of the Chico State College Foundation. Both foundations, or auxiliary organizations, had as their purpose the leadership and management of programs and activities that were not funded by the state and could only function with extensive administrative flexibility.

Beginning with the Fresno campus in 1922, student associations were established on all of the campuses. The Associated Students at Chico State College had a general manager, Paul Byrne, who was politically active. In 1942, Byrne took a pioneering step and led the student body, reduced in size with the advent of World War II, to the incorporation of the Associated Students of Chico State College, under the education code. This pioneering venture would manage athletics, publications, food services, the bookstore, drama and music productions, and all student extracurricular activities. This was accomplished with the creative leadership of the dean of students at the time, Hugh Bell, a pioneer among California deans who served for thirty years in that role. Byrne was elected to the California State Senate in 1946, moving to that role from his position as general manager of the Chico State Associated Students.

Pushed by both the San Luis Obispo and Chico campuses, legislation in the 1930s and 1940s provided a structure within which auxiliary organizations or foundations could operate. The legislation was in bits and pieces with no comprehensive structure or set of mandates. It would be up to the campuses for some years to build upon this, with the growth of enrollments and the establishment of new campuses from 1945 to the early 1950s. A consensus built in Sacramento that the operations of these auxiliary organizations needed to be within some understood and agreed-upon parameters. Thus, the Department of Finance informed the Department of Education in 1953 that auxiliary organization lease agreements to operate on the campuses (required by legislation in 1933), would no longer be renewed until a "set of guiding principles was developed and agreed upon by Finance and the Department of Education" (essentially, the presidents).

Auxiliary organizations were of great importance to all of the campuses by this point. The institutions had grown, in both size and function, but state management and statutes had not kept pace. Auxiliary organizations were widely used by the campuses simply to make the operation of certain programs possible. A working group of presidents and others from the campuses, and staff from the Department of Education and the Department of Finance addressed the Finance request over almost three years, and the two departments agreed to a set of principles in 1956.[27]

Auxiliary organizations, often called foundations or, in recent years, campus corporations, exist fundamentally to provide flexibility, both fiscal and managerial. Understandably, the state general fund budget structure is not a flexible one. Increasingly, however, flexibility is needed to operate a comprehensive university. On occasion, functions can be moved from an auxiliary to the state side of financial management, and more flexibility has been secured in financial administration since passage of the Master Plan.

Bookstores, food services, computer stores, and other commercial enterprises on all campuses are operated either by a campus auxiliary or on a contract basis between an outside corporation and a campus auxiliary. These enterprises, not unlike their counterparts in any marketplace, need flexibility on a day-to-day basis.

The Associated Students organizations on the campuses are without exception incorporated, and have substantial financial and administrative operational discretion. The Chico model, developed in 1942, is the most comprehensive. The operation of the bookstore and food services by the Associated Students Corporation on that campus has been at times controversial. In the more recent years, some Associated Students organizations have opened programs such as recreational opportunities for public use. The student organizations are substantial business enterprises, and as campus enrollments grow, the multimillion-dollar character of the organizations grows. Basic funding for the Associated Students auxiliaries comes from student fees that are voted on by students and are subject to approval by the campus president and the chancellor.

Student unions similarly are governed, and created, by auxiliary organizations. Most campus student unions are the creatures of a single-purpose auxiliary. Over the years, especially at the beginning of student unions on campuses, there was conflict about whether the governing structure and the board of the union should be student controlled. The division of programs between student unions and Associated Students auxiliaries varies from campus to campus. The student union auxiliaries build the buildings and operate them. In recent years, some campuses have developed student recreation or wellness facilities in addition to student unions. Similar to Associated Students auxiliaries, student union base funding comes from fees determined in student body elections.

Every campus has at least one auxiliary that handles grants, contracts, and a large variety of educational or campus-related programs. Some campuses have several auxiliaries, and divide programs among these. Auxiliaries to operate public radio and public television are found on campuses, as are auxiliaries that develop and operate student and, most recently, faculty housing. The importance of the use of auxiliaries for property acquisition is coming to the forefront in recent years.

In the early 1980s, the first auxiliary corporation specifically devoted to fundraising and development was established on the Northridge campus, followed by a similar auxiliary on the Sacramento campus. As the trustees have placed great emphasis on fundraising and development, beginning with the early 1990s, more campuses have moved to this model.[28]

The Master Plan had been silent on the subject of auxiliary organizations. From time to time legislative interest would be piqued by a specific matter, but for the most part state government did not interfere with auxiliary activities, and the legislature, over the years, enacted statutes authorizing their activities.

One of the first actions of the newly established board of trustees was taken shortly after Glenn Dumke became chancellor in the spring of 1962. The trustees adopted a "statement concerning auxiliary organizations," which encouraged the use of auxiliaries. The trustees faced the rapid growth of the system, new campuses, and many additional students. An office was established to work with the auxiliary organizations on the campuses and to bring some order and consistency to their functions. The auxiliaries were not only necessary to support the academic and educational programs of a campus, but they could be used as a cutting edge for the development of new programs. Auxiliary and Business Services (ABS, as it was known for thirty years) became the unit in the chancellor's office that worked with the campuses. The staff had to be grown. The first head of ABS was brought in from the private sector, as there was no comparable organization in higher education. Special legislation would be needed to provide for the orderly growth of auxiliaries and for new functions that would grow over time. Auxiliaries acquired a bonding function for the construction of facilities such as student unions, buildings for research and other academic purposes, and eventually housing.[29]

The statute authorizing auxiliaries was clear—auxiliaries existed only to support and further the educational programs of a campus. Auxiliaries could function only with the approval of the campus president, not only at the point of their establishment, but in their ongoing operations. The trustees developed a policy requiring that auxiliary organizations be in good standing with the chancellor's office and the board. This would be important over the years as the inevitable would happen, and an auxiliary would move beyond its campus mandate.

In 1962, the trustees established a systemwide auxiliary, the California State College Foundation. Its purpose was "furthering and enhancing the educational effectiveness of the California State Colleges, and the administrative effectiveness of the Trustees and the Chancellor of the California State Colleges in the discharge of responsibilities appropriate to the educational objectives of the colleges and the administration, both severally and as a System of Colleges, and for no other purpose." The incorporation documents continued to define "the specific and primary purposes for which the corporation is formed are to promote and assist the education, administrative and related services of the California State Colleges, and the Trustees and Chancellor thereof, and to receive and apply exclusively funds and properties coming into their hands. . . ."[30] The foundation has persisted over the years, with name changes consistent with those of the system, and is now the California State University Foundation. Given the tensions of bringing the campuses together in the immediate aftermath of the 1960 Master Plan, campus and presidential resistance could have been expected, and it did happen. The presidents, almost to a person, were concerned that the CSC Foundation would take over the campus foundations, particularly the generation and receiving of income. It is clear that a takeover was neither the intention, nor the result.[31]

As of 2008, the California State University Foundation holds a ten-million-dollar endowment. Most of this endowment supports scholarships and fellowships administered on behalf of the trustees, with awards open to students from all campuses. From time to time, the CSU Foundation has been used to make possible research and entrepreneurial activities such as the University Services Program, which operated from the late 1970s to the end of the century. These are multicampus activities. In 2006, the chancellor's office established an office of research initiatives and partnerships to support and promote research, scholarship, and creative activities that are multicampus or systemwide in those instances in which this is a useful approach. The CSU Foundation is used in these instances.[32]

The governance of auxiliary organizations is defined both in statute and in trustee policy. Auxiliaries are nonprofit corporations operating under California statutes. The trustees have a specific responsibility for them. Each auxiliary has a board. Trustee policy has required, since shortly after the trustees became responsible, that auxiliary corporate boards include at least one faculty member, one student, one community member, and the president or a designee. The exception is the corporate board of Associated Students auxiliaries. These boards are wholly composed of students, and the campus president or representative is a nonvoting member.

From time to time, there have been runaway auxiliary boards, or management, or both. These have largely been a product of presidents or administrations that were simply not paying attention. Eventually, an issue forces the attention of a campus administration or the chancellor's office, and the matter is necessarily resolved. The touchstone is the statutory requirement that auxiliaries must serve the educational program of a campus. Styles on the campuses varied about membership on auxiliary boards. One extreme is to have membership principally from the community, with one student, one faculty member, and the president or a designee on the board. The other extreme is to have the membership principally from the campus administration, with one faculty member, one student, and one community member. On at least one campus, the faculty captured the two major auxiliary organizations, and there was one student, one community member, and the president's designee.

The period from the 1960s to the 1990s can be understood as the adolescence of auxiliaries. With the 1990s came a substantial change in the financial administration of the California State University. The ABS office and function was terminated. Overall policy remained with the chancellor's office and the trustees. The trustees and chancellor made clear that the operational responsibility was on the campuses. More important, some campus leaders began to explore new uses for auxiliaries and the role that auxiliaries could play as cutting edge instruments for campus growth, not only in numbers, but in program. The auxiliaries were gradually required to reimburse the state for all services received, such as administrative support, telephones, and maintenance, and, simultaneously, they acquired the freedom to be adventurous. Fundraising became a major activity, even for student unions.

Auxiliaries in several instances manage campus endowments in excess of one hundred million dollars. Auxiliaries are becoming developers using the assets of a campus to move to a new level. For example, on the San Francisco campus, the foundation has been used to acquire major portions of a large apartment community adjacent to the campus on one side, and apartments in a major apartment—shopping mall community adjacent to the campus on the opposite side; the apartments are used for faculty, staff, and student housing. There is a certain irony to this acquisition. There was a bitter battle in 1947 over the selection of the site for the San Francisco campus. The strong San Francisco State president, J. Paul Leonard, prevailed. He had received active support from students (many of them veterans) who had demonstrated repeatedly at the San Francisco City Hall. The opponents, the Stoneson brothers, received zoning for adjacent property, which became Stonestown, a major apartment complex and regional shopping mall. The apartment portion was purchased by the university as noted above. The San Diego campus has used an auxiliary corporation for major property acquisition.

The California State University auxiliaries have always been important to campus development. In the nineteenth century, and for the first two decades of the twentieth century, the campuses had financial freedom to do what was necessary for educational programs and for campus development. Beginning in the 1920s, as the campuses became more enmeshed in state procedures and bureaucracies, creative campus leaders developed campus auxiliary corporations. As the Master Plan unleashed the campuses and the California State Colleges to grow, qualitatively and substantively, auxiliary corporations became significant to the development of the campuses. With the maturing of the California State University in the 1990s, auxiliary corporations are a major instrument for growth, and the establishment of new programs and services.

* * *

Fundraising and development are major activities in American higher education, public as well as private. Private colleges and universities in the United States have been heavily dependent on fundraising from their beginnings. Historically, the public sector was different for the most part, being funded by state and local governments.

The California State Colleges were funded by the state almost from the beginning. The first normal school, opened in 1857 in San Francisco, was funded in its early years by the city and county of San Francisco. By the time it moved to San Jose, it was state funded. In the nineteenth and early twentieth centuries, local communities and groups would make some modest funds available, not as part of a base budget, but as supplemental funding. Most often this was done to secure the location of a campus in the community. Many of the normal schools were established on land donated by communities or individuals. This practice continues to the present, with transfers of land from other public entities.

Presidents and others on the campuses, up to the time of the Master Plan, would accept funds for particular purposes. Student scholarships were sponsored by donors. Some presidents were more aggressive than others in pursuing outside funding. On the Chico campus, President Glenn Kendall undertook a quiet campaign in 1957–58, to secure funding for a program he and others wished to develop and grow. Word of the campaign circulated in the state. Kendall had been strongly supportive of a growing program in agriculture at Chico State. In 1958, Kendall received a letter from J. Burton Vasche, the associate superintendent of public instruction and head of the Division of State Colleges and Teacher Education. Vasche, writing on behalf of Superintendent Roy Simpson, stated that he knew Kendall to be a strong and effective president. It had come to Superintendent Simpson's attention that Kendall was seeking outside funding. Vasche was certain, so he wrote, that Kendall would want to follow state college custom and terminate his fundraising activities.[33] This did not necessarily happen, but the effort to gain support was tempered.

The Master Plan was silent on fundraising. The independent colleges and universities were involved in the writing and negotiating for the Master Plan. The Master Plan noted that California's ability to support public higher education was dependent on three factors: the size of the state's economy; the effectiveness of the states taxing instruments; and "the will of the people of the state to devote adequate funds for these purposes." The state was judged to be more than adequate with respect to the first two criteria. The report concluded that only the legislature could determine the will of the people, but the report clearly assumed that adequate public funding was available and would be provided.[34] Among those involved there was a quiet understanding that neither the University of California (which had for years accepted outside support, but never conducted major campaigns) nor the state colleges would compete with the independent colleges and universities in fundraising.

The advent of Glenn Dumke to the state colleges initiated a quiet, low-key change. Dumke's entire professional experience was in the independent Occidental College. As president of San Francisco State, he soon established a scholarship program. With the coming of federal student aid after Sputnik, he expanded the office to include all financial aid. The dean responsible for the office (whose background was also in a private university) was asked to be available for potential donors. Other presidents followed the example; but this was only really a modest effort.[35]

Dumke became chancellor in the spring of 1962. Louis Heilbron, when he was serving as the first chair of the board of trustees, observed that he did not believe that the state colleges needed to embark on fundraising, as they would be adequately supported by state funding.[36] In 1965, Dumke sounded out the presidents about fundraising. He set up a meeting with the presidents and a consultant with considerable experience in outside fundraising. The discussions with the presidents were not well received and the matter was dropped.[37]

The University of California quietly stepped up fundraising in the 1960s. The state colleges did not. Douglas Patino, who became the first vice-chancellor formally responsible for fundraising in the early 1990s, became aware of a "gentleman's agreement," or quiet understanding, between the UC and the CSU, that the CSU would not undertake a fundraising program that would compete with the University of California.[38]

Fundraising and development were dropped as a system priority almost until the year of Glenn Dumke's retirement as chancellor. Dumke remained supportive of those campuses that did pursue some level of fundraising activity. Many campuses did initiate or step up the development of alumni associations. At the San Luis Obispo campus of Cal Poly, a program to build alumni association membership was initiated in 1976. President Robert Kennedy sought outside money from a wealthy friend of the campus to pay for the alumni membership program. Kennedy recalled the opposition of longtime president Julian McPhee to state college fundraising as inappropriate competition with independent institutions. Kennedy's interest in fundraising was piqued as he learned of growing fundraising at UCLA. Kennedy reasoned that state auditors would force recovery of any state funds used to build alumni membership or other fundraising. The alumni program and the funds to support it were placed in the campus foundation.[39] Kennedy's successor, Warren Baker, who took office in 1979, questioned Dumke about his desire to do fundraising. Dumke's response was to go ahead with fundraising and be careful with the use of state funds.[40]

Over the years, Baker and his colleagues at San Luis Obispo have been the most successful fundraisers among all the CSU campuses. A few campuses undertook capital development projects despite some difficulty in working through administrative processes. In a final statement to the board of trustees (which in reality meant the entire California State University community) Dumke addressed four themes. The final theme was the inevitability of fundraising, as he projected economic and political trends. His argument, strongly stated, was that the CSU could not avoid or step aside from fundraising and maintain the university's mission.

The campus presidents in the late 1970s and 1980s were alive to the coming of development and fundraising programs in public higher education in California. There was no consensus among the presidents. The topic was not seriously addressed in the meetings of the Council of Presidents, but it was discussed in the presidents' informal gatherings. The presidents were in disagreement. Some believed that state universities should be wholly state supported on principle. Some believed it to be inappropriate to use state money to gain private support or raise private funds. Some believed, with varying degrees of strength, that it was time to get active fundraising underway with the use of state general fund dollars.

Active interest in fundraising increased in the 1980s. In 1986, Chancellor Ann Reynolds proposed a position of vice-chancellor to work with fundraising, but no appointment was made. In 1987, Governor Deukmejian appointed William Campbell to the board. Campbell proved to be a key figure in raising the sights of the trustees about fundraising, as he would also be in securing state funding for research. Shortly after becoming a trustee, Campbell was invited to meet with an advisory group at the San Luis Obispo campus. State Senator Gary Hart was also present at the meeting when the subject of fundraising surfaced. The San Luis Obispo campus was one that traditionally had not used general fund money for development. In the meeting, Senator Hart expressed his surprise about reservations concerning the use of general fund support, and promised to join the issue and look into the matter.[41] Campbell was a catalyst, and he was joined by other trustees in a discussion about fundraising.[42] This led to a study in the late 1980s and a practical consensus, and a resolution was subsequently adopted by the board in January 1991. The resolution settled the matter about using state general fund dollars. It recognized "the legitimate role of fundraising in the context of institutional advancement," and went on to urge "the presidents to use their authority and best judgment in allocating resources to increase their fundraising efforts."[43]

A major task for the trustees in the 1990–91 year was a search for a new chancellor following Ann Reynolds' resignation. The trustee committee that was formed took firm charge of the search and made the capacity to build a fundraising and development program an essential criterion. The search committee included faculty and presidents and a student. The trustees were firm, and they were successful. Barry Munitz, the new chancellor, was from the corporate sector, and he also had substantial academic and administrative credentials.[44]

Munitz gave attention to fundraising from the beginning of his chancellorship. As he described financial support for the California State University, he began to use the metaphor of a three-legged stool. He had assumed the chancellorship at a time when state revenue was in decline. The three legs were state funding, student fees, and extramural support, including fundraising. Fundraising was a topic for trustee and presidential—executive council discussion.

In the 1992–93 year, the trustees commissioned a major study and employed Ketchum, Inc., a consulting firm with considerable higher education consulting experience. The Ketchum staff completed a comprehensive and focused report, interviewing all campus chief fundraising officers (many of whom had fundraising among other responsibilities, and most of whom at that time had no fundraising background), presidents, trustees, relevant chancellor's staff, and others, but not faculty. The failure to interview faculty was a mistake for the longer run.[45]

The Ketchum report was presented to the board of trustees at the July 1993 meeting. The first sentence set the tone. "Fundraising is no longer an optional activity for the University."[46] The report gave strong support to the development of a fundraising arm on every campus and in the chancellor's office. It recommended the creation of a vice-chancellor position reporting to the chancellor (at that time the vice-chancellors for various specific areas reported to the executive vice-chancellor). A number of matters proposed by Munitz were addressed and endorsed, essentially setting a tone of strong support for the establishment of a serious fundraising capability. The report acknowledged that budgets were tight, and that campuses would have difficulty making funds available to establish "university advancement" offices. The report also addressed the work and organization of the California State University Foundation, and proposed that the new vice-chancellor also be the president of the foundation. The new activity would be defined as "university advancement."

The trustees and others received the report favorably, and implementation proceeded. Two groups were commissioned to prepare the way for the introduction of fundraising in the basic structure and life of the California State University. A presidential ad hoc committee, chaired by Robert Corrigan of San Francisco State, addressed the internal politics of introducing fundraising to the culture of the CSU. The report of this group noted that "recommendations for a subject as comprehensive in scope as university advancement be broadly stated, allowing flexibility in their implementation, and thereby accommodating the circumstances of each campus." A group of six chief campus development officers addressed the details of implementing campus programs, staffing, budgets, initial ground rules, and the like. A second Ketchum report encompassing the work of these two groups was presented to the trustees in January 1994 and contained analyses of the roles of presidents, the work of the chancellor's office, and specific implementation recommendations. The board of trustees was called upon to set policy for campus fundraising and to define presidential roles, and was asked for evaluation criteria to be used in addressing presidential accountability. The first mention of a 10 percent target for each campus surfaced: "achieving private sector giving that approximates 10 percent per annum over and above . . . their net general fund allocation (exclusive of fees and other income)."[47]

Douglas Patino, then the CEO of the Marin Foundation, was selected after a search and appointed as the first vice-chancellor for university advancement. In 1994, the trustees implemented the 10 percent rule: each campus was expected to raise a minimum 10 percent of its net general fund budget each year. The vice-chancellor for university advancement implemented annual reporting to the board of trustees, always in a public session with media and others present. Presidents were evaluated about campus fundraising every year informally, every three years with input collected from campus and community people, and every six years in a full formal review process with a visiting review team. The annual report to the board, presented by the vice-chancellor, became a real review. Campus fundraising performance came to be presidential fundraising performance.

Fundraising among the campuses varied substantially. The amount raised by each campus was a function of a number of variables, the two most important being academic programs and the maturity of the campus. Certainly location was a factor for some campuses, as was campus size. The age of a campus and both the number and achievements of alumni were factors. Young campuses had few alumni who were affluent. The socioeconomic mix of student bodies was a factor, and this mix changed over time on some campuses. Finally, the commitment and involvement of presidents and the size and skill of the development staff were inevitably factors. Some campuses had cultures open to fundraising, even supportive for the most part. Others had cultures that were resistant, at least in the early years.

For the most part, the role of the vice-chancellor was to give leadership to the fundraising efforts of the campuses, help develop staffs, and create a CSU culture that would be supportive. It was a building role and one that was important for the first ten years. The vice-chancellor, Douglas Patino, was also president of the California State University Foundation. He was succeeded as vice-chancellor after seven years by Louis Caldera, an attorney, a former California Assembly Member, and most recently, secretary of the army in the second Clinton administration. Caldera remained in the vice-chancellorship two years, and then moved to the University of New Mexico.

The campuses began early to fall into three groups in terms of annual fundraising. A small number of campuses easily achieved their designated target, and consistently went beyond the 10 percent goals. A larger number of campuses reported about 10 percent each year, and a slightly larger number of campuses struggled. All campuses, however, were significantly more successful with fundraising than they had been prior to the trustees' initiatives of the early 1990s.

When Barry Munitz left the chancellorship at the end of 1997, he was shortly succeeded by Charles Reed. Reed was as supportive of fundraising as Munitz had been. He became involved with fundraising as a cheerleader. Fundraising was incorporated into the life of the California State University. The role of a president changed, as emphasis was placed on fundraising. This too would require maturing. There was concern among some of the presidents, even ten years after fundraising began, that it detracted from the academic role of the president. The experience of both great universities and liberal arts colleges in the private sector would suggest that this is not necessarily inevitable, but rather that a new set of intellectual traits and interpersonal skills would be sought in presidential leadership over time.

In 2003, the vice presidents for advancement commissioned a study of the impact of the Ketchum report, and the trustees' actions of 1991 and 1994. It was recognized that there were varying fundraising patterns of the campuses. As a result, a proposal was made to the trustees to modify the 10 percent rule for expected fundraising with the recommendation and adoption of a three-tier rule. Tier-one campuses were those, eleven in number, "striving to build the capacity to raise gift commitments equivalent to 10 percent." Tier-two campuses, eight in number, had succeeded over the years with the 10 percent quota, and were defined as seeking to raise 10 percent to 15 percent of the state general fund allocation. Tier-three campuses attempted to raise 15 percent to 20 percent, and consistently accomplished or exceeded that goal. The trustees also initiated a planning process: each campus president would prepare a set of specific goals and submit these to the chancellor each year and, in turn, be measured against them.[48]

In 2003, the vice-chancellor position for advancement became vacant and a decision was made to not fill it. The responsibility was shifted to the executive vice-chancellor and chief financial officer, Richard West, and all financial operations were consolidated with him. An associate vice-chancellor position was created. This position, occupied by Lori Redfearn, was a redefinition of the chancellor's office role, and cast the role as one supportive to the campuses and coordinating their efforts. The California State University Foundation was stable at this point, and the associate vice-chancellor assumed the presidential role.

Endowments on the campuses had been modest over time. The campuses manage their endowment funds. Virtually every campus had endowed scholarships. Beginning in the 1970s, endowed professorships began to appear in modest numbers. The new emphasis on external support that began in the 1990s, and the resulting buildup of professional development staffs brought an increase in endowments. In the 2006–07 year, the value of endowments on all of the campuses and in the chancellor's office reached $874 million. In only the previous three years, the endowment value had increased 32 percent. There is some correlation of the sizes of campus endowments with the tier structure. The sizes varied in fiscal 2007 from $1.8 million to $181.7 million.[49]

As the trustees address external support, grant and contract income is also included, though the responsibility for this is almost solely on the academic side of the house. This too has grown substantially over the years. On most, but not all campuses, grants and contracts are administered through auxiliary organizations. At the time of the Master Plan in 1960, the number and value of grants and contracts was modest. The capability of faculty and departments was limited. In the years immediately after the Master Plan, a sizeable grant or contract was an occasion for major excitement on a campus. As the strengths of faculties have grown, so have faculty and institutional involvement in applied research, community development, and projects of all character, from soils research in agriculture to the involvement of students in the state legislative process to substantial international development ventures. In the 2007 fiscal year, total grant and contract revenue amounted to $1.128 billion. The largest amount was in Federal money, $717.6 million, with $342.3 million in state grants and contracts, and $69 million in nongovernmental grants and contracts. Campuses varied from $147.6 million to $2 million in the amount of activity.[50]

At the November 2005 meeting of the board of trustees, the discussion moved to the $524 million in cuts from the state budget in the 2002–05 years. The trustees concluded at a subsequent meeting that the time had arrived to revisit "alternative revenue sources." An Ad Hoc Committee on Alternative Funding Sources was formed. Three trustees, one of whom chaired the group, and two presidents and the executive vice-chancellor—chief financial officer met over several months and reported to the trustees in September 2006. The report addressed philanthropic income, sponsored contracts and grants, and a variety of approaches, including exclusive provider arrangements, the creation of a systemwide investment trust fund, and the more intensive use of CSU land for revenue-producing purposes.[51] The report and ensuing discussions did not result in any policy changes, but did serve to underscore the importance of development and fundraising programs.

* * *

The 1960 Master Plan was lacking regarding two major issues. The first had to do with the financing of public higher education, and the second with a mechanism, short of the legislature, for the orderly growth and development of public higher education, and indeed all of higher education, in California. The Master Plan did address financing of higher education. The horizon at that time was 1975. The Master Plan simply stated that, at least to 1975, public financing would be adequate as long as the will remained—represented by the legislature and governor. The document assumed that "will" would prevail, and said so. There was no anticipation of the changes in the states economic circumstance, nor was it reasonable that there could have been. Likewise, there was no anticipation of the emergence of major and rising competition for public funds from health care, elementary and secondary education, prisons, the state's infrastructure, or the like. In fact, public policy about the financing of public higher education in California has been made for some years by circumstance and indecision.

General fund support for the California State Colleges in 1960–61, the year of the passage of the Master Plan and the establishment of the board of trustees, was $79.85 million. Net state general fund support, after the deduction of income from student fees and other sources, was $68.20 million. The comparable figures for 2005–06 were $3.625 billion and $2.206 billion. Self-supporting fund expenditures (including reimbursed activities, housing and parking, continuing education, the lottery, federal financial aid and trust funds, and auxiliary organizations) totaled $2.614 billion. These two figures, along with some small expenditures from other sources, total $6.441 billion.

In the spring of 1985, David Benson was inaugurated as the fifth president of Sonoma State University. Benson was a CSU veteran, a faculty member at the Northridge campus who became a dean and then vice president for academic affairs. In the vice president's group, and subsequently in his eight-year presidency, he was known and respected as a serious and thoughtful expert on finance and budgets. Benson caused a quiet stir in the audience and beyond when in his inaugural address, he talked about California State University campuses moving from state-supported institutions to state-assisted institutions. He suggested that the time to rethink the financing of CSU campuses had come; serious development and fundraising were in the offing.

An unasked question: Is the California State University—indeed all of public higher education—a good place for the state to invest? Can the people of California afford not to invest in higher education—in themselves?

Notes

[1] Focus group on finance (Boyd Horne, Patrick Lenz, John Richards, Rodney Rideau, Richard West), October 9, 2006, 1.

[2] Ellis McCune, interview by Lawrence de Graaf, May 5–6, 1995, CSU Archives.

[3] Louis Messner, interview by Lawrence de Graaf, February 8, 1995, CSU Archives.
[4] Harry E. Brakebill, interview by Lawrence de Graaf, July 9, 1987, CSU Archives.
[5] A more full account of these events can be found in Chapter 3.
[6] Brakebill, interview, 36ff.
[7] *A Master Plan for Higher Education in California, 1960–1975*, 172–74.
[8] *Sacramento Bee*, February 26, 1967.
[9] Ellis McCune, interview by the author, June 23, 2005, CSU Archives.
[10] Louis Messner, interview, 3–4.
[11] This period is addressed in Messner, interview 27–28; focus group on finance, 25ff.; James D. Dwight, Chief Deputy Director, Department of Finance, testimony to the Subcommittee on Ways and Means, California State Assembly, March 31, 1971; David Provost, chair of the academic senate of the California State Colleges, "A Critique of the Teerink Report," addressed to Senate Finance Committee and the Assembly Ways and Means Subcommittee on Higher Education, June 8, 1971; D. Dale Hanner, interview by the author, June 21, 2004; William Mason, interview by the author, February 13, 2007; all sources are in the CSU Archives.
[12] Focus group on finance, 30.
[13] McCune, interview by de Graaf, 213ff., Messner, interview, 29ff.; focus group on finance.
[14] *San Francisco Chronicle*, December 15, 1978.
[15] Hanner, interview, June 21, 2004, 12ff.; focus group on finance, 34–37; Messner, interview, 12–13.
[16] Focus group on finance, 29ff.; McCune, interviews by both de Graaf and the author; Hanner, interview.
[17] Barry Munitz, interview by the author, November 18, 2005, 1–2.
[18] Munitz, interview, 3–4.
[19] Munitz, interview, 10, 13–14.
[20] Munitz, interview, 10, 13–14; focus group on finance, 6, 41–42, 58–59; CSU presidents' focus group, (Warren Baker, Robert Corrigan, James Rosser, and John Welty); Richard West, interview by the author, October 23, 2006, 2–4.
[21] Focus group on finance, 33–41.
[22] Elizabeth Hill, Legislative Analyst for the State of California, interview by the author, April 18, 2007.
[23] Focus group on finance, 43ff.; Elizabeth Hill, interview; Mary L. Robinson, memorandum to the author, March 15, 2006; all sources are in CSU Archives.
[24] See the chapter on teacher education programs.
[25] Office of Planning and Analysis, *Higher Education Compact: Agreement between Governor Schwarzenegger, the University of California, and the California State University, 2004/05 Through 2010/11*, the California State University, Long Beach, May 2004.
[26] Agendas and minutes, board of trustees, March 15–16, 2005, November 14–15, 2006.
[27] These paragraphs about the early history draw on *Auxiliary and Business Services Report on Auxiliary Organization,* the Office of the Chancellor, the California State University, March 5, 1973.
[28] Minutes, board of trustees, Committee on Finance, "Separate but Related Auxiliary Organization Supporting the California State University," March 11–12, 2008.
[29] Focus Group on auxiliary organizations and development (John Hillyard, Thomas McCarron, George Pardon, Peter Smits, Brad Wells, Richard West), November 1, 2006.

[30] Ketchum, Inc., *A Report on the Office of the Chancellor and the California State University Foundation*, report for the board of trustees of the California State University, July 1993 (hereafter cited as the Ketchum report.

[31] The author was a member of the chancellor's staff when the issue was a major concern of the presidents.

[32] Lori Redfearn, email to the author, September 8, 2008; Elizabeth Ambos, telephone interview with the author, September 11, 2008.

[33] J. Burton Vasche to President Glenn Kendall, June 18, 1958, Kendall Papers, California State University, Chico Archives.

[34] California State Department of Education, *A Master Plan*, 182ff.

[35] The author was the dean; responsibilities included admissions, recruiting students, and student financial aid.

[36] Trustee focus group, April 28, 2006, 33.

[37] Les Cohen, governmental relations focus group, January 24, 2006.

[38] Douglas Patino, interview by the author, July 25, 2006, 1–2.

[39] Robert Kennedy, interview by the author, October 24, 2006, 36.

[40] Presidents' focus group, October 23, 2006, 43.

[41] William D. Campbell, interview by the author, May 18, 2006.

[42] Trustee focus group, 32; presidents' focus group, 18–20.

[43] Minutes, board of trustees, January 16, 1991; see the Ketchum report, 3.

[44] Trustee focus group, 32–34, William D. Campbell, interview, May 18, 2006, 1–2.

[45] Presidents' focus group, 41–43; Munitz, interview, November 18, 2005, 15.

[46] Ketchum report, 2.

[47] Presidents' focus group, 41–43; Munitz, interview, November 18, 2005, 15.

[48] Agenda, board of trustees, Committee on Finance, September 19–20, 2006.

[49] The California State University, *Annual Report on External Support for the CSU, 2006–07*, CSU Archives.

[50] The California State University, *Annual Report*.

[51] Agenda, board of trustees, Committee on Finance, September 19–20, 2006.

Chapter 13

Capital Outlay: The Building Program

The California State University's building program, commonly known internally as the capital outlay program, has been vital to the achievement of the CSU mission and an important vehicle in bringing together from over the state the historically autonomous California State College campuses. The capital outlay program was a significant part of the decentralization moves of the later 1990s and in recent years has been a central component in creating a new financial culture and development and fundraising activities.

The two-stage implementation of the Master Plan in 1960 and 1961 provided an occasion for the board of trustees and senior administrators at the system level to begin to pull the campuses together and create a coherent whole. The capital outlay program was a major tool used by trustees and top administrative leadership to accomplish this. This was also a time to establish a new set of working relationships with state agencies in Sacramento, and between a newly created chancellor's office and the campuses. Common understandings and common definitions were established.

In the years prior to the Master Plan, capital outlay, or building programs, originated from each campus. In the nineteenth century, the campuses were independent of each other. When authority was legislatively given to the State Department of Education and the State Board of Education (as discussed in preceding chapters), this responsibility was not seriously assumed by either. In the years after World War II, when campuses were growing, each campus developed its own set of relationships with the State Department of Education and, most importantly, with the Department of Finance, the Legislative Analyst's Office, and legislative delegations. Typically these relationships involved the campus president and one or two other administrators. The relationships were parallel to those involved in the general fund support budget and sometimes involved the same individuals. Almost without exception, the campus president was central to the process.

Campus capital outlay budgets included proposals for buildings, minor construction and repairs, and land acquisition. They were coordinated through the State Department of Education and then advocated by the campuses, initially with the Department of Finance for inclusion in a governor's budget proposal. The Department of Finance had on its staff experts on building programs, and the review was comprehensive. Those campus initiatives that were eventually included in a governor's budget proposal went to the legislature for review and adoption. A customary first stop was the Legislative Analyst's Office, which would analyze every detail of every proposal and prepare a careful and very comprehensive analysis. Campus representatives would meet with Legislative Analyst's Office staff, as they had with Finance staff. The Legislative Analyst's Office would present a book of analyses to the legislature; it would often recommend deletion of a specific building proposal for whatever reason. Most often, when the Legislative Analyst's Office advised support, reductions or alterations were also recommended. There was no comprehensive framework or outline of academic programs or mission or structure against which proposals could be measured by the Department of Finance or the Legislative Analyst's Office. Finance staff did complete studies and publish these on particular aspects of capital outlay and support budgets in the 1950s. Analyses and recommendations were simply the judgments by Finance and Legislative Analyst's Office staffs based on experience.

The most effective president and campus was Julian McPhee of Cal Poly (during that time, both Cal Poly campuses were administered as one institution on two sites). In 1948, McPhee developed an architectural master plan, as he called it, for the two campuses. He also had an academic plan from which to advocate the building proposals. Funding to develop both plans came from the campus foundation. When Cal Poly was founded as a technical institution in 1901, dormitories were first built. McPhee secured funding for additional student housing in 1941, and then again in the postwar years, to accommodate an influx of veterans. California State College campuses as a whole only initiated a very modest student housing construction program in the late 1950s, as a result of a united presidential effort. McPhee was president from 1933 to 1966 and he used the applied programs in agriculture and technical fields, and engineering as well in later years, as a base from which to build a statewide network of support, and to advocate for campus student housing. He defined Cal Poly as a statewide, not a regional, campus, based upon its relationships to agriculture and industry over the state. Many of the Cal Poly programs, applied in character, were unique in the state.[1]

Student housing, in a variety of styles, goes back to the very earliest years of the state normal schools. The majority of students during those years were young women, and housing was perceived to be a moral necessity, under the guidance of a preceptress.[2] The student housing units gradually disappeared with age, other than at the two Cal Poly campuses. In 1957, shortly before the Master Plan, the legislature authorized the construction of residence halls on the campuses. Thirty-eight residence halls, each accommodating two hundred students, were constructed on eleven campuses. Financing came in part by a loan from the federal government, and the remainder was to come from anticipated rental fees.

In the years after World War II and before the Master Plan, construction flourished on the state college campuses. In 1948, the Strayer report, a study of California public higher education, was completed. The report addressed enrollment on individual campuses and the need for a coordinating mechanism for development and growth of the campuses. The presidents, responding to this dimension of the Strayer report, created a committee including the executive dean from each campus and representation from the Department of Finance, the Legislative Analyst's Office, the State Division of Architecture, and the State Department of Education. This group developed procedures for handling campus construction proposals and a number of "understandings" or formulae about campus entitlements. An office in the Department of Education, the State College Planning Office, worked with all of the participants and eventually staffed the presidents in their monthly meetings, as a priority list was built for the Department of Finance and the Legislative Analyst's Office. The Department of Finance then determined what the governor would propose.[3]

At this point, the presidents and their staffs went into action with an advocacy effort, although in reality, they had been involved all along the way. Most presidents did not feel limited to advocate only for proposals on the governor's list. Essentially, each president and his team were responsible for organizing the capital outlay program for the campuses. Presidents negotiated an understanding about academic programs, new ones to be developed, and rough understandings about a land-use plan.[4]

This established process was changed on July 1, 1960. On that date the board of trustees assumed responsibility for planning. In September 1960, Dr. Donald Leiffer became administrative officer. When Leiffer established an office in Sacramento and a small team to plan the transition to the board of trustees, he included an individual to begin to work on capital outlay.[5] The board itself, as it created its own structure, organized a Committee on Campus Planning, Buildings, and Grounds.

Harry Brakebill had been business manager and, more recently, executive dean at San Francisco State College from the late 1940s to 1960. He was clearly the most respected and informed financial administrator in the state colleges; his integrity was unquestioned, and he was a known and respected figure in Sacramento. Leiffer invited Brakebill to come to Sacramento to address the development of an agenda and framework for the use of the trustees and for the establishment of a chancellor's office unit dealing with capital outlay. Brakebill accepted the offer and (on loan from San Francisco State) became acting chief of facilities planning in January 1961.

Brakebill accomplished both goals, an agenda for the trustees and creation of a unit to work with capital outlay. He proposed an initial working relationship with the board and its Committee for Campus Planning, Buildings, and Grounds; he outlined the establishment of a unit within the chancellor's office to address capital outlay planning, both short and long range, and a building program. He did this with considerable skill and brought along most, if not all, of the presidents and other key campus figures. The chancellor's office unit was to be within the administration/business affairs function. Brakebill also created an agenda for the board and the chancellor to follow after July 1, 1961. He then returned to San Francisco State, and he subsequently declined an appointment to be vice-chancellor for business affairs, an offer made by Chancellor Buell Gallagher after the latter's arrival on July 1, 1961.[6]

In the autumn of 1961, recruitment began for a chief of facilities planning. As was the custom of the time, recruitment was by word of mouth. At that time each University of California campus had a sizeable in-house staff to shape its building program. Harry Harmon, a senior architect at UCLA, was responsible for building design and planning for all of the campus save the medical center. He reported to the campus architect. The UCLA campus architect was recruited for the California State College position, but ultimately declined an offer. Subsequently, Harmon was invited to visit the CSC headquarters, where he was interviewed by then vice-chancellor for business affairs John Richardson and by Don Leiffer, newly appointed as executive vice-chancellor. Three days after the interview, Richardson offered Harmon the position. Harmon had a dilemma, as he put it. He was not really looking for a job. He responded that he would think about the offer. The following week he asked to see Richardson once more, and Chancellor Gallagher. Harmon accepted the position and began as chief of facilities planning on January 21, 1962. Harmon did object to the title "chief." He had been a naval officer in World War II and had been recalled to active duty in the Korean War. He remained in the naval reserve until retirement. He did not want to be known as "chief."[7]

In his interim role, Harry Brakebill had hired a small staff. Brakebill brought on board four facilities planners to work with the campuses. Harmon appointed an architect to prepare contracts with project (i.e., for specific buildings, etc.) architects, and an experienced engineer to supervise construction inspections. Building design was done by the State Division of Architecture in Sacramento, and Harmon contracted with the Division of Architecture for construction inspections.

In 1961, the planning staff completed a study "Estimated Costs of Development and Role of Development of New State Colleges."[8] The study was predicated on existing programs and space requirements and utilization, and employed the many formulas that had been developed in previous years in negotiation with the Department of Finance and the Legislative Analyst's Office. But the study also recited from the Master Plan, stating that the total cost of a campus of twenty thousand full-time students would be eight-six million dollars, whereas the cost analysis employed in the study had resulted in lower figures. The major reason given by this new staff was that "the requirements for physical facilities will not lead the instructional program, but develop at the same rate as the other factors (approval of curricula, development of faculty, needs for specialized facilities by graduate students) that affect the education program development."[9] The trustees would soon take this reasoning to a much further point. Enrollment and growth estimates were calculated separately for each campus. The study was done to address the need for funding construction of new campuses proposed or already established by the legislature as the Master Plan was being enacted. The Department of Finance and the Legislative Analyst's Office accepted the results of this study and agreed with the statement about program leading the development of facilities.

The State Division of Architecture had for years designed and supervised the construction of California State College buildings and performed all architectural services for the campuses. There was a close connection among state government offices in Sacramento, the Department of Finance, the Legislative Analyst's Office, the Division of Architecture, legislative staff members, the governor's office, and other state agencies. Controls over CSC buildings were tight, and heretofore each campus had to protect and advocate for itself. Some examples are humorous. When the Division of Architecture staff designed a building for a program, that design was implemented on all campuses as enrollment growth necessitated new buildings. Thus, in the experience of this writer, once one learned the internal configuration of, for example, the social science building at San Francisco State College, that individual could be blindfolded and still navigate the social science building on any campus. A principal in the Legislative Analyst's Office had for some years a rule that he enforced: no more than two hinges on any door of three feet or less in width, no matter the weight of the door, for science laboratories and the like. When the campuses initiated a residence hall building program, a single architectural design was prepared. One campus, San Francisco State, had very limited land at that time (the late 1950s). The campus could have, by the reasoning of Sacramento agencies, two residence halls for men and two for women. The designs could not vary, so the buildings were stacked two and two.

Governor Pat Brown appointed the first trustees in the late spring of 1960. These individuals included the ten members of the State Board of Education and others for the remaining six seats. The first meeting of the new board was August 12, 1960. One of Brown's appointees accepted another position, in the 1960 presidential campaign, just before the August 12 meeting, a position that in his judgment made it imperative that he resign as a trustee. He attended the opening ceremonies of the August 12 meeting, announced his resignation, and departed. That appointee, Warren Christopher, had also agreed to accept an appointment to the new Coordinating Council for Higher Education. The governor then announced the appointment of Charles Luckman to the newly vacant seat. Luckman was present and was seated.

Charles Luckman was already a legend. Educated as an architect, he had graduated from the University of Illinois at the height of the depression, gone into sales for Colgate toothpaste, switched to Pepsodent, and moved up the corporate ladder to become president and CEO of Lever Brothers. An early global businessman, he had been the subject of a 1946 *Time* magazine cover story, "From Toothpaste to Soap to Skyscrapers. . . ." President Truman had named Luckman to head the food program for Europe, a Europe in recovery after World War II.

32. Charles Luckman.

In 1950, Luckman left Lever Brothers and moved to Los Angeles, where he and William Pereira, another widely known architect and a fellow University of Illinois alumnus, established a firm that overnight became one of the best known architectural firms in the country. A man of many talents, Luckman was to be central to the CSU building program, not only for the early period but for the next twenty-two years. He was a brilliant and forceful trustee, and a natural leader who could be very demanding.

Luckman was, from the beginning, the lead trustee for campus development. He was the first chair of the Committee on Campus Planning, Buildings, and Grounds. Harry Brakebill worked closely with him in 1961. Before Harry Harmon accepted the post of chief of facilities planning, he visited Luckman, whom he had come to know when Luckman's firm designed a building for UCLA. Harmon wanted assurance that Luckman would not interfere and micromanage as a trustee. Harmon received that assurance, and in both his oral history and his interview he affirmed that Luckman had honored that commitment.

Working first with Brakebill and then with Harmon, Luckman persuaded the trustees to put in place policies and practices about campus physical master plan development, site selections, responsibilities, and authority within the system at the campus, chancellor's office, and trustee levels for planning and approving buildings, appointment of campus master plan and project architects, and the like. Two early moves set the stage.

Luckman was convinced that the California State Colleges and its trustees and chancellor should select architects, select contractors for individual projects, and oversee its own building program. He and his colleagues at the Luckman-Pereira firm had done buildings for the University of California, and he thus had some experience with colleges and universities. Luckman personally negotiated, working with the state architect, an agreement that the trustees would pick architects and would most often pick private architects, both for the individual campus physical master plans and for specific projects and buildings. He had secured the governor's support for this. Part of this understanding was that the Division of Architecture would be eligible to compete with private architects for both campus master plan and project architect roles. One campus did have the Division of Architecture as the physical master planner for twenty years after the trustees assumed responsibility in 1961, and the division was on occasion selected in early years to do projects.[10] Doubtless others in state government were involved in these negotiations, most probably a few key legislators. Luckman's persuasions were successful.

The result was a highly centralized system. The power was in the board and the chancellor's staff. Campus Planning, Buildings, and Grounds Committee meetings were always well attended. The chancellor's staff prepared detailed analyses and recommendations, detailed agenda items for the board. The central staff was not large, so much of the preparation was done with the campuses. But there was no question about final authority. This shift of authority was widely regarded within the system as positive, and it was palatable because at least decisions were made within the state college family and not in the bureaucratic and political halls of Sacramento.

The second early move occurred at a trustee meeting. It had become a custom, from the establishment of the board, for presidents to review building programs and proposed projects first with the board committee and then with the full board. Beginning in 1961, unlike the mere pass through with the State Board of Education, the trustees actually reviewed projects and physical master plans in considerable detail. This was not simply an informative discussion. After the board had held full responsibility for a number of months, when a president was presenting a project to the board committee, trustee Luckman, the chair, quietly asked the president how this proposal related to the campus academic master plan. There was a silence. The president explained that he and his campus colleagues had thoroughly discussed the matter, but that he had no document that could be called a campus academic master plan. Other trustees joined the discussion. The result was an action moved by trustee Ted Meriam to declare a moratorium on approving capital outlay proposals until the individual campuses developed and brought to the board for approval, campus by campus, academic master plans and only subsequently physical master plans based on the academic plans. Thus began academic master planning in the California State Colleges.

This action was one of a small number of key moves made early on by the board and the chancellor to create a coherent system from a collection of campuses that had been quasi-independent (in earlier times totally independent).

> The physical master plan should not run a campus whose primary purpose is academics. An academic master plan should be developed followed by a physical master plan. It proved to be a sound basic planning premise. . . . The academic master plan was the key ingredient in the planning process. . . . As time went on, academic planning became more and more an important ingredient, and it ultimately became the lead activity that resulted in the buildings that we see today.[11]

The orchestration of this policy result is unclear. Evidence points to Luckman, Heilbron, Meriam, and Dumke. (Asked about this by this writer during an interview, Heilbron smiled.)

An uproar on the campuses immediately followed. This was the first clear and unequivocal sign that the days of autonomy were over. Presidents, deans, and faculty members expressed outrage. Cries of intrusion upon academic freedom came from many quarters. Presidents had to be a bit careful with criticism on this early issue at board meetings, but not necessarily when they were back on their campuses.

Academic planning is addressed in Chapter 4 in this work. But the overall context of the board using campus planning and building programs as an instrument for pulling the disparate campuses into a whole was complex. The role of faculty in decision making was not only on most minds, but an active issue. Faculty wanted to be involved in decisions about the buildings in which they would live. Enrollment was growing rapidly. The separate campus programs were consolidated into one system-building program and the trustees assigned a priority to each project.

The trustees were presented with "A Master Curricular Plan for the California State Colleges" on March 8, 1963. This plan incorporated an initial component for each campus. This was a first effort, and over time in a complex process, it became a central developmental tool for the CSU. As the emerging California State Colleges were coming together, a number of processes and planning approaches were developed. Some of these were unique in American higher education, and have been adopted as other states have grown university systems. In most states prior to the 1960s, higher education had not been thought of as a unified activity, related in important ways to economic and social development. This change over the years, and the California Master Plan, as well as the creation and building of the new CSC system, were major starting points.

As a new set of relationships was evolving with state government, the California State Colleges employed a representative in Sacramento. Members of the still relatively small chancellor's staff spent significant time in Sacramento. Presidents were encouraged, though not ordered, to stay away from Sacramento. Many did. All found staying away hard, whether they liked Sacramento activity or not. President McPhee of Cal Poly had been accustomed to visiting Sacramento often, and he had many friends in the legislature. To McPhee's credit, he used his relationships to support the proposals of the board in Sacramento. But it was the chancellor's staff that presented the trustees' building program to the Department of Finance, the governor, and the legislature, not individual campus presidents and faculty or administrators.

In the years before the Master Plan, enrollment capacities and targets and what came to be called enrollment ceilings were developed, often informally, by each campus, and were negotiated with the Department of Finance and the Legislative Analyst's Office. In 1961, the chancellor's staff initiated discussions with each campus, including the new ones, about enrollment ceilings. A rationale was developed to distinguish between urban and rural campuses. A common understanding was forged with the campuses, and trustee involvement was the final step. The norm for urban campuses was to be 20,000 FTE (full-time equivalent students). A common target for rural campuses, those outside of metropolitan areas, was set at 12,000 FTE. Some campuses had targets below the norm due to special circumstances—essentially, land limitations. In no instance was a target number set above the norm. Targets were set for each of the nineteen campuses, three of them, Dominguez Hills, San Bernardino, and Bakersfield, with later planned openings. The ceiling enrollments totaled 312,800 FTE. The actual enrollment in 1962–63 was 86,414 FTE and 118,201 individuals.

The financing of capital outlay projects has varied over the years since 1960. In the 1960s with Governor Brown, statewide bond issues, voted upon by the electorate, were the fund source. Brown permitted units of state government to borrow state funds against passage of bond proposals by the electorate. The state colleges were greatly assisted by this approach, as projects could be built to help with the very substantial increase in enrollments each year.

As the early capital outlay budget proposals were prepared by the campuses and the chancellor's staff, first attention was given to projects that would provide basic instructional capacity to address rapid growth. Some proposals were considered to be in the category of policy considerations. For example, would the state continue to fund the construction for performing arts facilities or for physical education buildings? These matters were not resolved, but as a practical matter such facilities moved down, far down, on priority lists for all but new campuses. Financing of the capital outlay program was a major public policy issue because of very sizeable amounts of money needed.

Ronald Reagan campaigned for office in 1966 on a "pay as you go" approach to financing of everything public, including building programs, and his administration began using general fund money for building in 1968. In 1969, the cash flow simply dried up. Projects not underway or deemed critical were halted and funds reverted to the state. A few projects that were absolutely essential to keep campuses in operation survived.[12] To resolve this stalemate, a bill originating in the assembly was adopted by the legislature and approved by the governor. Tidelands oil revenue came from land owned by the state; historically, the funds had gone to the city of Long Beach. In 1975, the legislature created the Capital Outlay Fund for Public Higher Education (COFPHE, known as the "coffee fund") to provide for higher education construction.

When Proposition 13 was adopted by California voters in 1978, public revenues at all levels of government in the state were affected. The Department of Finance adopted a policy of a one-third-each split of available money for capital outlay and construction and land acquisition among the community colleges, the University of California, and the California State University and Colleges. Heretofore, the split had been 20 percent, 40 percent, and 40 percent. This policy prevailed until the early 2000s.

Table 13.1 Higher Education Capital Outlay Facilities Bond Act: 1986 to the Present

Won	**1986:** Proposition 56 ($400 million over 2 years) For: 3,981,501–60% Against: 2,691,612–40%	Gubernatorial Primary (June)
Won	**1988:** Proposition 78 ($600 million over 2 years) For: 5,053,675–57.7% Against: 3,723,101–42.3%	Presidential Election (November)
Won	**1990:** Proposition 121, part 1 ($450 million over 2 years) For: 2,543,993–55% Against: 2,075,455–44.91%	Gubernatorial Primary (June)
Lost	**1990:** Proposition 143, part 2 ($450 million over 2 years) For: 3,183,710–49% Against: 3,349,708–51%	Gubernatorial General Election (November)
Won	**1992:** Proposition 153 ($900 million over 2 years) For: 2,812,027–51% Against: 2,706,811–49%	Presidential Primary (June)
Lost	**1994:** Proposition 1C ($900 million) For: 1,979,722–47% Against: 2,197,831–53%	Gubernatorial Primary (June)
Won	**1996:** Proposition 203 ($3 billion: $2.025 billion for K-12; $975 million for higher education) For: 3,258,669–61.9% Against: 2,010,050–38.1%	Presidential Primary (March)
Won	**1998:** Proposition 1A ($9.2 billion: $6.7 billion for K-12; $2.5 billion for higher education) For: 4,318,508–62% Against: 2,605,477–38%	Gubernatorial General Election (November)

Won	**2002:** Proposition 47 ($13.05 billion: $11.4 billion for K-12; $1.65 billion for higher education) For: 3,846,045–59% Against: 2,678,389– 41%	Gubernatorial General Election (November)
Won	**2004:** Proposition 55 ($12.3 billion: $10 billion for K-12; $2.3 billion for higher education) For: 3,239,706–50.9% Against: 3,130,921–49.1%	Presidential Primary (March)

This table was prepared by Dorena Knepper, director of governmental relations, emerita, at the Northridge campus.

Background Note: Prior to 1986, higher education capital construction was financed with tidelands oil revenues coming from royalties paid to the state for oil and natural gas extracted by oil companies from state-owned land. The legislature created the COFPHE (Capital Outlay Fund for Public Higher Education) to be the repository for these monies. When the price of oil dropped dramatically in 1985, revenue to the fund dropped to a quarter of what had been anticipated. The legislature proposed the first bond act to supplement the COFPHE. However, in subsequent years, it became clear that tidelands oil revenue was no longer a viable source for capital construction, and the legislature turned to bond act measures to fully fund higher education's needs.

Until 1996, separate measures were proposed for higher education and K-12. When two higher education bond measures failed passage, and private polls suggested that voters would be more likely to support higher education construction needs if they were combined into one measure with K-12, the legislature began proposing consolidated bond act measures.

Enrollment had not been a major pressure point in the 1970s. In the early 1980s, this changed. The use of revenue bonds, paid for by the recipient (the CSU) came into play. This approach was proposed in the legislature and approved by Governor George Deukmejian. Funding to pay off revenue bonds would have to come from the operating or general fund budget. In the mid-1980s, general obligation bonds, the first since the years of Governor Pat Brown, returned. Governor Deukmejian, who was generally friendly to higher education, supported this reintroduction. Governor Pete Wilson continued this approach, and the use of general obligation bonds continues to this day. In 1990 and 1994, voters did not approve bonds for higher education. Revenue bonds and funds remaining from previous bond issues were the only funds available for a time. This caused the three segments to join forces in a carefully defined joint political effort. Later in the 1990s and in the 2000s voters did approve bonds, and funding did become available for campus projects. The three higher education segments made common cause with the leaders of K-12 to assure passage of bond proposals.

Through 1998, the amount of bond revenue for higher education was split equally among the three segments, each getting one-third. In the November 2002 bond measure, the split was 40 percent for the community colleges and 30 percent each for the UC and the CSU. This split was maintained for the March 2004 ballot measure as well.

* * *

In 1975, Harry Harmon became executive vice-chancellor. He maintained an interest in campus physical development. Harmon's accomplishments were many. With the support of Luckman, he had built a process within the CSU that was highly centralized. This approach had been successful in capturing control, for the trustees and the CSU, of campus physical planning, the appointment of particular project architects as well as campus master plan architects, setting capital outlay priorities, and providing an important context for the establishment of a systemwide academic planning function. A common approach to master planning at all of the campuses was established. "Each master plan architect was required to produce a master plan document for the campus that included everything from light standards, building vocabulary, landscape improvements, and the complete envelope of what that campus should evolve to over time when the enrollments warranted bringing buildings online."[13] Each campus also had a mandated campus master physical plan committee with defined membership.

In the early 1980s, both Luckman and Harmon left the CSU stage. Luckman completed more than twenty years as a trustee in 1982. With the change in chancellors in 1982, Harmon offered to step down. He was asked to remain as executive vice-chancellor but agreed to do so for only one year, to assist with the transition.

When Harmon had become executive vice-chancellor in 1975, the position he vacated as a vice-chancellor had been filled with an appointment of an assistant vice-chancellor, James Westphal. A change quietly began. Westphal did not speak with the authority of Harmon with the trustees, the campuses, or in Sacramento. Campus and trustee dissatisfaction was substantial, with Westphal and with a process that increasingly came to be viewed as cumbersome. Westphal left in the transition of chancellorship from Dumke to Reynolds, and Sheila Chaffin was appointed as the assistant vice-chancellor. She did not work well in this role with the trustees, the campuses, or Sacramento. Dissatisfaction grew from the campuses, the presidents, and individual trustees to Sacramento agencies and even some members of the legislature. When Reynolds left the chancellorship in 1990 and subsequently went to the City University of New York, she took Chaffin with her.

For all practical purposes, the fifteen-year period from 1975 to 1990 was a period of quiet and sometimes difficult activity in preparation for a major transition yet to come. The campuses began to play a much more active role in the master planning and building process. The chancellor's office reacted within a framework built in earlier years. Campus master plans were redone as needed, buildings were built.

The campuses and the presidents became much more active in Sacramento during this fifteen-year period. Governor Deukmejian's Department of Finance backed away from detailed oversight of capital outlay projects and in a sense encouraged campus activity. Once the governor made a decision to include a project in the budget, it was supported by the Department of Finance. The Department of Finance and the Legislative Analyst's Office alliance for managing and micromanaging proposals through the legislature was broken. The legislature backed away from a major review of capital outlay proposals and, for the most part, approved the proposals advanced by the governor, who typically approved the proposals submitted by the trustees when it was possible to finance them.[14] A stage for a major change was being set for the CSU in its financial and building programs.

Over the years the University of California and the California State University had been treated similarly with respect to state-funded building programs. The roles of the Department of Finance and the Legislative Analyst's Office were similar. Thus the two systems made common cause to secure change. The State Public Works Board withdrew from active participation in the process; buildings for the two university systems moved from detailed and minute examination to the consent calendar. It is at least arguable that this approach by the Deukmejian administration helped to set the stage for the trustees to back away from their detailed involvement and chancellor's staff control of building programs on the campuses. Pete Wilson succeeded Deukmejian in the governorship in 1991, and his administration accelerated the moving of authority from state agencies "down" to the trustees. In turn, the trustees became more willing and interested in moving planning and proposals to the campuses.[15]

The most significant development in this period was the emergence of donor funds in the building programs. In 1980, the Dominguez Hills campus was offered four million dollars to participate in the 1984 Olympics in Los Angeles. A portion of the funds would be to build an outdoor velodrome. The facility was intended to be used later by the campus, not only as a cycling facility, but as an outdoor amphitheater, a track and field facility, and whatever other purposes the campus desired. Only after some discussion within the chancellor's staff, this proposal was advanced to the board, approved, and built. Later in the decade, the Los Angeles campus wanted to build a performing arts complex. The president of CSULA, James Rosser, and a few of his colleagues came together with former trustee Charles Luckman. The result was major funding by the Luckman family and the building of a far more adequate structure than would have been allowed using state funding only. The Harriett and Charles Luckman Center for the Performing Arts is a significant venue in Los Angeles and an anchor for the programs in the arts on the Los Angeles campus.

The emergence of fundraising and development as a major factor in the life of the CSU really occurred with the arrival of Chancellor Barry Munitz (this story is recited in Chapter 12). But as a result of the Los Angeles project, the trustees did consider giving priority—and have given priority—to building proposals that included donor funding. At first an effort was made to standardize this with a formula, for example, performing arts centers proposed with a one-third donor-match funding. As a practical matter, the availability of outside funding to advance a building project on the trustees' priority list is considered on a project-by-project basis.[16] This was the beginning of a new era for campus construction, in which outside funding for buildings traditionally provided by the state became more important each year.

In the very early 1990s a number of matters converged. There was a new assistant vice-chancellor, Jon Regnier, who had previous chancellor's office and campus experience, and he was widely regarded as a competent and helpful administrator. The difficulties of the 1980s with a willful assistant vice-chancellor who would sometimes impose changes on campus proposals, even against strong campus opposition and, some would argue, common sense, had departed. Relationships in Sacramento around capital outlay projects were rebuilt. The trustees elected Ralph Pesqueira as chair of the Campus Planning, Buildings, and Grounds Committee. Pesqueira began his tenure as chair by questioning the relative roles of the campuses, the chancellor's staff, and the trustees, and raising what he perceived as the desirability of decentralization.

When Ann Reynolds left the chancellorship in 1990, an experienced campus president, Ellis McCune, then retiring from the Hayward presidency, was appointed as acting chancellor. McCune's most significant accomplishments included addressing the centralization/decentralization issue, and his brief tenure began a period of reexamining these relationships and changing many. The appointment of Barry Munitz as chancellor ushered in, on many fronts, a time of redefinition of roles. Munitz's basic position on centralization/decentralization was that the chancellor's office should address broad policy matters: the mission of the CSU and the means to accomplish it, the budget, governmental representation, public understanding and support for the overall functioning of the California State University. Within this broad CSU framework, the campuses should be responsible institutions, governing and administering themselves. The board of trustees should address the encompassing policy issues, budgets, and the like, while retaining final authority for the life of the CSU. Many board members were heard to say that the most important thing they were immediately responsible for is the appointment of presidents, not the management of campuses.

This convergence of a new trustee approach and leader for the building program, a new chancellor, assistant vice-chancellor, and a newly developing atmosphere in Sacramento brought about substantial change in the way the building program functioned. Layered on top of all of this was the newly developing approach to joint state-donor-private funding.

***

In 1991, and then again in 1992, the California Postsecondary Education Commission staff did two studies about space needs and utilization in both the CSU and the UC. The two university systems collaborated successfully on pushing these reports through the commission. These studies paid more attention to the needs of both systems for educational space than had been the case in the past. At the same time, Barry Munitz, as a new chancellor, was successful in obtaining further delegations of authority from state agencies to the board of trustees for the capital outlay program.[17]

In 1990–91, the year that Ellis McCune was acting chancellor, the presidents and McCune had addressed the value of the Orange Book, the formulas that had generally governed the generation (not always, when money for the state budget was short) and the allocation/uses of resources for years. (The Orange Book is discussed in some detail in chapter twelve of this work.) One of the early acts of Munitz was to end the use of the Orange Book. Senior campus administrators then began to urge the restructuring of the capital outlay process. With the arrival of Richard West as vice-chancellor for business affairs in 1994, those who wanted change found a sympathetic ear. West commissioned a study by Coopers and Lybrand, a well-known accounting and management consultation firm. That study produced a map of the capital outlay process from an initial idea for a project, the work and proposal at the campus level, through the chance

Based on the study, West created, with the full support of the trustees, a systemwide task force to restructure the capital outlay process. The task force recommended a two-stage plan. The first was to move management authority for all capital outlay projects to the campuses. The second was to restructure the capital outlay funding and project delivery processes. The task force initially projected an implementation cycle over a four-year period.[18]

The Building Design and Construction Task Force report, *Restructuring the California State University Capital Outlay Process*, was completed in 1996. Trustee Ali Razi became a leader and advocate, along with trustee Pesqueira, for the changes recommended in the report. The report was clear and explicit: "By restructuring the current process, campuses will be given authority to directly manage the entire capital outlay process from budgeting through design and construction."[19]

The report's recommendations included moving funding for project feasibility studies from requests to the state, in the annual capital outlay budget, to the campuses; the individual institutions would be responsible for funding studies from existing resources. This was a trade-off. Campuses, not the chancellor's staff office of physical planning and development, would select project architects and engineers and enter into contractual arrangements with those they selected. Campuses would be responsible for pre-bid and bidding processes, and for construction management. The system office of physical planning and development would maintain only a small core staff to process the annual budget requests, work with and support the campuses, and provide a necessary measure of coordination and leadership. Working with the campuses and the trustees, the system office would especially address policy matters. The report stressed accountability, and was clear that campuses, in accepting delegated authority, from the board to the chancellor to the individual president, must demonstrate and maintain a capacity to manage a complex program. Processes to measure this were specified.[20]

The board approved the report. Immediately, attention turned to the second phase, "restructuring capital outlay funding and project delivery." The most important recommendation was to provide lump-sum project funding. Heretofore, for as long as anyone could remember, funding had been provided only in stages, each stage a part of an annual capital outlay budget request from the CSU to the governor: preliminary planning and working drawings, construction, and equipment.[21] Beginning in 1997–98, the CSU received from Sacramento a capital outlay budget, considerable streamlined budget authority, and lump-sum (i.e., for each project) funding.[22] The trustees were slower to react with respect to board–chancellor's office–campus relationships and division of authority. But after discussion, the board adopted the sense of the task force report and most of the recommendations. A few were modified.[23]

This evolution of the distribution of authority and responsibility settled into a new and productive pattern of centralization/decentralization after the changes of the mid- to late 1990s. The administration of Chancellor Charles Reed and the leadership of Executive Vice-Chancellor and Chief Financial Officer Richard West maintained a steady hand. The decentralization that occurred empowered individuals on the campuses to engage in creative thinking, and the campuses responded. The trustees and the chancellor's staff retained the authority and responsibility to oversee the standards set by statute and good practice, to approve campus master plans, and designs and contract amounts for projects, and these were strong controls. But the creative energy on the campuses was released.

For ten years, the experience with this distribution of authority and responsibility has been positive. The board and the chancellor's staff have not intervened in any regular or frequent way with campus proposals. Essentially, the central role is to assure that campuses have and follow master plans and that designs and contracts are acceptable within these frameworks. Presidents and campuses vie to secure priority positions for resources to fund campus projects; competition is substantial. Presidents have always done this. The years since the redistribution of responsibility are most accurately characterized as a time of changing ways of funding and building capital projects. The Luckman Center on the Los Angeles campus opened a door. The chancellor at that time, Ann Reynolds, urged a trustee to push for a policy that would assign first priority to project related to the arts in which there was a one-third donor match of funds to complete the projects. The trustees did move what came to be the Luckman Center to a first-priority position. The particular context for this was the performing arts, and the trustees adopted a task force report that assigned priorities to performing arts complexes on four campuses, all based on the assumption of a donor match.

Contributed funding from donors and public and private partnerships have become major factors in setting priorities for capital building projects. Each instance is considered on the merits of a proposal. It is fair to assert that in most instances donor funding and funding from partnerships are important in determining position on a priority list. One campus, CSU Sacramento, secured funding for a building by offering to provide the funding for equipping it—in this instance a major amount, as the building was entirely used for instructional technology. San Jose State constructed a large new library in partnership with the city on campus land. And again, on the Sacramento State campus, the federal government built Placer Hall, a geology building for US Geological Survey (USGS) research as well as for the geology program; this was initiated by a veteran faculty member in geology, Professor Gregory Wheeler. The building contains faculty offices, classrooms and laboratories, and the USGS laboratories and research space. Faculty members become USGS researchers, students are employed in projects, and the partnership is productive for all. Campuses are constructing athletic and student facilities with combinations of student fee and donor funds, totally nonstate funded.

Since the beginning in 1961, the trustees have had two capital outlay budgets and projections, one for state-funded projects and one for non-state-funded projects. Both have five-year time spans. Over the years, the five-year projection, or at least a two- or three-year projection was required for non-state-funded projects. The five-year projection time has been firmly required for projects that are in whole or in part state funded. As a practical matter, projects that are wholly non-state funded surface sometimes on six months' notice.

A strategic move made by the Reed-West administration in 2002–03 was to consolidate debt capacity from all campuses and the system. Historically non-state-funded buildings such as residence halls, parking facilities, student unions, and the like were built with borrowed money; the CSU sold bonds for residence halls and parking, campuses handled their student union financing through the chancellor's office and further bond sales. As financing of various projects became more flexible in the late 1990s and in 2000, campuses sought more bond funding. The Reed-West move was to consolidate debt capacity and then assign to each campus an amount. This has not created a problem for the campuses to date, as no campus is near debt capacity. In fact, with enrollment and budget growth, debt capacity is expanding faster than the use of debt.[24] The combined strength of the campus as in securing funds has resulted in a more flexible and lower cost for financing construction.

* * *

The story of the capital outlay program, of building the structures that the people of the California State University learn, teach, live, and work in, is in some ways the story of the organizational history of the CSU. The capital outlay program was used as an instrument by the early board of trustees and Chancellor

33. Artist's rendering of California State University Trustees and Chancellor's Building, 1998.

Dumke and a small staff, a tool to bring about quickly academic and enrollment planning among the campuses. In a very real sense, it was the instrument used to create the substance of the system in an organized and coherent way. That instrument was resisted by presidents and faculties over the state, but the trustees were firm.

If one looks at the CSU in terms of periods of development and the gradual maturing of the system, and inevitably associates these with the administration of individual chancellors, the capital outlay program was for about fifteen years an instrument to create a system. Subsequently, it was an essential and important, but by this time cumbersome, instrument for the orderly growth and operation of the system for another fifteen years. Then, a time of decentralization set in, beginning in about 1991. Once again the capital outlay program was a major factor in the repositioning the capacity of what is at the center—the trustees and the chancellor—and what is at the operating or substantive program focus of the CSU—the campuses. Simultaneously, the capital outlay program became a major factor in the restructuring of the financial base of the CSU.

In 1960, when the trustees assumed responsibility, the California State Colleges included 15,794,607 square feet in buildings on sixteen campuses. As of 2007, the California State University had 80,660,437 square feet on twenty-three campuses.[25]

Notes

[1] Robert Kennedy, president emeritus, Cal Poly San at Luis Obispo, interview by the author, October 24, 2006, 10, 24.

[2] Benjamin F. Gilbert, *Pioneers for One Hundred Years: San Jose State College 1857–1957* (San Jose, Calif.: San Jose State University, 1957), 54.

[3] Glenn S. Dumke, John Butler, and Arthur Hall, "Moving San Francisco State College to a New Site," pages 74–76 in "Sourcebook on Campus Planning and Institutional Development," U.S. Department of Health, Education, and Welfare, 1961.

[4] The information for these pre–Master Plan years comes from the author's works of 1963 and 1971, from "A History of the California State University and Colleges," the monograph coauthored by the author and Judson Grenier (Carson, Calif.: California State University, Dominguez Hills, 1981), and from detailed memoranda, in email form, from Jon Regnier and J. Patrick Drohan, prepared for a September 21, 2006, focus group discussion about capital outlay programs, to be found in the CSU Archives. Participants in the oral history focus group included J. Patrick Drohan, Jon Regnier, Elvyra San Juan, and Richard West.

[5] The comprehensive description of the transition is found in earlier chapters.

[6] Harry E. Brakebill, oral history, July 9, 1987, CSU Archives. Also personal knowledge of author. Brakebill became vice-chancellor for business affairs in 1965 and executive vice-chancellor in 1969; he retired in 1975.

[7] CSU oral history interview,[No interviewer name OK?] July 10, 1987; interview of the author, March 24, 2006; CSU Archives.

[8] "Estimated Costs of Development and Role of Development of New State Colleges," the California State Colleges chancellor's office, 1961, CSU Archives.

[9] *Ibid.*

[10] Harry Harmon, oral history, Lawrence de Graaf, July 10, 1987, interview by author, March 24, 2006; Arthur Hall, interview by author, March 2, 2005, CSU Archives; Charles Luckman, *Twice in a Lifetime: From Soap to Skyscrapers,* W. W. Norton, 1988, 348–52.

[11] Harry Harmon, Gerth interview, 11.

[12] Casper Weinberger, letter to Glenn Dumke, March 25, 1969, CSU Archives; Jon Regnier, memorandum to Donald Gerth, September 20, 2006, 10, CSU Archives.

[13] Harry Harmon, oral history and interview.

[14] Oral history group on capital outlay.

[15] *Ibid.*

[16] Gerald Beavers, retired principal, Legislative Analyst's Office, interview by author, March 26, 2007, CSU Archives.

[17] Focus group on capital outlay.

[18] J. Patrick Drohan, email to the author, August 30, 2006, CSU Archives.

[19] *Restructuring the California State University Capital Outlay Process*, final report of the Building Design and Construction Task Force, 1996, 6, CSU Archives.

[20] *Restructuring*, 6–18.

[21] *Ibid.*, 19–23.

[22] Drohan, email.

[23] Minutes, board of trustees, May and July 1999, CSU Archives.

[24] This segment of the manuscript heavily relies on the focus group on capital outlay, cited in note 4, above.

[25] Data from Capital Planning, Design, and Construction unit, Office of the Chancellor, April 25, 2008.

Chapter 14

In Sacramento and Washington

A persistent theme in the California State Colleges in the 1950s and 1960s was the change from a group of quasi-autonomous public colleges to a structure of institutions brought together by a shared overarching mission and a unified governance structure. One major dimension of this change that would affect institutional behavior was the relationship of the colleges to state government. Washington would be a new arena for the colleges, for there had been no representation by any of the campuses in the nation's capital, only individual contacts.

Sacramento

The state colleges were theoretically in a common governance structure, with the State Department of Education as the statewide encompassing administrative headquarters and the State Board of Education as the governing board for all campuses. As a practical matter, each campus had been founded separately and had its own regional political support base; the only exception was Cal Poly, where President Julian McPhee successfully used the fact of Cal Poly's uniqueness with programs in agriculture and other applied fields to define the constituency of Cal Poly as statewide.

Prior to July 1, 1960, each campus president, along with selected campus individuals chosen by the president to work with him, represented that campus in Sacramento. Shrewd presidents kept the small staff in the Division of State Colleges and Teacher Education informed of their activities; on occasion they would need support. The presidents not only worked with the state offices and agencies beginning with the governor's office and the Department of Finance, but also with their regional legislative delegations. On July 1, 1960, a process of change began.

The trustees and the newly appointed administrative officer for the transition from the State Board of Education to the board of trustees, Donald Leiffer, had no staff to work with the legislature and state government. Julian McPhee, who had a strong and working presence in Sacramento, offered his "man in Sacramento," Harold Wilson, as a temporary governmental relations person to work with Leiffer, and Leiffer accepted. Leiffer also knew Sacramento, as he had been a senior member of Governor Pat Brown's staff for the previous eighteen months, and he was politically experienced. He not only taught politics, he practiced politics. Wilson's routine for a number of years had been to drive from San Luis Obispo early on Monday, arriving in time for the noon start of the legislature, and return to San Luis Obispo late Thursday afternoon after the legislature ended its weekly scheduled session. Wilson was well known, and worked easily with the government community in Sacramento.

Leiffer brought to the transition staff three individuals experienced in working with state government, Harry Brakebill, then executive dean at San Francisco State, and two individuals from the Department of Finance. This group worked through the transition year and into the 1961–62 year, as the board began to make a number of senior appointments. Wilson worked with them.

Glenn Dumke was appointed chancellor in April 1962. One of his first moves, after consulting with faculty and presidents, was the appointment of a vice-chancellor to build a program of governmental relations and public affairs. The trustees appointed Don Muchmore, then director of the California Museum of Science and Industry and a former student of Dumke's at Occidental College, to a vice-chancellorship created by Don Leiffer's return to San Diego State. Muchmore's first two efforts were to create a Sacramento office, and organize a campaign to secure passage of a bond in November 1962 to support a higher education building program. He made two appointments, both individuals known to him, Les Cohen and Robert Reardon. Reardon, who had worked with Muchmore, was appointed to the position of director of public affairs, to work with the media and to assist Muchmore with the bond campaign for proposition 1A. Les Cohen, then assistant director of the museum, assumed the position of director of governmental affairs and moved to Sacramento.[1]

Cohen had to build on the history of the state colleges. Some good legislative and agency relationships existed, but there were issues on the table. At the time of the Master Plan two years earlier, Dumke, who was then president of San Francisco State, asked a member of his staff to do some background research on members of the legislature. This revealed that only three members of the eighty assembly and forty in the senate members were alumni of California State College. A plurality of members were alumni of private universities and colleges, and a lesser number were alumni of the University of California. Many members, particularly from regions where there were well-established state colleges, were deeply tied to their regional campuses, and not at all willing to see the autonomy of "their campus" diminished. The chancellor's office had moved from Sacramento to Los Angeles six months before Cohen's arrival, and the move from Sacramento was hardly a settled issue in the minds of many members.

The challenge for the small staff in the Sacramento office (Cohen and a very able all-purpose assistant, Sally Svilich) was to build an office that was credible with legislators and the executive branch. In a significant measure, the office was a service agency, helping legislators and others with matters about the state colleges, and helping the campuses and the chancellor and his staff with legislators and state agencies. In the early years of the newly established California State Colleges, discretionary money was virtually nonexistent for the chancellor's office and the trustees. The trustees did establish a foundation, or auxiliary corporation, following the model used on campuses for years. The foundation's income was modest. The Sacramento office had no discretionary money. In fact, the first director, Les Cohen, finally took out a second mortgage on his home so that he could function in his position. Consequently, the chancellor proposed to the board that it create an "education information fund" within the system foundation, specifically for the support of the Sacramento lobbying effort. Each campus was to contribute three hundred dollars per year to support the lobbying and representational efforts of the Sacramento office. Most campus presidents complied, but there were a few who delayed their financial support, some indefinitely. This practice continued until the early 1980s.[2]

The budget and the fiscal and administrative flexibility that the system needed were continuing concerns. The idea of a budget team would evolve over time. Individuals of the chancellor's staff in Los Angeles were the principal negotiators from the very beginning of the system. In the early years in the 1960s, the chancellor's senior staff would be joined by campus staff, and presentations and negotiations would be done campus by campus. The 1.8 percent issue (see Chapter 3) in the 1964–65 year was a major fiasco from the standpoint of the state colleges. The Sacramento office played only a small role in this, although experience suggests that it probably could have been helpful in bridging some of the personal and political divides that were really what the issue was all about, not an amount of money (just over two hundred thousand dollars).

In the spring of 1966, a rather remarkable event occurred. Julian McPhee was about to retire as the president of Cal Poly. He was just short of beloved in the legislature, and he was certainly credible and respected. He would be seventy on his next birthday, later that year. He had already received a five-year extension past the retirement age of sixty-five, and at that time further extension was not possible. The chancellor's office was anxious to separate the two Cal Poly campuses and had prematurely prepared legislation to do so. The bill eventually was heard in the Senate Finance Committee, chaired by George Miller. McPhee sent someone to testify against the bill—his message was that he would prepare a bill. Miller held the proposed bill in the air, tore it into pieces, and adjourned the hearing. McPhee wrote the bill.

Not long after that, a one-of-a-kind event occurred. The entire legislature gave a retirement dinner for President McPhee. The master of ceremonies was Senator George Miller. Most members were present, along with other colleagues and friends to honor McPhee for his thirty years of leadership. Nothing like it, a legislative event to honor an individual in higher education, had ever occurred before in the history of the state, nor has it happened since. Shortly before his last day in the presidency, McPhee learned that he had cancer. He lived a little less than one year, in retirement.[3]

Inevitably, the style of the chancellor and his immediate staff, have an impact on relationships and on the substance of issues in Sacramento. Glenn Dumke was an academic, not a political person. He was forceful about not wanting the state college headquarters to be in Sacramento, and that was not a secret. He did not want to spend any more time in Sacramento than absolutely necessary. Not only his staff, but individuals in Sacramento were aware of this, and the stories about his coming and going (last plane in, first plane out) were many. In his twenty years as chancellor he worked with three governors. He had excellent relationships with two, Pat Brown, and Ronald Reagan, and a poor relationship with the third, Jerry Brown. His relationships with Brown senior and with Reagan were important to building and supporting the system. His relationship to Jerry Brown was sometimes a problem, although the younger Brown's relationships with others, generally, were difficult. Dumke had a quiet style. Without question, he had no personal agenda for the Sacramento scene.

Almost as a counterbalance, one of Dumke's chief lieutenants, Harry Brakebill, vice-chancellor for business affairs from 1965 to 1970, and executive vice-chancellor until his retirement in 1975, was well known and very credible in Sacramento, largely due to his years as the business manager for San Francisco State and his work for more than a year in the 1960–61 transition. Brakebill recruited two very able career Sacramento staffers, Dale Hanner and Louis Messner; thus, a budget team for Sacramento was developing.

Cohen's more than five years as the director in Sacramento were the years of establishing a credible and useful office while building relationships. One of the important things that he did was to bring student leaders from the campuses to Sacramento. In early 1963, the student presidents had formed the California State College Student Presidents Association. Cohen invited them to participate in lobbying and to testify before the legislature to the advantage of the state colleges. When Dumke met with Reagan in December 1966, just after Reagan's election, only Les Cohen joined him. Cohen was responsible for seeing through legislation, and the first pieces of legislation that began to give some fiscal flexibility, largely a result of the quick action after the 1.8 percent debacle, occurred at this time.

The statewide Academic Senate and other faculty leaders were disappointed in Cohen's appointment, and they were very public about their disappointment. They wanted an academic, or at least someone with a graduate degree; Cohen had a baccalaureate degree. At one point, disappointment that Cohen had not yet in a legislative session produced a faculty salary increase, the Academic Senate voted no-confidence in Cohen. This caused an unanticipated reaction in the legislature ("He is our lobbyist, how dare you!"). The cost to the faculty was a deliberate six-month delay in an across-the-board salary increase. All of the actors in the state colleges were still feeling their way. Cohen resigned in 1968; his wife was seriously ill and he needed a somewhat less hectic lifestyle, not a regular commute to the system headquarters in Los Angeles. Cohen remained a lobbyist for a full career, and he continued to be supportive of the state colleges when asked.

By 1968, the central preoccupation of Sacramento with the state colleges was campus unrest, principally, but not solely, San Francisco State. A few years earlier the state colleges had opened a Washington DC office, largely focused on securing grants. The first director of the office of federal relations was John Kehoe, a congressional staffer. When Cohen resigned, Dumke invited Kehoe to come to Sacramento; he did. Inevitably, Kehoe came to know Governor Reagan and members of his staff. At the time of the Hayakawa appointment in the autumn of 1968, Reagan invited Kehoe to join his staff to be his informant at the San Francisco campus during those turbulent years. Kehoe consulted Dumke, who was agreeable, even enthusiastic about having a state college person on the governor's staff with direct access to the governor. Kehoe's assistant, William Storey, became acting director while Kehoe was on leave. Eventually, Kehoe decided to resign from the directorship.

With the end of the1960s and some restoration of peace on the campuses, a new era set in. This change, a sense of stability, affected the CSU's Sacramento Office of Governmental Affairs, as it did all of the California State College operations. The chancellor's office staff set about the recruitment of a new director for the Office of Governmental Affairs, and in November 1970, Dr. James Jensen was appointed as its director. Jensen brought to the role a background different from his three predecessors. He held baccalaureate and master's degrees from the University of Minnesota, and a doctorate in political science from the University of California at Berkeley. He had been an assistant dean of university extension for the UC (a statewide position, as UC extension was then a statewide operation), a legislative staff member, for one year acting executive officer for senate rules, and, most immediately, coordinator of legislation for the State Department of Education. Just as the system was moving into a new period, with an agenda of substance well beyond the initial organizational steps, so was the Sacramento Office of Governmental Affairs. It was time to build an agenda.

* * *

The California State Colleges were each named as they were founded, and their names associated with a city or county or a widely understood defined area, such as San Fernando Valley State College. The single exception was the original Cal Poly, understood from its beginning to have a statewide mission. With the establishment of the board of trustees and a system, an early question became the naming of campuses. At the July 1962 board meeting the president, faculty, students, and advisory board members of Orange County State College requested a simple change of name to Orange State College. The trustees approved unanimously. Herman Ridder, the chair of the trustee Committee on Gifts and Public Affairs and the publisher of the Long Beach Press-Telegram, then raised the question of "a uniform designation for the colleges." In the discussion that followed, the proposal was made "to explore the use of the name California State College to be followed by a clear designation of its locality in order to continue its local identity." The chancellor was instructed to do a study of the matter and gather opinions and recommendations from the campuses.[4] A survey of the campuses was completed in 1962–63. Not surprisingly, the campuses wanted to retain their original names. The trustees and chancellor concluded that only new campuses would be named "California State College," followed by a geographic designation.

The more complex political issue would arise in 1966, when an assembly member from San Diego, James Mills, proposed an interim study to consider designating the system the California State University. Much of the legislative leadership and pressure on the matter of naming and university status would come from the San Diego area over the next eight years. Mills' proposal was not adopted. The trustees had recently initiated a process to develop a legislative program each year in advance of the session. The legislative program for the 1967 session included a proposal to rename the system "The California State University." In the 1967 legislative session, two bills were introduced. Assembly Member Mervyn Dymally introduced a bill to name the system "The California State Universities and Colleges," and Assembly Member John Vasconcellos introduced a bill to name the system "The California State University." The bills were consolidated, and received serious consideration. There was discussion not only on the campuses and in the legislature, but around the state. In a lead editorial, the *Los Angeles Times* urged substantial additional financial support for the state colleges, while at the same time urging the defeat of the bills. The *Times* observed that the renaming would create confusion with the University of California, and would reinforce a campaign for the state colleges to grant the doctorate. The proposal passed in the assembly, and was defeated in the senate. The University of California regents and administration opposed the proposal strongly, for the same reasons the *Los Angeles Times* did, or perhaps, putting it another way, the *Times* published the position of the University of California; among the most powerful of the regents was Mrs. Dorothy Buffum Chandler, the wife of the publisher of the paper.

The experience of Les Cohen, then the director of governmental affairs in Sacramento, was useful in understanding the political climate surrounding the issue. The CSC campus presidents, to a person, supported the bill. Some faculty, principally education faculty, opposed the bill. Generally faculty were not strongly supportive; this was the time of significant campus unrest. The student body presidents were strongly supportive, and some testified on behalf of the bill. Cohen called campus advisory board chairs and found opposition, as many of the advisory board chairs and members were alumni of the University of California.

In January 1971, a new legislative session began. Assembly Member Richard Barnes of San Diego had been involved with the name change and university issue. He had earlier introduced a bill to change the name to "university." Barnes introduced Assembly Bill 123. Jensen worked closely with Barnes and monitored the bill from beginning to end. A major issue was whether the name change would cause a change in function and a departure from the Master Plan. The trustees, the chancellor, and other leaders, as well as Jensen in Sacramento, repeatedly made clear that this was not the purpose of the move. However, in fairness to the opponents of the bill, especially the University of California, it must be noted that some administrators and faculty continued to advocate for the independent doctorate and other substantive changes to the Master Plan. Opposition came from the University of California, even though the UC had said it would not oppose the name change. Jensen did everything from "holding off critical floor votes until the outlook for victory was fairly certain" to trading votes among members to orchestrating media support especially among smaller newspapers. Jensen secured forty-three coauthors of the bill in the assembly out of eighty members, and nineteen out of forty in the senate. It was a bipartisan bill.

The early support of the governor was secured. Dumke had worked hard to have a productive relationship with Governor Reagan. When Reagan had been on the Chico campus a few years earlier, Cohen had asked two Chico political science faculty members, Royce Delmatier and James Gregg, to ask the governor in an open meeting whether he would support the name change to university status. Reagan's response was that he would sign the legislation if it were to arrive on his desk.

A compromise was made as the bill was finally considered. The legislation introduced in the assembly was amended in the senate to require Coordinating Council for Higher Education establishment of criteria for moving campuses to university status. Each campus would be considered separately, and not all would become universities. Substantively this changed the proposed system name from "The California State University" to "The California State University and Colleges." This compromise was the result of a close working relationship between Jensen and George Deukmejian, then a senator from Long Beach. The senate vote was a tie; one vote was needed. Senator George Moscone wanted to avoid voting, as he planned to run for governor, and he did not want to incur the wrath of the University of California. He left the senate chamber. Deukemejian offered to exchange a vote for a local government bill that Senator Milton Marks badly wanted for a vote in favor of the name change.

The senate had amended the bill, so it needed to return to the assembly for concurrence on the amendment. The University of California in Jensen's words, "called in some chips." Assembly Member Barnes, a retired US Navy captain, was a quite conservative member. Assembly Member Robert Moretti, then the Democratic majority leader, approached Barnes and asked him to stay off the assembly floor. Barnes agreed, and Moretti carried the bill, with the senate amendment on the floor. The name change bill passed.

Governor Ronald Reagan signed the name change bill on November 29, 1971. He was joined at the signing by Assembly Member Barnes and by Jensen, Cohen, William Storey, and a student assistant in the governmental affairs of-

34. Governor Ronald Reagan signing legislation creating California State University and Colleges, November 1971.

fice, Martin Anderson. On the next day, a more ceremonial signing occurred with Reagan, Dumke, and others present. At the board of trustees meeting in Los Angeles a few days before the signing, Reagan appeared and issued a more lengthy statement than might be usual. An undertone in the statement was Reagan's impatience with the University of California, characteristic of his eight years as governor, and the progress that Dumke and others had made for support of the California State Colleges in the years of Reagan's governorship.

> Next Monday at a special ceremony in my office in Sacramento, I will sign into law an historic bill aimed at enabling California's well known and highly respected State Colleges to take their rightful place among academic institutions across the nation and become known as "State Universities."
>
> I say "take their rightful place" not in the sense that this legislation will change their function or responsibilities as teaching institutions. The fact is, the greatness they have achieved and the prestige they have earned is due in large part to the continued emphasis they have placed on their vital classroom teaching role.
>
> This bill is not intended to change that basic role, nor does it imply any change in function.
>
> What this legislation *does* represent is a dramatic acknowledgement of the excellence in teaching which the men and women of the State Colleges have achieved over the years.

During the past decade alone—so often characterized by turmoil and confusion at our institutions of higher learning—the leadership of the State Colleges has never lost sight of its primary purpose to provide the best possible education to its students, particularly at the undergraduate level.

The responsible—sometimes courageous—behavior of a vast majority of the faculty within the system also is deserving of great credit.

If there is anything lacking in this legislation, it is that under its provision, some campuses in the system could be designated "State Universities" considerably earlier than others. Because I am convinced that all of them are engaged in quality teaching, I am requesting that Chancellor Dumke, the Board of Trustees, and the Coordinating Council for Higher Education, move to bestow on each campus the distinction of "State University" as soon as possible.

To call some campuses "State Colleges" and others "State Universities" would imply differences in teaching standards which, in reality, do not exist within the system.

Subsequently, Dumke made a statement to both the media and to the students, faculty, and staff of the about-to-be California State University and Colleges:

The signing of Assembly Bill 123, which will create the California State University and Colleges, is an occasion of great moment for our system of higher educational institutions. I am absolutely delighted. The Trustees and I—as well as many others, including presidents and alumni— have pressed strenuously for this legislation for many years.

The passage of AB 123 by the Legislature, and its imminent signing by Governor Reagan, constitute recognition of the maturity and development of our system under the California Master Plan for Higher Education. This act underscores the responsibility we have accepted, and fulfilled with such success, under the Master Plan.

More than this, however, Assembly Bill 123 is a just recognition that, among our nineteen campuses, a number and, as the Governor said, perhaps all, are already in fact universities and full deserving of this description. I have utmost confidence that the Board of Trustees and the Coordinating Council for Higher Education, whose approval is properly required in developing the criteria and the renaming of individual institutions, will arrive at sound informed conclusions.

Assembly Member Barnes was defeated for reelection in November 1972. A coalition, including students from the University of California at San Diego, used a number of issues including the California State University and Colleges bill.

The saga of the name change did not end at this point. The board of trustees had on the January 1972 agenda the consideration of five criteria to be used in considering campuses for the change to university status. These had been developed by Dumke, personally working with two senior staff members, Vice-Chancellor William Langsdorf, and Assistant Executive Vice-Chancellor Lee Kerschner. The proposed criteria included:

1. Size of campus in total enrollment: a campus must be in the upper half of California's then twenty-two accredited universities (5,546);

2. Graduate enrollments: must be in the upper half of the same universities in graduate enrollment (1,317) or degrees awarded (99);
3. Complexity and diversity of range of baccalaureate and master's degree programs: again, these must be in the upper half (67) degree programs;
4. Quality measured by specialized accreditations held: must be in upper half—at least two programs must have recognized accreditations;
5. Quality measured by faculty possession of the doctorate in fields in which the doctorate is the usual terminal degree: must be at least 50 percent of full-time faculty.

The proposal recommended that four of the five criteria would need to be met, as only three public universities and two private universities in the state would meet all five criteria. The Coordinating Council adopted the proposal with only minor changes in April 1972.

On May 23, 1972, the trustees changed the names of fourteen of the nineteen campuses to "California State University" (followed by the campus's geographic designation). The only campuses that did not meet the criteria were the five founded in the 1960s. The two campuses that began at the same time that the trustees assumed the governance of the colleges were renamed California State College, Stanislaus, and California State College, Sonoma; the names of the remaining three campuses founded in the 1960s were each preceded by "California State College."

The statewide Academic Senate had supported this effort, going back to the initial legislation introduced in 1967. In the 1971–72 year, senate vice-chair Royce Delmatier of the Chico campus initiated a statewide referendum asking faculty about the name change. The faculties in eighteen of the nineteen campuses voted 3,634 in support of the name change, with 247 opposed. On the San Francisco campus, the campus senate executive committee did not send the referendum to the faculty, but approved the name change on behalf of the faculty.

The trustee action to create the common identification of all campuses as either "California State University" or "California State College" could be traced to the initial trustee discussion and survey in 1962. It caused a stir, and quickly became an issue at the San Jose campus. The president of San Jose at the time, John Bunzel, met with Assemblyman Alfred Alquist. Alquist, who would have a long career in both houses of the legislature, launched a strong, almost ad hominem, attack, not only against the issue, but against Chancellor Dumke. The San Jose campus resistance was soon joined by leaders, some faculty, some administration, some community at San Diego and San Francisco. The matter came up on every campus. At Chico, a former mayor in conversation with me proposed the name change to be Chico State University. When my response compared that suggestion to Riverside State University, the matter was dropped.

In introducing a bill to roll back the use of "California State University," Alquist attacked Dumke for empire building, for the size of the chancellor's office, and for central domination over minute campus matters. The argument became heated. The student newspaper at San Diego State carried the campus name San Diego State University on its masthead. Dumke appealed to the presidents for support. Most stayed away from the issue. Dumke's appeal encompassed a number of issues, including benefit to graduates and recruiting faculty for all but the very large campuses. In a sense, without using the language of marketing, Dumke was arguing the case for branding, essentially the case for the University of California, which had a campus known as the University of California, Riverside. This was one more manifestation of the difficult processes and length of time it would take to create a whole from disparate parts.

While Alquist's bill addressed only San Jose State, soon the San Diego and San Francisco campuses were included. Alquist went public with an argument that legislative intent only included the campuses at Los Angeles, Long Beach, San Diego, San Francisco, and San Jose for the name change, but this argument dropped from the debate. The Alquist bill passed and the governor signed it. A few years later the campuses in Humboldt and Sonoma counties successfully sought the same legislation.

By 1981, all but two campuses had become universities. Dumke announced his retirement in September of that year. The legislative leadership agreed that the issue was really moot, as the criteria had become less meaningful over time, and additional institutions had emerged as universities in California. The legislature quietly passed to the trustees the responsibility for naming campuses.

In 2005, a relatively new president of California State University, Sacramento went public with the idea of changing the name of the institution to Sacramento State University. Individuals at California State University, Chico and California State University, Stanislaus quickly proposed similar name changes. While the legal name remains California State University, Sacramento, the Sacramento campus is often now referred to as "Sacramento State, as it has been through its history." Just as quickly, the new president at Stanislaus rejected the proposal. The proposal soon disappeared.

In 1975, a history faculty member at the Chico campus, W. H. Hutchinson, wrote an essay, "Working for the Brand." Old Hutch, as he was known, was not a conventional historian. He had won a Pulitzer Prize in the 1960s, and then had been invited to join the faculty at Chico. His book *Oil, Land, and Politics* was a classic, as was Old Hutch. "Working for the Brand" had been at least in some small measure prompted by the name debate. In a very real sense, many in the academic world do not understand marketing, and more than often feel it unnecessary. The California State University and the University of California are powerful brand names throughout the world, but different brands with different goals. The supporters of the original local names for the most part, lacked vision and a sense of what the California State University would become.

Curiously, in 2007 a group of students at the San Jose campus initiated a referendum to change the name to California State University, San Jose. The students were supported by some alumni. The arguments were a replication of 1972–73, supplemented by assertions of the reach of the California State University name in the early twenty-first century. The referendum failed in the annual campus student elections, 1,729 against to 606 for (only 8 percent of the thirty thousand students on the campus voted, a not unusual percentage of participating voting members).[5]

* * *

Edmund G. Brown, Jr. (Jerry Brown) became governor of California on January 1, 1975. The world of higher education in Sacramento changed. Brown ushered in the "small is beautiful" rationale for government policy. He was a skeptic about the work of colleges and universities.

The first meeting of the trustees after Brown's inauguration was at the Sacramento campus. The trustees had moved most of their meetings to their headquarters in Los Angeles in the mid- to late 1960s, but they still held meetings in Sacramento at key times of the year, especially at budget time. They were in Sacramento hoping that a new governor would join them, for the governor was ex officio president of the board. At this meeting, Brown brought up two matters not on the agenda. He proposed, in the midst of a discussion about campus life, that the on-campus sale and use of alcoholic beverages be available, and he pushed that action through. The second item he initiated was the appointment of members of campus advisory boards, proposing that this be delegated to campus presidents.

Brown was consistently questioning practice and tradition. He and Dumke did not work easily together. Brown's appointments to the board of trustees were uneven. Some were excellent, and made a difference, while a number became known as single-issue trustees. Only one eventually became board chair. The tensions with Dumke were sometimes on issues, frequently budget matters, as Brown's general approach to public higher education was that it was too generously funded and often wasteful, and almost always on style. Brown was blunt and not given to debate. Dumke was a traditional academic in many ways, and preferred to talk issues through. Dumke, on the other hand, simply did not like Sacramento and the relationship of politics with higher education. In June 1975, he delivered a major address, "University Relationships with State Legislatures, State Education Departments, and State Coordinating Commissions," about what he regarded as the politicization of higher education, particularly public higher education, to the American Management Association at an American Council on Education conference. In interviews, Dumke's longtime director of governmental affairs (James Jensen) and the principal legislative analyst staff member, who was for many years responsible for higher education, (Harold Geoigue), commented about the relatively small size of the California State University and Colleges legislative program, contrasted with those of subsequent chancellors, the University of California, the community colleges, and other entities.[6] Dumke was not anxious to bring legislators and others into the system's affairs unless absolutely necessary.

The advent of Jerry Brown as governor brought about renewed pressure for collective bargaining. Some of the trustees appointed by Reagan fed the appetites of would-be faculty unions. In particular, Jeanette Ritchie, a 1972 Reagan trustee appointee, was advocating essentially a faculty retention program based on merit and minimizing the practical meaning of tenure. The Ritchie amendment galvanized both faculties and administrations. For faculty it was an assault on the established concept of tenure. For administrators on campuses it caused an unnecessary politicization of faculty and an unhealthy "we versus they" development. A former nursing faculty member, trustee Ritchie, was persistent, and the issue lived on at least two years. It helped to create an environment more supportive of collective bargaining than had been the situation prior to the Ritchie proposal.

The faculty organizations assumed correctly Brown's willingness to support collective bargaining. Brown had committed himself in the campaign for election as governor to support collective bargaining for public employees. There ensued four years of agitation and positioning among the faculty organizations for pre-eminence. The statewide Academic Senate was inevitably drawn in. If faculty collective bargaining came about, what would be the role of senates?

The trustees and chancellor were not unified. Dumke was generally viewed in the debate about collective bargaining as paternalistic about faculty and employees. This was not an inaccurate assessment. Dumke was simultaneously a major proponent of consultation and involvement of all, while in his behavior, he often came to a meeting with a solution to whatever issue was under discussion, and he expected everyone to support it. He did engage in give and take, but was more often than not convinced of a position. He was firmly opposed to collective bargaining, and just as firmly committed to what he saw as the role of faculty senates. The trustees ran the gamut of viewpoints, from absolute opposition and little sympathy for consultation, to a willingness to consider collective bargaining in some form and commitment to consultation.

Brown's initial first two appointments to the board included Dr. Mary Jean Pew, a political scientist and former president of Immaculate Heart College in Los Angeles. Pew was often the link between Brown and the board, keeping the governor informed of board and system activity, and on occasion conveying Brown's thoughts and preferences to other members. On the subject of collective bargaining, the most active trustee was Roy Brophy, a 1973 Reagan appointee who would later become board chair. Brophy was opposed to collective bargaining and took an active part in lobbying in the legislature, often without coordinating with the governmental affairs office. The board did not have a determined position, and sentiment changed. Brophy did have vigorous disagreements with the chancellor.

The statewide Academic Senate necessarily became involved. Some of the involvement was about matters internal to the system, and related to campus senates and positions. The statewide Academic Senate and its leadership had been engaged in the collective bargaining issue and its relationship to the faculty role in governance since the establishment of the senate and its first chair, Leonard Mathy, in 1963–64. Gerald Marley of Fullerton, chair from 1975–77, David Elliott of San Jose, chair from 1977–79, and Robert Kully of Los Angeles, chair from 1979–82, each played an important role, as did other faculty leaders. At issue were the definitions and roles of senates and the collective bargaining agent for the faculty. Senate chairs and other faculty leaders did not agree among themselves.

Collective bargaining in the California State University and Colleges was not only about faculty. The political efforts on the campuses and in Sacramento covered all employees, save only management. The potential of bargaining for the faculty received the most attention from the media as well as the trustees and senior management, just as it had over the years.

The drive toward collective bargaining entered the legislative arena definitively in 1977. Members of the legislature had been involved with the issue since the time of the Master Plan, and the establishment of the board and the system in 1960 and 1961. A prominent longtime member of the legislature, Senator Albert Rodda, had introduced unsuccessfully bills addressing the state colleges over the years. Rodda had been a Sacramento City College faculty member in economics for years before becoming an assembly member and later senator. Assembly Member Howard Berman introduced Assembly Bill 1091. Political infighting swirled not only around the basic concept and whether there should be collective bargaining, but around the details of the bill and the efforts of the various potential bargaining groups to gain advantages from legislation in their quests to be selected as bargaining agents.

The trustees and chancellor did not have a unified position. The two principal governmental relations staff members, Jim Jensen and his deputy, Scott Plotkin, were more influential in keeping the players informed and tracking all the activity than they were in affecting the outcome. The actual conversation with legislators was carried on principally by Roy Brophy, then a trustee. Legislative support among the Democrats, allied with Governor Brown, was not unanimous, but the outcome was made inevitable by Brophy and the board. Assembly Bill 1091 passed and set in motion a several-year process of implementation, and of a rethinking of roles not only about faculty and staff relationships but about governance. The governor signed the bill with enthusiasm. The process was completed before the November 1978 gubernatorial election.[7]

* * *

About the same time that the collective bargaining legislation was completed, another major issue arose. Property tax collections in California had been rising dramatically over the years, as the value of real estate climbed. This was especially true in urban areas. At the same time, a surplus in the state treasury had been accumulating in substantial amounts. Both the legislature and the governor ignored the surplus and the tax structure. Retirees, many living on fixed or mostly fixed incomes, were significantly affected. Some began to lose homes because of elevated property tax assessments. In the early spring of 1978, Proposition 13 burst upon the public, a bit like a bombshell. The media had for the most part ignored the matter, just as the governor and the legislature had. Two individuals, Howard Jarvis and Paul Gann, were the public figures leading the Proposition 13 initiative effort, which limited the increase in property tax assessments among other restrictions.

When the significance and potential impact of Proposition 13 finally got to the press and those in government, including public higher education, serious opposition arose, especially, of course, from those in the public service structure that would be affected most by loss of funds. The major media were split, some in support editorially, some opposed. But the die was cast. The week before the June primary election with "Prop 13" on the ballot, the governor semi-endorsed it. Proposition 13 passed with a very substantial margin.

The immediate impact of Prop 13 was on local governments, cities, counties, and special districts, all supported by property taxes. Proposition 13 both reduced and limited property taxes. The legislature and governor promised to make local government whole. The surplus in the state treasury at the time was in the range of six billion dollars, and it was expended to support local government services. The state's major initial effort was to address the needs of local government, not state operations, including higher education.

The impact of Proposition 13 on public higher education was substantial and immediate. It would take effect with the new fiscal year beginning on July 1, three weeks after the election. The chancellor's office and the State Department of Finance held meetings with campus presidents and financial officers. An immediate impact was in the final budget act for fiscal year 1978–79. For some years, the budget act had contained an automatic increase for both the State University and Colleges and for the University of California for additional enrollment. The provision was vacated, and would not be addressed again until the mid-1990s, when a different agreement was reached.

Proposition 13's impact varied on the campuses; campus administrations differed in their flexibility with respect to managing financial resources; campus size was a major factor. The small, relatively new campuses generally had more difficulty with the cuts than the larger campuses. There was discussion among some of closing one or two of the campuses. Stanislaus was the most frequently mentioned, but sometimes San Bernardino and Dominguez Hills were mentioned as well. The impact was not all bad, as necessity caused at least some of the campuses to move toward greater budget and even academic flexibility. A positive effect of the Proposition 13 cut was an agreement with Finance that the system and campus offices would decide where to cut, a major step for decentralized budget management.

Proposition 13 would have a longer-term impact on the California State University and Colleges. The campuses and the California State University and Colleges were funded based on long-established formulas and agreements about enrollments, programs, and the like. The short-term impact was not easy to address, but the campuses worked through it. Over the longer run, a process of erosion set in and the long-agreed-upon formulas and agreements began to disappear, one by one.[8]

The Dumke years drew to a close in 1982. Beyond the budget there were no major initiatives in Sacramento in his last few years as chancellor.

* * *

The year 1982 was an eventful one. The previous year had seen the change of the name of the system from the California State University and Colleges to the California State University. This had been accomplished in the legislature with little notice. A new chancellor, W. Ann Reynolds, took office on September 1, 1982. A new governor, George Deukmejian, was elected in November.

The role of the governmental affairs office and the role of the California State University itself in Sacramento are in many ways a function of the style and the policy agenda of the chancellor. The governor's interests and support certainly are extremely important. Ann Reynolds came to the role of chancellor from the position of provost of Ohio State University, a university in the state capital. She had not been a campus president, but she had considerable campus administrative experience at the University of Illinois at Chicago, as well as at Ohio State. Her experience at Ohio State whetted an appetite and interest in state government. In that sense and in many other matters of style, she was the opposite of the quiet, apolitical Glenn Dumke.

Ann Reynolds came to the role as chancellor and to California positively anticipating a role in Sacramento with the legislature and with the governor. Reynolds spent time in Sacramento and quickly developed an agenda that involved the state government. The budget and adequate financial support for the California State University were always central. The first budget developed during her administration was for fiscal 1983–84, and it was a difficult year. George Deukmejian took office as governor on January 1, 1983, four months after Reynolds's arrival. Deukmejian inherited a $1.4 billion budget deficit. The negative legacy of Proposition 13 lived on, and the funding stream for merit salary increases was lost, but the increases continued to be granted. Suddenly funding for both merit and the step increases for positions and cost of living adjustments simply were gone. A primary goal Reynolds set for herself was parity of funding with the University of California. Her definition of parity included both a percentage increase and a dollar amount equal or nearly equal to that which the University of California received, and this was partially accomplished.[9]

Another goal of Chancellor Reynolds was achieving authority for the California State University to grant an independent doctorate. A series of issues were joined. Reynolds wanted constitutional status parallel to the University of California for the California State University. She convinced Senator Alfred Alquist of San Jose to introduce a bill to accomplish this. Alquist had been a member of the legislature for many years, and there was great respect for him. Because of the respect he had attained, the constitutional status bill was heard in a number of committees. Jim Jensen, the CSU lobbyist, endured a beating each time. The bill went nowhere.[10]

Another review of the Master Plan began in 1985. It originated in the legislature. A primary concern of the legislature at that time was the community colleges. The governance structure of the community colleges had not been affected by the Master Plan or two subsequent reviews. The central issue with the community college governance structure is the fact that the governing boards with actual power are the district boards, not the statewide board of governors created in 1967 in the aftermath of the Master Plan. The mid-1980s review did not solve this problem either, though it did address a number of issues constructively. These included creation of the Intersegmental Coordinating Council and some efforts to address lower-division general education student-transfer issues from the community colleges. These set the stage for later efforts in the 1990s and, finally, more definitive action in the early years of this century. In the Master Plan review discussions, the issue of the independent doctorate for the California University again was raised. It was fiercely debated, but did not receive the support of the review commission.[11]

The independent doctorate remained an issue in Sacramento until almost the end of the 1980s. The chancellor pressed for and got hearings on the subject. The University of California remained strongly opposed. Leaders in the public schools, many superintendents, had been supportive in many discussions leading up to the legislative hearings, but failed to give support in the hearings.[12] Chancellor Reynolds unsuccessfully sought support from her predecessor, Glenn Dumke. She asked one of the presidents who had a close relationship and great respect for Dumke to request help. Dumke's reply to the request was that he had given his word in 1960 and did not believe it principled to change. A week later Dumke testified before a legislative committee and did not support the independent doctorate.[13]

The staff in the governmental relations office in Sacramento played a supportive role to the chancellor and her immediate associates; in a sense, they perhaps ran interference and kept communications open on the campuses. They were in a sometimes difficult situation, as they were not always kept informed of the chancellor's discussions with legislators and the executive branch. James Jensen remained as director of governmental relations, and he was very ably assisted by Scott Plotkin, a Sacramento State graduate and former president (in the 1970s) of the California State University and Colleges Student Presidents Association. Fiscal matters were handled by a three-person budget team that had developed in the mid 1970s: the vice-chancellor for business affairs, Dale Hanner; the assistant vice-chancellor, Louis Messner, whose office assembled the budget; and the assistant vice-chancellor for academic affairs, Anthony Moye, who was in charge of academic planning. These three worked well together and continued the march toward greater flexibility. The capital outlay program was handled by Sheila Chaffin, an assistant vice-chancellor who was close to Reynolds. Chaffin had a tendency to operate independently from campus judgments and was not well received in the legislature. Reynolds discouraged presidential contacts in Sacramento beyond structured legislative dinners each spring during budget season, but the Sacramento staff kept communication lines open.

There were some awkward moments with both the legislature and the executive branch. One key moment was in 1986 and pertained to the trustees raising executive salaries behind closed doors. At the time, Jensen wrote a letter to the members of the legislative committee promising that it would never happen again, only for it to be repeated in 1989–90. There were other strained issues. An assembly member from the San Fernando Valley introduced a bill to build a new science building at the Northridge campus. He was told in no uncertain terms that this was not his business, but that of the California State University. He retreated in order to avoid compromising the campus, but only after securing a commitment from the chancellor that the building would be in the next fiscal year budget and would receive full support from the chancellor's office.

There were positives to the relationship with Sacramento. Reynolds put a priority emphasis on three substantive educational issues: freshman admissions standards, teacher education, and student and faculty diversity. These were well received, although every year at the assembly budget committee hearings, the long-serving chair of the subcommittee that heard higher education budgets, Assembly Member Robert Campbell, would question whether the new freshmen admissions standards were having an impact on minority admissions.

As the 1980s drew to a close, significant tensions did arise in the Sacramento relationship with Chancellor Reynolds. The purchase of five Ford Taurus automobiles for vice-chancellors, which cost $99,900, just under the $100,000 limit necessitating state agency approval, aggravated relationships. Early in 1990, the board of trustees was asked to consider substantial raises for presidents, vice-chancellors, and the chancellor. This again happened in closed session. The trustees approved. A firestorm of anger developed in a legislative committee meeting, when members learned from a senior staff member of the Legislative Analyst's Office that the trustees had once again raised the salaries of the presidents and chancellor in a closed session. The analyst's staff member produced a letter signed by Reynolds after the first misstep; the letter stated that the use of a closed session was an error and would not be repeated. The analyst had been following the issue of California State University executive salaries for several years, and had developed a relationship with CSU unions around the matter.[14]

At about the same time Reynolds asked James Jensen, who had served as director of governmental affairs since 1970, to resign. Jensen had built many solid relationships in Sacramento; most believed he had almost single-handedly been responsible for the achievement of university status in 1971. Jensen quietly resigned, and he left Sacramento quickly. He accepted a position for one year, teaching political science at the San Bernardino campus, and then fully retired. He was succeeded as director by Jami Warner, a young woman whom the chancellor had come to know. Warner's background was in a modest role with a lobbying firm.[15] This change was not well received in Sacramento.

The spring of 1990 was a turbulent time within the California State University and in the CSU relationships in Sacramento. Ann Reynolds resigned in May 1990. The 1980s can reasonably be characterized, with respect to CSU—state government relations, as a time of the consolidation of working relationships between the campuses and the system staff and the legislative and executive branches, and the foundations were laid for the next period of development.

Once again, in 1990, changes in the chancellorship and the governorship coincided. In May 1990, after Reynolds resigned, the trustees appointed Ellis

McCune as acting chancellor. McCune had been deeply involved in the development of the California State University almost from the beginning; he had, as a faculty member, chaired the committee that created the statewide Academic Senate, and he had been the first dean of academic planning, from 1963 to 1968, when he became president of the Hayward campus, where he had served until 1990.

The governorship of George Deukmejian was also drawing to a close. As McCune became the acting chancellor, the gubernatorial primary of 1990 was about to be held. Deukmejian's term would end in December of 1990, and Pete Wilson, a former assembly member, mayor of San Diego, and US Senator, would become governor on January 1, 1991.

A first task for McCune as acting chancellor was to reassemble relationships in Sacramento. He asked the recently appointed director of governmental relations, Jami Warner, to step aside, and appointed Scott Plotkin as director. Plotkin, not unlike McCune, was a person of the California State University. He had been a student at the San Luis Obispo campus of Cal Poly, became president of the Associated Students organization on that campus, and then became the chair of the California State University and Colleges Student Presidents Association (CSUCSPA). This brought him to regular participation in trustee meetings and other activities. He was extremely effective and became well known to board members and presidents, the Sacramento scene, and in other arenas. At the end of his term as chair of CSUCSPA, he became a student lobbyist in Sacramento. At that time, the mid-1970s, the students were establishing a lobby in the state capital. Plotkin completed the baccalaureate at the Sacramento campus, continued as the student lobbyist for a time, and then was hired by Jim Jensen as his deputy. He brought rich experience to the role of director of governmental affairs. In his turn, Plotkin recommended to McCune the appointment of Karen Yelverton (later Zamarripa) as the deputy. Yelverton had come to Sacramento as a senate fellow, and then was a senate staff member on both sides of the aisle. She became a lobbyist for the California School Board Association, and remained there until she joined the CSU in January 1991.

McCune almost immediately began to spend significant time in Sacramento. Each chancellor has had a style about using the staff in the Sacramento office. Dumke generally kept the director with him in the meetings and negotiations, even with governors. Reynolds did not take the Sacramento staff into key meetings and tended to operate on her own; the staff in the Sacramento office and at times, even members of the board, often had not been not aware of what was underway. McCune's style was different. Not long after his appointment, he met with Governor Deukmejian about budget matters. He brought Plotkin with him.

McCune spent the year often in meetings with legislators and members of the executive branch. There were two issues. The first was the Sacramento establishment itself, as well as legislators and the governor's group. Relationships needed to be rebuilt and credibility established. The second had to do with collective bargaining and relationships with the unions. In particular, members of the legislature wanted peace with the CSU unions. McCune received a strong message. Hearings in the legislature had been dominated by acrimony between the unions and the chancellor's people. McCune eventually negotiated a new faculty union contract personally.

One of the issues that had troubled presidents and other campus administrators for years was the Orange Book. The Orange Book was a loose-leaf volume (some said the pages were not sufficiently loose) with formulas for everything from the number of square feet for which each custodian would be responsible to counselor—student ratios, and so on. These formulas had been developed over years and in a sense represented a kind of program approach to budgeting. They also were used by state agencies and the chancellor's staff as a control mechanism, and they were built upon an assumption that programs on all campuses were the same. Subsequent to the passage of Proposition 13 in 1978, the formulas were not fully funded, and funding had gradually declined. State agencies and particularly the chancellor's staff continued to use, or at least attempt to use, the formulas as a set of controls.

McCune had adopted the practice of meeting with the presidents on occasion by himself, without staff. One of the topics at most executive council meetings was the Orange Book. There was virtually unanimous agreement that the Orange Book should go. The final decision about this key financial link to state government was to be made in a new CSU administration.

* * *

Pete Wilson took office as governor on January 1, 1991. Shortly after that, McCune and Plotkin met with Wilson to review the CSU budget proposals for the next fiscal year, to begin on July 1. One result of that and other meetings was that Wilson quietly passed word to the trustees that he could easily live with McCune as chancellor; subsequently, Wilson would be involved and supportive in the selection of the next chancellor.

The year 1990–91 was a year of setting a stage for a new approach to relationships with state government. In early spring of 1991, the trustees selected a new chancellor, Barry Munitz, the former president of the University of Houston and a corporate executive with a large Texas conglomerate, the Maxxam Corporation. His appointment was not popular among many because of his association with Maxxam. Munitz took the flak, basically without fighting back. He knew how to lead. He made some very crucial changes for the campuses and worked well in Sacramento. As time went by and Munitz continued to lead the CSU in educational and public policy issues, the turmoil was left behind.

Munitz was no stranger to higher education leadership. He had worked for Clark Kerr when Kerr was with the Carnegie Commission on Higher Education and subsequently Munitz became a vice president of the University of Illinois. Although he would not become chancellor until August 1, Munitz immediately began quietly to meet individuals with whom he would work. He spent substantial time in Sacramento. The governor, Pete Wilson, had been involved in the selection of Munitz, and there was a relationship on which to build. Munitz worked with and built a relationship with the staff of the governmental affairs office and continued to work closely with them over his years as chancellor. He especially spent time with members of the legislature and built a firm friendship with the Speaker of the Assembly, Willie Brown.

The 1991–92 budget was in place as Munitz assumed the chancellorship in August, and preparation for the 1992–93 budget was well underway. In this context, one of the early moves was to make a decision about the Orange Book. To the applause of the presidents and others on the campuses, Munitz secured an agreement with the Department of Finance and, ultimately, the governor to do away with the Orange Book and, in return, achieve greater flexibility in budget administration. Essentially, the state university would receive a block grant. There was accountability and direction built in, as a product of negotiations to secure an amount with finance and the legislature.[16] The Orange Book was already dead as a generator of support. The Department of Finance had simply walked away from it. The approach Munitz and his newly appointed executive vice-chancellor, Molly Broad, took was to curtail enrollment in two successive tight budget years. In June 1992, Munitz, along with the UC president, David Gardner, and several CSU campus presidents, testified in a major legislative hearing, the budget conference committee of both houses. Munitz opened his testimony with the assertion that "California is in the process of tearing up the ticket to the American dream."[17]

This situation was both a minus and a plus for the state university in the long term. Enrollment was curtailed, although most campuses attempted to be as accommodating as possible, and many campuses overenrolled; students were often forced to curtail the number of courses they would take, thus prolonging the time to degree. On the other hand, the foundation was being laid for a new approach to budgeting.

Conversations about how to handle the state budget situation took place in Sacramento between Scott Plotkin, the CSU director of governmental affairs, and his University of California counterpart. Plotkin's deputy, Karen Yelverton, was to pay special attention to the budget. Munitz quickly became involved with this conversation.

In 1994, William Baker, whose portfolio as a University of California vice president included governmental affairs; Russell Gould, then Director of Finance for Governor Pete Wilson; and Munitz met for a long weekend in the wine country. The three of them, joined by William Hauck, a trustee appointed by Governor Wilson in 1993, had already met for a long dinner in Sacramento to address working relationships. Hauck, a former student body president at San Jose, had become a key figure in top-level Sacramento politics; he was trusted by both Democrats and Republicans, and would be chair of the board of trustees and among the most significant leaders of the trustees in years to come. In the first several years of the Wilson administration, Hauck was deputy chief of staff.

Baker had a home in the Napa Valley. The purpose of their meeting was to create a working relationship for state government support of the University of California and the California State University. From the vantage point of the CSU, some base of support or departure point for the annual budget cycle was needed, a replacement for the Orange Book. The result was something called "the compact." The compact was essentially an agreement about the factors and levels of support that constitute a starting point for the annual budget process, combined with an agreement about numbers and support for annual enrollment forecasts. It was eventually agreed to by the governor and accepted by the UC and CSU boards.[18]

The concept of the compact has remained through the 2007–08 budget year. With later Governors Gray Davis and Arnold Schwarzenegger, the details and numbers have changed, but the concept has remained. In the greatest measure this was a product of the Munitz administration. Though disagreements between the University of California and the California State University continued over the years, a capacity to work together had been developed. The compact was not binding on the legislature; it was really not binding on anyone. It was a reasonable framework within which reasonable people could work together. Despite frequent protests from legislators that "we were not part of the compact negotiation—we were not at the table," the compact has been generally followed over the years. Early in the Schwarzenegger years, the compact was suspended for a year, but the promise to resume it was honored.

Perhaps more important than the compact itself was the change it represented in the California State University presence in Sacramento. The CSU in 1960 clearly began as a junior partner (a very junior partner) in the Sacramento higher education scene. There are four players: the University of California; the independents, represented by the Association of Independent California Colleges and Universities; the community colleges, with very disparate leadership due to their governance structure; and the California State University. Each decade, however defined by a chancellorship or a governor or events, built the presence of the California State University. The 1990s saw the emergence of the CSU as a major player—some characterized it as CSU carrying the load for state senior higher education.

The 1990s and the Munitz administration saw the reemergence of the campuses and the presidents in Sacramento. In the late 1960s, the then new president of the Northridge campus, James Cleary, had designated a staff member, Dorena Knepper, as coordinator of government relations. This had not been well received by the chancellor's staff. As the years went on, more campuses began to designate someone, informally or formally, to work with matters in Sacramento. The Sacramento campus had a vice president for university affairs, Robert Jones, responsible for all dimensions of the public life of the university, including governmental relations. In the 1990s, it became essential for the campuses to have someone working with Sacramento and the governmental affairs office. The presidents were asked to help with Sacramento representation and they did so.

In the middle of the decade, affirmative action became an issue within the University of California. A newly named regent, Ward Connerly, an alumnus of California State University, Sacramento, introduced the issue of affirmative action to the regents' agenda. Essentially, he wanted to ban preferences, quotas, and the like, which had been put into use over time to achieve gender and racial balances in the UC staff, faculty, and student body. The issue migrated beyond the UC to the California ballot box, as Proposition 209. Munitz saw this coming and met with the presidents and legal counsel in a closed-door meeting in Sacramento. His objective was to have each campus modify its policies and procedures so that they would pass any constitutional test and, at the same time, continue toward equity for women and members of minority groups. There had been no system policy, but an attitude and values had been promoted, especially beginning with the Reynolds administration, as well as with some of the presidents long predating Reynolds. The campus efforts were successful, and the CSU stayed out of the line of fire during the Proposition 209 campaign. Two of the presidents joined in the public debate to defeat Proposition 209. It passed in the November 1996 election.

Three New Campuses and a Maritime Academy

The Bakersfield campus's founding in the late 1960s marked the end of a period of the establishment of new campuses that had begun with Fullerton in 1957 and followed with the creation of seven more.[19]

The focus of the board of trustees and the chancellor and staff went to consolidating the nineteen existing campuses and providing for the growth in students, establishing new undergraduate and graduate programs, recruiting of thousands of faculty and several score of presidents,[20] and attending to the emerging place of the California State University in California higher education. The system had no long-term growth plan.

In 1988, Chancellor Ann Reynolds initiated a discussion in the executive council about longer-term growth, and asked each of the campus presidents to address the question of the establishment of new campuses in his or her region. There was only limited discussion of the topic in the executive council. Some presidents addressed the topic willingly; some resisted the idea of establishing new campuses. Each president was asked to submit a growth plan for the campus region, and some plans did suggest new campuses. At least one plan included a careful analysis, not only of population growth, but also of transportation, freeways, and population density points; this plan suggested the establishment of no new free-standing CSU campuses, but rather the establishment of upper-division degree granting centers on selected community college campuses. This considerable effort and amount of work was lost in the transition of the chancellorship in 1990.

The campuses established in 1989 and the 1990s were established for varying reasons. San Marcos clearly met a present need in the 1980s and a long-term need with population growth in the San Diego-Orange County region. The Maritime Academy move into the California State University framework was simply the result of a long-overdue recognition of the character and mission of the institution and the manner in which it might fit in the overall structure of California public higher education, a recognition of the aphorism that "everything has to be someplace." It is arguable that the founding of the Monterey Bay campus was not unlike the founding of some campuses in the 1950s—a political solution to a perceived regional economic development issue. The establishment of a freestanding campus in the Ventura area was the fulfillment of a long-term popular regional cause ("our own college/university,") created in the 1960s by the state with the purchase of land for a campus, followed by the disappointment of the 1970s when the state sold the land. The Ventura campus—California University, Channel Islands—was an important economic development step for that region.

All of the campuses serve a useful public need, and will prosper over the years. Their establishment underscores the fact that neither the state of California, nor the California State University have long-term growth plans.

* * *

Community enthusiasm and support for a state college campus in northern San Diego County had been present as early as the 1960s. The San Diego campus of the California State Colleges had been a popular campus, with great pressures for admission and enrollment growth since the years after World War II and certainly since the 1960 Master Plan. Two apparent reasons were its location and the enthusiastic embrace by the San Diego faculty and campus leadership of the opportunities created by the Master Plan. In 1969, the chancellor's office forwarded a report to the Coordinating Council for Higher Education asserting an "ultimate need" for an additional state college campus in the area. In the early 1970s, the board of trustees increased the enrollment ceiling for San Diego State from 20,000 to 25,000 FTE. In 1978, Assemblyman William Craven carried a bill in the legislature to create a satellite facility for the San Diego campus. In 1979, the North County Center of San Diego State University was established in Vista and opened with 150 students. The center moved in 1982, from the rented facilities in Vista to rented quarters in San Marcos. Business and civic leaders had been working for a state university in the north county since the 1960s. The San Diego campus was growing and growth outstripped capacity, adding to enrollment at the San Marcos center.

In 1984, Chancellor Ann Reynolds created a group to examine the need for new state university facilities and services in the San Diego region. That group recommended a full off-campus center in northern San Diego County, but no new four-year campus. In 1985, Senator Craven introduced legislation to finance a comprehensive study of the educational needs of the north county. The study was completed, and legislation was introduced in 1987 to support property acquisition for a center. The California Postsecondary Education Commission was the statutory gatekeeper for new centers and campuses. CPEC added a paragraph to the legislative proposal, virtually inviting the chancellor's office to submit a proposal for a full-service campus by 1989. Senator Craven wanted this; it was to be his legacy. Chancellor Reynolds wanted the creation of a new campus during her chancellorship. The San Diego State administration opposed strongly the establishment of a freestanding campus, and urged support for the North County Center. Nevertheless, the legislation passed, was signed by the governor, property in San Marcos was purchased, and the San Marcos campus was assured.

The trustees appointed Bill W. Stacy as the founding president in 1989. The campus start-up was fast, no three-year planning period like the San Bernardino, Dominguez Hills, and Bakersfield campuses had in the 1960s.[21] As the institution was established—initially in rented quarters for two years, before the move to the newly constructed buildings on the campus—the statewide Academic Senate became involved. A process for selecting faculty was established. The Statewide Academic Senate created faculty selection advisory committees in the various broad disciplinary and applied fields, such as social sciences and business. Two questions are reasonable to ask in the regard: while there would be some assurance that the faculty selected (many from beyond the California State University) would learn about and share in the values of the California State University, does such an approach compromise the capacity of a founding president to shape a new campus initially? In addition, to what extent is it desirable that new CSU campuses be created in the image of existing campuses? The San Marcos campus opened with 448 students in the term of 1990. Ten years later, in the 2000 fall term, 6,256 students were enrolled.

The founding of California State University San Marcos can be noted for two additional facts. CPEC had inserted in the language, doubtless at the urging of a chancellor's office staff member, that the requirement that California State University campuses meet the 1972 criteria for university status be vacated for all new campuses. More importantly, the establishment of the campus did not vary procedurally in any significant way from the external politics surrounding the establishment of California State College campuses in the 1950s.[22]

Finally, in part related to disagreements between the then chancellor, Ann Reynolds, and the president of San Diego State at the time, Thomas Day, the momentum that had been building for a full campus came to fruition. William Craven, by the late 1980s was successful with legislation creating a new campus, and Governor George Deukmejian signed the bill formally creating California State University San Marcos. The campus opened in 1990 with 551 students.

* * *

Founded in 1929, the California Maritime Academy went in and out of a relationship with the California State Colleges for many years. From 1960–61, the time of the Master Plan, the academy was not within the California State Colleges or, subsequently, the California State University until 1995, when legislation formally made it the twenty-first CSU campus.

The California Maritime Academy had been related to the state colleges and then to state university for many years, from its founding in 1929. For some of the years since its founding, the president of the Maritime Academy had participated in the meetings of the presidents, but, formally, the academy was related to state government through the State Department of Education. For many purposes it operated as a semi-autonomous institution.

In 1991, the state experienced a downturn in revenues. The governor's office asked the head of each state agency to submit budgets with 5 percent, 10 percent, and 15 percent reductions from the previous year. The letter from the governor to agency heads was specific; the governor had two priorities that he hoped to save from cuts. Higher education was one of them. A new president, Mary Lyons, had taken office at the Maritime Academy in 1990; Lyons responded to the request for budget reductions with a call to the Department of Finance, to state the fact that the Maritime Academy was a higher education institution. The Finance response was that the Maritime Academy was not a part of either California public higher education systems. At the same time, President Lyons requested positions for student affairs. The academy had not had any student affairs staff. The Finance response to the request was that reserve prison staff could be borrowed. It was time for a change.

President Lyons went to the then newly appointed CSU chancellor, Barry Munitz and proposed that the Maritime Academy become a California State University campus. Munitz agreed and took the matter to the trustees for approval. Vice-chancellor Lee Kerschner was then assigned the task of working with President Lyons to secure the necessary legislation. A bipartisan bill was introduced to accomplish the transfer and passed easily, only to be vetoed by Governor Wilson, at the request of labor unions. The chancellor's staff and President Lyons redrafted the legislation to provide specifically for the transfer of employees to unite under the Higher Education Employee Relations Act, the collective bargaining legislation of 1978. The legislation passed for a second time, and the governor signed it. Enthusiasm for the move was high. The California Maritime Academy opened in the fall of 1994 as a campus of the California State University, with an enrollment of 422 students.

* * *

Each CSU campus is unique, and California State University Monterey Bay has its particular story within the CSU's history. Fort Ord was a military base on Monterey Bay, with a long history dating from 1917 and a US Army training program for World War I. For many years, it was a military basic training site. With the end of the Cold War, a decision was made in 1991 to close Fort Ord, and the base was formally closed in 1994. This was a circumstance of enormous economic consequence to the Monterey area. The congressman from the area, Leon Panetta, immediately formed a community task force to address the matter. Over the years, there had been interest expressed in the community about the establishment of a college or university.

San Jose State University had operated a center in Salinas for years. By 1991, the center needed larger quarters. Gail Fullerton, the retiring president of the San Jose campus, and Handel Evans, who had already been named as interim president at San Jose (and who would remain in that role for four years) and Academic Vice President Arlene Okerlund initially explored the idea that a new California State University campus in the Monterey area would be a sensible solution, rather than expansion of the San Jose center.

After Munitz had assumed the office of chancellor in August 1991, Evans wasted no time in bringing the idea of CSU acquisition of all or part of Fort Ord to the new chancellor. The San Jose State University Salinas Center (an easy half-hour drive) to the Fort Ord site, then had an enrollment of roughly five hundred students. The center's site was leased, and the lease was to expire in less than four years. The San Jose leadership envisioned the possibility of a full campus that could eventually accommodate fifteen thousand students. Coincidentally, Henry Hendrickson, the San Jose State director of operations, design, and construction had been the base commander at Ford Ord prior to his 1989 retirement from the army.

Munitz thought the idea worth exploring and suggested that Evans explore it with Congressman Leon Panetta and State Senator Henry Mello. Both were interested. Two trustees, Anthony Vitti and William Campbell, present and former board chairs, respectively, visited Fort Ord and encouraged the idea. They visited Fort Ord in mid-September, met with the state senator from the area, Henry Mello, and Congressman Panetta. Both were interested. Munitz invited staff from CPEC to join the meeting, given CPEC's role in the establishment of new campuses and centers. The meeting addressed both the move of the San Jose satellite center and the establishment of a new stand-alone CSU campus on the Fort Ord site. After discussion with board members, Munitz directed a member of his staff, David Leveille, who served as director of institutional relations, to open formal conversations with CPEC about both a center and a full campus. Evans was given the task of securing the site, and many trips to Washington ensued.

The Fort Ord site included twenty-eight thousand acres. The CSU was interested in only one thousand to twelve hundred acres, much of this included homes to house the military, and old but salvageable classroom buildings. Munitz moved quickly, secured a trustee resolution endorsing the concept of acquisition of a part of the base, and secured the support of the legislature and then Governor Pete Wilson. The legislature appropriated one million dollars in 1992, and a planning office was established at Seaside, the community nearest to Fort Ord, with retired Colonel Hendrickson in charge.

The Department of Defense agreed to transfer a segment of Fort Ord, with its many buildings and resident housing to the California State University. California State University, Monterey Bay was born and opened in the fall of 1995 with 717 students. The actual formal transfer of property to the California State University occurred in 1994, as did CPEC's formal approval, a statutory requirement. In September 1994, Governor Pete Wilson signed legislation creating the Monterey Bay campus.

Support in California was easily and quickly secured. Support in Washington was far more difficult, and essentially was only secured through political means. Congressman Norman Mineta of San Jose was an important player. A name for the campus was identified, California State University, Monterey Bay. Leon Panetta has remained a key figure in the development of the Monterey Bay campus. Panetta secured a fifteen-million-dollar planning appropriation from Congress.

In March 1993, Munitz appointed Steven Arvizu as provost. His task was to develop an academic plan for the new campus. An anthropologist, Arvizu had been a faculty member at the Sacramento campus and, since 1984, a dean at the Bakersfield campus. The goal was to have a planning faculty in place for the 1994–95 academic year. The process developed for the San Marcos campus, of using faculty committees established with the statewide Academic Senate was used. The California Faculty Association also became part of the process to hire new faculty. Arvizu also worked with a group established jointly with the statewide Academic Senate to develop a "Vision Statement for California State University Monterey Bay."

The first president of the campus was appointed in October 1994, after a national search. Peter Smith, a former member of Congress and lieutenant governor of Vermont, came from the deanship of the College of Education and Human Development at George Washington University. Steven Arvizu was appointed executive vice-president; he would move to a community college presidency after a year. Smith's approach to curriculum was a departure from the routine, both in the heavily interdisciplinary character and in the grouping and scheduling of courses. In many ways Monterey Bay was an improbable location for a campus, but a combination of curriculum and location attracted the first student body.

California State University Monterey Bay opened with 654 students in the last week of August 1995. On Labor Day, September 4, 1995, the campus was formally dedicated by President William Clinton. Leon Panetta, who would become chief of staff to the president in his second term, accompanied Clinton, as did a number of members of Congress, state legislators, and others. In the fall of term of 2005, ten years later, 3,773 students were enrolled. The creation of the Monterey Bay campus, unlike any other, was a product of politics at a very high level. Community development and economics was the beginning point. Handel Evans, in his role as interim president at San Jose, recognized the possibilities. Barry Munitz caught the idea and moved quickly, opening doors along the way. Evans was a skillful, quiet negotiator as he shepherded the idea and the institution through the establishment process. Evans left the presidency of San Jose campus in 1995 and became a vice-chancellor. He was not to remain on the chancellor's staff for long; another campus was to be founded.

* * *

Ventura County had been identified for the establishment of a new campus by the trustees and Sacramento officials in the 1960s. A site for a campus was purchased along with sites for two additional campuses in Contra Costa and San Mateo counties. As state finances tightened in the late 1960s, and '70s, the sites were sold. But local and regional pressure remained for the establishment of a campus in Ventura County.

Assemblyman Robert Lagomarsino had attempted to establish a campus at that time. The legislature appropriated funds for a site purchase, the Taylor Ranch. In the mid 1970s, Governor Jerry Brown ordered the site sold. At the same time, the University of California and the California State University and Colleges jointly opened a center in Ventura. This was staffed from several campuses in each system. In 1977 the Northridge campus became responsible for the state university segment of the operation and the University of California began a gradual withdrawal. In the mid-1990s, Assemblyman Jack O'Connell responded to actions of the Ventura City Council and initiated exploration of the establishment of a California State University campus. In late 1995, Chancellor Barry Munitz phoned Handel Evans and forthrightly asked Handel Evans to found a campus. Evans, upon leaving the interim presidency of the San Jose campus, had become a vice-chancellor and acted for Munitz in moving along the establishment and early operation of Monterey Bay.

State college classes had been taught in Ventura County since the 1960s at a number of sites. In 1974, the University of California and California State University and Colleges Learning Center opened in Ventura. This joint venture of the UC and the CSUC was administered initially through the central offices of both systems. It was possible to earn baccalaureate and master's degrees from campuses in both systems. The degree programs were administered by individual campuses; by 1976, eighteen degree programs were offered. Only upper-division and graduate classes were available, and students received residence credit, not extension credit, an important distinction. Though this was a joint venture of UC and CSUC with multiple campuses involved, the primary campuses were the University of California Santa Barbara, and California State University Northridge.

The number of students grew, and a measure of stability ensued in the 1980s. The UC Santa Barbara campus gradually withdrew from the learning center, and the Northridge campus quietly expanded. The first Northridge commencement ceremony, caps, gowns, and tradition, was held at the Ventura site in 1994.

The story of the actual development of a freestanding campus in Ventura County is a political story, centered in Sacramento. The two main CSU actors are Chancellor Barry Munitz and Handel Evans. The legislature and governor formally established a state university for Ventura County in 1996. The Northridge Center would remain, and the graduates would continue to receive degrees from California State University, Northridge until 2002. At the same time Handel Evans —as president of California State University Channel Islands, essentially a planning president—was focusing on the state hospital site at Camarillo and its development. The site and use of the buildings with their Spanish architecture were enhanced by Evans's professional talent as an architect, and the campus benefited from the successful fundraising efforts of the Evans administration.

Handel Evans, while president at San Jose State from 1991 to 1995, had brought the Monterey Bay campus into existence, and was to play the role again. Handel and Carol Evans attended a dinner meeting with Munitz, O'Connell, and a few Ventura civic leaders. The decision was made that a campus would be founded. There would be no state dollars spent, but the 260-acre Taylor Ranch, owned by the county, would be the site. Munitz took the proposal and Evans's appointment to the trustees, and the trustees approved. A new California State University campus was born; but the story was only beginning.

Munitz and Assemblyman Jack O'Connell held a press conference in January 1996 to announce a new state University. In the same month, the governor announced the close of the Camarillo State Hospital. Soon the story developed that the hospital closing was to be done to provide a site for the new university. This was not the case at the time, but it did turn out to be the fact. The Camarillo site was deemed practical. The legislative delegation from the area became involved. O'Connell had moved on to the state senate. Assembly Member Cathy Wright became the leader of a move to transfer the 600-acre hospital site to the trustees.

By the end of 1996, the small state university planning staff moved on to the hospital site. As the patients left, the state university moved in. Evans had a small development group, with two academic planning staff and a business officer. He had little money. He leased some of the buildings in order to have money to provide the security officers for the property.

Controversy developed about the name of the university. While it was located in Camarillo, civic leaders in Ventura and Oxnard likewise wanted the name of their individual communities attached. Ventura County leaders wanted the county's name to be used. In a discussion, Carol Evans jokingly suggested the offshore Channel Islands, populated only by goats. The idea caught on, and Barry Munitz presented it to the board with a smile. The board named the institution California State University Channel Islands.

The citizenry and leaders of Ventura County were more than pleased to have the university. The university leadership was very successful in raising money. Two gifts of five million dollars were received, one for a library and one for general purposes. Two capital outlay appropriations were received; ten million dollars for conversions of classrooms, and ten million for a science building.

Evans saw his work completed as the founder, and announced his retirement from the presidency, to be effective in 2001. The trustees and the chancellor initiated a national search which resulted in the appointment of Richard Rush, president of a Minnesota State University campus. For Rush, this was almost a homecoming. He had been a faculty member and administrator at the San Diego campus before moving to the Minnesota presidency. Rush assumed the Channel Islands presidency in 2001.

When California State University Channel Islands opened in the fall of 2002, enrollment was limited to upper division students for the first year. CSUCI registered 771 students who would work toward a Channel Islands degree. In addition, there were 1,509 students enrolled at the campus who elected to continue working toward Northridge degrees. By 2006, the Northridge degree candidates were finished and more than 3,000 students were enrolled for Channel Islands.

* * *

The Office of Governmental Affairs became of greater importance in the 1990s. Scott Plotkin, the director, worked directly with the chancellor. Karen Yelverton, the associate director, worked often with Molly Broad, the executive vice-chancellor. Early in the new legislative session of 1997, Plotkin was asked to become chief consultant for the Senate Education Committee. Plotkin's background was not only in higher education politics but included K-12 experience; he had been a school board member for a number of years, and he was president of the California School Board Association. Munitz's reaction to the offer to Plotkin was positive, provided that Plotkin would take a leave from the position of director of governmental affairs for two years, and then return. Plotkin moved and Karen Yelverton became acting director. She reported to a triumvirate of the executive vice-chancellor, the vice-chancellor for business affairs, and the vice-chancellor for university advancement. Shortly after this, Molly Broad resigned as executive vice-chancellor to become president of the University of North Carolina system. A few months later, in July 1997, Barry Munitz resigned to become president of the J. Paul Getty Trust. It became necessary to rebuild the system relationships in Sacramento.

The trustees' search for a new chancellor lasted five months. Their choice, Charles Reed, was then chancellor of the Florida State Universities. Reed had been in that position for a dozen years, and prior to that had been chief of staff for the governor of Florida. His experience as chancellor of the Florida system and in state government was a fit for the CSU.

The Sacramento governmental affairs office had been in something of a transition for a year, with Scott Plotkin's departure and the acting appointment of Karen Yelverton. Shortly before leaving the chancellorship, Munitz, with Reed's agreement, commissioned a study of the Sacramento office. William Baker, then retired from the vice presidency of the University of California, where his responsibilities included oversight of UC activity in Sacramento, was selected to do the study. Baker recommended a change of reporting relationships and an aggressive style for the Sacramento office. Reed was doing some reorganization in the chancellor's office, and he created the position of executive vice-chancellor and chief financial officer. Richard West, who had been vice-chancellor for business affairs, assumed the redefined role. The Sacramento governmental affairs office and its director would report to West.[23]

Plotkin had decided to remain with the legislature. The office was redefined, as the Office of Advocacy and Institutional Relations, and assigned the additional responsibility of working with alumni statewide. Karen Yelverton became director, and the Baker recommendation about an active approach in the Sacramento office was adopted. The role of director was later retitled as assistant vice-chancellor for advocacy and institutional relations, and Karen Yelverton, now Karen Yelverton Zamarripa was named assistant vice-chancellor.

Reed's approach to Sacramento was one that built on the openings that Munitz had created. Following his appointment by the board, Reed had returned to his hotel room. He received an unanticipated call; where Governor Wilson called him to welcome him to California. Wilson and Senator Robert Graham, for whom Reed had been chief of staff when Graham was governor of Florida, had served in the US Senate together, and Wilson had talked with Graham about Reed. A month later, in December 1997, Wilson invited Reed to Sacramento to spend an hour; he wanted to talk about the budget for the coming year. Wilson addressed the topic of teacher education; he had forcefully proposed a class-size reduction for the early elementary school grades. He wanted the California State University to increase the number of graduates with teaching credentials. Reed agreed and asked for four or five million dollars. Wilson agreed. As the conversation went on, Wilson asked about other issues and agreed to add twenty million dollars, to adjust faculty salaries. So Reed began his work in Sacramento.[24] Reed assumed the chancellorship in March 1998.

Reed was, and is, his own chief lobbyist. He works closely with his staff, and keeps them fully informed about his conversations, activities, agreements, and the like. At the same time, he often schedules meetings with the governor, legislators, and others by himself. Reed is seen by his staff as an implementer and a leader. He has developed personal relationships with many legislators and worked on a one-to-one basis with Governors Wilson and Schwarzenegger. The relationships with the Davis administration were not close, even perhaps strained, although there were good relationships with many senior staff in the governor's office.

The team of Barry Munitz and Molly Broad stressed the uses of technology. This was particularly an effort spearheaded by Broad. She worked closely with a group of presidents and then with the entire executive council, in a group identified as the Technology Steering Committee. Toward the end of the Munitz administration, this effort attracted some negative attention in Sacramento. In 1997–98, technology in the state university was a legislative issue in terms of costs, bids, and corporate selection, but the attention dissipated. At least part of the attention related to collective bargaining and the concerns of some unions about the impact of technology on jobs and the costs of technology. With the change in the chancellorship, this effort took on a new life. Chancellor Reed was determined to bring the California State University to state-of-the-art technology, with respect to both academic programs and administration. (See Chapter 8 for the story of the development of technology.)

The issue of technology and its cost surfaced in the legislature. Reed, Executive Vice-Chancellor Richard West, and Assistant Vice-Chancellor David Ernst worked with a group of presidents and with chief technology officers on campuses. A plan emerged, and it was costly: four hundred million dollars, at an early estimate. Controversy, much of it related to conflict with the faculty union, the California Faculty Association (CFA), propelled the matter into legislative hearings. The hearings were lengthy and brutal. Members who were close to CFA leadership were aggressive. The state auditor was brought in. The hearings and reports produced nothing of significance. The technology initiative and the vocabulary of the Common Management Strategy, introduced in the Reed administration, continued. It was a prolonged and angry set of events, characterized by one participant as "very, very painful."[25] CMS became Common Management Systems; CMS was implemented over a number of years.

Beginning in the late 1990s and continuing to the time of the anticipation of severe budget cuts in late 2007, California Faculty Association relationships were explosive and difficult. This condition quickly emerged in the legislative arena, and it did affect CSU initiatives and budget discussions. There was no unity among the chancellor's staff and the presidents, the unions, especially the CFA, and others. The student lobby, in some ways, was caught in the middle. The contentious issues went substantially beyond technology and included salaries, not only of faculty, but others, such as protests about administrative salaries, and many substantive matters beyond the traditions of unions addressing salaries and wages and working conditions. Many of these battles were fought in the legislative arena. While they were not conclusive, this continuous friction and hostility did impact relationships, negatively, and the toll on staff, especially faculty enthusiasm for the CSU, was significant.

The Master Plan had been reviewed in the late 1980s. The principal objective of that review was the community colleges, and the impact of the review was modest. With the turn of the century, State Senator Dede Alpert, the chair of the Senate Education Committee, introduced a resolution to create a joint legislative committee to create a comprehensive Master Plan for Education in California, an effort to address all of education. The joint legislative committee created task forces to work on topics ranging from the substance of education to finance to governance. The state university was well represented in the task forces.

The principal objectives of this review were K-12, preschool education and, to a lesser extent, the community colleges. The task forces labored for two years. There was some cynicism among state university leaders about a useful product. The most important issues for the state university members vis-à-vis the substance of education related to cooperation with the community colleges in addressing secondary school curriculum. The products of all of the task forces were consolidated, and the report went to the joint legislative committee. The joint committee removed or changed many of the recommendations. The task force members had in many instances resisted the pleadings of special interests. The joint legislative committee did not do so. Senator Alpert had given strong, even visionary leadership to the effort. The product in the form of legislation was modest. There was no impact on the state university.[26]

Soon after Reed took office as the sixth chancellor of the CSU, he consulted with various groups and appointed David Spence as executive vice-chancellor and chief academic officer. Spence had been vice-chancellor for academic affairs with Reed in Florida. Spence was a soft spoken and skilled academic diplomat who worked well with the statewide Academic Senate, the student leadership, and individuals in the Sacramento scene. Unlike Munitz, who had simply left the issue of the CSU awarding the doctorate alone, Reed and Spence together quietly laid the groundwork for the doctorate and then addressed the capacity of the CSU to award an independent doctorate. The statewide Academic Senate became an ally.

The Sacramento staff, campus presidents, Reed and Spence, and the statewide Academic Senate and trustees were of a single mind on the doctorate. Reed's lobbying style is intense and personal. He succeeded in getting the votes in both houses of the legislature for the CSU to award the independent doctorate in education. Once again the University of California opposed it. Reed met with Governor Gray Davis, who told him that he had a personal letter from Clark Kerr urging a veto, and that he would veto a bill authorizing the independent doctorate. Reed and the trustees dropped the issue.[27]

In 1994, voters in the Pasadena area elected Jack Scott to the assembly. Scott was the president of Pasadena City College and a veteran community college leader. He soon became chair of the Assembly Higher Education Committee. A good working relationship between Scott and CSU people of all categories developed. Scott moved on to the state senate, to which he was elected in 2000 and reelected in 2004. Scott became a significant figure in higher education legislation.

With the change in the governorship in late 2003, and the emergence of a positive working relationship between Chancellor Reed and newly elected Governor Arnold Schwarzenegger, the time had come to readdress the issue of the independent doctorate. The statewide Academic Senate published a major study and report in September 2004, *Rethinking Graduate Education in the CSU: Meeting the Needs of the People of California for Graduate Education for the 21st Century*. The group that prepared the report included campus graduate deans, chancellor's staff members, and senate members experienced with graduate programs; it was chaired by Cristy Jensen, a senior faculty member at the Sacramento campus who had founded a department in public policy on that campus that granted only graduate degrees. The senate had released a document in 2001 that addressed the work of the CSU in the new century, and the graduate report grew from that. This was used in the legislative arena as support for the CSU effort.[28]

In January 2005, Senator Scott introduced a bill to authorize the California State University to grant independent doctorates related to "professional practice." The fields in which this could be used were not specified, but degrees related to "university practice and teaching" were specifically included. Essentially the bill would authorize doctorates in applied fields, excluding the professions of law and medicine.[29] To no one's surprise the University of California strongly opposed the bill. The state university mounted a massive lobbying effort, and it seemed clear that the CSU had the votes and the support of the governor. Ultimately, the president of the UC, doubtless after conversation with the regents and campus chancellors and others, agreed to a compromise; the UC would support legislation for the state university to award independently the education doctorate. The bill passed in the assembly committee, which was key to its final passage. The chair of the assembly committee, Carol Liu, who was actively involved with the Berkeley campus of the University of California (her husband had been a CSU trustee in the late 1970s and early 1980s), was strongly opposed and voted against the bill, but it passed. The governor signed the bill on September 22, 2005. The plan was for the first students to begin their work for the EdD at selected campuses in the fall of 2007.

In January 2008, Senator Scott, who would be term-limited out at the end of 2008, introduced legislation to authorize the awarding of the degree of doctor of nursing practice. The fact that licensure requirements for some fields in the health professions (such as audiology, speech pathology, and physical therapy) are moving to require a doctorate, combined with the insufficiency of applied doctorates in the University of California, gives an impetus to this.[30] The 2008 proposal was not adopted. Legislation was reintroduced in 2009. The California State University will soon award the doctorate in a number of applied fields.

Scott played a major and useful role in bringing to a head a number of higher education issues that required legislation and that had been mired in the status quo for years. Perhaps the most important of these related to the movement of students from lower-division programs in the community colleges to the upper-division of state university campuses, and bringing about some common agreement on how courses transfer. This is an example of an issue that could and should have been settled within the educational establishment, but because faculty and academic administrators could not reach agreement, it was not addressed. Vice-Chancellor David Spence played a major role in this; he actually wrote the legislation.[31]

The compact that had been negotiated by Munitz and others with Governor Wilson was renegotiated by Chancellor Reed, with minor variations, with Governors Davis and Schwarzenegger, and remained intact as a concept through the 2007–08 fiscal year. There were complaints over the years. Legislators complained they were not at the negotiating table. Union leaders and others complained that the UC and CSU had settled for too little. The compact had provided a base from which to build a budget. The compact did not provide a student fee policy, a major matter.

* * *

In the 1950s, the independent colleges and universities were the most significant higher education institutions in Sacramento; in the 1960s, the University of California became a dominating force. By the mid-1990s and the first years of the twenty-first century, the California State University and the University of California were equal in strength in Sacramento, each with its own set of factors at play. For a number of years, since the turn of the century, the CSU chancellor was the higher education leader most listened to. The 2008–09 academic year saw changes in the leadership of the University of California and the California Community Colleges, and substantial strengthening of that leadership. The Regents of the University of California appointed Mark Yudof, the president of the University of Texas, to the presidency. The chancellorship of the California Community Colleges was filled by Senator Jack Scott as he was term limited from the legislature. For the first time since the Master Plan, all three public segments had strong leadership.

The Sacramento scene for the state university is a complex one. Students have emerged as a force, with their statewide organization and a budget, principally on those issues that have a direct bearing on students. The regional character of each campus is still a factor for most of the campuses, though this is not a card that can be played easily. To some extent the presidents, depending on their political talents, are a force, or can be. Trustees individually can play a role. In the very early years, the chair of the board had a major role. At some points along the way individual trustees have played both positive and negative roles. Some trustees, most notably William Hauck, because of his long relationship with the state university, his relationship to successive governors, and his chairmanship of the Business Roundtable, have played major roles.

Over the years since 1960 and the creation of the Master Plan, the legislature has become much more fiercely partisan. Initiatives passed by the voters have significantly narrowed the percentage of the state budget that is discretionary with the legislature and the governor. The constitutional requirement that the budget vote requires a two-thirds majority has had a negative impact on funding the California State University, the University of California, and the California Community Colleges. What is clear is that the world of Sacramento for all of higher education is a very different world in 2009 from that in 1960, when the California State Colleges were assembled into a system.

In Washington

In January 1966, Chancellor Dumke and Les Cohen, the director of governmental affairs in Sacramento, presented to the board of trustees a proposed action to establish a Washington office for the California State Colleges. The proposal posited the need for a Washington office based upon the increasing federal support for colleges and universities: "the federal government will become the largest single source of funds for American higher education." It quoted a Council of State Governments statement about federal liaison and coordination that noted California as the first state to establish a state office in Washington in 1959; the University of California had established a Washington office in 1963. The purpose of the state colleges' Washington office would be to "assist in developing and maintaining the closest possible relationship with the legislative and executive branches of the federal government." The office would be part of the governmental affairs unit headquartered in Sacramento and be staffed on a full-time basis. The Department of Finance had informally stated support for the proposal, and state funds were proposed for the fiscal year beginning July 1, 1966. The board supported the proposal unanimously.[32]

The legislature in its final action on the budget did not fund the proposal. The University of California opposed the establishment of a state colleges' office in Washington. The issue became a partisan one, essentially because of the University of California, with Democrats opposed and Republicans in support. The chancellor, his staff, and the trustees believed the office to be essential. They went ahead with the plan and decided that the office would be funded by the campus auxiliary organizations—"the foundations." The funding was immediately controversial and was resisted by many of the presidents and their staffs; all of the campus auxiliary organizations resisted. The trustees and the chancellor held firm. Some of the presidents and auxiliary organizations initially simply refused to forward financial support. The trustees had a full agenda, so the chancellor simply had to work this through with the campuses over time. The campus foundations were eventually assessed based on campus enrollments.

The Washington office was established later in 1966. James Corley, the recently retired vice president for governmental relations of the University of California, was retained to recruit a director for the CSU Washington office. John Kehoe, not a Californian, was appointed. Kehoe had had brief experience as a governmental intern in Hayward. He was then serving as an executive assistant to the chair of the House Science and Space Committee.

The early months of establishing the Washington office were full ones. There was a cooperative effort to group a number of California entities together. In the debate in the legislature about the office, the state colleges had agreed to a compromise over the University of California efforts not only to not fund the office but to prohibit its establishment. The compromise provided for the establishment, with state support, of a Washington office for the Coordinating Council for Higher Education, as a supposed counterbalance. Together, the University of California, the Coordinating Council, the legislature (using the Legislative Analyst's Office), and the state colleges rented an old brownstone on 19th Street near Dupont Circle, the headquarters of the American Council on Education and other national higher education organizations. The building, leased from Congressman James Symington, was modified to place legislative offices on the top floor, the University of California on the second floor, the state colleges on the first floor, and the Coordinating Council in the basement.

Kehoe moved to build relationships in Washington both on Capitol Hill and in the executive branch, and with higher education organizations. A few years prior to the 1966 establishment of the Washington office, five state college presidents had worked together to establish the American Association of State Colleges and Universities (AASCU). Two of the five were Californians, Glenn Kendall of Chico and Arnold Joyal of Fresno. Actually, the interim executive director of AASCU as it was being established was a longtime San Francisco and Chico faculty member, Professor Joseph Smith. The AASCU office was fully established by 1966, and its executive director, Allan Ostar, invited Kehoe to participate in a weekly meeting of Washington representatives. The California State Colleges, along with representatives from other institutions (not a large number in 1966), were participants. The Brookings Institution had also initiated periodic meetings of Washington representatives, and these meetings included representatives of established major universities, private institutions, and the whole range of American higher education; Kehoe participated regularly with Brookings.

The Washington office was not popular with the campuses. Both Kehoe and the office had been received with some hostile reaction; the campuses were supporting it financially. Kehoe remembers the first time a CSU campus dean came to his office to visit while in Washington for another meeting. The dean came through the door, introduced himself, and asked, "[H]ow can I help?" Kehoe was amazed and welcomed this friendly gesture. It was not the norm. Despite the opposition of the University of California in the Sacramento debate, a good and helpful relationship developed between Kehoe and the UC Washington representative, Mark Ferber.

The Washington office was created in 1966 during the Dumke years. Chancellor Dumke did not like Washington politics any more than he liked Sacramento politics, but he clearly understood the growing needs of CSU's students for financial aid, and the state of California's needs in seeking grants for support of higher education. He was articulate, and he was effective about educating the congressional delegation, the U.S. Office of Education staff, and national higher education groups about the newly formed California State Colleges. Members of the California delegation were largely removed from the politics of organizational infighting that were present almost daily in Sacramento. One of the two California senators, George Murphy, was on the Senate Committee on Education, and he went out of his way to be helpful.

In the first year of the Washington office, grants totaling twenty-four million dollars came to the CSU through the office. Only a few of the campuses used the office aggressively, notably San Diego, San Francisco, and Los Angeles. Negotiations with federal agencies were complex, as these initial grant activities were affected by an early UC insistence that the Master Plan did not permit state colleges to do research other than that specifically related to instruction. Thus, most grants had to be awarded to individual faculty members or departments, not to the colleges as institutions. This interpretation disappeared after a few years.

After two years as director in Washington, Kehoe was asked to come to Sacramento to head the governmental relations unit, and he accepted the position.[33] Meanwhile, as the Washington office was developing, the role of AASCU became more important to the state colleges. AASCU established an office to assist campuses with grants, and cooperative relationships developed. AASCU was effective particularly at this early stage, as it assigned staff to individual member campuses. Chris Bitting was the staff member assigned to the California State Colleges campuses, and she worked effectively and productively with faculty and deans on the campuses. Bitting later became a vice president of AASCU. As time passed, national organizations grew both in numbers and activities in which campus faculty, presidents, and administrators became more involved and began to look to the Washington office for help.

In the 1970s, the Washington office made a major step forward. A new director was appointed in 1975, Sheppie Abramowitz. She had previously worked for the State University of New York. Abramowitz was experienced in the ways of Washington. Her husband was a senior career foreign service officer, albeit at a younger age than most. In the last years of the Carter administration he would become ambassador to Thailand; in the Reagan administration he would be the ambassador to the International Atomic Energy Commission, located in Vienna, and the US representative in conversations about nuclear weapons and atomic energy. Sheppie Abramowitz became director just as Saigon fell in the Vietnam

War; her first major task was to respond to a chancellor's office request about students from Vietnam. Some were anxious to find out about their families, some about their finances and sources of support, some did not want to return to Vietnam. Her State Department contacts and experience helped immensely. Abramowitz continued at the Washington office until 1979.

The office was still supported in part by the campuses, and this continued to have an impact on campus relationships. By the mid-1970s most state college campuses had research directors or coordinators, someone actively working on grants. Some of the research coordinators used the Washington office and AASCU extensively and productively; some campuses attempted to work with Washington agencies and Congress directly. A few campuses developed the practice of employing a Washington professional representative, a practice that was in some measure a function of the presidential relationship to the chancellor's office.

The thrust of the Washington office in these years was twofold: to explore opportunities for the campuses to gain support for academic and other projects, and to make first steps toward a policy agenda. Each year, in conjunction with the Washington offices of other institutions, the office would carefully go through the budget and other documents to develop a comprehensive picture of opportunities for campuses to follow. In a sense, the office informed the campuses what was being funded. Some important gains were made in placing faculty and academic administrators on national panels and in the national organizations. Individuals began to assume leadership positions in national organizations.

A policy agenda at the national level was not on the agenda for the chancellor's office or the trustees. Perhaps the most important move made by Sheppie Abramowitz was a major step in that direction. The most important support the state colleges received (and continues to receive, as the CSU), from the federal government is student financial aid. The state colleges had in the chancellor's office a staff member, Sumner Gambee, who was nationally acknowledged as a leader and an expert in student financial aid. Abramowitz introduced him to Washington as an expert in testimony before Congress. Gambee became a regular in congressional testimony. The California State University and Colleges had made a first move toward a national policy agenda.[34]

Sheppie Abramowitz left the Washington office in 1979 for Thailand. The momentum of the office carried it into the 1980s. The chancellorship changed in 1982. With the arrival of Ann Reynolds, the stance toward the Washington office also changed. Ann Reynolds was interested in the national scene. She wanted to be personally involved. She brought into the role of director Clyde Aveilhe, a former advocate for the College Board in Washington. At the beginning of the Reynolds years, the legislative analyst took exception to the balance of funding for support of the Washington office. The funding had been split between a general fund item for the chancellor's Office and the campus foundations. The analyst's pressure resulted in moving a greater percentage of funding to the campuses.

Reynolds faced the same problem that Dumke had faced in 1966, the need to obtain support from the presidents. The resistance of some of the presidents was fierce.

The California State University, despite funding difficulties, maintained a Washington agenda through the 1980s. One of the most important occurrences was the emergence of a number of CSU presidents on the national scene. Thomas Day of San Diego State and Warren Baker of Cal Poly at San Luis Obispo both became members of the National Science Board. James Cleary of Northridge and Stephen Horn of Long Beach were both chairs of the AASCU Board during the decade. Aveilhe was active on the Washington scene and helpful to the campuses. Reynolds was not a major presence in Washington, but she was influential on some specific issues. Activity about student financial aid stepped up. Sumner Gambee retired and was replaced by Allison Jones on the chancellor's staff. Jones had been director of student financial aid at the Fullerton campus. He picked up where Gambee left off, and the influence of the CSU nationally continued to rise.

When Ann Reynolds left the chancellorship in 1990 to move to the City University of New York, she soon took Clyde Aveilhe with her. Thus, when Barry Munitz was appointed to the chancellorship, the Washington office was vacant. He moved quickly to appoint Allison Jones as an interim director. Munitz wanted the presidents to be involved nationally, and he made that clear as he entered the scene. One of his early moves was to negotiate membership for a number of California State University campuses in the National Association of State Universities and Land Grant Colleges; in California, only University of California campuses had been eligible to be members of NASULGC.

A tone for the 1990s was set by Munitz and Molly Broad, in effect the chief operating officer for the system. Both valued the Washington activity, and a new director for the office of federal relations was recruited. Beth Buehlman was an experienced legislative staffer in Washington. Munitz encouraged the use of the office for gaining grants and contracts, for aiding campus administrators and faculty with Washington contacts as well as moving to national leadership positions, and certainly for positioning the CSU on policy. The Washington office assisted Handel Evans, the president of San Jose State, along with Leon Panetta, the point person, in securing the Monterey Bay campus site, formerly Fort Ord. Leon Panetta was a congressman, later director of the Office of Management and Budget in the Clinton administration and chief of staff for the White House in the second Clinton term.

Munitz was elected to the board of the American Council on Education (ACE), the Washington umbrella organization for all of American higher education. He soon became chair of the ACE Board. He began the practice of aggressively encouraging presidents to be involved in Washington. The role of the California State University in national policy for student financial aid continued to grow. Essentially, the California State University was beginning a major repositioning.[35]

In 1998, the chancellorship changed once again. Munitz left the CSU in December 1997; Charles Reed became chancellor the following March. A new director came to the office, Barbara Bennison. Reed's personal approach to Washington was not unlike his manner in Sacramento, but he had had a head start in Washington. Twelve years as chancellor of the Florida State University system, and a close professional and personal relationship with a powerful senator, Robert Graham of Florida, gave Reed a knowledge of Washington and a set of well-developed personal relationships.

Reed's first years concentrated heavily on issues internal to the California State University, but he did not ignore Washington. He set in motion an annual California State University pilgrimage to Washington in the spring. All of the campus presidents and their chief governmental affairs officers and staff, the vice-chancellors, other key staff, and trustees who wished to come, joined Reed in a visit to Washington for several days. Every California member of Congress was visited, and there were substantive discussions. A grand reception for the Congressional delegation was held. All of the participants engaged in two very full days, from early morning into the evening hours. What perhaps began as a formality became a set of developing personal relationships.

Reed brought in a new vice-chancellor for advancement, Louis Caldera. Caldera is an attorney, a former member of the California Legislature, and had been secretary of the army in President Clinton's second term. Reed initially defined the reporting relationship of the Washington office within the responsibilities of Caldera. Caldera replaced Douglas Patino, who left in the year 2000. Caldera in turn brought into the Washington office a longtime staff colleague, James Gelb. Gelb had been on Caldera's staff as a member of the California State Assembly, and he went with Caldera to Washington when Caldera became secretary of the army. Gelb moved to the Washington office in 2001; in the spring of 2002, he became acting director. Gelb described the situation as an office being reborn, as there was a total turnover in staff, and he had to rebuild. Caldera left the vice-chancellor role in 2003 and was not replaced. Gelb was soon named director.

Gelb reports directly to the chancellor. Funding for the office had been stabilized in the Munitz years; the office is funded from the general fund appropriation to the chancellor's office and has remained stable. In June 2002, Gelb prepared an eleven-page memorandum to Caldera and Reed, "The Future of the CSU Office of Federal Relations," which became the blueprint for the Washington office.

Gelb has built a federal agenda process. Each fall he solicits items for a federal agenda from each campus and the chancellor's office. This is reviewed by the presidents, vice-chancellors, and the chancellor, in the executive council, and then presented to the board of trustees for review and action at the January meeting. Gelb began the practice of frequent participation in executive council meetings and attendance at some board meetings. Gelb's position was retitled assistant vice-chancellor for federal relations. Two points are important, here. There was a planned integration of the Washington staff and office into the activities of the system. The Washington office was no longer a distant activity that was not on the screen for most. There was the clear establishment of a federal policy agenda. The CSU was to be at the table in the Washington higher education policy discussions and actions.

The restructured Washington office is small. There are two professional positions and one staff position; the experience of this restructured office is that having the professional positions occupied by one Democrat and one Republican, each with Capitol Hill ties, is useful. The office is located near the Capitol and has conference facilities available. The office has established routine and regular communication channels with the campuses and the chancellor's office, and current technology keeps both the campuses and the chancellor's office in virtual daily touch with Washington and unfolding opportunities and issues.

Earmarks in legislation have been a fact of life for years. Reed has no problem with using earmarks, a very limited number, to support state university agendas. Earmarks have been successful for agriculture and for coastal issues. Reed also has no problem with campuses pursuing their own earmarks. The system's posture toward campus involvement in Washington is supportive. Reed's style is such that he welcomes presidential and faculty involvement. In a sense, given both distance and the substantive difference in issues between Sacramento and Washington, it is easier for the system to encourage Washington activity than Sacramento activity. Activity in Sacramento, especially given the budget process, needs a fair measure of centralization. A major ground rule is that campuses, presidents, and others, keep the Washington office informed. In turn, the Washington office is helpful. It can be, and often is, the base from which campus individuals operate. One of the expressed goals of the office is to help the campuses.

On the whole, the Washington offices of the California State University and the University of California work well together. For the most part, the agendas are complementary, not competitive. The role of the CSU in national financial aid policy continues to be a major one; Allison Jones is a nationally known figure on this front. Financial aid is a big figure for the CSU—well over one billion dollars each year.

The role of CSU presidents and the chancellor and others on the Washington scene has changed greatly, building in the 1990s from the initial activities of a few in the 1980s. There is not a national higher education group addressing public higher education that does not include California State University people in its leadership. The American Council on Education, the National Association of State Universities and Land Grant Colleges, the American Association of State Colleges and Universities, the Council on Higher Education Accreditation, and international groups such as the International Association of University Presidents, the United Nations University and its American Council, and many other groups have had California State University people in a leadership role.

The chancellorship of the state university has developed a major role in Washington. Reed built on Munitz's leadership of ACE and his own twelve years of activity as the Florida chancellor in Washington. There is seldom a national committee formed that Reed is not asked to be a member of. In the work of the Spellings Commission, Reed made a major impact when he used the Early Assessment Program, developed by the CSU in the first decade of the twenty-first century, and the state university outreach to K-12, as examples of what works in higher education: K-12 relationships. Gelb makes the point in his analysis of the CSU on the Washington scene that the personality and style of a chancellor is a major variable in Washington. The state university directors of the Sacramento office have made the same point.

One piece is missing in the Washington operation, at least in the minds of some. The state university has no student or research academic presence in Washington. This has been at least discussed in a low-key way over the years. Whether this would be a desirable activity or not, the major factor is money. Some campuses have used the Washington Center, an organization that makes available Washington experiences of several kinds. A few campuses have used, on occasion, placements of various kinds in congressional offices. The Center for California Studies annually places one individual in the California Institute in Washington. Gelb, in his 2002 analysis of the future of the Office of Federal Relations, addresses the desirability of examining "at some point ... the viability of having an academic presence in Washington." He notes the value of the programs of the Center for California Studies and the Sacramento Semester.

* * *

The state university role in Sacramento and Washington, essentially, the system's program for governmental relations at the state and national levels, is a story of building. Dumke's administration, for its time, did what was needed to establish a presence and secure support. A first task was to build upon the independent work of the campuses prior to the Master Plan. The campus roles were modest, but essential. The mission of the newly formed California State Colleges had to be articulated. Support was secured, not only financial support. Perhaps the two most important actions by the state government in this area were the name change from the California State Colleges to the California State University, and the authorization for granting an independent doctorate. And after steady progress over the years in governmental relations, the California State University is a major factor in state and national higher education programs and policy.[36]

The Center for California Studies

In November 1983, I was appointed to the presidency of California State University, Sacramento, after serving as the president of the Dominguez Hills campus for eight years. In conversations with trustees leading up to the appointment, I had been asked about moving (the original suggestion that I move had come from a trustee, Willie Stennis, who was then vice-chair of the board) and about my thoughts concerning the Sacramento campus. My response to trustees, and to the campus-trustee committee when I met with them, was about two specific matters: address the role of the state university in the state capitol, attend some specific matters internal to the campus, and of course listen and learn.[37]

Often in my then twenty-six years in the California State University on three campuses, with a year in the chancellor's office early in the life of the system, I had taken part in discussions about the Sacramento campus and the fact that it had not engaged, in its programs of teaching, scholarship, and public service, the work and policies of state government. The fact that I am a political scientist and was active professionally may have added to the number of such conversations in which I participated. Not until I interviewed the first chair of the board of trustees, Louis Heilbron, in December 2003, did I learn that in its first year of responsibility, 1961–62, the board had a discussion about giving some, if not all, campuses special support for programs in which they showed, for whatever reason, particular advantages. Cal Poly was an already existing example. Humboldt, and programs associated with oceans, fisheries, and forestry were examples that Heilbron used. But he went on to say that the board had decided to use the Sacramento campus as the first such recipient, to demonstrate the point that the campuses were not meant to be all alike, and that special programs could be developed and supported. Heilbron proposed to the then president of Sacramento State College, Guy West, that the campus receive special support for a program addressing state government. West, after consulting colleagues, thanked Heilbron for the offer but said the campus would not be interested.[38]

On a scheduled Washington trip in the spring of 1984, and prior to my beginning date of July 1, 1984, as president of the Sacramento campus, I had planned some side trips, to the State University of New York at Albany; Rutgers University and its Eagleton Institute; the University of Wisconsin–Madison; and the University of Illinois at Springfield. When in Washington, I visited Sacramento Congressman Robert Matsui. We spoke about the role of a state university in a state capital. He was firm that the campus was missing both an opportunity and an important educational need. I later spent some time on the CSU Sacramento campus, and it was then that I learned that the government department (the department I belonged to as a faculty member) had established a Center for California Studies in 1983. Elizabeth Moulds, a new chair but a longtime member of the department, and John Syer, a state government expert and a relatively recently recruited senior member of the department from the San Luis Obispo campus, had cofounded the center.

Legislative fellows programs originated in California in the mid-1950s. The original idea came from Professor Joseph Harris of UC Berkeley. He interested a number of colleagues from Berkeley, UCLA, Stanford, and Pomona College, along with key legislative members, in the idea of better staffing for the legislature. At that time, the only staff was clerical, and only when the legislature was in session. There were small offices of the legislative counsel, the legislative auditor (later to be the legislative analyst), and the auditor general. The Berkeley campus had a bureau of public administration, and UCLA had a bureau of governmental research. The state library had a small law and legislative reference section. Often the research staff was what was then frequently called the "third house," the unregulated corps of lobbyists.

Harris was instrumental in calling a conference on state government, which was held at Stanford in September 1956. Participants in this conference were both academics and members of the legislature, in about equal numbers. Out of this conference an informal group of academics and legislators decided to explore internships for recent college and university graduates. A group of academics, led by Professors Harris and Peter Odegard (also of Berkeley, and a friendly mentor to me when I was a young faculty member at San Francisco State), and representing Berkeley, Stanford, UCLA, the University of Southern California, and the Claremont Graduate School, proposed to President Robert Gordon Sproul that the regents take the lead in securing Ford Foundation support for the creation of a small group of legislative interns. Some regents were cautious, but Sproul moved ahead. Ford Foundation money was secured. Berkeley also invested funding to start a program.

The first legislative fellows program began in the assembly in September 1957. The program was a success from the beginning. There were problems, and there was hesitation on the part of some members, but the quality of service given by the fellows greatly extended the capability of members. A by-product of the fellows program was Ford Foundation support for faculty research fellows. This was a program for young faculty; it began in 1962 and ended in 1965. There was competition for these positions. The first year, 1962–63, the three faculty research fellows were from Fresno, Sonoma, and Sacramento State Colleges.

The senate did not quickly follow the assembly's lead. The first senate fellows program began in 1969 with only three participants. The senate program gradually developed, and in 1976, the Senate Rules Committee developed the internship program to the point that it roughly paralleled the assembly program. Both programs, over the years, became fully funded in the annual appropriations to the legislature. The original group of five universities simply drifted away from the programs.[39]

On July 1, 1984, I assumed the presidency at the Sacramento campus. Almost immediately, within the first week, I received a call from Senator Robert Beverly. Bob Beverly and I were friends. His district included the Dominguez Hills campus from which I had just come. His wife and their two sons were Dominguez Hills graduates. Beverly told me that the senate was reeling financially from the passage of Proposition 24 in early June by the California voters. This proposition required a 30 percent reduction in the legislative budget effective on July 1. Beverly was a member of the Senate Rules Committee, the governing body of the senate. They had been advised by Cliff Berg, the executive officer of the committee (essentially the chief administrative officer of the senate), that the senate fellows program had to be terminated. Beverly asked if CSU Sacramento could take the program, but with no funds. My immediate response was that I would very much like to do so, but I needed to speak with the chancellor, then Ann Reynolds, and I promised to be back to Bob Beverly within the day.

The idea of an internship program having to do with state government was not new on the campus. In 1976, three faculty members in the government department, Gary Wilhelms, who originated the idea, Richard Krolak, and Jean Torcom, had initiated the "Sacramento Semester," which Torcom led until her retirement in 2003. This was a program open to upper-division undergraduates from all California State University campuses (and University of California students on occasion, as the UC had no comparable program). These undergraduate student participants intern in the legislature, the executive branch, and in lobbyists' offices. The program is, as titled, one semester in length.

For me, Bob Beverly's offer was a gift or, at least, a potential gift. I was determined to address the role of the state university in the state capital, and I had a number of thoughts from my explorations of the previous months. This was a solid, known, and important program. First I talked with Betty Moulds, the chair of the government department. The Center for California Studies already existed; it needed a solid program. Betty agreed to the idea. Then I phoned Ann Reynolds. Fortunately, she was available, as I needed to move quickly. Ann and I had developed a productive working relationship in the two years she had been chancellor. I told her about the Beverly proposal, said that I very much wanted to do it, and said I would not ask for money. She agreed. I would have to find funding. The money necessary for that fiscal year, which had begun only a few days earlier, would be about $275,000, or so I estimated. Then I phoned Bob Beverly and told him we looked forward to doing it, and together we set a transition in motion.

The money was found a bit at a time, wherever we could scrounge. Being new to the Sacramento campus and the presidency had its plus and minus sides. The plus was that many would give some room to move, and my colleagues and I had to be creative. Certainly, the minus was being new to the community. I did not know potential donors, and we had no fundraising staff apart from athletics, nor did I know well the campus pattern of allocations. Little by little and with a fair amount of scrambling, we found money, allowing us to put together the Senate Fellows Program to begin on time in November 1984. An academic component was developed by the faculty. The academic component was at the graduate level, and credit was awarded. The faculty member who developed the academic component and worked with the senate fellows for a number of years was John Syer; his administrative counterpart in the senate, essentially, the operational administrator, was Nettie Sabelhaus, and she would remain with the program for fourteen years. The faculty role soon became formally known as "faculty advisor," but it is an instructional role.

In October 1984, I received a phone call from a friend of many years, a political scientist at UC Berkeley who had been in a very senior position in the UC administration when Clark Kerr was president. It was a very personal and critical call. Essentially, the message was, "Don, how could you do this? Running the senate fellows program is not something the state university does; this is what the University of California does." (Here, I am paraphrasing from notes. I had not recalled this incident until I was reminded by Elizabeth B. Austin's book, *To Be the Change You Wish to See: A History of the Assembly, Executive Judicial Administration and Senate Fellows Programs*, that the UC vice president for governmental relations, William Baker, had written at about the same time to David Roberti, president pro tem and chair of the Senate Rules Committee, to ask that the University of California "assume administrative and academic responsibility for the fellowship program through a cooperative effort among the UC Davis Extension Program, the UC systemwide California Policy Seminar, and the Senate Rules Committee." The letter noted the UC role in creating the original program in the assembly. I forwarded a copy of the Baker letter to CSU provost William Vandement with the comment that "the program has been settled with California State University, Sacramento administering it.")[40]

Early in 1985, Michael Galizio, chief of staff to Assembly Speaker Willie Brown, phoned to ask about CSU Sacramento assuming responsibility for the Assembly Fellow Program. Michael told me that many of the assembly fellows had learned of the opportunity that the senate fellows had to participate in an academic component and receive credit for it. The Speaker wanted to know if Sacramento State would take on the assembly program, and said that the assembly had money and would fund the program; I accepted the offer before the call ended. The first faculty advisor, who developed the academic component and was responsible for instruction in the program, was Dr. Cristy Jensen; she remained with the program until 1989, when she became the founding chair of the Department of Public Policy and Administration on the campus.

Governor George Deukmejian and I had known each other since the late 1960s. At that time I was at Chico State and had responsibility for two years for an entity known as The Institute for Local Government and Public Service. The institute's major activity was an annual weeklong conference in June for local government officials, civic leaders, and the like from northern and northeastern California. Each day a different topic was covered. Deukmejian, then in the legislature, was always invited to be on the program the day that law enforcement was the topic. My wife and I moved to California State University, Dominguez Hills in 1976; Deukmejian was then in the senate, and his district was contiguous to the campus. He visited the Dominquez Hills campus and welcomed me.

In the spring of 1985, I received a call from Governor Deukmejian. The governor had learned of the move of the senate and assembly fellows programs to the CSU, and the incorporation of an academic program. He was, of course, familiar with the legislative fellows programs, as he had served in both houses. He asked if the CSU would be interested in developing a fellows program for the executive branch, something like the White House fellows. He offered twenty-five thousand dollars from the 1985–86 budget to develop the program. I agreed, and he designated his education assistant, William Cunningham, to be his person to work with the establishment of the program. The actual budgeted amount turned out to be somewhat larger than twenty-five thousand dollars. I asked Richard Krolak, a political scientist and faculty member in the government department, to take on the responsibility. Krolak had been a key member of the campus administration and knew both program development and budgeting. Krolak built the program from the ground up. The legislative programs had a history. The Executive Fellows program had to create its history. The Executive Fellows program took its first class of fellows in September of 1986. Krolak remained with the program for two years.

By the opening of the 1985–86 academic year, funding for the Senate Fellows Program had been secured from the legislative budgets, though it was not sufficient to cover all of the costs. The early years of the three fellows programs were years when the programs had to be renegotiated annually between the campus and the chancellor's office. This is something I did personally, as I did not want the programs to be lost in administration, either on the campus or in the chancellor's office. The CSU had never had anything resembling the financially complex relationship that was involved with the fellows programs and the legislature. The fellows received stipends, a practice that began with the initial development of the program. It was important to avoid involvement of the legislative or executive staff in the negotiations with the chancellor's office, lest we lose the programs. There was considerable resistance to these programs. While the chancellor's staff did not necessarily understand the programs' importance, there was certainly goodwill and benefit seen in the offices in which the fellows served. Both members of the legislature and legislative staffs appreciated the work fellows were doing, and close university-legislature relationships developed.

The Center for California Studies was in the government department. By 1986, the three fellows programs had become a significant administrative operation, particularly because this was a new venture for the CSU. We decided the center should have a director, and we recruited nationally. Dr. Bernard Shanks was appointed director and arrived on the campus with the opening of the 1986 academic year. Bern Shanks was not a career academic; his career was in public service. He had been recently on the staff of Governor Bruce Babbitt of Arizona, in a position at the cabinet level. Shanks stayed with the center for three years.

On July 1, 1987, my wife and I were moving into a new home we had built. My task that day was to check off the numbered boxes and pieces of furniture on an inventory we had made, as the movers unloaded the truck. Bev took a phone call. Chancellor Ann Reynolds was on the phone and insisted that she speak to me. Chancellor Reynolds explained that she wanted me to accept as a faculty member an individual for whom a key member of the legislature, John Vasconcellos wanted to find employment. I demurred, as there had been no faculty consultation. This was simply not my style. She insisted, and said her office would pay the salary. The individual was Jeffrey Lustig, a political scientist who had at one point been a lecturer at the Humboldt campus. I met with Jeff and was positively impressed with his abilities. After a bit of thought, I told him that his work would be to do a major report about academic programs throughout the state that had to do with California Studies, and I assigned him to the Center for California Studies. He was not placed in a tenure-track faculty position at that time. Jeff quietly came on board and did the study well.

This study became the trigger for a series of conferences about California. The first conference was held in Oakland and addressed the feminization of political power in California. In 1989, the conference used the title "Envisioning California," and the title stayed with the conference series. Each year the "Envisioning California" conference addresses a different theme and set of related issues. It has become a major California conference. When Shanks left the directorship in 1989,

Lustig took over. He was everyone's logical choice. Subsequently, he founded the California Studies Association, as part of the Center for California Studies. In 1992, Lustig moved to a full-time professorship in the government department. The California Studies Association moved from the Center for California Studies and became independent. Donna Hoenig-Couch, a former senate fellow and the director of the Executive Fellows Program, served as interim director through a full and demanding year.

Barry Munitz became chancellor of the California State University in 1991. Beyond the usual interest a president might have in a new chancellor, I wanted especially to speak with him about the Center for California Studies, and the work of the fellows programs—essentially, the campus role with state government in Sacramento. We met at the Hyatt Hotel across from the Capitol. Munitz's reaction to my description was that this could be the most important tool we have to level the playing field with the University of California. He may have been exaggerating, but clearly he understood, and was on board.

In 1992, Assembly Speaker Willie Brown invited the center to take responsibility for new member orientation. The center continued with this responsibility through 1998, when, after term limits set in and the speakership began to turn over frequently, a new Speaker decided to move the program to his alma mater, UCLA, which wanted the program. Members rebelled, but this only caused the program to become an in-house program with the assembly.

In the spring of 1984, as I was looking at programs of state universities in state capitals and what they did, the thought occurred to me that it might be useful for some kind of continuing conversation among universities with strong state programs. In 1993, the center sponsored a conference, the first of its kind, inviting all public universities in the United States located in state capitals or with a major capital presence to participate in three days of learning from each other. The conference was a major success. The conference used the term "LINKS." The group, mercifully, did not form a new national organization, but did continue to meet annually in state capitals, returning to Sacramento in 1999. Understandably, the group ran out of steam in 2001 or 2002. Sometime, in the not too distant future, the generational turnover in leadership and staff in state universities across the country will create the sensible desirability for another conference or two or three. The LINKS conferences served their useful purpose for the time.

Dr. Timothy Hodson became the executive director of the Center for California Studies in 1993. Hodson had a conventional academic background and had taught at Claremont McKenna College and at the University of Southern California, both institutions that pay attention to California government. For many years he had been a staff member in the senate, and he was responsible for the staff work in two legislative and congressional reapportionments. Hodson rather quickly brought leadership to the center that resulted in the maturing of the center both in the life of the CSU and in the capital and state government. The governance of the center was settled. The director would report to the president. The center had two advisory groups. The campus advisory board includes faculty and staff members. The statewide advisory council was important to the development

35. Capitol Fellows Alumni, June 8, 2007.

of the center; its chairs included California Journal founder Tom Hoeber; former assembly member and head of the California Cable and Television Association Dennis Mangers; and former Assembly Speaker and lieutenant governor Leo McCarthy. The advisory council was discontinued in 2004.

The year 1994 brought two new activities to the center. A Faculty Research Fellows Program was established. Beginning with the 1994–95 fiscal and academic year, there has been an annual appropriation creating three accounts for research, one each for the assembly, the senate, and the executive branch. Members or authorized individuals in the executive branch may draw on the account. They ask for research to be done. The center circulates a Request for Proposal (RFP) among all twenty-three CSU campus faculties, asking for responses; typically, it receives several, and the individual asking for the research selects the proposal judged to be most useful. Thus, faculty from throughout the state university can be drawn into the Sacramento scene.

Michael Galizio, still the chief of staff to Speaker Willie Brown, called Tim Hodson with a proposal from the Speaker. LegiSchool each year brings ten thousand high school students from over the state into televised Town Hall meetings, online dialogues, essay contests, and summer internships. Members from both houses participate in the Town Hall meetings, and these focus on specific legislation. The first year the legislation used was a bill authorizing high school district boards to require high school students to wear uniforms. Hodson and Sacramento State professor Kenneth Futernick developed the program. It has been administered for years by center staff member Kolleen Ostegaard.

The center continued to develop new programs. In 1995, an annual statewide journalism conference and awards for media coverage of state government was established. The center collaborated with the campus Institute for Social Research in the creation of the California Election Database. The California secretary of state joined this effort in 1997 that office continues to support it.

In 1997, Hodson approached California's then new chief justice, Ronald George, and proposed the creation of a Judicial Administration Fellows Program. George liked the idea. There had been no ready source for court administrators in the state. Governor Pete Wilson and the legislature responded positively, and funding was provided in the budget. Donna Hoenig-Couch became the founding director of the program, and Patricia Clark Ellis, a faculty member in social work who is also an attorney, became the faculty advisor.

Discussions about developing a doctoral program for community college administrators had been ongoing with David Spence, the executive vice-chancellor and chief academic officer in the Reed administration. We started conversations around the year 2000, encouraged by some community college colleagues. David and I shared this interest. The doctoral program was not to be a reality until 2007, but a spin-off was the creation of a higher education policy research capacity. I knew that I would retire within the next few years since I had turned seventy in December 1998. I thought it important for the California State University to have a policy research capacity focusing on higher education. I asked David, and then chancellor Charles Reed, about sharing initial funding to create an institute between the chancellor's office and the campus. They agreed. The Institute for Higher Education Leadership and Policy was created in 2001, as a unit within the Center for California Studies. Dr. Nancy Shulock was invited to be director; Dr. Shulock had been associate vice president for academic affairs, responsible for planning and the academic budget for a number of years, and, prior to that, had been a member of the legislative analyst's staff; she is also a faculty member in the

Department of Public Policy and Administration. The institute and Shulock have been major and productive entities, and like the center itself, have national reputations.

As of the 2007–08 year there were sixty-four fellows, eighteen in each of the assembly, senate, and executive programs, and ten in the judicial program. Competition for places in the fellows programs is national. Typically, the number of applicants exceed one thousand. Some of the applicants have graduate degrees, some have significant work experience. The fellows programs remain the core of the center, but the center has grown and developed in extraordinary and unanticipated ways.[41]

The Center for California Studies is important for the California State University. It is an academic link to state government, and a piece of the state university presence with state government. Moreover, given California's role in the nation, it is a reasonable expectation that the California State University in the state's capital city be preeminent in the country in the study and teaching of public policy and administration at the state level.

Notes

[1] This chapter, especially the first section about Sacramento, draws upon two four-hour focus groups on governmental relations, held on January 24, 2006, and February 14, 2006. Participants were Les Cohen, the first director of the governmental affairs (Sacramento) 1962–1968; John Kehoe, the first director of federal relations 1965–1968 and, subsequently, director of governmental affairs (Sacramento); Dorena Knepper, the first campus-based (Northridge) director of governmental relations, from 1972–2005; Scott Plotkin, a student lobbyist, president of the California State University and Colleges Student Presidents Association, and subsequently associate director and director of governmental affairs (Sacramento) from 1975–1996; and Karen Yelverton Zamarripa, the associate director and then director for governmental affairs from 1997 to the present. In addition, the following individual interviews were used: Louis Messner, D. Dale Hanner, Glenn Dumke, Alan Post, Harold Geoigue, John Smart, Keith Sexton, Patrick Callan, John Kehoe, Ellis McCune, Ann Reynolds, Barry Munitz, Elizabeth Hill, Charles Reed, Dede Alpert, Murray Haberman, J. Handel Evans, Mary Lyons, and Timothy Hodson. All interviews are in the CSU Archives. Papers and records from the CSU Archives, and the papers of the author were also used.

[2] William L. Storey, memorandum to Glenn Dumke, July 31, 1970, CSU Archives. Storey, then acting director of the Sacramento office, proposed almost doubling the campus contribution, but that idea was rejected.

[3] The author accompanied President Glenn Kendall of Chico to this event.

[4] Minutes, board of trustees, July 13, 1962.

[5] The information on name change is from the two focus groups on governmental relations (see note 1, above); James Jensen, oral history interview by Judson Grenier, March 19, 1997; Sarah Motley, "What's in a Name," term paper, graduate course in political science, cited in Jensen interview; Les Cohen, January 24, 2006, focus group 25–29; Board of Trustees of the California State University, news release, November 23, 1971; minutes, board of trustees, May 23, 1972; Lynn Smith (assistant to the chairman, statewide Academic Senate), memorandum to campus senate chairman, March 31, 1972;

State Hornet, CSU Sacramento, various issues, September–October, 2005; San Jose State University, news releases, March 2007; *San Francisco Chronicle*, March 10, 2007.

[6] Glenn S. Dumke, "University Relationships with State Legislatures, State Education Departments, and State Coordinating Commissions," address to the American Management Association and American Council on Education Joint Conference, June 18, 1975; Harold Geoigue, interview with the author March 15, 2007; Jensen, interview, March 19, 1997.

[7] The full story of union and management activity and the implementation and impact of collective bargaining is written in Chapter 10 of this work. The information in these paragraphs comes from the two focus groups on governmental relations, the oral histories of Ellis McCune, James Jensen, and Glenn Dumke, and the papers of the author.

[8] A more detailed discussion of California State University finances is found in Chapter 12. This segment about Proposition 13 relies upon the February 14, 2006, focus group and upon papers of the author; McCune, interview.

[9] W. Ann Reynolds, interview by John Fowler, June 14, 2001; W. Ann Reynolds, interview by the author, August 19, 2004.

[10] Focus groups on governmental relations.

[11] Lee Kerschner, interview by the author, June 9, 2006.

[12] John Smart, interview by the author, March 6, 2007.

[13] I was that president. This was to be the last time I saw Glenn Dumke. He died in his sleep a number of weeks later.

[14] Focus groups on governmental relations.

[15] Focus groups on governmental relations; Jensen, interview, March 19, 1997, 44.

[16] Focus group on governmental relations, February 14, 2006, 22, 25; Kerschner, interview, June 9, 2006, 37–38; Louis Messner, interview by Lawrence B. de Graaf, February 1995, 4ff.

[17] Office of Governmental Affairs, legislative report, the California State University, June 5, 1992, 1–2.

[18] Munitz, interview by the author, November 18, 2005; focus group on governmental relations, February 14, 2006, 23–24, 31. Richard West, interview by the author, August 14, 2006.

[19] The eight new campuses were Fullerton (1957), San Fernando Valley (Northridge, 1958), Hayward (East Bay, 1957), San Bernardino (1960), Stanislaus (1957), Dominguez Hills (1960), Sonoma (1960), and Bakersfield (1965).

[20] Actually, sixty-eight presidential appointments were made between 1960 and 1988. (CSU Statistical Abstract to July 2006.)

[21] California Postsecondary Education Commission, "The Twentieth Campus: An Analysis of the California State University's Proposal to Establish a Full Service Campus in the City of San Marcos in Northern San Diego County," Sacramento 1989.

[22] Judith Hunt, Dean of Faculty Affairs, CSU, memorandum to Harold Chernofsky, statewide Academic Senate, September 9, 1989, CSU Archives

[23] West, interview, August 14, 2006.

[24] Charles Reed, interview by the author, December 20, 2006.

[25] Focus group on governmental relations, February 14, 2006, 19.

[26] Dede Alpert, state senator, interview by the author, April 18, 2007; Joint Committee to Develop a Master Plan for Education, *California Master Plan for Education*, California State Legislature, 2002.

[27] Reed, interview, 11, 17–18.

[28] Cristy Jensen, phone interview by the author, April 13, 2008.

[29] SB 724, February 22, 2005; amendment to Education Code 66010.4, relating to the California State University.

[30] Jack Scott, state senator, interview by the author, April 18, 2007.

[31] Scott, interview; focus group on academic programs, March 30, 2005.

[32] Minutes, board of trustees, January 23, 1966.

[33] The recitation of the establishment and first years of the Washington office is based on the author's interviews of John Kehoe, March 10, 2006, and February 6, 2008; focus group on government relations, January 24, 2006, and papers of the author.

[34] Sheppie Abramowitz, interview by the author, April 4, 2006.

[35] Munitz, interview, November 18, 2005; West, interview, August 14, 2006; papers of the author.

[36] James Gelb, memorandum, "The Future of the CSU Office of Federal Relations," June 18, 2002 (the quotation is from page 8); James Gelb, interview by the author, April 5, 2006; Reed, interview, 27; West, interview, 2, 10–11, 14; focus group on government relations, January 24, 2006, 4–6.

[37] I was appointed to the presidency of California State University, Sacramento in November 1983 and assumed office July 1, 1984. Given my level of involvement with the center and the programs related to California state government, I am writing some portions of this section in the first person.

[38] Louis Heilbron, interview by the author, December, 2003.

[39] These paragraphs about the early development of the fellows programs are heavily dependent upon Elizabeth B. Austin's *To Be the Change You Wish to See: A History of the Assembly, Executive Judicial Administration and Senate Fellows Programs* (Berkeley Public Policy Press, Institute of Governmental Studies, University of California, 2007). Austin's work has been helpful to me in recreating the work I did affecting the fellows programs.

[40] Elizabeth B. Austin, *To Be the Change*, 74.

[41] The staff of the center has prepared three brief papers with information about the center, and I am indebted to the staff for sharing these.

Part Five
The Mission, Master Plan, and an Agenda for the Future

Chapter 15

The Promise of the People's University: Promises Realized, Promises to be Fulfilled

In 1960, only a few saw the promise of the California State Colleges. Certainly Governor Pat Brown understood that there was a potential for change and growth, and that becomes clear in the decision he made in March 1960 to not place the state colleges in California's constitution.

Brown's stand was a great disappointment to both Glenn Dumke and Clark Kerr, for very different reasons. Kerr wanted to channel and limit the growth and development of the state colleges; he wanted to preserve the role of the University of California as the state's sole public research university, and that meant protecting a monopoly on research and the doctorate by fixing a limited state college role in the constitution. Dumke wanted to provide the freedom of constitutional autonomy for the establishment of excellent public institutions focusing on the liberal arts and professional programs through the master's degree. He had no interest in building a system of research universities, though he did see the role of faculty undertaking scholarship— research and creative activity—as important to the academic strength of the state colleges as teaching-centered and student-centered institutions.

A safe generalization is that none among the architects of the new California State Colleges or the Master Plan had in mind the California State University of the twenty-first century. What set Pat Brown aside is that he understood the need for making moving room to allow for addressing change. His position was bolstered by the absolute unwillingness of the legislative leadership, most notably Senator George Miller, to allow the state colleges to secure the autonomy that the University of California had.

The task for the 1960s for the state colleges was to build a system, even if Chancellor Glenn Dumke did not want to use the word *system*. The remarkable accomplishment of the 1960s was to be found in surviving the decade, despite all of the turmoil with students and faculty, despite a lack of consistent support from many of the presidents, only some of whom really understood the significance and potential of the system, and despite the pendulum swing of state government from the moderate liberal leadership of Pat Brown to the conservative leadership of Ronald Reagan. The 1960s was a decade for strong leadership. The trustees were fortunate to have strong chairs throughout the decade, and the members of the board, consciously or otherwise, created solidarity.

The board itself would be an interesting study. Many, if not most, college and university governing boards are not unified with a spirit of working together to address issues. The question is not whether board members always or frequently agree; rather, the important point is whether board members work together from whatever points of view. The members of the board were not unified or together in the 1970s or early 1980s, despite some very strong and able trustees. The strength of the early board of the 1960s was regained quickly after a lapse in the 1970s, and has remained constant over the years.

The promise of the California State Colleges in 1960, as the Master Plan was adopted for the people of California, was a very practical one. For years, the California State University—and, earlier, the California State Colleges—have used three words as practical descriptors of the system and of the campuses: access, affordability, and quality. The California State Colleges of the Master Plan offered access, affordability, and increasing quality to programs in the arts and sciences, a sound and sturdy undergraduate education, and study in professional programs, including teacher training through the master's degree. This was not an idle promise. It was real, and it was the most substantial promise that any society had ever made to its people.

* * *

Implicit in the Master Plan for many faculty and leaders, and for most trustees, as the system began to function, was a change of designation—almost a labeling issue—from colleges to university. Thus, it was not surprising that an initial effort was made in 1968, followed by more intense efforts in the early 1970s, to have the California State Colleges become the California State University. This was successful, and the name of the system did change to the California State University and Colleges in 1972, with clear criteria that each campus would have to meet to secure the university designation. This change was followed almost ten years later, as Glenn Dumke's announced retirement from the chancellorship in the summer of 1982 approached, by legislative action to change the name of the system to the California State University.

The story of the name change is told elsewhere in this work, as is the story of the resistance of three campuses, followed by two others, to the change to California State University (followed by each school's city, county, or other location, for example, California State University, Los Angeles, or California State University, Sacramento). San Diego State University, San Francisco State University, and San Jose State University, followed later by Humboldt State University and Sonoma State University, secured legislative action to retain their campus names as primary parts of their titles. In 2005, an effort was made to change the name of California State University, Sacramento to Sacramento State University, and individuals on two other campuses probed the possibility. In 2006, some presidents raised the possibility of changing the name of the entire system to the California State Universities.

Universities and colleges have market positions, just as do commercial enterprises, manufacturers, charities and philanthropic organizations, and even governments, whether local, regional, or national. Market positions have to do with public understanding and support, as well as the understanding and support of groups with particular interests. A key element of marketing is "branding," establishing recognition. Thus, there is an importance to whether an institution might be named Desert State University (in Arizona, California, New Mexico, or, perhaps, Morocco) or California State University in the Desert. Marketing and branding are basic to understanding and support. In a public university, legislative and executive support are strengthened by successful marketing and branding. Student and parental interest and enrollment; the ability to recruit faculty, staff, and administrators; and success in attracting and gaining private support are enhanced by effective marketing.

The importance of marketing and branding is underscored by the ratings and rankings that are a feature of higher education nationally and worldwide. The annual *U. S. News & World Report* ratings, decried by many in higher education, are nevertheless followed by educators and read by many. The *Times of London Higher Education Supplement* rankings, and in more recent years those of Shanghai Jiaotung University, are followed by educators over the world.

The California State University campuses in well-known cities and other areas have substantial marketing positions. San Francisco and San Diego, for example, are known throughout the world. Sonoma is known over the country and among wine connoisseurs throughout the world. The question that has never been addressed is whether all of the campuses and, indeed, the strength of public higher education in the state, would best be served by understanding the whole and the parts together.

The 1960s and 1970s, and, to a substantial extent, the 1980s, were a time when the California State Colleges and the California State University were not known over the world. Some of the campuses were known in the United States for particular programs. The California State Colleges, and then the California State University, were building not just quantitatively, but in strength of programs; the campuses were emerging. The California State University has become known and respected over the nation and is understood for its character and its mission. There are still some, even in education, who cannot distinguish between the twenty-three campuses of the California State University and the ten campuses of the University of California. Likewise, there are those who do not understand that the system leader of the California State University is titled chancellor and the leaders of the individual twenty-three CSU campuses are presidents, compared to the system leader of the University of California, who is titled president, and the leaders of the ten individual UC campuses, who are titled chancellors. But this too will eventually end. There is seldom a national commission or other body that is representative of American higher education in which someone from the California State University is not in a leadership or governing role. The CSU is represented on governing boards and executive committees, and individuals hold chairs in numerous national groups, while faculty and professional staff members are in leadership positions of professional organizations.

The politics of higher education and the pride of communities make it unlikely that this matter will be attended to by the legislature in the near future. Nevertheless, the naming of the California State University campuses and the uses of naming should be addressed. The chancellor and the presidents, the faculty and alumni, need to address the matter, followed by a discussion with the board of trustees about strategy. This matter will become more important as the strength of the California State University and its potential, both for an impact on public policy and its continuing development of a nationally and internationally important model, grow. The names of the campuses and their identification are important to the faculty, staff, students, and alumni; they are about how we understand ourselves and our campuses. This cannot be casually resolved, but it should be resolved, so that the California State University is understood as an entity. The California State University has standing in the world of higher education and in the world at large; all of the campuses should be identified with the California State University.

An International Evaluation

The California Master Plan received worldwide attention soon after its adoption. Over the years, delegations from other states and nations visited California to study the structure and functioning of higher education in California. For a week, a month, or even a year, individuals came to study, and sometimes participate in the California higher education enterprise. In 1987, the leadership of the Organization for Economic Cooperation and Development (OECD), a group of economically mature nations, selected California and its higher education for one of its periodic studies.[1] The OECD has a tradition of performing policy studies on subjects of interest to member nations in terms of their national development. One series of policy studies addresses higher education. Up to 1987, all of the policy studies had been at the national level. California was chosen because as a state it is larger in population and area than some of the OECD members and, at the time of the study, the sixth largest economy in the world.

OECD followed its custom of selecting three examiners, eminent and recognized figures in higher education. A. H. Halsey was professor emeritus of social and administrative studies at Oxford University and professorial fellow of Nuffield College; he served as rapporteur, and was effectively chair of the group. Pierre Tabatoni was former rector of the academy and chancellor of the Universities of Paris. Michio Nagai was a former minister of education of Japan and, at the time of the California project, an eminent scholar at the United Nations University. In preparation for the visit and the subsequent review, the leadership of higher education in California asked Dr. Clive Condren, a staff member in the University of California president's office, to prepare a detailed study. Condren's study, which was essentially descriptive, was completed under the auspices of the California Postsecondary Education Commission.[2] The study identified a number of areas that needed attention, an agenda in a broad sense, including "achieving equity while maintaining excellence," working relationships with the schools, faculty replacement, teacher education, student aid, economic development, and the community colleges.

The visit of the examiners occurred in April 1988. They were accompanied by a senior staff member from OECD headquarters in Paris. The visiting group spent three weeks in California with students, faculty, administrators, legislators, public policy figures, and the like. They prepared a lengthy report that was widely circulated among those in California higher education and public policy leaders. Subsequently, in May 1989, leaders from California, the review group, and others met in Paris. The entire effort, including its product, was known simply by its OECD label, the "Review."[3]

The report, and, indeed, the effort of several years, was only marginally productive. The report, as have many analyses of California public higher education in earlier years, saw the California State University and its campuses in a middle ground between the University of California and the California Community Colleges. The community colleges received significant attention. This should not have been surprising. Developed in the United States only a century earlier, with a focus on curricula preparatory for university attendance, and brought to a new level in California in the twentieth century, with attention to vocational education and work force development, the concept of a junior college had an important economic potential for OECD member nations.

The Review was not without importance to the role of the California State University and the then nineteen campuses (the San Marcos campus came into being as the Review was coming to a close). The first question posed for the CSU addressed the role of elementary and secondary schools in the preparation of candidates for university and college work and the composition of the pool of candidates—the matter of diversity. Moving on, the reviewers asked about the curriculum and the extent to which this should reflect the multicultural composition of student bodies. What balance should be sought in undergraduate curriculum—liberal in contrast with vocational orientation, fundamental skills versus employment skills? To what extent should the three segments work together to achieve a common core in the first two years of undergraduate education?

The Review panel members posed some very specific questions to the CSU; regarding faculty, for example, they asked, "Are reforms necessary in the evaluation and pay of academic staff (faculty) so as to emphasize the value of teaching?"

They also asked probing questions about budgets and the work of the most recent assessment of the Master Plan. The report recognized the lack of authority vested in the California Postsecondary Education Commission, and raised the question of vesting some authority in that body for budget planning. The Review became specific about the lack of any "pricing policy," and implicitly urged that a student fee policy be developed. The essentially political nature of budgets for public higher education did not escape the panel, and the members grasped the significance of California's constitutional processes that made possible voter decision making about budget allocations and the shrinking portion of the state budget, from which support for public higher education and, specifically, the California State University and the University of California must be drawn. "Without modification ... , it will be impossible for the two public segments of higher education, CSU and UC, to accomplish their mission and reach stated goals. Most affected are the goals associated with accommodating projected enrollment and educational equity."[4]

The May 1989 Paris meeting, in which all of the major leaders of California higher education, public and private participated, was an interesting conversation. The event was extensively documented. There were no conclusions as such for the California group either as a whole or singly. The assistant for education to the governor was also a participant.[5] Subsequently, the University of California secured funding for a conference following on the Review and the May 1989 Paris meeting. This two-day conference, held at the UC Berkeley campus in May 1990, was invitational and included influential individuals from the public policy and higher education arenas in California. The heads of the three public segments of higher education spoke; CSU vice-chancellor John Smart addressed the conference in place of Chancellor Ann Reynolds, as the 1990 transition in the chancellorship was underway. Major papers were presented over the two days, none by anyone from the CSU. One of the most interesting comments was made by Clark Kerr, president emeritus of the University of California. For the first time, Kerr publicly acknowledged the Master Plan of 1960 as a treaty. "The Master Plan has been called 'The California Dream.' We were not dreaming the California Dream; we were trying to escape the nightmare that was otherwise facing us. What we were really engaged in was negotiating a treaty among the constituent parts of higher education in California."[6]

The OECD project was either an interesting interlude that had no impact in California and provided for conversation among students and scholars of higher education, or it was an opportunity missed. Within the California State University, only a few key staff were involved along with the chancellor. At the May 1990 conference in Berkeley, only one CSU president participated. In fairness, none of the leaders in the other segments of higher education engaged the major themes or issues identified by the Review. The California State University was in the midst of a complex transition in the chancellorship, and the continuing press of a growing and maturing system. By the time the transition in the chancellorship was completed and a new chancellor had assumed office in 1991, California was in a recession that would put stress on all public sector budgets. The Review sent a clear signal, perhaps grounded in the experience of European nations: access and quality are difficult to achieve together—perhaps impossible, in the minds of the visiting group. This message was to the point of the missions of both the California State University and the California Community Colleges. While the focus of the Review was clearly not on the CSU, there were messages for the CSU about relationships with the schools, about teacher education, and about changing demographics. The issues raised in the Review have remained issues into the twenty-first century.[7]

Issues on the Table

California's population has tripled since 1960. There is every reason to believe that soon the population will reach fifty million, and then sixty million. There must be a limit, but that issue belongs to the global population strategists. For the present, California public higher education and the California State University need long-term coherent growth plans. With the new campuses of the 1990s came an emerging sense, particularly among the CSU presidents and chancellor and the vice-chancellors, that the time of establishing new campuses had ended, that there should be no additional campuses. No single occasion or individual triggered this view, it just became a part of the common wisdom. As campuses reached their enrollment ceilings (twenty-five thousand full-time equivalent students, for the most part, which would mean the number of individuals was well over thirty thousand), several campuses requested an increase in their enrollment ceilings. There remains no substantial growth plan beyond increasing existing campus sizes. A number of campuses do have room for growth in the acreage they have. A few could easily add acreage. A few have room for additional students in existing facilities. Through the more efficient use of Friday and weekend classes, campuses could increase capacity by simply making use of the facilities already available, even without adding new buildings. Neither faculty nor students like Friday classes, and there is limited student interest in Saturday classes. The CSU campuses have not, since the Master Plan, made aggressive use of facilities for "extended-day" or weekend classes. In the short term, the CSU is subject to the general lack of public funding in California, and the constitutional inhibitions about increasing public funding. But there is no reason to expect California's population growth to end.

One assumption is basic to a consideration of enrollment. The percentage of California's population needed to complete at least a baccalaureate degree must grow if California is to maintain its economic position and its sociopolitical health. The changing demographics of the state dictate this, as do national and world economies. A recent study by the Public Policy Institute of California makes clear that it is unlikely that California's education structure can produce an adequate number of university and college graduates to meet California's workforce needs in 2025. Strong efforts to increase admissions and enrollments, to increase transfer rates from community colleges to public and private universities, and to address completion rates to the baccalaureate degree all would be beneficial to accomplish this goal. A massive effort is called for.[8]

With this assumption, the choices narrow. Decreasing the percentage of the population at the university level by artificial means through fees, tightening admissions standards, or a simple lack of space are not options. New CSU campuses could be created, raising the number of campuses to thirty, perhaps thirty-five. Existing campuses could be supersized; to an extent, this is already underway. The curriculum could be narrowed. Portions of the curriculum could be moved to technology—whole degree programs could be moved, in numbers, to technology. Nonresident enrollments could be curtailed. The 1960s' idea of restructuring public higher education into regions, each region with one or two UC campuses, several CSU campuses, and numbers of community colleges, could be reopened and pursued; the regions would be of reasonable enrollment sizes to make sensible leadership and management possible.

The greatest enrollment pressures will be experienced in the CSU and the community colleges, if rational planning is followed. The state's need for additional research universities is limited. Six or seven of the University of California campuses are major research universities. Three or four UC campuses are more akin to CSU campuses and remain to be developed. There will be, without question, efforts made to convert some of the community colleges to degree granting institutions or to CSU campuses. This would rupture the Master Plan and inevitably create the chaos that the Master Plan was designed to prevent.

Clearly, the key issues include funding to provide for expansion, not only for construction or technology, but for continuing operations, equipment, administration, the faculty to work with students, and all the varied serious aspects of the contemporary university. At least equally important to expansion is a review and careful, courageous analysis of the components and structure of the baccalaureate degree, and exploration of possibilities such as the three-year baccalaureate and the like.

Higher education in the United States has in the last several decades become increasingly costly. In California, the time has come to assess costs of higher education and develop a serious financial plan. There is no firm student fee policy, nor is there a thought-out financial plan. Moreover, the question of what is essential to the maintenance and growth of higher education and, specifically, public higher education, is not addressed. Substantial funding is allocated to athletics, to student centers of various kinds, in recent years to wellness centers, to a new generation of residence halls, and the like, while not to classrooms.

The argument is made that many, if not all, of these costly expenses are financed by students. But at the same time, increases in student fees to support the academic program and the mainstream of the university are decried. Money is money. Student fees, which are mandatory for a variety of nonacademic programs, are a component of the affordability issue. Students assessing themselves (with only a miniscule number of students voting) fees that support an intercollegiate athletic program are increasing the cost of attendance, essentially for the students who follow in subsequent years. It is not possible for sound public policy to move in opposite directions simultaneously, for taxpayers and students to have it both ways—for student fees to be kept low and for students (in collaboration with administrators and faculty) to develop extra fee schedules that have nothing to do with education and academic programs and the basic costs of attending the CSU. The time has come for a probing review of all student fees and university programs to consider whether there are nonessentials universities and students can do without in order to reduce costs.

Year-round operations (YRO), the use of campuses for twelve months a year rather than eight or nine, has been on and off the California State University agenda since the 1960s. A serious effort was made to address this shortly after the turn of the century. It is a difficult issue to address because it was very poorly handled in the 1960s, and that memory has lingered. The most recent effort to address year-round operations foundered on the downturn of financing the CSU. The costs of conversion were estimated to be substantial. Again, this is a matter that needs serious attention and strong leadership.

The use of instructional technology has not been addressed as a system issue in the CSU, but rather as an issue for each campus. Addressing instructional technology as a systemwide issue means having a comprehensive set of the degree programs that can be offered using technology available to students. To make this realistic, either the CSU must develop a freestanding institution with the educational characteristics of a campus—a noncampus campus, an "Open CSU"—or develop a planning and coordinating mechanism that provides for offering academic programs among existing campuses. Technology at the system level has been primarily for administrative purposes and the acquisition of equipment. Technology has been made to work for specific academic programs with strong faculty involvement and program-oriented marketing; it is not an answer to a comprehensive approach addressing the educational needs of the state. The impact of technology will be limited for California's higher education needs until there is a comprehensive statewide approach. Several issues are outstanding. To what extent will one state university campus accept courses from another state university to fulfill degree requirements? Is it possible to create a statewide institutional capacity to offer degrees? (This had been tried before with limited success, in part due to the tradition of campus resistance to systemwide programs; see the discussion of the Consortium in chapter four.) Could campuses agree to the assignment of specific degree programs offered by technology to specific campuses?

Unless population growth trends reverse, California's population will surely grow to fifty million or sixty million. Unless California's economic and social goals change— and there has been negative change—enrollments surely need to increase. The California State University needs a long-term growth plan. There is certainly reason to believe that a CSU growth plan in isolation from the other segments of higher education (the UC, the community colleges, and the private institutions) is not practical. And there is certainly reason to anticipate that waiting until a more serious problem becomes visible in the public sector and to policy makers, is neither sensible nor realistic.

* * *

Collective bargaining has had a major influence on the culture of the California State University, the influence ranging from benign and negative—sometimes very negative. The issue of collective bargaining is among unfinished matters.

The establishment of collective bargaining in the CSU was not well handled, largely by management. It is important to make a distinction in addressing collective bargaining among the employee populations within the CSU. Bargaining for the nonacademic units has been, for the most part, comparable to bargaining generally within the US economy. Bargaining for the faculty has been another matter, and it has been characterized, increasingly over the years, by serious and debilitating conflict. One of the employee groups, that of many professional individuals within student affairs, has sometimes found itself positioned in the middle, between the faculty and the other employee groups. It is faculty bargaining that needs attention.

The history of collective bargaining in the CSU, which is addressed in earlier chapters, suggests the development of bargaining that was dominated at times on all sides—labor and management, faculty, administrators and trustees—by "true believers." The cacophony of voices supporting, at times demanding, faculty collective bargaining at the time of the Master Plan and through the 1960s was persistent—though not representative of a significant number of faculty—but did not produce results, either in the legislature or with the trustees. The trustee position through the 1960s was dominated by founding chair Louis Heilbron. He was resistant to bargaining because it would interfere with the traditions of academic community and governance, and he was committed to an academic senate model.

The 1970s brought a role reversal, and that has had a lasting impact on bargaining and governance. The faculty interest in collective bargaining became more temperate, dominated by statewide Academic Senate leaders and individuals with conventional union values. The trustees were in a period dominated by values that often were perceived as anti-faculty positions on a variety of matters, academic and professional. The chancellor backed away from the opportunity to have competent and knowledgeable staff work with the issue; it was clear that the trustees did not want any position other than absolute opposition to bargaining, as serious consideration began with the 1974 election of Governor Jerry Brown. The Academic Senate and the potential faculty union leadership dominated the field. Later, the implementation of collective bargaining was made awkward by the transition in the chancellorship and especially the vice-chancellorship for faculty and staff affairs. Nevertheless, though bargaining with the faculty unit, the California Faculty Association (CFA), was complex, it was manageable through the 1980s and early to mid-90s. The trustee ideological position relaxed as new individuals were named to the board, and the chancellor's staff had individuals with collective bargaining experience. The CFA leadership was strong, but temperate, but this varied over time.

The 1990s saw the emergence of strong bargaining positions on both the labor and management sides. During the almost twenty years from the implementation of bargaining to the beginning of the twenty-first century, faculty politics and governance continued to develop with no uniform pattern on the campuses. On some campuses, the CFA controlled the academic senate. On others, there was a clear distinction, not to the point of conflict, but simply regarding agendas. Approaching the turn of the century, CFA-management relations deteriorated. It is at least arguable that the faculty union and management's worsening relationship and resulting tensions created a situation in which each side fed off the other, to the detriment of a healthy and productive collective bargaining relationship. The anger level on both sides grew. It is a mistake to identify the union and its leadership with the faculty, particularly in a structure as large as the California State University, with more than twenty thousand faculty members. Similarly, it is an error to identify management as fundamentally hostile to faculty, for that would suggest hostility toward the purposes of a university. The deterioration of California's budget, as the first decade of the century has worn on, has brought the union and management together on occasion, while exacerbating conflict at other times. The fundamental conflict has not been resolved.

Collective bargaining with the faculty in the California State University needs a new and healthy beginning. Someone needs to call a time-out. It is simply counterproductive for a state of angry conflict to exist between the faculty and management, however defined. In a book he authored after leaving the board of trustees, Louis Heilbron, board's founding chair, wrote, "[A] board in conflict with its faculty is a board at war with itself."[9] One could paraphrase Heilbron and note that a faculty in unending conflict with its governing group, however defined, is a faculty at war with its own university. A healthy university is one in which a sufficient measure of harmony and civility is extant to assure reasonable people of reasonable support. This is a matter on the unfinished agenda of the CSU.

* * *

Core values are a framework that pertains to purpose rather than precise substance at any given moment. Seeds of the core values of the California State University are in the first one hundred years of the campuses. The preparation of elementary and secondary school teachers who would reach out to all the youth of the state; the idea that vocational and technical education of teenagers would build productive lives; the preparation of educational materials for teachers over the state; the establishment of California's first junior college with a state normal school—all these are elements that lead to the CSU of today. Similarly, the campuses founded in the years soon after World War II—Sacramento, Los Angeles, Long Beach, and others—expanded opportunity for Californians to prepare for living in a state and a world markedly different from the past. The core values are inherent in the history of the CSU.[10]

The California Master Plan of 1960 provided the circumstance for rethinking the nature of the state colleges and the re-creation, over the years ahead, of the core values of what has become the California State University. The succeeding generations of faculty, students, trustees, and administrators have built these core values and helped to further their meaning. Over the years since 1960, the most often recited values of the CSU are access, affordability, and quality. These need explication to be meaningful. Some things are clear and understandable about the context of the Master Plan. The architects of the plan did not foresee the changing demography of California, already quietly underway in 1960, nor did they anticipate the great growth in population. The Master Plan was intended only to pertain to the period from 1960 until 1975. Its designers did not forecast in any meaningful way the impact of technology, not just on education, but on the economy and the fabric of the total society—the changing economics of the state and nation, and the fact of globalization. But it was a framework higher education in California could build on.

The California State Colleges were understood as "the system in the middle," between the University of California and the California Community Colleges. In the 1960s and 70s, and probably even into the 1980s, there was not an appreciation or understanding of the meaning of this middle region, its potential and its importance to the state and people of California, but programs were built, and students were educated.

One core value of the California State University consistently over the years is that of broad-based access. This idea has translated into access for a wide range of high school graduates ready to move on to university-level work. With the changes that have occurred in elementary and secondary education, the California State University has needed to respond to qualitative issues such as remedial work. On the unfinished agenda of the CSU is the need to draw ever closer to the elementary and secondary schools of the state, and to be a part of the enormous transition the schools are undertaking as the state's demographics continue to change. Broad-based access includes the community colleges with the greatest number of community college transfer students moving to the CSU campuses. At the graduate level, access concerns the many professional programs, all with an applied character, and students in the traditional arts and sciences who wish to undertake further study but not in the context of a research university. The California State University advances knowledge to a broad and increasing segment of the population, providing experiences and a capacity to aspire to a good life.

Broad-based access is a general concept. The implementation has been and is pragmatic. The Master Plan provision for admissibility of the top one-third of high school graduates was not the result of scientific investigation, but rather an analysis of economic capacity, and the architecture of a set of relationships with the other two segments of higher education. Given the Master Plan, it made sense.

The California State University is a key element to a learning society, a knowledge-based society. That translates not only to broad-based access, but to the nature of society and the higher education needed in that society. The concept of differentiation of functions is what makes California public higher education a cohesive whole rather than a heterogeneous mixture of institutions pursuing a variety of goals and wishes. The California State University educates undergraduates for productive lives, lives that are productive civically, and culturally, economically enriching, and satisfying. At the heart of undergraduate education for all students is general education. General education in the California State University is an unfinished agenda item. The general education program on most campuses is more akin to distributive education than it is to a cohesive and coherent general or liberal education. This is not surprising, as budget and allocation procedures at the campus level encourage this. Budget allocations commonly reward enrollment numbers, and, in some instances, courses may be designed more to attract enrollment than to be an integral part of a coherent and careful intellectual design for general education.

The nature of the idea of core values is such that while values of the California State University and its campuses have a constancy, the precise meaning and translation of these values into what students and faculty do will change over time. Core values are like a good constitution, a statement of principles that are constant while their implementation changes with societal changes. By way of example, it is perfectly sensible that the mandate that the California State Colleges received in the 1960s to develop master's degree programs in applied fields (clearly, other than medicine, law, veterinary medicine, and dentistry) should, over time, transform to the inclusion of doctorates in applied fields—for example, education, nursing and other health-related fields, public administration; licensure and professional standards, as well as the breadth of available knowledge in many fields, lead to this. Similarly, it is sensible that the mandate the California State Colleges received to reach out to the people and communities of California should have translated into the 1,000 Mile Campus of the 1970s and the continuing potential of that idea.

Perhaps the most important value of all is that students are at the center, the reason for being. This has translated over the years to the oft-repeated statement that the California State University is a teaching university. It has taken years—arguably into the early years of the present century—for the faculty and especially some administrators as well as others in higher education to understand that this *does not mean* that faculty and students do not engage in research; rather it means that research has a goal: the education of students and the ever-increasing capacity of faculty to enrich their work with students as well as applicability to the greater society. For the most part, faculties and administrators understand this, and understand that useful research and scholarly and creative activities develop "organically in a faculty member's career, not because it is mandated."[11]

The cultures of the California State University and those of the campuses cannot be expected to be maintained without effort. Again the analogy of a society's constitution is useful. The constitution of a healthy society does not maintain itself; people have to work at it. The changes virtually all societies are experiencing in this time are extraordinary in the perspective of history, and the challenges to many, if not all, social institutions are great; the participants have the task to maintain and adapt. A healthy society has a process to make the environment for changes positive, and the legitimacy of changes accepted. This is yet another reason why a coordinating/planning mechanism is needed for higher education in California. In the years leading up to 1960 and perhaps for a decade thereafter, there was significant faculty sentiment toward becoming like the University of California. This desire has abated for the most part, as faculty members understand and advocate the richness of the mission of the CSU. Most, but not all faculty, come at the beginning of their careers from research universities. The CSU campuses do not look or act like research universities. Thus, the challenge to recruit faculty who want to be part of a unique public university, an institution not interested in imitating research universities, is a substantial one, and this is not always understood. For the most part, faculty become committed to a new California State University—one that includes an emphasis on teaching and research, mostly of an applied nature, and a level of involvement both in the greater community of the region and state and in the broader academic community—to an institution that properly could be called a "people's university." Most faculty understand and accept that they are making a difference in California. The recruitment of presidents is even more important because presidents can set a tone and a spirit on a campus. Trustees represent the public interest, and they hold the institution in trust, for what it is and what it can become. At the heart of the mission of the California State University are the students, from all walks of life and in large numbers. These students, the graduates, animate the economic and cultural life of the state.

Who has responsibility for maintaining the core values of the CSU? One definition of the center of the CSU includes the board of trustees and the chancellor, just as presidents are inescapably at the center of the life of a campus. But that is too simple an answer. Faculty, particularly senior faculty, are in the higher education world of today the permanent party (to use a military expression) on the campus, and they are at the heart of maintaining core values. Without question, students, not all perhaps, contribute to the campus culture. The culture of a campus can be a significant educational instrument.

The values and culture (and these overlap) of the campuses and the system are not identical. The role of the system is to provide for an overarching set of values, understandable and few in number. The people of each campus, in the varied ways of the campuses, fill out the values and culture. There can be values that hold people apart; what are the values that bring people together? These are conversations that presidents, chancellors, faculty, students, and others need to have, and they are continuing conversations, for out of these conversations grows the strength of the California State University.

A healthy university is a community. The California State University is a community of more than five hundred thousand individuals, all preparing themselves for their individual futures, whatever that may be. Each campus is a community, and there are inevitably and necessarily differences in these communities. Each university has its distinctive character, and there are twenty-three university campuses within the CSU. All share in valuing broad-based access, the sense of students being at the center, and a commitment to excellence in teaching and in sound programs. Hopefully, students in the CSU learn how to make a life, not just a living; and in this context, students define and refine values. Healthy universities create within students a capacity to address values.

* * *

The programs of the California State University reflect the core values and the cultures both of the system and the campus. As the CSU has reached a level of maturity, essentially in the 1990s and the first decade of this century, faculty, students, presidents, and trustees have increasingly asked questions that need to be asked—and answered. The Organization for Economic Cooperation and Development (OECD) study and review did this for the late 1980s, and posed questions still to be answered. The Cornerstones project of the mid-1990s did this, and the Access to Excellence plan is undertaking this.

The system and most of its leaders focused for many years on access and, to some extent, on retention of students. Only in the years after 2000 has that focus broadened to include graduation. Graduation rates have always been calculated. Low rates are often defended, principally on the grounds that the socioeconomic backgrounds of many students make degree completion, especially timely degree completion, difficult. The issue of degree completion and graduation rates has been opened, and it is being addressed in accountability processes of the last decade, introduced in the implementation of Cornerstones. This is on the unfinished list for the immediate years and is being addressed.

The capacity to award the doctorate in education, legislated in 2005, opened a new and important chapter in the California State University. The EdD is limited to the field of educational administration, but that needs to be understood as only the beginning. A move to award doctorates in applied fields needs to be initiated, as a next step in the development of curriculum and graduate programs. It is a logical and sensible extension of the Master Plan, as these are programs growing from existing master's degrees, programs for which there is a clear societal need, and programs that are not adequately addressed by the University of California.

The campuses of the CSU have always been involved with their communities and their regions. This was essential for the normal schools from day one; it is among the things that teacher education institutions do, though limited to their own field of education. In the California State University of the last fifty years, the role of campuses has varied. Examples of community outreach and interweaving abound, ranging from the desire of the first administrator responsible for building programs to create the borders of a campus like an open hand—with the fingers and thumb weaving in and out of the surrounding community—to the work of faculties in business and economics in regional economic development.

Prior to 1960, a number of campuses were very active in their regions. The San Diego, Chico, and both Cal Poly campuses developed strong regional constituencies, and the Cal Poly San Luis Obispo campus spread its programs in agriculture statewide. With the formation of the California State Colleges and the gradual developing freedom from microcontrols of budgets, campuses became more active. In the 1970s, efforts having to do with economic development were undertaken on most campuses. Working with the community has tremendous educational potential. This is realized by some departments and academic units, and totally ignored by others. Programs in social work, in all of the helping professions, and in many of the traditional disciplines, can be and are developed by the campuses.

In many ways since the 1960s, students have been the leaders in outreach to the communities. In the CSU, the hours devoted to community development and the many creative projects that students relate to their fields of study and their social values run into the millions each year. This is a timely area for development, and there is, among some faculty and administrators, an increasing appreciation of the potential. The regional role of comprehensive public universities is often overlooked. California State University campuses have deep roots, and each campus has strengths that relate to its region or to the state as a whole. These are points from which to build program and curriculum strengths for students, and to enhance the impact and work of the 1,000 Mile Campus. This too is on the agenda of unfinished business.[12]

The most important area for community involvement and development in which the CSU faculties have a special and historic competence is in the schools. The public schools of California, albeit with some fine exceptions, need help and attention. This should not be a surprise. California has experienced extraordinary demographic change and this has impacted the schools massively. The California State University has a capacity to help and to intervene. This is not easy to do. As noted in Chapter 6, the schools and teacher education are subject to extraordinary and continuing political intervention, but without change in the schools of the state, neither the California State University, nor the economic and societal life of the state, can function properly.

* * *

The Master Plan for Higher Education is a social contract among the three segments of public higher education and the government of the state and the people of California. It was designed as a time-limited contract, from 1960 to 1975, and it has lived on. The Master Plan was a recognition that the most important investment any society makes is in its people: Investment in learning is the creation of wealth. Investment in education is the creation of a good society. In the twenty-first century, higher education is the quintessential common good.

The most important concept in the Master Plan is the differentiation of function. Like many aspects of the Master Plan, the concept was developed within the realities of state government and the existing educational enterprise of the late 1950s, as well as the certainty of population growth in the 1960s and 1970s. The concept of differentiation of function was and is pragmatic public policy making at its best. The Master Plan was not a construct based on theory, but a framework, like a good constitution, built on reality. It has withstood the test of time. One can reason and argue that differentiation of function is an important concept related to social structure and the needs of the contemporary world for higher or further education, for education beyond the secondary schools. In fact, the roots of the concept of differentiation of function go back to the legislative debates inspired by Senator Anthony Caminetti in the 1880s and the first decade of the twentieth century. Caminetti initially tried to bring greater focus to the normal schools, and two decades later he gave leadership to the legislation creating the junior colleges, now the community colleges. Differentiation of function placed the faculty, what were then soon to be nineteen campuses, and the presidents, chancellor, and trustees in a position to build a system then unique in the United States and in the world.

The uniqueness of the California State University is to be found in its mission and the core values that are more nearly in the classic tradition of what a university is all about than the modern research university. The research university, as it is known in the contemporary economically developed world, is a product of big government, big enterprise, and big economies. The undergraduate students are important, and the graduate students are more important, but students are not always at the heart of the research university. The model that the California State University has built over the past fifty years is in the great tradition of universities, scholars working with students in an environment in which excellence and egalitarianism converge. The model has clearly not been perfected; witness the degradation of many public K-12 schools, without which universities cannot function.

The Master Plan has two major shortcomings. These have been noted elsewhere in this work, but their importance needs to be stressed again. Short of the legislature and the governor, there is no public body charged with the coordination and planning and orderly growth of higher education—all of it, including the private sector and the three segments of the public sector. The California Postsecondary Education Commission (CPEC) does valuable and necessary studies. These, however, do not constitute an agenda for public higher education or a growth plan for all of higher education. The three public higher education segments, the California State University, the California Community Colleges, and the University of California, all live in their own worlds, or "silos," as some call them. The 1990s saw the emergence of some of the same conditions that prevailed in the 1950s, with the emergence of two campuses in areas with relatively low populations, campuses brought into existence simply by the political process. Neither the California State University, Monterey Bay, nor the University of California, Merced fit a model of orderly growth; both will in time fill out with enrollment, simply to help cope with the need for student spaces. The more recent actions of the University of California to modify freshman admissions standards would increase the pool of students invited to apply to the University of California from 12.5 percent to more than 21 percent.[13]

The history of the top leadership of the three public segments, the presidency of the University of California, the chancellorship of the California Community

Colleges, and the chancellorship of the California State University, is not a history of close cooperation and a sharing of leadership for all of higher education in California. In part, this may be due to the widely varying roles the individuals in these positions are expected to play nationally and in higher education. It may also be due to the stereotyped understanding that many—legislators, some of the governors of the last fifty years, frequently the media, and some of the public—have about the three segments, and what they do; in many minds, there is a "pecking order" among the segments. Finally, it may also be a result of the unevenness of the strength of the leadership at any given time. At no time in the past fifty years has the strength and capacity for leadership among the individuals occupying these three positions been evenly matched, until the present moment, in which there are three strong individuals, each with a firm base. This situation of balance creates an unusual opportunity for the three segments of California's public higher education to work together equally for the good of the citizens of the state—the intent with which the Master Plan was designed—and to advocate the cause and role of higher education.

The second major shortfall of the Master Plan is money, the financing and support of public higher education in California. The Master Plan assumed adequate support up to 1975, its assumed expiration date. At the time of the Master Plan, the principal concern of the state for financing addressed the University of California and the California State Colleges. The community colleges later entered the scene in a major way with the passage of proposition 13 in 1978, and the resulting legislative shift of major financial responsibility from local districts to the state (though with the local boards retaining the major governance authority). There is no California public policy about financing public higher education, nor has there been; there are expectations and hopes and realities, both in higher education and the public arena. No one is asking questions about the uses of funds in higher education. For example, there is no policy discussion about money being spent on programs that are not really among those that are educational per se, but rather customs, such as conference athletics which have been around for years (as distinct from students generally participating in sports, which has been around for many more years). There are policy discussions to be had in a world that deals with reality, and these go way beyond athletics.

California needs an update in the Master Plan for Higher Education. The issue is not that the concept of differentiation of function has become outworn; it is still sound and essential as basic public policy recognizing the structure and substance of higher education and the needs of California and its people. The issue is the lack of order, the reemergence of politics in some decisions. The issue is the need for a rational growth plan; the Master Plan was a rational growth plan, and it worked, even beyond its 1975 date. The issue is the need for a mechanism, a body, to attend to the evolution of higher education in California. Economic, technological, demographic, and sociocultural circumstances change with time, and higher education adapt just as the general society must adapt.

Readdressing the California State University and all of higher education in the current environment, particularly the economic environment, will be very difficult.

It will be difficult to get the attention of decision makers even to talk about whether higher education or all of education needs serious attention. The world of public policy in California (and beyond) is a world of competing interest groups, and this reality impacts educational policy as it does all areas of policy. Pursuit of the common good may be hard to come by, but it cannot be impossible.

It may be almost trite to assert that higher education, indeed all of education, in California is in crisis, but it is accurate. By any reasonable measure, California is slipping—in the preparation of students for college and university work, in the percentage of the college-age cohort participating in higher education, and in the percentage of individuals at various age levels holding degrees. In a sense, Californians and those in higher education are living off past achievements. The three words used for many years to characterize the California State University—access, affordability, and quality—are each in jeopardy, and the reasons converge around the need for a new look at the Master Plan, the need for a capacity for orderly growth and a plan for the years ahead, and the need for a policy about financing education. The social contract with the people of California cannot be driven only by the economics of the day.

Promises Realized

The California State Colleges of 1960, as the trustees, the chancellor, and reinvigorated faculties, staffs, and presidents assumed responsibility for what was then a group of fifteen institutions, promised the people of California access to affordable, genuine, quality education, education that would prepare individuals for meaningful and productive lives. In the years from that time until 2008, 2,650,973 individuals have received degrees from the California State Colleges and the California State University. This total includes 2,170,804 baccalaureate degrees, 479,133 master's degrees, and 1,036 doctorates; to achieve a sense of the work of the CSU over a longer span of years, a total of degrees conferred since the 1935, date of the redefinition of the teachers colleges to state colleges to state universities, reaches 2,764,106. In addition, hundreds of thousands of individuals, more likely millions, have attended CSU campuses for a portion of their higher education, though these enrollment figures have not been netted. These are the most basic promises realized.[14] The California State University is a network of campuses with programs reaching to every corner of the state, and with graduates throughout not only all of California but the nation and the globe. The CSU is fundamental to the economic life of the state and to the maintenance of California's civic culture. It is a base for the social structures of the state.

In 1960, educational leaders, legislators, a governor with foresight created from a rich past of service to people an entity known as the California State Colleges to partner with the University of California and the California Junior Colleges, It has become a custom to label some colleges and universities as "world class." The California State University is a "world-class teaching university." As students are the core mission of the California State University, perhaps a "world-class learning university" is more accurate.

"The California State University stands on its own because it has a unique mission."[15] To understand the evolution of the California State University and its maturing over the last nearly fifty years, it is useful to recall Alden Dunham's statement at the 1976 dedication of a new building for the trustees and chancellor's office in Long Beach. Dunham had characterized universities and colleges like the California State University and Colleges campuses of that time as being "in the middle."[16] Given the role that the California State University plays in the life of California and beyond, it is now accurate to characterize the California State University as being at the center, the center of educating a workforce for California's economy and educated citizens for California's civic culture.

Promises to Be Fulfilled

Promises to be fulfilled are, without exception, the orderly and reasonable outgrowths of the maturing of the California State University and the core values of the CSU moving into a changing world, a changing California, and a changing higher education structure. These promises fit into three broad categories, and they are interrelated.

The California State University will benefit from a growth plan, as will the state and people of California. Growth and financial support are inevitably coupled. It is reasonable to assume that the contemporary state of public finance in California and in the US will not lead to a return to a time of more generous and full support of higher education. Demands upon the public fisc resulting from social, technological and political change have modified the reasonable percentage of public funds that higher education can expect. These changes are inevitable and occur over time as they always have, and they are not and will not always in the future be negative to higher education. In the meantime, higher education, including the California State University, must deal with reality and, in doing so, build the strength of the higher education enterprise. There are two certainties that the California State University must address: the absolute necessity to increase the "production" of university graduates at all levels, most immediately the baccalaureate level, and do so with enhanced, not diminished quality; and the recognition that the state's capacity (and governmental capacity generally) is not keeping pace with CSU needs as these are presently understood.

Two initiatives logically follow, and these must and can be consistent with the history and mission and values of the CSU. The first is to address expenditures and budget needs, and ask the question that will be unwelcome by many: what activities within the CSU, all of which cost money, can be reduced or eliminated because they are marginal or peripheral? Certainly, activities and even programs can be identified within administrative programs, more general campus programs, and some dimensions of instruction and academic programs. To do so will not be easy, but arguably, it will be essential; the alternative is diminished quality, reduced enrollment, or both. Greater use of campus facilities, weekend use, and year-round operations all can be productive in these instances, to reduce demand and needs for capital outlay. A clear and meaningful student fee policy, one accepted not only within the CSU, but accepted politically as a part of the civic culture of California, is overdue.

California's economic and workforce needs have been of growing concern for some years. A recent study referred to earlier, published by the Public Policy Institute of California (PPIC), has underscored the economic need for a greatly increased number of baccalaureate graduates. The PPIC projects a massive shortage. "If current trends persist, California will have one million fewer college graduates than it needs in 2025—only 35 percent of working adults will have a college degree in an economy that would otherwise require 41 percent of workers to have a college degree."[17] The California State University must be the principal source of college and university graduates; there is no alternative. This is a matter of both public and sound educational policy.

The uses of academic technology have been addressed earlier in this chapter and at length in Chapter 8. While creative and of substantial quality, California State University campus uses of technology have been modest, in comparison to the potential of academic technology. Much can be learned about the quality, strengths, and weaknesses of academic technology from institutions in and out of the United States, including institutions as disparate as the British Open University and some proprietary universities, as well as the experiences of CSU campuses. Short of very substantial increases in traditional campus capacity, technology offers one reasonable, sensible, and academically sound route to increased enrollments and graduates. Two paths are apparent: a comprehensive CSU-wide approach to offering baccalaureate degrees in all possible disciplines and applied fields among the twenty-three campuses, or the establishment of a new institution, California State Open University. Either path will be politically difficult, the separate institution more so, difficult given the internal history of the CSU regarding efforts to cut across campus boundaries. The establishment of a separate twenty-fourth California State University with its own president and faculty (possibly with some faculty from the twenty-three existing campuses holding joint appointments) would seem a practical route. Such an initiative would capture the imagination of California's people and its leaders, would be significantly less costly than a conventional campus, would move some distance toward encompassing more of California's changing population within higher education, and would assume the responsibility of the California State University to be the principal vehicle to secure an adequate, perhaps even more than adequate, college and university graduate population.

As the people of the California State University look to the future, the work of Cornerstones and Access to Excellence can be built upon.[18] An important effort of the first decade of the new century has been to emphasize undergraduate degree completion and the award of the baccalaureate. A piece of this issue is certainly how a campus and faculty and staff relate to students one by one, and this is being addressed. The matter is not an easy one. The substance of general education, whether it is general education or distributive education, should be a campus matter, but there may be a time to force the development of some standards about the intellectual and analytical content of what general education is thought to be beyond the range of subject matters to be covered. It is arguable that general education is the defining component of a baccalaureate degree; the task is a complex one for any CSU campus, as a heavy percentage of baccalaureate graduates are transfer students who have completed general education before attending the CSU.

The proposal to consider a three-year baccalaureate degree is an ever-emerging topic, not frequently, but periodically. A rigorous review of the meaning and components of the baccalaureate may well be timely. The objective obviously cannot be any diminution of the quality and results, for any individual graduate, of the undergraduate experience or the meaning, perhaps the enhanced meaning, of the baccalaureate. Such a review could be accompanied by a reexamination of the master's degree and consideration of defining the master's as a two-year degree.

* * *

As I finish this manuscript, it is appropriate to share thoughts about the meaning of the history of the California State University. The California State University is an important social invention. It is a driver of the California economy, it is among the creators of the culture and the many cultures of the state, and it is an essential ingredient of the political and social health of the state and its people. An important question addresses the maintenance of the California State University, with its core values and mission, while at the same time, a capacity for adaptation and change as California and the world of California change.

There are some both within and without the California State University who think that the Master Plan was a contest, a zero-sum game, and that the University of California won. But it is arguable that the California State University and the people of California won, if not the "whole thing," a major vehicle for building the future. The Master Plan of 1960 created a finely balanced structure of higher education, the greatest investment any society had ever made in its own people. The California State University was the new element in that creation. It was not the system in the middle, as some characterized it in the 1960s and 1970s; rather, it became what no single CSU campus could be, an agent for progress in the state and an agent to build for the future. This work should have made clear that the first meeting of the board of trustees on August 12, 1960, reset in motion development of a group of campuses that together made twenty-first-century California possible. The building of the California State University has been complex; it has not been easy, and the problems have been many. The time has come to look to the future.

The California State University is a "world-class teaching and learning university," and it is at the center of California's future. There is an enormous responsibility borne by the faculty, the trustees, the leaders, and all the people of "the people's university."

Notes

[1] Founded in 1960–61, the OECD included twenty-four countries in 1990, including Australia, Austria, Belgium, Canada, Denmark, Finland, France, Germany, Greece, Iceland, Ireland, Italy, Japan, Luxembourg, the Netherlands, New Zealand, Norway, Portugal, Spain, Sweden, Switzerland, Turkey, the United Kingdom, and the United States.

[2] Clive P. Condren, *Preparing for the Twenty-First Century: A Report on Higher Education in California*, California Postsecondary Education Commission, Sacramento, 1988.

[3] *Review of National Policies for Education, Higher Education in California*, Organization for Economic Cooperation and Development, Paris, 1990.

[4] David E. Leveille, memorandum, "OECD Question Responses," April 3, 1989, CSU Archives. Leveille was at the time the director of institutional relations for the California State University.

[5] Peter Mehas would in 2007 become a trustee of the California State University.

[6] Sheldon Rothblatt, ed., *The Master Plan and the California Dream; A Berkeley Conversation* (Center for Studies in Higher Education, University of California, Berkeley, 1992).

[7] In addition to the preceding citations, other material relevant to the OECD project and available in the CSU Archives include: John Smart, "Summary of OECD Examiner Draft Report," memorandum to Chancellor W. Ann Reynolds and Vice-Chancellor Lee Kerschner, September 20, 1988; interviews by the author of David Leveille, December 20, 2006, William Pickens, June 25, 2007, John Smart, March 6, 2007.

[8] Hans Johnson, and Ria Sengupta, *Closing the Gap; Meeting California's Need for College Graduates* (San Francisco: Public Policy Institute of California, 2009).

[9] Louis H. Heilbron, *The College and University Trustee* (San Francisco: Jossey Bass, 1973).

[10] The section about core values benefits greatly from a focus group of March 20, 2007 with Professors Juanita Barrena and William Dorman of CSU Sacramento, and Dr. Herbert Carter, a member of the board of trustees, former executive vice-chancellor, and former interim president of CSU Dominguez Hills.

[11] William Dorman, "Livingston Lecture," California State University, Sacramento, fall 2006.

[12] Robert Fountain, Professor Emeritus of Business, CSU Sacramento, interview by the author, January 22, 2007.

[13] Steven D. Boilard, Director of Higher Education, Legislative Analyst's Office, "University of California Eligibility Proposal," memorandum to Interested Legislative Staff," January 7, 2009.

[14] The California State University, Statistical Abstract to July 2008, 243ff.

[15] Charles B. Reed, CSU Legislative Day address, April 3, 2000.

[16] See Chapter 4.

[17] Johnson and Sengupta, *Closing the Gap*, 5.

[18] See Chapter 4.

Appendix 1. Timeline: The Years of the CSU

1849	• California Constitutional Convention—provision for common schools, an eventual university, and an elected superintendent of public instruction
1852	• Establishment of State Board of Education; members: governor, state superintendent of public instruction, surveyor general
1857–1871	• Establishment of Minns Evening Normal School, San Francisco; moved to San Jose in 1871, now San Jose State University
1860	• Minns Evening Normal School becomes San Francisco Normal School
1861	• First State Teachers Institute, San Francisco
1862	• San Francisco Normal School becomes California State Normal School to prepare teachers for elementary schools
1864	• State Board of Education reconstituted: removal of surveyor general, addition of five major county superintendents of schools (all northern California)
1868	• Founding of the University of California, Oakland; moved to Berkeley in 1869
1870	• Legislature authorized moving State Normal School to San Jose; cornerstone laid at One Washington Square (current address)
	• State Board of Education reconstituted: addition of one northern county superintendent, principal of Normal School, two teachers
1871	• California State Normal School opens in San Jose; first student housing with a preceptress
1875	• California Teachers Association founded in meeting organized by and at California State Normal School, San Jose

1878–1879	• Second California Constitutional convention, provision for normal school in constitution, definition of the University of California as "a public trust," in Article IX, section 9
1881	• Legislature provided for "Southern Branch" of State Normal School, opened in Los Angeles in 1882
1883	• Legislature provided for a Northern California Normal School
1886	• Southern Branch became Los Angeles State Normal School; San Jose campus renamed San Jose State Normal School
1889	• Chico State Normal School opened
1890	• State Board of Education includes principals of three normal schools, added president of University of California
1896	• Principals of normal schools become presidents; presidents appointed by local boards
1897	• Legislature established San Diego State Normal School, classes opened 1898 • California Supreme Court ruling that legislature could define requirements for teacher certification
1898	• Legislature established San Francisco State Normal School; classes opened 1899
1899	• First summer school in any California public higher education institution opened at San Diego State Normal School • First study of public higher education in California; recommended boards for each campus appointed by governor and split authority with State Board of Education; institutional boards appoint presidents and faculty, approve budgets; State Board to address curriculum
1901	• Legislature established California State Polytechnic School, San Luis Obispo, classes opened 1902; students, faculty, director live in dormitories initially
1909	• Legislature established Santa Barbara State Normal School of Manual Arts and Home Economics, classes opened that year • First international travel study program; San Jose president, faculty, students in Europe

1910	• First junior college in California established in Fresno, two year "post-graduate course" at Fresno high school
1911	• Legislature established Fresno State Normal School including authorization to prepare secondary school teachers in some subjects • Fresno Normal school and junior college integrated with one faculty, one administration, a single curriculum including lower division of University of California curriculum
1912	• Legislature established Humboldt County State Normal School, classes opened in 1914 • Constitutional amendment, State Board of Education, seven members appointed by governor, responsible for all state education except University of California; superintendent of public instruction is administrative head
1913	• Legislature authorized normal school programs for secondary school teachers in subjects not addressed by the University of California and private colleges and universities, including art, music, physical education, and all commercial, technical, and industrial subjects
1914	• Normal schools placed under State Board of Education for all matters except appointment of presidents and faculty and allocation of budgets
1917	• State Board of Education assumes responsibility for appointment of presidents and faculty, and allocation of budgets; local boards gradually disappear.
1919	• Los Angeles State Normal School becomes Southern Branch of the University of California as the result of legislative and gubernatorial action • State Superintendent Will Wood initiates a study "meeting needs and furnishing support for schools and educational needs of the state;" Senator Herbert Jones and a legislative committee sponsor the study; Stanford professor Elwood Cubberly completes study which recommends that normal schools become four year teachers colleges and confer degrees.
1921	• Legislature establishes state superintendent as ex-officio Director of Education • Legislature renames normal schools as state teachers colleges

	• Fresno State Teachers College and Fresno Junior College formally merge
1922	• First associated students organization established at Fresno State Teachers College
1923	• State teachers colleges authorized to confer bachelor of arts in education • All colleges except San Francisco are de facto junior colleges awarding certificates of completion for first two undergraduate years and transfer admission to the University of California
1929	• Legislature establishes California Nautical School
1932	• Carnegie Foundation for the Advancement of Teaching, the Suzzalo Report, completed 1934, study of higher education in California
1934	• Constitutional amendment to create state civil service; teachers colleges not included, but comparable system created.
1935	• Legislature and governor renamed teachers colleges to state colleges and authorized degree programs in any subject matter commonly taught in secondary schools
1936	• Council of State College Presidents established by the presidents
1938	• Voorhis School for Boys in Pomona acquired by Cal Poly President Julian McPhee; this later determined to be official founding date of California State Polytechnic University, Pomona; classes began September 1938
1939	• Legislature renamed California Nautical School as California Maritime Academy
1944	• Santa Barbara State College becomes Santa Barbara College of the University of California
1945	• State Board of Education established Liaison Committee with Regents of the University of California • Explosion in student enrollments with end of World War II • San Luis Obispo campus named California Polytechnic State College

	• State colleges authorized to offer 5th (graduate) year of instruction
1946	• State colleges authorized to award general secondary (high school) teaching credential
• Liaison Committee first study: need for state college or University of California campus in Sacramento
• Constitutional amendment adopted; prohibits transfer of state college campuses to University of California
1947	• Sacramento State College created July 1; classes began September
• Los Angeles State College created July 2; classes began September
• Liaison Committee recommended statewide study of the organization of public higher education
• Division of State Colleges and Teacher Education created in State Dept.; position of associate superintendent to head division established
1948	• "Report of a Survey of the Needs of California in Higher Education" published (Strayer Report)
• State Colleges authorized by legislature to grant master's degree in conjunction with a credential
1949	• Authorization of a state college to be in southwest Los Angeles or northern Orange Counties; Long Beach State College classes began September
• President Julian McPhee acquired Kellogg property adjacent to Voorhis in Pomona; Kellogg-Voorhis branch of Cal Poly established
• Legislature authorized creation of campus advisory boards at all campuses except Cal Poly
1950	• State college presidents requested Department of Finance study of state college campus (including Maritime Academy) organization
1951	• "Department of Finance Report 828" (Chandler Report) published; established model administrative structures for campuses with prescribed specific positions
1953	• State colleges placed within jurisdiction of State Personnel Board (civil service)

- Adoption of "60–40" rule—60% upper limit on full and associate professor appointments (this disappeared with collective bargaining—not firmly observed in 1970s)

1955
- "A Restudy of the Needs of California in Higher Education" under auspices of joint staff of Liaison Committee
- Legislature authorized branch of Los Angeles campus in San Fernando Valley; students enrolled in 1956
- "A Study of the Need for Additional Centers of Public Higher Education in California," Liaison Committee
- Master of science authorized for vocational fields

1957
- Legislature authorized campuses in Orange and Alameda counties
- State college faculty staffing formula implemented
- Legislature authorized purchase of sites for campuses in Stanislaus County and North Bay (north of San Francisco Bay)
- Legislature authorized student housing financing, loans from federal government

1958
- San Fernando Valley State College established—from branch of Los Angeles State College
- State Board of Education authorized master's degrees without credential
- Campus associated students presidents establish Student Presidents Assn.
- The cast changes: Glenn Dumke appointed president of San Francisco State College (1957); Robert Gordon Sproul retires, Clark Kerr appointed president of the University of California; Edmund G. "Pat" Brown elected governor, teacher education a campaign priority

1959
- Orange County (Fullerton) State College opens
- Alameda County (Hayward, now East Bay) State College opens
- March 14—joint meeting State Board of Education and Regents of University of California
- April 15—second joint meeting, governor presides
- April—Assembly Concurrent Resolution 88, Dorothy Donahoe and Walter Stiern, Liaison Committee "to prepare a Master Plan for the development, expansion, and integration of the facilities, curriculum, and standards of higher education in junior colleges, state colleges, the University of California, and other institutions of higher education of the State . . ."

- June—Master Plan Survey Team begins to meet
- December 7–9 final meeting of survey team, Master Plan agreed upon
- December 18—joint meeting of State Board and Regents

1960
- February 29—Governor Brown calls special session of legislature to consider Master Plan
- April 14—Governor Brown signs Donahoe Higher Education Act
- August 12—first meeting of Board of Trustees of the California State Colleges, a transitional board
- September—trustees appoint Dr. Don Leiffer as administrative officer; office established at 11th and "L" St., Sacramento, across from capitol
- November—voters approve constitutional amendment separating the California State Colleges from the State Board of Education and providing eight year terms for trustees
- Legislature funds site purchase for Sonoma State College
- Legislature authorizes campuses for San Bernardino—Riverside counties and South Bay (Los Angeles County)
- Stanislaus State College opens

1961
- Sonoma State College opens
- April 6—Buell Gallagher appointed as chancellor
- July 1—Board of Trustees assumes responsibility for the California State Colleges
- December, CSC system office moved to Inglewood (near Los Angeles airport)

1962
- February—Buell Gallagher resigns chancellorship after 7 months
- April 6–7–Board of Trustees meets at San Fernando Valley State College, Glenn S. Dumke, president of San Francisco State College, appointed chancellor
- April—Chancellor Dumke convenes presidents, creates Council of Presidents; Dumke convenes campus faculty/academic senate chairs, sets in motion the creation of Statewide Academic Senate
- Trustees request establishment of international programs
- Trustees adopt policy for auxiliary organizations, create California State Colleges Foundation
- May—trustees require campus academic plans to support budget proposals for construction of buildings
- Sacramento governmental relations office established

1963
- March—statewide faculty vote overwhelmingly approved establishment of Statewide Academic Senate; first meeting in May; officers seated at board of trustees meeting
- Office of General Counsel established
- Dean of Academic Planning position established
- International programs office established at San Francisco State College; first programs in five countries: France, Germany, Spain, Sweden, and China (Taiwan)
- Feldheym report on campus administrative organization, implemented July 1 with new budget year
- Legislature initiated requirement for faculty salary studies with comparison institutions
- California State College Student Presidents Association (CSCSPA) recognized as representative of all students, seated at Board of Trustees meetings
- Enrollment ceilings defined by Board of Trustees for urban and nonurban campuses

1964
- Trustees removed prohibition re requiring a foreign language for the baccalaureate

1965
- Freshmen admission standards implemented, top 1/3 of high school graduates
- Bakersfield campus authorized; land donated by Kern County Land Company
- Error in calculating budget, temporary salary reduction, 1.8%
- California State College San Bernardino opens for students
- California State College Palos Verdes (location and name changed to California State College Dominguez Hills in 1966) opened for students
- CSC systems office moved from Inglewood to Wilshire Blvd., in Los Angeles, again in rented quarters
- Chancellor creates Committee on Fiscal Responsibility

1966
- Committee on Fiscal Responsibility report to Board of Trustees and legislature
- Establishment of government relations office in Washington, D.C.
- Increased student and faculty activism on state college campuses, notably San Francisco State College
- California State Polytechnic College southern campus at Pomona becomes a separate polytechnic State College campus

1967	• Joint doctorate programs initiated; chemistry, San Diego State College and the University of California San Diego; special education, San Francisco State College and the University of California Berkeley • California Community Colleges created as a formal statewide entity, chancellor in Sacramento
1968	• Legislature mandates administrative unit for technology connecting all campuses to central data system in chancellor's office • Preparation of "Orange Book" (budget formulas) initiated in chancellor's office
1969	• Campuses initiated student computer systems, each independently
1970	• California State College Bakersfield enrolls students • First four joint doctorates awarded • Student Presidents Association establishes advocacy office in Sacramento
1971	• Chancellor Glenn Dumke, "New Approaches to Higher Education . . . for The California State Colleges"; establishment of Commission on External Degree Programs; conference on 1000 mile campus • Alumni Council (statewide) organized, seated at Board of Trustees • Common admissions program implemented
1972	• Consortium of the California State University and Colleges established • Continuing education unit established in chancellor's office • International programs office moved from San Francisco campus to chancellor's office and consolidated with other system offices • Name change authorized by legislature and governor; 14 of 19 campuses become California State University campuses
1973	• Establishment of system affirmative action office • Residence for chancellor donated in Bel Air location of Los Angeles
1974	• Coordinating Council for Higher Education becomes California Post-Secondary Education Commission

- Senate Bill 381 changes names of four campuses to Humboldt State University, San Diego State University, San Francisco State University, and San Jose State University

1975
- Legislature passes and governor signs bill to define faculty grievance procedures, AB 804 (Berman)
- Trustees consider measure for faculty layoff by merit and competency

1976
- First student trustee appointed
- Chancellor's office moves to Long Beach, building dedicated September;
- Assembly Bill 3063 changes name of Sonoma campus to Sonoma State College

1977
- First alumni trustee appointed
- Annual faculty comparison salary studies expanded to include presidents
- Assemblyman Howard Berman introduces AB 1091 to authorize collective bargaining in California State University and Colleges (and the University of California)
- University status attained at Dominguez Hills campus, "A New U"

1978
- AB 1091 passes, signed by governor in September (Higher Education Employee Relations Act, HEERA)
- University Services Program established
- Proposition 13, limiting taxation and thus impacting budgets, passed by electorate
- First teacher educator appointed to chancellor's staff since 1961
- University status attained at Sonoma campus
- Trustees authorized first joint doctoral program with a private California university, (Ph.D. in education, San Diego State University and Claremont Graduate School)

1979
- Student Presidents Association becomes California State Student Association (CSSA)
- Chancellor's Council of Presidents restructured to become Executive Council
- Freshman admission requirements modified to require three years of college preparatory English and two years of college preparatory mathematics, implemented in 1985

1981	• California Faculty Association (CFA) selected over United Professors of California as faculty bargaining agent; margin of victory very narrow
1982	• State University and Colleges system designated "The California State University" • Glenn Dumke retires from chancellorship • W. Ann Reynolds appointed chancellor • First collective bargaining contracts signed
1983	• Collective bargaining contract with California Faculty Association is signed • Management Personnel Plan adopted • First faculty trustee appointed
1984	• California Legislature Senate Fellows program moved to California State University Sacramento, Center for California Studies • University status attained at San Bernardino campus
1985	• Assembly Fellows follow Senate move to Sacramento campus • Freshman admission standards change to require college preparatory high school curriculum adopted by Board of Trustees, to be implemented over time • University status attained at Stanislaus campus
1986	• Governor Deukmejian requested Executive Fellows program at Sacramento campus
1987	• University status attained at Bakersfield campus
1990	• California Education Code amended to support research; trustees secure $2.5 million annual appropriation for faculty research • W. Ann Reynolds resigns chancellorship • Ellis McCune appointed acting chancellor • Board of Trustees adopts policy framework for information technology • California State University San Marcos opens as a result of 1989 legislation, the 20th campus
1991	• Barry Munitz appointed chancellor • Chancellor's residence (State University House) in Bel Air sold; new State University House acquired in Long Beach

- Commission on Learning Resources and Instructional Technology (CLRIT) established

1992
- Board of Trustees adopts policy on fund-raising, and major study on fund-raising/development initiated (Ketchum Report I)
- Chancellor's office reorganization/reorientation initiated

1993
- Trustees create position of vice chancellor for advancement
- Major initiative on technology begins; executive vice chancellor and small group of presidents provide early leadership
- Board of Trustees adopt policy framework for student fees
- Joint meeting of Board of Trustees and Board of Regents in state capitol

1994
- First Higher Education "Compact"—agreement among leadership of the California State University and the University of California and the governor about levels of funding
- Position of State University Dean for Teacher Education created;
- Chancellor establishes Institute for Educational Reform at Sacramento campus
- Chancellor presents Integrated Technology Strategy to Trustees; Technology Steering Committee of six presidents and two vice chancellors established
- Ketchum Report II presented to Trustees, fund raising target of 10% of general fund budget set for each campus
- Major report "International Programs is a Tree" to Board of Trustees
- California Maritime Academy formally joins the California State University as the 21st campus

1995
- Cornerstones project initiated
- California State University Monterey Bay admits first students, 22nd campus
- California State University Institute established
- Joint meeting of Board of Trustees and Board of Governors of the California Community Colleges at California State University Sacramento

1996
- Proposition 209 adopted by voters; eliminates "affirmative action" with respect to students and faculty
- Technology Infrastructure Initiative adopted by Board of Trustees

- Freshman admissions standards requiring college preparatory program fully implemented
- Chancellor announces establishment of 23rd campus to be located in Ventura County; campus eventually named California State University Channel Islands at former site of Camarillo State Hospital
- Building design and construction task force report to trustees; authority and responsibility for capital outlay programs delegated to all campuses

1997
- Executive Vice-Chancellor Molly Broad resigns in June to assume the presidency of the University of North Carolina system
- Chancellor Barry Munitz resigns in July for the presidency of the Getty Trust
- California Educational Technology Initiative selected to implement technology strategy
- Trustees appoint Charles Reed, chancellor of the Florida State University System, to the CSU chancellorship in November

1998
- January -Cornerstones adopted by Board of Trustees; Statewide Academic Senate Report "Baccalaureate Education in the California State University," complements Cornerstones
- Charles Reed assumes the chancellorship March 1, 1998
- May—Task Force on Globalization report
- June—California Educational Technology Initiative ends

1999
- March—Trustees adopt Cornerstones implementation plan
- November—Trustees approve CSU accountability process
- Common Management System proposed and adopted as a technology strategy; oversight from Technology Steering Committee
- Legislation signed by governor to implement agency shop for collective bargaining in the CSU

2000
- Trustee policy on campus enrollment impaction adopted
- Second student trustee position created
- California State Student Association policy statement approved by Trustees, "Shared Responsibility: Enhancing Institutional Effectiveness by Encouraging Student Participation in CSU Policy-Making"

2001
- CSU Center for Teacher Quality established on Sacramento campus; annual evaluation of all CSU graduate teachers

- Statewide Academic Senate report—"The CSU at the Beginning of the 21st Century; Meeting the Needs of the People of California"
- Trustees affirm CSSA 2000 policy statement and reaffirm CSSA official role with the Board of Trustees
- Institute for Higher Education Leadership and Policy established at Sacramento campus

2002
- California State University Channel Islands formally opens

2003
- Trustees modify policy on expectations of campus fund-raising from 10% to 15% to 20% based on assessment of campus performance and capability
- Move to integrate Washington office and staff operations with system, chancellor's office and campuses; development of federal policy agenda with presidents, chancellor's office and trustees

2005
- Senate Bill 724 authorizes CSU to confer doctoral degrees in the field of education narrowly defined; implemented with first students in 2007
- California State University Hayward renamed California State University East Bay

2006
- September—Board of Trustees comprehensive evaluation of achievements of Cornerstones
- Board of Trustees initiated "Access to Excellence," a successor agenda to Cornerstones
- Legislature restores graduate differential in budget
- Treasury function established within CSU, a major positive step for financial management
- Position of assistant vice-chancellor for research initiatives and partnerships established

* * *

The book's comprehensive treatment of the history of the California State University ends with 2006. In some chapters, selected matters are addressed beyond 2006.

The years after 2006 were inevitably and necessarily dominated initially by collective bargaining matters and massively by declining state financial support for the California State University and all of public higher education in California.

Appendix 2. Interviewees, Participants in Focus Groups, and Contributors

Sheppie Abramowitz
Roberta Achtenberg
Wallace Albertson
Dede Alpert
J. Theodore Anagnoson
Warren Baker
Juanita C. Barrena
Gerald Beavers
David Benson
Colleen Bentley
Robert O. Berdahl
Howard Berman
Sandra Bernard
Robert O. Bess
Molly Corbett Broad
Patrick M. Callan
William D. Campbell
Herbert Carter
Robert Cherny
Raymond Clark
James Cobble
Les Cohen
James Connor
James Considine
June M. Cooper
Robert Corrigan
Kathryn Covington
William D. Crist
Patricia Cuocco
William Dermody
Karyn Domich
William Dorman
J. Patrick Drohan
Dorothy Dumke (Elliott)
Lyle Edmison
David H. Elliott
David Ernst
J. Handel Evans
Julia Fahrenbruch
Martha Fallgatter-Walda

Phil A. Fitch
J. Robert Fountain
John Francis
Spencer Freund
Marian L. Gade
Patrick Gantt
Harold Geiogue
James M. Gelb
Harold Goldwhite
Steven Gregorich
Judson Grenier
Murray Haberman
Arthur Hall
Gary Hammerstrom
D. Dale Hanner
Harry Harmon
Brice W. Harris
Robert Harris
R. William Hauck
Gerald Hayward
Louis Heilbron
Elizabeth Hill
John Hillyard
Timothy Hodson
Boyd Horne
Kibbey Horne
Judith Hunt
Cristy Jensen
J. W. Jiminez
Allison Jones
Robert G. Jones
Kathleen Kaiser
Jacquelyn Kegley
John Kehoe
Robert E. Kennedy
Lee Kerschner
Michael W. Kirst
Archie Kleingartner
Dorena Knepper
Dorothy Knoell

Robert Kully
Thomas P. Lantos
Teven Laxer
Patrick Lenz
David Leveille
Charles L. Lindahl
A. Robert Linscheid
Shaun Lumachi
Sara Lundquist
Thomas McCarron
Jackie McClain
Peter McClory
Ellis McCune
Scott McGown
Rosario Marin
William Mason
Leonard Mathy
Ralph D. Mills
Ann I. Morey
Allen A. Mori
Anthony Moye
Barry Munitz
Caesar J. Naples
Thomas Nussbaum
Morgan Odell
Doris Ozuna
George Pardon
Douglas X Patino
Thomas Philo
William Pickens
Scott Plotkin
A. Alan Post
Charles B. Reed
Jon Regnier
Gary Reichard
W. Ann Reynolds
John Richards
Rodney Rideau
James M. Rosser
Christine Ribeiro Rubin
Jack Samit
Elvyra San Juan
Henrietta Schwartz
Jack Scott
Jolayne Service

Keith Sexton
Richard Shek
Nancy Shulock
John M. Smart
Glenn P. Smith
Peter N. Smits
David A. Sommers
David Spence
Nancy Sprotte
Samuel Strafaci
Richard L. Sutter
Leo Van Cleve
John Vasconcellos
David Viar
Virginia Watts
Bradley Wells
John Welty
Richard West
Thomas West
Helene Whitson
Sandra Wilcox
Gregory Williams
William Wilson
David Wright
Beverly Young
Brian Young
Karen Y. Zamarripa

Appendix 3. Trustee Appointments

The Trustees of the California State University include sixteen persons appointed by the governor and confirmed by the Senate, and nine statutory trustees, including the governor, lieutenant governor, speaker of the Assembly, superintendent of public instruction, chancellor of the California State University, two students and one faculty member (each appointed by the governor from lists of at least three persons submitted by the California State Student Association and the Statewide Academic Senate), and one alumna or alumnus selected by the Alumni Council of the CSU. They are as follows:

Original Trustees

Original Trustees	**Appointing Governor**
Byron H. Atkinson (1960–1961)	Edmund G. (Pat) Brown
Peggy Bates (1960–1962)	"
Thomas Braden (1960–1963)	"
William Coblentz (1960–1964)	"
Raymond J. Daba (1960–1962)	"
Donald M. Hart (1960–1968); (Chair 1967–1968)	"
Louis H. Heilbron (1960–1969); (Chair 1960–1963)	"
Mabel E. Kinney (1960–1962)	"
Charles Luckman (1960–1982); (Chair 1963–1965)	Edmund G (Pat) Brown, Ronald Reagan and Edmund (Jerry) Brown
Mickey B. Mathiesen (1960–1962)	Edmund G. (Pat) Brown
Theodore Meriam (1960–1971); (Chair 1968–1969)	"
J. Philip Murphy (1960–1961)	"
Thomas L. Pitts (1960–1965)	"
Herman H. Ridder (1960–1962)	"
Paul Spencer (1960–1969)	"
Allen J. Sutherland (1960–1964)	"

Subsequent Trustees

John E. Carr (1961–1965)	Edmund G. (Pat) Brown
Albert J. Ruffo (1961–1971); (Chair 1965–1967)	"
Phebe B. Conley (1962–1972)	"
Trevor Gardner (1962–1963)	"
Dan Kimball (1962–1963)	"
Daniel H. Ridder (1962–1975); (Chair 1969–1970)	Edmund G. (Pat) Brown and Ronald Reagan
E. Guy Warren (1962–1972); (Chair 1970–1972)	Edmund G. (Pat) Brown

Gregson E. Bautzer (1963–1968) "
George D. Hart (1963–1974); (Chair 1972, "
   1973–1974)
George Thatcher (1963–1964 "
James Thacher (1964–1970) "
Victor Palmieri (1964–1967) "
Simon Ramo (1964–1967)   Edmund G. (Pat) Brown
Chester Bartalini (1965–1966) "
Alex Cory (1965–1973) "
Edward O. Lee (1966–1974) "
William Norris (1966–1972)
Earle M. Jorgensen (1967–1970)   Ronald Reagan
Dudley Swim (1968–1972) "
Karl L. Wente (1968–1976); (Chair 1972–1973) "
E. Litton Bivans (1969–1971) "
William O. Weissich (1969–1977); (Chair 1974,
   1976–1977)
Robert A. Hornby (1970–1978); (Chair 1974–1976) "
Phillip V. Sanchez (1970–1971) "
Gene M. Benedetti (1971–1978) "
Winifred Lancaster (1971–1977) "
William F. McColl (1971–1972) "
Wendell W. Witter (1971–1979) "
Frank P. Adams (1972–1981) "
Robert F. Beaver (1972–1977) "
Roy T. Brophy (1972–1980 and 1983–1986);   Ronald Reagan and
   (Chair 1977–1979, 1985–1986)   George Deukmejian
Richard A. Garcia (1972–1979)   Ronald Reagan
Jeanette S. Ritchie (1972–1980) "
Dean S. Lesher (1973–1981 and 1985–1993)   Ronald Reagan and
   George Deukmejian
Claudia H. Hampton (1974–1994);   Ronald Reagan,
   (Chair 1979–1981)   Edmund (Jerry) Brown,
   and George Deukmejian
Yvonne W. Larsen (1974–1975)   Ronald Reagan
Mary Jean Pew (1975–1981)   Edmund (Jerry) Brown
Willie J. Stennis (1975–1991)   Edmund (Jerry) Brown and
   George Deukmejian
Juan Gomez-Quinones (1976–1984)   Edmund (Jerry) Brown
Kathleen A. Carlson (student); (1976–1978) "
John F. O'Connell (alumni) (1977–1984);   –
   (Chair 1981–1984)
Blanche C. Bersch (1977–1984)   Edmund (Jerry) Brown
Michael R. Peevey (1977–1985) "
John F. Crowley (1978–1985) "

Wallace Albertson (1978–1986); (Chair 1984–1985)	"
Eli Broad (1978–1982)	"
Kevin Gallagher (student); (1978–1980)	"
Donald G. Livingston (1979–1987)	"
Celia Ballesteros (1979–1987)	"
Jason E. Peltier (student); (1980–1981)	"
Lynne Wasserman (1980–1988)	"
August Coppola (1981–1984)	"
Jeremiah F. Hallisey (1981–1982)	"
George M. Marcus (1981–1989)	Edmund (Jerry) Brown
Roland E. Arnall (1982–1998)	Edmund (Jerry) Brown and George Deukmejian
Thomas J. Bernard (1982–1989)	Edmund (Jerry) Brown
Dixon R. Harwin (1982–1990)	"
Jennifer A. Oropeza (student) (1982–1983)	"
Blaine B. Quick (1982–1983)	"
Daniel J. Bronfman (student) (1983–1984)	"
Robert D. Kully (faculty) (1983–1987)	George Deukmejian
Dale B. Ride (1984–1989); (Chair 1986–1988)	"
Tom C. Stickel (1984–1988)	"
Marian Bagdasarian (1984–1996)	"
Lee A. Grissom (alumni) (1984–1990)	-
William L. Crocker (student) (1985–1987)	George Deukmejian
Marianthi Lansdale (1985–1993); (Chair 1988–1990)	"
Theodore A. Bruinsma (1986–1988)	"
John E. Kashiwabara, M.D. (1986–1994)	"
William D. Campbell (1987–2003); (Chair 1990–1992)	George Deukmejian and Pete Wilson
Martha C. (Fallgatter) Walda (1987–2003); (Chair 1996–1998)	George Deukmejian and Pete Wilson
Lyman H. Heine (faculty) (1987–1991)	George Deukmejian
John F. Sweeney (student) (1987–1989)	"
Ralph R. Pesqueira (1988–2004)	George Deukmejian and Pete Wilson
Ted J. Saenger (1989–1997)	George Deukmejian
J. Gary Shansby (1989–1992 and 1993–1995)	George Deukmejian and Pete Wilson
Scot Vick (student) (1989–1991)	George Deukmejian
James H. Gray (1990–1999)	George Deukmejian and Pete Wilson
Gloria S. Hom (1990–1992)	George Deukmejian

Anthony M. Vitti (1990–2005); (Chair 1992–1994) — George Deukmejian and Pete Wilson
Terrance W. Flanigan (1990–1993) — George Deukmejian
R. J. Considine, Jr. (alumni) (1991–1999); (Chair 1994–1996) — Pete Wilson
Bernard Goldstein (faculty) (1991–1997) — "
Arneze Washington (student) (1991–1993) — "
William Hauck (1993–); (Chair 1998–2000) — Pete Wilson, Gray Davis, and Arnold Schwarzenegger

Joan Otomo-Corgel (1993–2000) — Pete Wilson
Rosemary Thakar, appointment not confirmed (1993–1994) — "
Michael J. Stennis (1994–2000) — "
Christopher A. Lowe (student) (1994–1995) — "
Stanley T. Wang (1994–2002) — "
Frank Y. Wada (student) (1995–1997) — "
Ali C. Razi (1996–2001) — "
Laurence K. Gould, Jr. (1996–2002); (Chair 2000–2002) — "
Eric Mitchell (student); (1997–1999) — "
Robert Foster (1997–2005) — "
Maridel Moulton (1997–1998), appointment not confirmed — "
Alice S. Petrossian (1997–1998), appointment not confirmed — "
Harold Goldwhite (faculty) (1998–2003) — "
Frederick W. Pierce IV (alumni) (1999–2004) —
Dee Dee Myers (1999–2004) — Gray Davis
Roberta Achtenberg (1999–); (Chair 2006–2008) — Gray Davis and Arnold Schwarzenegger
Debra S. Farar (1999–); (Chair 2002–2004) — Gray Davis and Arnold Schwarzenegger

Neel I Murarka (student) (2000–2001) — Gray Davis
Murray L. Galinson (2000–2007); (Chair 2004–2006) — "
Shailesh J. Mehta (2000–2005) — "
Daniel Cartwright (student) (2000–2002) — "
Kyriakos Tsakopoulos (2001–2009) — "
Richardo F. Icaza (2001–2008) — "
Erene S. Thomas (student) (2001–2003) — "
M. Alexander Lopez (student) (2002–2004) — "
Eric Guerra (student) (2003–2005) — "
Kathleen Kaiser (faculty) (2003–2005) — "
Jeffrey L. Bleich (2004–); (Chair 2008–) — Arnold Schwarzenegger
Herbert Carter (2004–) — "

Carol R. Chandler (2004–) "
Moctesuma Esparza (2004–2007) "
George G. Gowgani (2004–) "
Melinda Guzman Moore (2004–) "
Raymond W. Holdsworth, Jr. (2004–) "
Corey A. Jackson (student) (2004–2006) "
Larry Adamson (alumni) (2004–2005) -
A. Robert Linscheid (alumni) (2005–) -
Craig R. Smith (faculty) (2005–2009) "
Andrew LaFlamme (student) (2006–2007) "
Kenneth Fong (2006–) "
Lou Monville (2006–) "
Glen Toney (2006–) "
Jennifer Reimer (student) (2006–2008) "
Peter Mehas (2007–) "
Curtis Grima (student) (2007–2009) "
Henry Mendoza (2008–) "
Russell Statham (student) (2008–) "
Margaret Fortune (2009–) "
Linda Lang (2009–) "

Appendix 4. Chancellors of the California State University

*36. Donald Leiffer (Administrative Officer)
1960–1961*

*37. Buell Gallagher
1961–1962*

*38. Glenn S. Dumke
1962–1982*

*39. W. Ann Reynolds
1982–1990*

40. Ellis E. McCune (Acting)
1990–1991

41. Barry Munitz
1991–1998

42. Charles B. Reed
1998–

Appendix 5. Enrollment in Five Year Intervals from 1935-36 to 2008-09

Year	Students Enrolled	FTE Students	Average Units per Student
1935-36	8,131	7,422	13.6
1940-41	11,874	10,866	13.7
1945-46	7,907	6,967	13.2
1950-51	30,502	24,610	12.1
1955-56	54,618	40,134	11.0
1960-61	94,837	69,089	10.9
1965-66	154,825	116,689	11.3
1970-71	251,434	203,700	12.2
1975-76	312,989	235,727	11.3
1980-81	317,505	239,035	11.3
1985-86	328,869	248,456	11.3
1990-91	376,741	278,502	11.1
1995-96	330,695	253,827	11.5
2000-01	376,262	290,554	11.6
2005-06	432,816	334,343	11.6
2008-09	466,075	372,392	11.9

An "FTE" is a full-time equivalent student. An FTE is a unit of measure equal to fifteen semester or quarter units per term. FTE is reached by dividing the total semester or quarter hours by fifteen. College year FTE (the numbers used on the table above) includes fall and spring semesters (and summer terms if applicable) for campuses operating on the semester calendar, and summer, fall, winter, and spring quarters for campuses with a quarter calendar. FTE and student enrollment numbers do not include enrollments in extension (extended education, continuing education) which are self supporting. For a few years in the 1960s, some graduate students were counted for FTE purposes on a basis of ten units. This "graduate differential" was reinstated mid 2000 for a limited number of graduate students.

The enrollment, FTE numbers, and definitions are from the *CSU Statistical Abstract*, a volume published each year by the Chancellor's Office. The purpose of this table is simply to outline the magnitude of growth within the CSU over almost seventy-five years. It does tell another story; many students in the CSU are not full time enrollees. Part-time students are more numerous on the urban campuses.

Appendix 6. Statewide Academic Senate Chairs

Year	Faculty	University
1963–1964	Leonard Mathy	CSU Los Angeles
1964–1965	Samuel Wiley	CSU Long Beach
1965–1966	John Livingston	CSU Sacramento
1966–1967	Jesse Allen	CSU Los Angeles
1967–1968	Sol Buchalter	CSU Northridge
1968–1969	John Stafford	CSU Northridge
1969–1970	Jerome Richfield	CSU Northridge
1970–1971	Levern Graves	CSU Fullerton
1971–1972	David Provost	CSU Fresno
1972–1975	Charles Adams	CSU Chico
1975–1977	Gerald Marley	CSU Fullerton
1977–1979	David Elliott	San Jose State University
1979–1982	Robert Kully	CSU Los Angeles
1982–1984	John Bedell	CSU Fullerton
1984–1987	Bernard Goldstein	San Francisco State University
1987–1990	Ray Geigle	CSU Bakersfield
1990–1993	Sandra Wilcox	CSU Dominguez Hills
1993–1995	Harold Goldsmith	CSU Los Angeles
1995–1998	James Highsmith	CSU Fresno
1998–2000	Gene Dinielli	CSU Long Beach
2000–2003	Jacquelyn Kegley	CSU Bakersfield
2003–2004	Robert Cherny	San Francisco State University
2004–2005	David McNeil	San Jose State University
2005–2007	Marshelle Thobaben	CSU Humboldt
2007–2008	Barry Pasternack	CSU Fullerton
2008–	John Tarjan	CSU Bakersfield

Index

AASCU, 233-234, 284, 575-578
AB 1091, 364-365, 367, 381
AB 123, 547
Abramowitz, Sheppie, 576, 577, 633
Academic affairs, 124-125, 128,130, 136-137, 169, 173, 182, 192-193, 195, 198, 212-213, 222, 229-230, 252, 256, 260, 266, 270, 278-279, 281 288, 290, 314, 317, 329, 333, 342, 345-346, 351, 357, 400-401, 403, 414, 416, 421, 424, 439-441, 443-445, 449, 452-453, 456, 471, 479, 487-490, 516, 555, 571, 589,
Academic Communications Network Committee, 294
Academic Council on International Programs, 272, 276, 278-280, 282
Academic Information Resources Council, 294
Academic Master Plan, 138, 190, 285, 525
Academic planning, 118, 125, 136-139, 143, 181, 189-194, 200, 208, 218-219, 222, 248, 254, 256, 272, 289, 355, 403, 441, 452, 486, 489-490, 526, 530, 555-556, 568
Academic Senate, 137, 139, 141-143, 146, 152, 165, 169, 171-173, 175, 179-181, 190, 193, 195, 197-198, 200-207, 209, 212-213, 217, 222, 225-226, 228, 230, 234-237, 249, 263, 265-266, 272, 279-281, 292, 296, 299, 330-331, 333, 348-349, 352, 356-360, 362-368, 373-375, 379, 382-386, 395, 399-409, 411-412, 420, 435, 440, 445, 452-454, 469-472, 476-477, 484, 488, 517, 542, 548, 551, 556, 563, 566, 571-572, 604-605
Access, 40, 53, 84-85, 182, 197, 199, 210, 215, 216-219, 223, 227, 230, 236-238, 269, 281-283, 309, 310, 316, 320-321, 332, 399, 470, 496, 596, 601, 606, 609, 613, 615
Access to Excellence, 216-219, 236-238, 399, 609, 615

Accountability, 33, 210-211, 215-218, 281, 295, 303, 313, 378, 465-466, 470, 501, 513, 534, 559, 609
Accreditation, 41, 61, 73, 190, 213, 255, 266, 275, 277, 441-442, 548, 580
Achtenberg, Roberta, xxi, 216, 217, 476, 479, 633, 638
ACT, 148, 326
Ad Hoc Committee on Alternative Funding Sources, 515
Ad Hoc Committee on Development of Policies and Administrative Procedures, 167
Administrative Information Management Systems (AIMS), 293-294, 304, 306
Administrative tenure, 343
Admissions Advisory Council, 329, 331, 333, 406, 444, 470
Admission standards, 18, 28, 54, 88-91, 110, 113, 173, 197, 325-326, 402, 459
Admissions, 15-18, 27-29, 54, 57, 63, 85, 88-91, 95, 99, 125-126, 135, 140, 145-146, 148, 163, 167-168, 193, 195, 210, 213, 224, 230, 258, 266, 302, 310, 312-313, 322-331, 333-335, 338-339, 344, 374-375, 386, 402, 404, 406, 439, 441-442, 444, 447, 452, 459, 460, 463, 464, 467, 470, 478, 495, 518, 557, 563, 602, 611
Affirmative action, 312-314, 332-33, 338, 359, 374-375, 405, 444-447, 454, 561
Affordability, 227, 312, 596, 602, 606, 613
Agency shop, 379-380
Ahmanson, Howard, 156
Allaway, William, 269
Alquist, Alfred, 548, 549, 554
Alternative admissions, 328-329, 339, 404,
Alumni Council, 212, 337, 395, 396, 399, 412, 627, 635

647

American Association of University
    Professors, 88, 345, 358, 360, 362,
    363, 403
American Council on Education
    (ACE), 5, 277, 284, 321, 450, 550,
    575, 578, 580
Angel, Myron, xvii, 10, 19, 26, 29, 30,
    40, 41, 45, 47, 56-57, 80, 126,
    127, 133, 136, 144, 154, 156-158,
    258, 262, 318, 338-339, 358, 361,
    401, 437, 456, 493, 531, 544
Applied fields, 20, 210, 229, 231-232,
    266, 344, 442, 468, 472, 487, 540,
    564, 573-574, 607, 609, 615
Appropriation, 7-8, 10, 16, 19, 58, 60,
    78, 116, 118, 151, 162, 191, 201,
    207, 231, 233, 236, 262, 299, 305,
    321, 425, 428, 484-485, 490-491,
    493, 501-502, 504, 567, 569, 580,
    584, 590
Arcata, 25-26, 65
Arciniega, Tomas, 260, 332, 420
Articulation, 84, 467-469, 473
Arts, 9, 20, 21, 23-24, 33-34, 37, 41,
    44, 48, 52, 54-58, 60-63, 87, 96,
    193, 232, 318, 320, 329-332, 369,
    406, 444, 447, 493, 504, 527, 531-
    532, 534,
Assembly, 11, 16, 25-56, 75, 79, 81,
    95, 97, 106, 110, 115, 172, 200,
    229, 235, 238, 250-252, 258, 299,
    305, 314, 356, 359, 364, 368, 386,
    405, 447, 455, 458, 461-463, 470,
    479, 514, 517, 544-549, 553, 557,
    560, 563, 568-569, 573, 580, 585-
    589
Assessment, 213, 216, 230, 255, 263-
    264, 435
Associated Students, 209, 299, 312,
    371, 407, 408-411, 435, 499, 505-
    506, 508, 557, 622, 624
Association of California State College
    Professors, 88, 92, 115, 132, 141,
    182, 360, 361
Association of Independent California
    Colleges and Universities, 79, 80,
    560
Audiology, 229, 574
Audit(s), 208, 272-274, 289, 300, 488,
    511, 571, 583

Automobiles, 35, 56, 423, 557
Autonomy, 50-51, 82, 89, 96, 102-103,
    105-106, 111, 142, 190, 211, 216,
    400, 472, 491-492, 526, 541, 595
Auxiliary and Business Services
    (ABS), 507-508, 517-518
Auxiliary organizations, 162, 234, 297,
    407, 427-428, 430-432, 449, 502-
    509, 515-517, 541, 575-576
Axelrod, Joseph, 156

Baccalaureate, 35, 37, 44, 47, 61, 63,
    85, 91, 122, 153-154, 157, 182,
    195-199, 212-213, 215, 221-222,
    269, 272, 281, 315, 323, 468, 471-
    473, 549, 568, 601-602, 613-616
Baker, William, 289, 290, 443, 477,
    479, 495, 511, 517, 518, 559, 569,
    578, 584, 633
Bakersfield, 57, 74-75, 98, 122, 161-
    162, 196, 201, 204, 260, 294, 332,
    415, 421, 461, 527, 562, 564, 567
Barnes, Richard, 544-545, 547
Barrows, David Prescott, 17, 30, 140,
    331
Bartlett, Washington, 11
Beck, Julian, 56, 57
Bell, Hugh, 297, 411, 505
Benson, David, 192, 219, 238, 516, 633
Berman, Howard, 356, 362-368, 419,
    492, 553
Bess, Robert, 260, 329-330, 332-333,
    339, 444, 633
Beverly, Robert, 262-264, 267, 583-
    584, 634
Bidwell, John, xi, 11, 12
Bierman, Arthur, 114, 171, 355
Bilingual credential, 255
Board of Admissions and Relations
    with Schools (BOARS), 331
Bond, James, 267, 420, 528
Bonds, 107, 301, 454, 502, 507, 527-
    530, 535, 540-541
Braden, Thomas, 78, 85-86, 108-109,
    119-120, 127, 132, 246-247, 249,
    635
Brakebill, Harry, 112, 151-152, 181,
    454, 484-488, 517-518, 521-522,
    524, 537, 540, 542

Broad, Molly, 5, 193-194, 211, 219, 280, 293-294, 297, 314, 406, 418, 424-425, 448-450, 453, 494, 500, 559, 569-570, 578, 606, 631, 633, 637
Broesamle, John, 56
Brophy, Roy, xii, 358, 364-365, 367, 381, 384, 396, 430, 492, 551-552, 636
Brown, Governor Edmund "Jerry," 254, 258, 276, 356, 358, 362-363, 367-368, 384, 395, 404-405, 409, 421, 423, 490, 497, 542, 550-552, 567, 604
Brown, Governor Edmund G. "Pat," 59-60, 62, 64, 71, 74, 76-78, 85-86, 91-93, 96-99, 122, 124, 126, 130, 132, 135, 148, 151-152, 155, 157-158, 161, 163, 164, 224, 227, 244, 246, 248-249, 271, 336, 343, 368, 392-393, 414, 458, 476, 488, 490, 523, 527, 529, 540, 542, 595-596
Browne, Arthur, 78, 80, 86, 89, 94
Budd, James, 15, 16
Burchard, George, 25
Burk, Frederic, 18, 19, 32, 167, 232, 241, 413
Bush, George H. W., 320
Buttelman, Michele, 298
Byrne, Paul, 407, 505

Cain, Leo, 117, 155, 156, 158, 204, 206, 254, 415-416
Caldera, Louis, 455, 514, 579
California Administrative Code, 54, 342, 357
California Basic Educational Skills Test (CBEST), 258-259, 268
California College and University Faculty Association, 114, 141, 358, 360, 362
California Conference on Higher Education, 38
California Constitutional Convention, 9, 619
California Education Code, 182, 385, 387, 505, 629

California Education Technology Initiative (CETI), 297, 298, 299, 300-301, 304-306
California Faculty Association (CFA), 298-299, 302, 362-363, 367, 369-370, 372, 375-376, 378-382, 387, 397, 409, 433, 445, 492, 500, 504, 566, 570-571, 604-605, 629
California Junior College Association, 80, 467, 479
California Maritime Academy, 33, 49, 369, 563-564, 622, 630
California Master Plan for Higher Education, xiv, xvi, xvii, 229
California Master Plan, for Higher Education, 5, ix, xi, xiv, xvii, xviii, xix, xx, xxi, xxii, xxiv, xxv, 4, 24, 50, 56, 61, 63-64, 70-71, 73-76, 78-81, 83-100, 105, 107-108, 111, 115-116, 118, 123-125, 131, 135, 138-140, 142, 145-147, 150-151, 155-156, 159-160, 163, 165-168, 172, 190, 193-194, 200, 205, 209-210, 218-219, 221-222, 225, 227-228, 230, 232-233, 235-237, 241, 244-246, 248-249, 265, 269, 272, 279, 283, 289, 296, 310, 315, 316, 318, 320-321, 323-326, 328, 333, 335-336, 338-339, 341, 343, 345, 348, 350, 354, 355, 359, 368, 383-384, 391-393, 396, 398-400, 402, 407-408, 413-416, 422, 426-427, 436, 438-439, 441-442, 445, 449, 457-468, 470, 473, 475-476, 478-479, 481, 483, 485-486, 495-497, 499, 502, 506-507, 509-510, 515-522, 524-526, 530, 534, 537, 540, 545, 547, 552, 554, 562-563, 571, 573-574, 576, 581, 593, 595, 596, 598, 600-602, 604, 606, 609-613, 616-617, 624-625
California National Guard, 157
California Nautical School, 32, 622
California Polytechnic State College, 37, 160, 622
California Postsecondary Education Commission CPEC, 326, 346, 380, 428, 462-466, 475, 479, 562-563, 565

California State College Foundation, 507
California State College International Programs, 273
California State College Student Presidents Association, 164, 542, 626
California State Department of Finance, xx, 45. 48, 51, 60-61, 82, 90, 109-111, 125-127, 136, 150, 163, 168, 189, 191, 202, 204, 208, 231-233, 272-273, 289-291, 296, 316, 324, 342, 344, 346, 348, 351, 354, 414, 427-428, 459, 482-484, 486-489, 491, 495, 497, 501-502, 504-505, 517-518, 520-523, 526-527, 531, 540, 553, 559, 564, 574, 623
California State Employees Association, 92. 298, 358, 360, 361-363, 371-372, 378, 380, 386-387
California State Federation of Teachers, 114, 141
California State Normal School, xvi, 5, 7-11, 17, 241, 619
California State Polytechnic College Foundation, 505
California State Scholarship Commission, 316
California State Student Association (CSSA), xii, 212, 298-299, 318, 330, 338-339, 395, 399, 409-412, 477, 479, 500, 628, 631-632, 635
California State Teachers Colleges, 34
California State University Foundation, 507-508, 513-515, 518
California Student Aid Commission, 316
California Teachers Association (CTA), 9, 15, 114, 132, 141, 241, 251, 258
Callan, Patrick, 211, 462-465, 475
Camarillo, 567-568
Caminetti, Anthony, 10, 22, 611
Campbell, William D., 235, 332, 406, 476, 479, 512, 518, 556, 565, 633, 637
Campion, Howard, 80

Campus Information Resource Plans (CIRP), 291, 292, 304, 306
Capital outlay, 51, 82, 107, 112, 121, 125, 136, 143, 213, 297-298, 301, 402, 416, 496, 501, 519-536, 555, 568, 615
Capital Outlay Fund for Public Higher Education (COFPHE), 527, 529
Carlson, Kathleen, 16, 395, 409, 636
Carlson, William, 16, 395, 409, 636
Carnegie Foundation for the Advancement of Teaching, 34, 39, 41, 84, 243, 448
Carr, John, 109, 115, 635
Carson, 158-159
Carter, Herbert, xi, 255, 293, 312, 317, 338, 339, 374, 431, 445, 447-448, 478-479, 494, 576, 617, 633, 638
Center for California Studies, xxvii, 334, 581-582, 584, 586-587, 589-590, 629
Centralization 111, 142, 169, 342, 475, 532, 534, 580
Certification 242, 249-50, 331, 353, 362
Chandler report 482
Chaffin, Sheila, 530, 555
Champion, Hale, 156, 157
Chandler, Everett, 49, 267, 482, 544, 623, 639
Channel Islands 195-196, 562, 567, 568
Chapel, Charles, 154
Chico 11-12, 19, 24, 26, 31, 33, 42-4, 47-49, 54, 58, 64, 66, 95, 119, 146, 149-150, 153, 156, 158, 162, 165, 181, 192, 196, 205, 207, 226, 233, 247, 269-270, 290, 299, 310, 314-315, 318-320, 322, 328-330, 338-339, 344, 357, 361, 371, 381, 395, 407, 411, 427, 434, 443, 478, 488, 505-506, 510, 518, 545, 548-549, 575, 585, 590, 609
Childs, Charles, 15
Christopher, Warren, 108-109, 143, 458, 478-479, 523, 638
Churchill, Jordan, 141-142, 400
Civil service 51, 125, 341-343, 349, 358, 370-371, 373, 376, 427, 432
Civil War, xvii, 3, 9, 11

Index 651

Clark, Raymond, xii, 18, 62, 73, 75, 84-85, 125, 131, 143, 145, 150, 164-165, 222, 227-228, 237-238, 295, 304-306, 325, 348, 398, 417, 438-439, 448, 456, 467, 478-479, 494, 558, 572, 584, 589, 595, 600, 624, 633
Clucas, George, 125, 483, 486
Cobb, Jewel Plummer, 329, 351, 446
Cohen, Les, xi, 154, 163, 408, 477, 479, 518, 540-545, 574, 590, 633
Collective bargaining 83, 131, 133, 172-173, 179, 341, 346, 348, 350, 352, 355-356, 359-365, 367, 368-373, 377-379, 381-382, 384-385
College preparatory 89-90, 110, 145-147, 313, 324-326, 329-331, 335, 339, 470
Collins, John J., 42
Commission on Education Reform 252
Commission on External Degree Programs, 206-207, 329, 404, 499, 627
Commission on Institutional Management (CIMIT), 295, 304, 306
Commission on Instructional Technology (CIT), 292, 304-306
Commission on Learning Resources and Instructional Technology (CLRIT), 293, 295, 304, 306, 630
Commission on Teacher Preparation and Licensing 251-253, 256, 258
Commission on Telecommunications Infrastructure, (CTI), 295, 304, 306
Committee on Alternative Admissions Criteria, 328, 339, 404
Committee on Campus Planning, Buildings, and Grounds, 521, 524
Committee on Educational Policy 271, 361, 460
Committee on Fiscal Responsibility, 205, 484, 487-488, 490, 502, 626
Committee for Improving Teacher Education (CITE) 244
Committee on Selection and Retention of Students, 324-325
Committee on State College Entrance Requirements, 323

Commission on Teacher Preparation and Licensing 251-253, 256, 258
Common Management Systems (CMS), 302, 303, 304, 306, 571
Community Colleges 22, 31, 41, 154, 195-197, 209-213, 225, 227, 229-231, 235, 252, 260, 321, 323, 334, 375, 395-396, 398-406, 452, 461-463, 465, 467-8
Community service learning, 214
Compact, 210-211, 215, 227, 481, 495-496, 500-501, 559-560, 573
Comparison institutions 345, 346, 428, 433, 463
Connerly, Ward, 314, 560
Considine, R. James, 395, 476, 479, 633, 638
Coolidge, Belle, 42
Coons, Arthur, 61, 80, 85, 86, 93, 222, 244
Cooper, June, 32, 378, 386, 387, 449, 451, 454, 633
Consortium, 202-203, 207-208, 283, 450, 603, 607, 611
Constitution, 3, 9-11, 15, 17, 22, 26-27, 31, 39, 50, 62-64, 82, 93-101, 106, 108, 142, 151, 181, 227, 242, 400-402, 406, 412, 457-8, 466, 595, 600
Constitutional status, 82, 85, 88, 91, 97, 100, 554
Continuing education, 117, 203, 205-207, 210, 215, 225, 227, 234, 277, 283, 290, 461, 487-488, 499, 516
Controversial 118, 129, 131, 138, 152, 170, 200, 253, 274, 314, 325, 373, 380-381, 423, 450, 506, 539
Coordinating entity, 466
Corley, James, 74-75, 575
Cornerstones, 154, 227, 236-237, 281, 303, 310, 325, 398, 406, 444, 452-453, 501, 609, 615
Corrigan, Robert, 339, 477, 479, 513, 517-518, 633
Council of Library Directors (COLD), 292, 295, 304, 306
Council of State College Presidents, 37, 50-51, 55, 95, 134, 148, 622
Counselors 83, 250, 352, 369, 558

CPEC 326, 346, 380, 428, 462-465, 475, 479
Credentials 23, 210, 222, 258, 262, 421, 512, 570
Crist, William, 363-364, 367, 369-370, 386-387, 633
Crowley, Gerald, 116-117, 636
CSSA 330, 409, 410-412, 377, 500
CSU-ERFA 383-4
Cubberly, Ellwood, 31, 621
Culture(s) 100, 119, 140, 184, 208, 214, 233-234, 236, 237-238, 254, 256, 281-283, 303, 311, 313-315, 318-319, 322, 330, 334, 349, 382-383, 375, 392-393, 407, 416-417, 438, 474, 513-515, 519-520, 580, 604, 607-610, 613-16
Curriculum 5, 7, 10, 15-21, 23-24, 27-28, 31, 33, 36, 41, 43, 54, 63, 79, 86, 89-90, 101, 129, 138, 140, 145146, 153, 157, 159, 189, 187-199, 201-202, 204, 210, 228, 244, 254, 264, 266, 270, 279, 281, 292, 298-299, 310, 311, 313, 320, 323-326, 328-332, 334-335, 339, 354, 401, 402, 444, 447, 467, 469-473, 566, 571, 599, 602, 609-610

Daba, Raymond, 77, 247, 635
Davis, Gray, 19-20, 84, 223, 228, 261, 379-380, 396, 464, 473, 476, 479, 497, 500-501, 560, 570, 572-573, 585, 638
Day, Thomas, 290-291, 563, 566, 578, 617
Dean, James, xxvi, 22, 48, 80, 85, 117, 190, 222, 241, 421, 461, 464, 499, 518, 617, 626, 630, 636
Decentralization, xx, 121, 211, 213, 219, 424, 449, 454, 474, 501-502, 519, 532, 534, 536
Demographics, 318, 601, 606
Desmond, Earl, 42, 43
Deukmejian, George, xii, 235, 259, 371, 375, 377, 379, 395-396, 429-430, 470, 476, 479, 493, 497, 512, 529, 531, 545, 554, 557, 563, 585, 629, 636-638
Dewey, John, 18
Dickson, Edward, 29, 30

Differentiation of function, 53, 56, 58, 79, 84-85, 89, 91-94, 96-97, 123, 457, 607, 610, 612
Dilworth, Nelson, 58
Diversity, xiii, xviii, 257, 281, 314-315, 318, 401, 548, 556, 599
Division of Information Systems (DIS), 288-289, 290-291, 304, 306
Division of State Colleges and Teacher Education, 42, 46, 55, 62, 80, 116, 189, 244, 248, 255, 510, 539, 623
Doctorate, xi, xviii, 18, 57, 72, 80, 83, 85-89, 91-95, 98-100, 122, 147-148, 152, 161, 215, 221-232, 236-237, 249, 260, 263, 265, 270, 275, 336, 343, 354, 374, 401, 406, 438-439, 442, 448, 451, 453, 464-465, 504, 543,-545, 548, 554-555, 571-573, 581, 595, 609, 627
Dodd, Paul, 165-167, 169-171, 175-176
Dominguez Hills, xi, xiv, xxi, xxv, xxvi, xxviii, 64, 117, 143, 154-158, 196, 201, 204, 206, 219, 224, 226, 254, 262, 267, 305-306, 312, 318-320, 329, 338-339, 342, 406, 415-416, 419, 430-431, 434, 488, 493, 527, 531, 537, 553, 563, 581, 583, 585, 617, 626, 628, 645
Donahoe Act, 105-106, 110, 138, 163, 345
Donahoe, Dorothy, xi, 74, 75, 77, 78, 81, 83, 91, 95-98, 105-106, 110, 138, 160, 163, 345, 458, 461, 624-625
Donnelly, Hugh, 115
Dorer, Fred, 294
Douglass, Aubrey, 42, 46, 73, 414
Dumke, Glenn S., xi, xii, xiv, xviii, xxiii, xxiv, xxv, 61-62, 72-73, 80, 85-95, 97, 99-100, 106, 112-113, 117, 123, 125, 129-141, 143-148, 151, 155, 159, 162-167, 169, 172-176, 178-182, 190, 192, 198-206, 208, 210, 219, 222, 224-225, 237, 248, 254, 257, 269-270, 273, 276-277, 282, 290, 313, 316, 322, 324-326, 328-329, 333, 339, 342, 344-345, 348, 355-356, 358-360, 363, 365, 367-368, 371, 373, 382, 385-386, 387, 397, 399, 400-405, 412,

414-422, 426, 428, 430-431, 434-435, 437-443, 445, 447-448, 455-456, 459-461, 463-464, 468, 476-479, 484, 486-489, 492-493, 507, 510-511, 526, 530, 536-537, 540, 542-543, 545-551, 553-555, 557, 574, 576-577, 581, 590, 595-596, 624-625, 627, 629, 633, 641
Dutton, Fred, 107

Early Assessment Program (EAP), 198, 215, 264, 303, 333, 335, 452, 469, 473, 580
East Bay, 58-60, 155, 196, 282, 424, 464, 617, 624, 632
Eastin, Delaine, 314
EdD, 227, 230, 238, 336, 453, 572, 609
Education Round Table, 225, 314, 463, 469
Education, Board of, xviii, xxv, 26-27, 29, 32-34, 38-39, 42, 45, 50-51, 54-55, 57-58, 63, 73-79, 85, 90, 92-94, 96-99, 106-108, 110, 113, 115-116, 131, 140, 145, 159, 166, 198, 215, 221, 242-249, 251-253, 255, 323, 333, 341-342, 360, 383, 385, 387, 392, 400, 413-414, 452, 457-458, 462, 469, 484, 502, 519, 523, 525, 539-540, 619-622, 624-625
Education, Department of, xix, 31, 33, 42, 45-46, 50-52, 55-57, 60, 63, 72-73, 75, 77, 82, 84-86, 89, 91, 110, 116, 125, 137, 241-244, 246-247, 249-252, 255-256, 258, 269, 312-313, 330, 334, 339, 341, 393, 468, 478-479, 482-484, 486, 505, 518-521, 539, 543, 564
Educational Opportunity Program (EOP), 173, 312, 444, 461
Educational Policies Committee, 138, 217, 260
Eligibility, xviii, 88-90, 95, 135, 167, 326, 330, 439, 460, 463-464
Elliott, David, xii, 207, 365-368, 386-387, 404-405, 477, 479, 551, 633, 645
Endowments, 36, 504, 508-509, 515
Enochs, James, 125, 137-139, 190, 248, 256

Enrollment ceilings, 53, 324, 526-527, 562, 601
Epstein, Norman, 143, 144, 354, 355, 385, 387, 441, 478-479
Ernst, David, 287, 296, 302, 570, 633
Evans, Handel, 564-568, 578, 590, 633
Extension, 162, 206, 585
External degree programs, 182, 203, 206-207

Faculty staffing formula, 199, 354-355, 482, 487, 489-491, 495, 497, 624
Faculty trustee, 209, 235, 383, 395, 405-406, 409, 476, 479, 629
Fallgatter, Martha, xii, 321, 450-451, 476, 478-479, 633, 637
Federal Advisory Committee on Student Financial Assistance, 317
Fees, 60, 80, 174, 210-211, 223, 230-231, 272, 278, 299, 316-317, 320, 409-410, 459, 483, 485-486, 491, 497, 499-501, 503, 506, 512-513, 516, 518, 521, 602, 630
Feldheym, Lois, 143, 343-344, 350-351, 383, 385, 387, 477, 479, 626
Fenton, Frank, 62, 165
Finance, Department of, xx, 45, 48, 51, 60-61, 82, 90, 109-111, 125-127, 136, 150, 163, 168, 189, 191, 202, 204, 208, 231, 233, 272-273, 289-291, 296, 316, 324, 342, 344, 346, 348, 351, 354, 414, 427-428, 459, 482-484, 486-489, 491, 495, 497, 501-502, 504-505, 517-518, 520-523, 526-527, 531, 540, 553, 559, 564, 574, 623
Financial aid, 213, 217, 271, 274, 302, 313, 315-318, 320-322, 333, 369, 374, 410, 452, 497, 510, 516, 518, 576-578, 580
Finch, Robert, 163
Fisher Bill, 166, 246-251, 258, 267
Fitzgerald, Oscar, 8, 148, 238
Fort Ord, 564-565, 578
Fowler, Laura, 18, 219
Framework, 24, 42, 63, 148, 166, 200, 204, 210-212, 214-215, 218-219, 227, 230, 237, 271, 282, 284, 292, 295, 345, 360, 382, 401, 436, 442,

454-455, 520-521, 530, 532, 560-561, 605-606, 611, 629-630
Francis, John, 141-142, 633
Fremont, John, 117
Fresno, xvii, 16, 21-24, 26, 28, 30, 33, 39, 41, 44, 47-48, 58, 72, 92, 113-114, 140-141, 143, 149, 160, 173, 193, 196, 201, 203-204, 213, 230, 235, 243, 263, 270, 297, 299, 318, 330, 336, 358, 362, 402, 421, 449, 467-468, 504-505, 575, 583, 621-622, 645
Fresno State Normal School, xvii, 23-24, 30, 44, 72, 467, 621
Fresno State Teachers College Association, 504
Freund, Spencer, 287, 294, 633
Fringe benefits, 345, 428
Frisen, Carl, 90
Fullerton, 47, 59, 62, 181, 192, 195, 196, 198, 230, 234, 263, 267, 276, 317, 330, 344, 350-351, 358, 362, 365, 386-387, 402, 442, 445-446, 453, 487, 551, 561, 564, 578, 617, 624, 645
Funding, xx, 9, 16, 25-26, 63, 71-72, 79, 81-82, 88-89, 91, 100, 121, 143, 163, 166, 189-190, 194, 199-201, 204, 210, 214-216, 223-226, 229-231, 233, 235, 260, 262, 264, 274, 291-294, 296-297, 299, 301, 334, 337, 349, 375, 377, 379, 383, 392, 400, 406, 411, 425, 430-431, 436-438, 459-461, 464, 475, 482, 493, 495-496, 500-501, 504, 506, 509-510, 512, 520, 523, 529, 531-535, 554, 558, 574, 577-578, 583-584, 586, 589, 600-602, 630
Fundraising, 193, 215, 296, 316, 397, 399, 411, 425, 449-450, 454-455, 457, 493, 506, 509-516, 519, 531, 567, 584

Gage, Henry, 19
Gallagher, Buell, xi, xii, xxv, 106, 114, 120-130, 132-133, 135-137, 140-141, 144, 145, 151-152, 165, 179, 182, 270, 325-326, 342-343, 350, 400, 414-416, 438-441, 455, 459, 478-479, 483, 522, 625, 637, 641

Gambee, Sumner, 317, 577-578
Gann, Paul, 491, 552
Gantt, Pat, 381, 386-387, 633
Geisler, Gene, 290
Gelb, James, 579-581, 633
General education, 22, 35, 58, 152-154, 161, 196-197, 199, 249, 311, 328, 336, 401, 461, 468-469, 471, 555, 607, 615
GI Bill, xvi, 38, 42
Gillette, James, 21
Gilmore, Paul, 155
Girvetz, Harry, 92, 244
Glenny, Lyman, xxiv, 87, 96, 99
Globalization, 281, 283, 606
Gould, Russell, 495, 559, 638
Governmental relations, 135, 305-306, 440, 477, 479, 495, 518, 529, 540, 552, 555, 557, 560, 575-576, 581, 584, 590, 625
Governor, xvii, xxiii, xxv, 3, 4, 7, 8, 11, 15, 18-21, 23, 25-28, 30-35, 38, 40, 45, 48-49, 51, 55, 59, 60, 63, 64, 71, 74-75, 78, 83-85, 89, 91-92, 94, 97, 99-100, 106-110, 112, 114, 122, 124, 130, 132-133, 150, 152-153, 155-157, 161-162, 164, 166-167, 173-175, 178, 180, 189, 202, 204-205, 211, 216, 224, 228, 230, 234-235, 245-246, 251-252, 259, 261, 264, 276, 278, 334, 336-337, 342-343, 345, 350, 352, 356, 358-359, 363, 371, 378, 380, 392, 394-396, 404, 409, 413, 421, 423, 427-428, 451-452, 456, 458, 462-464, 466, 474, 476, 479, 485, 488-493, 495-497, 500-503, 516, 520-521, 523, 525-527, 531, 534, 540, 543, 545-546, 549-554, 557-560, 563-564, 566-570, 572, 574, 585, 588, 600, 611, 613, 619-, 622, 624, 627-628, 630-631, 635
Graduate programs, xviii, 83, 91, 210, 221, 228, 231, 236-237, 292, 352, 561, 572, 609
Graduation rates, 212, 214, 216, 302, 609
Graham, Robert, 228, 500, 570, 579
Grants, 214, 233, 299, 506, 515, 543, 576-578

Index

Gregg, James, 157, 545
Grievances, 167, 353, 355-356, 363
Guy, Wilfred, xxiii, 16, 42, 582, 635

Hall, Arthur, 125, 128, 145, 165, 326, 339, 509, 535, 537, 589, 633
Hammerstrom, Gary, 331, 333, 339, 633
Hampton, Claudia, xi, 260, 394, 419, 636
Hanner, Dale, 193, 293, 444, 447-448, 454, 488, 493-494, 503, 517-518, 542, 555, 590, 633
Harcleroad, Fred, 60, 401, 415
Harmon, Harry, 125, 137, 156, 419, 434, 443, 483, 522, 524, 530, 537, 633
Harper, William Rainey, 22
Harrison, Mernoy, 448, 494
Hart, Gary, 160, 177-178, 224, 258, 261, 264, 512, 635-636
Hauck, William, xii, 408-409, 476, 478-479, 495, 559, 574, 633, 638
Hay, Joe, 409
Hayakawa, Samuel, 161, 175-180, 252, 352, 421, 543
Hayward, xii, 59-60, 117, 143, 155, 191-192, 200, 226, 299, 312, 351, 361, 401, 403, 415-416, 419, 424, 446, 464-465, 479, 486, 493, 532, 557, 575, 617, 624, 632-633
Heilbron, Louis, xi, xxi, xxv, 78-79, 85-86, 97, 108-110, 113-114, 119-120, 124, 127-130, 132-133, 135, 137-138, 140, 142, 144, 146, 148, 166, 168, 177-179, 182, 190, 219, 222, 224, 232, 238, 244, 246, 271, 360-361, 386-387, 392, 400, 402, 439, 476, 479, 510, 526, 582, 604-605, 617, 633, 635
Helwick, Christine, 314, 449
Henry, Allen, 5, 11, 19, 34, 80, 253, 279, 565, 639
Hensill, John, 137
Hertlein, Grace, 290
Hicks, Howard, 486
Highsmith, James, 299, 645
Hill, Robert E., 47, 157, 164, 192, 284, 478-479, 517-518, 575, 580, 590, 633

Hodson, Timothy, xxvii, 587, 589-590, 633
Hoff, Peter, 195, 279-280, 424, 449, 452
Holy, Thomas, 52, 80, 385, 387
Horne, Boyd, 275-276, 278, 280, 481, 484, 486, 517-518, 633
Humboldt, 25, 26, 28, 33, 43-44, 47-48, 54, 58, 95, 138, 146, 190, 196, 203, 344, 350, 361, 393, 415, 427, 549, 582, 586, 597, 621, 628, 645
Humboldt County Normal School, 25
Hutchins School of Liberal Studies, 119

Impaction, 327, 332-333, 631
Information Systems, 202, 300, 449
Institute for Higher Education Leadership and Policy, 589, 632
Institute of California, 601, 615, 617
Institutional research, xxiii, 125-126, 145-146, 318, 326
Instructional Television Fixed Service (ITFS), 290, 292, 304, 306
Integrated technology initiatives, 216
Integrated Technology Strategy (ITS), 295-306, 630
Interdisciplinary, 156, 207, 210, 252, 566
International programs, xviii, 269, 271-272, 277, 279, 281, 432, 490, 625
Intersegmental, 225

James, Henry, 5, 15, 21, 48, 64, 74, 111, 125, 137-138, 157, 177-178, 190, 219, 238, 248, 250, 253, 256, 258, 267, 287, 290, 297-299, 303, 305-306, 363, 374, 381, 395, 420-421, 432, 442-443, 446, 476-477, 479, 517-518, 530-531, 543-544, 545, 550, 555-556, 560, 575, 578-579, 590, 633-634, 636-637, 645
Jarvis, Howard, 491, 552
Jensen, James, 229, 363-364, 391, 432, 446, 479, 543, 545, 550, 552, 554-557, 572, 585, 590, 633
Jespersen, Chris, 35
Johnson, Hiram, 23-24, 312, 322, 346, 617

Joint doctorate, 93-94, 124, 221-224, 226-228, 232-233, 265, 354, 439, 442, 627
Joint Legislative Budget Committee, 150, 233, 345
Jones report, 31, 84
Jordan, David Starr, 22, 141-142, 400
Joyal, Arnold, 72, 92, 141, 149, 160, 575

Keene, C. Mansel, 125, 143, 173, 179, 342-343, 345-346, 350-351, 358, 385, 387, 415-417, 420-421, 477, 479
Kehoe, John, 25, 477, 479, 543, 575-576, 590, 633
Kellogg, W. K., 36, 127-128, 158-160, 200, 623
Kendall, Glenn, 149, 161, 247, 510, 518, 575, 590
Kennedy, John F., xi, 120, 135, 147-148, 158-159, 359, 416, 511, 518, 537, 633
Kennedy, John Fitzgerald, xi, 120, 135, 147-148, 158-159, 359, 416, 511, 518, 537, 633
Kennick, Joseph, xi, 154, 437
Kerr, Clark, xii, 62, 73-77, 79-81, 84-87, 92-94, 97-98, 100, 125, 131, 143, 145, 150, 164-165, 222, 227-228, 237-238, 325, 398, 438-439, 448, 456, 460, 467, 478-479, 494, 558, 572, 584, 595, 600, 624
Kerschner, Lee, 193, 225, 238, 278, 350, 359, 363, 386-387, 424, 445, 448, 477-479, 547, 564, 617, 633
Kerschnew, Lee, 279
Kersey, Vierling, 34-35
Kessler, Warren, 362, 367, 369-370
Ketchum report, 512-514, 518, 630
Ketchum Report, 512-514, 518, 630
Kirst, Michael, 339, 473, 479, 633
Knight, Goodwin, 57-58, 60
Korean War, 488, 522
Kramer, Robert, 159-160
Kully, Robert, 383, 395, 405, 477, 479, 551, 634, 637, 645

Lange, Alexis, 22

Langsdorf, William, 58-59, 62, 135, 141-142, 181, 195, 198-202, 219, 401, 453, 487, 547
Lantos, Thomas, 270-271, 274-275, 634
Layoff, 357, 359, 449, 628
Learning society, xiv, 100, 413, 606
Lecturers, 348, 369, 376
LegiSchool, 334, 589
Legislation, xi, xii, 7, 9-10, 16-17, 22, 25-26, 29-32, 39, 42-43, 47, 57-60, 92, 97, 111, 115, 152, 154-155, 159-160, 166, 208, 228-231, 233, 242-243, 246, 249, 251-254, 262-263, 265, 288, 334, 337, 341, 356, 362-367, 370, 372, 379, 381, 383, 386-387, 392-393, 395-396, 403-404, 407, 409, 416, 419, 422, 458, 462-463, 468, 470, 472-474, 492, 502, 505, 507, 541-543, 545-549, 552, 562-565, 571-573, 580, 589, 611, 629
Legislative Analyst's Office, 224, 233, 346, 414, 428, 520-523, 527, 531, 537, 556, 575, 617
Legislature, xvii-xviii, xxiii, 3, 5-11, 15-16, 18-19, 21-24, 26-32, 34-35, 38-41, 43, 45-55, 57-59, 61, 63, 72, 74-79, 81-84, 89, 92, 95-96, 98-100, 105-106, 109, 111-112, 114-116, 118, 121, 130-131, 136, 141-142, 150, 152-153, 155, 158-160, 163, 166-167, 171, 182, 189, 191, 198, 202, 204-205, 216, 224-225, 227-231, 235, 238, 242-246,b 248-251, 261-262, 264, 266, 274, 276, 278, 288-289, 296, 299, 303, 312, 321, 334, 336, 342, 345, 350, 355-356, 359, 361-364, 366, 368, 372, 377, 379, 384-387, 395, 400, 404, 408, 415, 423, 426, 428, 433, 458-459, 461-464, 466, 468, 470, 471, 473-474, 478-479, 481-482, 484-486, 488, 490-491, 495-497, 500-502, 504, 507, 510, 516, 520-521, 523, 526-527, 529-531, 540-542, 544, 547-549, 551-555, 557, 559-560, 562, 565, 567, 569-570, 572-575, 579, 582-586, 589, 598, 604, 611, 619-629, 632

Leiffer, Donald, xi-xii, xxv, 91-92, 107-113, 118, 120-121, 124-126, 129-130, 135, 144-145, 182, 244, 342-344, 438-440, 455-456, 483, 521-522, 540, 625, 641
Levit, Burt, 60, 78, 115, 488
Liaison Committee, 40, 45, 50, 52, 56, 58, 74, 76-79, 81, 86, 88, 91-93, 96, 115, 118, 341, 385, 387, 457, 466, 622-624
Library Automation Project, 291
Licensure, 229, 242, 245, 251, 255, 573, 607
Lindahl, Charles, 195, 280, 309, 314, 333, 339, 452, 634
Long Beach, xiii, 41, 47, 58-59, 148, 168, 195-196, 207, 226, 230, 238, 255, 263-264, 277, 294, 297, 300, 305, 316, 338-339, 351, 367, 374, 379, 399, 418, 420, 422-424, 426, 431, 437, 442, 444, 448-449, 453, 456, 476, 479, 517-518, 527, 543, 545, 549, 578, 605, 614, 623, 628-629, 645
Los Angeles, xvii, 4, 10-12, 19, 26, 29-30, 35, 40-41, 43, 45-48, 56-58, 61, 63, 73, 77-78, 80, 82, 88, 124-129, 133, 136-137, 140, 143-144, 149, 154-157, 162, 164, 168, 176, 180, 196, 201, 214, 222-223, 226, 233, 254, 258, 262, 267, 270, 273-274, 288, 290, 293, 297-300, 303, 312, 318, 336, 338-339, 342, 356, 358, 361, 369, 374, 380, 383, 394-395, 401, 403, 419, 421, 431-432, 437, 439, 441-442, 446, 448, 455-456, 482-483, 493-494, 524, 531, 534, 541, 543-544, 546, 549-551, 576, 597, 605, 620-621, 623-627, 645
Los Angeles Board of Education, 40
Los Angeles City College, 40
Los Angeles State College of Applied Arts and Sciences, 41, 56-57, 61
Los Angeles State Normal School, xvii, 4, 11, 29-30, 41, 63, 620-621
Lottery, 374, 481, 503-504, 516, 518
Love, Malcolm, 72, 79-80, 86-87, 92, 95, 130-131, 135, 168, 222, 415

Lower division, 24, 90, 95, 100, 324, 461, 468, 471, 621
Luckman, Charles, xii, 109, 124, 129, 138, 146, 148, 155-156, 168, 358, 393, 523-526, 530-531, 534, 537, 635
Lumachi, Shaun, 309, 338-339, 410, 634
Lustig, Jeffrey, 586-587
Lyons, Mary, 564, 590

Mann, Horace, 6
Marin, Rosario, 336, 338-339, 358, 513, 634
Maritime Academy, 48-49, 195-196, 261, 561, 563-564, 623
Marketing, xxviii, 159, 549, 597, 603
Marley, Gerald, 358, 365, 551, 645
Marvin, J. G., 5
Mason, William, 192, 219, 347, 486, 517-518, 634
Master Curricular Plan, 137, 139, 190, 193, 526
Master Plan, 5, ix, xi, xiv, xvii-xxii, xxiv-xxv, 4, 24, 50, 56, 61, 63-64, 70-71, 73-76, 78-81, 83-100, 105, 107-108, 111, 115-116, 118, 123-125, 131, 135, 138-140, 142, 145-147, 150-151, 155-156, 159-160, 163, 165-168, 172, 190, 193-194, 200, 205, 209-210, 218-219, 221-222, 225, 227-228, 230, 232-233, 235-237, 241, 244-246, 248-249, 265, 269, 272, 279, 283, 289, 296, 310, 315-316, 318, 320-321, 323-326, 328, 333, 335-336, 338-339, 341, 343, 345, 348, 350, 354-355, 359, 368, 383-384, 391-393, 396, 398-400, 402, 407-408, 413-416, 422, 426-427, 436, 438-439, 441-442, 445, 449, 457-468, 470, 473, 475-476, 478-479, 481, 483, 485-486, 495-497, 499, 502, 506-507, 509-510, 515-522, 524-526, 530, 534, 537, 540, 545, 547, 552, 554, 562-563, 571, 573-574, 576, 581, 593, 595-596, 598, 600-602, 604, 606, 609-613, 616-617, 624-625
Masters, Warner, 56
Matheu, Gustav, 276

Mathy, Leonard, xxi, 168-169, 401, 402, 477, 479, 551, 634, 645
McCabe, George, 118, 206-207
McCallum, G. W., 168-169
McClain, Jackie, 379, 381, 386-387, 454, 634
McClatchy, Leo, 168-169
McConnell, T. R., 52
McCune, Ellis, xii, xxv, 139, 141-142, 189-194, 200, 219, 226, 400, 403, 416, 419-420, 424, 432, 443, 446-447, 455, 479, 486, 493-494, 517-518, 532-533, 557-558, 590, 629, 634, 642
McDonald, Howard, 41, 56-57
McGrath, Thomas, 128, 206
McHenry, Dean, 80, 85-86, 90, 93, 222
McLane, Charles, 21-24, 30
McLaughlin, Donald, 77, 93, 97
McPhee, Julian, xi, xx, 35-36, 46, 49, 55, 72, 112, 127, 135-136, 149, 158-160, 168, 189, 311, 411, 415, 505, 511, 520, 526, 539, 540-541, 622-623
Meisenhelder, Susan, 380
Meriam, Theodore, xi, 49, 109, 119-120, 129, 138, 146, 174, 176-178, 525-526, 635
Merit Salary Adjustments (MSA), 378, 387
Merrill, George, 483
Messner, Louis, 193, 447-448, 486, 488, 493-494, 517-518, 542, 555, 590
Miller, George, xi, 57, 75, 79, 83, 91, 95-99, 150, 233, 361, 458, 541, 595
Milliken, Robert, 38
Minns Evening Normal School, 5, 8, 17, 619
Minns, George Washington, 5, 8, 17, 241, 619
Mission, xiii, xvii, xix, xxii, 4, 34-35, 37, 44, 46, 54, 56, 62, 64, 76, 84, 86, 99-100, 105-106, 113, 117, 137, 139, 144, 148, 152-153, 176, 189, 191, 209, 214, 217, 219, 222, 224-227, 233-237, 241, 243, 265-266, 281-282, 289, 293, 299, 310, 312, 317, 333, 335, 337, 354, 382, 384, 393, 402, 412-413, 415-416, 428, 433, 436, 439, 442, 450, 454-455, 466, 470, 473, 475-476, 481, 511, 519-520, 532, 539, 543, 561, 581, 597, 600, 608, 611, 614, 616
Monterey Bay, 196, 561, 564-567, 578, 611, 630
Morey, Ann, 248, 255-257, 259-260, 267, 634
Morrill Act, xvii, 3, 9, 35
Mosk, Stanley, 144
Moulder, Anrew, 6, 7
Moulds, Elizabeth, 582, 584
Muchmore, Donald, 135-136, 540
Muldoon, Thomas, 301
Multicultural, xx, 257, 260, 320, 599
Munitz, Barry, xii, xxv, xxvii-xxviii, 192-195, 209-213, 219, 226-227, 238, 260-261, 279-280, 284, 293-299, 303, 314, 317, 322, 331, 333, 339, 375, 378, 397-398, 406, 410, 418, 424-426, 432-433, 435, 437, 442-443, 448-453, 455, 470, 478-479, 490, 492, 494-497, 500, 504, 512, 514, 517-518, 531-533, 558-561, 564-571, 573, 578-580, 587, 590, 629, 631, 634, 642
Murdy, John, 58

Naples, Caesar, 372, 375, 382, 386-387, 444, 448, 478-479, 634
National Council for Accreditation of Teacher Education (NCATE), 255
National Defense Student Loan Program, 271
Nava, Julian, 421
Nelson, Hans, 25-26, 58
New Approaches, 106, 181, 198, 200-203, 205, 208, 241, 257, 290, 355, 365, 386-387, 404, 417, 437, 487-490, 627
Nichols, Ambrose, 118-119, 142
Normington, George, 109, 112
Northridge, 56, 173, 180, 195-196, 298, 305-306, 333, 383, 419, 437, 443, 477, 479, 506, 516, 529, 556, 560, 567-568, 578, 590, 617, 645

OECD, xxiii, 279, 284, 598-600, 609, 617

Index

Office of Administrative Law (OAL), 371, 386
Oliver, Lew, 269
Orange Book, ix, 424, 449, 481, 487, 490-491, 493-496, 533, 558-560, 627
Orange County State College, 58-59, 543
Out-of-state fees, 278
Outreach, 17, 136, 210, 214, 216, 313, 332, 447, 461, 580, 609-610
Oviatt, Delmar, 57

Panetta, Leon, 564-566, 578
Patino, Douglas, 455, 511, 513-514, 518, 579, 634
Pauley, Edwin, 77
Paulson, Stanley, 169-170
Peltason, Jack, 314
Pereira, William, 524
Perkins, George, 10
Pesqueira, Ralph, 197, 215, 399, 472, 532-533, 637
Peterson, P. Victor, 40-41, 47
Pfau, John, 152-154, 415-416
Plotkin, Scott, 364, 409, 477, 479, 552, 555, 557-559, 569, 590, 634
Pomona, 35-36, 58-59, 127, 158, 160, 196, 200, 270, 318, 415, 582, 622-623
Pomona Junior College, 36
Post, Alan, 78, 81, 91, 96-97, 125, 238, 276, 288-289, 304, 306, 488, 590, 627, 634
Power, 5, 28-29, 51, 63, 84, 113, 131, 141, 146, 164, 266, 352, 380, 402, 412-413, 458, 525, 555, 586
Prator, Ralph, 57, 89, 141-142, 324-325
Presidential homes, 427, 431
Privilege, xxi, 413
Probation, 323, 342
Professional degrees, 72, 222
Proposition 13, 208, 355, 376, 425, 464, 474, 490-493, 497, 503, 527, 552-554, 558, 628
Proposition 209, 314, 322, 374-375, 561, 630
Proposition 98, 225, 497
Public policy, xiv, xvi, xxiv, 9, 83, 85, 99-100, 166, 190, 197, 210, 236, 250, 320, 324, 360, 421, 451, 481, 497, 516, 518, 527, 558, 572, 590, 598-600, 603, 611-613

Quality, 5, xiv-xv, xix, 18, 153, 167, 181, 215, 217, 226, 230, 236-237, 241, 244, 255-256, 258-259, 291, 295, 301, 304, 309, 319, 333, 337, 348-349, 365, 374, 384, 401, 413, 416, 442, 470, 495, 547, 583, 596, 601, 606, 613-616
Quarter system, 142-143, 153, 402

Randall, Ambrose, 15
Ratigan, Joseph, 118
Ravine, Chavez, 41
Razi, Ali, 533, 638
Reagan, Ronald, xii, 162-164, 177-179, 181, 251-254, 276, 327, 352, 358, 362-364, 368, 384, 394, 415, 443, 476, 479, 485-486, 489-490, 497, 527, 542-543, 545-547, 550-551, 576, 596, 635-636
Redfearn, Lori, 515, 518
Reed, Charles B., xi-xii, xiv-xxv, xxvii, 194-195, 197, 211-213, 216, 218-219, 227-228, 230, 262-264, 282, 284, 299-302, 305-306, 317, 322, 333, 335, 338-339, 347, 379-381, 398, 410, 418, 425-426, 433, 435, 450-455, 471-472, 478-479, 500-501, 514, 534-535, 569-573, 578, 579-580, 589-590, 617, 631, 634, 642
Regnier, Jon, 532, 537, 634
Remedial, 197-198, 215, 265, 324, 329, 398-399, 452, 469, 472-473, 606
Research, xiv, xvi, xxiv, 44, 53, 71-73, 79-81, 83, 85, 87-89, 91-95, 99-100, 113, 125, 135, 145, 210, 214, 216-218, 221-222, 229, 23-237, 256, 266, 290-291, 293, 303, 328, 346, 349, 354, 369, 383, 401, 406, 416, 428, 438, 446, 451, 465, 469, 493, 507-508, 512, 515, 535, 540, 576-577, 581-583, 589, 595, 602, 606-608, 611, 629, 632
Retention, xix, 81, 89, 113, 214, 216, 234, 264, 302, 325, 345, 348-349, 367, 433, 458, 550, 609

Reynolds, W. Ann, xii, xxv, 193, 219, 225-226, 259-260, 278, 292, 313, 322, 329, 331-333, 335, 339, 371-375, 382, 395, 422-424, 427-428, 430-432, 435, 442-448, 455, 464-465, 470, 478-479, 493-494, 511-512, 530, 532, 534, 554-557, 561-563, 577-578, 583-584, 586, 590, 600, 617, 629, 634, 641
Richards, Richard, 154, 458, 460, 478-479, 481, 517-518, 634
Richardson, John, 21, 32, 35, 124-125, 129, 151, 483-484, 522
Richter, Bernard, 314, 339
Riles, Wilson, 252-253, 358
Riverside Agricultural Experimental Station, 152
Roberti, David, 584
Roberts, Alexander, 33
Robinson, Maynard, 297, 499, 517-518
Rodda, Albert, 142, 249-250, 253, 363, 366, 368, 552
Rohnert Park, 118
Romberg, Paul, 161, 181
Roosevelt, Theodore, 20
Rosser, James, 287, 290, 297, 299, 303, 306, 374, 421, 477, 479, 517-518, 531, 634
ROTC, 44, 90, 124, 146, 172, 312, 320-321
Ryan Act, 252, 254-255, 258
Ryan, Leo, 250-255, 258, 267
Rydell, Raymond, 128, 136-139, 168, 181, 190, 192, 219, 270, 385, 387, 403

Sacramento, ix, xiv, xx, xxiii, xxv-xxviii, 7, 11, 18, 24-27, 35, 40-43, 45-48, 51-52, 58, 60, 72-74, 77, 83-84, 87-88, 92-93, 96, 109, 112, 115-117, 119, 125-126, 129, 132-133, 135-136, 142, 149, 151, 153, 161, 163-164, 166, 180, 189-192, 195-196, 200-201, 209, 213-214, 225, 227,-230, 234-235, 238, 241, 244-247, 249, 255, 260-262, 264, 267, 273-274, 276, 290, 294, 297-298, 302-303, 314, 316, 318-321, 329, 330, 332, 334, 337-339, 341, 360, 363-365, 368, 375, 381-382, 387, 391, 393, 398, 404, 406-410, 413, 415, 419-420, 422-424, 426, 432, 437, 439-441, 443, 446-448, 454-455, 457, 459, 462-464, 467, 473, 477-479, 482-484, 486, 488, 491, 494-495, 500-501, 505-506, 517-519, 521-523, 525-526, 530-532, 534-535, 539-546, 549-560, 566-567, 569-574, 576, 578, 580-585, 587, 589-590, 597, 605, 617, 623, 625, 627, 629-632, 645
Sacramento City Unified School District, 41
Sacramento Junior College, 41-42, 467
Salary, 11, 23, 109, 114, 150-151, 163, 172, 180, 205, 345-346, 348-349, 370-372, 375-378, 423, 427-428, 432-433, 446-447, 463-464, 484-485, 487-488, 502, 542, 554, 586, 626, 628
Salary savings, 487-488
Samit, Jack, 386-387, 634
San Bernardino, 58, 78, 152-153, 155, 158, 196, 230, 287, 342, 361, 380, 415-416, 431, 527, 553, 556, 563, 617, 625-626, 629
San Bernardino Valley Community College, 153
San Diego, xi-xii, 16-17, 19, 26, 30, 33, 38, 44, 47, 58, 72, 78-80, 91-92, 95, 107, 109, 118, 121, 130-131, 135, 137, 140, 148, 166, 168, 193, 196, 222-224, 226-227, 230, 232-234, 244-245, 247, 250, 252, 256, 267, 270, 290-291, 298-299, 318, 328, 330, 332-333, 338-339, 354, 415, 421, 439-440, 442, 449, 455, 465, 509, 540, 544, 547-549, 557, 561-563, 568, 576, 578, 597, 609, 617, 620, 627-628
San Francisco, xiii-xiv, xvi-xvii, xx, xxiii-xxvi, xxviii, 3, 5-9, 11, 17-19, 24, 26-27, 32-33, 35, 38, 47, 58-62, 64, 72, 78, 80, 83, 86, 92, 95, 109, 112, 114, 117-119, 122-127, 130-132, 137, 141, 145-146, 151, 155-156, 158, 161-162, 164-181, 191-192, 196, 201, 203-204, 206, 214, 222-223, 226, 229-230, 232-233, 235, 241-242, 248-250,

252, 261, 263, 267, 269-271, 273-274, 276, 282, 290, 310-311, 316, 318-320, 322, 325-326, 329, 333, 338-339, 344, 348, 351-352, 355, 357, 359, 361-362, 367, 369, 385, 387, 393, 399-400, 403, 413, 415, 421, 430, 439, 444, 459, 461, 467, 472, 482-484, 486, 509-510, 513, 517-518, 521-523, 537, 540, 542-543, 548-549, 575-576, 583, 597, 617, 619-620, 622, 624-628, 645
San Francisco Board of Education, 5, 7, 18
San Francisco State Normal School, 17, 18, 203, 232, 241, 620
San Francisco State Teachers College, 33
San Jose, xi, xvi, 3, 8-15, 17-19, 21, 26, 31-33, 40, 44, 47, 58, 60, 64, 72, 92, 95, 110, 122, 124, 126, 129, 136, 162, 168, 178, 180, 196, 201, 203, 207, 222, 241, 267, 288, 299, 345, 348, 351, 355, 358, 360-361, 365, 386, 408, 417, 462, 509, 535, 537, 548-549, 551, 554, 559, 564-567, 578, 597, 619-620, 628, 645
San Jose State Normal School, xi, 3, 11, 13, 15, 17, 21, 620
San Luis Obispo, 19-21, 35-37, 125, 127, 155, 158-160, 165, 196, 290, 311, 318, 321, 327, 332, 359, 361, 365, 409, 415-416, 427, 443, 486, 504-505, 511-512, 540, 557, 578, 582, 610, 620, 622
San Marcos, 196, 333, 415, 561-563, 566, 599, 617, 629
Santa Barbara State Normal School of Manual Arts and Home Economics, 21, 620
Santa Rosa Center, 118, 204, 206
Scholastic Aptitude Test (SAT), 146, 258, 326
Schwarzenegger, Arnold, 227-228, 230, 334, 338-339, 396, 476, 479, 497, 501, 517-518, 560, 570, 572, 573, 638
Scott, Jack, xxvii, 228-231, 364, 409, 472-473, 477, 479, 552, 555, 557, 559, 569, 572-573, 590, 634
Secor, Kenneth, 161

Sedgwick, Harold, 79
Semans, Hubert, 52, 385, 387
Senate, xxi, 75, 96-97, 106, 139, 141-143, 146, 150-151, 161, 164, 168, 170-172, 174, 178-179, 190, 193, 195, 197-198, 200-202, 205-207, 209, 212-213, 217, 222, 225-226, 228-231, 234-238, 245, 249, 253, 263, 265, 272, 279-281, 292, 296, 299, 305, 330-331, 333, 348-349, 352, 356-368, 373-375, 379, 382-383, 385-387, 391, 395, 399-409, 411-412, 435, 440, 445, 452-454, 458, 462, 470-472, 477, 479, 484, 488, 505, 517-518, 541-542, 548, 551, 557, 563, 566, 569-572, 576, 583-584, 586, 604, 617, 628-629, 632, 635
Senate Education Committee, 97, 229, 253, 472, 569, 571
Senior Commission of the Western Association of Schools and Colleges (WASC), 213, 255, 277
Sexton, Keith, 81, 458-459, 461, 478-479, 590, 634
Shaw, Stanford, 152
Sherriffs, Alex, 252-253, 256-257, 394, 405, 443, 456
Siemens, Cornelius, 138, 415
Simpson, Roy, 39, 42, 57-62, 73, 76-80, 84, 86-87, 93-94, 97-98, 100, 109-111, 113, 116, 118, 182, 246-247, 416, 510
Smart, John, 198, 200-201, 219, 238, 478-479, 590, 600, 617, 634
Socioeconomic, 259, 318, 320, 336, 513, 609
Sommers, David, 336, 338-339, 350, 634
Sonoma, 27, 115, 117-119, 125, 129, 139, 142, 152, 155, 182, 192, 196, 201, 206-207, 248, 254-255, 280, 299, 318, 344, 351, 361, 420, 457, 488, 516, 548-549, 583, 597, 617, 625, 628
Southern Branch of the University of California, xvii, 30, 41, 621
Southern Branch State Normal School, 11
Spalding, Willard, 459, 461

Spence, David, 195, 197-198, 212-213, 215-216, 219, 230, 238, 264, 301, 333, 452-453, 469, 471-472, 478-479, 571-573, 589, 634
Spencer, Paul, 271, 287, 294, 633, 635
Spindt, Herman, 89, 324, 325
Spreckels, John, 16
Sproul, Robert G., 30, 36, 38-39, 41, 62, 73, 75, 140, 438, 456, 467, 583, 624
Stahlburg, Ernest, 160
Stanford, Leland, xxiv, 7, 18, 22, 24, 31, 38, 80, 152, 209, 249, 258, 339, 342-343, 458, 473, 479, 582-583, 621
Stanislaus, 62, 77-78, 115-117, 119, 155, 182, 193, 196, 297, 318, 344, 363, 424, 448, 548-549, 553, 617, 624-625, 629
State College Revenue Bond Act, 502
Statewide Academic Senate, x-xii, xxi, 168, 202, 226, 362, 386-387, 405, 563, 625-626, 631-632, 635, 645
Stiern, Walter, 160, 461, 478-479, 624
Strafaci, Sam, 377, 379, 381, 386-387, 454, 634
Strayer Report, 40, 43-45, 50, 56, 64, 84-85, 92, 145, 323, 521, 623
Student fee policy, 215, 501, 573, 600, 602, 615
Student trustee, 209, 217, 337, 395-396, 409-500, 628, 631
Student unrest, 164, 170, 310, 403, 479
Study abroad programs, 269-270, 278, 281
Summer session, 17, 29, 91, 136, 152, 203-206, 212, 274, 344, 484, 487
Summerskill, John, 169-173
Super Sunday, xi, 214, 317, 322
Superintendent of Public Instruction, xii, 358, 465
Sutter, Richard, 275, 278, 280, 634
Suzzalo, Henry, 34, 41, 622
Swett, John, 5, 17-18, 242
Syer, John, 582, 584
Systemwide Internal Partnership (SIP), 296-297, 304, 306

Taiz, Lillian, 381, 387

Task Force on Student Affirmative Action, 313, 332, 339
Teacher education, xiii, xvii, 7, 10, 18, 34, 37, 43, 48, 54, 57, 62, 72-73, 76, 83-84, 86, 113, 118, 123, 130, 141, 149, 166, 193, 195, 210, 221, 232, 241-245, 247-256, 258-267, 325, 335, 344, 348, 351, 383, 414, 417, 426, 442, 444, 447, 452, 467, 489, 500, 517-518, 556, 570, 599, 601, 609-610, 624
Teachers Association of Southern California, 29
Teachers college, xxii, 4, 21, 24, 26, 31, 32, 33, 34, 37, 39, 41, 47, 49, 50-51, 59, 63, 84, 118, 203-204, 218, 221, 241, 243, 259, 272, 310, 323, 336, 341, 344, 442, 493, 504, 613, 621-622
Teale, Stephen, xi, 154
Technology, xv, xix, 189, 193, 201-203, 205-206, 210, 214, 287, 289, 290-306, 311, 322, 369, 380, 399, 418, 425, 437, 454, 456, 477, 479, 495, 535, 570-571, 580, 602-603, 606, 615, 627, 629, 630-631
Technology Infrastructure Initiative (TII), 296-297, 301, 304-306, 630
Technology Steering Committee (TSC), 295-297, 303-304, 306, 418, 425, 570, 630, 631
Teerink Report, 489-490, 517-518
Telecommunications, 281, 290-291, 293-294
Tension(s), xvii, 164, 254, 257, 382, 423, 507, 550, 556, 605
Thomas, Vincent, 52, 78, 80, 85, 108, 119, 128, 154, 206, 209, 229, 246, 270, 287, 290-291, 301, 371, 382, 470, 479, 518, 563, 578, 634-635, 637-638
Three-legged stool, 496, 512
Three-year baccalaureate, 602, 616
Tidelands oil revenue, 527
Title 5, 342, 371
Transfer(s), 150, 195, 197, 471, 510
Treasury function, 632
Truman, Harry, 36, 523
Trustee professor, 430, 433, 446, 448
Trustee professorship, 446, 448

Tuition, 9, 22, 100, 274, 483, 485-486, 499
Turlock, 115-116
Tyler, Henry, 80

Uniform Code of Military Justice, 320
Unions, 88, 133, 298, 352, 366, 369, 370, 373, 377-379, 381-382, 409, 492, 500, 506-507, 509, 535, 550, 556-557, 564, 570-571
United States Department of Agriculture, 36
University of California, 3-4, xii-xiii, xvii-xix, xxvi, xxviii, 3-4, 8-10, 15, 17, 19-22, 26-31, 33-39, 41, 44-45, 49, 52-55, 58-59, 62-63, 71-75, 78-84, 87-88, 90, 92-94, 96-100, 106-110, 112, 122-124, 133, 135, 139, 142-143, 145, 148, 150, 152, 162-166, 205, 211, 213, 221-223, 225, 227-228, 230-233, 237, 242-244, 252, 255, 261, 264, 269, 274, 276, 279-280, 288, 291, 296, 314, 325-326, 329, 331, 335, 342, 345-346, 348-350, 363-364, 375, 381, 383, 385, 387, 392, 398, 400, 402, 406, 421, 428, 437-439, 443, 448, 453, 456-457, 459-470, 473-474, 478-479, 481, 484, 486, 491-492, 495, 500-501, 503, 510, 511, 517-518, 522, 524, 527, 531, 540, 543-547, 549-550, 553-555, 559-560, 567, 569, 572-576, 578, 580, 584, 587, 595, 598-600, 602, 606, 608-609, 611-613, 616-617, 619-624, 627-628, 630
Unruh, Jesse, 78-79, 127, 132-133, 155, 250, 479
Upper Division Written English Test (UDWET), 169

Vallejo, 8
Van Cleve, Leo, 280, 634
Van Matre, Nelson, 25-26
Vasche, J. Burton, 73, 87, 116-117, 510, 518
Vasconcellos, John, 200, 209, 235, 462, 479, 544, 586, 634
Ventura County, 566-568, 631

Vietnam War, xvii, 164-165, 170, 310, 362, 577
Visual and Performing Arts (VPA), 329
Voorhis School for Boys, 35, 622
Voorhis, Jerry, 35-36, 158-160, 622-623

Wagner, Marjorie Downing, 341, 351, 371, 387, 420-421
Wahlquist, John, 72, 92, 348, 417
Wang, Stanley, 282, 638
Ward, Mary, 19, 35, 314, 560
Warren, Earl, xii, 39-40, 42, 47, 49, 108-109, 143, 290, 362, 367, 369, 370, 443, 458, 477, 479, 511, 517-518, 523, 578, 633, 635
Washington office, 440, 455, 574-580, 632
Weaver, Henry, 279-280
Weintraub, Royd, 290, 305-306
Welty, John, 263, 297, 477, 479, 517-518, 634
Western Association of Schools and Colleges (WASC), 213, 255, 277
Westphal, James, 530
Wheley, Lloyd, 47
Whitsell, James, 111
Wickson, E. J., 20
Wilbur, Ray Lyman, 22, 38
Wilcox, Sandra, 226, 406, 477, 479, 634, 645
Wiley, Samuel, 168, 645
Wilson, Pete, 112, 194, 211, 227, 252-253, 261-264, 358, 377, 379, 395-396, 451, 476, 479, 496-497, 500, 529, 531, 540, 557-559, 564-565, 570, 573, 589, 634, 637-638
Winkler, Maria, 290
Woo, Chia Wei, 421
World War I, xiii, xvi-xvii, xxii, 3-4, 20, 24, 26, 30-31, 34, 36-38, 42, 51, 56, 63, 64, 71-72, 85, 87, 92, 105, 112, 117, 122, 124, 139, 145, 162, 204, 221, 232, 243, 270, 310, 342, 365, 407, 438, 505, 519, 521-523, 562, 564, 605, 622
World War II, xiii, xvi-xvii, xxii, 4, 24, 26, 34, 36-38, 42, 51, 56, 63-64, 71-72, 85, 87, 92, 105, 117, 122, 124, 145, 162, 204, 221, 232, 243,

270, 310, 342, 365, 407, 438, 505, 519, 521-523, 562, 605, 622

Year-round-operations (YRO), 143, 210, 402, 603

Young, Clement, xxiii, 32, 56, 262, 263-264, 267, 305-306, 386-387, 513, 634